A
THIRST
FOR
EMPIRE

A
THIRST
FOR
EMPIRE

HOW TEA SHAPED THE
MODERN WORLD

ERIKA RAPPAPORT

PRINCETON UNIVERSITY PRESS
PRINCETON AND OXFORD

The Library of Congress has cataloged the cloth edition of this
book as follows:

Names: Rappaport, Erika Diane, 1963– author.
Title: A thirst for empire : how tea shaped the modern world / Erika
Rappaport.
Description: Princeton : Princeton University Press, 2017. | Includes
bibliographical references and index.
Identifiers: LCCN 2016044343 | ISBN 9780691167114
(hardcover : acid-free paper)
Subjects: LCSH: Tea—History. | Tea—Social aspects—History. |
Imperialism—Social aspects—History. | History, Modern.
Classification: LCC GT2905 .R26 2017 | DDC 641.3/372—dc23 LC
record available at https://lccn.loc.gov/2016044343

British Library Cataloging-in-Publication Data is available
This book has been composed in Adobe Caslon Pro

For ANDY & BEN

CONTENTS

ABBREVIATIONS

ATDL   Anti-Tea-Duty League

CAL   Ceylon Association London

CTPB   Ceylon Tea Propaganda Board

EIC   British East India Company

HCM   *Home and Colonial Mail*

ITCC   Indian Tea Cess Committee

ITDA   Indian Tea Districts Association

ITMEB   International Tea Market Expansion Board

ITA   Indian Tea Association

LMA   London Metropolitan Archives

M-O   Mass Observation

NA   National Archives

TCTJ   *Tea and Coffee Trade Journal*

TGA   Tetley Group Archive

VOC   Dutch East India Company

ACKNOWLEDGMENTS

This book has taken me on a long journey in which I have gained an immense appreciation for the people who labor to produce one of life's true pleasures: a cup of tea. Along the way, I have drunk a great deal of tea and coffee with many colleagues, students, family members, and friends, all of whom have given me more support, or one could say sympathy, and inspiration than they are aware. Though I began this book many years after I finished graduate school, my conviction to write world history came from the time I spent at Rutgers University. Victoria de Grazia and John Gillis taught me to paint on a large canvas, while Judy Walkowitz and Leonore Davidoff (who taught at Rutgers at a crucial point in my career) demonstrated that historical change happens at an intimate and local level.

I began researching and writing this book, however, after I became a member of the history department at the University of California, Santa Barbara. Although the mistakes I have no doubt made are my own, this book could not have been written without the generosity and intellectual nourishment I have received at UCSB. My entire department had faith that one day I would complete this "tea book," and several colleagues read drafts and listened to me talk endlessly about commodities, food history, and the British Empire. First on this list has to be Lisa Jacobson, a fellow traveler who also made the move from the study of consumer culture to the history of food and drink, though her drinks are precisely those that tea advocates so despised. Lisa's knowledge of business history and the intricacies of trade publications and her own ability to find meaning and humor in even the most tedious source have been an incredible inspiration. She has been a careful editor who read the entire manuscript and I believe made it a better book. I have also been very lucky to have several colleagues who know a great deal about food, leisure, capitalism, and colonialism. Stephan Miescher and Mhoze Chikowero introduced me to many books and people working in African history and frankly gave me confidence to focus on Southern Africa as one of the sites in this book. Though she only recently moved to UCSB, Sherene Seikaly's knowledge of colonial political economy, her passion for politics, and her generous reading of portions of this manuscript allowed me to see more clearly the role of race and power in this story. Gabriela Soto-Laveaga stimulated an excitement for the history of science and showed how seemingly mundane plants can open the door to fascinating global histories. Nelson Lichtenstein, Mary Furner, and Alice O'Connor have read and commented on several portions of the manuscript and helped me wrestle with developments in U.S. historiography.

I also offer gratitude for the food, friendship, and sheer rigor from my colleagues in Santa Barbara, especially Hilary Bernstein, Eileen Boris, Patricia Cohen, Adrienne Edgar, Sharon Farmer, Sabine Frühstück, Bishnupriya Ghosh, Anita Guerinni, Terence Keel, Mary Hancock, Toshi Hasegawa, John Majewski, Harold Marcuse, Kate McDonald, Sears McGee, Cecilia Gastelumendi-Mendez, Ken Mouré, Ann Plane, Luke Roberts, Bhaskar Sarkar, Paul Spickard, Jack Talbott, and Xiaowei Zheng. Carol Lansing has been a mentor and friend who has kept me healthy and happy for nearly two decades.

Over the years, many wonderful graduate students have patiently read portions of the manuscript and discussed this book in seminars and office hours. Nancy Stockdale, Sandra Trudgen Dawson, Jason Kelly, Justin Bengry, Bianca Murillo, Jean Smith, Nicole Pacino, Sarah Watkins, and Charlotte Becker have all graduated and published books and articles that shape my approach to history. Sandra introduced me to the pleasures of twentieth-century history and the study of working-class leisure. Jean was a tireless research assistant who taught me how to take clear digital photographs in the archive, and she generously translated advertising that I found in Afrikaans. While learning Burmese in Wisconsin, David Baillargeon found (and digitized) a treasure trove of materials from the Earl Newsom Archives. His work on international business and mining in colonial Burma has also influenced my thinking about the multinational nature of nineteenth-century colonial business. Kashia Arnold, Masha Fedorova, Brian Griffith, Julie Johnson, Laura Moore, Tim Paulson, Josh Rocha, Sergey Saluschev, Elizabeth Schmidt, and Stephanie Seketa have all expanded my ideas and approaches to these topics. Julie and Elizabeth generously also stepped in at the end of this journey to help with the tedium of checking notes. Finally, this book literally could not have been completed without the help of Caitlin Rathe, who read the entire manuscript, dealt with the intricacies of copyright laws, managed and organized dozens of images, and all the while kept me interested in the history of food policy in the United States and UK. I hope she knows just how much I have appreciated her assistance and friendship.

Beyond UCSB, I have learned from a large network of people. Melissa Caldwell, Carolyn de la Peña, Charlotte Biltekoff, and Julie Guthman, and the many others who regularly participated in the UC MultiCampus Research Program on Food, Culture, and the Body, supported by the UC Office of the President, provided an interdisciplinary home and a great deal of feedback, particularly on chapter 2. In addition to those who listened and responded to many conference papers and talks, I have especially learned from those I have met at the North American Victorian Studies Assocation, the North American Conference on British Studies, the American Historical Association, and Berkshire Conference on Women's History. I'd like to give special thanks, however, to a number of faithful colleagues who have consistently advised and responded to my work in these and other settings: Emily Allen, Anneleen Arnout, Jeffrey Auerbach, Jordanna Bailkin, Prithwiraj Biswas, Alister Chapman, Lisa Cody, Becky Conekin, Brian Cowan, Mark Crowley, Donica Belisle, Antoinette Burton, Arunima Datta, Joy Dixon, Durba Ghosh, Nicoletta Gullace, Peter Gurney, Dino Felluga, Kate Flint, Douglas Haynes, Anne Helmreich, Dane Kennedy, Seth Koven, Lara Kriegel, Thomas Laqueur, Marjorie Levine-Clark, Shinobu Majima, Thomas Metcalf, Maura O'Connor, Susan Pennybacker, Stefan Schwarzkopf, John Styles, Lisa Tiersten, Michelle Tusan, and Amy Woodson-Boulton. Amy's friendship, collegiality, and willingness to read and comment on my work have sustained me for years. Jayeeta Sharma graciously shared the maps she had made for her book on colonial Assam, a work that has been very influential in shaping my thinking on the place of tea and India in world history. Geoffrey Crossick, Paul Deslandes, Nadja Durbach, Philippa Levine, Abigail McGowan, Steven Topik, Frank Trentmann, and James Vernon read all or significant portions of the manuscript and helped me wrestle with a massive amount of material and the diverse histories I encountered while writing this book. At Princeton University Press, Brigitta van Rheinberg has been a careful editor who has encouraged me to try to write for many audiences.

A book like this cannot be written without the help of many librarians and archivists. At UCSB Sherri Barnes has been especially invaluable. I would also like to thank the many people at the Bancroft Library at UC Berkeley, the British Library, the National Archives (UK), the archive at the Centre for Studies in Social Sciences, Kolkata, the Mitchell Library, Glasgow, the London Metropolitan Archives, the Guildhall Library Archives, the Mass Observation Archive, the Typhoo Corporate Archives, the History of Advertising Trust, the Wisconsin Historical Society, the Hagley Museum and Archives, and so many others in Ireland, New Zealand, Australia, Sri Lanka, India, and South Africa who have sent me materials to complete this book.

The generous financial support from a number of granting agencies has also made this book possible. I would especially wish to thank the National Endowment for the Humanities and the UC President's Fellowship program for providing two years of much-appreciated sabbatical. A wonderful summer at Birkbeck College, University of London, was supported by a grant from the Cultures of Consumption Research Program directed by Frank Trentmann. I also received support from the Hagley Museum and Library to work in the Dichter papers, and a generous grant from Robert and Christine Emmons funded a research trip to India. The Interdisciplinary Humanities Center and the Academic Senate at UCSB as well as the UC Regents have supported a number of research trips and paid for research assistants and the reproduction of the many images for this book.

I have also been lucky to have friends and family who have helped make my life a pleasure while I wrote this book. I would especially like to thank Dana O'Neil for her infecting vivacity and enthusiasm that continues to inspire me. This book owes an immeasurable debt to my husband, Jordan Witt, who has shared housework, child care, and many a research trip with me. He has read virtually everything I have ever written no matter how busy he becomes and somehow has maintained his optimism and love for me even as I became engrossed with writing this book. I have dedicated this book to my two sons, Andy and Ben Witt, who have lived with this project throughout their childhood. I began writing this book when Andy started elementary school and I was pregnant with Ben. Both of them have displayed a patience and wisdom beyond their years, and yet they have encouraged me to play with toys, listen to music, read fiction, and watch a great deal of sports; and, most important, Andy and Ben have kept me laughing.

A portion of chapter 2 appeared as "Sacred and Useful Pleasures: The Temperance Tea Party and the Creation of a Sober Consumer Culture in Early Industrial Britain," *Journal of British Studies* 52, no. 4 (October 2013): 990–1016. A section of chapter 8 appeared as "'Tea Revives the World': The Decolonization of Tea Advertising during the Depression," in *Moving Around: People, Things and Practices in Consumer Culture*, edited by Hiroki Shin, Shinobu Majima, and Yusuke Tanaka (Tokyo: Forum for History of Consumer Culture, 2015), 27–41. "Drink Empire Tea: Conservative Politics and Imperial Consumerism in Interwar Britain," a section in chapter 8, was published in *Consuming Behaviours: Identities, Politics and Pleasure in Twentieth-Century Britain*, edited by Erika Rappaport, Sandra Trudgen Dawson, and Mark Crowley (London: Bloomsbury, 2015), and finally part of chapter 5 appeared as "Object Lessons and Colonial Histories: Inventing the Jubilee of Indian Tea" in the wonderful new online platform *BRANCH: Britain, Representation and Nineteenth-Century History* in 2016, which was started and is edited by Dino Felluga and can be found at http://www.branchcollective.org/?ps_articles=erika-rappaport-object-lessons-and-colonial-histories-inventing-the-jubilee-of-indian-tea.

Santa Barbara, California
August 2016

A
THIRST
FOR
EMPIRE

INTRODUCTION

A Soldiers' Tea Party in Surrey

O n a cold Friday evening at the end of November in 1941, an unknown photographer captured a quiet moment when a group of Indian soldiers came to Woking, Surrey, to rest, pray, and drink tea. These men and the residents of this unassuming town in southern England had been fighting Nazi Germany and its allies for just over two years. Germany had reduced whole neighborhoods of London to rubble, had conquered much of the European Continent, had invaded the Soviet Union, and Japan was about to attack Pearl Harbor. Although things looked very bleak at this point in the war, Great Britain was not alone in its struggles. In 1941 it was not an island nation but a multinational empire able to marshal and supply a huge military machine. Men and women from the Indian Subcontinent, from Africa, Canada, Australia, New Zealand, and so many other regions in the empire were fighting this war. American money, munitions, and supplies had also already been deployed against the Axis powers. Millions of people and a great deal of tea sustained the nation at war in 1941. Like so many other nation-states, Germany, Japan, and the Soviet Union included, twentieth-century Great Britain was a global creation. Its history cannot be separated from the multiple worlds with which it interacted, whether in periods of war or times of peace. By tracing the rise and fall of tea's empire that stretched from western Canada to eastern India, *A Thirst for Empire* reveals the belief systems, identities, profits, politics, and diverse practices that have knit together and torn asunder the modern "global" world.[1]

If we take time to look closely at the photograph of the soldiers' tea party on the front of this book, we can discern a multilayered, racially and socially diverse community that is all too often conveniently forgotten in contemporary politics and public debate. Although the picture looks as though it could be anywhere in the Muslim world, this tea party took place in front of the Shah Jahan mosque in Woking, a modest-sized English town roughly thirty miles southwest of London. The Indo-Saracenic style building that opened in 1889 is the oldest purpose-built mosque in Great Britain and indeed in all of northern Europe.[2] Though quite small, the mosque rapidly became an important place of worship and social center. Its history reminds us that migration and cultural exchange were as common in the 1880s as in our own day. W. L. Chambers, a British architect, designed the building. The Nizam of the princely state of Hyderabad provided funds for the land. Her Highness, the Begum Shah Jahan ruler of Bhopal and a number of Muslim donors financed the building. Dr. Gottlieb Wilhelm Leitner, a brilliant linguist born in a Jewish family in Budapest in 1840, inspired and oversaw the project. A naturalized British citizen who worked for the colonial state, Leitner was proficient in nearly fifty languages, served as an interpreter during the Crimean war, studied in Turkey, received a doctorate from Freiburg University in Germany, and at the age of twenty-three became Professor in Arabic and Muslim Law at King's College, London. He then moved to British India to take up the position as principal of the new Government College in Lahore in 1864 and contributed to several literary and educational projects in India and Britain before building the mosque. Without romanticizing this world that was also rife with racial, religious, and social tensions as well as intellectual debate, we need to acknowledge this history.

One way to begin is to take a second look at the photograph of the soldiers' tea party. While the mosque is a tangible reminder of Britain's global past, so too were the YMCA volunteers who drove their mobile canteen to Surrey, the soldiers they served, and the unseen businesses, planters, politicians, and workers who manufactured tea *and* the markets for this imperial product. This book is their story. The tea these soldiers were drinking was grown primarily in India and Ceylon but also in British colonial Africa. Tea planters and their publicists first encouraged the YMCA and other similar agencies to manufacture, stock, and drive hundreds of tea cars to serve those in need. Why did so many work so hard to serve tea to Indian soldiers in wartime Surrey? The simple answer, and one that so many Britons would easily reach, was that tea was energizing, soothing, and boosted morale. "Tea is supposed to be the favourite drink of the privileged sex," recalled Admiral Lord Mountevans, Regional Commissioner for Civil Defence in London during the war, but then he mused: "believe me, men became tea-drinkers in all our services, especially Civil Defence. It gave us courage and that matey feeling which gets the best effort out of us to help our fellow humans."[3] The notion that good tea would comfort the weary and support the weak seems so natural to those of us who drink caffeinated beverages that it is almost impossible to consider a time when anyone would suggest otherwise. Yet such reminiscences, the photograph on the front of the book, and the soldiers' tea party in Surrey were instances of commercial propaganda that the colonial tea industry disseminated virtually everywhere the Allies were training, fighting, or working for the war effort.

A nurse who had treated the wounded after Rommel had "punched" the Eighth Army "hard on the nose" and taken Tobruk in Libya in 1942 recalled how though the men could barely talk, the first thing they asked for was a cup of tea.[4] An Egyptian State Broadcasting Studio radio program that featured the military hospital recognized that the ubiquitous presence of tea in public life was in fact commercial propaganda, but this did not make the tea any less appreciated. Speaking about the care of the soldiers, the announcer remarked: "Many of the men are of course suffering from loss of blood and shock," but they no doubt would recover because "the Army Medical Authorities have found that hot sweet Tea has, in such cases, very great value as a stimulant and restorer." The speaker went on to reflect, "This seems like a battlefield adaptation of the advertising slogan 'Tea Revives You.' But it must, I was told be *hot* and it *must be sweet.*"[5] The observation that the Army Medical Authorities were sounding a great deal like an advertising slogan was apropos. The slogan "Tea Revives You" had entered the popular lexicon because British and Dutch tea planters had advertised tea in this way in key markets around the world for decades. And it did not abate in wartime. To give just a few examples, during the war tea's public relations machine screened films on tea and "National Defence" and lectured on the "proper" way to brew up a good pot of tea at the Port Said Rotary Club, Cairo's Police Schools, and countless other venues. It slapped posters on hoardings that declared: "There is Health in Good Tea."[6] An industry leader explained in March 1942 that, although the Japanese occupation of the Netherlands East Indies had cut off supplies from Java and Sumatra, Tea was fighting back. He was not referring to the tortuous experience of tea garden laborers from Assam who had been conscripted to build roads to defend India and, it was hoped, recapture Burma from the Japanese.[7] He was rather describing the huge public relations effort that planters had mounted to raise awareness of "the magnificent part that Tea is playing in the War Effort all over the world."[8] *A Thirst for Empire* traces the origins, significance, and foreseen and unexpected consequences of, as well as opposition to, this effort to create a world market for the British Empire's tea.

We must begin this history long before the twentieth century, for the ideas behind such propaganda were nearly as old as tea itself. Although the plant's origins are still somewhat unclear, archaeologists have recently discovered 2,100-year-old tea in western China, proving that tea was ingested in some fashion before any textual or previous archaeological evidence of its existence.[9] Scholars will no doubt delve into how the tea buried in an emperor's tomb was used, but we know that the Chinese understood that tea had restorative properties centuries before the German scientist Friedlieb Runge discovered caffeine in 1819.[10] Virtually all cultures that enjoyed an infusion of the plant that Western science has named *Camellia sinensis* recognized that it fought off sleep, and many believed it could cure headaches, constipation, and other more serious disorders.[11] Such benefits and the caffeine that creates a mild biological and psychological compulsion have preserved tea's hold on its users, but there are many other ways to consume this substance and people often live quite happily without caffeine. Addiction has played an important part of the history of drugs, drink, food, and capitalism, but it cannot explain individual or social differences, diverse modes of preparation, changing preferences, or brand loyalty.[12] Economics plays a role to be sure, but all things being equal, consumers still make countless culturally, socially, and politically informed choices when they purchase, prepare, ingest, and think about foods and drinks, even those that are addictive in nature. Chemistry, biology, and economics simply do not determine the social and commercial worlds that have inserted tea and similar commodities into the daily life of millions of individuals and the political economies of so many nations.

While there were always those who disliked its taste or who called tea a poison, a waste of money, and a dangerous foreign import, virtually every culture that has been in contact with tea has described it as an agent of civilization and a temperate pleasure. Such ideas first appeared in China more than a thousand years ago, but, in the seventeenth and eighteenth centuries, European scholars, merchants, and missionaries translated and reframed Chinese ideas about tea (and similar commodities) and made them a core part of European culture.[13] Incorporating a strand of early modern social thought that proposed that consumption and foreign commerce were positive forces that produced civility and social harmony, tea's advocates contended that it balanced the economy and produced a healthy and temperate self-controlled consumer.[14] This notion that tea was a civilizing force was critical to its success and its failures. We often think of temperance as a reaction against mass marketers' push to urge us to buy more, overeat, and shop till we drop. This, however, is a very contemporary understanding of the relationship between restraint and consumption.[15] Temperance did not reject the material world. It developed a morality of consumption that demonized certain commodities and consumer behaviors while promoting others. Thus, as we will see here, the nineteenth-century transnational temperance movement transformed the food and drink industry, contributed to the making of the modern diet, and legitimized consumerism as a positive social force.[16]

Even in the midcentury United States, during a time when consumers were beginning to prefer coffee, an American merchant professed:

> No other production of the soil has, in equal degree, stimulated the intercourse of the most distant portions of the globe; nor has any other beverage, with equally alloyed benefit, so commended itself to the palates of the people of the more civilized nations, or become so much a source of comfort, and a means of temperance, healthfulness, and cheerfulness; whilst it may be doubted if any other is equally restorative and stimulative of the intellectual faculties of man.[17]

This merchant's description of tea applied a core idea of nineteenth-century liberalism, the faith that commerce was a civilizing agent, to a single commodity. Such ideas were not the exclusive property of the West, however. For example, in 1906 the Japanese-born curator of Oriental Art at the Boston Museum, Okakura Kakuzo, published *The Book of Tea*, a small but widely read English-language history, which celebrated what the author called "the Cup of humanity." "The Philosophy of Tea," Kakuzo believed, was not mere aestheticism, but it

> expresses conjointly with ethics and religion our whole point of view about man and nature. It is hygiene, for it enforces cleanliness; it is economics, for it shows comfort in simplicity rather than the complex and costly; it is moral geometry, inasmuch as it defines our sense of proportion to the universe. It represents the true spirit of Eastern democracy by making all its votaries aristocrats in taste.[18]

The cosmopolitan Kakuzo traveled widely but settled in the United States and joined the wealthy and artistic circle surrounding Mrs. Isabella Stewart Gardner. It was at her home at Fenway Court that Kakuzo first publicly read his history of tea and encouraged the consumption of Japanese culture in wealthy America. In myriad histories such as Kakuzo's tea serves as a diplomat bridging the gap between East and West, rich and poor.

At almost the same time that Okakura Kakuzo was writing his history, Indian tea planters proposed that the true tea of democracy, health, and civilization was not from Japan or China but from the British Empire. For example, in October 1914 one of several publicists dedicated to promoting Indian tea, A. E. Duchesne, published "Tea and Temperance" in *The Quiver*. It is fitting that Duchesne should publish in this non-sectarian evangelical journal started by John Cassell, a temperance reformer and tea and coffee merchant who created a major publishing house.[19] These social worlds ensured that tea would be identified with Britishness and Britain's civilizing mission. This piece repeated the adage that "the temperance reformer's most valuable ally" had sobered up the British nation. Tea, Duchesne wrote, had eliminated the "drunken nurses and bibulous coachman" of Dickensian times, had eradicated the need for every businessman to "clinch his bargain over a glass," and expelled the belief that "drunkenness was the test and evidence of British manliness."[20] The hot beverage had in a positive way feminized twentieth-century Britain by evoking "delightful associations of home . . . the innocence of childhood, the sacredness of the mother, the love of the wife, the fascination of the daintily feminine." Free of "vulgarity," "rowdyism," and "obscenity," this simple good was "a factor in civilization." Tea drinking was moreover a democratic habit enjoyed equally by the "fashionable dame," "the businessman," "the clerk and the typist," the "factory hand, the toiling sempstress and washerwoman, the navvy, and the soldier."[21] This celebration of domesticated Britishness especially took hold after the devastation of the war years, but tea's advocates had been selling elements of this story since the seventeenth century.

In 1914, however, tea was much more than a national symbol. It was a protagonist in a tale about commerce and Christianity, democracy, civility, and empire. On the surface, Duchesne's and Okakura Kakuzo's texts seem very similar, but while Kakuzo saw tea as an example of Eastern civilization, Duchesne contended that "the energy and business capacity of our British planters in India," not Chinese farmers, had transformed the "luxury of the rich" into the "everyday drink of the poor."[22] Duchesne thus argued that British imperialism enabled mass consumption and spread civilization. In truth, Chinese farmers and an international merchant community had cultivated the Chinese tea that Victorians so appreciated, and it was not until very late in the nineteenth century that most Britons drank or even knew about their empire's tea. In Duchesne's interpretation, tea justified imperialism. Critics of empire have made the same point and noted how, instead of being a diplomat easing relationships between peoples and nations, tea was a thief or pirate, appropriating Eastern treasures for the benefit of the West.

The humanist and imperial interpretations of tea's historical role differ in their attitudes to the impact of global economic and cultural exchange, but they similarly employ tea as a device to relate a story about human nature and global relationships. The humanist has tended to rely on a comparative model in which many diverse people participate as consumers in a shared pleasure. This approach typically has emphasized consumer rituals and experiences rather than labor and unequal profits. Those who created our global economy and wrote its history, for example, often celebrated consumerism as a universal human trait, yet used commodities to enforce inequalities and difference. By contrast, what we could call the imperialist model has tended to highlight those inequalities and the environmental and human costs of plantation-based colonial economies. Though academic histories have fallen more often into this category, both models have been around a long time and have been used to illuminate global connections and comparisons and reveal the intersecting histories of culture, economics, and politics. I also employ tea as a device to write the history of globalization but do so without assuming that this process is inevitable or natural or that it has produced greater equality or homogeneity.

By lifting the lid on a pot of tea and really looking at its contents, studying where it was grown and *who* bought, sold, and consumed this commodity, we can explain why British women and Indian soldiers drank tea together in wartime Woking. We can also see how the British Empire exerted power over land, labor, tastes, and the daily habits of millions of people living in so many parts of the globe. Using both a wide angle and a focused lens, this book demonstrates how advertising, retailing, and other forms of distribution created and were shaped by the history of the British Empire and the integration of the world economy since the seventeenth century. This commodity-centered approach to world history highlights the fantasies, desires, and fears that motivated buyers' and sellers' attitudes and behaviors. While I have revisited many themes that will be familiar to scholars of empire and commodities, those in the tea business, and aficionados, I have built this history of tea from the ground up.[23] I have explored a wide variety of corporate, colonial, advertising, associational, and personal archives in several countries to uncover the experiences and attitudes of the people who labored to make, sell, brew, and drink tea. Tea's massive archive illustrates that there was nothing straightforward about its history, and at no point since the seventeenth century has this history been untouched by the history of capitalism.[24]

Many of the firms or brand names that we still associate with tea, such as Lipton's, Brooke Bond, Twinings, and Tetley, and many we are less familiar with today, such as the Assam Company, Billy Brand Tea, or Horniman's, play a pivotal role in this history. Rather than assuming the corporation is the driving force behind globalization, however, I argue that early modern trading monopolies, particularly the British East India Company, the merchant firms of the nineteenth century, and multinationals of the twentieth have overlapping histories, and all of these types of corporations participated in and benefited from belonging to a web of interconnected transnational and local relationships.[25] All these businesses were part of political, religious, familial, and industry-based communities that moved within but also well beyond the official boundaries of the British Empire.[26]

This history starts in the seventeenth century, at the beginning of a long-term shift from a Chinese to European and then a British-dominated global trade. Chinese and other Asian and Near Eastern people had manufactured, traded, and consumed tea long before Europeans encountered the beverage. Early modern Europeans played a relatively minor part in the trade compared to that of other tropical commodities such as sugar, tobacco, coffee, and cocoa. Nevertheless, in the seventeenth century, the Dutch, French, and Portuguese acquired a taste for the rare luxury and introduced the British to the drink. Over time a small but influential group of aristocratic and cosmopolitan Britons began to view and promote tea as a panacea capable of curing most mental, physical, and social disorders. The British East India Company entered the trade and its efforts, and those of smugglers, private merchants, shopkeepers, medical experts, and temperance enthusiasts, enabled tea to become a regular feature of social life and diets of people in England, Scotland, and Wales, parts of Ireland, North America, and other areas of the British Empire and British World in the late eighteenth and early nineteenth centuries.

Tea was very useful to state revenue and the creation of a sober society, but in an era of mercantilism, the mass consumption of foreign things bred dependency and weakness, or so theorists believed. As is well known, the British began to exchange Indian-grown opium for Chinese tea as a way to stop the drain of silver from the nation's coffers. The Chinese addiction to opium and British addiction to tea became so intertwined that in both places myths developed about the similarities between the two substances. This anxious relationship shaped the history of retailing, advertising, consumption, and colonial conquest in India and the nature of tea production throughout the nineteenth century. The opium trade was one solution to trade imbalances and fears of dependency. Another was the search for alternative sources of supply. Beginning in the late eighteenth century, the British contemplated growing their own tea within the boundaries of the Raj. In the 1820s, during a war with Burma, and with the help of local elites seeking a new source of money and power, a British soldier of fortune found tea growing wild in Assam, just outside the borders of the empire. Growing "British" tea thus began with the violent appropriation of land and labor and a good deal of subterfuge in Assam and China. However, the new generation of planters who launched the tea industry in Assam encountered enormous resistance and made many errors. It was not until the late 1870s that the industry was on a sure footing, but markets were not forthcoming. People simply preferred Chinese tea. Indian teas did not find a significant market in Great Britain until the 1880s, nearly fifty years after the first plantations had been laid out. Promoters of these new teas secured those markets by stoking anti-Chinese sentiment and claiming that Indian tea was modern, healthy, pure, patriotic, and, most important, "British," thereby transforming a foreign thing into a familiar object. Pure food activists, retailers, and Indian tea growers asserted that Chinese teas were adulterated with dangerous chemicals and bore the residue of sweaty and dirty Chinese laborers. Such stories and the blending of India's leaf with that of China accommodated palates to the new British teas. By the 1890s, Britons, the Irish, and Australians were primarily drinking the empire's produce. Yet British markets never seemed capacious enough, and planters felt compelled to conquer vast new colonial and foreign markets. They formed powerful and long-lasting trade associations that lobbied governments and raised taxes that paid for massive, and often repetitive, global advertising campaigns. Planters, their allies, and associations thus cultivated many of the technologies and ideologies we associate with the history of modern consumer society.

We need to pay special attention to the role of the planter in global history. If we follow planters as they moved through time and across space, we will see how they shaped the political and cultural economies surrounding tea. By cultural economy, I mean the attitudes, sets of behaviors, and rituals around the growing, trading, and consuming of tea. Planters included the owners and managers of large-scale agricultural operations known as estates, gardens, or plantations, but the "Planter Raj" also included the investors and members of agency houses and cognate industries who may or may not have lived in India, Ceylon, British East Africa, and Dutch-controlled Java and Sumatra but who identified with this business. There were never very many European planters living in the empire. In the 1850s and 1860s, planters were a tiny fraction of the ten thousand non-official Europeans—merchants, traders, and missionaries—in British India.[27] The vast majority came from Scotland, but the early planting industry was more multifarious than has been supposed and there were many mixed-race individuals and families who financed and grew tea. Some indigenous planters owned tea plantations, but white Europeans and major corporations controlled the industry.[28] Wives, sisters, mothers, and daughters also helped erect the colonial hierarchies that sustained the planter class. Women invested in the growing and trading industries, spread knowledge about and sold the commodity, but with a few notable exceptions they typically did not manage plantation agriculture.[29]

The Planter Raj invented many of the advertising and marketing techniques that similar industries still use today. Decades before Coca-Cola refreshed the world or McDonald's served fast food to millions, tea growers combined propaganda, politics, and ideas derived from preexisting consumer and commercial cultures to create tea drinkers in places as diverse as Glasgow, Cincinnati, and Calcutta. Although they met with a great deal of resistance, planters were nevertheless able to alter retail and consumer practices, design new drinking habits, and transform bodily experiences. Business and family connections, politics, and religion, as well as gender, class, and racial ideologies, helped cement far-flung commercial and consuming communities, as did fiscal, land, and other state policies. Planters relied on the many new technologies that inspired globalization in the nineteenth century, including the railway, clipper and steamship, telegraph, chain provision shop, cooperative society, tea shop, newspaper, magazine, and exhibition.[30] They also readily used radio, cinema, popular music, market research, public relations, and television in the twentieth century. Additionally, trade associations and journals were critical to their social power and global reach and provided the skeleton upon which planters created a new kind of global political economy and consumer culture. The Indian Tea Association (ITA), for example, founded in the late nineteenth century, is one of several key protagonists in the second half of this book. This body and similar institutions in Africa, Ceylon, and elsewhere sustained the class, gender, and racial hierarchies of colonial rule and yet also produced mass markets for tea in Europe, North America, Africa, and South Asia.

To put it simply, planters did not stay on the plantation. Starting as early as the 1850s and 1860s, planters traveled around and beyond the British imperial world, seeking diverse pathways to the consumer. They forced collaborations and engaged in numerous small and large conflicts within and beyond political empires. When they moved to London, Glasgow, Dublin, Chicago, or Cape Town, they did not leave behind their colonial mentality or connections. In fact, they often conceived of creating markets as akin to colonial conquest. They explored unknown lands, gained local knowledge, and acquired territory and subjects for their commercial empire. Frequently, planters imported the rhetoric and methods of colonial conquest into the spheres of market research and advertising, and they influenced the politics of consumption and production everywhere they traveled and resided. However, the British never completely controlled the flow of ideas, capital, and commodities. Men and women from India, Ceylon, the Netherlands, Africa, the Middle East, and the United States also stimulated a thirst for the empire's tea. Ultimately, the creation of mass markets was a varied and contentious political, economic, and cultural process that required a great deal of money, labor, power, and persistence. The history of this evergreen with lovely white blossoms demonstrates the fluctuating global dimensions of empires and the racial and ideological underpinnings of transnational business and advertising; it garners for us an intimate social and cultural history of global capitalism.

It is often supposed that tea's commodity chain, especially in the past, was divided into separate gender, racial, and class spheres.[31] Since at least the nineteenth century, it is most common to find portrayals of white male planters, non-white female tea pickers, and middle-class or poor white female consumers. The Victorians thought in these terms and though they knew that men drank tea they often assumed that tea was a particularly feminine drink consumed most often in the private sphere, at home or in dainty tea shops. For example, in 1874, a well-regarded food scientist, Dr. Edward Smith, quipped: "If to be an Englishman is to eat beef, to be an Englishwoman is to drink tea."[32] Tea allowed women to in effect become British, though what that meant varied over time and in different locations. In *A Thirst for Empire* I ask, how did such ideas emerge and impact consumer cultures, business practices, and political debate? I argue that tea's purported femininity and its association with Britishness was not so much a reflection of the sociology of markets but a result of deeply embedded and long-lasting ideologies that at times benefitted sales but also became an obstacle to profits. As we will see, the industry spent a good deal of time debating how and whether to brand tea as feminine, masculine, national, or imperial. Such considerations provide a window into when and how global business constituted the gender of consumers and producers, but as we will see the feminine and domestic image of this commodity allowed some women to declare themselves as business experts and own and manage tea shops, groceries, and specialty shops and some gained real prosperity and political clout selling imperial commodities. Of course, their activities helped solidify tea's femininity and undercut efforts to capture the male market. Gender and race also informed producers' identities and actions. Planters, retailers, and advertisers, for example, forged masculine trade-based identities that helped them gain power and make profits.

The general outline of tea's history is quite well known in part because growers, manufacturers, and retailers wrote accounts of the commodity's past to shape markets, and they continue to do so today.[33] We have countless general histories that tend to rely on published sources and rarely delve into the rich archival record that tea has left behind.[34] We can learn a great deal from some of these works and at times I have found it necessary to rely upon them, but I have also studied the origins and uses of this well-worn history. Indeed, the fact that the industry has been so involved in writing its own history is one of the most fascinating and telling aspects of this commodity's culture. The Indian and Ceylon tea industries wrote versions of tea's past to distinguish their product from Chinese and Dutch supplies, to discredit alternatives such as coffee and soda, and to maintain power even during the upheavals of decolonization in the mid-twentieth century. While it has been hard to look underneath the official story, I have been able to build upon the work of a number of historians who have diligently and creatively charted the diffusion of caffeinated beverages in Europe and colonial North America.[35] Sidney Mintz's seminal work on sugar, Jan de Vries's more recent examination of what he called Europe's "industrious revolution," and the work of numerous other scholars have demonstrated how tea became a highly profitable commodity in early modern global trade. Tea became a much-appreciated aspect of an "Enlightened" consumer revolution, contributing to the growth of slavery in the Caribbean and the making of an industrial working class in eighteenth- and nineteenth-century Great Britain.[36]

Yet, for all this attention, European and American tea markets were much smaller than those in Asia at the time.[37] Using region rather than nation as a category for comparison, scholars have demonstrated that parts of China, Japan, India, Africa, the Middle East, and the Americas had much larger and more developed market economies and tea cultures than Europe prior to the nineteenth century and that the expansion of European-dominated capitalism did not always destroy local meanings or these economies.[38] Much of this work in some way or other has contributed to the larger question of the so-called rise of the West. Instead of contributing directly to this debate, I take a step back and ask why, despite the diverse nature of the people, capital, and technologies that have shaped the global economy, it has been so easy to frame modern history as the rise of the West. *A Thirst for Empire* questions such grand narratives by paying as much attention to the local and personal as the global. Consideration of the intimate and regional especially clarifies the power dynamics that have produced the broad patterns, gaps, edges, and borders that have made the contemporary world.

In the nineteenth century, tea's history does indeed look quite a bit like an epic battle between the British and Chinese empires. In one of the most dramatic episodes in the history of this commodity, British soldiers, scientists, and colonial officials engaged in outright violence, bribery, drug dealing, and stealing, and they imprisoned, executed, and expropriated the property of their South Asian allies and employees.[39] Slavery was abolished in the empire at virtually the same time that tea plantations were laid out, and over the course of the nineteenth century European beet sugar replaced slave-produced Caribbean sugar, but forced labor remained an important ingredient in the Victorian cup of tea.[40] Tea cultivation in British India and other colonies thus exemplifies what historian Sven Beckert has called "war capitalism." In his study *Empire of Cotton*, Beckert argued that in the nineteenth century capitalism relied on state power and violence to expropriate immense tracts of land, enslave whole populations, and reorganize "economic space" on a global scale.[41] This seemingly "relentless revolution," as Joyce Appleby has described the historical development of capitalism, repeated itself in many different regions around the globe, but as she also proposed there was nothing "inexorable, inevitable, or destined" about this history. Capitalism was a historical creation shaped by coercion, culture, and contingency.[42] It was also an "irresistible empire" that fashioned new wants, new identities, new ideologies, and new things. Victoria de Grazia has used this phrase to describe the American market empire that reached its greatest power in the second half of the twentieth century.[43] As we will see in this book, war capitalism and an irresistible empire often went hand in hand, and indeed U.S. business and markets played an important if subordinate role in building the British empire of tea throughout its long history.

One of my central aims in this book is to demonstrate the precise connections between the formation of markets in Great Britain, its colonies, and its trading partners.[44] While I could have traced the planters from Ceylon who forged markets in Russia, in France, or within their own colony, I have particularly written about the process of market formation within what the late Victorians called the British World, especially focusing on the British Isles, India, Ceylon,

South Africa, and the United States, and with some comparisons to Australia and Canada. At various moments all of these places were important markets, despite the fact that so many people could not afford to or did not want to drink tea. Comparing how similar institutions developed in each of these places offers a unique prism through which we can examine the global production, rejection, and perpetual reinvention of an imperial commodity. It also reinforces our growing sense of South Asia's role in influencing the Indian Ocean arena and connecting that region of the world with Europe and the Americas.[45]

Researching and writing the history of commodities is not in fact a new phenomenon, but our increasingly connected world and the global economic crisis of the early twenty-first century has led to a flurry of studies on the global circulation and meaning of things. Anthropologist Arjun Appadurai inspired much of this work when he urged scholars to write the global biographies of objects and commodities, to "follow the things themselves," and detect how "meanings are inscribed in their forms, their uses, their trajectories."[46] Appadurai defined the commodity very broadly as *"any thing intended for exchange."*[47] The "commodity turn" in the historical profession has usefully questioned the centrality of the nation in historical writing, the modernity of globalization, and the European nature of modernity.[48] It has expanded our understanding of the motives for empire building and the nature and consequences of the colonial encounter. It has helped us see imperialism as something that happens in the metropole and in the colonies, and to regard colonialism as a form of exchange between the colonized and colonizer.[49] Following particular commodities also reveals how transnational encounters, exchanges, and agencies worked within but also outside of formal imperial borders. Instead of regarding commodities then as quantifiable evidence of the value of colonies, we can examine things as carriers of meaning, sites of contestation, and lenses through which we can see the making and unmaking of imperial, subimperial, and transimperial relationships.

In contemporary social science and the multidisciplinary field of food studies, scholars and activists have frequently employed the heuristic device of the commodity chain to demonstrate the institutions that bring a commodity from factory to market or farm to table. This method can clarify what is hidden by packaging and supermarket culture and thereby reveal the labor and/or hidden additives that produce our daily bread. Historians have used this model as well to research how things become commodities, where conflicts arise along the supply chain, and how different labor and retail systems have come into being.[50] These studies have brought a historical perspective to contemporary issues, including the environmental, labor, and health consequences of the global food system, and emphasize how workers, distributors, and consumers make history.[51]

A commodity-centered history of capitalism is not perfect, even if it is popular. The model makes it difficult to chart change over time or capture what I see as the messy, unpredictable, and highly volatile nature of nineteenth- and twentieth-century capitalism. It also typically positions the consumer as passively responding to the work of others. Another problem is that it has tended to produce artificial categories that did not actually exist in reality. Even relatively simple commodities such as tea are not stable entities, and like the nation-state their borders have to be shored up over and over again. Moreover, manufacturers often produce and sell many types of items together; shops are situated within complex retail systems, and consumers also buy many things at once.

Capitalism, nevertheless, creates categories and knowledge systems that make commodities and industries appear singular and unique even when they are not, a problem I am especially concerned with in this book. Advertising, one such knowledge system, is central to the process of making products appear special; this capacity goes a long way to explain why advertising has become such a phenomenally successful global business, even when it is hard to prove the effectiveness of a particular advertisement or campaign.[52] Like advertising, packaging and branding also both produce and suppress knowledge about the production of goods, and all of these processes can shift markets, alter commodity chains, and inspire consumer-based politics. As many food activists today will readily note, advertising is just as likely to quash knowledge as to inform consumers about the nature of goods. Just to give one example, currently Kenya is one of the top two exporters of tea in the world and there are significant producing areas in Uganda, Malawi, Tanzania, Rwanda, Burundi, Zimbabwe, and South Africa.[53] Because of the nature of advertising, branding, and packaging, however, most consumers are unaware that African leaf is in their "English" breakfast tea. Of course, not all commodities rely heavily on consumer advertising, but if we consider the broader history of trade advertising then we will see more fully how distribution and publicity in their broadest sense need to move from the periphery to the center of commodity studies and world history.

Tea's history is in fact inseparable from that of advertising, and this has a great deal to do with the nature of the plant. While tea can grow in many climates, it thrives in tropical and subtropical areas with warm temperatures, high humidity, and a great deal of water, sunlight, and well-drained and nitrogen-rich soil. Once mature, the freshly picked leaves must be processed quickly to prevent spoilage and thus whether produced on large-scale plantations or small farms processing typically happens near growing areas. Tea can be made into bricks, pounded into powder, and dried and fermented in various ways to become green, black, oolong, and other varieties. However, ideally all leaf teas should be transported from the field to the cup relatively rapidly or they will lose freshness, flavor, and value. Tea cannot languish in warehouses; it must be purchased quickly. Thus while this simple commodity has been enjoyed as a luxury item, in the nineteenth and especially in the twentieth century it has most often been blended, branded, and retailed as a very inexpensive mass consumer good. It can be served hot and iced, with added flavorings and spices, prepared in urns, samovars, and pots, sold in tea bags and even freeze dried, but unlike corn, soy, sugar, oils, cotton, or even diamonds, it has no appreciable industrial uses. Wherever it is grown and manufactured, tea is basically a beverage. These facts are very significant to tea's commercial history.

Manufacturers have of necessity primarily dealt with surpluses through the production of more consumers rather than the creation of new uses for tea. Very early on producers became aware of the need to find, create, and maintain domestic, colonial, and overseas markets. They became early adopters of advertising and market research, and experimented with many different forms of publicity and distribution. We know a fair amount about how the big companies introduced brand advertising, but we know very little about the kind of cooperative, generic, or group publicity that planters' organizations paid for and conducted to create new tastes in the first place. One of the leading transatlantic practitioners of generic campaigns, Sir Charles Higham, explained in 1925 that direct brand advertising was a "reaping process," with immediate results, but "group publicity is more a process of fertilization—the courageous effort of farmers who intend to do everything possible to endure a good harvest later on."[54] Higham insisted that generic product advertising produced new desires, educated public tastes, and created the demand that retailers would later satisfy. At the time he was developing his theory of collective advertising, Higham was hired by the Indian Tea Association to teach Americans to drink the British Empire's tea. India's planters were not as patient as Higham hoped and they fired him after they could not detect rapid results. Nevertheless, this sort of advertising fashioned many of the cultural and institutional frameworks that enabled the British Empire to determine the flow of ideas, goods, and knowledge, commonly labeled as globalization.

There are many definitions for this broad and yet vague concept, but rather than apply a contemporary definition, I trace what the global meant to consumers, business people, politicians, and others in diverse locations in the past. I thus tease out different "global" imaginations and consider where and how people gained, used, and lost global knowledge. African historian Frederick Cooper proposed that historians must disentangle the differences between "long-distance" and "global," recognize the limits to a global framework, and avoid characterizing globalization as a unitary or inevitable process.[55] I have followed his suggestions by focusing on the commercial and consumer cultures of a single commodity as it moved and failed to move from one site to another. In addition to using both a comparative and connective approach to world history, I emphasize continuities and discontinuities between early modern and modern empires and today's global world.

The notion of thirst has been helpful here. I have employed "thirst" in two ways in this book. It is a metaphor for desire that is inherent in imperialism and mass marketing, two forces in world history that share an unquenchable desire for people and resources. It is also a sensual experience. While we can never obtain a pure view of how an individual experienced his or her cravings and satisfactions, we do know that thirst has a history.[56] We can trace the forces that produce thirst and its satisfaction and examine why people acquire and lose tastes for food and drinks, and how this might be different from how people sell and use clothing, toiletries, furniture, entertainment, and so on. For example, food and drink habits tend to change slowly and are highly influenced by habit, tradition, and environment. Religious and scientific cultures often determine what is eaten, how it is prepared, and the spatial and temporal histories of consumption. In general, drink cultures are deeply connected to the formation of social groups and identities. As one scholar has explained, they "give rise to a whole set of graded consumption patterns" and uses that are "based on the perceived oppositions such as between wine and beer, tea and coffee . . . inebriant versus stimulant, cold versus hot, silver versus ceramic."[57] Drink cultures therefore have often become associated with multiple and overlapping identities. They can bolster regional or national cultures and class, gender, and racial identities at the same time.[58]

While the empire of tea I describe was largely the work of Scottish and English planters and colonial officials, generally speaking, these men and their families used the term "British" to describe their identities, their home, and the products they produced. The term was not inert; it took on different meanings within diverse contexts. At times, for example, "British" had a racial connotation and was often a stand-in for a cluster of attributes associated with "whiteness," but this was not always the case.[59] It was also a common term used to brand the new teas from the colonies. At the same time, I have avoided when possible the term "Indian" or "Sinhalese" to define people that did not define themselves in this way. Yet, as we will see, it became common to describe teas and industries as having "national" characteristics long before these nations actually existed. This demonstrates how economic theories, methods, and rhetoric, particularly that of political economy, helped produce ideas of nation often well before places such as India or Ceylon/Sri Lanka became political realities.[60] To explore this process, it is critical to pay attention to and unpack the language and actions of historical subjects, considering why they employed particular words and phrases, why they traveled where they did, and how they interacted and understood diverse people.

In one of his well-known lectures on globalization, the cultural theorist Stuart Hall thought about how commodities, slavery, empires, and immigration were interconnected forces that shaped his identity and that of modern Britain:

> People like me who came to England in the 1950s have been there for centuries; symbolically, we have been there for centuries. I was coming home. I am the sugar at the bottom of the English cup of tea. I am the sweet tooth, the sugar plantations that rotted generations of English children's teeth. There are thousands of others beside me that are, you know, the cup of tea itself. Because they don't grow it in Lancashire, you know. Not a single tea plantation exists within the United Kingdom. This is the symbolism of English identity—I mean, what does anybody in the world know about an English person except that they can't get through the day without a cup of tea?
>
> Where does it come from? Ceylon—Sri Lanka, India. That is the outside history that is inside the history of the English. There is no English history without that other history.[61]

As a Jamaican who moved to Britain in the 1950s, Hall perceived how a variety of British identities and colonial relationships became personified in a cup of tea and in the rituals and histories surrounding its production and consumption. Hall asked how "foreign" yet everyday objects revealed the "outside history" that is English history. He asked, how does the history of a commodity illuminate the intimate and social experience of imperialism? I have placed this question at the center of this book but extended it to consider how tea exposes as well the outside that produces African, South and East Asian, and American history.[62]

This book is a study of a global commodity that foregrounds intimate yet public settings, individuals, institutions, and recurrent practices. It investigates key episodes that illuminate the underlying ideologies and cultural norms and political and economic thinking that shaped the behaviors of a transnational business. I especially zero in on times of collaboration and conflict between disparate groups for a number of reasons. First, these are moments when the unspoken becomes uttered, when implicit ideas about people, bodies, places, and economy become explicit. Second, a close-range analysis highlights how the actions and concerns of men and women who lived far from one another collectively produced global capitalism. Third, my method acknowledges the centrality of gender, race, and class in the construction of global capital flows and ideologies, or what I have labeled as cultural economies. Moving between micro- and macrolevels of analysis allows us to see the way in which these markers of difference manufactured the culture of global business.

This study is organized chronologically and thematically in three parts. Each chapter delineates broad developments in production, distribution, marketing, and consumption before turning to analyses of important episodes, such as the conquest of Assam, the history of temperance tea parties, and the racial underpinnings of food science and packaging. The first part of the book, "Anxious Relations," traces how Chinese tea was absorbed into British imperial culture and its economy between the seventeenth and nineteenth centuries. This was not a straightforward process, and it was always shaped by fears of foreign things entering the British nation and bodies. This part demonstrates how trade and colonialism, importing, retailing, and exporting defined and redefined nations and citizens. The second part, "Imperial Tastes," continues these themes but focuses on how the producers of the new imperial teas from India and Ceylon overcame a great deal of resistance to find and maintain markets in Britain and in colonial and foreign settings between the late nineteenth and mid-twentieth centuries. This part traces the emergence of a dedicated group of tea publicists and shows how they used politics and propaganda to make imperial tastes and markets. Rather than a political entity colored pink on a map, the empire they created was a material and cultural space defined by countless acts of production and consumption. The third part of the book, "Aftertastes," examines the impact of decolonization on this imperial industry and tea's consumer culture. As nations struggled to determine the place of tea, advertising, and foreign capital and corporations in their new polities, they redefined tea not as an imperial commodity but as a global industry critical to national development. At the same time, young consumers in many locations also began to eschew this imperial brew as they became addicted to new American and European tastes and consumer cultures. Young consumers traded one form of empire for another when they abandoned tea in favor of coffee and Coke. I end this book in the 1970s, when both India and Sri Lanka made concerted efforts to kick out foreign businesses, but even then they could not cast off the many inequalities and problems of the colonial era. As we will see, it is striking the degree to which today's food conglomerates originated in Victorian and even Georgian companies, but the intensive growth and globalization of the food and drink industry in the last quarter of the twentieth century is another story.

A Thirst for Empire: How Tea Shaped the Modern World thus charts the history of several interconnected transnational communities that were united by a powerful belief that tea was not just a plant or a beverage but a civilizing force that healed bodies, nations, and world problems. With a missionizing zeal, these communities argued that by spreading the habit of drinking tea they were ending social conflict, elevating the intellect, fueling the tired body, and calming strained and overexcited nerves. The Chinese and Japanese, Russians and Central Asians have viewed tea in this way for centuries, but as it became an article of global trade, tea's civilizing properties became one of most long-lived and dominant advertising appeals in history. There were many who disagreed with such ideas, but nevertheless they helped build, maintain, and eventually destroy a vast empire defined by numerous exchanges and long-distance relationships. This empire inevitably encountered resistance from rival empires, from small and large-scale insurgencies, from consumers, workers, and other producers. Like all empires, it exerted power. The empire of tea has shaped the modern environment, food and agricultural systems, diet and leisure habits, nations, and other polities.

PART I

Anxious Relations

1

"A CHINA DRINK APPROVED
BY ALL PHYSICIANS"

Setting the Early Modern Tea Table

I n 1667 Samuel Pepys thought it noteworthy to write in his diary that he had
returned home to find his "wife making of tea; a drink which Mr. Pelling,"
the apothecary, had explained, would be "good for her cold and defluxions."[1]
Seven years earlier, on September 25, 1660, Pepys recorded that he had first
tried the new "China drink" at the end of a busy day in his new job as the navy's
clerk of acts.[2] Pepys likely drank his tea in one of the new coffeehouses that
were opening in London, while his wife took her medicine at home. Both paid
a great deal for their tea. What propelled the couple to try this foreign substance
and to imagine that it could cure a cold or revive one's energy after a long day at
the office? I argue that these episodes mentioned in passing by the great diarist
illustrate how European consumers embraced a Chinese practice and began to
make it their own. Momentous and mundane, these two moments in the history
of consumption open up new ways of thinking about Great Britain's position
in the early modern world.

In 1660 few Britons had ever heard of tea, but over the course of the next
century economic and cultural exchanges that transpired in Asia, the Near East,
Europe, and the Americas produced Britain's craze for trading, growing, and
drinking tea. Pepys's tea represented a major shift in European material, medical,
commercial, and culinary cultures, but it was hardly the first foreign good to make
its way to the British Isles. For centuries, spices, salt, silk, silver, gold, and other
goods traveled extremely long distances, but, in the sixteenth and seventeenth
centuries, Europe's wealthy began adorning their bodies, satisfying their palates,
and decorating their homes with a wider variety of foreign commodities.[3] While
most people's material world was unquestionably local, long-distance trade
had altered diets and medical and consumer cultures around the world. Social
interactions within communities and between people from diverse backgrounds
transformed tastes and habits. Between the 1500s and 1700s, however, merchants,
missionaries, soldiers, and medical experts were the primary conduits of cultural
diffusion, even as they also denigrated the indigenous cultures they encountered

away from home.[4] In addition, a small group of educated elite eagerly studied books, treatises, maps, advertisements, and other texts that conveyed knowledge about foreign commodities.[5] Consumers and sellers altered the meanings of new substances; thus exchange was never straightforward but an amalgam of economic, cultural, political, and violent practices that occurred in intimate and public spaces in several continents at the same time.

Europeans did not always initiate or dominate these exchanges, but they certainly profited from them. Initially Europeans were importers who possessed little direct control over the production of eastern commodities, whether Javanese pepper, Indian cotton, Arabian coffee, or Chinese tea. Over time, however, they replicated and exported their own versions of these desired luxuries, providing stimulus for the shifting manufacturing and sales techniques that came to be associated with Europe's industrial and commercial revolutions.[6] Atlantic slavery made such transformations possible. Slave labor enabled the mass production of cotton, sugar, tobacco, and the like, but it also generated wealth that underpinned the refined culture of consumption that emerged in early modern Europe and the Americas.[7] Slavery was moreover a site of cultural exchange in which millions of Africans brought culinary and agricultural knowledge with them to the Americas.[8] Slavery was hence at the heart of European and American consumer society, often hidden in plain sight.

Tea was unique, however, in large part because the Chinese prevented the transfer of its seeds, plants, and knowledge to the West. Europeans were unable to transplant production to regions under their control until the early nineteenth century, and it took another half century to compete successfully with the Chinese in world markets. This did not preclude the growth of a highly profitable commerce, but it did mean that China influenced tea's global commerce and consumption until the twentieth century. Unlike previous studies, I argue that early modern Europeans imported what they believed were Chinese beliefs and practices along with their tea and tea ware. They adopted and adapted the Chinese conviction that drinking tea led to bodily health, psychic contentment, and a more poetic, productive, and sober self. Tea was not without its critics, but in these attacks we see a profound sense that ingestion, and by extension consumption, was a nearly magical act that had the power to remake the self. This is a basic ideology of consumer society. Tea was not the only commodity that was understood to possess such power, but tracing its history allows us to see the global forces that produced Europe's faith in the healing power of commodities and their circulation and consumption, and Great Britain's particular investment in the notion that tea could cure all manner of evils and discomforts.

This chapter builds on the work of a generation of scholars who have shown the diverse ways that Asian, African, and American cultural practices made their way to Europe and established new forms of power and authority, social identities, and tastes. Coffee, for example, became a hallmark of the Enlightenment project of "improvement" and sustained a new type of rational, "masculine" individual who adopted a cosmopolitan appreciation of and knowledge about other cultures.[9] Elite men and women also demonstrated their cosmopolitanism through the consumption and display of foreign art and objects, especially Chinese tableware, furniture, and ornamentation. The craze for Oriental-styled goods or chinoiserie was so pervasive that it left its mark on decorative arts, household and garden design, clothing, and culinary cultures in much of Europe, the Americas, and parts of the Middle East.[10] Chinaware became so associated with overseas trade and new forms of shopping and socializing that observers used this foreign fashion to criticize consumer society itself. This was particularly true in Britain where the taste for China and its things had reached unprecedented heights in the middle of the eighteenth century.[11] Consumers did not import Asia's culture wholesale, however. For one thing, there was no single "Chinese" style and Chinese manufacturers adjusted designs to cater to European tastes. Depending on context, chinoiserie could represent refinement, beauty, elite social status, and politeness or signify pretentiousness, licentiousness, and the feminizing effects of luxury and foreignness.[12] While scholars have recognized that European aesthetics reflected an appreciation and also a repulsion for Asian design, we have not sufficiently acknowledged that beyond its material and artistic practices, European tea cultures also had Chinese roots.

Everywhere communities spawned local modes of preparation and meanings, but there was a similar tea culture that stretched from China to the Americas in the early modern world. Men and women living in many lands endowed the China drink with extraordinary healing and civilizing properties. Long before food scientists discovered caffeine, early modern experts proposed that tea could cure many ailments, increase longevity, counter drunkenness, stimulate one's libido, and help one live a spiritual, intellectual, and productive life. Nearly everywhere tea was said to bring balance to the self and to society. Such philosophies originated in China and Japan and moved overland through Central Asia and via maritime trade to ports, cities, and hinterlands around the Indian and Atlantic oceans.

The faith in tea's temperate and civilizing nature crossed political borders, social divisions, and historical epochs. Although prevalent and enduring, tea cultures were not a mere force of habit. They were a product of a history. New attitudes toward foreign things and people compelled exploration and colonization and created novel understandings of health, the economy, the polity, and the household. Consumer and capitalist fantasies, desires, and anxieties wove together the modern world, but similar tastes did not lead to equality of conditions. Rather, tea's global culture produced new social hierarchies and inequities. We have to take seriously people's desire to feel less pain and anxiety and to find pleasure in acts of ingestion. We also have to recognize that such aspirations brought a great deal of pain to those who labored to produce modernity's palliatives.

EAST AND WEST

In Asia, the Near East, Europe, and North America, tea was a powerful medicine, a dangerous drug, a religious and artistic practice, a status symbol, an aspect of urban leisure, and a sign of respectability and virtue. State and military revenues derived from its use waged war and paid for colonial expansion. Cultivation of the plant transformed the environment and generated servitude. Tea was a tool of empire and a mode of protesting imperial power. And everywhere tea drinking was said to fuel the body, stimulate the mind, calm the soul, and civilize the consumer. Travelers' accounts, ship manifests, tax and probate records, government and court documents, art and literature, scientific and religious texts, and the voluminous archives of merchant trading companies have told us how tea spread from East to West, but we have less evidence about how attitudes and consumer practices moved with the commodity. The first half of this chapter begins to investigate this question by considering the multiple sites and people who translated Asian, Middle Eastern, and European practices and traditions. The second half then examines how Europeans came to profit from and think about the tea trade and tea drinking. Tea was highly desired in France, the Netherlands, and parts of central, southern, and eastern Europe, but in Britain and its North American colonies a tea culture developed that rivaled that of China and Japan. Yet, everywhere Western tea culture was an interpretation or translation of East Asian practices and ideologies.

Tea arrived in Europe later than coffee and chocolate, but its history parallels these other hot beverages.[13] Europeans encountered tea, much like New World foods and drinks, as an unintended consequence of attempts to best Arab merchants who had come to dominate the whole of the Eastern spice trade. By the fifteenth century, Arab states and traders had gained firm control of a limited number of trade routes and impeded direct contact between Europe and India and China. Alexandria reigned as the center of the spice trade, a situation that benefited Venetians and the Genoese but meant that most Europeans depended on Arab middlemen to satisfy their desire for spices and other "Eastern goods."[14] This problem prompted the age of exploration, but for some time Europeans were much more interested in spices than tea.

Medieval Europeans desired spices for their ability to cure, astonish, and impress. They sought spices for their intense flavors, colors, and aroma. Spices were also redolent of heaven and the Garden of Eden. They signified the divine and offered a momentary taste and scent of paradise. Their price and rarity also meant that these sacred condiments served as ideal status symbols. Pepper, ginger, cinnamon, and other spices were also regarded as powerful drugs. Generally thought to be hot and dry, spices balanced the dangers of wet and cold foods and treated illnesses such as melancholia. Some spices such as ginger, both "hot and moist," enhanced sexual desire.[15] Europeans often thought of the new beverages in a similar way, as hot, moist, and stimulating, but medical theory was divided on their effects.

It was in truth difficult to place chocolate, coffee, and tea into the reigning medical theories of the day. The theories of Galen, the Greek physician who developed the predominant European thinking about health and diet in ancient Rome, were experiencing a revival in early modern Europe, just as Europeans began to encounter new foods and drugs from Asia and the New World.[16] Throughout Europe, Galenic principles determined notions of health, personality, and diet. The body and mind were considered a cohesive whole, and foods and drugs balanced the four humors: blood, yellow bile, black bile, and phlegm. All ingested substances were designated as wet, hot, dry, or cold because like all matter they consisted of the four elements: water, fire, air, and earth. Foods could therefore be either healthy or harmful depending on how they were prepared, what they were consumed with, and the nature of the consumer. There was no hard and fast line between foods and drugs, since a healthy diet was one that matched the particular needs of the person. But while humoralism was significant, Europeans also adopted many Eastern notions about tea's impact on the body and society. This should not be surprising since it was in Japan, China, Persia, India, and Java that a handful of seventeenth-century Europeans first tasted tea.

Tea was indigenous to the monsoonal district of southeastern Asia and the Chinese grew and drank tea for thousands of years before Europeans. From its first appearance in Chinese myth tea grew into an article of intra-Asian trade and warfare, state building, religion, art, and connoisseurship.[17] Climate, soil, and rainfall determined the plant's territory, as did the migrations of animals, people, and religious and cultural practices. The Chinese first used tea as a medicinal herb and drink during the Western Han period (c. 206 BC–AD 9), and it found a place in the broader culture during the Tang era (618–907).[18] Initially people simply picked fresh leaves, dried them in the sun, and infused these in water. Without processing, only the leaves could not last and would have necessarily been consumed locally. During the Tang dynasty, however, cakes made of unfermented leaves that were steamed and mixed with a binding substance allowed tea to be stored and traded. Through the Yuan (1279–1368) and Ming dynasties (1368–1644) modern forms of processing emerged. Freshly picked leaves were pan-fried, rolled, and dried. This procedure prevented immediate oxidation and produced what is commonly known as green tea.[19]

Leaf teas slowly replaced cake and powdered varieties, and these would become the primary teas of commerce. Green tea was the earliest leaf tea to be used, but in the sixteenth century fermented black teas became popular. These were chiefly souchong, congou, and bohea, a bastardized European term for tea from the Wuyi Mountains. Black teas were fermented before roasting, whereas green teas were roasted immediately to prevent fermentation. After roasting all leaves were rolled by hand to extract their juice, and quality teas such as souchong could go through this process up to four times. Congou was made from thinner leaves and was roasted and rolled fewer times. The best teas were then dried over a slow-burning fire and the very finest were then put through a sieve to discard any burnt or coarse leaves. In the eighteenth century, oolong, a semi-fermented tea that originated in South Fujian, was a very profitable cash crop in Formosa and pekoe became especially popular in the export trade to Russia.[20]

Production methods varied with region, and this along with the growing conditions accounted for many of the differences in type and quality. By the eighteenth century tea was cultivated in at least twelve provinces, but Anhui and Fujian supplied the majority of the crop consumed in Europe.[21] Production was dispersed on smallholdings of between one and five acres employing perhaps only a few dozen workers each. Peasants processed the raw leaves before selling them on the open market or mortgaging them in advance to buyers who then resold the leaves to manufacturers for processing and packing.[22] Some of the larger merchants, however, employed up to three hundred workers and the whole operation was, according to one study, similar to a kind of assembly line production.[23]

Green, black, and the semi-fermented varieties all came from the same plant, though Europeans did not recognize this fact until the nineteenth century. There were dozens of types of green and black teas. Hyson, which included some of the finest green teas and was in great demand in eighteenth-century Europe, consisted of some thirteen qualities. Another green tea produced for export known commercially as singlo or twankay came from the T'un-chi or "Twankay" region of Anhui province. In contrast to the care taken with hyson, these teas were produced quickly and were picked and manufactured in a more haphazard manner and thus were considered an inferior product, selling in London for about half the price of superior hyson. By the end of the eighteenth century, bohea was the poorest-quality black tea, picked and processed quickly and on a mass scale. For example, one merchant could roast as many as 70,400 pounds at a time and pack it into chests of 170 pounds or more. Manufacturing methods improved after the Napoleonic wars, and by the 1820s bohea was the third largest selling tea in London.[24]

All of these teas passed through many hands and each exacted dues, fees, and taxes. Theoretically, the government granted a small number of Canton-based hong merchants the monopoly to trade with the West, but trade practices were quite fluid by the latter half of the eighteenth century. The British East India Company (EIC) was the main buyer and thus it influenced production standards. Yet Chinese producers also shaped the actions of company directors. For example, Chinese manufacturers pressured the company to purchase large amounts of hyson, though the prices varied in London, by threatening to uproot tea plants and thus create shortages. Cooperation and consultation between Chinese merchants and the EIC buyers were necessary to guarantee steady markets and prices.[25] A growing private trade and smuggling in China and Britain also meant that no one entity, let alone the EIC, was in total control and the "flow of influence was never one-way."[26] All of this is well known and well studied; what is less understood is how consumer practices and cultural ideologies flowed from China.

An elaborate consumer culture and trade in tea emerged during the Tang period when poetry, plays, histories, treatises, and other texts endowed tea with religious and cultural significance. Around 780 Lu Yu compiled his famous *Classic of Tea*, a book that described the herb's history, cultivation, and consumption.[27] The book proposed that tea stimulated the mental faculties, promoted a temperate lifestyle, and cured the diseased body. Poetry similarly described tea as aiding "the liveliness of poetic feelings" and provided a means to transcend the mortal world, though the drink had become a central aspect of feasting and sociability.[28] The intellectual Lu Wen wrote, tea "does not cause men to get drunk, but subtly awaken to pure thoughts."[29] In addition to producing a temperate body and soul and artistic turn of mind, this medicine also cured headaches, fought fatigue, countered intoxication, aided digestion, eliminated anxiety and toxins, and generally invigorated the mind and body.[30] Buddhism, Taoism, and medicine developed such beliefs and insisted that tea acted as a filter that absorbed impurities in the body.[31] Art, poetry, and religion spread these ideas and also implied that tea healed social conflict, thereby unifying China's diverse populace.

By the Southern Song era (1127–1279), observers began to describe tea as a mass commodity, and they used terms like "necessity" when noting how both rich and poor alike partook of the drink. In 1206, one writer opined, "Everyone, high and low, all drank tea, especially the farmers [and] tea shops at the market places were numerous."[32] Consumers did not drink the same tea in the same manner, of course. The rich could purchase expensive varieties with names such as "Dragon Buds of Ten Thousand Year Longevity," exquisitely wrapped in packages of silver, bronze, bamboo, and silk.[33] Pricing, preparation, and connoisseurship emphasized rare and expensive ingredients, and an early system of branding helped produce distinctions between teas and consumers, even as tea was becoming widely known throughout China. Mass consumption and distinction thus went hand in hand.

Celebrations of tea's marvelous purifying and medicinal powers, not to mention lovely wrapping, contained a more violent story of forced labor and state aggrandizement. When the Tang dynasty had collapsed and nomadic people invaded northern China, the Chinese state harnessed tea production and trade to shore up its borders and military strength. In 1074, the government established a state monopoly, known as the Tea and Horse Agency, which controlled trade and production in Sichuan in order to purchase Tibetan war horses. This agency forced farmers to sell at low prices and produced misery for the farmers and "coolies" who transported the tea across dangerous terrain. The monopoly failed to strengthen defenses, but it did enrich the state and create a new class of bureaucrats. Some merchants and entrepreneurs grew rich, while the masses became impoverished.[34] Aspects of this dynamic continued into the Ming dynasty (1368–1644), when soldiers were required to cultivate tea, peasants were whipped if they failed to sell to merchants, and smugglers who traded with nomads were executed.[35]

During this time consumption and production altered considerably. Both leaf and cake tea had typically been pounded into a powder and placed in a warm shallow bowl, to which hot water was added and the drink frothed with a bamboo whisk.[36] Zhu Yuanzhang, the first Ming emperor, demanded that whole leaf teas be used as tribute instead of the labor-intensive cake teas. Leaf teas brewed in teapots thus grew in popularity. This simplified preparation meant that tea could be served in roadside stalls. Enthusiasts still emphasized that skill, quality ingredients, and the type of vessels one used signified refinement and taste.[37] Connoisseurship reached new heights at this time when China's elite was especially concerned with the relationship between the material world and the social order.[38] Writers and artists continued to extol tea's virtues, and religious figures and medical experts promoted its use in Chinese culture and daily life. For example, the scholar and statesman Xu Guangqi authored *Nong Zheng Quan Shu* (*The Complete Book of Agriculture Administration* [1639]), which celebrated the "divine herb" for its ability to purify the spirit of one who drank it, to bring profits to one who "plants it," and to provide an "asset for the fiscal prosperity of the state."[39] Such ideals of balance, civility, and profitability spread the taste for the beverage and advanced the belief that tea was an asset to the state and a pleasure for the body. The unanswered question is: How did these ideas travel from the Celestial to the British Empire?

Many have argued that Buddhist monks were early adopters who spread the cultivation and use of the beverage to other Asian cultures, most notably to Japan.[40] While some believe the plant was indigenous to Japan, and we know it was in use there by the ninth century, it was not until the twelfth century that the Buddhist monk Myōan Eisia (1141–1215), who had studied in China, returned to develop and propagate Zen Buddhism and tea's place in that culture. "Tea is a transcendent drug for nourishing life and a miraculous technique for extending one's lifespan," began Myōan Eisia's text, *Kissa yōjōki* (roughly translated: *An Account of Drinking Tea to Preserve Life*).[41] Translating Chinese medical knowledge in Japan, the book provided precise guidelines about tea's medical uses.[42] Over the next several hundred years, the tea ceremony (*chanoyu*), with its special rules, utensils, tea houses, art, and poetry, developed into a complex cultural practice. *Chanoyu* animated the material world and endowed it with spiritual, social, and political significance. By the nineteenth century, tea consumption more broadly and *chanoyu* in particular came to be acknowledged by outsiders and Japanese alike as a defining element of Japanese culture and "national" traditions and heritage.[43] It was much earlier, however, that Europeans first learned of *chanoyu*.

The tea ceremony was developing just when European traders and missionaries first arrived in Japan. The Portuguese Jesuit missionary João Rodrigues arrived as a teen in the 1570s and may have met the famed tea master Sen Rikyū. Rodrigues left a long account of the tea ceremony and had a tea room built in the Jesuit residence at Nagasaki.[44] In 1610 Matteo Ricci, the famous Jesuit who spent many years in China, also published a very detailed account of Chinese and Japanese tea rituals.[45] It was, however, a long time before these texts made an impact on European culture. Nevertheless, in the 1660s, the Japanese government became eager to push teas upon Dutch traders, who seemed to have little sense of what to do with the commodity and were unhappy about being forced into the tea trade. Soon, however, they realized the commodity's potential and began to purchase Chinese teas in Batavia on the island of Java.[46]

Before maritime trade developed, however, the commodity moved west via the Eurasian silk (or tea) roads, a fact noted in several European travelers' accounts in the mid-sixteenth century.[47] The first known mention of tea in a European text appeared in the multivolume collection of travel accounts *Della Navigationi et Viaggi* (1550–59) (*Voyages and Travels*), translated and edited by the geographer and secretary to the Venetian senate, Giovanni Battista Ramusio.[48] This Venetian declared to have learned about an herb called *Chiai Catai* from a Persian merchant, Hajji Mohammed.[49] Venice had been a very important commercial center and contact zone between East and West and a place where Arab merchants and travelers introduced Asian drugs, foods, and foodways to Europeans. Tea and coffee were already staples in the Middle Eastern coffeehouses, and the Mongols may have brought tea to Iran as early as the thirteenth century.[50] Tea appears in a limited number of key texts, and the fact that the Persian word *chay* is similar to the Mandarin *cha* points to tea's early travels across Asia and the Near East.[51]

In the seventeenth century, a select few Europeans encountered the hot brew in Persia, the Indian Subcontinent, Southeast Asia, China, and Japan. Adam Olearius, the secretary to an embassy from the Duke of Holstein, witnessed tea at the Persian court in the 1630s. He described it as a common beverage that was often mixed with "Fennel, Anniseed, or Cloves, and Sugar."[52] Johan Albrecht de Mandelslo, who accompanied Olearius on this embassy, recalled that in Surat, the great trading port on the western coast of what is now in the Indian state of Gujarat, "at ordinary meetings every day, we took only *Thé*, which is commonly used all over the *Indies*, not only among those of the Country, but also among the *Dutch* and the *English*, who take it as a Drug that cleanses the stomach, and digests the superfluous humours by a temperate heat particular thereto."[53] Missionaries and merchants then adopted and transformed humoralism and local practices as they traveled between Europe, Central Asia, the South China Sea, the Indian Ocean, and the Arabian Peninsula.

Merchants traded and drank tea in the mercantile centers of Surat, Madras, Banten (also known as Bantam), and Batavia.[54] One of the fullest European accounts of this world comes from John Ovington, an Anglican chaplain in the employ of the EIC, who wrote about his life in Surat in the early 1690s. Ovington was born in Yorkshire to a family of yeoman farmers. He studied at Trinity College, Dublin, and Cambridge before being ordained and receiving a position as a chaplain on the *Benjamin*, one of the EIC's ships. Ovington lived in Surat for over two years, hoping to Christianize the indigenous and minister to company employees and other Europeans living in the city.[55] Just as the company was entering the tea trade, Ovington described how tea was a universal drink in Surat and was especially popular among the *bannians* or Hindu merchants, who "are not restrain'd from the liberal Draughts of Tea and Coffee, to revive their wasted Spirits, any part of the Day." He further noted, however, that "Tea likewise is a common Drink with all the Inhabitants of *India*, as well *Europeans* as Natives; and by the *Dutch* is used as such a standing Entertainment, that the tea-pot's seldom off the fire, or unimploy'd."[56] In addition to identifying consumers, Ovington described consumer practices, such as the fact that Indians, like Persians, drank their tea with sugar candy and conserved lemons. Such evidence raises the question of where Europeans might have learned to sweeten their tea. We need to be careful not to read too much into Ovington's work, since his "India" was limited to Surat and its surroundings. However, his account is very similar to those of Adam Olearius and Johan Albrecht de Mandelslo. It is possible that he borrowed from these earlier writers, and a history of Surat during this period makes all of these accounts plausible.

Surat was the commercial center of the Mughal Empire in the seventeenth century and one of the most important sites of cultural contact in the early modern world.[57] The EIC established a factory there between the 1620s and 1660s, where it made hefty profits from supplying coffee markets in western India and Persia.[58] Europeans did not control this trade, however. A small number of enormously wealthy men, such as Virji Vora, had business interests in Mokha, western Asia, Malaya, and Sumatra, and his agents purchased goods throughout the Subcontinent.[59] Surat's markets were filled with gold, silver, and textiles from the eastern coast of Africa and the states around the Red Sea, Arabian Peninsula, and Persian Gulf. Ovington was unrestrained in his excited account of "the most fam'd Emporium of the *Indian* Empire, where all Commodities are vendible," and arrive "not only from *Europe*, but from *China, Persia, Arabia*, and other remote parts of *India*. Ships unload abundance of all kinds of Goods, for the Ornament of the City, as well as inriching of the Port."[60] Stimulating his readers' appetites, Ovington described the velvets, taffetas, satins, silks and calicos, pearls, diamonds, rubies, sapphires, gold, and many types of coin that could be had in this city that was more populous and much richer than London at the time. Relative to these other goods, tea was unimportant but it was sold and consumed in this Indian Ocean port.[61] It is not clear whether tea drinking spread beyond the city, but Hindu, Persian, Arab, Jewish, Dutch, British, and other European merchants who lived and worked in Surat enjoyed both tea and coffee.[62] Surat went into decline, however, just as tea gained economic and cultural significance.[63] The Dutch East India Company, or Vereenigde Oost-Indische Compagnie (VOC), chartered in 1602, brought the first tea to Europe from Japan and China in 1610. In the 1630s, the VOC began to purchase tea in Batavia (Jakarta), but it was only a small part of a much more profitable commerce in silks, gold, and porcelain.[64] Batavia became the capital of the Dutch East Indies, and like Surat it was a major hub of commercial and cultural exchange.

During the next decades tea made its way to the European Continent, but only aristocrats, monarchs, and society's wealthiest consumers could afford this status symbol. In France, Louis XIV became devoted to the luxury and heightened its symbolism by brewing his tea in a golden teapot. In 1648 a Parisian physician called the drink "the impertinent novelty of the age."[65] Cardinal Mazarin took tea for his gout, while Racine was also a devotee. Tea then was both a desired object of conspicuous consumption and the cure for the diseases that came with lavish living. A pan-European elite and learned culture soon spread French notions of taste and refinement. But not everyone liked these tastes. The German duchess Élisabeth Charlotte d'Orléans nicely described her disgust in a letter. "Tea," she wrote, "makes me think of hay and dung," coffee of "soot and lupine-seed," and chocolate was "too sweet" and gave her a stomachache.[66] Tea, coffee, and chocolate were thus acquired tastes. Instead of paradise and Eastern pleasures, these drinks could evoke the taste of soot, animal fodder, and excrement. Despite many such reactions, Europeans slowly gained a great liking for the beverages and the profits from the trade in these drug-like substances.

In contrast to the French, Dutch, and Portuguese, the war-torn, politically divided, and relatively weak English nation was slow to adopt the drink. Small amounts arrived in the 1650s and some Britons encountered tea overseas, but it was not until the 1660s and especially after the Glorious Revolution of 1688–89 that a new tea culture began to take hold in the British Isles and parts of North America. Within the next several decades, tea came to comprise an important part of what one historian has recently called the "material Atlantic."[67] Asian ideas about the body, materiality, health, and spirituality traveled with the commodity throughout much of the Atlantic world.

CHANNEL CROSSINGS

John Ovington returned to England with great enthusiasm for tea. In a treatise on the beverage that he published in 1699, Ovington unreservedly endorsed the "Eastern" habit by illuminating how the drink's powerful healing and temperate properties would be good for the English. If the custom were "Universal here, as it is in the Eastern Countries," Ovington proposed, "we should quickly find that Men might be cheerful with Sobriety, and Witty without the Danger of losing their Senses." Tea drinkers could also expect a long and enjoyable life, "exempt from several painful and acute Diseases."[68] This panegyric was especially well timed since the EIC was just then establishing direct trade with China. Others had similarly championed tea as therapeutic, sobering, and cheerful, but Ovington had the audience of the court and was a trusted authority on the East. Such ideas were also quite appealing in a country that had lived through revolution, civil war, plague, and a fire that had nearly destroyed its capital city. When Ovington published his essay, however, he implied that "the Drinking of it [tea] has of late obtain'd here so universally, as to be affected both by the *Scholar* and the *Tradesman*, to become a private *Regale* at *Court*, and to be made use of in places of *Publick Entertainment*."[69] Ovington exaggerated tea's universality in 1699, but he was right that scholars, tradesmen, and aristocrats were drinking the beverage at court and within a new public sphere of coffeehouses, intellectual societies, and pleasure gardens.

With the restoration of the monarchy in 1660 and especially after the Glorious Revolution installed the Dutch stadtholder William and his Protestant queen Mary on the throne the tea habit grew; yet the social, economic, and political divisions of the day shaped popular accounts of tea's appearance and acceptance. One story that branches into several subplots claims that the émigré royalists living in Europe during the English Civil War of the 1640s and Interregnum in the 1650s were the first English tea drinkers.[70] Royalists did drink tea in the fashionable courts of Europe and some carried the cherished treasure home in their baggage after the Restoration in 1660.[71] At the same time, tea was used to solidify new political alliances in Britain. For example, the EIC supposedly gave two pounds of the rare substance to Charles II in 1660 in order to secure his good will.[72] Rather than interpret this as a form of bribery and influence, most historical accounts instead emphasize how Charles II's Portuguese-born queen, Catherine de Braganza, established the fashion in England after her marriage in 1662. In 1663 the royalist poet Edmund Waller was the first to establish this story when he penned "On Tea," a poem in honor of the queen's birthday that championed "the best of queens, and best of herbs."[73] The poem endorsed tea, monarchy, and the consumption of Eastern productions as feminine and domesticating forces.[74] It thereby transformed a Catholic and Portuguese queen and a Chinese drink into lauded symbols of Britishness.

Subsequent histories credit the queen's initiative, but it is just as likely that her Portuguese servants and other foreign chefs who came to England with her introduced the brew. The most cited source about the queen's role is Agnes Strickland's *Lives of the Queens of England*, which she wrote in the 1850s.[75] Offering little evidence for her claims, Strickland argued that the Portuguese princess used the temperate brew to tame the dissolute and rakish habits of the British courtiers. As Strickland explained, Catherine introduced tea to civilize the British "ladies as well as gentlemen" who "at all times of the day heated or stupefied their brains with ale and wine."[76] Strickland's portrait of Catherine looked uncannily like contemporary views of the sober Queen Victoria and followed the plot of many a Victorian temperance tract. Early modern Britons did regard tea as an antidote to alcohol, but Strickland's history highlighted women's moral, social, and cultural authority in a typically Victorian manner. This story also celebrated the British Empire for the marriage dramatically expanded Great Britain's overseas territories. Catherine's famous dowry included Tangiers, the right to free trade with Brazil and the East Indies, and the island of Bombay.[77] Bombay was not considered much of a prize at the time, but the impoverished Charles II was very pleased with the £500,000 that Catherine also brought to the marriage. Empire and feminine influence thus were already chapters in the history of tea in the seventeenth century and later generations frequently repeated such tales.

A very similar history, also written long after the fact, recalled how the Catholic Italian Duchess of York, Mary of Modena and future queen of England and Ireland as wife of James II, drank tea while exiled in The Hague and then introduced the refreshment at Holyrood Palace in Edinburgh in the 1680s.[78] The royal couple very likely drank tea in the Netherlands, but the drink certainly made its way to Scotland before this time.[79] Like the story of Catherine's tea table, this account emphasized how royals and aristocrats introduced the beverage and played down the cosmopolitan world of scholars, tradesmen, and missionaries who resided in Surat, London, Oxford, and other commercial and intellectual centers. In England, Oxford and London provided the social spaces for tea's appreciation.

From the 1650s on, tea quenched the thirst of many men (and a few women) who inhabited what theorist Jürgen Habermas described as a new public sphere, or arena that emerged between the court and the household in the early modern period.[80] While profits from overseas trade and investments aided the growth of the public sphere, the press, the coffeehouse, and intellectual societies enabled the expression of political critique and artistic production. The public sphere promoted witty sociability and celebrated an ideal of openness but also depended upon and produced new notions of gender, racial, and class differences.[81] While technically "open" to all who could afford a cup of coffee or a newspaper, the public sphere gave rise to social practices that produced and reinforced local and global hierarchies.[82]

Instead of a demarcated sphere, however, I prefer the phrase "public culture," a concept scholars have used to emphasize the movement of images, ideas, and people across geographic and social spaces. Early modern public culture can best be seen as a "zone of cultural debate," in which national, commercial, mass, and popular cultures interacted in "new and unexpected ways."[83] This public culture included the merchant company, retail shop, coffeehouse, shopping street, tea garden, tea shop, newspaper, advertisement, play, and broadside. It often divided men and women, but some arenas encouraged social mixing even as spaces were increasingly being segregated by gender. Yet, we must remember that the early modern household was not sealed off from worlds of work and economy and it too could be part of public culture.[84]

Seventeenth- and early eighteenth-century public culture characterized cosmopolitan knowledge and tastes as exemplifying polite or civilized society, but such ideals also inadvertently instigated acquisitiveness and imperialism. English elites, for example, consumed fashion and foods to demonstrate their knowledge of classical antiquity, the Italian Renaissance, and the wider world. They collected and displayed rare specimens, had a great appetite for "natural wonders and mechanical inventions," and appreciated an aesthetic of rarity.[85] In their societies and in urban coffeehouses they sampled coffee, tea, and chocolate, and discussed other new foreign things. The Royal Society, a very prominent social and scientific organization, sponsored innovations, the acceptance of domestic and foreign luxuries, and a global thirst for a Christian empire. As one scholar has written, Royal Society members had "capacious interests" and were keen cultural borrowers. They encouraged "new desires and identities for the well-to-do . . . [and provided] new artifacts that underpinned this identity."[86] Many of its members held that commerce and Christianity were central to Britain's civilizing mission.

The career of a founding member of the Royal Society, Thomas Povey, illustrates tea's place in the commercial and political culture of the early modern empire. Povey came from a very wealthy merchant family with interests in sugar plantations in Jamaica and Barbados, where Povey's two brothers served as colonial officials. Povey's cousin was lieutenant governor of Massachusetts and Lord Chief Justice of Ireland, and in 1647 Povey sat in Cromwell's Parliament. By the 1650s Povey was an expert on colonial affairs. In 1655 he was appointed to the council of trade, a new body he likely had recommended. He then invested in various colonial trading schemes and his wealth and power grew. After the Restoration, Povey managed to invent and then be appointed to the position of receiver-generalship for the rents and revenues in Africa and America. He also obtained other related appointments, including treasurer of Tangier and surveyor-general of its victualling department.[87] Samuel Pepys later gained this position, sharing the wealth from that job with Povey, who later proposed Pepys for membership in the Royal Society. Povey was thus an architect of the seventeenth-century empire with a vested interest in the sugar trade and colonial plantation crops. He promoted tea most likely to benefit the West Indian sugar industry. Povey's advocacy included his translation of a Chinese text that listed twenty health benefits, claiming tea purified heavy blood, vanquished heavy dreams, and cured giddiness and "paines in the heade." The text also claimed that tea prevented dropsy, dried moist humors, cleansed and purified a hot liver, helped the bladder and kidneys, eased pains of the "collick," and prevented consumption. Tea also sharpened memory and strengthened the will.[88] Other texts acknowledged similar powers. For example, in 1690, a broadside titled "The Virtues of Coffee, Chocolette, and Thee or Tea" advertised "an Herb that growth in *China* and *Japan*," which since it was "moderately Hot and binding . . . preserveth in perfect Health till very Old Age."[89]

John Chamberlayne, another tea enthusiast, was elected a fellow of the Royal Society in 1702. At the age of sixteen Chamberlayne translated Philippe Sylvestre Dufour's *The Manner of Making of Coffee, Tea, and Chocolate*. He had just matriculated from Trinity College, Oxford (where he likely drank tea, coffee, and chocolate), and he dedicated this book to Sir Thomas Clayton, who had served in the Restoration Parliament and was Regius Professor of Medicine and Warden of Merton College at Oxford. Dufour's treatise acknowledged tea's Asian origins but also stated that tea was a work of "Divine Providence." He then asserted that it was a Christian duty to "draw out of the bosom of the Earth many sorts of Medicines," which can "ease and cure of those that are infirm or crazy."[90] Dufour thereby placed the Chinese drink within a Western Christian framework. As a zealous Protestant and one of the founding members of the Society for the Promotion of Christian Knowledge, Chamberlayne no doubt agreed with Dufour's Christian vision of tea.

In his own text, *The Natural History of Coffee, Thee, Chocolate and Tobacco* (1682), Chamberlayne acknowledged tea's Asian provenance but also believed native Floridians and "the Inhabitants of Carolina prepare a Liquor out of the Leaves of an *American* Tree, which is very like *Thee* and equal to it in every respect."[91] Chamberlayne wanted to promote the value of the North American colonies, but his interest in tea also came from his fascination with Chinese culture. He believed that Chinese "Noblemen, Princes, and Persons of Quality" drank tea "at all hours of the Day," preparing it themselves at "every Palace, and House, being furnished with convenient Rooms, Furnaces, Vessels, Pots and Spoons for the purpose," which "they value at a higher rate than we do Diamonds, Gems, and Pearls." He adhered as well to Chinese medical theories that proposed that tea cured headaches, gout, and blocked urinary passages, prevented drunkenness, and was useful after a "Debauch." Finally, Chamberlayne related Asian recipes, noting how the Chinese used "one teaspoonful" of leaf tea to brew "one quart of boyl'd water." He further acknowledged that "a Chinese boy might drink such tea with a little sugar," and that the Tartars have been observed to "boyl their tea in Milk with a little Salt."[92] These translations of Eastern modes of consumption may well have been the origin of the British habit of drinking tea with sugar and milk. The common recipe that the British would later enshrine—one teaspoon for each tea drinker and an additional one for the pot—may also have been a Chinese preparation.

Men such as Povey and Chamberlayne discussed the China drink at meetings of the Royal Society and similar bodies and in the new coffeehouses that opened in Oxford and London in the 1650s.[93] Connected to the early stock exchange and insurance and banking industries, and the forerunners of elite men's clubs, the coffeehouses were masculine institutions that in their public nature posed a threat to established hierarchies and power.[94] Charles II even tried to suppress these resorts of "idle and disaffected persons," but a vocal backlash forced the king to rescind his edict banning the institutions.[95] Unable to suppress them, the government decided to tax the coffeehouses, and in 1658 it issued an excise duty of eight pence on every gallon of tea, chocolate, and sherbet sold in the coffeehouses. Since the duty was on brewed tea, excise men regularly visited coffeehouses to measure and inspect the tea before it was drunk.[96] The tea had to be made in large quantities and sit around until this was done, so it is probable that the taste of the brew left something to be desired.[97]

Coffeehouse proprietors often played up tea's Oriental origins and curative properties. For example, the earliest known newspaper advertisement for tea appeared in September 1658 in *Mercurius Politicus* and explained in a few short lines that one could buy a "China Drink" approved by "All Physicians" at the Sultaness Head.[98] Two years later, Thomas Garraway published a broadside declaring to have first sold tea in 1657 at his coffeehouse down the street from the Sultaness Head. The broadside informed readers that this drink from China and Japan was held in "high esteem" and had of late been much used by "Physicians and knowing men in France, Italy, Holland and other parts of Christendom." It also explained how tea could cure headaches, aid digestion, help one "overcometh superfluous Sleep," and "maketh the body active and lusty." This was especially true for "men of a corpulent Body" who are "great eaters of Flesh."[99] In other words, tea would make fat men feel energetic and "lusty."

Merchants gathered in coffeehouses to drink the new beverages, trade stocks, and invest in and buy these new commodities. Susanna Centlivre's comedy *A Bold Stroke for a Wife* (1717) set one act within Jonathon's Exchange Ally coffeehouse. With rapid-fire dialogue, serving lads interrupt the cries of stockjobbers selling South Sea stock and East India bonds with cries of "Fresh coffee gentlemen!" and "Bohea tea, Gentlemen?" In the play, as in the actual coffee shop, the gentlemen who invested in stocks, bonds, and hot beverages were a cosmopolitan crowd of English, Jewish, and Dutch merchants and traders who eagerly awaited news about the market prices and Spanish maneuvers in the European war.[100] This play satirized these stockjobbers, but it also advertised tea, coffee, and the coffeehouse.

Men and women also took their tea in the outdoors, especially in the pleasure or tea gardens that opened on the south side of the Thames. In 1728 Jonathan Tyers hired artists, designers, architects, and landscapers to construct Vauxhall Gardens, a resort for aristocrats and the newly prosperous middle classes.[101] Those who could afford the price of admission promenaded through sculptured gardens and gazed upon water features, illuminations, and painted transparencies, and spent too much money on the "notoriously overpriced refreshments."[102] These gardens opened on the Continent as well, but in England a weak court and church allowed for the flowering of these staged spaces for social performance.[103]

The American colonists founded their own coffeehouses and tea gardens, and took readily to the China drink. In Dutch-owned New Amsterdam, tea was drunk with sugar, saffron, or peach leaves. It was in Massachusetts as early as 1670, and William Penn brought tea into the Quaker colony shortly thereafter. When the English took over New Amsterdam in 1674, coffeehouses and tea gardens named after the London resorts became popular. Ladies and gentlemen listened to concerts, watched fireworks, enjoyed walking through well-tended shrubbery, and drank tea at any hour of the day.[104] Until the Revolution, the prosperous and governing classes served tea to signify their social position and sense of being part of a global British identity, even as they purchased Dutch tea.[105]

Throughout the Atlantic world in the late seventeenth and early eighteenth centuries, the educated and wealthy regarded tea as an Asian medicine and status symbol. Scientific treatises, broadsides, and advertisements promoted this Chinese herb that could heal, energize, strengthen, and balance European bodies. Court cultures, pleasure gardens, and coffeehouses reinforced tea's foreignness, while making health and foreign cultures fashionable and pleasurable. Whether in England or Pennsylvania, British tea cultures were an amalgam of European, Asian, Near Eastern, and diverse local customs and ideologies.

A MOST REVOLUTIONARY DRINK

A rarity in the seventeenth century, tea drinking greatly expanded with the growth of an Atlantic consumer culture in the eighteenth century.[106] There was something revolutionary about common folk and their social betters imbibing similar substances. For good or ill, the mass consumption of foreign and often smuggled goods disrupted traditional hierarchies, trade routes, businesses, and social customs. As a heavily taxed and smuggled item, tea made and then broke down the political and economic monopolies of the old regime. Eighteenth-century monopolies were never as absolute as critics implied, but social observers increasingly believed that the widespread consumption or abstention from consumption of tea, sugar, tobacco, and other similar goods could challenge the stranglehold of monopolistic power. Whether they liked it or not, people began to discuss consumption as revolutionary and universalizing. Thus, even before the American Revolution, tea was a most revolutionary drink.

The rivalry between European merchant companies, particularly between the Dutch and British, the growth of semilegal "private trade," smuggling, the expansion of shops, and new fiscal policies increased supplies and lowered prices, thus laying the foundation for the growth of mass consumption in parts of Europe and America.[107] In the 1750s the Dutch started buying directly in China rather than Batavia, decreasing costs and increasing the scale and value of the tea trade.[108] At this time, the VOC sold its goods at public auctions in several cities, but Amsterdam was the most significant tea mart in Holland.[109]

After buying at auctions, wholesalers and large retailers would then sell to small retailers, who typically offered customers samples of dry leaves to chew and evaluate, before preparing samples of hot tea, which was also tried before the buyer made a final purchase.[110] As sales grew, so too did government taxation. Owing to the heavy costs of war with Louis XIV's France, the Dutch issued a tax on "All the people" who sold "coffee, tea, chocolate, sorbet, mineral water, lemonade, or some other suchlike beverage which has been prepared with water, whey, or milk, by infusion of sage or other spices."[111] This tax did not distinguish between hot and cold drinks or foreign imports and homegrown brews, but it inadvertently encouraged the export of tea. Through legal and illegal channels, Dutch teas found continental and Atlantic markets, defying the Navigation Acts, which required goods from Africa and Asia to travel on British ships from Britain.[112] Ultimately, this profitable trade collapsed in the 1780s when the British government passed the Commutation Act of 1784, which we will discuss further. It is important to note, however, that the Act significantly brought down the cost of the EIC's teas, making it harder for the Dutch and other Europeans to compete.

The EIC had officially entered the tea business in a very small way in the 1660s, but at the time they had to pay almost double the rate of teas on sale in Dutch-controlled Batavia.[113] The British, however, benefited from changing Chinese policies. In 1685 China's emperor liberalized trade policies with Europe in order to attract silver to the empire. In 1713 direct trade opened between China and Britain, and within a few years a consistent annual trade grew in absolute terms and value.[114] The EIC first entered the tea trade as a "complement to sugar," which was suffering from a surplus in the English market in the late seventeenth century.[115] The EIC was also equally concerned about the Dutch and other European companies supplying tea to the home market.[116] This rivalry increased the scale of the trade, with tea eventually accounting for between 70 and 90 percent of all cargo outbound from Canton, something well recognized by a French merchant who commented that "it is tea which draws European vessels to China; the other articles that comprise their cargoes are only taken for the sake of variety."[117] While the English came to dominate this business, French, Flemish, Swedish, and other companies also satisfied European markets. Russia imported via overland routes, and all the while the Chinese still made up the greatest single market for tea.[118] During the eighteenth century, however, the EIC increasingly specialized in tea. From only a few hundred pounds in the 1690s, by 1757 the company imported twelve million pounds a year and stored another seventeen million in its London warehouses.[119]

Founded in 1600, the EIC was a political and commercial power that cast a long shadow over the history of Europe, the Americas, Asia, and Africa. As one scholar has eloquently explained, the EIC was a "form of early modern government" that was not so different from other forms of corporate power, including the monarchy itself.[120] Along with the Bank of England, the EIC became the driving force behind Britain's "fiscal-military" and imperial state.[121] It was also a highly flexible business that never possessed a true monopoly, despite the long-lasting and vociferous claims of its "free trade" critics.[122] It often suffered from financial difficulties and was frequently the subject of scandal and criticism, but it maintained a degree of political and financial power, and thus contributed to what has famously been described as "gentlemanly capitalism."[123] However, the company was not so "gentlemanly," nor was it entirely British.

The EIC raised capital from stock and bondholders, loans, profits from trade, and, after the 1760s, revenue collection in India. Stockholders, who earned a handsome dividend of between 7 and 10 percent, came from the elite and the "middling" classes, and remarkably by 1756 women owned almost a third of the stock accounts and over a quarter of all stock.[124] Female representation later declined but EIC stock remained popular with spinsters and widows. The shipping interest and members of Parliament were so heavily invested in the company that Horace Walpole even suggested in 1767 that one-third of the House of Commons was "dipped in this traffic."[125] Before the American War of Independence, Dutch stockholders also accounted for over a third of the total, but this dropped precipitously thereafter. A few investors also came from Antwerp, Brussels, Geneva, Leghorn, North America, and the West and East Indies. At frequent stockholders' meetings, women with enough stock could vote on policies and on the company's directors. Balloting was especially feverish in the 1760s and 1770s, when the company's finances were in a state of crisis. Noting this situation, Robert Walpole commented in 1769 that from the West End "people trudge to the other end of town to vote who shall govern empires at the other end of [the] world."[126] At these meetings male and female Britons quite literally debated the meaning of empire. As the EIC became a land-based and revenue-collecting empire, however, foreign and female representation declined and the company became increasingly a masculine and "British" entity.[127]

During the eighteenth century, tea paid for war, but war also paid for tea. Robert Clive's victory over the Nawab of Bengal in the Battle of Plassey in 1757 brought political power and tax revenues, both of which aided the company's sale of tea in Britain and its American colonies. The company's new power over Bengal encouraged its development and control of opium, which it used to pay for Chinese tea, thereby stemming the flow of the nation's silver reserves to China. Bengal's tax revenues also enabled the company to purchase more, lower-priced black teas.[128] More work is needed to understand the EIC's decision to trade in mass-market goods such as bohea, but China's and the Indian Subcontinent's

FIGURE I.I. *East India House*, by Thomas Malton the Younger, c. 1800. (Paul Mellon Collection, Yale Center for British Art, Yale University, New Haven, Connecticut/Wikimedia)

economies were utterly transformed by this decision. In the second half of the eighteenth century, such changes helped the British East India Company become an Asian power that influenced material and culinary histories virtually around the world.

Architecture demonstrated the company's global power. In London, massive warehouses and palatial headquarters indicated its intensifying role in the China trade and political influence in the Indian Subcontinent. With each new addition and refurbishment, the Leadenhall Street headquarters showcased an empire that was part fantasy and part reality. In the 1720s, a Palladian-style, four-story building replaced an original wooden structure, but over time, and even with a William Jones addition, the building was still inadequate. In the 1790s, the entire building was redeveloped and expanded, and a new frontage indicated an opulent Asian Empire (fig. 1.1). Designed by Richard Jupp and then Henry Holland, the new façade was 60 feet high and 190 feet in length. Its neoclassical style evoked the might of the Roman Empire, and the frieze that stood above six large ionic columns left no doubt as to the building's meaning and purpose. The decoration presented Asia laying its riches at the feet of George III clothed in Roman attire and shielded by Britannia and Liberty. Commerce, embodied by Mercury and attended by Navigation, stood to the left of the king. An Elephant,

FIGURE 1.2. *India House, the Sale Room.* Thomas Rowlandson and Augustus Charles Pugin, 1809. East Henry Payne, *The Microcosm of London in Miniature*, 1904. (Wikimedia)

the Ganges, and a camel represented the East, while a horse, the Thames, and a lion signified Britain.[129] The interior, too, projected dreams of wealth and empire. Tea, coffee, and other commodities were auctioned in a salesroom decorated to signify the military and imperial underpinnings of capitalism. Statues of Lord Clive, Lord Cornwallis, Sir Eyre Coote, and other major military figures literally watched over the feverish buying that took place in this lavish room (fig. 1.2). This building projected a sense of stability when, in fact, the EIC faced several severe crises. Until the 1780s, the Dutch were still major competitors, and a thriving "private" (or what was known as country) trade was also growing. Private trade, the trade allowed to ship's commanders and officers, made up 4–7 percent of the total tea market but could be much higher, as much as 75 percent of the total of expensive teas such as souchong.[130] And all the while, smuggling helped build the mass market for tea and, by extension, capitalism itself.[131] British fiscal policies made teas much more expensive in Britain than on the Continent, and this encouraged smuggling especially in lower-cost teas. Smuggling may have accounted for as much as two-thirds of annual imports and perhaps a higher rate in colonial America.[132]

Tea was smuggled in a variety of ways. Wealthy ladies and gentlemen hid teas and other treasured goods on their person or in their luggage when they returned home from continental sojourns. In a letter sent in 1772, for example, Lady Elizabeth Montague instructed her sister-in-law in Paris on the art of smuggling tea, taffeta, and other contraband goods. She bragged about her "good luck in smuggling" and hoped her relative would bring her two pounds of "that excellent tea," which she believed to be as "good as that which costs me sixteen shillings a pound in London." Montague was well versed in more traditional methods as well. In 1777 she asked another relative to get her "a couple of pounds of good smuggled tea at Margate."[133] Such tea typically came from European ships. The Swedes and the French were known for the best quality, while the Dutch acquired a reputation for awful tea.[134] After smaller ships transferred the tea ashore hawkers distributed the commodity with remarkable speed and efficiency. Some journeyed to London in the middle of the night and put the tea into warehouses in places like Stockwell, known as "Smugglers' den." Dealers would then buy between 1,000 and 2,000 pounds, which they could disperse throughout the British Isles within little more than a week. According to Uriah Creed, a smuggler from the famed Hawkhurst gang, "persons called duffers, who go on foot, and have Coats in which they can quilt a quarter of a hundred weight of tea, and bring it to London, in that manner, undiscovered; and these duffers supply the hawkers, who carry it about the town, and sell it to the customers."[135] Like many smugglers, Mr. Abraham Walter set up shop as a "Dealer in Tea." An expert in this clandestine business, Walter surmised that there were some 20,000 smugglers at work along the Sussex Coast in the 1740s "importing" more than 3,000,000 pounds annually.[136] By the 1770s, the system had grown to such an extent that hundreds of large, well-financed, and heavily armed vessels brought teas that ended up being sold by some of the most prestigious London, Edinburgh, and Glasgow retailers.[137] In addition to bringing vast quantities of relatively cheap tea to consumers, smuggling also brought tea and capital to "villagers far removed from the influence of the fashionable world."[138]

However, this was a bloody business. Smugglers sometimes murdered officials, and excise officers and other local law enforcement officials tried and hanged captured smugglers. In general, this trade also publicly flaunted landowners' authority and destabilized social hierarchies.[139] Further research is needed to uncover the meaning of "importing," selling, and drinking smuggled goods, but it is likely that consuming contraband may have brought its own pleasures. Rather than aping their social betters, lower-class consumers may have regarded the consumption of smuggled goods as a means to signify their independence from the Hanoverian state. This certainly was the case in the colonies, where smuggling could serve as a form of political protest. For example, one Philadelphia merchant argued that the colonists sought out Dutch and other smuggled supplies because the British imported so little Pennsylvanian wheat.[140]

By the 1780s, the "legal" trade felt so threatened by smuggling, however, that its members organized and effectively pushed the government to pass the famous Commutation Act of 1784, which reduced the duties to 12.5 percent ad valorem.[141] The government had previously attempted to reduce and reallocate the duties to combat smuggling, but the exigencies of imperial wars meant that the tea duties had reached nearly 110 percent of the sale price of tea just before the Commutation Act. This Act dramatically lowered the cost of EIC tea and put many smugglers out of business. It stabilized the EIC's finances and enabled a dramatic surge of consumption by lowering the price of legal teas by approximately 50 percent.[142] Between 1791 and 1823, per capita consumption increased by an estimated 44.7 percent.[143] Political economists saw the surge in consumption as demonstrating the law of supply and demand and proving that low taxes made markets. However, the duty soon rose again, and the Commutation Act introduced a new level of government regulation when it charged the excise commissioners with supervising the landing, storage, and sale of tea and required the licensing of tea dealers. The Act also obligated the EIC to maintain at least a year's supply in its warehouses, to hold four auctions a year, and to sell at a price that did not exceed the prime cost and the freight and charges of importation. It also required the company to sell to the highest bidder. The Act thus put the smugglers out of business and placed the tea trade more thoroughly in the hands of the British state. It also coincided with a rapid expansion in shops and shopping.

A RETAIL REVOLUTION

The growth and transformation of shops, which some historians have called a retail revolution, generated competition, lowered prices, and transformed the gender dynamics of buying and selling tea.[144] In the eighteenth century, standalone businesses developed as distinct from households and workshops. Retailing and wholesaling began to separate physically and ideologically, and specialty shops with fancy showrooms serving rich clientele also became a force in the marketplace. Small shopkeepers, many of whom were women, also entered the tea trade. But this was not a straightforward process.

Tea shops, that is, eateries serving light refreshment, did not appear until the second half of the nineteenth century, but the first specialty shops to sell tea in Britain were designed as elite female spaces. Apothecaries, grocers, and other types of shops sold tea, but bourgeois gender ideals made it difficult for wealthy women to feel comfortable within the coffeehouses where dry and brewed teas were primarily sold at this time. In what is an apocryphal tale, Thomas Twining claimed to have recognized this and created separate shopping venues for women. After he opened a coffeehouse in 1706, Twining maintained that he became aware that ladies would not enter his establishment, preferring to wait outside in their carriages while their footman went inside to shop. In 1717, the same year that the British East India Company began a consistent annual trade in tea with China, Twining purchased the house next door to his coffee shop and opened a retail tea shop for female shoppers. If we look at this story too quickly, we might conclude that an enterprising man invented a space for female consumers. However, Twining also acted as a wholesaler, selling to other coffee-house proprietors, milliners, innkeepers, apothecaries, and grocers. Heretofore, petty retailers could have acquired lower-quality cheap tea from smugglers, but expensive teas were sold in very large lots at the EIC auctions.[145] This system encouraged the growth of large, well-financed retailers. Petty dealers formed associations to purchase tea together, but Twining established another route for people of smaller means to become retailers, and tens of thousands of men and women chose to do so by the end of the century.

Twinings was also not the only firm to open tea shops at this time. Several women in fact founded notable firms in the early eighteenth century. We know from a court case in 1720, for example, that a Mrs. Horne had made a sub-stantial fortune selling tea and tea things at her "tea-shop" near the Bishop of London's House in Aldersgate Street.[146] In 1725 Mary Tewk (Tuke), a spinster from York, established a tea shop in Eastcheap and left the firm to her nephew in 1742. The company grew into a very successful financial business in the twentieth century.[147] Even Twinings owed much to female entrepreneurship. Mary Twining, the widow of Daniel, Thomas's grandson, managed the shop in the 1780s before leaving it to her two sons, Richard and John.[148] Mary carried the firm through an extremely competitive era, when, according to Richard, there were about thirty thousand "tea dealers" in the United Kingdom.[149] We do not know whether women managed their businesses differently, but we have to acknowledge their role in such important capitalist enterprises.

Chemists, booksellers, ironmongers, linen drapers, milliners, and even toyshop proprietors sold tea, but grocers specialized in this and other "exotic" or tropical goods.[150] According to *The London Tradesman*, a guide for young men considering a career in trade published in 1747, earthenware and grocers' shops dealt in "Tea, Sugar, Coffee, Chocolate, Raisins, Currents, Pruens [*sic*], Figs, Almonds, Soap, Starch, Blues of all sorts, &c. Some of them deal in Rums and Brandy, Oils, Pickles, and several other Articles fit for the Kitchen and the Tea-Table."[151] Such shopkeepers commonly used credit, loss leaders, advertising, and free samples to outdo their rivals.[152] Some initiated cash sales to lower costs. In one typical advertisement from the 1790s, T. Boot's Tea, Coffee and Chocolate Warehouse at no. 212 Piccadilly told the "Nobility, Gentry and others" that they might be supplied with "fine fresh Teas, Coffee and Chocolate, on the most reasonable terms for Ready Money Only."[153] Many retailers who dealt in countless other goods also served the beverage to their customers to stimulate desires, enhance the pleasurable and sociable ambiance in their shops, energize flagging customers, and introduce them to a new lucrative item.[154]

Retailing was different in the colonies where there were far fewer shops and regional variation was pronounced. In the Chesapeake, tobacco planters purchased supplies from London firms and sold these "stores" to their neighbors (hence the use of the term "store" instead of "shop" in America). After the middle years of the century, Scottish and English mercantile houses began to open chain stores along rivers and in the interiors of Maryland and Virginia.[155] One of the biggest firms, John Glassford and Company of Glasgow, opened shops in Fairfax County, Virginia, primarily selling to white male customers who purchased goods but also sold their crops for cash.[156]

Throughout the Atlantic world, however, retailers contributed to the growth of the mass consumption of tea, coffee, and other similar commodities.[157] Shop inventories, probate, and legal records suggest that, as one scholar put it, the "consumption hierarchy was not exactly the same as the social hierarchy."[158] Between 1700 and 1725 we know that many elite and middle-rank English households commonly drank tea, coffee, and chocolate. Yet, national patterns were not established, and region and occupation were as important as income and social status in shaping the rates of adoption and meanings surrounding these new beverages.[159] Geography and the nature of the local economy also often influenced consumer preferences. For example, those involved in the transport and the dealing trades were early adopters of the new beverages.[160] Hot drinks utensils first appeared in London inventories around 1700, and by 1725, 60 percent of London households owned such things.[161] However, Cumbria and Hampshire had virtually no material traces of a hot drink culture in these years.[162] Nearly 74 percent of Kentish households had tea and coffee equipment in the 1740s, while only 12 percent of Cornish households possessed such housewares.[163] We see similar patterns in Scotland, colonial America, Antwerp, and Amsterdam.[164]

In general, good harvests in the 1730s and 1740s lowered food costs, freeing up discretionary income for rural and urban residents in England.[165] But even as incomes fell later in the century, the consumption of tea and sugar continued to rise and tea began to gain on coffee. In Britain around 1700, coffee consumption was approximately ten times that of tea, but by the 1730s, the pattern was reversed and tea continued to outpace coffee for the remainder of the century. For a variety of reasons, the British tended to export coffee, particularly to German markets, and retain tea for domestic and colonial markets.[166] Europeans began to grow coffee in their colonies, and an integrated global coffee market was coming into being, but the British did not govern this trade.[167] The Dutch East

India Company first managed to break the Arab monopoly when they planted coffee on the island of Java. Coffee then moved to Surinam and the French islands of Réunion and Bourbon, and later to Martinique, Guadeloupe, and Saint-Domingue. The British planted coffee in Jamaica in 1728 and exported about a decade later, but sugar growers had better land and the imperial tariff system benefited sugar over coffee.[168] British coffee planters complained as well that the tax system favored tea and explained why, as a contemporary saw it, "our consumption of coffee decreases as that of tea increases."[169]

Relative price differentials created by fiscal policies privileged tea.[170] However, until the 1680s at least, the data are insufficient to be able to draw conclusions, especially since prices were highly volatile. It is also difficult to compare what a cup of either beverage would have cost because pound for pound dry coffee and tea do not make the same amount of liquid, and preparation of the brews varied. The best evidence does suggest, however, that the highly organized West Indian sugar lobby and the EIC used political pressure to create a cheap market for sweet tea at the expense of coffee, with the result being that the British Isles consumed more than 60 percent of all the tea shipped to Europe and sugar consumption was ten times higher than that of the rest of Europe.[171]

By midcentury prices were low enough for plebian consumers in many regions to become avid tea drinkers. In the 1750s, the Frenchwoman Madame du Boccage wrote that even the "poorest country girls drink tea" in the farmers' cottages near Oxford.[172] In 1759, a Delaware clergyman found that "tea, coffee, and chocolate . . . are so general as to be found in the most remote cabins, if not for daily use yet for visitors, mixed with muscovado or raw sugar."[173] In 1749 the Dutch settlers in Albany, New York, enjoyed tea for breakfast, though they continued to drink buttermilk at dinner.[174] In New Jersey some colonists made "an infusion" of hot water and white cedar chips, which they regarded as more wholesome than "foreign tea."[175] But sweet tea from China was the norm. An Iroquois woman who lived along the river Mohawk had drunk so much tea (and presumably sugar) that, according to one observer, she developed "a violent tooth-ache."[176] While there is more to learn about the meaning of tea in these diverse communities, European settlers and indigenous people were drinking as much if not more tea than metropolitan Britain.[177] The tea-drinking colonial population was not restricted to the Americas, however. In Asian colonial cities, European, mixed-race, and indigenous elite drank tea, though we do not know whether this was seen as a local, Asian, or European practice.[178]

By the end of the century, social observers repeatedly described how tea had nearly found its way to the bottom of British and colonial society. In his well-known analysis of the English poor in the 1790s, Sir Frederick Morton Eden explained, for example, that "any person who will give himself the trouble of stepping into the cottages of Middlesex and Surrey at Meal times, will find that, in poor families, tea is not only the usual beverage in the morning and evening, but is generally drunk in large quantities even at dinner."[179] The tea and coffee habit had spread quickly, but it is worth remembering that not everyone took part in this drinks revolution, and growth was not always sustained.

We have little evidence of mass consumption on the Indian Subcontinent for these years, and most Irish laborers, a good many Scottish and Welsh, and quite a few English workers did not incorporate tea into their diet until well into the nineteenth century, despite common perceptions.[180] In Scotland in the 1840s, the beverage was much more popular in Edinburgh and along the English border and was almost entirely unknown in the north and especially in the Highlands. Irish farm laborers typically drank milk at most meals. The Irish middle and upper classes, domestic servants, and Ulster weavers were tea drinkers in the eighteenth century but abandoned the habit as they faced economic distress in the nineteenth century.[181] In the 1880s, those living in the Kerry mountains lived on "potatoes and porridge; seldom eat bread, meat never; wine, beer, tea, coffee are to them unknown luxuries."[182] The vast expansion of cultivation in India and Ceylon at the end of the nineteenth century, however, would lower costs, and by the late nineteenth century most Irish families could afford to subsist on a steady diet of "bread and tea."[183]

Dietary changes thus did not occur in a sudden consumer revolution. The tea habit increased dramatically after the 1784 Commutation Act, but by the early 1800s, tax increases, growing impoverishment, mounting troubles with China, and perhaps even the cultural backlash against the brew meant that consumption in Britain stagnated. Between 1801 and 1810 British per capita consumption was at 1.41 pounds a year. It fell to 1.28 in the next decade and did not recover its earlier consumption rates until the 1840s.[184] Given the prevalence of smuggling, however, per capita statistics are estimates at best and obscure much regional diversity. Nevertheless, we can conclude that by the end of the eighteenth century tea was sold and consumed in urban and rural settings by a large segment of Britain's population throughout the empire. Efficient modes of production in China and competition between the merchant companies, and among private traders, smugglers, and retailers, lowered costs and brought tea to consumers across the British World. This phenomenon was lauded and denigrated, but it could not be ignored. Many moralists became concerned, arguing that working-class and female consumption of foreign things indicated a dreadful and irreversible corruption of the body politic. Men such as John Ovington championed tea's potential to eradicate disease, lengthen life, and produce happiness. Critics, however, contemplated the negative consequences of tea being drunk by every "Lady, Lord, and common Punk."[185]

"OUR LADIES HAVE A FOREIGN TASTE"

An escalating number of essays, books, and pamphlets laid out both the untold benefits and ills tea brought to Great Britain and its colonies. Medical men, religious figures, and merchants were unable to agree on whether tea was a godly substance or a slow poison. All assumed that tea had dramatic powers to heal or harm, but promoters and detractors relied upon different conceptions of the consumer and the consequences of importing and ingesting foreign goods. On both sides of the Atlantic, however, critics used gender and racial stereotypes to condemn the mass consumption of tea, proposing that this foreign substance enfeebled men, overexcited women, and demoralized nations. Tea, they charged, brewed dependency and effeminacy, a concern that Americans could never quite forget. At stake was the degree to which the consumption of a foreign commodity damaged or augmented one's ability to be an independent citizen and nation.

Concerns about tea stemmed from several developments: the scale of smuggling and adulteration may have tarnished the commodity's status as a moral good; the EIC's so-called legal trade also came into disrepute as political economists began to condemn monopolies as corrupting influences; and mercantilists worried about an excessive drain on the nation's wealth. New notions of racial and national differences increased anxieties about consuming foreign substances as well. Abolitionists raised doubts about the ethics of consuming sugar produced by slave labor, and new gender ideologies censured many forms of female authority, including dominance of the tea table. Finally, a growing distaste for the sort of cosmopolitan, aristocratic masculinity that had embraced foreign cultures also threatened tea's growing status. The wealthy nabobs who donned local garb and indulged in Eastern pleasures became increasingly suspect, for example, while the credit-worthy, family-oriented, Christian middle-class man became a new model of British masculinity.[186] Whereas Europeans had once appreciated Chinese knowledge and culture, in the eighteenth century such admiration faded.[187] These changes fed social anxieties and stoked anti-tea sentiment. Supporters would eventually detach the commodity from its Chinese origins, but not before decrying the growing use of the China drink.

In his lengthy *Dissertation Upon Tea* (1730), for example, Dr. Thomas Short, a Scottish physician resident in Sheffield, charged that John Ovington's expertise was not systematic, was based on travelers' observations of "*Eastern* Countries," and reflected the self-serving views of merchants trying to sell their "importations."[188] Short was something of an eccentric, known to have stuck "to the diet of his native land [Scotland]," but he was a recognized expert on beverages and published several books on milk, wine, mineral waters, and tea. Rather than trusting the French or the Chinese, he conducted his own experiments in his kitchen with "cups and saucers full of mixtures" of all sorts.[189] Short recognized that "this little crumbled Leaf" had returned such a revenue to "the Crown of *England*" that "the general Taxes are so much lessened to the Poor." He also acknowledged tea's widespread use at "assemblies" and coffeehouses, which advanced "business, Conversation and Intelligence" and prevented "Expense and Debauchery."[190] Tea was thus popular, profitable, and beneficial, but he cautioned that one should not expect "that any Medicine or Diet should always have the same Effect on different Ages, Sexes, Constitutions, &c."[191] He then delineated why and for whom tea was helpful or harmful, and how it could safely be used. He introduced gender into the conversation when he suggested that because they possessed "more lax and delicate Fibre, [and] they are more liable to a *Plethora*, or Fulness of Juices," the fair sex should consume only modest quantities. Anyone, however, who possessed "very sensible and elastic Nerves" or who was "seized with *Tremor*, or shaking" should steer clear of the brew.[192] Short advocated moderation, he resisted Chinese knowledge, and he introduced the idea that male and female bodies would react differently to the same substance.

Others went much further in their denunciations and raised the specter of gender inversion, social upheaval, and racial degeneration. They charged that tea, like coffee and the coffeehouse, was a foreign import that could turn British men into impotent feminine creatures. In 1733 John Waldron famously satirized "Female *Ovington*" in his burlesque, *A Satyr against Tea*. Waldron portrayed all tea consumers as luxury loving and thoughtless females impoverishing the nation:

> Our Ladies have a foreign Taste,
> They glory in excessive Waste,
> And take great Pride, and vast Delight,
> To send their Money out of Sight,
> T'enrich all climes, beside their own.

After many more verses making fun of Ovington's health claims, the author concludes, "Tea cure the Megrim of the Head? It rather helps to — p—ss the Bed."[193] Far from curing headaches and improving lustiness, tea turned a man into a women and a bed-wetter. Gendered and sexualized critiques were stock features of a wider debate on the consumption of luxuries in Europe and not a reflection of the sociology of the tea market per se. That being said, critics suggested that tea was so powerful that it threatened one's masculinity, independence, and health.

Denigrators also opined that tea-drinking ladies allowed the masculine British nation to be penetrated, emasculated, and even cuckolded. Jonas Hanway's nearly four-hundred-page diatribe against tea famously developed this argument. Hanway was a merchant who had spent many years of his young life in Lisbon and

St. Petersburg before returning to London in 1750. He conducted business in John's Coffee House, just east of the Royal Exchange. He thus lived in the same world that many tea advocates inhabited. During the second half of his life, however, he became a noted philanthropist and thoroughly rejected the consumption of foreignness. In 1756, the same year that he published his lengthy condemnation of tea, Hanway donated a significant sum to the London Foundling Hospital and was elected one of its governors. Thereafter he worked to improve the conditions of the poor, especially prostitutes and sailors, and developed what one scholar has described as an ideology of "Christian Mercantilism."[194] Hanway's *Essay on Tea* reiterated the basic mercantilist belief that the widespread importation and consumption of foreign goods weakened the domestic economy of the nation.

Though he addressed female readers and acknowledged the power of the elite female consumer, Hanway relied on gendered and racialized arguments when, for example, he described the Chinese as an "effeminate people" who were incapable of performing "any manly labor."[195] Hanway was especially concerned about how the Chinese drink could weaken Britain's "PLEBIAN order."[196] He believed that the mass consumption of tea by chambermaids and others had encouraged the Chinese to produce an adulterated and unhealthy product and placed Britain in a weakened position. Tea was "an idle custom; an absurd expense; tending to create fantastic desires, and bad habits, which must render us less happy, or more miserable, than we should otherwise be."[197] Tea shortened one's life and rendered the poor unfit for labor at home or abroad. "What an ARMY has GIN and TEA destroyed!" he exclaimed.[198] "Were they the sons of TEA-SIPPERS, who won the fields of CRESSY and AGINCOURT," Hanway asked, before asserting that this "EPIDEMICAL disease" was irrevocably weakening average Britons, even the nation's beggars.[199] Tea simply created a "SICKNESS in the body politic."[200] Writing a year after Britain had entered what would become known as the Seven Years' War, such concerns were very real. Tea may not have debilitated soldiers, but the war set off a chain of events that would weaken the British Empire. It so disrupted imperial finances that the British state felt it had to prop up the East India Company. The way it did this ignited the American Revolution.

In both Britain and North America high taxes and mercantilist policies led to consumer and other protests, but in the colonies these actions stoked political tensions that had been simmering for some time. The so-called Boston Tea Party has been enshrined in American political culture as a symbol of a taxpayer revolt and individual resistance to a monopolistic government. In part, colonial taxpayers did protest Lord Grenville's Stamp Act passed in 1765, which among other things imposed a tax on tea. The Act was repealed a year later, but not the tax on tea, which was reaffirmed with the passage of the Revenue Act in 1767.

As in the British Isles, taxation led to a brisk smuggling trade in which colonists purchased tea from the Dutch rather than from the EIC. Worried that they were losing the colonial market and concerned with selling some seventeen million pounds of surplus tea, the company appealed to Lord North to grant them a monopoly to export directly to the Americas, something they had not previously done. The Tea Act of 1773 accomplished this, lowering the cost of tea by eliminating the English and American middlemen and reducing the actual tax to three pennies a pound. However, as is quite well known, American merchants and their allies exhorted fellow colonists to abstain from importing, buying, and drinking tea, with the latter injunction focusing on individual responsibility and everyday consumer choices.[201] American tea traders and smugglers resented the way colonial policy had granted the EIC a new monopoly at their expense, and they launched what later came to be known as Tea Parties in Boston, Greenwich, Charleston, and Philadelphia.

Consumer boycotts and organized protests such as the Boston Tea Party generated a new view of the average consumer as a political subject. American political culture recognized the public significance of consumers and called upon them to reject their status as colonial subjects. Americans attended meetings and wrote articles and pamphlets, which labeled tea as "*enslaving* and *poisoning* ALL the AMERICANS."[202] The protest surrounding tea in the 1770s repeatedly admitted that the tea habit was no "mere Luxury." One critic asserted on the eve of the Revolution that the drink was so cheap and plentiful that it had "become a necessary and common diet for the *poor*."[203] Others emphasized that drinking tea was a political sin. "A Woman" made this point in a Massachusetts journal when she wrote, "The use of tea is considered not as a *private* but a *public* evil."[204] Men and women celebrated their new American identities by holding tea bonfires or exhorting the colonists to give up this "slow poison which not only destroys our constitutions, but endangers our liberty, and drains our country of so many thousand pounds, for teas of our own *American Plants*."[205] Some drank "herbal teas" of sage, rosemary, and Labrador tea, which was made from the leaves of red root. Others took to coffee. In an apocryphal story of the birth of the nation as coffee drinkers, John Adams wrote to Abigail in 1774 that after making a long ride through the interior of Massachusetts, he asked the lady of the house where he was resting whether "it was lawful for a weary Traveller to refresh himself with a Dish of Tea provided it has been honestly smuggled, or paid no Duties?" To which the lady shockingly responded, "No Sir . . . we have renounced all Tea in this Place. I can't make Tea, but I'le make you Coffee." Whereupon Adams confessed to Abigail that he had thereafter drunk coffee every afternoon and that he had "borne it very well."[206] This compelling narrative enshrined the political power of the individual consumer and the housewife.

Adams learned to be a citizen from a woman far removed from the center of political or economic power. He claimed that revolutionary politics were also pleasurable since he enjoyed his new coffee habit.

The boycotts and other consumer protests leading up to the Revolution condemned tea but did not denounce consumption per se. In truth this movement was premised on faith in the power of the mass market. Many Americans would later refer to the Revolution as the moment the country lost its taste for tea. This was not the case. A year after the signing of the Treaty of Paris in 1783, the first American ship, *The Empress of China*, set sail from New York bound for China. It returned in May 1785 with seven hundred chests of bohea, one hundred chests of hyson, and a large amount of porcelain.[207] The voyage's success set off a veritable scramble for China, and hundreds of American ships made their way to Canton in the next thirty years. Merchants like William Morris, John Jacob Astor, and Stephen Girard became enormously wealthy China traders.[208] In the late nineteenth century and throughout the early twentieth century, British tea planters remembered this era when American consumers and merchants were passionate about tea, and they longed to recapture this transatlantic culture.

Jonas Hanway and colonial revolutionaries understood that intimate acts could have widespread public, political consequences. Critics stimulated fears about imports and trade imbalances, and argued that the desire to take in without being able to export created dependency, weakened the state, and was emasculating. North Americans called tea a degrading foreign substance in the hands of the monopolistic EIC. As we will see, many in Britain and the empire would similarly denounce the company, but they would take the opposite position on tea. Hanway and the American Revolutionaries relied upon different notions of tea's foreignness. Hanway worried about an Asian substance; Americans feared a nefarious British product. Instead of desiring a sobering and healthful Chinese herb, eighteenth-century critics denounced an enfeebling foreign temptation.

This chapter opened with Samuel and Mrs. Pepys and Mr. Pelling because they represent the type of characters who transformed this foreign exotic substance into a mass commodity and daily habit in Europe and the British Isles in the seventeenth and eighteenth centuries. European merchants, missionaries, and aristocrats first encountered the drink in China, Japan, the Indian Subcontinent, and the Near East. They saw this Chinese plant as a powerful medicine, an aristocratic fashion, an intellectual curiosity, and an urban pleasure. The longing for tea inspired Europe's and especially Britain's thirst for new tastes, global trade, empire, and conquest. This thirst reshaped local cultures and environments, but it began with the belief that ingesting foreign substances could make Europeans healthier, stronger, and more civilized. With time, however, the British in the metropole and the colonies began to disavow tea's foreign nature. The tension between attraction and repulsion characterized attitudes toward the beverage until well into the nineteenth century.

A circular process developed in which global trade altered consumer practices and then desires and wants became a driving force in the world economy. Retailing, consumption, and taste increasingly linked Europe with China and other faraway regions, something especially clear if we examine what a noted historian has called a "consumption bundle," or group of commodities that were purchased and consumed together.[209] As we will look at more closely in the next chapter, tea drinking involved consuming multiple items including sugar, milk, porcelain, furniture, and a host of other commodities, as well as time and space. The demand for tea encouraged a corresponding market for British manufacturing in Asia and helped stimulate British industrialization. But given the growing critique of cosmopolitanism in Britain and its empire, these desires had to be tamed, domesticated, and transformed into safe, healthy, and moral wants. Middle- and working-class consumers accomplished this and invented a new temperate culture of consumption surrounding tea, sugar, wheat, and cotton in the early nineteenth century.

2

THE TEMPERANCE TEA PARTY

Making a Sober Consumer Culture

in the Nineteenth Century

In the decades following the American and French revolutions, war, economic dislocation, industrialization, and the many radical and conservative ideologies that circulated throughout and beyond the Atlantic world transformed the nature and meaning of the consumer and mass commodities such as tea. In addition to these changes, in Britain the growth of class and mass cultures, political reform, evangelicalism, and new family and gender ideals also altered the nature of free time. For the middle classes the home became idealized as a space that banished work, while the hidden labor of an army of domestic servants upheld the fiction of the "leisured" lady.[1] For both the working and middle classes, however, time off work became more organized, commercialized, and understood as leisure.[2] Tea adapted to this new world of leisure, yet its history was profoundly shaped by political debate, religious passions, working- and middle-class aspirations, and dramatic alterations in the location and nature of the workplace. Evangelical Christians and their allies in a growing temperance movement championed tea as a sacred good. Political economists argued that it was among a handful of key commodities that were essential to controlled economic growth and peaceful social interaction. Together, these intellectual currents and social movements secured tea's reputation as the most moral and useful of commodities. In early industrial Britain especially drinking tea came to be seen as a rational recreation that transformed lower-class individuals into predictable consumers. In diverse and often contradictory ways, tea became a source and symbol of a moral, liberal empire and productive nation.

In the eighteenth century tea did not inevitably evoke national passions, except perhaps in North America, where rejecting this symbol of British imperialism became critical to the making of new American identities. As we saw, some Britons adored their tea but others rejected this taxed poison that increased Britain's dependence on China. Yet despite such concerns, during the first half of the nineteenth century, a growing number of Britons embraced what they saw as this temperate, civilizing, and healthy "British" brew. Liberal merchants and cotton industrialists in the north of England and in Scotland fostered this vision of tea as they attacked the East India Company's monopoly of the China trade, yearned for Chinese markets, and desired a sober and productive workforce. Lower-middle-class artisans and shopkeepers also presumed that tea drinkers would spend their money wisely rather than on wasteful pleasures. Political radicals, socialists, and feminists saw tea and sobriety as a route to citizenship and gender equality in the political sphere and at home. Tories reasserted social hierarchies and evangelicals made good Christians at the tea table. However diverse, these communities agreed that the trade in and consumption of tea underwrote moral and political stability.

Yet this ostensibly moral commodity was also a tool of empire. British, Chinese, Dutch, American, and indigenous elites exploited workers and conquered new lands for tea. To be sure, cotton was the commodity of the day. Slave labor in the Americas, industrialization, and global merchant networks shifted the concentration of profits to Britain and other industrializing regions.[3] However, tea, cotton, and sugar developed a shared history. Anthropologist Sidney Mintz highlighted this when he showed how the mass consumption of tea flavored with slave-produced sugar helped fuel Great Britain's Industrial Revolution.[4] He maintained that British workers found in a cup of sweet tea a cheap and convenient fuel necessary for a long shift in the factory. Sugar and bread, Mintz proposed, constituted the industrial meal that quickly and efficiently fed a machine-like industrial body.[5] I argue here that these commodities are also connected in ways that Mintz had not perceived and the notion that tea and sugar was good for workers was not always readily understood by either workers or their employers. Indeed, as we will see in this book, the idea that tea was the ideal workers' drink was manufactured in many of the same ways that raw cotton was transformed into a marketable good. The concept that sugared tea aided workers' productivity was first asserted in industrializing Great Britain, but it became one of the most notable and recurrent themes in tea's history. In early nineteenth-century Britain, tea was not always cheap or easy to prepare and it was not self-evident that it provided more energy than beer and other foods that workers consumed. However, temperance advocates, free traders, and evangelicals developed the idea that tea made good workers, reliable consumers, stable societies, and healthy economies. These communities steadfastly maintained that sober forms of ingestion and socializing made the frivolous thrifty, the indolent productive, and the rebellious compliant.

As we will see in this and the next two chapters, the making of the British industrial working class, the creation of plantation agriculture and indentured labor systems in South and Southeast Asia, and new modes of buying, selling, and drinking tea worked together to produce a new global economy. To really understand this history, we have to look at how and why tea came to be consumed in industrial Britain and who specifically promoted its uses. By using this focused lens, we can see how similar beliefs and communities built Britain's imperial and industrial economies and created new moralities associated with importing and exporting commodities, tastes, and consumer practices. This chapter interrogates how particular Protestant ideals of food and the body, working-class notions of community as socially and spiritually elevating, and a liberal faith in the civilizing power of commerce came together to create tea's mass market in Britain. These forces met in the Victorian temperance movement. Temperance created a cross-class, mixed-gender public culture in which workers came to see themselves as consumers and businessmen learned to appreciate working-class markets. The workers and owners, merchants and industrialists, and men and women who joined the movement endorsed and ultimately sold tea as a Christian and liberal commodity that could bring an end to the many crises that plagued this era of rapid urbanization and social and political change. All of these ideas gathered at the temperance tea table and transformed an industrial working class into a mass market.

"THERE IS NO USEFUL STRENGTH IN IT": THE MORAL AND POLITICAL ECONOMIES OF TEA

In the early nineteenth century, tea's presence in so many shops and larders and its centrality to foreign trade and government finances meant that it garnered a great deal of public attention and various individuals weighed in on its place in British society, political economy, and households. Attitudes did not fall into clear groupings and some radicals, liberals, and conservatives still insisted that tea was a wasteful commodity that consumed time and money without providing true energy. Many even went so far as to argue that tea was an intoxicant and no different than other nefarious substances that depleted working-class resources and bodies. Others saw tea as simply bad for the working classes, a sign of their political and social oppression.

One problem, which had also so upset the American colonists, was taxation. During and after the wars with France, tea, coffee, and alcohol were all heavily taxed items and some radicals urged abstention from buying, selling, and drinking all of these commodities.[6] The Bath Union Society for Parliamentary Reform thus "earnestly recommended" that their members not spend "Money at public houses, because half of the said Money goes to Taxes, to feed the Maggots of Corruption."[7] Glasgow reformers abstained from whiskey, ale, tobacco, and tea. A Scottish radical association even produced a "sinecure teapot . . . with the gudwife's compliments to be smashed by the leader." Women activists carried "inverted gill stoups (whiskey glasses) and teapots at demonstrations along with placards proclaiming 'No luxuries.'"[8]

Others used their pen to develop a thorough critique of such wasteful "luxuries." In the 1820s the radical journalist William Cobbett condemned the working-class use of tea in his household guide *Cottage Economy* (1822). Making tea wasted women's labor and men's time, Cobbett opined. He demonstrated this point by describing how brewing tea involved numerous repetitive acts that turned the rural housewife into a domestic slave. It also transformed men into idlers, who wasted hours "hanging about waiting for the tea." Tea was also expensive. The price might be low in the shop but its cost was high if one calculated the time, space, and price of the whole cluster of commodities needed to support the tea habit, including milk, sugar, fuel, and "tea-tackle." Cobbett also denied that tea provided energy. Rather, the drink was "a destroyer of health, an enfeebler of the frame, an engenderer of effeminacy and laziness, a debaucher of youth and a maker of misery for old age." Furthermore, he insisted, "there *is* no useful strength in it—it *does not* contain anything nutritious—and, besides being *good* for nothing, it has *badness* in it . . . it communicates *no* strength to the body," and thus "it does not in any degree assist in affording what labour demands."[9] Tea was thus unhealthy, unproductive, effeminizing, and unsuited to the lifestyle of the farm laborer. Relying on an imagined past that privileged local goods, self-sufficiency, and low taxes, Cobbett's anti-tea tirade was in part a means to gain support from estate owners who produced grain used to brew beer.[10] Yet as a perceptive witness of plebian domestic labor in the agrarian areas of southern England, Cobbett perceived just how difficult and expensive it would have been for working-class Britons to make tea in the 1820s.

Some evangelicals were in total agreement with Cobbett. Esther Copley, the daughter of a Huguenot silk manufacturer and wife of a Baptist minister, offered her opinion in *Cottage Comforts* (1825), a book that also sought to instruct the "labouring classes" on how "to provide themselves with decent habitation, wholesome food, and suitable raiment."[11] Copley plagiarized more than Cobbett's title. She shared many of the journalist's worries, but she was really of two minds about tea. Though she recommended "a good copper tea-kettle" as the most durable type for the working-class larder, she nevertheless insisted that "tea *is* a luxury and the less of it there is used in a cottager's family, the better it will be for their pockets, and certainly not worse for their health." She also bemoaned the decline of the older breakfast of bread and cheese, beer and porridge. Like Cobbett, Copley longed for a time of rural and domestic self-sufficiency, represented by home-brewed beer and warm "infusions of mint, roasted grain," and other "British herbs," which were "just as good and pleasant as the foreign tea."[12] Cobbett and Copley were both concerned with farm laborers' shifting diets in commercializing southern

England, formerly prosperous communities known to enjoy prodigious amounts of beef and beer.[13] They also defended local produce rather than foreign imports and thus developed new ideals of locality and nation—which in this case did not include tea, a symbol and cause of national decay.

A number of prominent liberals also bemoaned the new working-class diet of bread and sugar, tea and coffee. William Rathbone Greg, for example, wrote that poor quality, weak tea was "fatal to the constitution of all working men" and but a temporary means to relieve "internal languor and depression." Even worse, it often "calls for another and stronger stimulus . . . the work people who have been long habituated to the use of tea as a frequent meal, are at length reduced to mix a large proportion of spirits in every cup they take. This pernicious practice prevails to an inconceivable extent among our manufacturing population, at every age, and in both sexes."[14] A number of critics of the factory system agreed with such views. Dr. James Phillips Kay-Shuttleworth, Peter Gaskell, and radical socialist Friedrich Engels all insisted that weak tea mixed with spirits and other stimulants signified poverty rather than prosperity.[15] Dr. William Alcott, a temperance enthusiast, similarly called tea a "narcotic" that provided only a "fictitious strength." As he put it: "The female who restores her strength by tea and the laboring man by a glass of spirits, and the Turk by his pill of opium are in precisely the same condition; so far, we mean, as the matter of stimulation is concerned."[16] Another warned, "*Tea-drinking* visits open the floodgates of various temptations."[17] Tea was not alcohol's antidote but a gateway drug that depleted incomes and bodies. All of these writers associated tea and alcohol with the decline of the working classes. So too did sympathetic historians such as E. P. Thompson, who famously quipped that the workingman's "share in the 'benefits of economic progress' consisted of more potatoes, a few articles of cotton clothing for his family, soap and candles, some tea and sugar, and a great many articles in the *Economic History Review*."[18] Tea, Thompson insisted, did not make up for the long and tedious hours of factory life, the loss of traditional forms of leisure, and intense political and social repression.

However many suspected tea's worth, the idea that this drink was healthy and temperate and a cure for alcoholism and other dangerous pleasures won this fight because tea acquired powerful and dedicated champions from across the political, religious, and social spectrum. Many evangelical churches developed what could be described as an addiction to the China drink. The founder of Methodism, John Wesley, personally renounced the brew in the 1740s but by 1761 he had commissioned the famous potter to the world Josiah Wedgwood to make him a one-gallon teapot. Other Methodists also became avid tea drinkers.[19] The well-known evangelical poet William Cowper immortalized the temperate vision of tea in his poem *The Task* (1785) when he penned the most famous paean to tea, which originally was written as "cups, That cheer but not inebriate."[20] Countless versions of Cowper's line became shorthand for evangelical ideas about the brew, the home, and the power of consuming moral goods. In the empire, missionaries and colonial officials reinforced such ideas when they served tea to civilize and convert indigenous people and teach them to appreciate working hard and spending a wage. In metropolitan Britain the temperate vision of tea assuaged anxieties about industrialization, international trade, and the consumption of this Chinese product.

As we saw in the last chapter, many early modern cultures assumed that tea inspired temperance, self-control, and rationality. In the early nineteenth century, free traders and evangelicals felt the same way and argued that tea aided temperance, and temperance was a defining characteristic of Britishness.[21] As a mode of achieving temperance, cheap tea was not only moral, it was also critical to national belonging and development. Temperance was also a gendered concept that helped spread new ideas about marriage and family. Temperance pamphlets, sermons, and political utterances described how sober husbands and wives created healthy families and communities. They rewrote the meaning of British masculinity in particular, when arguing that a sober man was a domestic being who needed to retreat to a temperate home to cleanse himself of his tainted contact with the public world.[22] Temperance thus sanctified the family, the household, and its contents. However much they celebrated the private sphere, as we will see in this and following chapters, temperance communities built many of the public spaces that became the foundation of a new kind of mass consumer society. They also developed the ideological framework that made consumption productive and moral rather than wasteful and sinful.

Before it became an organized political and social movement, temperance as an ideology fueled political debate. Early nineteenth-century liberals, for example, condemned mercantilism as an immoral economic system and one of their primary examples was the fact that the East India Company's monopoly bred intemperance by restricting the trade in moral goods, especially tea. The company in turn claimed that it was a temperate force that balanced the passions that were stimulated in a free-trade economy.[23] Historians have paid much attention to this struggle between the company and free traders to explore the influence of business on politics and the growth of extra-parliamentary lobbying.[24] However, what has been overlooked is the way in which liberal businessmen living in Manchester, Liverpool, and Glasgow envisioned the mass consumption of tea in Britain as critical to their ability to do business with China and India. Organized in various chambers of commerce and merchant associations, these men argued that the growth of working-class tea consumption was necessary to the functioning of the global economy.

During the key years of debate over the renewal of the EIC's charter, in 1812–13 and again between 1829 and 1833, and in later fiscal struggles, free traders did two important things. They connected the consumption of tea in Britain with the sale of cotton and other Manchester goods in China, and they suggested that any obstacle to the growth of this moral commerce was aiding and abetting immorality since tea promoted temperance and good behavior. During these years, Glasgow's and Liverpool's merchants and Manchester's cotton manufacturers and others involved in the East India trade repeatedly attacked the company as an unscientific, inefficient, and archaic institution that had stymied legitimate and moral "temperate" desires, particularly a free trade in tea.[25] Entering into the debate, a correspondent who wrote to the *Glasgow Chronicle* in 1812 argued that by keeping the price of tea high the EIC was immorally keeping tea, that "enemy to *strong drink*," from the people.[26] Glasgow merchants may have truly believed in temperance, but this was also a useful argument for men who had been excluded from the lucrative China trade.

Kirkman Finlay (1772–1842), a Glasgow cotton industrialist and influential lobbyist for free trade, was a leader of this movement.[27] Finlay and his colleagues were partly successful and the company's charter was revised in 1813, opening all but the tea trade to competition. This was only the beginning of the fight, however.[28] When the EIC's charter was again debated in the late 1820s and early 1830s merchants and manufacturers in Manchester, Liverpool, and Glasgow passed resolutions and printed numerous pamphlets and articles spelling out how monopoly restricted home and foreign markets for tea and cotton.[29] Finlay's father James had founded James Finlay and Company in 1750. The company became the leading textile firm in Scotland, was heavily involved in creating Asian markets, and eventually developed tea cultivation in the British Empire. Finlays is still one of the largest producers of tea in the world.[30] We now know that the last decades of the EIC's monopoly of the China trade was more open and more efficient than critics like Kirkman Finlay suggested, but acknowledging this would have hurt the power of their argument.[31] By the 1820s "private" trade had gained a place within the Canton system and at the time the EIC lost its charter more than half of the trade was already in private hands.[32] Qing policy recognized the legitimacy of foreign trade and both Chinese and British merchants were able to bend the rules to fit their needs.[33] Nevertheless, many liberals insisted that the EIC monopoly was as yet powerful and restrictive.[34]

The Oriental traveler, liberal reformer, temperance and peace activist, and believer in women's rights James Silk Buckingham led the struggle against the company and drunkenness in the early 1830s and created a vision of a moral society built upon free trade. Buckingham's life reads like fiction, but, like Kirkman Finlay, he represents a wider segment of the new liberal middle classes. Buckingham was born in Cornwall in 1786, a region that experienced the fervor of evangelicalism and became a Methodist stronghold during Buckingham's childhood. Jacobinism and anti-Jacobinism took hold as well, particularly after war with France inspired patriotic fervor. Cornwall was also awash with commodities and ideas coming from America, Europe, India, and China. On the western reaches of the British Isles, Falmouth, the region's main port and commercial town, was home to a thriving legal and illegal global trade. Merchant ships and warships anchored in its harbor on their way across the Atlantic or to other lands, and it was often the first port of call upon arriving home. American timber, rice, and grain, Spanish and Portuguese wool, and West Indian sugar were just a few of the foreign goods that landed in Falmouth. In addition, there was such a lively business in contraband goods that one observer noted in 1800 that virtually every "man, woman, and child in the town, except the revenue collectors . . . were in commercial enterprises of questionable legality."[35] As we saw in the last chapter, tea was at the heart of this illicit economy and Buckingham's family and the young Buckingham himself could have also traded in this illegitimate pleasure. Yet he devoted his career to legitimizing free trade and goods such as tea.

Buckingham went to sea at the age of ten, following in the footsteps of his father, who had been a sailor before becoming a farmer. On Buckingham's second voyage, a French privateer, manned with many English mutineers, captured his ship and took him and his fellow sailors to a prison in Spain, where he fell in love with the prison keeper's daughter.[36] After his liberation by the Spanish government, he separated from his first love to return home in 1797 and then worked for a dealer in nautical instruments, studied the law, married, and returned to the sea in 1806. This time, Buckingham encountered foreign ideas about temperance. On a trip to Nassau in the Caribbean his captain forbade swearing and the drinking of spirits and encouraged the sailors to keep themselves and their berths clean.[37] It is difficult to say whether this shockingly stern discipline influenced Buckingham's beliefs about temperance, for he also claimed to have been inspired by his direct observation of Muslim dietary and temperance habits. In addition to sailing to the Caribbean and the United States, he sailed through the Mediterranean to Egypt, learned Arabic, advised Mehmet Ali and even developed a plan to dig a canal between the Mediterranean and Red Sea. Becoming a well-known Orientalist, that is, a Western figure who purported to study and have knowledge about the East, Buckingham traveled to India and back, journeyed overland through Palestine, Syria, Mesopotamia, and Persia in 1816, and returned to India in 1817.[38]

Arriving in India just four years after the East India Company had been forced to open up trade with the Subcontinent, Buckingham became a leading critic of the company, which he condemned as a despotic regime. He advocated for a free press and in September 1818 established the *Calcutta Journal*, a liberal paper that included international news, literature, and praise for English radicals.[39] Seeing the press as a check on government power, Buckingham allowed the correspondence pages to become a platform for criticizing the company. Buckingham thus became a critic of "Old Corruption" in India at the same moment that political unions were demanding the reform of Parliament and the expansion of the suffrage at home. But India was not Britain and Buckingham's radical journalism eventually led to his deportation in 1823. Not surprisingly, when he returned home, Buckingham continued his attack on the company, and he furthered his career as a writer and journalist, establishing, among other journals, the *Oriental Herald and Colonial Review* in 1824 and the *Athenaeum* in 1828. He also became involved in national politics and temperance.

Elected to the first reformed Parliament representing Sheffield in 1832, Buckingham led the fight for many social reforms, including temperance, the rights of women, the Irish, and the working classes. He certainly believed that drunkenness was one of the leading social problems of the day. He personally gave up drink in 1826 and formally took "the pledge" of total abstinence in 1832.[40] Two years later he chaired a parliamentary select committee to investigate the causes of drunkenness and became a vice president of the British and Foreign Temperance Society. In a speech given in the House of Commons in 1834, Buckingham concluded that there was the "most irresistible proof . . . that Intemperance, like a mighty and destroying flood, is fast overwhelming the land."[41] His struggle against the EIC had brought temperance and free trade together, a fact that British teetotalers well recognized at the time. At a temperance meeting in Liverpool in October 1834, just months after the EIC lost its tea monopoly, a leading teetotaler professed that "in opening the China trade Mr. Buckingham had rendered greater service to the country than any other man or body of men in England. The reform of drunkenness was of far greater importance than the reform of parliament."[42] Free trade, this advocate imagined, would create a temperate nation not simply because commerce was civilizing but because tea was now free. Over the next several decades, Buckingham continued to support liberal causes; among other things, he argued against the use of force in Ireland, for the abolition of slavery, and for the reform of the navy.[43] Buckingham resigned his seat in 1837, enabling him to embark on a lecture tour to the United States and Canada, campaign for temperance and against the Corn Laws, and attend the World Peace Congress in Brussels in 1848.[44] Throughout his life Buckingham remained dedicated to the belief that peace and free trade went hand in hand and were anathema to war and imperial conquest.

Buckingham and his colleagues successfully brought about the abolition of the company's monopoly of the tea trade in 1833, but he and other free traders continued to complain that government policy was restricting the free flow of tea and cotton.[45] For one thing, the Chinese market did not materialize as expected and tea became momentarily more expensive with the onset of free trade. Fearing the loss of approximately £3,300,000 in revenue derived from tea, the British government had introduced a new three-tiered duty that increased prices for the lowest-quality tea largely drunk by the working classes.[46] This much-hated policy created new alliances as tea traders, cotton merchants, and working-class and middle-class temperance enthusiasts joined forces to fight these and other new duties. "If government were really alive to the true interests of the labouring classes," the *Preston Temperance Advocate* opined in 1836, it "would, from considerations of a moral character, reduce the duty on tea, coffee, and sugar."[47] In a somewhat dramatic gesture, a radical grocer and Chartist teetotaler, J. J. Faulkner, protested these duties by dressing in a Chinese costume while selling tea and other groceries in his Oxford shop. He later stopped selling them altogether with the explanation that he would not become the government's tax collector.[48]

Throughout the 1830s and 1840s, tea's temperate nature became central to arguments about free trade and fiscal policy. After the resolution of the first Opium War in the early 1840s, manufacturers and merchants grew even more committed to the fantasy that "now, China, with her almost countless millions, is ready to receive from us our manufactures . . . she is also ready to give us in return her Tea."[49] At a meeting of the Liverpool Committee to Reduce the Tea Duties in 1846, the 2nd Earl of Harrowby, known as Viscount Sandon, who then represented Liverpool in Parliament, proposed that low taxes would increase the British workingman's "consumption of a wholesome, agreeable, and unintoxicating beverage" and also "extend commercial intercourse with China." Making a similar argument, William Brown, who represented South Lancashire, professed: "I am interested in promoting the social comfort and domestic happiness of the people," and this means "substitut[ing] the moral teapot in the place of the demoralizing ale-jug."[50] "Why tax tea and coffee, which are the antidotes to spirits, and a free and cheap use of which would in all probability, supersede the use of spirits?" asked tea broker Edward Brodribb, in a speech he gave on taxation before the Financial Reform Association in Liverpool in 1849.[51] When arguing for lower taxes, Brodribb employed rhetoric common to both early nineteenth-century free traders and temperance activists, and he entered a broader conversation that claimed that free trade in itself was a sobering force.[52] Similar arguments shaped imperial fiscal politics as well.[53] They also had staying power. In 1882, when William Gladstone proposed in his budget speech, "the domestic use of tea is a powerful champion able to encounter alcoholic drink in a fair field," he was simply reiterating arguments that had been around for decades. We will also see the temperance argument as part of fiscal battles surrounding tea in the early twentieth century. Underlying such rhetoric was the very real sense that the mass consumption of tea in Britain was the key to the ever-elusive Chinese market. Liberals fighting for low taxes referred to the moral teapot then to reference their faith in the morality of global commerce.

Of course, tea was by no means the only temperate brew. Coffee was always popular and many advocated the moderate drinking of beer, wine, and cider. Colonial Americans and Georgian Britons actually viewed wine and tea in strikingly similar ways. Like tea, wine was used as a medicine, a sign of hospitality, and a health drink.[54] Many also argued that a free trade in beer would combat excessive spirit consumption.[55] Beer was of course a local product closely tied to an agrarian economy. Lord Brougham, the Whig statesman who favored political reform, abolition, and temperance, thus denounced tea as a foreign substance that unlike beer did not lead to "the cultivation of one single acre of English land." Though politically similar to Buckingham, Brougham preferred beer, "a good sound, wholesome, constitutional beverage."[56] Founding editor of the *Edinburgh Review*, Anglican cleric, and temperance advocate Sydney Smith expressed the same idea when he asked, "What two ideas are more inseparable than Beer and Britannia!"[57] Throughout the early part of the century, then, many radicals and liberals toasted Britannia with a pint of ale and were as yet unconvinced about the merits of the Chinese brew. The new type of temperance societies that appeared in the late 1820s changed all this because they wanted followers to drink no alcohol at all.

FOOD AND FEASTING IN A SOBER SOCIETY

On 11 July 1832, 540 workingmen and women from the northern industrial town of Preston attended a new type of public banquet that became known as a temperance tea party or tea meeting.[58] This meal was held in the Cloth Hall of the Corn Exchange in the middle of race day, traditionally a time of excessive drinking.[59] The location, menu, decorations, and table equipage, the speeches and songs performed, and the interpretations of these events brought to mind the promises of sobriety and free trade. Tea was the star of the show, but the piles of bread and butter, cakes and fruit, and cotton decorations also flavored the affair. A reporter for a temperance journal described a feast for the eyes and stomach and proof of the civilizing effects of cross-class and heterosocial forms of leisure. The walls, this sympathetic observer pointed out, were "entirely covered with bleached calico, tastefully arrayed, and decorated with various emblems." The food and drink were "good" and the tea "served up with so much order and regularity as to astonish the visitors." Men who "had never been absent from the races, usually intoxicated, [were] now seated at the table with their wives and friends!" After tea was served, various speakers addressed the audience, and the next day the speeches continued at a field meeting on Preston Moor. This had surely been, the journalist concluded, a "feast of reason."[60]

Beginning in the late 1820s and increasing in the 1830s, hundreds and even thousands of plebian and middle-class communities attended similar gatherings in factories, barns, tents, schools, churches, and commercial halls in England, Scotland, Ireland, the United States, Canada, Australia, India, Jamaica, and Southern Africa. Organizers laid out tables with pure white cotton cloth, brewed up gallons of hot tea, and baked all manner of cakes, breads, and other sweets. They decorated halls with floral arrangements and reams of cotton shirting printed with aphorisms that interpreted the meaning of these meals. The writing on the wall literally explained that these meals were about religion and abundance. Abstinence did not imply renunciation of the sensual or the material. Rather, temperance addressed their followers as consumers whose desires could become moral and profitable.[61] In the British Isles temperance tea parties demonstrated the civilizing potential of free trade and Christianity. At such affairs the working and middle classes developed a new kind of heterosocial consumer culture that did not revolve around the public house and tavern. Temperance teas held out the promise of a better life to those who struggled to earn a living wage and make ends meet during a period of recession, high taxes, political repression, and the extraordinary disruptions of industrialization and rapid urbanization. The middle classes were drawn to these events primarily to assert their new social and political authority vis-à-vis corrupt elites and rebellious workers. Once there, they were struck by the spectacle of their troublesome workers quietly consuming religion, cotton, sugar, and tea. Witnessing the calming effects of consumption firsthand, the middle classes came to believe that if coupled with religion, consumerism could transform the working-class mob into a civilized market. Temperance tea parties were thus multilayered oral, tactile, and visual performances that demonstrated the moral and economic benefits of the consumption of tea, coffee, sugar, wheat, and cotton, not to mention religion.

It was likely, however, that socialists and other early radical groups invented this new social practice. In the 1820s the Utopian Socialist followers of Robert Owen hosted mass tea parties to raise money, promote their cause, and indicate their deep commitment to gender equality.[62] During the next decades, other radical communities hosted tea parties at which they too preached gender and social equality within radical families, politics, and society at large.[63] For these radicals, temperance tea parties demonstrated their vision of an equitable and abundant world. On such occasions several hundred men, women, and children ate and drank temperate beverages, listened to and made speeches, and danced into the late hours. In early spring of 1831, for example, a Belfast Co-operative Society hosted a tea party, which included many "respectable well dressed females."

"No spirituous liquors" were served so speakers toasted their radical heroes and heroines over cups of tea and coffee. They honored "Working people, the source of all wealth," and looked forward to "the withering blight of competition" giving way to the "rising sun of Co-operation." They toasted feminist heroines and ideas, including "Miss Frances Wright, Mrs. Wheeler, and the Rights of Women."[64] Frances or Fanny Wright was the Scottish-born freethinker and feminist socialist who moved to the United States, became an abolitionist, and was friends with American, French, and British radicals across the Atlantic world. Figures like Wright invested tea and temperance with the power to bring about political as well as social citizenship for men and women. While drinking tea, they organized against class oppression and unjust legislation. For example, an all-female tea party held in Brighton in 1836 protested the class privilege inherent in the New Poor Law (1834), the law that created the new workhouse system, which was so reviled in working-class communities that it came to be known as the Starvation Act.[65] These radical communities thus revised earlier radical thinking about tea. Rather than see tea as a tool of oppression, socialists saw tea drinking as emancipatory.[66] As we will see, Christian-inspired teetotalers held a very different view, but they drew upon Owenite and cooperative social practices and especially the early socialists' commitment to heterosociality.

Also inspired by the formation of the American Temperance Society in 1826, new temperance organizations began to appear in Scotland, England, Wales, and Ireland in the summer of 1829, and by 1830 most major cities had such a society, including Glasgow, Preston, Manchester, Leeds, Dublin, Birmingham, Bristol, Newcastle, Bradford, and London.[67] These societies held mass tea parties to recruit followers, raise funds, and provide alternative forms of pleasure and leisure for their members. Incorporating the public nature of radical and reform politics with Methodist-style tent meetings and the use of personal testimony in the conversion experience, the temperance tea party became a material and culinary expression of popular liberalism and evangelical revival.[68] None was entirely committed to free trade, however.[69] For example, advocates opined that the passage of the "liberal" Beer Act of 1830, which no longer required beer sellers to obtain licenses from magistrates, increased the sin of drunkenness. In fact, the passage of the Beer Act and the failure to achieve universal suffrage with the passage of the Reform Act in 1832 actually convinced many radicals that they had to reform working-class culture in order to create a class ready for the vote.[70]

Total abstinence societies spread especially quickly in the industrial areas of England, Scotland, Ireland, and Wales in the early 1830s and 1840s. Preston, a cotton town in the heart of industrial Lancashire, reputed to be the model for Charles Dickens's Coketown in *Hard Times*, was the center of the new teetotal movement. Like Coketown, Preston was a smelly, noisy, and monotonous town, rattling and trembling to the sound of the steam engine. Its population grew from 11,887 in 1810 to 69,542 in 1851, with over sixty textile firms employing nearly 40 percent of girls and 25 percent of boys in their teens.[71] Young and famously rebellious, these operatives went on strike many times in the 1830s, 1850s, and 1860s. While these factory workers often clashed with managers and large merchants over wages and working conditions, they were nonetheless united by nonconformity and their agreement to eschew the glass.[72]

Dickens and others derided temperance as an oppressive tool of self-serving factory managers, but the teetotal movement was in many respects a cross-class endeavor. Joseph Livesey, a self-educated handloom-weaver-turned-cheese-factor, and several other Lancashire merchants and workingmen founded the crusade and spread it beyond Preston.[73] These men had been involved in political reform and would later become active in the Anti-Corn Law League and similar liberal causes. Whig newspapers and cotton manufacturers and their wives and daughters joined societies and hosted and spoke at meetings.[74] For these middle-class adherents, temperance was a practice of self-improvement and allowed them to inculcate thrift and good behavior among their workers. Beyond encouraging a compliant and productive workforce, temperance culture provided a space for the middle classes to affirm their own "social aspirations and identity."[75]

The term "teetotal" did not refer to tea drinking even though teetotalers were especially fond of tea. Richard Turner, a stutterer, was rumored to have coined the term when he inadvertently pledged "t-t-t-total" abstinence. The word came to mean the total rejection of buying, selling, or consuming all alcohol, including wine and beer. The more radical and socially marginal dissenting churches may have influenced this total renunciation since some, such as the working-class Salford Bible Christian Church, had already promoted a diet that abstained from "the use of animal food and intoxicating liquors."[76] However, while denouncing alcohol, advocates created a temperate lifestyle that promoted tea, coffee, and other nonalcoholic drinks. Believing in the power of education, moral suasion, and substitution as the best means to fight alcohol and the public house, teetotalers built a sober consumer culture.

Teetotalism was, as one historian put it, permeated with "popular evangelicalism," and the movement used propaganda techniques and methods of organization learned in both American and British revivalism.[77] The first meeting of Preston's society was presided over by a Wesleyan minister and held in a Wesleyan chapel. Livesey was a Scotch Baptist who sought to model his conduct on the "charitable and forgiving spirit of Jesus."[78] Anglicans and many Wesleyans were ambivalent or even hostile to total abstinence, but the Congregationalists, Primitive Methodists, Bible Christians in the west of England, and Calvinistic Methodists in Wales were quite enthusiastic. Quakers were also prominent, though they were not total abstainers. They banned believers from making, selling, or drinking hard alcohol but they saw nothing wrong with beer. Notable Quaker families like the Cadburys built business empires selling temperance brews, a theme that we will explore in later chapters.[79] Nonconformist ministers, who were gaining professional status and becoming spiritual and cultural leaders in industrial cities, frequently preached at these events, while self-proclaimed former drunkards confessed how religion had helped them give up the "love of the glass," as one pensioner put it during a Bolton tea party in October 1833. Since joining the New Temperance Society, this pensioner explained how it had been fourteen weeks since he had tasted anything stronger than "tea or coffee." He now believed he would "be able to live more consistently as a professor of our holy religion."[80] Such confessions sanctified tea and other temperance drinks as the symbol of and path to a holy life.

Organizers nearly always declared that they were promoting "sobriety, industry and religion."[81] The first tea parties were often held at Christmas and helped transform this once raucous holiday into a consumer-oriented family affair.[82] Whenever they were held, however, the tea party provided a brief taste of the sweet life and showed how the rejection of immoral pleasures would bring an everlasting world of copious food and domestic happiness. Temperance journals described such affairs in delicious detail. At one of the earliest of these affairs, 1,200 men and women attended a temperance tea on Christmas Day in 1834. Organizers draped the walls and windows of Preston's Cloth Hall in the Corn Exchange with white cambric decorated with colored rosettes and evergreen garlands. The same material covered 630 feet of tables and the forty former drunkards who served tea dressed in white aprons printed with the word "temperance" on the front. The *Preston Temperance Advocate* explained that "the tables were loaded with provisions, and plenty seemed to smile upon the guests." "Plenty" was certainly the party's official message, as it was printed on the festooned walls, along with the words "Temperance," "Sobriety," "Peace," and "Happiness." The party ended quietly with the singing of temperance hymns, accompanied by a small band that played softly.[83]

The location of this tea party was important to its argument. Preston's Corn Exchange was a public market and saleroom that had only recently opened in 1824, and it and other similar venues became popular spaces for many religious, civic, and business associations to gather and create shared values and a sense of community (fig. 2.1). Year after year, temperance made good use of these new public spaces. In 1836, Preston's Cloth Hall was once again "elegantly decorated with evergreens, rosettes, artificial flowers, [and] fruit trees." Fifty-six windows were also "tastefully festooned" and "900 yards of white cotton shirting" covered the tables and walls, which again were printed with the words, "temperance,"

FIGURE 2.1. Dinner for Wesleyan Methodist Church, 29 May 1856. The Corn Exchange, Preston. (Courtesy of the Preston Digital Archive)

"sobriety," "peace," "happiness," and "plenty." The latter motto appeared directly above tables loaded with mountains of bread and butter. The themes of plenty, regularity, cheerfulness, and social harmony were carried through in the mode of description of such events as well. The writer who described this affair made sure to note, for example, how "75 sets of beautiful tea and coffee services" and "34 tea kettles holding about 250 gallons of water" served between 1,200 and 1,300 at precisely "half-past four o'clock." He also noticed that Preston's mayor, "his lady, and son" were "gratified with the splendid scene, and the cheerful and happy countenances of those who were partaking a liquor which cheers but does not inebriate."[84] Sympathetic observers wrote about rational, cheerful, and disciplined occasions. This interpretation was not just a statement of fact but a political and economic argument.

In 1836, when this tea party took place, Preston's operatives were on strike, protesting declining wages.[85] Livesey explained to the operatives how sobriety could help them in their struggle. "Masters are continually inventing new machinery in order to dispense with manual labour," he proposed, because they are not "able to depend on their men, in consequence of their drinking."[86] He argued that sober workers would make machinery unnecessary. Tea thus was a useful commodity because it prevented the waste of labor and this in turn would improve living standards.[87] Livesey also believed that through abstinence workers could improve their own material conditions regardless of whether managers raised or lowered wages. He was suggesting then that religion, personal reform, and social and gender harmony rather than violence and activism would lead to plenty, peace, and happiness. This argument spread with the temperance movement, and everywhere tea came to be associated with social harmony.

Within a short time, Preston's tea parties became highly ritualized, varying little from their original script.[88] *Livesey's Moral Reformer* noted this in 1838, writing that the city's Christmas Day tea party "has been regarded as the PATTERN," followed year after year in Preston and across England.[89] This was not a coincidence. Livesey and his colleagues embarked on what they called "temperance missionary" tours to spread the word. On one such tour in the summer of 1833, they visited Blackburn, Heywood, Rochdale, Oldham, Stockport, Manchester, and Bolton ringing a bell, announcing meetings, and waving a small white silk flag exhorting others to "touch not, taste not, handle not, drink not, buy not, sell not, brew not, distil not intoxicating liquors."[90] But many of these towns had already hosted tea parties. On Guy Fawkes' Day, 5 November 1832, 300 sat down to tea in Oldham's Methodist School Room.[91] On 22 December about 100 persons held a party at the Brown Street Sabbath schoolroom in Chester.[92] On 12 January, 450 took tea in "the large room of a mill belonging to Mrs. Scholfield" at Heywood. The village clergyman, a Baptist minister, a Wesleyan minister, the schoolmaster, and the leader of the Anti-Corn Law League, John Bright, all drank tea with the workers that day.[93] In Liverpool 2,500 of the town's "wealth, beauty and intelligence" listened to "an Englishman, a Welshman, and a Scotchman," and 500 immediately signed the pledge of total abstinence at one meeting in 1836.[94]

Sunderland, Middlesborough, Bradford, Gloucester, Birmingham, and Nottingham and several towns in Wales also hosted such affairs.[95] Some lasted for days. In Wilsden, near Bradford in the West Riding region of Yorkshire in April 1835, a party began with a procession through the town's streets, and then at precisely "twelve o'clock the doors of the church were opened and the multitude entered and arranged themselves in the pews." The teetotalers said prayers, sang hymns, and listened to speakers before moving outside to feast under "a splendid tent" erected outside the church. Writing thirty years later, the temperance historian Samuel Couling repeated the themes of calm abundance, and he and others were struck by how so many people could quietly eat together without any confusion. Couling described in detail the size, scale, and feel of the affair. In a tent measuring "135 feet in length by 54 feet in width . . . supported by three rows of pillars, eight in each row, and adorned with flags, evergreens, and artificial flowers," this party began at exactly five o'clock, with the greatest of order, each seat was occupied, and 1,400 partook of tea and its accompaniment. No sooner had the company received sufficient then "with an orderly and simultaneous movement," they made way for 1,100 others, who had been patiently waiting without. At the departure of this second company, the conductors, officers, and others, to the number of 200, regaled themselves. Thus, 2,700 persons sat down to tea on this grand occasion.[96]

Not all parties were as large as those in Wilsden and Preston.[97] But the food and drink, decorations, and moral messages were quite similar whether copper miners in Kendal were hosting a tea in a barn and farmhouse or Londoners "partook of the exhilarating but not inebriating beverage" in a large room in Theobald Road.[98]

Participants came to look at, smell, and experience the gustatory pleasures of tea, sugar, bread, butter, and cake. Livesey claimed that such feasts drew on historical and biblical examples, and he especially pointed to the marriage supper in the New Testament as a moral yet public feast. The tea party, Livesey argued, was a form of rational feasting that usefully superseded "the sumptuous and riotous *eating and drinking* much too prevalent in this country."[99] However, temperance consumed vast quantities of bread and cake, butter and cream, fruit, sugar, tea, and coffee. At one festival, 1,400 persons consumed "700 pounds of currant bread, 364 pounds of common bread, 130 pounds of lump sugar, 60 pounds of brown sugar, 81 quarts of cream, 30 pounds of coffee, 10 pounds of tea, 50 pounds of butter, 84 dozen oranges, [and] 800 pounds of apples, &c."[100]

Food thus became spectacle. Temperance processions carted oversized foods through urban streets as symbols of the "fruits of teetotalism." In Manchester, for example, a temperance cart loaded with a sack of flower, a 65-pound ham, 85 pounds of cheese, and a loaf of bread weighing in at 60 pounds evoked a sober yet bountiful version of the mythical Land of Cockayne, that place where peasants stuffed themselves and lived a life of ease.[101] Making a spectacle of food was actually common at the time, and retailers often paraded around oversized hams and cheeses through city streets on carts.[102] And even the most average of grocers delighted in piling mounds of food and provisions in their windows.

Feasting and fantasizing about food were very old traditions, but tea parties were modern banquets serving up new foods that were purchased in shops and public eateries rather than baked or brewed at home.[103] Sugar was very prominent, baked in cakes and sweet breads, added to hot and cold drinks, and appearing in its natural state in the many fruits that graced the temperance table. Sweet drinks such as cocoa, aerated and spiced waters, ginger beer, and lemonade and coffee were also common.[104] Low duties on West Indian coffee and the expansion of cultivation in Ceylon after 1815 led to falling prices and very rapidly expanding markets in the 1840s. In 1847 London had between 1,500 and 1,800 temperance coffee rooms serving tea and coffee at affordable prices and providing space for meetings and organizing.[105] The temperance coffee shop and tea party were thus two new forms of mass catering that encouraged the creation of sober workers and rational consumers. The coffee shop targeted male workers in urban settings, while the tea party was designed to "prevent young persons of both sexes from going to public houses and beer shops."[106] Declining prices and other factors abetted the spectacular increases in sugar consumption during these years; however, temperance certainly stimulated the British sweet tooth.[107] Quite simply, temperance helped create the modern diet, as it aided the broader dietary shift from alcohol and grains such as oats to caffeine, sugar, and wheat.

Tea parties were held in public settings, but they also demonstrated the new gender and domestic ideologies associated with evangelicalism. In addition to sobering the working classes, the tea parties redefined wealthy women's consumerism. Eighteenth-century critics had often labeled elite women's tea drinking as frivolous gossipy affairs that were but an idle waste of time.[108] Tea parties turned this private pastime into a public good.[109] Wealthy women often led this change. While Livesey and his merchant friends founded the movement, women from the local elite donated money, food, space, and time to the cause. They legitimized their own consuming habits and carved out a space for themselves in the public sphere by reforming the consumerism of others. Philanthropic and reforming ladies particularly liked to argue that a well-behaved, cross-class, shared culture of consumption could bring social understanding and end class conflict. Mrs. William Cooke Taylor, who was married to a prominent apologist for the factory system, described tea parties as evidence of "good feeling between masters and men" and "cordiality and good fellowship between the operatives and their employers." She especially pointed out that although the event took place in a "large room crowded with persons of both sexes, all from the mills . . . [yet] everything went most orderly. . . . [And] the whole affair went off with as little breach of propriety, or even etiquette, as if it had been a fashionable dining room; no noise or confusion of any kind."[110] Catherine Marsh, a well-known evangelical philanthropist and writer, organized parties for navvies, factory workers, villagers, and Sunday school children.[111] Marsh believed that sharing food and drink, particularly tea and cakes, created cross-class friendships and common Christian behaviors that would obviate the deep class divisions that plagued Victorian society.[112] Evangelical women understood that sharing food was a deeply Christian act that demonstrated bourgeois forms of bodily discipline and etiquette and forms of eating and drinking.

Workers came to the tea table, however, because it spoke to their own concerns and fantasies. Eighteenth-century workers were already invested in looking good and eating well; thus consumerism was not necessarily a middle-class value foisted upon plebian communities.[113] Working- and lower-middle-class organizers both believed in the civilizing power of women's presence, and many "honest lads and bonnie lasses" came to tea parties seeking sober life partners.[114] This was not an insignificant promise. Heavy drinking was associated with the more violent aspects of masculine artisanal culture, and it ate up paychecks, instigated domestic violence, and crystallized competition over scarce resources within the working-class family.[115] At a party held in Wigan's Commercial Hall on Christmas Day in 1838, however, we begin to see ways in which temperance objectified women. One writer intimated the sexual pleasures underlying these events when he wrote: "The Ladies who had undertaken tea services on the occasion, amounted to thirty in number, arranging themselves, forming a decoration not less beautiful, and infinitely more interesting than the perishing productions behind them."[116] Such descriptions indicated the commercial nature of heterosexual courtship and companionate marriage that were becoming popular ideals during these years.

Perhaps most important for the history of consumer society, the tea parties transformed how managers saw their workers. According to social theory and much popular sentiment, managers saw workers as naturally rebellious and idle. Schooled in the economic theories of Thomas Malthus and David Ricardo, these manufacturers also assumed that higher wages brought more drunkenness, larger families, and a faster path to utter poverty. Instead of leading to economic growth, these theorists imagined that immorality and an inability to control one's passions made it impossible to sustain healthy mass markets. Their focus, however, was on work and how to develop institutions—the factory, the workhouse, and the plantation—and policies to make good workers. Liberal-minded temperance advocates picked up on such concerns but provided a new morality of consumption and economics. They contended that the consumption of the right kinds of goods in the right kinds of places solved the Malthusian trap and instead of creating poverty produced an industrial labor force. Tea became one of those special commodities that stimulated the senses without igniting uncontrollable passions and, even more important, enabled one to make rational decisions in the marketplace. It essentially made "liberal" subjects, or the notion that a person was not governed by his or her passions but instead was at liberty to make free choices. While there were many facets to liberalism and many temperance advocates would certainly not have defined themselves as liberals, they all believed that civil persons were self-governing and able to control their bodily desires. Desires must then be redirected to productive aims. To put it in the simplest terms, consuming good things prevented the attraction to bad things.[117] In this formulation, tea, like commerce itself, became a mild passion that literally sweetened the self and the nation. Merchants and manufacturers learned about the civilizing power then of consumption when they witnessed hundreds and even thousands of workers calmly ingesting mountains of goods and surrounded by the reams of cotton that decorated every public tea drinking. It was not a coincidence that anti-spirit societies especially flourished among the nonconformist textile manufacturing communities in Ulster, Glasgow, Preston, Bradford, and Leeds and that mill owners hosted and spoke at meetings and were common on subscription lists.[118] These manufacturers needed mass markets.

The temperance movement specifically addressed such issues and argued that temperate individuals learned how to marshal scarce resources and become good, that is, predictable, shoppers who had some discretionary income. As one Irish campaigner explained it, "Ale houses, spirit shops, &c. will be substituted by the . . . baker, the soup shop, the coffee house." Abstinence provided funds for "clothing, good food, all the comforts of life, in a word, shall well reward the grower and manufacturer."[119] Livesey urged shopkeepers to support his cause since "nearly all the money spent at public houses ought to be, and if tee-totalism prevailed, spent at YOUR SHOPS."[120] Livesey was connected to many of Preston's liberal causes, and he resolutely believed that far from depressing trade and hurting agrarian interests, total abstinence turned workers into consumers. He also revealed the connection between home and foreign markets when he posited that tea rather than alcohol would create more income for clothing and other commodities. Temperance thereby furthered foreign as well as local markets.[121]

The new temperance movement thus concluded that the mass consumption of tea solved the central conundrum of an industrializing and expanding imperial economy—that is, how to make modern efficient laborers *and* consumers. They addressed followers as consumers and believed that the reform of dietary, material, and other consumer practices would lead to earthly and spiritual rewards, bodily and psychic health, social and for some even political citizenship.[122] Temperance developed a moral narrative about the sensual and spiritual, social and political rewards that would come with disciplining one's consumer desires. Advocates articulated and demonstrated these ideas through serving specific foods and drinks in particular settings decorated with meaningful decor. The commodities and consumers present at a temperance tea were then the mise-en-scène that constituted a spatial and material, visual and culinary performance. Ultimately, the tea party promoted and managed the culture of consumption taking shape in the early nineteenth century. Not everyone became teetotalers, but temperance nevertheless became a dominant political ideology and social practice. It influenced economic theory and culinary tastes and habits.

Temperance encouraged workers to fantasize about a spiritual yet consumer-oriented lifestyle that revolved around the home and domesticity. It also taught retailers and employers to fantasize about male and female workers consuming reams of cotton and pounds of sugar, butter, wheat, and tea. The idea of a sober working-class market became visible in temperance halls in the 1830s.

THE TRAVELS OF THE TEA PARTY

Preston was the center of a new kind of global economy and culture, but it was only one center in a much larger movement.[123] A Victorian temperance historian, P. T. Winskill, believed that only God could have planted the "seed" of such a rapidly growing global movement.[124] Who other than the Creator could have spread such a phenomenon across vast oceans? However, the same forces that spread the use of global commodities in these years also spread temperance and its foodways. Literacy, popular writing, and a vast network of missionaries, soldiers, businessmen, merchants, and philanthropic "ladies" linked North America and the British Empire and helped create a shared temperate consumer culture.[125] Before the telegraph and other modern systems of communications, mobile and like-minded individuals distributed a set of ideas and habits over large geographic distances. Temperance was an example of early nineteenth-century global flows and circuits of exchange that moved in multiple directions at once. Similar practices nevertheless were shaped by diverse racial and class, gender, and colonial politics.

Total abstinence societies started in the United States and crossed the Atlantic with ship captains who were docked in Liverpool in the autumn of 1829. They distributed American tracts and inspired the founding of the movement in the port city. A Liverpool iron merchant with business dealings in Preston then personally "reformed" his drunken business associate, the aptly named Thomas Swindlehurst, who would become one of the original founders of Preston's teetotal society. At virtually the same time, a Miss Allan and a Miss Graham heard of the movement in America and founded a society for women near Glasgow.[126] Many Americans traveled to Glasgow and Liverpool and from there, ideas also spread to imperial locales. However, it is also likely that Americans learned about total abstinence in these cities. For example, in 1819 a Mr. James McNair, president of the Greenock Radical Association, a group that abstained from all intoxicating liquors, tea, coffee, and tobacco, founded a total abstinence society in Scotland before moving to New Zealand to promote teetotalism among the Māori and English colonists in the early 1830s.[127]

Evangelical missionaries were also at the forefront of this global movement, and they were hosting tea parties in the empire at the same time that radical

socialists were doing so in the UK.[128] This is not to suggest that American organizers did not inspire British abstinence societies but that evangelicalism and
socialism were transnational movements that helped spread temperance ideals
and practices. Tea parties were part of the missionary's arsenal everywhere but
they were especially popular in Southern Africa. Though diverse European missionaries encountered multiple ethnic groups, languages, systems of land use, and
economies in Southern Africa, British missionaries had an abiding faith that a
cup of tea would soothe any colonial encounter.

In the 1820s and 1830s, the British were hoping to liberalize and monetize
the economy and encourage white settlement of the Cape Colony in Southern
Africa.[129] Missionaries in this era tended to be from the middle classes and
they increasingly believed that British-style domesticity, the desire for clothing,
household comfort, and similar rational comforts were critical to conversion.[130]
As in Preston, they believed that tea symbolized and created a Christian material
world. Describing his experiences in the Cape in the spring of 1820, the Reverend
John Campbell, who was a London Missionary Society inspector, wrote about
an African "king" who brought "his two wives into the tent and introduced
them; but they appeared chiefly to have come to see our tea-pot, the fame of
which had reached them. They viewed it with great attention, and expressed their
astonishment with uplifted hands."[131] Samuel Broadbent, who had started the
Wesleyan Missionary Society in Ceylon before moving on to Southern Africa,
was also fond of tea and in 1823 he too first approached the Tswana in Southern
Africa with the offer of a cup of tea. He later recalled in his diary that when
"two women came into my hut . . . I let them taste my tea and presented each of
them with a needle, thread and thimble."[132] Through such means missionaries
tried to inculcate new gender and domestic practices. For missionaries tea was
symbolic of European domesticity and a means to transform Africans' material
and culinary cultures.[133] In such accounts, tea became a Christian and domestic
commodity, a point of contact between male missionaries and indigenous women.
Such stories show how missionaries, not necessarily Africans, invested tea and
tea things with sacred significance.

Almost everywhere they went, missionaries used food, material culture, table
manners, and tea to inculcate Christian and commercial moralities and practices.
For example, in 1825, the *London Evangelical Magazine* reported that in the South
Sea Islands, a Reverend Tyerman and his brother witnessed "parents, children,
chiefs, and people, upwards of 1,000 in number," eat dinner

> in the English fashion, off tables, sitting on sofas. The sofas were upwards
> of 200 in number, and tables in proportion. All took tea together in the
> same manner. The tables were arranged in rows, in a spacious place in the

midst of the settlement, and screened from the sun with native cloth. Joy
beamed in every countenance, and we trust gratitude ascended from every
heart to the God of all grace, for the blessings of the "gospel of peace."[134]

There are several very important elements to this account. The description of this
episode is nearly identical to the way in which missionaries and total abstainers
would later describe the British tea parties. We see here the importance of the
arrangement of tables and the discussion of a cross-class and mixed "mass" of people.
The "joy" that beamed on "every countenance" announced that these South Sea
islanders felt God's grace and blessing while eating and drinking tea. In other
words, it was at such collective meals that "heathens" were converted to Christianity.
Underlying much of the discourse of the tea party is the idea of the gift. At large
Baptist tea parties in Spanish Town, Jamaica, in 1855, the American abolitionist
newspaper *The Liberator* made a point of noting how the "tea, coffee, ices, cakes,
[and] tarts" were "freely" handed out and "freely" consumed."[135] The gift is not
opposed to commerce for it implies the notion of liberty or free choice that was
also critical to emerging notions of liberalism and market cultures. In the first
half of the century, giving and sharing tea and numerous sweets thus became
elements of Christian culture and missionary practices in Britain, Jamaica, South
Africa, and the South Sea Islands, among other places.

This culture also extended to India, where it became part of military economies and cultures. Army officers, many of whom were evangelical, spread tea and
temperance in the Indian army. For example, a colonel who opened a temperance
coffee room in Kurnaul (Karnal), India, in 1837 hosted mass tea parties for his
and other regiments claimed that he had been inspired by reading American and
British temperance literature.[136] The military was thus also civilized by tea and
helped spread the culture of sobriety in an Anglo-American world that stretched
from the Americas to the Indian Subcontinent. As we will see, the tea industry
came to regard armies as providing excellent marketing opportunities and missionaries as loyal allies.

Of course, temperance became a huge movement and major force in U.S.
politics, and throughout the nineteenth century, mass tea parties often raised
funds for temperance and other causes. For example, a small group of Primitive
Methodists from Derbyshire who settled in the township of Albion in Dane
County, Wisconsin, hosted tea meetings to raise money to build their church
in 1849.[137] Another group of Primitive Methodists in Platteville, Wisconsin,
who charged twenty-five-cents admission to a tea meeting on New Year's Eve
in 1851, raised fifty dollars "towards liquidating the debt" on their church and
had enough food left over to treat the children of the Sunday school the next
day.[138] In Pennsylvania, the fashionable hosts who raffled prizes were accused

of breaking a state law against gambling, despite the fact that the funds were "devoted to religious purposes."[139] In Massachusetts abolitionists held large tea meetings to support the cause and make visitors from England feel at home. At times tea parties reached truly spectacular proportions. In 1843, for example, the ladies of Cincinnati hosted former president John Quincy Adams at a temperance tea, which was attended by over five thousand persons. The Executive Committee of the American Temperance Union found the whole proceeding had reached a "scale of great magnificence."[140] John Quincy's father may have renounced tea during the Revolution, but by the 1840s American business was heavily involved in the tea trade and the beverage no longer carried any threat to American independence. Throughout the century, tea remained an adjunct to many political, religious, and social meetings in urban and rural states across the land.[141] It is true, however, that the American temperance movement was especially fond of coffee.[142]

In all of these locations, it was common for social and economic elites to serve food and drink to their social inferiors, inverting social norms and hierarchies. Chiefs dined with children, and mill owners sat down with their hands. This inversion must have been quite meaningful for people who, because of their race, class, and gender, had often been relegated to the status of servant. The implications of this could be read many ways. For some it may have meant that material blessings came with and from a Christian lifestyle. Others may have seen such moments as a time to gain power and authority. The tea party itself, as already mentioned, shifted meanings as it crossed political as well as geographic borders.

Like any public event, tea parties could be adopted for many uses and promote any number of causes. The Chartists, Rochdale Co-operators, and Anti-Corn Law League were, for example, fond of tea parties.[143] Conservative organizations liked them too. The Birmingham Loyal and Constitutional Association even followed the radical ceremonial calendar when it held a mass tea party to commemorate its second anniversary on 26 December 1836.[144] In his diary in 1846 the Earl of Shaftesbury recorded that he had chaired a tea party at the new evangelical organization, the YMCA. He remarked it was "a very striking scene" to see four hundred "shopmen, with their mothers and sisters, attending really in a religious spirit."[145] Tea parties simply became standard ways to raise money, socialize, and reform the working class or colonial subjects in the nineteenth and twentieth centuries.

Faith also turned into big business, especially for Britain's relatively small community of Quakers. These advocates of plain dealings saw nothing morally wrong in making money, and they were especially adept at using new forms of publicity and retailing to create mass markets. John Cadbury, founder of the Birmingham Auxiliary Temperance Society, was a tea and coffee merchant in

Birmingham in the 1820s.[146] He was the first to purchase the cocoa-processing machine invented in Holland by C. J. van Houten that eliminated the need for starchy additives, such as potato starch and sago flour, and allowed Cadbury to boast the purity of his product.[147] Like many food manufacturers, Cadbury happily mixed religion, social reform, and business.

The publishing giant John Cassell also exemplifies the mutually satisfying relationship between religion, reform, and the mass market. Born in 1817 in Manchester, Cassell first worked at the loom before becoming a carpenter. In 1836 Joseph Livesey won him over and Cassell became one of the teetotal movement's leading "missionaries."[148] He traveled through much of Britain preaching the gospel of abstinence as a lecturer for the National Temperance Society. By 1839 he became an agent for the new British and Foreign Temperance Society and gave countless lectures at temperance meetings and tea parties.[149] Cassell soon realized that "cheap tea and coffee would not only promote temperance in the masses but put money in the purse of the man who purveyed them; and he resolved to be that man if ever capital came his way."[150] Marriage brought him that capital. As the story goes, he launched what became a famous publishing house by printing tea advertisements and packages, as well as temperance tracts and journals such as the *Teetotal Times*.[151] After he became a successful publisher, Cassell was still lecturing on the tea party circuit into the 1850s.[152] The biographies of men like Cassell have exaggerated truths and suppressed facts, but they tend to emphasize how moral earnestness created the mass market. Men like Cassell learned from moral reform and they traded upon the good name they had built in these communities.

As time went on, however, temperance simply became a business. Refreshment contractors catered for any group that wanted to put on a tea party, and a few enterprising retailers branded "temperance teas," to be served at any public affair or in the home.[153] After liberals began to regulate the drink trade in the 1870s, publicans, brewers, and distillers looked to the Tories to defend their interests. Still, liberals and conservatives agreed that tea achieved good will between the classes and the sexes, advanced international commerce, and created jobs and profits for workers and manufacturers alike.

———

The temperance movement had introduced new tastes and eating habits, contributing to the long-term shift from beer and spirits to caffeinated beverages, even as the public house remained an epicenter of British working-class life throughout the nineteenth century.[154] It is also possible that temperance communities invented the social ritual of afternoon tea. Standard histories of this "meal" assert that Anna Maria, the Duchess of Bedford, conceived of this meal in the 1840s to offset hunger and fatigue in the long afternoon hours between luncheon—also a new meal—and dinner, which was moving later.[155] Tea had certainly been drunk in the afternoon prior to this time, but private tea parties were typically held in the evening after dinner. The duchess was said to have introduced the idea of light refreshments with tea in the afternoon, and thereafter ladies in particular began to gather together in the afternoon for gossip, tea, and snacks. The working-class meal of tea, in contrast, became simply the evening meal and when possible consisted of meat, fish, and other proteins with tea and bread and butter.[156] Perhaps rather than moving down the social ladder, however, the lighter and sweeter version of tea may have started in temperance communities. At least a decade before the duchess turned the evening tea party into an afternoon affair, workers, shopkeepers, merchants, missionaries, and manufacturers began to drink tea and eat sugary foods in the evening and the afternoon in schoolrooms, factories, and meeting halls across Britain and its empire, as well as in the United States.[157] The duchess was an evangelical and she surely knew about, attended, or even hosted temperance teas. Much more work is needed on how religious and other social networks made such habits fashionable among different segments of British and imperial society. However, as we have seen, socialists, liberals, evangelicals, and organized temperance advocates began to serve sweets with tea and proposed that this meal carried religious, political, class, gender, and racial connotations. This new consumer culture bestowed tea drinking with moral and pleasurable meanings about the self and the sacred, and it demonstrated how drinking tea rather than alcohol would bring domestic happiness, class and gender harmony, political citizenship, and a heavenly home.

Of course, people joined temperance movements for a variety of reasons and did not always accept the values that leaders envisioned or promoted. When working- and middle-class men and women drank tea together they were nevertheless shaping the social, physiological, and spiritual consequences of industrialization, long-distance trade, and consumer society. They were absorbing foreign substances into "local political and cultural economies."[158] Tea parties were not just demonstrating Christian and liberal values, they were also creating a new kind of promotional culture. They were akin to an advertisement or any other mass cultural form that legitimated certain commodities while denigrating others as irrational, wasteful, and harmful. Yet, like advertisements, the tea party was understood and misunderstood differently by the workers, shopkeepers, manufacturers, and merchants who attended these affairs. Cotton operatives who were experiencing the shift to the factory and facing reduced wages and restricted leisure no doubt appreciated the abundant food and drink served up at a tea party. These communities were also starting to believe that abstention from drink would bring domestic happiness, social improvement, and political citizenship. Small shopkeepers who helped found and were eager followers of the teetotal movement wanted to mark their place in respectable society, but they also assumed that they would accrue profits that were typically spent at the public house. Large manufacturers were religiously inspired, but they also believed that temperance would create a sober workforce *and* stable domestic and foreign markets. Mill owners imagined that by stimulating the mass consumption of tea in Britain, which was still entirely sourced from China, they would produce a mass market in China for British manufactured goods.[159] Evangelicals frowned on worldly pleasures and avoided dancing, drinking, and other stimulating and ungodly pastimes, but they were invested in promoting certain forms of material comfort and consumer habits and choices. Whatever their politics, religion, and social position, these diverse interests came together at tea parties and thus shaped the history of consumer culture. Religion and liberalism sought to manage the consumer but also promoted desire and pleasure. Restraint and pleasure were ever intertwined.

As time went on, tea moved beyond class and party and became the nation's drink. It is well to remember, however, that in the 1830s many still suspected the brew of all manner of evil effects, and it was temperance advocates and liberals who were convinced that tea was a social and spiritual good, a sacred taste and useful pleasure. They advanced such notions at mass tea parties, public meals with private, political, and economic significance. As we will see in the next chapter, tea was being showcased as a moral good at the same time that it contributed to war with China and colonial conquest in India, and created new forced labor systems that came in the wake of the abolition of slavery.

3

A LITTLE OPIUM, SWEET WORDS,
AND CHEAP GUNS

Planting a Global Industry in Assam

In 1838 the East India Company pursued endorsements from British royals, aristocrats, and merchants for their newest product, tea grown in Assam. Reactions were mixed, but those with imperial interests professed their delight with a beverage grown in one of their country's most recent colonial acquisitions. A very young Queen Victoria enthusiastically declared that she was "much pleased" with the tea's "quality and flavour," and she prophesied that "this Experiment" would "exercise an important influence over the prosperity of the British Empire in the East."[1] After sipping this new "treat," Princess Sophia Matilda likewise wrote that her "national feelings . . . [were] much gratified by the prospect of Tea being brought to perfection in British India."[2] Andrew Melrose, the wealthy Edinburgh grocer and tea wholesaler, ranked this new commodity among the highest class of China black teas.[3] Another batch brought more endorsements. Lady William Bentinck, the spouse of the governor-general of India, asserted that she liked it very much. Sir Robert Peel's wife, Lady Julia, also raved about Assam's "superior and excellent quality." In January 1840, Lord Richard Wellesley, a former governor-general of India and brother to the Duke of Wellington, pronounced that he had enjoyed a "most excellent" beverage.[4]

We cannot say whether these elite consumers actually enjoyed their tea, but we do know they were motivated to declare publicly that Assam's tea was sweet indeed. This tea auspiciously arrived just as the British and Chinese governments were exchanging a series of belligerent gestures that would soon lead to full-scale war. As another privileged consumer put it after sampling the Indian harvest, the prospect of a tea being produced in India that could "supply the home market" would "make this great country independent of China."[5] If tea could be grown in a British colony, Britain could chastise the Celestial Empire, improve its ever-worsening trade deficit, and find a new source of imperial revenue and legitimacy after the EIC lost its monopoly of the China trade. These testimonials thus endorsed a new commodity and an expanding empire.

Tea had grown and been consumed in Assam long before the British arrived, but the British Empire transformed the region into a vast tea garden able to satisfy world markets.[6] This was a sordid business. Between the 1820s and 1870s, the British and their allies fought, threatened, and rewarded local leaders to secure the land and labor for tea.[7] Many never capitulated, and their resistance prompted planters to use the law, the state, and the military to secure their industry and expand into Cachar and Darjeeling and so many other regions. Assam's conquest and reworking into a plantation economy is thus not unique; rather it exemplifies the connections between imperial expansion, international conflict, and the making of mass markets. As we move from Preston to Assam, we can observe the stark colonial power and racial violence that enabled Britain's consumer revolution.

"AN OBJECT SO DECIDEDLY NATIONAL"

At the exact moment that temperance and free-trade enthusiasts sat down to tea together in Preston on Christmas 1834, an official Tea Committee in British India pronounced that Assam's tea was the real thing, that is, the same plant that grew in China.[8] On two sides of the world at the same time, Britons were making tea British. This is not to say that indigenous landowners, rulers, entrepreneurs, and investors did not play their part, but as we will observe, white male planters dominated this industry and defined it as British.[9] This act of appropriation reveals a complex dance in which the British contended with their desires, fears, and fantasies about Asia. Assam and its tea were valued, as William Robinson, the author of *A Descriptive Account of Assam* (1841), saw it, as a means to break China's monopoly and prevent "the merchants of Great Britain" from having "to submit to innumerable restrictions, and insults, and occasional suspensions of trade." Robinson thus called upon the British government to support Indian tea because it was "an object so decidedly national."[10] Attitudes about China had shifted a great deal since Pepys's day, but even as the British and Chinese increasingly viewed each other as barbarians, the British could no longer live without tea. China's control of the tea trade thus endangered Britain's national honor, the liberty of its merchants, and the daily habits of its populace.

Assam's fate was inextricably tied to interactions and tensions among China, Britain, Burma, and local powers. The region was a work of the colonial imagination, shaped by consumer desires, merchants' fears, and international relations. The British described Assam as near China, like China, a path and yet also a barrier to China. It was also a site in need of protection from another growing Asian empire, Burma. British soldiers first found tea in Assam while fighting the Anglo-Burmese War of 1824–26 and as a consequence of allying themselves with some members of the Singpho, the local people who lived in the area of Assam where tea grew abundantly. The Singpho claimed sovereignty over the tea lands and used tea as a resource to battle both the Burmese and the British. The British government nevertheless referred to them as stateless, nomadic "tribal" people who did not lay claim to the land they inhabited. Multiple perceptions of diverse Asian people determined Assam's fate and that of its tea.

In 1833, the newly reformed British Parliament abolished the EIC's monopoly of the tea trade. Immediately, in January 1834, India's governor-general, Lord William Bentinck, established a twelve-person Tea Committee to investigate where and how the plant could be grown in the Raj and to substantiate rumors that the tea plant already grew in a wild state in Assam.[11] Although stories had circulated about this tea since the 1820s, the EIC previously had no financial incentive to develop an alternative tea industry. Things changed in the 1830s, however. In addition to their loss of the China monopoly, the Americans were becoming a notable force in the tea trade, the Dutch were starting to grow tea in Java, and the Chinese were threatening to cut off British supplies. The directors of the EIC believed that "Indian" tea would give the British more control of this trade and it would provide a new way to make money in their Indian empire. In office until 1835, William Bentinck introduced liberal reforms to establish a secure economic footing in the wake of the collapse of the agency houses, credit crisis, and economic depression of 1830–33.[12] By 1834 the company had also incurred a large debt in part as the result of the war with Burma. Bentinck cut the costs of government and made sure that Indian revenues paid for Indian administration.[13] The second son of the Duke of Portland, who had twice been prime minister and was a leader of the Whigs, Bentinck was linked through marriage to leading Evangelicals and also came to support the abolition of slavery.[14] Although socially superior to the community described in the last chapter, Bentinck shared some of their sympathies and no doubt saw tea as a moral drink and profitable crop. Yet he was also eyeing Britain's old rival, the Dutch.

Like the British, Dutch liberals were pressuring for free trade in the colonies, and they too were looking for new ways to make their colonies profitable. In 1824, the Dutch East India Company's head functionary in Japan shipped plants and seeds to Batavia. In 1826 and 1827, seedlings sprouted at a botanical garden and an experimental tea garden, under the control of a new chief commissioner of agriculture, Jacobos Isidorous Lodewijk Levien Jacobson. Born in Rotterdam, the son of a tea and coffee broker, Jacobson had worked for the Netherlands Trading Company as their expert tea taster in Canton. On his last sojourn to China, he managed to leave with an astonishing 7,000,000 seeds and fifteen workmen, among them planters, tea makers, and box makers. The Chinese authorities had placed a price on his head, but Jacobson absconded with his loot in part because his interpreter was captured in his stead.[15] It is no wonder that the Chinese grew guarded in their affairs with Europeans.

The first sample of Dutch colonial tea was produced in the spring of 1828, though there is also evidence that Chinese immigrants had already cultivated tea in their home gardens on Java. The Dutch encountered many problems, however, including an uprising of their Chinese workers.[16] The colonial government remained heavily involved in this business, and the era of private ownership did not really begin until the early 1860s. After that time, Dutch- and English-owned plantations expanded rapidly in the highlands of West Java and later in northeast Sumatra, and planters sought out technical assistance from India and London. They eventually introduced modern processing methods and the Assam *jat* (variety).[17] Indigenous smallholders also grew green and scented teas for local markets. The "Dutch" tea industry was thus a multinational project with several forms of production, but plantation-grown black teas dominated the export trade.[18]

When Bentinck established the Tea Committee, he was thinking about the Dutch and the Chinese, and he was aware that the British lacked the necessary agricultural and manufacturing knowledge to produce an alternative to Chinese tea.[19] He expressly resented the way that the Chinese limited European access to their country and prevented the export of knowledge about growing and processing. Even the most learned European botanists remained fairly ignorant about this plant, though European knowledge was growing. As early as 1778, the famed naturalist Joseph Banks had suggested that tea could be grown in India, and he traveled to China with Lord Macartney in 1793 to learn about tea.[20] In the 1780s, Colonel Robert Kyd of the Bengal Infantry had planted tea in his private botanical garden in Calcutta, and a few plants had sprouted in Brazil and Malabar.[21] Others hunted for tea outside of China. In 1815 one British officer claimed that he had heard that the Singpho people gathered and ate a wild tea. The next year, the resident at the native court of Nepal, Edward Gardner, also reported that he thought tea was growing in the palace garden at Kathmandu. He sent specimens to Dr. Nathaniel Wallich, then superintendent of the Royal Botanical Gardens in Calcutta, but Wallich dismissed them as not true tea but rather a plant known as *Camellia kissa*.[22]

In the 1820s, Britons' desire to plant an Indian tea industry grew as the Chinese increased restrictions on foreign business and refused to buy British manufactured goods. Free traders desperately had wanted to increase trade with the Celestial Empire, but the Chinese, as is well known, were not particularly interested in British manufactured goods. China was purchasing a good deal of Indian opium. Yet officially the British interpreted the restriction of merchants to particular ports, the attempts to curb the importation of opium, and the refusal to export knowledge about tea as rejecting natural law and impeding merchants' liberty.[23]

For some the only answer was war. Historians have debated whether or not the first Opium War (1839–42) was launched to defend trade interests or to avenge Britain's national honor.[24] These concerns were inseparable. For several years before war broke out, British free traders popularized a degenerate and immoral view of the Celestial Empire. The opium and tea traders Jardine and Matheson, for example, developed a corrupt vision of China in their "free trade" journal, the *Canton Register and Price Current*, in the late 1820s and early 1830s. The paper described China as a site of profit and of danger, for Europeans and Chinese alike. Readers could learn of tea merchants being robbed and of horrific floods that "carried away houses, people and brute animals."[25] The paper also revealed China as a world of disease, disorder, and sexual violence.[26] It became a venue for airing grievances and developing a sense of moral superiority. In 1831, for example, one merchant wrote in a letter to the editor of the *Register* that the British should cut off the tea trade altogether rather than submit to repeated Chinese insults. He threatened, "The Chinese must be undeceived, and must be taught that England, in the character of a prude merchant, will calculate accurately the cost of what she buys, and will not consent to purchase Tea at the high price of national disgrace."[27] Britain, a careful shopper, would not let her thirst for tea come at the expense of national honor. Free traders thus used nationalism and gender to devise moral arguments to criticize China's economic policies and to promote free trade.[28]

It is in this atmosphere of growing animosity between China and Britain that Indian tea came to be seen as appealing. In 1828, John Walker, a tea trader who had lived and worked in Canton, wrote a long memo to the government describing how Indian tea could "annihilate the China monopoly."[29] This memo shaped government policy but also left its mark on later understandings of tea and its history.[30] Walker contended the uncertain state of commercial relations with China was not "consistent with the dignity of the British Empire." He especially condemned the "jealous policy of the Chinese Government in her intercourse with all nations," which had

> confined us for the present to the port of Canton, (in former times we had access to other ports) situated at the western extremity of the empire, and furthest from Peking, the seat of Government; even in the city of Canton, barriers are fixed beyond which no Englishman can pass; so that all commercial men who go to China, see about as much of China as a Chinese would of England, or of London, if we were confined to Wapping, and not permitted to go beyond the Tower.[31]

Walker thus described China's attempts to maintain its sovereignty as insulting to British manhood. He argued that doing business in China felt like a form of imprisonment that was demeaning and emasculating. In Walker's memo China became a potent symbol of monopoly and despotism.

"We must not deceive ourselves," Walker explained, "the empire of China is the greatest, most extensive and most populous that exists in the world, or has existed in ancient or modern times, and contains everything necessary within itself." The Chinese were formidable enemies who were well aware of Britain's growing Asian power. As he explained it, "The fears of the Chinese government have lately been excited by the brilliant and rapid progress of our arms, and the prodigious extension of our Indian empire, which in the North and North-East has its boundaries almost upon the very frontiers of China."[32] The victor in this struggle was yet to be determined, but Walker worried that Britain's insatiable thirst for Chinese tea could tip the balance in favor of Asia. He recognized that tea earned the government approximately £4,000,000 per annum in taxes and that its use had become "so intermingled" with British "habits and customs that it would not easily be dispensed with."[33] For Walker and others, the mass consumption of Chinese tea had become the foundation of British power and its problems.

While other nations certainly enjoyed their tea, Britain was by far the greatest market for the Chinese import at this time. As can be seen in table 3.1, Great Britain imported 40,000,000 pounds annually in 1834, all of which came from China. British settlers in the colonies, including India, consumed another 2,750,000 pounds. This British World was willing to fight for its tea. In February 1839, at one of the first meetings of the newly formed Assam Company (the first private company to grow tea in India), a speaker explained the situation to the company's board of directors:

> It is well known that, on the slightest pretense, and indeed, without even the excuse of pretense, the Chinese authorities have frequently suspended our trade, and ordered the "Barbarians," as Englishmen are still publicly and officially styled, to quit the country—a proceeding which has often occasioned considerable inconvenience and embarrassment and Every Merchant who is engaged in the Tea Trade, must feel that it is carried on under the most humiliating circumstances, and be desirous of getting rid of a dependence on the "Celestial Empire" by a submission to which he is alone enabled to carry on a profitable Trade in an article, which was once a luxury, but is now become a necessary of life—An opportunity now, for the first time, presents itself to the English Merchant to render himself and his country independent of China in the Tea Trade.[34]

This speech was delivered only a month before British traders were confined to their warehouses in Canton for six weeks and just months before hostilities

TABLE 3.1. EUROPEAN AND AMERICAN TEA MARKETS,
APPROXIMATE NATIONAL ANNUAL CONSUMPTION
IN POUNDS, 1834

MARKET	POUNDS (MILLIONS)
Great Britain	40.0
United States	10.0
Russia	6.5
Holland	3.0
Germany	1.0
British America and West Indies	1.5
British Settlements in India	1.0
British Australian Colonies	0.25
France	0.25

Source: Report on Tea Duties, Ordered by the House of
Commons, printed 25 July 1834, *Westminster Review* 22, no. 44
(April 1835): 369–70.

broke out between the two nations. The Chinese were embarrassing and humiliating British merchants. Indian tea offered a noble alternative that could satisfy consumer desires without generating merchants' shame.

Indian tea's advocates were not just thinking about the British market, however. Walker and others who promoted the industry guaranteed investors almost limitless global markets. Walker assumed that the "whole Continent of Europe . . . Canada, the United States, and the Barbary Coast and India itself" would buy the Subcontinent's tea. Indeed, he claimed that a substantial market already existed in the East India Company's territories, particularly in Calcutta. And, relying on the health claims popular among free traders and temperance enthusiasts, Walker asserted that the Indian consumer, especially "Hindoos" whose "only drink is water," would find moderately priced tea "a most refreshing addition to their domestic economy, as well as a salutary beverage in those fatal febrile affections to which the oppressive heat of the climate predisposes them."[35] Indian tea offered another reward as well. Walker argued that Bengal's "native [cotton] weavers," who had been ruined by competition with the factories in Manchester and Glasgow, would happily migrate to tea-producing regions in Assam.

Thus in the 1820s and early 1830s, Indian tea came to be regarded as a solution to a series of interconnected global problems. Assam could satisfy the world's thirst for an inexpensive and healthful beverage, could provide the British government with steady revenue, and would teach China once and for all that Britain was the more powerful of the two empires. Such ideas had circulated before, but they grew in significance when China threatened to cut off Britain's supplies. In the 1820s, however, much of Assam was not technically within the borders of the British Empire, and the British state had not officially recognized its tea as the real thing. Ten years later the situation would be very different.

WAR IN THE BORDERLANDS AND THE EUROPEAN "DISCOVERY" OF TEA

*A discovery has been made of no less importance
than that the hand of Nature has planted the [tea]
shrub within the bounds of the wide dominion of
Great Britain; a discovery which must materially
influence the destiny of nations.*

—G. G. SIGMOND, *TEA: ITS EFFECTS MEDICINAL AND MORAL*

This account of the "discovery" of tea growing wild in Assam was published in 1839, just a few months after the British removed all pretense of local autonomy in this region. When the author suggested that "Nature" had planted the tea shrub within the "wide dominion" of Great Britain and that this would "influence the destiny of nations" he was correct. Assam was now officially British. However, this was not quite the case five years earlier when on Christmas Eve 1834 the Tea Committee publicly announced that "the tea shrub is beyond all doubt indigenous in Upper Assam," and this "discovery" was "to be by far the most important and valuable that has ever been made on matters connected with the agricultural or commercial resources of this empire."[36]

The conquest and cultivation of tea in Assam were two parts of the same process. War and trade brought the British to Assam and allowed them to "discover" tea in its jungles. Military might and colonial power enabled the conquest of the land and labor necessary for production, and this inspired resistance that lasted into the twentieth century.[37] Most histories of Indian tea acknowledge aspects of this imperial story.[38] Political and economic accounts of annexation have also recognized the role of tea.[39] However, until recently local involvement has been downplayed, with one scholar commenting: "In the discovery of tea the Assamese had no important role."[40] All too often, Assam has served merely as a backdrop for the adventures of soldiers and naturalists, who struggled to nurse China plants or courageously explore dangerous jungles in

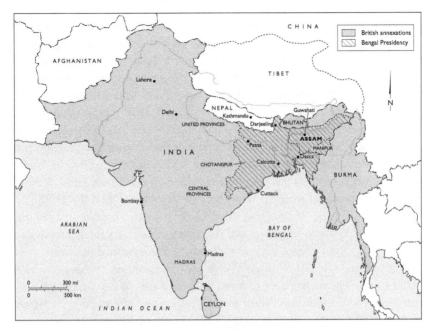

MAP 3.1. British India, showing the Bengal presidency and Assam.

search of tea.[41] In reality, several nationalities and people of mixed-race descent transformed the political economy of these northeast borderlands. Politics and racial and gender ideologies also influenced the history of this complex region.[42] As one important new study has argued as well, the monsoonal climate and ever-shifting river systems shaped administrative practices, notions of sovereignty, economies, and social and cultural histories. Though far from the center of British India, this borderland was central to the colonial and postcolonial history of the Subcontinent (map 3.1).[43]

Though its boundaries shifted throughout the eighteenth and nineteenth centuries, the kingdom of Assam was situated along the Brahmaputra River and was about four hundred miles in length and about sixty miles in width. Its soil is exceptionally fertile, enriched by the flooding Brahmaputra and its many tributaries. It is also one of the wettest places in the world, with an especially long and heavy rainy season. There are hilly regions, but the area is largely flat and covered with dense jungle. For about six hundred years, the Ahoms, a group of Shan who had migrated from Upper Burma in the thirteenth century, ruled the kingdom. Except for a brief period of Mughal rule, and until the 1760s, the Ahom government had been exceptionally stable.[44]

Although understood today as on the edge of India, Assam was an important region in the commercial and migration routes known as the South-West Silk

Road, or the overland commercial networks that connected China with India and Southeast Asia.[45] The Ahom kings had promoted trade with neighboring regions, especially Bengal, Tibet, Bhutan, and China. Some of the principal exports to Bengal and Tibet were muga silk, lac, elephant tusks, cotton, pepper, and mustard seed. From Bengal Assam imported salt, copper, English woolens, and spices. From Tibet came Chinese goods, such as silk and smoking pipes. Assamese merchants also went to Yunnan directly, through Sadiya and across several mountain ranges. The hill communities traded spices, cotton, salt, and silver between China and South Asia. The EIC became interested in Assam precisely because of its position between Bengal and China and hoped to establish commercial relations with these "frontier tribes" and through them directly with China.[46] Assam was also thought to be rich in gold. In 1792, for example, J. P. Wade wrote to a friend, "Assam is not a country for diamonds, but it is for gold dust. I think I shall do well in it."[47] Wade penned this letter while accompanying Captain Thomas Welsh on an expedition to Assam, which Lord Cornwallis had launched to assess the possibilities of commercial relations between Assam and Bengal. These men found a potentially valuable landscape, rich in sugarcane, pepper vine, poppy, indigo, mustard seed, tobacco, betel nut, ginger, and rice. They also found iron and saltpeter, and gold in the sands of the Brahmaputra and the other mountains and streams.[48] They did not notice or were uninterested in the tea growing in Assam's jungles.

British colonization of Assam was a long, drawn-out, and bloody process, whose history parallels that of some areas of the American Southwest. Though the EIC officially followed a policy of nonintervention in the region, it was attracted to Assam's riches and its trading networks and ultimately contributed to its political and social instability.[49] The company began to be involved in Assam in the 1760s, a period typically described as a time of social conflict, "weak" kings, "evil" ministers, and court intrigue.[50] During the last years of Ahom rule, from approximately the 1760s to the 1820s, the region went from being a stable polity to a borderland in which various groups possessing different assumptions about landholding and authority vied for control.[51] Empires and smaller indigenous groups fought for power, but Assam's fate was not determined until the Burmese invaded and occupied the region in 1817.[52]

The Kingdom of Ava or Burmese Empire, growing in power and confidence, was concerned about the East India Company's increasing interest in the region. The two powers went to war in 1824. At the opening of hostilities, the British sought to reassure the Assamese that they had no interest in conquering them. Addressed to the "Inhabitants of Assam," the British issued a proclamation that began:

It is well known to you that some years ago the Burmese invaded your territory, and that they had since dethroned the Rajah, plundered the country, slaughtered Brahmins, and women, and cows, defiled your temples, and committed the most barbarous outrages of every kind, so that vast numbers of your countrymen have been forced to seek refuge in our dominions, where they have never ceased to implore our assistance.[53]

The British had in fact ignored Assamese calls for help for some years. Now they claimed to be Assam's protector, as the proclamation went on to explain: "We are not led into your country by the thirst of conquest; but are forced, in our own defense, to deprive our enemy of the means of annoying us." "You may, therefore rest assured," the proclamation continued, "that we will never consent to depart until we exclude our foe from Assam, and re-establish in that country a government adapted to your wants, and calculated to promote the happiness of all classes."[54] Though it is unlikely that most Assamese ever heard this declaration, one contemporary local ballad expressed that "The hearts of the people became glad at the coming of the English."[55]

The British presented themselves to the Assamese as a friend and protector who would rout Burma, which they described as a despotic brutal kingdom engaged in a reign of terror.[56] Popular reports and histories repeated how the Burmese plundered the region, murdered men, raped women, and tortured children. Maniram Dewan, an Assamese nobleman who would help establish tea in Assam, gave this account of the Burmese occupation:

> In attacking the house of a rich man they would tie him with ropes and then set fire to his body. It was dangerous for a beautiful woman to meet the Burmese even in the public roads. Brahmins were made to carry loads of beef, pork and wine. The Gossains were robbed of all their possessions. Fathers of damsels whom the Burmese took to wives rose speedily to affluence and power.[57]

Maniram described the Burmese as sexually and morally depraved, not honoring religious or gender norms, and devoid of respect for property.[58] He likely used such rhetoric to elicit British support, and his interpretation became the official story. In his study of the region in the 1850s, Major John Butler indignantly described "the barbarous practices of the Burmese, who, in their invasion of Assam, massacred great numbers of inhabitants in cold blood." He characterized the Burmese as inhumane cannibalistic savages, who "cut off the lobes of poor victims' ears and choice portions of the body, such as the points of the shoulders, and actually ate the raw flesh before the living sufferers."[59] Butler then wrote about the EIC's rule right after his account of Burmese cannibalism: "I will turn now from these cruelties, so revolting to humanity, and with pleasure place on record the improvements that have taken place in Assam under British rule."[60] The contrast between Burma and Britain thus justified British involvement in the region and led to the sense that Assam was empty and ripe for British conquest. In one account written "to afford information to the shareholders of the new Assam Company," Lord Amherst described the Ava war (as the struggle with Burma was known) as emancipating the "Assamese and other tribes on our northeast frontier, from the Burmese yoke."[61] The British styled themselves liberators, and this view was repeated in various accounts of the discovery of tea. The British interest in Assam thus appeared to be a humanitarian gesture. Rather than a bold move of colonial expansion and search for new sources of commerce and revenue, the British East India Company's annexation of Assam looked like a means to contain the evil Burmese Empire.

In truth, the costly and difficult war destabilized the EIC and other polities in the region. In addition to the Burmese, the British battled local communities, particularly the Singpho, a far from harmonious group that was also vying for power in the region. Some of their leaders took advantage of the general chaos of this period, raiding villages and enslaving the inhabitants.[62] Though not officially allied with the Burmese, the Singpho lived in Burma and Assam, and they occasionally joined the Burmese on their raids. Slavery was an important part of the Singpho economy so when the British released their prisoners and ended slavery in the company's territories in India in 1843, this disrupted the local economy and inspired rebellion. It was in this territory that the British discovered tea seemingly growing in a wild state.

In late February 1826, the Burmese ministers signed the Treaty of Yandabo, in which the king of Ava renounced his claims on Assam and the neighboring states of Cachar, Jayantia, and other conquered provinces (map 3.2). The British announced that they wished to revive the Ahom system of government and to make the lands productive. David Scott, the agent to the governor-general for the eastern frontier, had urged the reestablishment of the native dynasty.[63] However, the British could not decide upon the rightful line of succession, leading many Assamese nobles and commoners to remain in open rebellion.[64] After years of unsettled rule, the British government installed Purandar Singha as raja of Upper Assam in the spring of 1833 (map 3.3). However, the British exacted an extraordinarily high tribute of 50,000 rupees, and they reserved the right to remove Singha if he proved an ineffective ruler. Lower Assam remained directly under British control.[65] Within a few years, the British charged Singha with all

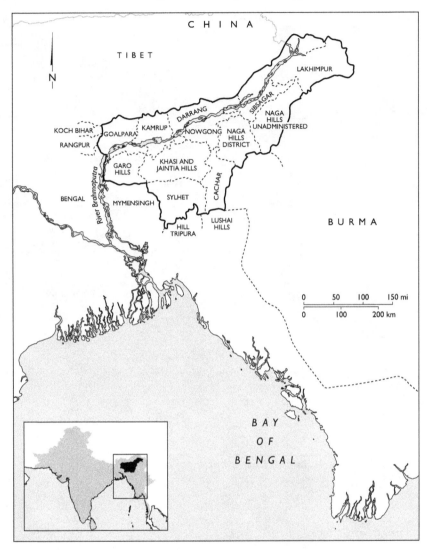

MAP 3.2. District map of British Assam.

manner of crimes and in 1838 they summarily dismissed him and annexed all of his former territory.[66] Before this happened Purandar Singha and his main advisor, Maniram Dewan, helped launch the plantation economy.

During the unsettled years immediately before and after the Treaty of Yandabo, several individuals "discovered" tea in Assam. The indigenous communities drank tea, but it was "discovered" only when outsiders declared Assam's tea trees were the same as the China plant. While contemporaries and later historians

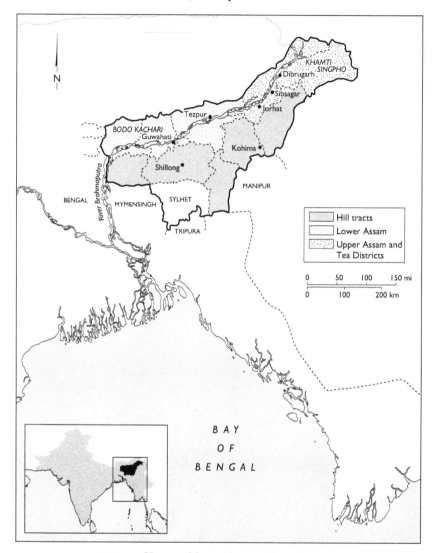

MAP 3.3. Upper and Lower Assam with main towns.

debated which European protagonist made this scientific "discovery," in fact
many figures were involved in a long process. The Tea Committee credited
the "indefatigable researches" of Captain Jenkins, the agent to the governor-
general of the Northeast Frontier, and Lieutenant Charlton of the Assam Light
Infantry, who in 1831 found tea trees nearly fourteen feet high growing near
Beesa at the foot of a low range of hills.[67] Charlton was the officer in charge of

this region, and according to an Assamese chronicle, he first encountered this tea while pursuing the Burmese. The same chronicle noted that Charles Bruce, Captain Neufville, Lieutenant Kerr, Captain Bedingfield, Maniram Dewan, and Baloram Khargharia Phukan were also with Jenkins and Charlton.[68] The disagreement has been over whether Charlton or Robert Bruce (Charles's brother) should be regarded as the true discovers of Assam's tea, and whether this momentous event happened in 1823 or 1831. This debate has reinforced the idea that outsiders discovered tea in a single moment instead of seeing this as a story of conquest and colonization.

Major Robert Bruce came to Assam as a merchant and soldier of fortune and he had already been fighting the Burmese before the British were officially involved. In 1821 Bruce procured arms and ammunition from the EIC and led a command of Purandar Singha's forces against the Burmese.[69] In 1823, while on a trading expedition, Maniram introduced Bruce to a Singpho chief, Beesa Gaum (gaum translated roughly meant chief or clan leader), who lived in the region of vast tea tracts. Beesa Gaum agreed to supply Bruce with tea seeds and plants. Robert Bruce died soon thereafter, but first he told his brother Charles about the tea. Beesa Gaum followed through on his agreement and sent Charles both seeds and plants in 1824.[70]

Another important figure in this history is Dr. Nathaniel Wallich, director of the government's Botanical Gardens at Calcutta and secretary of the Tea Committee. Wallich was born Nathan Wolff, a Danish Jew, who had come to Bengal as a surgeon with the Danish East India Company. Wallich at first claimed that Assam's tea was not the real thing. However, reports came back from Assam that convinced Wallich and the others that this was in fact a species of *Camellia sinensis*, the Linnaean name given to the China tea plant.[71] Wallich supported Charles Bruce's claim and proposed Bruce be hired to turn Assam's wild plants into working plantations. "It was Mr. Bruce, and his late brother, Major R. Bruce, at Jorehath, who originally brought the Assam tea to public notice, many years ago, when no one had the slightest idea of its existence," Wallich contended. He also liked Bruce's local knowledge, his morality, and his physical stamina:

> His long residence in Assam, his intimate acquaintance with the customs, languages, prejudices, etc. of the many tribes that inhabit the province and adjoining countries, his excellent moral character . . . his extraordinary strength of constitution, which has enabled him to encounter the fiercest jungles, at seasons when it would be fatal to anyone else to come near them; all these considerations combine to render him eminently qualified for the duties in question.[72]

Wallich thus characterized Bruce as a heroic figure whose ability to battle the jungle made him the best person to nurture a young industry. Later histories often presented planters similarly as bellicose and nurturing.[73]

Charles Bruce saw himself as on a solitary quest to bring pleasure and profits to the British and the Assamese. When he recommended himself to the Tea Committee, Bruce described how at sixteen he left England as a midshipman, how he had twice been captured by the French "after two hard-fought actions; [and] was marched across the Isle of France at the end of the bayonet . . . until that island was taken by the British." In captivity he "suffered much, and twice lost all I possessed, and was never remunerated in any way." Once freed, he became an officer on a "troop ship against Java, and was at the taking of that place." Then at the outbreak of the war against Burma, he offered his "services to Mr. Scott, then agent to the governor-general, and was appointed to command gun-boats." This position was fortuitous since his command was at Sadiya in the extreme northeast, the very place that his brother had told him tea was growing "wild." Bruce asserted that he "was the first European who ever penetrated the forests, and visited the tea tracts in British Suddiya, and brought away specimens of earth, fruit, and flowers, and the first who discovered numerous other tracts." He also claimed that he had defended the tea against the Singpho chief "Duffa Gaum, and his followers, who threatened to over-run the frontier, and it was my good fortune to expel him twice with my gun boat from two strong positions."[74]

In 1836, after the Tea Committee appointed Charles Bruce as superintendent of Tea Culture, he explored jungles, discovered tea tracts, seduced and threatened the Singpho, and figured out how to grow and manufacture tea. Bruce's memoranda and letters to his superiors and the Tea Committee reveal, however, a complicated account of local complicity and resistance. Bruce, Wallich, and others went on numerous forays through the jungle looking for tea. Most wrote of these adventures as arduous but exciting work. Wallich, for example, described how traveling through the Muttock country in February 1836 was horrible. He complained of "incessant rain day and night," which was "awfully distressing, considering the rough mode of traveling which we are obliged to and the horrid jungles we have to pass through. . . . Such is Assam!"[75] William Griffith, also on this expedition, was not as disgusted by the climate and published a detailed description of the landscape, vegetation, and people of Upper Assam. His account from January 1836 is typical: "This morning we crossed the small streamlet Maumoo, ascended a rather high bank, and within a few yards from it came upon tea; which as we advanced farther into the jungle increased in abundance; in fact within a very few yards, several plants might be observed."[76] They also desired what they saw as extraordinarily fertile land; though it was watery and difficult to navigate, it simply needed "a settled government" to become "a highly valued acquisition to the British Government."[77] Such writing made colonization a European and masculine project of opening and penetrating the dark secrets of a far-off yet fertile landscape.[78] Nature had to be conquered to make tea. Major Butler, who had been an officer with the Bengal Native Infantry and later became an administrator in Assam, began his memoir with a powerful image of the flooding Brahmaputra sweeping away his newly built house, which had sheltered his wife and young child. Nature was both abundant and dangerous. It provided apple, peach, oak, fir, and coffee trees, as well as tea, but Butler also saw a "dreary, gloomy, desolate wilderness."[79] Planters' memoirs were laced with the "metaphor of redemption," in which a barren but potentially abundant landscape was brought under cultivation and hence made useful and godly.[80]

Published descriptions tended to ignore or downplay the fact that the local inhabitants did not welcome the British and their allies with open arms. In truth, the British had entered into a rivalry between two groups of Singpho, led by Beesa Gaum (their ally) and Duffa Gaum (their enemy). Duffa was so troublesome that Bruce wrote in 1836: "I have little hope of making anything in that quarter as long as the Duffa Gaum is at large."[81] Burra Senpattee of the Muttock country, in the center of Upper Assam, was an ally of Duffa Gaum who also tried to block Bruce's efforts.[82] In Bruce's words, Senpattee was "reluctant" to give Bruce "an elephant and a few coolies" and had tried to stop his people from revealing the whereabouts of the tea. Bruce believed he won over the "villagers" with "kindness and presents, and by free access to my person of all the village people who came flocking in to see me." They then told him about "one tea tract after another, although they had been strictly prohibited from giving me any information whatever."[83] Bruce evidently "reconciled" with Senpattee, who, as Jenkins described it, had "evinced a good deal of jealousy in regard to our occupation of the tea forests."[84]

This colonial archive is highly revealing. Jenkins, Bruce, and their colleagues refused to see Senpattee as exercising sovereignty. Rather, they called him jealous, reluctant, childish, and greedy. In a letter to Jenkins, Bruce wrote, "I would like to go back to the Singpho country to make a few presents to those gaums who may be favourably disposed to our objects, I therefore hope the guns and pistols are on their way up, the very sight of which would make them promise anything." Bruce explained to Jenkins that he had told "all these people that I had come to do the country good, by instructing them how to cultivate and manufacture tea." The next part of this sentence is illuminating, for he also wrote, "I do not think any of them believed me, so strongly had they been prejudiced and assured to the contrary." Nevertheless, he felt assured that he could bring them round "to study their own interest," and soon "all of Upper Assam [would become] a tea-garden."[85] Bruce thus realized that he was not believed, but that didn't stop him from his mission. These letters describe conquest from the conqueror's position, but they do tell us that while some resisted the British outright, others used the British and their presents to gain power and allies in an unstable period.

The Tea Committee backed up Bruce and described him as a hero, who had gained access to the tea tracts cheaply, with the promise of "a little opium, and the use of a 'few soft words,'" and a few "cheap" guns. In Nigrew the gaum "denied at first that he knew of any more tea in that neighbourhood" until Bruce "made him a small present of opium, and told him how much he would be thought of by the commissioner if he forwarded his views." After smoking a Singpho pipe and addressing the chief as "elder brother," the chief then picked up Bruce's double-barreled gun and "begged" Bruce to ask the commissioner if he could have one. Bruce promised the gun in return for information about the whereabouts of tea. The Tea Committee praised Bruce for thus establishing "friendly feelings in the minds of the rude tribes, amongst whose villages the indigenous tea is found."[86] Bruce asked for more guns and traded these for compliance.

The Singpho capitulated perhaps out of a combination of fear, the anticipation of rewards, and the desire to use the British to gain power over their neighbors. There is no doubt that Bruce played one group off of another and gunboats always lurked behind his sweet words. While the Tea Committee described a solitary British hero, both brothers had local wives and eight children between them. Charles's mixed-race nephew, Captain Bruce, was often by his side and was also in command of Purandar Singha's militia.[87] The Bruce family, Beesa Gaum, Purandar Singha, and Maniram Dewan lived, worked, and fought together, and it was this mixed-race community that launched the Indian tea industry in Assam. Purandar Singha, for example, believed that commercial production would help his people and bring him "a handsome profit."[88] He helped the British procure "the best laborers in Assam" and started his own plantations as well.[89] He divided the tea tracts between the British and himself and expected that the British would "instruct his people in the management of the plant and manufacture of tea." Captain Jenkins supported this plan because it would secure the "goodwill of all the native chiefs" and the raja's "zealous assistance in the undertaking."[90] The tenuous partnership was short-lived, however, and the British removed Singha from the throne in 1838 as soon as they no longer needed his help.

A similar fate befell Maniram Dutta Barbhandar Barua, known as Maniram Dewan. For several decades, Maniram had a very successful career working with the British and thus is a controversial figure, remembered as a collaborator and as an early nationalist leader. A noble and modernizer, Maniram helped transform the region from a "native feudal economy to the alien colonial plantation economy."[91] In the 1820s and 1830s he worked for the EIC and was chief advisor to Purandar Singha. He reorganized the local administration, collected revenues from a destitute peasantry, helped the British defeat the hill tribes, and thus worked to establish the plantation economy. Maniram had close connections with both Indian and European businessmen and imagined that a plantation-based economy would help modernize Assam and provide him with a substantial income, thereby replacing lost revenues that came with British conquest. Reduced to a "commoner," he lost no time in making the new regime work for him.[92]

In 1839, the newly created Assam Company hired Maniram Dewan as a chief executive and gave him a very high annual salary of six hundred rupees. He managed accounts, convinced the Naga and Singpho to work on the company's plantations, and established a local market for tea.[93] He was so successful in helping this new company overcome a host of obstacles that one of the directors wrote in 1841, "I find the Native Department of the office is in its most beneficial state under the excellent directions of Muneeram, whose intelligence and activity is of the greatest value to our establishment." He also commented, "The marts which he is establishing at and around our location will, he declares, become of considerable importance.[94] In other words, Maniram helped cultivate the Indian market.

Maniram's success led to his eventual downfall, however. The Europeans in the Assam Company began to challenge his authority and conflicts erupted between Maniram and the European officers, one of which involved an unproven charge of murder. Maniram resigned his post in 1845 and started two plantations, Cinnemara at Jorhat and Selung at Sibsagar.[95] He recruited Chinese and native labor, produced a high-quality tea, sold it in Assam and abroad, and displayed samples at the Great Exhibition in 1851. In 1858, Cinnemara was producing 70,000 pounds annually.[96] Maniram did not profit from this success, however, since that year he was hung for his supposed involvement in the "Indian Mutiny."

Nevertheless, local elite and foreign nationals had worked with the British to bring capitalism to Assam. The Tea Committee also included one Chinese and two "native" gentlemen. Wallich was a Danish Jew and the Bruce brothers were Scottish and their children were half Assamese. The early Assam Company was also initially a "racially hybrid business." For example, Dwarkanath Tagore served on the board and Marwaris made loans to tea estates.[97] By midcentury, however, heightened racial tensions and sheer greed encouraged white Britons to enact laws and systems of land distribution that permitted only the wealthiest local elites to remain in this new industry.[98] Europeans, especially the Scottish, came to dominate the planting industries, but Indians also invested in tea and helped establish the new capitalist enterprise.

On 10 January 1839, twelve chests, approximately 350 pounds, of Assam tea went to auction in the London Commercial Sale Rooms. This sample was from the same source as the tea that had so pleased Queen Victoria, her courtiers, and retailers, such as Andrew Melrose. Despite the fact that it had actually arrived in a damaged state in Calcutta, a publicity-seeking retailer by the name of Captain Pidding purchased all the tea for unheard-of prices, with the last lot reaching 34s. per pound. Much like the queen's endorsement, this auction was about publicity. According to the EIC Court of Directors, it created "a great excitement and competition," as did the "fancy price" for a product of "novelty and curiosity."[99] In February, the Assam Company formed in London, with a capital of £500,000 divided into 10,000 shares. Europeans and Indians also formed the Bengal Tea Association, another joint-stock company with a capital of Rs 10,000,000. The two firms eventually merged, and in 1866, the Calcutta board was abolished and London controlled the company.[100] By that time, the Assam Company and other private and joint-stock companies thought they had found El Dorado on the northeast frontier of the Indian empire.

"THEY WILL NOT CLEAR THE JUNGLE": MAKING TEA MAKERS

After the EIC proved tea could be grown in Assam, it transferred most of its plantations into private hands, primarily to the Assam Company. But state support did not recede. Government agents surveyed and mapped the region, instituted wasteland rules that granted land on liberal terms to Europeans and a few wealthy indigenous elite, and bestowed planters with police powers to protect their land and compel laborers to work. State revenues helped build transportation and communication systems that linked the plantations to the outer world. As we will see in later chapters, the colonial state also funded global advertising and market research and helped planters forge agreements with major retailers. In these and countless other ways, then, the colonial government facilitated the creation of the plantation economy and global markets.

The Assam Company's archive illuminates planters' mind-sets during these early years and clarifies how migrant workers and local communities also structured this industry. The company was launched amid great optimism as company directors and investors were led to believe that "the process of Tea manufacture is considered to be peculiarly suited to the peaceful habits of the Assamese."[101] Soon, however, the Assam Company discovered it could not induce local people to work for a wage and that the hill populations, namely the Singpho, Lushai, Mishmi, Khasi, and Naga, constantly attacked planters and their families.[102] The British responded in kind and between 1835 and 1851, for example, they launched ten military expeditions against the Naga alone, and even then the area was not completely incorporated into the Raj until 1898.[103]

It is well to remember that large-scale plantations were not necessary for the mass production of tea. In China peasant proprietors grew tea on smallholdings, which they sold to collectors, who resold tea to the factories that transformed the leaves into manufactured teas for the home and export markets.[104] The British might have adopted this system, but they lacked the workers, knowledge, and efficient systems of transport that would have enabled them to ensure freshness and quality. They imported Chinese seeds, plants, and technical knowledge, but not the system of peasant proprietors.[105] Instead, the Raj imported the plantation model in use in the Americas and the Caribbean. Also known as "estates" or "gardens," tea plantations required an abundant supply of cheap labor. In India, experts determined that plantations should be at minimum about five hundred acres with at least one laborer per acre if not more.[106] Workers cleared and prepared the land, planted, weeded, and tended young plants (fig. 3.1). In the spring they plucked new leaves and brought them to a factory that was on or near the plantation, where the leaves would be sorted and then undergo a process by which they were transformed into a marketable commodity. European or mixed-race managers supervised the process, which in these early years was all done by hand.[107] The plantation and factory were structured not just for efficiency and economies of scale but to supervise a very unenthusiastic labor force.

FIGURE 3.1. Tea garden workers, Assam. Sir Bampfylde Fuller, *The Empire of India* (Boston: Little, Brown, 1913). (Courtesy of the Library of Congress/Internet Archive)

In Assam, decades of war, civil strife, and the first years of British rule had brutalized and decimated Assam's population.[108] Instead of focusing on why Assam had so few people and why so many did not want to work on the plantations, Bruce and his colleagues repeatedly justified their failures by racializing and denigrating "the miserable Opium-smoking Assamese."[109] For example, in 1837, Charles Bruce frustratingly reported: "I cannot get the Singphoos to do as I wish; they work how and when they please. They are under no control, and do not wish to work at all." Bruce could not get them to clear the jungle and felt that "as long as they have sufficient opium and rice of their own" they simply would not work for pay. He worried the country could not be made profitable, "unless we import men to make the Singphoos more industrious."[110] They were not just resistant; they were rebellious.

In 1839 Bruce despondently wrote that the "troubles in which this frontier has been unfortunately involved" had made it difficult for him to commit his "thoughts to paper."[111] He begged the government to make this frontier safe for British business: "Muttuck is a country that abounds in Tea, and it might be made [into] one extensive, beautiful Tea garden"; but "Our Tea," he admitted, "is insecure here. . . . It was but a month or two ago that so great an alarm was created, that my people had to retire from our Tea gardens." He continued, "We have to have the means of defending ourselves from a sudden attack, ever since that unfortunate affair at Sudiya."[112] This "unfortunate affair" referred to the Khampti revolt, in which Major A. White, political agent in Upper Assam, and several others were killed. Bruce's writing suggests that although he thought of tea and the region as British, the local communities did not. He called on the government to protect "British" interests. The use of force only worsened the situation, however, and in January 1843 the Singpho attacked British outposts at Nigrew and Beesa. All the chiefs had joined in this attack, including Beesa Gaum, who had, it will be remembered, previously helped the British find tea in the first place. The British interned Beesa Gaum and took other measures to suppress the local population.[113] At least one planter, Francis Bonynge, fled the country and ended up in the southern United States where he began to plant tea and other tropical commodities with African slave labor.[114] Worker rebellion thus spurred the globalization of production and labor.

As in so many other plantation societies, the planters began to import indentured labor from communities that were far removed from growing regions.[115] Between the 1860s and 1947, over three million migrants from other areas of India were transported to work in Assam's tea gardens.[116] The mass consumption of tea could not have existed without this extraordinary movement of people. Initially the British wanted Chinese workers, but this soon changed after a famous incident involving a particularly rebellious group from Singapore in 1841. A large group of these workers had become involved in an affray with the local Bengalis "in which death ensued." The British magistrate jailed fifty-seven of the Chinese men, but there were "so many difficulties" that their trial was delayed and eventually no proof was offered against them. Those who were not imprisoned refused to go to Assam without their countrymen and evidently "when they were released, they demanded a further advance of pay, and supplies of opium and provision." The report suggested that they still "would not yield; we had little power over them, and they were consequently discharged on the spot."[117] The workers then went on a rampage in Calcutta before being exiled to Mauritius. Another report, trying to explain this same incident, commented, "These men turned out to be of a very bad character—They were turbulent, obstinate, and rapacious."[118] The Assam Company relied on racial and cultural stereotypes to explain their problems. While the Chinese were "turbulent," the local Assamese were repeatedly described as indolent.

Bruce acknowledged that Assam's peasants believed it was "mean and servile" to take "service for payment," and they preferred "to cultivate a small patch of ground which barely yields a subsistence." Yet, rather than see these people as independent-minded peasants, he called them lazy and ultimately blamed their behavior on an affinity for opium.[119] Opium cultivation was widespread in nineteenth-century Assam.[120] When Europeans first described Assam, they included opium, along with minerals, timber, and fruit, as a useful and potentially profitable crop.[121] Planters and officials began to call Assamese opium a morally dubious luxury, not a commercial crop under peasant control, only when it threatened tea production and posed a threat to Bengal's opium trade.

Bruce had traded opium for information about tea, but without any sense of contradiction he repeatedly argued that opium had ruined the region and its people. In a passionate plea for the government to outlaw its cultivation, Bruce surmised that "the Opium mania,—that dreadful *plague* . . . depopulated this beautiful country, turned it into a land of wild beasts . . . and has degenerated the Assamese from a fine race of people, to the most abject, servile, crafty, and demoralized race in India." Opium had made the Assamese unfit for work and rendered its workforce unable to reproduce itself. "The women," he argued, "have fewer children compared with those in other countries" and the men are so "enfeebled" that they are "more effeminate than women."[122] When explaining their failures to investors and government officials, other tea planters also argued that opium drained off available labor supplies and corrupted workers' bodies and morality. John Butler, agent to the governor-general in Assam in the late 1830s, regretted that "two-thirds of the population are addicted" to opium, that the drug made the Assamese "licentious" and accounted for their degeneration.[123] The Assam Company's annual reports told the same story.[124] One report from May 1857 (just before the outbreak of the Indian Rebellion) concluded: "the unrestricted cultivation of Opium in the province of Assam has an injurious effect on the Assamese, and considerably diminishes the supply of labour."[125] Such accounts made tea planters the victims of unruly indigenous consumer behaviors and highlighted, through opposition, tea's morality. This negative view of opium was never entirely endorsed, and some colonial administrators argued that opium produced better, more docile workers who were able to endure physically demanding tasks.[126] The nascent Indian tea industry, however, saw opium as an indigenous-owned industry that was in direct competition with tea and with British-controlled opium in Bengal, and in 1861 the state banned opium cultivation in Assam.[127] Like tea, opium was profitable and had medicinal properties, but it became a convenient scapegoat for tea's myriad problems.

All the excuses in the world could not cover up the fact that during the 1840s, Charles Bruce and his colleagues made many mistakes and the Assam Company tottered on the brink of financial disaster.[128] Labor shortages and discontent, indigenous resistance, and sheer ignorance hampered the company's ability to turn a profit.[129] Shareholder and other reports remained optimistic, however.[130] Romanticizing failure as part of the experience of pioneers, an 1843 report, for example, explained that "the novelty of the undertaking, the wild character of the country, the necessity, at first, of bringing at great cost a large number of labourers from a distance, the unhealthy state of the locations, until clearances were made, have all concurred to swell the first dead outlay of our establishment in the province."[131] After the financial crisis of 1847, the Assam Company's fortunes began to turn around. Its tea was awarded a prize medal at the Great Exhibition in 1851 and a few favorable articles appeared in the popular press.[132] Yet there were still complaints about the ill-managed company and the "coarse flavour" of its teas.[133] At this point as well, the Assam Company also found it was no longer the only show in town.

In 1849 the East India Company sold most of its remaining plantations to a Chinese employee, but his crop was stolen on its way to Calcutta and he was forced to sell the plantation, known as Chubwa, to James Warren, one of the founders of the Assam Company. Warren's business thrived, and he was recognized as one of the industry's pioneers.[134] Lieutenant Colonel F. S. Hannay, another "pioneer," opened a garden in 1851 and several other colonial administrators, officers, and planters soon did as well. George Williamson senior and his cousins arrived in 1853 and began establishing gardens and leasing parts of others, including Cinnemara, the plantation first begun by Maniram Dewan. By 1859 there were fifty-one tea gardens in private hands and a new major competitor, the Jorehaut Tea Company, was incorporated, making it the second limited liability company to enter this business.[135] Government labor and land policy was instrumental to this expansion, especially when in 1854 it extended its previous wasteland rules. As with an earlier 1838 rule, land designated waste, that is, uncultivated, was granted rent free to anyone who would agree to survey and plant the land. The 1854 rule insisted that the grants should not be less than five hundred acres. This encouraged the development of large plantations and sparked a land frenzy as people acquired property that they could not possibly cultivate.[136] Yet during the 1850s acreage, outputs, and profits grew. The Assam Company, for example, planted 2,921 acres and produced 366,687 pounds of tea in 1853. By 1860, 4,726 acres produced 880,154 pounds.[137] In 1862, the wasteland rules were simplified, and large lots were offered at 3,000 acres and individuals could purchase more than one lot. Applications poured in and soon there were 160 plantations in Assam owned by five joint-stock companies, fifteen private companies, and a number of private individuals.[138] This frenzy, coupled with the labor shortage and resistance, led to the development of the horrific "coolie" trade that many have compared to Atlantic slavery.

The use of indentured labor was triggered by the problems cited above but also by the fact that local workers demanded high wages. Wage rates doubled between the 1850s and 1860s, and company managers felt they had to import a large, cheap, and obedient workforce to maintain profitability.[139] After 1850, and especially in the 1860s, extremely poor and illiterate workers were encouraged to migrate to Assam. A local folk song captured the promise that Assam offered workers: "Come let's go to Assam my girl, as there is great misery in our country, let's go to Assam the land of lush green tea plantations."[140] These "girls" and male workers as well did not realize that the terms of their labor contract would effectively mean that they could never return home. According to one recent scholar, the "'Coolie Trade of Assam' was reminiscent of the slave trade conducted between Africa, America and the West Indies."[141]

Labor recruiters came from all over the British Empire to scour impoverished villages in Bengal, Orissa, the Northwest Provinces, and Oudh.[142] Both Europeans and Indians set up businesses as coolie raiders who were much feared by villagers. Although the government introduced a licensing system, many recruiters were not registered and fraud was rife. Even licensed recruiters (*sirdars*) were often known as the "scum of the country," burglars, thieves, and other "bad characters" who had little interest in the welfare of the people they recruited.[143] Recruiters tempted workers with loans, liquor, and women. Young girls were kidnapped and then married off at recruiting stations in what was known as "depot marriages."[144] Once "recruited," workers had to survive the long and dangerous trip to the plantations, where they encountered long hours, hunger, and diseases, such as cholera and malaria. Mortality rates could be as high as 50 percent on some plantations.[145] Writing about a later period, one company doctor made excuses about the high death toll; he asked, if a "debilitated and sickly class of coolies" were "imported into an unhealthy district can any physician keep them alive by pouring medicine down their throats?"[146]

Planters also had enormous power over their workers. Indeed, with the passage of the Assam Contract Act VI of 1865, the Bengal government made it legal for planters to arrest runaway workers without a warrant and mete out extreme punishments.[147] Though there were several government investigations into the state of tea labor, particularly in 1868 and 1873, and laws passed to curb the grossest abuses, workers were frequently flogged, imprisoned, and sexually and physically abused. Many were not paid, and working and living conditions remained appalling. By the 1880s, the industry argued that it was the early, "unqualified" planters that committed abuses, and that experience and state regulation improved the situation. This is not the case. During and after the 1880s workers were essentially enslaved and high death rates, low birthrates, disease, and countless abuses continued.[148]

Throughout these years, however, workers defied their labor conditions and at times joined or were inspired by full-scale political insurrections. In 1857, during the year of the Indian Rebellion (or Indian Mutiny as the British called it), the Assam Company was particularly upset with "turbulent and dissatisfied" workers who "absconded," were caught, and ran away again.[149] Company reports never suggested that the workers who ran away were resisting the establishment of the tea industry or British rule in India; they were just bad workers. As one report noted in 1863, "The Kacharrie and Dhangha Coolies appear to brave the climate and the difficulties of the locality, while the Bengallee Coolies become disheartened, fall sick, are unable to work and earn the means of buying sufficient food—gradually sink and die."[150] This report at least acknowledged that those from Bengal became disheartened in Assam.

When the sepoys and much of northern India erupted in rebellion in 1857, British confidence was shaken. But in many areas the post-mutiny government continued to build upon economic trends begun under the Company Raj.[151] The Crown assumed direct authority over India and, in the words of one scholar, "sought to aggressively . . . standardize market practice and organization."[152] Commercial and property laws, tariff policies, and labor legislation encouraged the large-scale cultivation of cotton, jute, coffee, wheat, and oil seeds, which, like tea, were geared toward export.[153] Irrigation projects, road building, steam navigation, and the railway lowered the costs and increased the output of Indian agriculture. Assam did not have a railway until much later, but steamships on the Brahmaputra and its many tributaries transported tea to Calcutta. After the Calcutta tea auction opened at the end of 1861, some of the tea was sold directly to buyers; most, however, was loaded onto clippers to make its journey to London and a few other major markets. By the late nineteenth century, then, changes in transportation, labor, and the environment meant that Indian produce, like that grown in other areas of Asia, Africa, and the Americas, increasingly stocked the industrializing West's larders and fed its factories.[154] Peasant systems of landholding and subsistence agriculture thus gave way to heavily capitalized monocultures irrevocably dependent on the severe fluctuations of the global economy.

"ALL THE WORLD IS INTENT ON SUPPLYING ALL THE REST WITH TEA"

The mid-Victorians were very excited about tea as a drink, a crop, and an investment. Growers and capitalists around the world dreamed of almost limitless possibilities. Chinese production boomed, Japan and Formosa began to export, and experimental plantations appeared in Ceylon, Southeast Asia, Southern Africa, Brazil, the Caucuses, California, South Carolina, and Georgia. By the 1880s and 1890s, India and Ceylon dominated world markets, but this was not apparent in midcentury when tea fever infected governments, companies, and private individuals in Asia, Africa, the Americas, and Europe. Indian tea thus represented a wider phenomenon in which, between the 1850s and 1914, the scale, speed, and significance of plantation agriculture and commodity exchange grew at phenomenal rates, and foodstuffs were at the forefront of this new globalizing world.[155]

For a time, the tea shrub became regarded as a "veritable Eldorado."[156] Assam's story was repeated in Cachar, Darjeeling, Dooars, Chittagong, Nilgiris in southern India, and other districts as well. Darjeeling's growth was very rapid, and by 1874, the district's 113 gardens produced 3,928,000 pounds annually.[157] In some places there was a good deal of local investment and ownership. In 1863, for example, there were 78 plantations in Kumaon, Dehra Dun, Garhwal, Simla, Sylhet, and the Kangra Valley; of these, Europeans owned 37 and Indians, including the maharaja of Kashmir, owned 41.[158] Bengali lawyers and clerks started the first Indian-managed firm, the Jalpaiguri Tea Company, in 1879. Two others formed within two years.[159]

Colonial policies, growing dividends, and a flurry of favorable publications encouraged a gold rush mentality. In the 1880s, J. Berry White, an expert on Indian tea, gave a speech in London in which he described the tea mania as an addiction: "Although tea has the reputation of furnishing a beverage that cheers but does not inebriate, its cultivation in new districts exercises the most strangely intoxicating influences of those engaged in it, equaled only by the sanguine dreams of explorers." The early 1860s, White remembered, was an era of "wild excitement and speculation."[160] Organizations such as the Royal Society of Arts, Manufactures and Commerce awarded prizes and medals to the new teas, feeding tea fever.[161] Robert Fortune, already famous for stealing seeds from China, had pushed Indian tea's expansion, but he also worried that "in India every man seems to think himself qualified to undertake the management of Tea cultivation without having any knowledge of the subject, whatever. I have even heard it stated that a lady had, at one time, offered herself as a candidate to manage one of the Government Plantations." Fortune was not really anxious about female planters, but he was alarmed that the "charm" associated with "our national beverage" misled the unqualified to feel they could strike it rich growing tea in India.[162] Perhaps he was also worried about Indians starting gardens. The metropolitan trade journal *The Grocer* explicitly stated in 1865 that "native" planters should not be trusted. Even though "native capitalists" could not "of course, be excluded from the right to purchase these [waste] lands . . . some means should certainly be adopted to prevent their being sold to any but men who intend *bona fide* to cultivate them."[163]

Experts worried too that the wrong sort of white men were becoming planters. After analyzing the industry in 1863, agricultural expert William Nassau Lees confidently concluded that Indian tea was "pregnant with promise," but he too disapproved of the way that the industry had become a wild frontier, which like the American West had lured out disreputable characters with the dream of quick and easy riches.[164] In 1873 A. J. Ware Edgar, the junior secretary to the Government of Bengal, wrote that the years 1863–65 had exhibited "a dangerous spirit of speculation," in which "a rush took place to secure waste lands as quickly as could be, to bring portions of them under nominal cultivation, and then to dispose of them at enormous profits to newly formed companies." Even worse, he wrote, "enterprising traders" persuaded "shareholders to invest in tea gardens that were actually not in existence at all." Edgar worried that many a young British man had been lured to Assam on false pretenses, only to find himself "suddenly turned adrift in a most inhospitable country without a penny or a friend; some died, others had literally to bet their way out of Assam, most had to regret impaired constitutions, and all the loss of some of the best years of their life."[165] The speculative bubble had furthermore created a lust for labor as contractors and recruiters in Calcutta sent up anyone who "had sufficient vitality to walk or crawl on board the steamers employed to convey to Assam . . . the blind, the insane, the hopelessly diseased—in fact the refuse of the bazaars, were all alike drafted to Assam at a certain rate per head, which yielded a handsome profit to recruiters and others interested in the trade."[166] This situation damaged "legitimate" growers, their workers, and investors and meant that little consistently good tea was produced in India during the 1860s. Former planter-turned-tea-expert Edward Money summarized this view as well when he explained: "People who had failed in everything else were thought quite competent to make plantations." He recalled that "in those days were a strange medley of retired or cashiered army and navy officers, medical men, engineers, veterinary surgeons, steamship captains, chemists, shop-keepers of all kinds, stable-keepers, used up policemen, clerks, and goodness knows who besides" took up the occupation.[167] The crash inevitably came in 1865–66, and by 1867, as Money put it, "Tea could not pay at all. Everyone wanted to sell, and down went all Tea shares to a figure which only increased the general panic. Many companies, and not a few individuals, unable to carry on, had to wind up and sell their estates for whatever they could fetch . . . and the very word 'Tea' stank in the nostrils of the commercial public."[168]

Tea fever was not merely an Indian malady, however. The Chinese also suffered from the disease. Foreign and native banks backed Chinese merchants who mobilized "land, labor, and money" to produce tea at "unprecedentedly high levels."[169] Changes in land utilization and the extension of acreage met the world's growing demand, but some Chinese officials nevertheless condemned the tea-planting mania, believing as Fujian's governor did that tea brought with it foreign corruption, a ravished environment, and a shaky future:

> From the time of [Fujian's] opening to commerce, foreign ships have flocked here and merchants have been corrupted by profits. More and more mountains have been planted over. Verdant cliffs have been cut down to the red soil, and clear streams have become yellow-flowing [because of] reckless cultivation.[170]

This official denounced irrational speculation and forecast the dangers of overproduction. This was an astute assessment.

Japan too caught tea fever. In 1853, even before Japan was officially opened to world trade, Madam Kay Oura, a female tea merchant from Nagasaki, had already sent samples via a Dutch firm to America, England, and "Arabia." In 1856 an English buyer purchased Oura's teas and soon thereafter Jardine, Matheson and Company opened offices in Japan, as did American firms, which along with their Japanese allies eventually captured this market. Formosa, now known as Taiwan, also began selling its teas in world markets. In 1861, the British consul reported about the industry's possibilities, and a few years later another Englishman established Dodd and Company and started buying Formosa's tea. In 1869, this firm sent a trial shipment to New York, and by 1879 Americans purchased fifty million pounds of Formosa Oolongs. Foreign firms controlled the firing and packing of Formosa's growths, though the Chinese community eventually entered the field as well.[171] In Java, too, government sponsorship gave way to private enterprise and its teas began to find markets, especially in Holland and northern Germany.[172]

Growers and investors also planted in Southern Africa, South America, the Caucasus, the Azores, Jahore, Fiji, and even coastal California.[173] As early as 1866, when writing about Brazilian tea, *The Grocer* quipped: "All the world is intent on supplying all the rest with tea."[174] Brazil, of course, became coffee country, but in the 1860s it looked like it would also grow tea. North Americans were also starting plantations. After the Singpho destroyed his four tea gardens in Assam, Francis Bonynge moved to Georgia to grow tea, coffee, mangoes, dates, lychees, melons, and indigo.[175] Junius Smith also planted tea near Greenville, South Carolina, in 1848 and became a leading advocate for Americanizing this Asian crop.[176] Smith had been an early promoter of transatlantic steam navigation and is thus a significant figure in the history of globalization. Originally from Connecticut, this Yale graduate moved to England where he became a shipping merchant, married an Englishwoman, and in the 1830s became the owner and promoter of the British and American Steam Navigation Company. By the 1840s he had the resources to delve into other new ventures.

Smith acknowledged, however, that tea was his daughter's idea. Miss Lucinda Smith had married an Englishman, Rev. Edward K. Maddock, in 1840, a chaplain in the East India Company's army, and the couple moved to Meerut in northwest India. Like many a colonial wife, the young Mrs. Maddock summered in the Himalaya, and on one of her trips home she sipped some of the East India Company's tea grown in its botanical gardens. In a letter home, she wrote to her father, "We hear it surpasses the China tea and is likely to become a most valuable speculation to the East India Company. Some of the tea has been sent to London and sells there for $1.50 a pound."[177] "No sooner had I perused the letter," Smith wrote, "than the idea burst upon me, that if the tea-plant could be successfully cultivated upon the mountains of the Himalaya, there would be nothing in the ordinary course of vegetation to prevent its growing in the United States."[178] Smith wrote to experts, read voraciously, and studied in the library of East India House in London.[179] Smith acquired seeds from several sources, including the Assam Company and his own daughter who had purchased seed from one of "her shopkeepers." She sent seeds home with a female acquaintance so they would reach her father faster than if they had arrived via "public conveyance."[180] This tea thrived in South Carolina until 1853, when Smith died after a violent assault. Before his untimely death, Smith had inspired others to take up the crop in the United States.

Smith, his daughter, and their friends were thus making a global economy that stretched from the Indian to the Atlantic oceans. Transnational families transferred commercial knowledge across what some historians have called the British World.[181] Such individuals moved tea and its knowledge around the British World that reached beyond the formal boundaries of the British Empire. As we will see in later chapters, Anglo-American families and colleagues often worked together in the tea trade in the British Empire throughout the second half of the nineteenth century and into the twentieth.[182] At this point, however, men such as Smith believed that tea could actually grow in the United States. When writing about the possibilities of planting in Texas, for example, Smith proposed that it was much easier to transport goods from Texas to London than it was to do so from Assam through Calcutta to the metropolis. As an owner of a transatlantic shipping company writing before the opening of the Suez Canal, he understood that "distance, like time, is long or short by comparison."[183]

While Americans tried to plant tea, quite a few "British planters" moved to the United States to grow and sell tea and shape American policy. A manager of the Scottish Assam Company, for example, established tea gardens in Georgia and lobbied the U.S. government to give support to this new industry.[184] After the Civil War, the Department of Agriculture actually distributed numerous plants to farmers in South Carolina, Georgia, and California.[185] Already in 1864 the British trade journal *The Grocer* reported that in San Francisco, "nurseries near the Mission Dolores had succeeded in raising several thousands of the tea plant during the last twelve months." "There can be little doubt," the journal suggested, "that before long it [tea] will be cultivated hereafter for household purposes at least on every farm in the State."[186] A few years later, growers transplanted Japanese tea to Calistoga in the heart of the Napa Valley; and in 1872 the wealthy and innovative landowner Colonel W. W. Hollister introduced 50,000 plants at his ranch in Santa Barbara.[187] Today California is hardly known for its tea. However, English grocers, Indian planters, and American businessmen assumed that because the state had a ready supply of "Celestials" to work on the plantations it would soon be covered with tea gardens.[188] By 1880, the New York correspondent for the *Home and Colonial Mail* anticipated that quite soon "hundreds of thousands of plants will be growing in this country." This journalist quipped that the introduction of tea cultivation into America was one of the "pet hobbies" of General Le Duc, the commissioner of agriculture.[189] American labor costs were higher than in China or India, but experts imagined that "inventive" Americans might "by the use of machinery" make the industry pay.[190] These planters also placed their faith in an expanding domestic market. Per capita tea consumption in the United States was small but growing.[191] The tea trade argued that Americans were natural consumers whose tastes had simply veered off course since the Revolution. As we will see, they embarked on a concerted effort to recapture this lost market.[192]

While so many tried to grow tea, it was Ceylon, a relatively small island off India's southeast coast, that eventually rivaled India. Ceylon had been the stopping point for global traders for centuries and had experienced waves of European conquest. The Portuguese first came as traders in 1505 and their influence grew over the course of the century. In the mid-seventeenth century, the Dutch obtained all of the former Portuguese possessions, introduced plantation agriculture, and maintained a tight monopoly on cinnamon, which was then the island's most significant export. The British East India Company gained control in the late 1790s, and on the first of January 1802, Ceylon became a Crown colony. Ceylon possessed its own administrative structure and was not incorporated into the British Raj. Nevertheless, the EIC was granted the profitable cinnamon monopoly until 1833 and coffee soon became the most lucrative crop.[193]

During the early part of the century, Ceylon's coffee enjoyed preferential tariff protection, and the industry and British coffee drinking surged.[194] The British coffee habit may have stayed strong had not a fungus, *hemileia vastatrix*, arrived in late 1869. Popular histories praised tea for saving coffee planters from utter ruin, but in fact the fungus took several decades to destroy coffee, and tea was grown on a commercial scale two years before the fungus first hit.[195] As early as 1839, Dr. Nathanial Wallich, then head of the Calcutta Botanic Gardens and member of India's Tea Committee, sent seeds from "indigenous Assam plants" to the Royal Botanic Gardens at Peradeniya, near Kandy. The plants thrived, proving that tea could be grown in Ceylon's climate.[196] Some coffee planters also grew tea on their plantations, but it was the Scot, James Taylor, who first grew commercial tea on his estate known as Loolecondera in 1867, the very year of the tea crash in India. Tea succeeded because it could be cultivated at a greater range of altitudes and because the island's heavy rainfall did not endanger the tea plant as it did the coffee crop. Tea had greater start-up costs than coffee because it required immediate processing, but because Ceylon's tea, unlike that in China or India, was plucked year-round rather than seasonally growers could realize profits more quickly.[197] As a result, sickly coffee plants were uprooted to give way to tea in the 1870s and 1880s.

"Ceylon has been known to the world as a coffee producing country," wrote the *Planters' Gazette* in 1878, but the journal predicted that it might very soon become "no mean rival to Assam."[198] Ceylon first exported a mere twenty-three pounds in 1872, but the amount shipped to London in 1884 was twenty times that sent in 1880.[199] When Edward Money published a fourth edition of his best-selling textbook in 1883, he was astonished by the recent and very rapid globalization and industrialization of tea production and was especially impressed with Ceylon. Money was not sanguine, however, for he foretold inevitable recession and bitterly asserted "there is too much tea already."[200]

———

A diverse community of British, Assamese, and other local people launched the Indian tea industry in the first half of the nineteenth century. Many nationalists would later label tea a prime example of a European colonial enterprise, but local landowners, rulers, and workers vacillated between resistance, resignation, and profit seeking. Assam was not unique but its history proved to others that tea could be grown on a commercial scale outside of China. By the 1850s and 1860s, tea cultivation moved to other parts of India, South and Southeast Asia, and even the Americas. It especially thrived in colonial conditions, however, because colonial states fertilized this industry with cheap land, labor, and other requirements.

By the 1880s, British planters and companies had conquered the land, labor, and technical knowledge to grow tea in Assam and in many other parts of their empire on a mass scale. They established families and built bungalows, which they decorated with a mixture of local objects and things from home. They dressed for dinner and enjoyed drinking tea in their gardens, surrounded by servants, pets, and the paraphernalia of bourgeois domesticity (figs. 3.2 and 3.3). While they called themselves British, most were Scottish, and we know that many married or had children with local women. Their offspring returned home to be educated, to marry, or to recover from the stresses of imperial life, but we tend to imagine these planters and their families as a world apart from the metropole.[201] They were literally far away, and as we can see from the portraits of these unknown planters, no amount of tea could banish a sense of loneliness, fear, and anxiety that came from living in the empire and trying to turn a profit in a globalizing economy. Such emotions often instigated racism and a perpetual cycle of violence, as well as extreme efforts to control workers, governments, and the landscape. It also, as we will see in the following chapters, compelled some planters to leave their gardens, organize and assert political

FIGURE 3.2. Victorian planter family taking tea in front of their bungalow, c. 1880s.
(By permission of LIFE Picture Collection/Getty Images)

FIGURE 3.3. Tea planter having tea in his tea garden, c. 1880s.

power, and become salesmen and develop cultural expertise in order to conquer global markets and transform tastes. Though we see them here alone or with their families in India, the Planter Raj was also a global phenomenon. Along with advertisers, exhibition experts, and other impresarios, these planters built a new consumer culture around "British" tea. These planters never worked alone, however, and they inevitably sought out friends, relations, and allies to help them build a thirst for the empire.

4

PACKAGING CHINA

Advertising Food Safety in a Global Marketplace

I n 1826, Quaker, abolitionist, temperance enthusiast, and parliamentary reformer John Horniman began selling tea in preweighed and sealed packages.[1]
Packet tea took some time to become established, but within a few decades
this innovation secured Horniman's position as a leader in the trade. By the 1880s,
the practice became the norm when mass-market companies began to sell tea
in this way. At that time, as we will see in the next chapter, these firms began to
add small amounts of the new Indian and Ceylon teas to their packaged blends,
unbeknownst to consumers. John Horniman, however, first packaged tea in the
early part of the century, as a response to mounting concerns that the Chinese
were routinely adulterating tea, especially green tea, with unwholesome and even
poisonous materials. Though their countrymen also adulterated the nation's tea
supply, opinionated Britons blamed the Chinese for practicing this trickery,
which most assumed had grown after the end of the East India Company's
monopoly of the tea trade in 1833, and especially after the forcible "opening"
of China at the end of the first Opium War in 1842. Free trade had in truth
inspired a free-for-all as inexperienced and easily fooled merchants could now
sail to China and purchase whatever "tea" the Chinese offered. The transition
to this new mode of doing business had far-ranging consequences, including
mounting suspicions about Chinese imports. The British invented a variety of
ways to assuage their growing fears, but their solutions tended to spread panic
even as they sought to contain it.

In the previous chapter, we saw how the growing animosity between China
and Great Britain inspired the conquest of Assam and the establishment of the
Indian tea industry. Similar anti-Chinese attitudes stimulated the use of packaging and branding and encouraged the development of food science and state
regulation of the food system. Fears about ingesting foreign imports such as tea
set the framework for how we still discuss food safety in a global marketplace.[2]
During the mid-Victorian years, merchants, scientists, and state officials promised to defend the British public from perilous Eastern pleasures and from the
more unruly aspects of the marketplace. These authorities claimed they could
draw boundaries between good and bad commodities, modes of production,

distribution, and consumption. Horniman and Company's advertising took the lead in popularizing this culture of expertise, quoting extensively from chemists and China scholars, explorers, and government documents. Ultimately, Horniman sold a great deal of tea, but the adulteration scare and its legal response destroyed the British taste for Chinese green teas and set the conditions for the public to appreciate what they believed were the pure, modern, British teas from South Asia. The volatile economic, diplomatic, and cultural relations between China and Great Britain from the late 1830s through the 1870s thus fashioned new tastes, attitudes, and markets.[3]

VICTORIAN FOOD SCARES: "THERE IS MUCH THAT IS NOXIOUS IN THE THINGS THAT WE EAT"

Adulteration was physically harmful, but it also exposed imperfections in the principles of a laissez-faire economy.[4] Food has always been dangerous, but it is only since the nineteenth century that food scares have become public events. In our current times, food-reforming journalists, writers, and filmmakers highlight the dangers that lurk in our foods to trigger emotional responses from their audiences and to gain support for what they hope will be lasting political, economic, and social change.[5] Following in the footsteps of writer-activist Upton Sinclair, Michael Pollan and Eric Schlosser, for example, have produced compelling exposés intended to raise awareness about the threats posed by a globalized and industrialized food system.[6] We are not, however, the first generation to condemn the globalization and industrialization of food. At the very moment they were creating the global industrialized food system, the Victorians also set the terms for our criticisms and the way we think about solutions.[7] They were convinced that science, technology, branded goods, and colonialism would protect consumers from dangers lurking in their food supply.

Food scares are especially useful for historians. As examples of revulsion entering public consciousness, they illuminate the subtle processes of how tastes change. All foods can produce either pleasure or disgust, especially when they are imagined to be unclean or polluting.[8] Ingestion reminds us that our bodies are fragile and vulnerable.[9] Food preferences, cooking, and table manners are some of the cultural responses to deep-rooted fears about absorbing impurities into the body. I argue, however, that food scares highlight the connections between the self and the social, the body and the market. They illuminate how tastes are cultural, social, and historical, even though they are also shaped by biology.[10]

Perhaps to an even greater degree than today, foods and drinks evoked public concern in mid-Victorian Britain. Legislation, high-profile court cases, popular exposés, and advertising alerted consumers that many if not most of the products that lined grocers' and bakers' shelves were adulterated with a wide variety of spurious items.[11] This situation was by no means new, but the meaning and extent of this activity shifted with the growth of mass consumption and intensified retail competition, the lifting of controls on international trade, and the advancement of scientific methods for detecting additives in food. Considering some of these changes, the prominent food scientist Dr. Edward Smith surmised in the 1870s that the "increased intercourse with distant countries" as well as other issues had attracted "public attention to the subject of Foods and Dietaries."[12] In other words, Smith believed that the public recognized and was interested in the fact that they consumed foods that were produced on the other side of the world.

Attention to such issues peaked in the middle of the century, paralleling the devastating cholera epidemics that swept through Britain in these years. Indeed, several of the same individuals who were involved in identifying cholera studied the food supply.[13] Though it would take decades for scientists to accept this idea, in the second half of the century these experts came to understand that ingestion of contaminated water or foods spread illnesses such as cholera. Cholera sufferers were struck with intense speed and became dehydrated, and most died within a few days. The disease left a visible mark upon the body of its victims. Food adulteration killed more slowly and invisibly, but nevertheless it raised similar worries about the efficacy of science and the state to manage the public's health.[14] Not all foods and drinks raised similar concerns, however. Tea's adulteration signified the dangers of doing business with China and the difficulties of policing national borders in an era of free trade.

Since the thirteenth century, laws had been in place to deal with adulterators. Eighteenth-century legislation even punished the adulteration of tea and coffee specifically.[15] Yet these laws had proven ineffective in the face of increasingly widespread and dangerous examples of adulteration.[16] In the early nineteenth century, analytical chemists declared they had the tools and the knowledge to detect the constituent elements of foods, drinks, and drugs.[17] By the 1850s and 1860s, many became noted food experts who served as witnesses before government committees and shaped the science and laws surrounding food adulteration, claiming that they could safeguard a healthy and ethical marketplace. If adulteration and other forms of commercial trickery disguised the commodity, chemistry promised to reveal the true nature of things.

In the 1820s, the chemist Friedrich Accum published a best seller asserting that adulteration, an "unprincipled and nefarious practice[,] . . . is now applied to almost every commodity which can be classed among the necessaries or the luxuries of life, and is carried on to a most alarming extent in every part of the United Kingdom."[18] Though he was later disgraced for defacing books in a science library, Accum was very influential, and soon others promised that chemistry would "erect a barricade against the cupidity of fraudulent tradesmen" and would "put it into every man's power to ensure his health and wealth against the ravages of adulteration and disease." In doing so, this author asserted that chemistry had direct applications in "common life" and was not a "frivolous and fruitless pursuit, which many consider it to be."[19] Household guides described and popularized this science, and explained how chemical tests and the microscope rendered visible that which the producer and distributor had hidden.[20] Of course, as food processing changed, the problem of what was a harmful additive remained up for debate, but chemists successfully claimed food as an area of expertise.

Social reformers concurred with the chemists' basic conclusions and especially worried about what the urban poor were eating and drinking. In 1831, for example, William Rathbone Greg warned that inadequate, adulterated food was one of the factors leading to the great suffering of the manufacturing classes in England. As he described it, the poor drank "tea, diluted till it is little else than warm water, the materials of which never came from China, but are the production of one of those innumerable frauds which are practiced upon the poor."[21] A series of newspaper articles and salacious publications, such as *Deadly Adulteration and Slow Poisoning Unmasked, or, Disease and Death in the Pot and the Bottle*, likewise told how "unprincipled and diabolical adulterations of foods" were killing people.[22] In such texts, the commercial classes appeared particularly malicious and secretive.[23]

Soon the public began to demand solutions. One "English Churchman," for example, advocated that the state should create "a class of trustworthy men," or food "detectives," who would detect the purity of "the commonest necessaries of life." Maintaining a patriarchal view of the state typical of Tory social reform, this Churchman argued that Britain's "Paternal Government" must protect plebian consumers from the immoral market.[24] Working-class consumers did not wait for official food detectives, however, and in the 1840s they began to form co-operative retail societies that professed to sell pure foods and eliminate the fraudulent middleman and dishonest petty retailer.[25]

During the 1850s, Dr. Arthur Hill Hassall, known as the "Apostle of Adulteration," led the fight for food reform.[26] Hassall was best known for his work on cholera and his great skill with the microscope.[27] He argued that the instrument could "detect" adulteration better than the chemical tests used at the time. Such tests were not abandoned, but Hassall and his followers made the microscope an important tool and declared it enabled them to see, and hence define, the constituent elements of substances more clearly. In the early 1850s, Hassall embarked upon an extensive investigation into the quality of the nation's food, conducted under the auspices of the esteemed medical journal *The Lancet*.[28] His work, and the public outcry it inspired, led to the establishment of a Parliamentary Select Committee in 1854–55 and the passage in 1860 of the first comprehensive law against the adulteration of food, drink, and drugs. In the summer of 1855, Hassall and his colleagues spent several days before the committee laying out evidence that nearly every ingestible substance was adulterated.[29] Hassall reported that the most common products of domestic consumption—sugar, honey, bread, milk, potted meats, tinned vegetables, spices, mustard, pickles, vinegar, and every conceivable beverage—contained numerous, and in his estimation unwholesome, additives.[30] His work and that of the many hundred microscopists and chemists "scattered all over the parts of the country" proved that Britain's food was very tainted indeed.[31]

Not all imitations were deadly, of course, but Hassall insisted that adulteration was a health issue, a moral failing, and a crime. He declared adulteration simply a fraud caused by the "desire of increased profit."[32] Adulterators asserted that they were defending "freedom of trade" and the "liberty of the subject," but Hassall contended that these were not the assertions of principled liberals but were mere "bugbears" used "to frighten the timid." "Effective scientific organization for the discovery of adulteration, and the adequate punishment of the offense," he argued, would clean up the nation's food.[33] The scientist and the state could thus defend "the consumer [who] is extensively robbed through adulteration."[34] This was, Hassall believed, "a great national question, closely affecting the pocket of the consumer, the revenue, and the health and morals of the people."[35]

Throughout this period the legal definition of adulteration remained vague, but it incorporated two somewhat distinct ideas. It was seen as an inadvertent but nonetheless criminal act, which could sicken its victims. It was also a civil crime, which defrauded the consumer through violating the basic contract implied when one purchased goods in a shop. The 1860 pure food law expressed both facets of this definition when it stated that an item was adulterated by "the infusion of some foreign substance . . . other than that which the article purports to be." A food or drink was also considered adulterated when it contained "any ingredient which may render such article injurious to the health of the consumer" or if it was mixed with "any substance that sensibly increases its weight, bulk, or strength, or gives it a fictitious value."[36] Adulterated foods were essentially fictional commodities or at least products that contained elements that added a fictional value.

The idea of disguise was central to popular understandings. George Dodd, who published an extensive survey titled *The Food of London* in 1856, asked, "Are the commodities such as they seem. . . . Is a pound of nominal coffee a pound of authentic coffee? The tea or chocolate, the wine or beer, the milk or vinegar, the bread or the flour—do these, as purchased and consumed, correspond with their names?"[37] An 1871 poem titled "Poisoning and Pilfering: Wholesale and

Retail," which exposed the prevalence of adulteration, fittingly began, "Scarce an article bought—or so it seems to me—is the substance they'd have you believe it to be. There is hair sold as wool, there is cotton for flax. There is sugar for honey, and tallow for wax. . . . There is much that is noxious in the things that we eat."[38] Adulteration thus articulated a central Victorian problem, that of distinguishing the real from the artificial.[39]

In *Capital*, written during the peak of the adulteration scare, Karl Marx quoted Hassall when making the point that fraud was an inherent part of an unregulated capitalist marketplace. Marx regarded adulteration as a form of capitalist "sophistry" that demonstrated "that everything is only appearance."[40] In the early twentieth century, Walter Benjamin returned to this problem when he explained how visual technologies such as cinema fundamentally disrupted the perceived relationship between the original and the copy.[41] There is, however, an international and racial dimension to such concerns. Consumers, retailers, and interested experts wondered how could they trust foreign goods produced by racial others in the frenzied mid-nineteenth-century economy?

CHINA: THE "HOTBED OF ADULTERATION" IN THE ERA OF FREE TRADE

Tea's adulteration was a real problem and a metaphor for miscegenation and the disruption of boundaries inherent in international commerce. Nearly all mid-Victorian experts agreed that "China" was the "real hotbed of adulteration."[42] The "Chinese vendor and the Chinese artist" were masters in this art, noted one authority.[43] Another described how dangerous chemicals were introduced "in the Chinese ports."[44] While there is a long history here, anxieties about Chinese adulteration peaked in the 1850s when Britain, China, and the United States were plagued with internal upheavals and imperial rebellions and animosity ran high. Western nations were worried about both drinking China's tea and being unable to do so. Such fears propelled the global expansion of tea cultivation and cemented the image of the Chinese as a dishonest people. The mid-Victorian hysteria surrounding Chinese tea reveals the bodily, cultural, and scientific consequences then of the "imperialism of free trade."[45]

Free trade had vastly complicated the journey from field to cup and removed the older controls that had operated during the age of the chartered companies. Gone were the days when the EIC servants in Canton had inspected supplies and ensured quality control.[46] In the 1830s, the end of monopoly brought a veritable scramble for tea, and it seemed as though "every merchant and ship-owner who had ever seen a chest of tea immediately turned his attention to China."[47] Merchants with little knowledge of the tea trade began exporting all kinds of low-quality teas.[48] Shifting fiscal policies in Britain and the United States also contributed to a rash of fraud and adulteration. The British government had initiated a new system of taxation that caused the duty on low-quality teas to peak between 1834 and 1853.[49] At the same time, free traders and temperance advocates pushed the U.S. government to abolish all taxes on imported tea in 1832–33. This tax returned in little more than a year, but in the meantime demand surged. American firms sent a large number of ships to China in 1833 and 1834 and they were especially interested in green tea, the favorite of American consumers.[50] Supplies could not keep pace with demand.[51] The Chinese solved this problem by turning black into green tea through the use of coloring agents. "There is not a single box of tea . . . that is not opened and extensively be-rubbished by the Canton dealers before it is allowed to get into the hands of the Christian barbarians," opined one American trader. He admitted, however, that there was also a "liberal be-Yankification before it reaches our tea-rooms."[52] The rapid and uneven nature of the shift to free trade in the Anglo-American world thus increased the incentives to produce and sell false goods. The Chinese adulterated green tea for a variety of reasons, but the most important factor was that they were responding to the changing nature of markets in this new era of free trade. Like smuggling, adulteration was a quasi-illicit practice that helped create the mass market, but Western nations rejected economic motivations and relied on racial ideologies to explain adulteration.

The Chinese "adulterator" amplified the negative racial stereotypes emerging in much of the West in these years. Whereas many early modern Europeans had admired Chinese civilization and culture, the Victorians imagined the Chinese as a lazy, dirty, and dishonest people who delighted in selling false goods. During the first half of the nineteenth century, the emergence of racial science as a reputable discipline contributed to such beliefs and made race a fixed characteristic rather than a cultural attribute. Declining international and commercial relations did not help matters. At the end of the first Opium War, the British gained Hong Kong and access to five treaty ports, Canton, Amoy, Foochow, Shanghai, and Ningpo. British merchants were granted reparations and the Chinese were forced to accept the concept of extraterritoriality. Many British assumed, as one writer put it, that this meant that the resources of the "mighty empire" were now "open" to British consumers.[53] High expectations did not come to fruition, even though the China trade was extensive and growing in value. Britain imported 44 million pounds of tea in 1835 and just over 86 million in 1856.[54] The problem for the British, as is well known, is that they were running a substantial trade imbalance of well over £8 million sterling by 1854.[55] The government did not wish to restrict tea imports because the profits and taxes from tea had become so important to Britain's industrial and global economy. In 1836 the taxes paid on Chinese tea were enough to cover over 112 percent of the Royal Navy's annual expenditure. It declined thereafter but then climbed again so that by 1850 it could once again offset all the costs of operating the navy.[56] And this was despite the fact that naval expenditures soared in these years. The government thus felt it needed to maintain a healthy tea trade and had to find other means to offset the trade imbalance.

During the 1840s and 1850s, the British sought to renegotiate the terms of their treaty in the hopes that they could obtain access to the interior of China, and to freely navigate the Yangtze River, legalize the opium trade, and eliminate transit duties on foreign goods. Access to the Yangtze basin would enable the British to purchase directly from tea-producing regions, thereby lowering costs. When negotiations failed, Palmerston, who was then prime minister, seized upon a flimsy excuse and once again went to war with China. The *Arrow* War, or second Opium War (1856–60), was in part conducted in the interest of furthering the tea trade.[57] Some committed free traders such as Richard Cobden suffered politically for opposing Palmerston, but many merchants and tea importers supported military force to achieve their commercial aims.

Rampant jingoism and anti-Chinese feeling ran high. Newspaper accounts and illustrations by the likes of George Cruikshank depicted the Chinese as an especially barbaric people who committed untold atrocities on others as well as on their own people.[58] Though the British committed numerous "barbaric" acts before and during the war, the mass media focused on Chinese barbarism. The figure of the Chinese poisoner especially gained credibility in 1857 after the public learned that an attempt had been made to poison the foreign community in Hong Kong by baking arsenic into their bread. The incident occurred in January but the public learned of the poisoning in early March in the midst of the House of Commons debate on the war. *The Times* printed a short notice on 2 March, and the next day the *Morning Post* gave a fuller account, supporting Palmerston's bellicose China policy and lashing out against the "noxious animals" behind the poisoning.[59] This event influenced debate on the war and stoked fears of tea adulteration as well. The specter of poisoned bread in a bakery in Hong Kong thus reverberated at home. In the early months of 1857, just before northern India erupted in rebellion, a hysterical British public would have had good cause to be fearful that the Chinese might be lacing their tea with deadly substances.

In 1860, after the end of the war, the British once again expected that they would at last be able to penetrate Chinese markets. The Treaty of Tientsin promised to open up the interior and many assumed that British manufacturers would gain access to a "huge market of four hundred millions."[60] An essayist marveling at Shanghai's tea gardens similarly wrote, "China is no longer a sealed book to the traveler."[61] Yet from the merchants' perspective access was partial at best. Military victory brought trade concessions but also undermined the stability of the Qing dynasty and contributed to violent and long-lasting civil war. The Taiping Rebellion that swept through southern China in the 1850s and early 1860s heightened Anglo-American fears that their tea supply would be cut off.[62] It also forced the Qing government and local authorities to impose a host of new duties that significantly increased the overhead cost to the trade. In China, as in Britain, the tax on tea was used to pay for war and became a significant source of revenue.[63] Worried that the rebellion and the responses to it would seriously harm the tea trade, *The Grocer* warned its readers in 1862: "The condition of China is most unsettled. Every successive mail from the East brings intelligence of further bloodshed, insurrection, and extension of civil disturbances."[64]

At the same time China was so unsettled, American firms were starting to threaten British dominance of the tea trade. North American merchants had long been involved in this business, but the repeal of the Navigation Acts in 1849 made it possible for U.S. companies to sell tea in Britain and other markets. In Fujian the Taiping Rebellion disrupted internal trade routes, but the American agency house of Russell and Company used their longstanding connections with an ex-hong merchant to be the first company to export tea from Fuzhou. Other British and American companies followed suit, helping to launch the Fujian tea boom.[65] Americans had also invented the swift "Boston clippers," which cut the journey between China and the United States and Europe dramatically in midcentury.[66] The voyage from the Chinese ports to London typically took between 100 and 130 days, but some runs were made in less than three months. The clippers, modern marvels that symbolized technology's conquest of distance, also evoked a shifting world order in which the United States was becoming a real competitor in the China trade. Scottish and other British shipwrights copied American designs and built many of the era's most famous vessels, but American shipbuilding prowess nevertheless threatened British dominance of the newly "freed" tea trade.

Famous tea races captured the sense of speed and intensity of global trade. Innovations in ship design, betting agents, fan clubs, and premiums for winners transformed the tea trade into an international sporting event.[67] Between the 1840s and the opening of the Suez Canal in 1869, an interested public eagerly waited for the clippers' return with the freshest crop of new spring teas. Remarkably competitors often arrived within hours of each other. The trade journal *The Grocer* captured the thrill of this sport when, in 1866, it reported that "the excitement at Lloyds has been immense, and the betting ran very high." The paper was referring to one of the most famous races, which ended with the *Taeping* landing in London only minutes before its rival the *Ariel*, followed closely by the *Serica*.[68] The tea races celebrated the shrinking distance between East and West. Technology, government policy, and military force had ended monopoly and encouraged speed, but these achievements prompted concerns over oversight and authenticity.

The Chinese were not the only ones of course to produce "counterfeit" teas, nor did free trade create the problem. In 1818 a prosecutor who charged a grocer with manufacturing such tea explained to a jury, "At the moment [the public] were supposing that they were drinking a pleasant and nutritious beverage, they were, in all probability, drinking the produce of the hedges round the metropolis."[69] Excise officers arrested at least ten others for the same crime that year.[70] These prosecutions and publications taught consumers that their "tea" was in reality a mixture of pigments added to beech, elm, oak, willow, poplar, hawthorn, and sloe leaves and genuine tea or tea dust.[71] According to an Inland Revenue Office report in 1843, at least eight manufacturers in London revived tea used by hotels, coffeehouses, and other public places. Once dried, used leaves were "faced," that is, mixed, with gum, rose pink, black lead, or similar items and then resold as new.[72] Rose pink was a dye made by infusing logwood in a carbonate of lime. Black lead, a product commonly used by Victorian domestic servants, contained both carbon and iron.

These chemicals gave used leaves a deep color and simulated the curled shape of new leaves.[73] The ever-perceptive journalist Henry Mayhew calculated that approximately 78,000 pounds of such old tea were "converted into new" in London alone.[74] As an early issue of the *Anti-Adulteration Review* described it, the "poor man's teapot is often little else than a dustbin for all sorts of rubbish." Cheating the poor consumer was big business, and many were doing "a roaring trade in the art of filling the stomachs of women and children with used up tea-leaves, willow-leaves, spent leaves, steeling-fillings, and dirt."[75] Plebian housewives also manufactured their own imitations, fooling unsuspecting family members. Poor mothers stretched tea by mixing it with burnt bread crusts, burnt barley cake, and similar concoctions. Mint tea was also a cheap and appreciated summertime drink.[76] Though producing these imitations was not illegal, workers nevertheless remembered them as a sign of hard times.[77] For much of the nineteenth century, the working classes were often drinking either an infusion of London's hedges or a more dangerous recycled version of the very leaves first drunk by the wealthier classes in places of public resort. No wonder some social reformers were so concerned about the negative consequences of drinking tea.

While adulteration was a widespread practice throughout the century, the Chinese were said to produce the most dangerous concoctions. Chemist Robert Warrington relied on both chemical tests and travelers' accounts to support his argument that the Chinese "glazed" or faced their export with unwholesome materials.[78] He later wrote that a typical sample of Chinese tea contained the following:

> A mixture of tea-dust with dirt and sand, agglutinated into a mass with a gummy matter, most probably manufactured from rice-flour, then formed into granules of the desired size, and lastly, dried and coloured, according to the kind required by the manufacturer, either with black lead, if for black tea, or with Prussian blue, gypsum, or turmeric, if intended for green.[79]

The Chinese frequently turned low-quality black tea into green with the help of Prussian blue, an iron salt that according to Hassall was "not absolutely poisonous" but was "capable of exerting an injurious action."[80] Pigments such as mineral green, verdigris, and an arsenate of copper, which was a very dangerous poison, and chemicals such as chromate of potage and bichromate of potage were known to produce inflammation of the bronchial and nasal mucous membranes, convulsions, and paralysis, and in the worst cases their ingestion could be fatal.[81]

Chinese green tea was so adulterated that it came to be understood as "slow poison." Famed botanist and explorer Robert Fortune wrote that all green tea was "the result of a dye" and joked that "the Chinese, I doubt not, could substitute for that colour either red or yellow, should our tastes change and lead us to prefer more glaring tints!"[82] A year later, Samuel Ball, a former East India Company tea inspector, proposed, "Fictitious means are now generally or almost universally adopted to imitate or to increase the effect of the natural colour."[83] When he returned to China in the early 1850s, Robert Fortune disguised himself as a "Chinaman" in order to "obtain" tea seeds and a deeper knowledge about Chinese manufacturing. On his adventures, he wrote that the Chinese used so much pigment that the "hands of the workmen were quite blue." Fortune could not help but think "that if any green-tea drinkers had been present during the operation, their taste would have corrected."[84]

Fortune's resort to disguise reminds us that Europeans still lacked a great deal of knowledge about the tea plant. In much the same way that men such as Charles Bruce were frustrated by Assamese obfuscation, European scientists despaired about the Chinese monopoly of knowledge about the growth and manufacture of tea. In 1830, for example, food scientist Dr. J. Stevenson angrily condemned the Chinese for inhibiting the development of Western science when he wrote, "While the present narrow and jealous policy of the Chinese continues, many interesting particulars respecting the natural history of this particular plant must remain unknown to Europeans."[85]

In 1839, Dr. G. G. Sigmond, professor of Materia Medica to the Royal Medical-Botanical Society (and great supporter of Indian tea), similarly complained that "for a number of centuries the character, the manners, the customs, and the institutions of the Chinese, from whom alone could be gathered any information upon the subject of the tea-plant, were veiled in the deepest curiosity."[86]

As late as the 1840s, European botanists were unsure about whether green or black teas came from the same plant (which they do), but they were universally starting to suspect that green tea was a potentially unhealthy drink.[87] Virtually all experts believed that green was stronger than black tea and could have "severe effects" if drunk by "those popularly known as nervous." For such weak people, green tea could give rise to "tremor, anxiety, sleeplessness, and most distressing feelings."[88] Dr. Sigmond cautioned that for some, green tea acted "almost as a narcotic poison."[89] Medical reports, too, occasionally described the fate of individuals who suffered from their green tea habit. In one such case an "English traveller who [after having] walked some distance during a hot summer's day under the stimulus of green tea" began feeling faint and had an irregular pulse, difficulty breathing, and heart palpitations.[90] Doctors believed that the physical and psychological condition of the consumer needed to be considered when assessing tea's effects on the body. Green tea's dangers, however, were also a sign of Chinese duplicity.

Anglo-American fiction publicized such concerns by highlighting how Chinese green tea corrupted the souls and psyches of Western consumers. While much fiction celebrated the comforting domesticity of a cup of tea, green tea symbolized the dangers of commerce. In Elizabeth Gaskell's novel *Cranford* (1851–53), for example, the sale of green tea stresses the moral quandaries of a middle-class woman thrust into the marketplace. The impoverished spinster Miss Matty Jenkyns decides to sell tea to her neighborhood, believing this to be a respectable employment. She soon confronts the problem faced by all shopkeepers who sell ambiguous goods. Should she simply meet the public demand or does she have a moral duty to protect her customers from a hazardous product? Miss Matty adopts a middle ground. Though she sells green tea, she also explains to vulnerable customers that it is "slow poison, sure to destroy the nerves and produce all manner of evil." She especially feels compelled to warn customers who are "too young and innocent to be acquainted with the evil effects green tea produced on some constitutions."[91] Green tea is a source of satire and amusement in *Cranford*, but in other works it is more menacing.

J. Sheridan Le Fanu, the Irish gothic writer, turned the brew into a sinister and addictive Oriental drug in "Green Tea: A Case Reported by Martin Hesselius, the German Physician." In this ghost story the drink is a dangerous psychoactive

Eastern substance that unravels the mental health of a respectable, wealthy bachelor. The protagonist, Reverend Jennings, is a prosperous author who has a special fondness for green tea. But he describes this passion as an addiction that produces a morbid state of mind and delusions that include the haunting illusion of a monkey.[92] In this text, green tea reduces a morally upright and respectable man to a lost soul haunted by the East.

American author Mrs. Nancy Smith develops similar themes in her 1861 essay "Confessions of a Green-Tea Drinker." The title plays on de Quincy's well-known novella and thus already posited a likeness between opium and green tea. Smith identifies herself as a nervous woman who uses green tea to help her travel in "that border region which lies between the spirit world and the natural." The author's doctor tries to convince her that the Prussian blue, indigo, and sulfate of lime contained in her tea are slowly poisoning her and producing an "exaltation of the senses." Smith abandons the brew as per doctor's orders, but she misses hearing her "voices of the night."[93] This sensational story of spiritualism and tea drinking seemed fanciful, but American experts did suspect that the "prevalence of nervous diseases among the women of the Northern States" was due to their "near universal use" of adulterated tea.[94] Green tea could be said to be deadly, but it also could allow one to commune with the spectral world.

The British and Americans were by no means the only nations to recognize the similarities between opium and tea. In 1850 the merchant magazine *Hogg's Instructor* published an article on the adulteration of Chinese tea that suggested that some Chinese believed opium and tea were in fact the same thing. "It is commonly reported," a Chinese informant told this English colleague, "that you buy our teas in order to convert them into opium and resell them in that form to us."[95] The Chinese, of course, regarded opium as more enervating than green tea, but both the British and Chinese believed that ingestion of these substances opened the door to foreign invasion.[96]

Anxieties about green tea were racialized fears associated with consuming commodities in an increasingly global marketplace. Indeed, the modern conception of addiction was emerging at this time in part because it expressed the power that a substance could hold over its consumer. As the Victorians were increasingly finding, making rational economic choices in a globalizing marketplace was not easy, if even possible. Addiction implied forces that were beyond the consumer's comprehension. Adulteration similarly expressed fears about trade, particularly long-distance trade, in which consumers no longer saw the actual labor producing their food and drink. Of course, many local foods, including milk, were also adulterated, but green tea illuminated the way in which foreign producers could influence the nation's health. Tea dealers had to find ways to overcome such anxieties.

ADVERTISING PURITY: JOHN HORNIMAN AND
THE RISE OF THE PACKAGED GOOD

In April 1860, the major importers met in Canton to discuss ways to ame-
liorate adulteration. These businessmen pledged to abstain from purchasing
all adulterated tea and gave an order through one of the ex-hong merchants,
Woo E-ho, that any persons selling adulterated tea would be punished. Like
the more general discussions of green tea in Britain, this effort at industry self-
regulation impugned and sought to punish the Chinese for tricking respectable
European merchants.[97] Such posturing on the part of companies such as Jardine,
Matheson, and others placed the blame wholly on the Chinese, when in fact the
Chinese government and merchants based in China regularly sought to control
and punish adulterators, not an easy task given the high volume and dispersed
nature of production.[98]

In Britain and in other consumer markets, such concerns gave rise to new
forms of retailing, advertising, and branding. Adulteration induced racial fears
and cast doubt on the civilizing power of international commerce, but business
found a way to turn anxiety into profits. The master of this strategy was the
trusted Quaker merchant John Horniman, who claimed to be the first to package,
brand, and advertise pure unadulterated tea. We can imagine his advertising as
a kind of global encounter, which invited buyers and sellers to contemplate the
foreign nature of their consuming passions.

Especially in the late nineteenth and early twentieth centuries, European and
American advertising was imbued with imperial ideology that produced notions
of racial difference and white supremacy. European consumers learned to gaze
upon the bodies of racial others, who often but not always were represented as
laborers who made the things Western consumers desired. Such racial imagery
also established new gender and class sensibilities.[99] Advertising was a place
then where national identities were made and sold. Advertising and the goods
themselves demarcated new kinds of state boundaries and created "imagined
communities" even as the goods regularly disregarded national borders, but
before the 1870s it often was quite limited.[100] Many foreign goods were not
advertised at all, and many Victorians regarded advertising as mere puffery
that like adulteration was designed to confuse the consumer about the nature
of the commodity. Well-known writers and politicians and lesser-known
journalists and pundits often agreed that advertising was but a ruse intended
to mislead the naïve consumer.[101] John Horniman's key innovation was not
to avoid Chinese goods but to convey trust in advertising, the brand name,
and packaged goods. Throughout all his advertising he relentlessly talked
about product safety and taught consumers that carefully wrapped, sealed,

and advertised products were pure of adulterants. This Quaker merchant took advantage of the anxieties about the Celestial Empire, advertising, and the market in general to brand himself as a paternalistic food reformer rather than a purveyor of poison and puffery.

Quakers, who introduced many new retail practices, were part of the large community of temperance, abolition, and other reform movements we examined in chapter 2. John Horniman's personal history and that of his family were squarely situated within this reform-oriented world. Born in Reading in 1803, John Horniman first went into business as a grocer on the Isle of Wight before moving to London around 1850. He established an honest reputation through his many religious and philanthropic commitments and ubiquitous advertising. By the time he died in 1893, Horniman had amassed a huge personal fortune. He was able to leave legacies to a variety of Quaker causes, including £10,000 to the Peace Society, £12,500 to the Friends' Foreign Mission Committee, another £11,000 to the Friends' Home Mission Committee, and £2,000 to the Friends' Temperance Union.[102] Whereas in chapter 2 we saw how temperance spread the taste for tea, Horniman's career reminds us that profits from tea also contributed to temperance, missionary work, and other similar causes.

John Horniman transferred his thriving company to his son Frederick, who, in addition to running the family business, served on the London County Council and became a Member of Parliament for Penryn and Falmouth in Cornwall in 1895. Frederick became a practicing Anglican, but like his father he supported social reform and temperance. He had also become a noted world traveler and ethnographic collector.[103] To house his imperial collection, Frederick built an exquisite Art Nouveau building in South London, which after it was bequeathed to the London County Council, became known as the Horniman Museum. Like James Silk Buckingham, Frederick was a liberal Orientalist and social reformer. Though a staunch opponent of the South African War, Frederick accepted annexation of the Boer Republics and, as one reporter explained it, "his patriotism is of the right sort."[104] Frederick's son Emslie John continued in the same tradition, becoming a Liberal MP for Chelsea in London. Frederick's sister Annie was more progressive than her brother. She advanced the cause of avant-garde theater and female artistic entrepreneurship. Among other things, she introduced the first plays of George Bernard Shaw to London, promoted W. B. Yeats and other Irish playwrights, founded the Abbey Theatre in Dublin, and developed the Repertory movement at the Gaiety Theatre in Manchester.[105] The Horniman family thus exemplifies the alliance between trade, philanthropy, and liberal imperial culture. Imperial profits supported this cultural and social world, and both John and Frederick promoted an "imperial gaze" in the metropole. At the same time, the Hornimans left a lasting legacy in the arts, social reform, and business in Britain.

John Horniman's firm produced an especially rich and diverse archive that included print advertising, shop cards, handbills, pamphlets, posters, circulars, and packaging.[106] His advertising was so ubiquitous that it infiltrated popular culture and inspired jokes and fictional characters.[107] Although he began packaging tea in the 1820s, Horniman started advertising in earnest in the 1840s and 1850s. Examples from this era are limited, however, since heavy duties were still levied on advertisements, paper, and newspapers.[108] By the 1860s, these so-called taxes on knowledge were lifted and changes in printing technology and the growth of literacy enabled the development of mass-circulation newspapers and magazines. Circulation numbers were still relatively low, however, so Horniman bought ad space in a wide variety of periodicals, including temperance journals and papers for wine merchants and connoisseurs.[109] *The Times*, the *Saturday Review*, the *National Review*, *The Critic*, and *The Athenaeum* (the paper Buckingham had started) advertised Horniman's tea.[110] The first ads were simple short inserts nestled in columns selling cures for the common cold, cheap and painless dentistry, moral publications, and early branded goods such as Lea & Perrins Worcestershire Sauce and Cross and Blackwell's "Oriental Pickle, Curry or Mulligatawny Paste."[111] Even when unremarkable, together such ads reflected the prosaic and global tastes of middle- and lower-middle-class Victorian consumers.

In magazines that accommodated illustrations, Horniman reproduced images of his famous tea package (fig. 4.1). The package itself was an advertisement and told the story of both adulteration and the value of trusting brand-name goods. In one typical example, from January 1863, the ad reassured readers that for "the last 15 years" Horniman's had supplied pure tea that had not been "faced" by the Chinese. Countless other ads warned the British public about the Chinese threat and then proclaimed Horniman's brand was imported "free from the Usual Artificial Facing Powders."[112] An ad from 1856 explained to readers of *England Wine Magazine* that "both merchants and scientific men have established as a fact, before a *Committee of the House of Commons*," that the Chinese "faced" common teas with colored powders, but Horniman and Company recognized that "the Public would prefer *Pure Tea*." Packaging and branding thus protected "the *purchaser from injury*."[113] The ads proclaimed that packaging was a barrier protecting the British consumer from the fraudulent retailer and the unclean Chinese producer. Packaging was a technology that made the Orient safe and palatable.

FIGURE 4.1. Horniman's tea advertisement. *Ragged School Union Magazine* 15, no. 169 (January 1863). (By permission of Proquest, Early British Periodicals)

Since their reputation was typically based on their blending skills, grocers cared little for this new technology and many refused to stock Horniman's tea. The company then simply turned to other retailers, including chemists, confectioners, booksellers, and other "agents."[114] It is not clear whether the agency system originated with the temperance movement or manufacturers since there was such a close connection between these worlds.[115] In 1873, a company known as the London Tea Association even hired Wesleyan preachers as agents to sell their 2s. tea, maintaining that this job would improve the finances of cash-strapped ministers. The trade journal *The Grocer* made fun of this venture and claimed that the misguided idea was "borrowed from America" and would likely not "go down in this country."[116] This was not strictly speaking an American idea, however, and the agency system became an industry norm. By the late 1870s and 1880s, Horniman had thousands of agents in the UK, France, Germany, Russia, Norway, Italy, Austria, Belgium, Switzerland, and Denmark. In all these lands, his ads emphasized the purity of his product and played upon and stimulated anti-Chinese fears.

Horniman's produced a veritable mountain of shop cards, handbills, pamphlets, circulars, and posters.[117] One Pimlico grocer jealously criticized his neighbor, "a baker," who "on every possible printed medium" advertised "Horniman's Tea."[118] Some advertising was admittedly quite spartan. J. Woodhurst, a Ramsgate confectioner and fancy bread and biscuit maker, simply announced that he was an agent for "Huntley and Palmer's and Robb's Biscuits, Celebrated Leicester Pork

Pies, Foreign Wines and Horniman's Packet Teas."[119] Other examples were lav-
ishly illustrated, but all assured consumers that they were safe when they bought
"Horniman's Pure Tea in packets."[120] Many ads featured food reformers, scientists,
and other experts, including French chemists, Robert Fortune, and Dr. Arthur
Hill Hassall, as well as Board of Inland Revenue Reports.[121] One typical example
from 1862 quoted Dr. Hassall, who assured the public that when he personally
visited London's docks he found "Tea, perfectly pure" in Horniman's stocks.[122]
Another version in the *National Review* similarly hinted that Hassall preferred
Horniman's brand tea.[123] Thus, Hassall seemed to be in favor of branding and
advertising, and Horniman looked like a progressive food reformer.[124]

Horniman's ads were also political documents that advocated free trade and
low taxes. Some quoted "The Great Political Economist, Dr. Adam Smith," and
urged Lord John Russell, who was then prime minister, to lower the tea duty.[125]
High taxes, the ad suggested, encouraged adulteration and ultimately limited
free trade. This argument would have made sense to retailers and consumers
who were following the politics surrounding the tea duty in the late 1840s and
1850s. Another ad went into great detail about this issue and the impact of the
transition from monopoly to free trade when it explained how since the "retir-
ing of the Honourable East India Company from commercial pursuits . . . the
Chinese commenced sending a counterfeit tea . . . [which] is now extensively
retailed in every Town and Village throughout the entire Kingdom."[126] Though
monopoly had eliminated quality controls, Horniman did not want to reassert
government controls. Rather he offered market-based solutions. He warned in
one ad, for example, that high taxes had reduced consumption in Britain and
threatened a sense of British national cohesion: "Tea no longer holds its own as
the national beverage. It cannot be questioned that the consumption of ordinary
tea does not increase in proportion to the population."[127] Using advertisements
as a political forum, John Horniman encouraged consumers to trust branded
and packaged products in the era of free trade.

While condemning high taxes and monopoly, Horniman also raised concerns
about gender and the family to raise the stakes of Chinese dishonesty.[128] A
newspaper advertisement, for example, explained that when "the Chinese face"
tea with poisonous color, they defrauded the British body and destroyed the
sanctity of the home. This advertisement appealed to women as shoppers who
had a duty "to purchase good food and tea" and thereby ensure "Healthy children,
and happy homes."[129] Linking domesticity and imperialism, one advertisement
admitted: "Every land under the sun is ransacked to provide the good things in
life for Englishmen and Englishwomen, and there is no other country in which
the women have such chances of making a pleasant happy home."[130] Both men
and women enjoyed tea and domesticity, but by characterizing tea drinking as

a female and private ritual Horniman's advertising domesticated this unruly product. Commodity-chain type advertising, that is, ads that demonstrated the travels of a commodity from production to consumption, did the same thing. Postcards, booklets, and trade cards, for example, all detailed how Horniman kept tea clean and pure as it traveled from a Shanghai tea farm to the Port of London and then to the British parlor.[131] Such ads reminded middle-class consumers that tea was a foreign product but one rendered safe by branding, packaging, and advertising.

In the 1870s and 1880s, Horniman's and many other brands depicted the consumer as a bourgeois woman or female child playfully enjoying a domestic pleasure. Such ads shifted purity from the commodity to the consumer, who was most commonly middle class, white, and feminine. A Horniman's almanac from 1887 surrounded a child's tea party with the tea flower and Chinese symbols (fig. 4.2). The ad reproduced a visually stunning, pastoral, picturesque, and premodern China that resembled a nostalgic preindustrial England, with small villages, farms, and hand production. This reassuring image packaged China as English, but not all ads celebrated pastoralism. Some highlighted how modern industrial British manufacturing enabled an ancient China to serve world markets.[132] China and the problem of adulteration disappeared from the almanac for 1888 (fig. 4.3). Yet the phrase "Horniman's Pure Tea" remained and lasted well into the twentieth century, long after adulteration was a significant problem and long after the British stopped drinking Chinese tea.

Horniman's never had a monopoly on images of China, of course. Victorian popular culture was saturated with positive and negative portrayals of the Celestial Empire. Chinese art and material culture, much of which had been war booty, were displayed in museums and similar sites throughout the midcentury.[133] Other firms also cultivated a variety of images of China. In 1839, Peek Brothers issued a circular that impersonated the form and content of a newspaper or gazette. It reported news of the war with China and the commercial "phrenzy" it had caused, concluding, "The trade with China hangs in vibrating uncertainty." The ad assured buyers that the firm did not go in for speculation and that it continued to engage in a "respectable, legitimate trade."[134] Other firms also transformed war and trade instability into publicity. An Oxford grocer and tea dealer marked the taking of the "City of Chin-Kiang-Foo" in 1842 with an illustration and description of this example of English bravery and prowess.[135] Merchants could turn almost any bad news into advertising copy. A Wandsworth tea and coffee warehouse, for example, issued an advertisement in 1857, which admitted that "**IN TIMES LIKE THESE** when Mutiny prevails in India, and War still going on in China . . . we strictly confine our attention to the finest

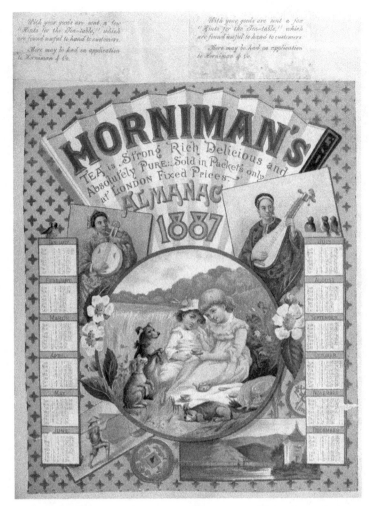

FIGURE 4.2. Horniman's Almanac, 1887. (Courtesy of Tetley Group Archive,
Acc#4364/01/002, London Metropolitan Archives)

qualities only, always refusing those weak and inferior kinds."[136] All of these
approaches roused interest in China and offered consumers a safe place to shop
in this global marketplace.[137]

On New Year's Day 1870, *The Grocer* admitted, "Packet Tea has become
an institution in the Trade."[138] It took several more decades before most teas
were sold in this way, but the growth of packaging and branding created new
supply chains and benefitted large importers and retailers who could afford to
alter the contents of the package to suit their needs. While John Horniman
no doubt believed he was acting in the best interests of consumers, packaging

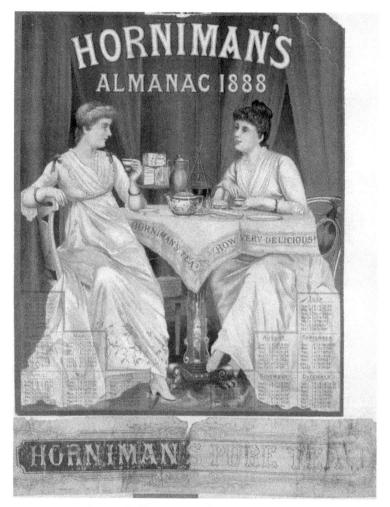

FIGURE 4.3. Horniman's Almanac, 1888. (Courtesy of Tetley Group Archive, Acc#4364/01/002, London Metropolitan Archives)

ultimately accrued power to the large importer. Ironically, pure food legislation also had the unintended consequence of securing the interests of big brands and Indian tea.

CHANGING TASTES: THE DECLINE OF GREEN TEA

The mid-Victorian hysteria over and responses to tea adulteration contributed to the general decline in the importation, sale, and consumption of Chinese green teas in Britain, Canada, and the United States.[139] Canadians and Americans continued to prefer green tea for the whole of the nineteenth century, but in general consumers on both sides of the Atlantic began to turn away from "the flavour of green tea."[140] Tea dealers believed that popular exposés, advertisements, parliamentary select committees, and pure food legislation that targeted shopkeepers rather than importers had led to the sharp decline in the use of green tea. Grocers felt they had been unduly targeted by the new legislation and they criticized government interference in their trade. They also argued that pure food legislation had escalated public fears, damaged markets, and altered tastes. They especially believed that the second 1872 Adulteration of Food Act hurt their reputations and magnified "the evil of adulteration in the public mind."[141] Augustus Thorne, a tea importer, bluntly explained the Act itself had caused the "public taste" to go "off green teas."[142] A former tea inspector who had worked in China for many years agreed that the Act had led to a sharp depreciation in the value of both green and scented teas in England.[143] A London tea retailer perceptively suggested "many paragraphs, taken from very popular journals, in which 'death in the pot,' 'grocers' poisoners', and all sorts of sensational headings" had changed his business, and in general had "had a very injurious effect upon the tea trade." He then joked that such articles probably "have been put in with the view the next day of inserting an advertisement in the same paper, that if people want a really good thing, they must come to their particular shop."[144]

The 1872 Act fined shopkeepers found guilty of selling adulterated teas, so they increasingly avoided green and scented teas, stocked packet teas such as Horniman's, and began to slowly sell the new Indian teas, which were also advertised as free from "Chinese" adulteration. At the same time, this legislation had a more limited notion of adulteration than the previous law and the intense fears of adulterants that had existed in midcentury had dissipated to a certain degree. Giving evidence before another select committee on adulteration, an alderman and sheriff of the City of London who had worked in the grocery trade for thirty-seven years even joked about the ill effects of green tea. When asked if green tea was unhealthy, he responded:

Certainly not; I remember a case 30 years ago; a gentleman came into my place of business, and asked for two pounds of black tea; and my assistant asked him, "Will you take any green tea," he said, "No green tea is slow poison." An old lady, 80 years of age was sitting by in a chair, and she said "Yes, it must be very slow poison, indeed, for I have drunk nothing but green tea for 60 years, and I'm not dead yet."[145]

Many medical experts had also shifted their position. One Scottish doctor explained that chemicals such as Prussian blue are "not so nice . . . but the proportion is so extremely small that it is not quite capable of proving injurious."[146] Another quipped that not all disgusting things found in tea were unhealthy. He had once found a "Chinaman's toe nail in some tea," but then stated, "I do not call it an adulteration."[147] The scientific community was far from unified on this point, however.

When the aging Dr. Hassall appeared before the committee, he reiterated his belief that the coloring of green tea was fraudulent *and* physically harmful to consumers. Additives such as Prussian blue were especially perilous, he noted, because they accumulated in the body. Furthermore, he felt that retailers should be held accountable for selling fraudulent goods. In fact, he called for an activist government that would "teach people the component parts of everything" they ate and drank.[148] Reaffirming the position he had taken twenty years earlier, Hassall contended: "The consumer entering a shop, asking for an article, has a right to expect that he will be supplied with that which he demands, and for which he pays."[149] Hassall felt that proper labeling could help ensure transparency and allow consumers to actually know what they were buying when they went shopping. Hassall's comprehensive understanding of government intervention and consumer protection would have appealed to many consumer activists and food reformers today. He was an early advocate of public health, market regulation, and labeling laws at a time when such ideas were not popular. Though in a minority, Arthur Hill Hassall believed that the government needed to maintain a sense of where and under what conditions food is produced and sold to consumers. Hassall and his contemporaries had great faith in a government that was responsive to science. He did not see global trade in itself as a problem, but he did feel that a liberal market had to have intelligent oversight. His vision lost out, however. In its report, the select committee concluded that the coloring of green tea was not particularly harmful, though it could potentially disguise poor quality goods. It noted that consumers should be protected but did not "consider that Parliament desires needlessly to hamper or fetter trade."[150] The 1875 Act that amended the 1860 and 1872 laws further narrowed the definition of adulteration.[151]

Similar laws influenced markets in the empire and in the United States. Following the British example, in 1883 the United States passed the Tea Adulteration Act, which was one of the first federal laws regulating imported foods.[152] Scientists and the Department of Agriculture had conducted their own investigations and concluded that most imported Chinese and Japanese tea was artificially colored.[153] The U.S. Tea Act, which was intended to prevent the importation of spurious or adulterated tea, came just after the passage of the 1882 Chinese Exclusion

Act. Both laws reacted to fears about Chinese invasion.[154] Influenced by a very heavy marketing campaign, American consumers increasingly turned to Japanese green teas, which were also advertised as pure and unadulterated. Adulterated tea did not disappear, but this scare did hurt the reputation of Chinese imports and increased the market share of British colonial teas. Pure food legislation, adulteration, and advertising thus shifted world markets, as Australian, British, Irish, and other tea drinkers acquired a taste for packaged brands that often contained supplies from British-owned plantations in India and Ceylon.

———

Mid-Victorian debates about adulteration were, as we have seen, a venue in which notions of consumers' rights, government responsibility, and scientific efficacy were contested and confirmed. Food reformers, like Dr. Hassall, and merchants, like John Horniman, asserted that consumers needed to know where and how goods were produced. The question was whether the state or industry would protect and inform consumers. A focus on tea adulteration in particular allows us to see the ways in which chemists and retailers defined healthy goods, consumers, and forms of production, distribution, and consumption. It also exposes the international concerns at the heart of domestic consumption. In early and mid-Victorian Britain, tea gained new meanings through such political, scientific, and popular debates about fraudulent forms of Chinese production. Europeans did not regard all teas as equally healthy, nor did they regard all of Asia as a unitary site. They did, however, agree that Western science and industry could make the East profitable, safe, and healthy for British consumption.

PART II
Imperial Tastes

5

INDUSTRY AND EMPIRE

Manufacturing Imperial Tastes in Victorian Britain

In the summer of 1881, the fashionable ladies in the West London neighborhood of Chelsea held a fund-raiser for their local hospital. That year they elected to put on a bazaar, nostalgically called an "Old English Fayre."[1] By the 1880s, no such gathering, even one pretending to be an early modern marketplace, was complete without the presence of brewed tea. But the tea on sale could not have been more modern. It was pure, unblended Indian tea supplied by a firm of planters who believed that London Society could help them find a market for their new product. This seemingly innocuous and long-forgotten episode in West London pinpoints the beginning of a new phase in the histories of tea, advertising, and planters' influence on metropolitan consumer culture. It represents the moment when a colonial business began intentionally to manufacture imperial tastes as well as commodities.

In the last third of the nineteenth century, India's and Ceylon's tea planters experimented with diverse means of selling their new "Empire teas" to British buyers and shoppers.[2] In the forty years since the Assam Company first auctioned their crop in London, Indian tea slowly made its way into packet brands and shopkeepers' blends, but in general retailers did not like the product. Indian tea had no significant price advantage and consumers typically found it distasteful. The tea bubble and crash of the 1860s and the revelation that, as an article in *Chambers's Journal of Popular Literature* on Assam published in 1880 clarified, planters had "treated their labourers as cattle, underpaid, overworked, badly housed, half-starved, mercilessly beaten" did little to encourage buyers or shoppers to prefer empire-grown teas. The article, however, was also part of what we would now call a public relations campaign that explained how a "conscientious and right thinking body of men" had replaced the early scoundrels who had exploited their workers.[3] This campaign took many forms and lasted for decades, and in addition to improving planters' soiled image, it taught buyers, consumers, and politicians who had long been satisfied with Chinese tea to prefer the British Empire's produce.

Especially during the last quarter of the nineteenth century, the peripatetic and transnational Planter Raj included those who grew tea and those who

sold it. I use the term "planter" for those who literally were involved in cultivating tea and for those who left the garden to sell their produce. As we will
see, planters became a formidable and capacious sales force, and in a variety
of ways they called upon "the consumer" to come to their aid in their battles against the Chinese, reluctant distributors, and a somewhat indifferent
metropolitan government. Collaboration and competition among planters,
particularly between those from India and Ceylon, spurred developments
in advertising, marketing, and retailing and provided the impetus for a new
kind of imperial politics. We will trace these developments through reading
planters' trade journals and listening to their conversations in new corporate
bodies and trade associations.[4] In these venues, "industries" came into being as
members developed a shared vocabulary, politics, and identity. Letters, articles,
and opinion pieces chronicled labor issues, legislative changes, commodity
and share prices, new technologies, and retail and consumer behavior. The
business press and trade associations provided an international framework
for parochial concerns, formalized what had been personal networks, and
became promotional arenas that helped manufacturers convince retailers to
buy their goods. Trade journals were thus tools of empire and instruments of
globalization, but they also reveal the ways in which these two forces could
be at odds with one another.

The empire's publicists developed a very simple and yet powerful national story
that went something like this: the British were brave and ingenious engineers
who had a predilection for "invention" and "improvement." Their improving
nature had built the steam engines, power looms, and factories that had mass-
produced cotton and other goods. In India and Ceylon, British men similarly
cleared jungles and invented machinery that produced a new high-quality and
cheap tea that could satisfy the world's thirst. This story about modern British
tea was well developed by the time Arnold Toynbee coined the term "Industrial
Revolution" in his famous lectures on the subject published in 1884. The key
elements of the cotton and tea revolutions were the same. Both included the
substitution of machines for domestic production and the belief that competition rather than regulation and monopoly naturally lowered costs and created
mass markets.[5] In the British Empire, plantations, machinery, and British men
were thus said to produce a pure, healthy, and civilized "British" brew. In the late
1880s, trade statistics supported this view by revealing that just over half the
tea consumed in the United Kingdom now came from the British rather than
the Celestial Empire.[6] It had taken a half century, but it appeared that Queen
Victoria's prophecy that one day Indian tea would enrich her empire in the East
had finally come true.

MAKING MASS MARKETS

Empire-grown tea, that is, tea that was cultivated and manufactured in British colonies, was a product of national and global developments in capitalism and working-, middle-, and upper-class consumer cultures.[7] Between the 1850s and 1914, the scale, speed, and significance of commodity exchange grew at phenomenal rates, and foodstuffs were at the forefront of this new globalizing world.[8] New methods of processing and refrigeration permitted perishables to travel much longer distances from the farm to the plate. The first shipments of frozen meat, for example, arrived in Britain in 1874, and by the mid-1880s Englishmen and women ate meat from Ireland, Australia, New Zealand, and South America. Processed products such as meat extract, condensed milk, and margarine also moved onto the grocer's shelf.[9] Together, the industrialization of agriculture and food production created new foods and transformed older products. But, as the food industry was well aware, getting a new product to market required the cooperation of countless middlemen and women.

Indian tea benefited from the numerous technological developments that defined this era. Steam-fueled railway, river, and ocean travel increased the speed of exchanges within nations and around the world. Well-engineered roads, bridges, docks, and warehouses enabled massive amounts of tea to move to primary markets in London, Liverpool, Amsterdam, New York, San Francisco, and elsewhere. Yet the centuries-old caravan trade still carried tea overland from China through Central Asia to Russia between the 1860s and 1880s. The 11,000-mile journey took sixteen months and typically involved sea and river travel and hundreds of people, horses, and camels that managed to traverse incredibly arduous terrain, including the 800-mile stretch of the Gobi Desert. The journey was transformed but not destroyed with the completion of the Trans-Siberian Railway in 1900.[10] The caravan trade nevertheless reminds us that while modern technologies were quite helpful in facilitating the movement of goods, the intensive use of human and animal energy also made mass markets throughout the nineteenth century.

Despite the diverse paths that tea took from field to table, Mincing Lane in the City of London became the recognized financial and physical center of the global tea trade.[11] With the end of the East India Company's monopoly, the tea auctions and tea dealers migrated to the street.[12] The metropolis offered concentrated access to capital, commercial information, storage and sales facilities, and a huge local market. During the 1820s a surge of dock construction served goods from around the world. Particularly critical for the tea trade, St. Katharine's Docks were an engineering marvel built with remarkable speed (fig. 5.1). Opened in 1828, these docks included six, elegant six-story warehouses with access to the

FIGURE 5.1. Engraving of St. Katharine's Docks, c. 1860, from Walter Thornbury, *Old and New London* (London: Cassell, Peter and Gilpin, 1873), 2:121. (Archive.org)

Thames via a 190-foot canal and handled up to 700,000 chests of tea a year.[13] Loading and unloading goods was an extremely efficient process. In 1864, for example, the 14,000 chests that the *Fiery Cross* had brought from China were unloaded in just six hours, between 4 and 10 am.[14] The opening of the Suez Canal in 1869 made the clippers obsolete and dramatically increased the speed of trade, lowered costs, and boosted imports.[15]

Once in port, laborers transferred the tea to warehouses, where it was weighed, inspected, sorted, tasted, smelled, taxed, and marked with signs that looked something like Egyptian hieroglyphics. Over a dozen strange symbols indicated the size, quality, and flavor, described in terms such as "woody," "flaggy," "dusty," "very dusty," "burnt," and "odd smell."[16] Tea tasters thus translated taste and smell into language and then into prices. These processes became infinitely more complicated as new teas from India and Ceylon and elsewhere were thrown into the mix. The markings nevertheless made diverse teas conform to quasi-scientific classification systems, and this tended to benefit the big London buyers who could afford to hire specialized tea tasters and blenders.

Most consumers remained ignorant of such details as they typically purchased very small amounts of tea from local shops. However, in the 1860s and 1870s, packet companies, department stores, the Co-operative Society, multiple shops, and chain tea shops altered distribution networks and introduced fixed, low prices, new shopping experiences, and social meanings surrounding the purchase and use of foods. Petty merchants, peddlers, and street and market vendors remained important aspects of distribution systems, but national brands grew and took over many pre-distributive processes. The chain stores and Co-operative Society particularly built up commercial empires by selling cheap tea and similar products to working-class markets.

In Britain the cooperative movement had a profound influence on the history of food distribution and working-class consumer culture. The movement began in the 1840s and was based on shared ownership and socialist principles, but it also pioneered many new forms of retailing. In 1863 the Co-operative Wholesale Tea Society (CWS) formed to act as a manufacturer and wholesaler to over 500 independent cooperative societies. The CWS lowered costs by introducing centralized bulk purchasing and processing. In 1882 it set up a tea-buying department and the following year it opened a large London warehouse in Lenman Street near Aldgate. The CWS initially imported direct from China, bypassing a bevy of brokers and middlemen, but soon it began importing from India as well, and in 1902 it purchased its own tea estates in Ceylon. By 1913 the society owned over 30,000 acres in both India and Ceylon and blended 25 million pounds of its own and other teas.[17] In terms of ownership and ideology the Co-op was unlike private corporations, but its business methods followed changes that were underway in other facets of the retail sector.[18]

Rather than grow by moving into diverse commodities as the Co-op and department stores were doing, other firms opened branches dealing in only limited goods. Individual shops might be small, but the scale of their operations was not, and many introduced bulk buying, fixed prices, standardization, and cash transactions, all of which lowered prices for consumers.[19] The International Tea Company, for example, had 100 branches in 1885 and double that number ten years later.[20] In Scotland and the north of England, Templeton's and Cochrain's initially purchased through buyers in Mincing Lane, but they soon began to mix, package, and advertise their own blends at numerous shops.[21] The Home and Colonial Stores also became a major player with 400 branches on high streets throughout the British Isles in 1900.[22] This firm lived up to its name in the 1890s when it opened buying offices in Colombo and Calcutta and increased its export business.[23] These multiples overlapped with the packet trade and also mixed and packaged their own teas. Independent retailers thus were forced to compete by lowering prices and giving away all manner of free gifts to their customers, including jewelry, books, teapots, butter dishes, and even live ponies.[24] In 1885 one Glasgow shop even gave away "Tea for nothing."[25]

Sir Thomas Lipton was the most famous grocer to exploit the mass market. His larger-than-life personality, showmanship, sporting career, faith in advertising, and desire to leave a lasting legacy has meant that Lipton has received a disproportionately large degree of historical attention. He was not unique, but his career does represent several key trends. Like the generation of planters that went to Assam, Cachar, Darjeeling, and Ceylon, Lipton was Scottish, but his imperial career came only after learning about plantations and advertising in the United States. Lipton's father had been a typical petty Glaswegian grocer with a pronounced distaste for innovation. Lipton might have followed in his father's footsteps had he not traveled to the United States as a youth and gained firsthand knowledge of food production and sales by working as a laborer on a tobacco plantation and on a rice plantation, and as an assistant in a high-class New York grocery store. It was in America, he claimed, that he embraced "modern" ideas of salesmanship and display. In 1871 he returned home and opened a small shop in Glasgow, selling cheap bacon, eggs, butter, and cheese, largely imported from Ireland and the United States. Within a few years he launched a major export business, and by 1878 Lipton's hams were selling as far afield as the West Indies.[26] While he specialized in cheap food, he did not neglect the middle classes. Lipton opened his first London shop directly across the street from Whiteley's famous department store in fashionable Westbourne Grove.[27]

Thomas Lipton only began selling tea in 1889, but he radically changed the market when, instead of charging two shillings a pound, Lipton priced standard teas at only one and seven pence. This stunt captured the attention of a group of London bankers who represented the proprietors of several Ceylon estates who wanted to sell up. Destroyed by fungus, coffee plantations were going cheap in the 1880s. When recalling his decision to buy a plantation, Lipton did not mention economics but wrote that he "rather liked the sensation" of being a tea planter. In his advertising and autobiography he then (falsely) asserted that he was the first "owner of tea estates . . . to act as his own retailer."[28] After purchasing his first plantation in Ceylon in 1890, Lipton flooded the press with images of tea plantations, factories, and phrases that claimed his teas were imported direct from the "Garden to the Tea Cup." Like that of John Horniman, Lipton's advertising presented a modern view of the tea trade and implied that consumers could place their trust in the brand name. Unlike Horniman, he suggested that packaging was not enough. Consumers needed to buy from the British Empire.[29]

Lipton succeeded not because he purchased plantations or advertised a great deal but because he recognized the buying power of the British working class.[30] The 1851 census revealed that there were over 27 million people in the British Isles, with 18 million of those living in England and Wales, 3 million in Scotland, and 6 million in Ireland. In 1911 there were 18 million more Britons, though Ireland's demographic catastrophe meant that it was now roughly equal in size to Scotland, with both at about 4.5 million each.[31] Living standards were profoundly uneven between 1850 and 1910, and dire poverty remained a

TABLE 5.1. TEA: AVERAGE PRICES, DUTIES, AND RATES
OF TEA CONSUMPTION IN THE UK, 1811–71

YEAR	AVERAGE PRICE PER LB.	AVERAGE RATE OF DUTY PAID BY THE CONSUMER	AVERAGE PER CAPITA CONSUMPTION (IN POUNDS)
1811	6s. 8d.	3s. 4d.	1.4
1821	5s. 8d.	2s. 9½d.	1.4
1831	4s. 7d.	2s. 2¾d.	1.4
1841	4s. 2¾d.	2s. 2¼d.	1.6
1851	3s. 4¾d.	2s. 2¼d.	1.15
1861	2s. 10d.	1s. 5d.	2.11
1871	1s. 10½d.	6d.	3.15

Source: "Consumption of Tea," *Journal of the Royal Society
of Arts* 20 (23 August 1872): 812.

very real experience for as much as a third of the population, but in general real wages increased. In working-class communities, money and foodstuffs were not evenly distributed, and men notably ate more meat while their wives survived on sweet tea.[32] Lipton especially catered to this working-class female consumer.

Low taxes helped create the mass market. After William Gladstone reduced the tea duty to 1s. in 1863 and 6d. in 1865, consumption and imports grew.[33] In good and bad times, tea imports increased from about 4 to 11 percent annually throughout the 1860s. The period 1866–67 was a disastrous time for the trade, but 10 percent more tea was imported in 1868 than in 1867.[34] Experts believed that Gladstone's liberal fiscal policies explained the growth of consumption between the 1850s and 1870s, and such increases excited retailers. "The statistics," the trade journal *The Grocer* proposed in 1863, "show that tea has not yet even reached the limit of consumption."[35] In this period, national statistics tended to diminish local differences and allowed observers to describe markets as possessing collective national appetites, identities, and corporal attributes, which could grow and shrink and have personalities.[36] Markets had needs and desires that could be unborn, unsatisfied, stimulated, or fully sated.[37] Allowing the Victorians to theorize and govern passions, quantification thus naturalized and nationalized consumer markets.

While the government and industry experts focused on measuring national consumer habits, British tea cultures reinforced class and gender differences. For example, the highly ritualistic meal of afternoon tea often symbolized the private social world of wealthy Victorian ladies.[38] Family teas could be very modest, private affairs, but by the late nineteenth century, afternoon tea had become a social performance in which the menu, arrangement of furniture, choice of gown, selection of entertainment, and, of course, one's guest list all reflected upon the breeding and refinement of the hostess. Anticipating the way in which theorists such as Pierre Bourdieu revealed how taste and cultural expertise became a class marker, Victorian writers pointed out how one's social position could be revealed through how one served tea.[39] The "difference between an ill- and well-bred person," one author noted, was in the "small details" and "courtesies."[40] One advice book, written "By a Member of the Aristocracy" in the late 1870s, identified at least three classes of "five o'clock teas." The largest of these typically had professional musical entertainment for as many as one hundred people. The next class consisted of between twenty and forty guests and often featured "amateur" talent, while the final class was considered the small and friendly tea in which five to fifteen friends and family members gathered for conversation rather than entertainment. There were numerous social nuances at each of these gatherings. The food, organization, equipment, decor, and dress needed to fit the occasion. At the larger events ladies maids and other female servants stood at the back of a buffet and poured tea and coffee from large urns, while at smaller events the hostess poured tea from fine china teapots. The usual refreshments included tea and coffee, sherry, champagne, claret, "ices, fruit, fancy biscuits and cakes . . . bread-and-butter, potted game sandwiches, &c."[41] The food was always abundant, expensive, and carefully arranged. Coffee and other drinks were also served and in summer the tea was often both hot and iced. The smaller more intimate afternoon tea party was much less involved and, as one author explained, "the preparations involve nothing more than a few extra teacups and a little more bread and butter."[42] Though savory dishes were common, especially at the meal known as high tea, the tea party was always a sugary affair. One society journalist even joked in 1887 that bonbon consumption was so fashionable at these tea parties that "we must be laying up plenty of future work for the dentist!"[43]

At larger teas, the hostess hired professional or amateur musicians and organized dancing, card playing, and other games such as charades.[44] At garden parties, croquet, badminton, lawn tennis, and archery often accompanied the tea drinking.[45] The central entertainment was always good conversation, especially since tea was thought to produce "sociability, cheerfulness, and vivacity."[46] To this end, the hostess had to attend to furniture arrangement. One's rooms should "look full," advised one authority, but furniture should not impede guests' movement, and tables and chairs needed to be arranged so "guests naturally form themselves into little groups, and can with ease pass from one knot to another.

A room stiffly arranged will destroy all the wish for conversation and mirth."[47] A beautiful gown, according to a fashion journalist, also made the tea "taste sweeter, and the cups look prettier."[48]

Whether large or small, the afternoon tea party was imagined as a female event. Men were usually greatly outnumbered and were said to "not care" for these gatherings.[49] The Victorians regarded tea as "essentially the ladies' meal," so when men attended a tea party, they needed to downplay their pleasure in this indulgence, lest they be considered effeminate.[50] Authors admitted, however, that "secretly" gentlemen took great pleasure in these affairs; and, as one authority explained it, "you see them swallowing a cup of tea on these occasions with all the relish of whisky and water, and like little Oliver eagerly asking 'for more.'"[51] A comic song, "Afternoon Tea," joked: "one doesn't care much for the bev'rage we drink, as the people we see . . . love and scandal is in full swing, at afternoon tea."[52] The objective of these parties was to use food, fashion, and flirtation to win male attention. The tea party thus was a visual, sexual, and tasty affair.

They could also be very childish events. Victorian girls delighted in playing hostess to a stuffed animal, family pet, friend, sibling, servant, or parent. At times, indulgent parents even hired "performing dogs or monkeys, or some other special entertainment" for their special child's tea party.[53] Painting, literature, poetry, and music illustrated the child's tea party as an innocent, pastoral experience embedded in the British countryside. In truth, with their toy tea sets, special songs, and games these consumer-oriented teas were not simply child's play.[54] And not all Victorian tea parties were private or innocent.

In the 1880s and 1890s, New Women and New Men held bohemian and artistic teas in museums and picture galleries, which were frequented by luminaries in the art, music, and literary worlds.[55] There were even "Exhibition teas," in which a group of friends had tea at their home before visiting one of London's many temporary exhibitions. Parties of "young men and maidens" enjoyed the air of "bohemianism" about them.[56] Whether bohemian or not, afternoon tea reimagined the once sobering brew as a centerpiece of a new culture of conspicuous consumption. Serving tea stimulated the purchase, display, and use of clothing, furniture, foods, advice literature, and tea things. It required servants, paid performers, and the type of house or public space that could contain these kinds of events. Apprehensive critics proposed that drinking tea had moved from a simple pleasure to a form of excess. Although he later retracted his position on tea, the Dean of Bangor even called tea a revolutionary agent in 1883.[57] In 1893 a Dr. J. Murray-Gibbes also worried about tea's radical nature when he asserted that there was a "distinct connection between the movement to secure women's rights and too great a consumption of congou." By overstimulating women's brains, tea had developed an unnatural desire to "enter the professions, and, in fact to take the place of man as bread-winners."[58] Making light of such accusations, the feminist press presented tea as a source of women's power.[59]

Much like its cousin the temperance tea party, afternoon tea mixed spending and leisure, created and sustained social hierarchies and gender identities, and made a relatively cheap beverage a special commodity. It also embedded foreign foods in local communities, class and gender systems, thus producing new meanings surrounding a global commodity. These meals made tea British, but they also sold the empire's tea and popular forms of imperialism. Before we turn to this history, however, we need to examine why planters enlisted women and other agents to help them sell their produce and their vision of empire.

"INDIAN TEA ALONE TASTES AWFUL QUEER"

Victorian Britons loved tea but until the 1890s they disliked the taste of that grown in their empire. Consumers who sampled pure Indian blends before that period typically complained that they had an awful taste, and thus it should not be surprising that retailers were reluctant to stock this new product. After mid-century a few packet companies began to sneak the new teas into their blends, but British tea planters called this practice and small vendors' disinclination to buy their tea treasonous and fraudulent acts that engendered consumer ignorance and passivity. Tensions mounted as more Indian tea became available after the 1860s, and by the early 1880s planters and grocers disagreed about how or whether to sell the empire's tea. Throughout their battle they blamed each other for being insufficiently imperialistic. Until the 1870s, shopkeepers had the upper hand, compelling planters to establish new distribution chains that bypassed grocers and to engage in a wave of consumer advertising and publicity that advanced a variety of political, economic, and health-based arguments in favor of the empire. The seemingly petty quarrel between tea growers and sellers over the practice of blending and introduction of branded goods cuts to the heart of how long-distance supply chains emerged, changed, and produced friendships, enemies, and transformations in retailing and shopping. In the middle years of the century, it was not clear what role consumers could and should play in shaping markets. It was also uncertain what form of retailing could manufacture imperial tastes and mass markets. Growers, large wholesalers, and smaller vendors did not trust one another and they resented the power that each wielded in the marketplace. Throughout these years, imperial rhetoric and competing visions of the consumer and commodity materialized during this debate about how to buy and sell tea.

Throughout the century experts admitted that Assam's leaf was "faultily plucked, faultily rolled, and faultily dried."[60] In addition, different climactic and soil conditions produced teas that looked, smelled, and tasted foreign and unpleasant.[61] Consumers grumbled that the new teas were too strong and bitter, while experts described India's tea as "acrid," and some worried about the health hazards of the "gummy, gaseous-looking coat of film" that settles on the top of a cup of Indian tea.[62] Others simply described a harsh, unrefined taste.[63] "One of the chief reasons that the China teas continue to keep in favour," wrote one expert in 1880, is that they possess "a roundness and mellowness," while Indian teas "do not assimilate well with milk, becoming herby," and "throw off a foreign weedy flavour."[64] One of the first "gentlemen" who had tried to sell pure Indian tea in London during the early 1880s remembered how radically different this product tasted:

> The consumer had been used to China teas, some of it highly scented and adulterated. I was therefore giving him something foreign to his palate too suddenly. I should have used a little China tea at first. At starting I had all kinds of complaints from my agents. My tea was not tea at all. . . . In vain I tried to persuade all concerned that my tea was the real thing, and that the malty flavour noticeable was one of the virtues of Indian tea. Some complained that it was nasty, others that it was too strong, a few that it was too weak.[65]

Generally speaking, the appellation "Indian" was not a selling point; and, as former planter Lieutenant Colonial Edward Money explained in 1883, until recently "Indian tea" was "not known to the [British] public." There had been, he pointed out, "only one or two shops in London and Glasgow that even sold pure Indian tea," and the fact that "India is even a Tea-producing country is scarcely known in England."[66] Money and his fellow planters set out to educate ignorant consumers and ignite their passion for their empire's produce.

Indian tea's notably strong flavor had some virtues that Money and his ilk were happy to point out. While small firms and shops with very intimate relations to their customers received swift and quite negative reactions to the new teas, large companies found that in blends the new teas strengthened and improved the taste of cheap weak China teas. These firms thus began to hire professional tea tasters to mix many grades and varieties to create what they claimed was a uniform and reliable product that looked and tasted the same wherever and whenever it was purchased.[67] Blending was not new, but individual shopkeepers had built their reputations on their unique and secret shop blends. Thus, when large firms began to blend and brand teas this eliminated a key talent that brought in regular custom and set small shops apart from their rivals. The large firms that sold blends eliminated this skill, and they defended their actions by claiming that little by little they were teaching consumers to appreciate stronger teas and were gradually creating what we could call an imperial palate.[68] Planters did not agree with this logic because they worried that blending and branding made it impossible for consumers to know what they were buying or drinking. Ultimately, this is what happened, but planters put up a major fight to prevent this development.

Tea growers fought the custom of blending by calling it an illegitimate trade practice that erased all "traces of the original importation."[69] When grocers blended China and India (and later Ceylon and other varieties), consumers could not discern differences, nor could they shop for the empire. There was a good deal of trickery going on here. Just to give one example, as early as 1872, William Stewart of Newcastle told consumers how "English Enterprise, Capital, and Industry, had made India the Finest Tea Garden in the world." India tea, this ad continued, was virile and strong and had "lasting power[,] . . . [and] increased satisfaction derived in drinking this life-sustaining Cup of Pleasure."[70] And yet Stewart's shop front included a diorama telling of tea's travels from East to West in a way that blended various Asian teas (fig. 5.2). The façade depicted the overland caravan trade, and both China and India as the source of tea. Much packaging and advertising did as well. This sort of indiscriminate Asian imagery

FIGURE 5.2. Stewart's Tea and Coffee Shop. Tyne and Wear, Newcastle upon Tyne, c. 1902. (By permission of Past Pix/SSPL/Getty Images)

incensed Indian planters who wanted to remove Chinese teas from the market and eradicate tea's association with China.

In a lecture to the Indian Section of the Royal Society of Arts in 1873, Dr. Archibald Campbell, who had been superintendent of tea cultivation in Darjeeling, bemoaned the problems that planters were facing in the "home market." He worried that grocers and the general public barely "knew anything about Indian tea."[71] In 1880 planters still made this point but they also began to complain that tea dealers were only using "Indian to back up and strengthen China tea." One planter insisted that "the interested lover of Indian tea, or the disinterested lover of this country would wish to see . . . the day when the British Empire shall be self-supporting."[72] "The Indian Tea Farce," published in the planters' journal *Home and Colonial Mail* in 1880, satirized this battle between planters and grocers:

DEALER: [after a man has asked for pure Indian tea]
Some planter chap, no doubt, no cause for fear:
Say Indian tea alone tastes "awful queer."
GROCER: I tell folks it's only grown to mix,
And then I palm off China "blend" at three and six.
DEALER: Of course; pure Indian tea is far too strong,
The public taste wants guiding, or it soon goes wrong.
GROCER: Let those who will sell Indian, I prefer to blend;
I don't pretend to be the Indian planters' friend.
Profit's my game.
DEALER: Pray let's go in, I'm grubbish.
GROCER: I want a rasping Indian tea to help that China rubbish.
[They wink and enter warehouse][73]

This satire illuminated planters' fears that they simply could not control distributors.[74] Blending, they repeatedly complained, disguised the product and confused consumers who would be unable to use their buying power to support their countrymen toiling in the British Empire.

Responding to such criticisms, grocers and packers publicly pledged fidelity to the British Empire and asserted they had not "entered into a sort of conspiracy to prevent Indian teas a fair trial."[75] They professed instead, "By the said mixture with China teas the public have, little by little, been educated to appreciate the Indian flavour."[76] Over time, they predicted that the public would acquire a taste for the strong black South Asian teas, even if they were unaware of this change.[77] Planters and dealers thus differed about the value and nature of consumer knowledge. Some vendors imagined that middle- and upper-class consumers would want to show their loyalty by purchasing empire teas, but they were not convinced that working-class consumers cared about such issues. In 1880, a trade expert captured this idea when he warned:

> Those who expect the average consumer to buy tea because it comes from India, irrespective of the value for the money, are imagining a state of things which does not exist at the present. A few people might purchase Indian tea upon the principle that it is useful to encourage trade with India rather than China, but this, we fear, will not be sufficient for our purpose.[78]

While making such assertions about consumers' imperialism, grocers repeatedly defended their own loyalty to the empire.

When *The Grocer* was founded in 1862, its editor called the grocery trade "one of the most indispensable wheels of the great machinery of social life of civilized nations, and most particularly of the British Empire and its vast colonial dependencies."[79] While there is much truth to this assertion, this was also a clever use of contemporary understandings of imperialism to elevate this much-abused trade. The journal frequently and explicitly championed imperialism but never promoted the idea of exclusively buying from and selling to the British Empire. In fact, this and other similar journals provided retailers with the skills and knowledge necessary to trade in a global marketplace.[80] *The Grocer* depicted the expansion of the British Empire as simply a means to increase choices in the global marketplace of goods and it was initially very supportive of the growing Indian tea industry. In the 1860s, for example, the paper recommended that its readers stock Indian teas, invest in plantations, and support military means to protect this new industry.[81] It also justified a "small" war in "Bhootan" because it would protect "the Assam planters" from their "unruly neighbours."[82] Colonialism was hard but gratifying work: "It is very true that in India, North and South, there are evils and difficulties to contend with. There are more tigers than miles of road in India—the coolies are there, but they do not flock readily to the planting districts—and the civilians of India have not in all cases lost the traditional dislike to interlopers," but "ultimately the thousands of miles of forest will be cleared and cultivated with coffee, tea, cinchona, and other useful products."[83] For this journal, empire and mass consumption went hand in hand.[84] However, after the tea crash came in 1866–67, the paper grew cautious and began warning readers against risky and unproven colonial ventures.[85] Echoing abolitionist sentiment as well, one article expressed worry about the conditions of plantation labor and asserted that "the coolie can no longer be housed miserably, fed wretchedly, and flogged unmercifully in India . . . he gets quite enough infamous treatment on board the floating dungeon that takes him from home to something very like slavery."[86]

Planters met such accusations about their industry and their tea head-on. In December 1868, for example, Charles Henry Fielder, who was the secretary to several Assam tea companies, gave a lecture to the Statistical Society in London in which he admitted the industry had an "an imperfect resume," but he also boasted of myriad improvements, including the support of the Government of Bengal, the introduction of machinery, "rigid" economies, and the migration of the right type of British man to manage the plantations.[87] Similar figures recast Ceylon's public image as well. In Ceylon during the late 1860s, the *Hemileia vastatrix* fungus effectively destroyed the coffee crop.[88] Many companies were ruined, but contemporary studies and later histories memorialized tea as the redeemer of this island colony. In truth, the first tea planter, James Taylor, had introduced Assamese tea on his estate in Ceylon in 1867, two years before the blight first appeared, but as tea grew and coffee failed Victorian histories personified the tea plant as the savior that offset the "great disaster that befell the island." The story took hold that "courageous," "wise," and determined British tea planters had saved Ceylon.[89] Statistics seemed to support this story. In 1875, Ceylon exported only 282 pounds of tea to Britain, but in 1885, 4,353,895 pounds arrived in London.[90]

Nowhere was a positive account of India's and Ceylon's tea's history more thoroughly developed than in the *Home and Colonial Mail*. Launched in 1879, this paper declared itself the voice "of the planting industry for readers at home and in India, Ceylon, and the Far East." It purported to offer "merchants, garden agents, shareholders and all interested in tea, news of sales, shares, machinery, and all necessary information."[91] An editor later admitted that the paper had been started as a sales tool to get "Indian tea on the market."[92] Its nod to the Far East illuminates the importance of formal and informal empire, but the paper increasingly promoted colonial produce. Nearly every issue traced the travels of Indian tea from garden to table, using the movement of the commodity to indicate the economic and cultural connections between metropole and colony.[93]

Tea planters also consolidated their power and forged a collective identity by joining trade associations. These bodies helped foster a "professional diaspora," a group of people who worked within and across the English-speaking world.[94] In the second half of the century, such bodies also became the backbone of a new kind of global economy.[95] They wielded a strong hand in politics, were deeply involved in labor questions, funded scientific research and product development, and, most important for this study, organized and supported global advertising campaigns.[96] They also tended to subsidize, as we will see in the next chapter, the growth of large-scale production and retailing.

The Planters' Association of Ceylon, started in 1854, dealt with land, labor, and related issues, and in the 1870s and 1880s it aided the shift from coffee to tea and developed other export-oriented plantation crops such as rubber.[97] A related body, the Ceylon Association in London (known as the CAL), was a lobbying group that, as one supportive writer boasted, served to "weld all the interests of the island together. It fosters enterprise, and imparts knowledge as to the resources of Ceylon, and forms a brilliant centre from which radiate energy, capacity, [and] hospitality."[98] The CAL and the Planters' Association united individual planters, tea companies, journalists, and politicians in the shared mission of advocating for the needs of British Ceylon.

The Indian Tea Association (ITA) was even more powerful.[99] It grew from two separate bodies, one of which was the Indian Tea Districts Association (ITDA). Originating in July 1879 in the Guildhall Tavern, Gresham Street in London, the ITDA saw itself as a "medium of intercommunication" for those interested in the "cultivation of tea in British India." It intended to "watch the course of legislation in India and England in so far as it affects the tea industry" and to "promote a fuller and freer stream of immigration" to help ensure cheap and obedient labor.[100] The ITDA represented about twenty-seven British firms and agency houses, which held about four-fifths of the total north Indian crop.[101] Original members included the directors and managers of virtually all the leading firms, including Samuel Bird, Alex Lawrie, James Warren, Dr. J. Berry White, and nearly two dozen others.

In 1894 the ITDA merged with the Calcutta-based Indian Tea Association, a group conceived at a meeting of tea estate agency houses held at the Bengal Chamber of Commerce in May 1881.[102] The new amalgamated organization became known as the Indian Tea Association, with centers in Calcutta and London. The London branch lobbied the British government and was in charge of creating markets, while Calcutta was especially concerned with production and labor issues. Its early chairmen, secretaries, and members were planters and/or colonial administrators. Directors were often born in England or Scotland and had come to India as employees of the East India Company, private companies, or the military. Sir Thomas Douglas Forsyth, for example, who had also been the ITDA's first chairman, was born in 1827 in Liverpool and served as a writer in the EIC. He then became assistant commissioner in the Punjab in 1849, commissioner in Lahore and then Oudh, member of the Legislative Council, and Order of Knight Commander of the Star of India in 1874. Forsyth was also appointed special envoy to Burma, and after his retirement he directed several Indian railway companies and helped form the Indian Tea Association, for which he served as chairman from 1879 until 1886.[103] Forsyth and so many others had careers spanning from the time of the Company Raj well into the twentieth century, providing continuity over time and space.

The ITA championed planters' racial, gender, and class privileges in a host of different ways.[104] In addition to gaining state support for a cheap and steady flow of workers, this body also defended the notion of white privilege even when this meant going against government policy. The organization took a prominent role, for example, in the fight against the famous Ilbert Bill, a measure proposed in 1883 that would have granted non-European judges in the *mofussil* criminal courts power to rule on cases involving Europeans. The bill received widespread reaction at home, and in India many believed it would "deal a 'death blow' to the tea, coffee and indigo planting industries."[105] This is but one example of many in which this industry used political means to defend their economic and social interests. What we have not acknowledged enough, however, is the degree to which such planters' associations invented and publicized a new idea of the empire as an economically bounded space united by multiple acts of buying and selling. India's and Ceylon's planters constructed this imperial vision when they argued that British buyers should prefer "British-grown" teas.

PLANTERS, PUBLICITY, AND THE CREATION
OF AN IMPERIAL SALES PITCH

The empire's tea planters developed an extraordinary publicity machine during the last third of the nineteenth century. Scholars have spilled much ink on the extent and significance of such imperial propaganda, but few have examined how Victorian business debated the value of imperialism as a sales pitch.[106] As we will see, transformations in the global political economy gave rise to specific forms of imperial propaganda, a development that is particularly clear in the late-Victorian tea trade. While one can find examples of businesses using imperial ideologies and imagery to sell goods long before the late nineteenth century, the conservative nature of consumers' tea tastes, retailer resistance, and the economic recession of this era caused tea growers to think more consciously about how to sell goods. They concluded that the most likely way to defeat the Chinese was to call upon consumers' patriotism. However, patriotism by itself proved a hard sell and planters had to rely on a host of explanations about why British teas were better for British consumers.

The issue of how to sell Indian tea in the home market did not emerge until the 1860s and 1870s. Prior to that time, colonial teas appeared at exhibitions but consumers were more or less ignorant of their existence until new descriptors such as "colonial," "British-grown," "Indian," or "Assam" began to appear in ads and on packages.[107] At the same time, firms with names such as Indian Tea Direct Company and the Pure Indian Tea Supply Agency began to sell unblended Indian teas direct to consumers.[108] These companies professed that all Indian teas were unadulterated, healthy, tasty, economical, and patriotic.[109] A Pure Indian Tea Supply Agency ad from early 1881 is illustrative. In bold capital letters the company proclaimed:

INDIAN TEAS ARE PURER. INDIAN TEAS ARE MORE
AROMATIC. INDIAN TEAS ARE STRONGER. INDIAN
TEAS ARE CHEAPER. INDIAN TEAS ARE MORE
WHOLESOME AND ARE THEREFORE BETTER
IN EVERY RESPECT THAN CHINESE TEAS.

The ad called upon "All Anglo-Saxons, having the prosperity of their own race at heart . . . [to] try Indian tea." The ad defined consumers as influential white men—clergymen, army and naval officers, lawyers, medical men, and teachers— and encouraged them to buy Indian tea and thus "assist in promoting the national welfare!"[110] In addition to encouraging patriotism, the company reiterated how the empire supplied a purer, stronger, more aromatic, wholesome, and cheaper product than that produced in the degenerating Chinese Empire. During an era when free trade dominated political discourse, such ads trod lightly. They were not asking for imperial tariffs or other preferences; rather they urged consumers and retailers to voluntarily use their buying power to shape the fate of the empire. In addition to appealing to influential men, planters often inspired working-class consumers and female shoppers to see the virtues of the imperial choice.

In the late 1870s and 1880s, place-of-origin advertising and imperial appeals became more common and nearly always set Backward China against Modern India.[111] India's planters and their allies stoked anti-Chinese sentiment and kept adulteration fears alive well after the problem had receded. Edward Money's sensational *The Tea Controversy: Indian versus Chinese Teas. Which Are Adulterated? Which Are Better?* (1884), for example, maintained that Indian tea was "grown and manufactured on large estates under the superintendence of educated Englishmen." In China, however, tea was produced near "the cottages of the poorer classes, collected and manufactured in the rudest way, with no skilled supervision." Cultivating racial fears about disease and infection, Money opined, "Indian Tea is a clean article, which Chinese is not." There were many reasons for this but essentially, Money continued, the "Tea of Hindustan is now all manufactured by machinery, but in China it is hand-made. The latter is not a clean process. . . . [It is] *a very dirty process.*" Rolling especially required much pressure and "necessitates hard muscular exertion, [which] is performed by nearly nude men bending over the tables on which the leaf is rolled. They perspire freely: the result need not be minutely described!" The China drink thus nearly always included the sweat of a naked Chinaman, while Indian tea "has

FIGURE 5.3. Sorting tea in Ceylon in the 1880s. C. A. Coy, photographer. (Wikimedia)

not been touched by hand at all." Building on preexisting notions of revulsion and fear about naked and dirty heathens, Money then reminded readers that while China tea is often adulterated, "*no other substances but Tea leaves have ever been found in Indian teas.*"[112] The trope of bare feet appeared again and again in both texts and illustrations. The implication, of course, was that a cup of tea was not so nice when it carried remnants of a laborer's body. In truth, all tea wound up on dirty floors and touched workers' feet. In London and in the colonies workers stood on tea to pack it into boxes, and as late as the 1880s sorting tea simply involved rotating tea in a sieve-like contraption, with smaller leaf falling to the factory floor (fig. 5.3).

Not surprisingly, those who manufactured processing machinery also peddled the benefits of technology. The career of Sir Samuel C. Davidson of Belfast illustrates the multifaceted nature of this history. Like so many young men, Samuel went out to India in 1864 to help his father run his tea estate. He prospered and bought out his father in the 1870s. In 1874 Davidson returned to Belfast where he invented a machine to use hot air to dry tea. His first machine appeared in 1877, followed by the famous Sirocco in 1879. By 1886, the Sirocco cured 50,000,000 of the 70,000,000 pounds of Indian tea imported into the United Kingdom. Davidson manufactured the Sirocco in his Belfast factory, where he also began to sell tea from his Cachar estates. He supplied friends and family and opened depots to sell tea at his factory and in Shaftesbury Square in the center of Belfast.[113] By the late 1880s, Davidson's Sirocco Tea was available through-out the north of Ireland, England, Scotland, the United States, and Europe.[114] Company advertising such as a "prettily illustrated" booklet from 1889 included drawings of the company's tea estate in Cachar and offered direct comparisons between Davidson's modern machine-made tea and that produced by "the feet and hands of dirty [Chinese] coolies."[115] Such methods turned Irish consumers especially into loyal fans of Indian tea; as early as 1881, 75 percent of all teas retailed in Northern Ireland were of Indian origin.

Like Davidson, other planters colonized urban spaces as they opened shops that sold only or primarily pure Indian teas in some of Great Britain's most fashionable shopping streets, particularly in London's West End. In early 1881 an Indian Tea Store, for example, opened in Oxford Street.[116] In March of that year a shop in Jermyn Street offered estate teas from Assam, Cachar, Sylhet, Chittagong, Darjeeling, Kangra, Kumaon, Dehra Dhoon, the Neilgherries, Ceylon, and Singapore.[117] Commenting on such developments, one planter who was visiting England found that it had become "impossible to walk London's streets without being informed of the virtues of tea of Indian growth."[118] By the end of the year, the *Home and Colonial Mail* went so far as to assert: "What a change has come over the situation! Indian tea is in high favor all around. Brokers, dealers, retailers and consumers all agree as to its excellence and value. . . . There is no longer difficulty in procuring it. . . . Not long ago there was but one shop in Oxford Street where Indian tea can be procured. Now it is placarded for sale everywhere."[119] Shops decorated with "artistic sketches of Indian planter life" also appeared in Manchester, Glasgow, and Birmingham.[120] In 1882, the *Home and Colonial Mail* excitedly wrote, "The eyes of the public have been opened to the importance of the Indian tea industry."[121]

Planters also turned to friends and family, particularly female relatives, to spread the taste for their product and increase its social and economic value. For example, the Countess of Cadogan, who presided over the "Indian" tea stall in Chelsea in 1881, came from an elite conservative family, and between 1878 and 1880 her husband had served as undersecretary to the colonies. The countess made India and empire fashionable by serving tea in a stall decorated with illustrations of tea gardens and the process of modern manufacture. Selling tea raised a good deal of money for charity while also, one reporter commented, "spreading the knowledge of, and stimulating inquiry for, the teas of our Indian Empire."[122] The Pure Indian Tea Supply Agency catered this and many similar events, supplying the tea and decorations.[123] At an exhibition in support of the National Eye and Ear Infirmary in Ireland, for example, the company hired two "doctors" and a "Parsee in his national costume" to serve hot cups of Indian tea. Another firm from Assam, the Hattibarree Tea Company, also sold the "pure unadulterated beverage" at this Irish fundraiser.[124] These events were marketing opportunities in which planters and wealthy women incorporated a heretofore much-disparaged imperial product into their world of fashion, luxury, and philanthropy.

So taken with the power of female influence, one firm even decided to pay a commission to ladies who would introduce Indian teas to their friends. The *Home and Colonial Mail* loved the idea because, of course, "in the tea trade the weaker sex are deemed useful allies."[125] Another planter made the same point when he wrote excitedly about the Colonial and Indian Exhibition to be held in London in 1886 because he assumed that "ladies will be there in numbers."[126] Some firms even began to hire female tea experts. For example, a Mrs. Innes, the daughter of Canon James Craigie Robertson, became a professional tea taster at this time.[127] Planters also supported women who began to open or manage tea shops. Not all such venues began with the stated idea of selling imperialism, but planters appreciated the marketing opportunities that such institutions provided and they recognized the advertising potential of women's taste.

Glasgow, the first place in Britain to form a temperance society, was closely linked to the planting and shipping communities and was also famous for its tea shops. The Cranstons, a family of temperance caterers and hoteliers, established Glasgow's most famous tea rooms. Stuart Cranston had worked in the wholesale tea business in the early 1860s as a subagent for Joseph Tetley before becoming a tea and coffee taster. In the 1870s he set up his own business and opened a chain of tea rooms. In 1878, Stuart's father, who was an early supporter of women's rights, helped his daughter Kate open the Crown Tea Rooms, while he also gave Kate's sister Mary and her husband a temperance hotel as a wedding present.[128] Kate was the most adventurous of all the siblings, and in the 1890s she famously patronized the Arts and Crafts Movement when she commissioned Charles Rennie Mackintosh to design the exquisite interior for the Willow Tea Rooms (fig. 5.4). "Those Glasgow tea-rooms were things of extraordinary beauty and originality, and one cannot find any restaurants in London to-day comparable with them," remembered American expatriate artist Muirhead Bone.[129] Temperance, women's rights, and modern art thus created an exciting tea culture in the heart of Glasgow.

Some tea shops, such as Hand's Afternoon Tea Company, specifically sought to popularize the empire's new teas.[130] In 1886, the Indian and Ceylon Tea Room and Art Exhibition opened at 18 Berners Street in the very center of female clubland in London's West End with this aim in mind. At this "elegantly furnished" shop "ladies" had the opportunity "to taste and try teas from India and Ceylon" while listening to musical recitals.[131] In late Victorian London, two single women, Misses Lambert and Bartlett, even decided they could act as

FIGURE 5.4. Charles Rennie Mackintosh's "Room de Luxe,"
Willow Tea Rooms, Glasgow, 1903. (Wikimedia)

"London agents for a friend of theirs who owned a tea estate in Ceylon." They rented a small room over a glove shop in Bond Street and began selling tea in "attractive packets."[132] But they soon realized that people liked to taste their tea before buying it, so they opened a tea room, and within a short time they purchased chairs and tables and found themselves serving up to two hundred customers a day. They named themselves the Ladies' Own Tea Association and were so successful that in 1892 the ladies went public with a nominal capital of £2,000 divided into 2,000 shares of one pound each.[133] In their "handsome establishment" at 90 New Bond Street the female owners purchased, blended, and served imperial teas. Even more remarkable, the ladies purchased a "large tea plantation in Ceylon."[134] The Ladies' Own Tea Association began training women in management, bookkeeping, buying, and other facets of the tea trade. These women thus had enough capital to pioneer vertical integration. Not all female businesses supported the British Empire, but most imperial growers buoyed female businesses and the social ritual of afternoon tea.[135]

A similar tea culture developed in continental Europe. The department store Messrs. Whiteaway and Laidlaw, for example, opened twenty "good class depots" in major European cities to sell brewed, packet, and bulk Indian tea.[136] In Paris, the British Dairy Company had three tea rooms in 1900.[137] As in England, planters believed tea shops allowed them to find individuals "of the right class, outside of the grocer clique," to act as their agents.[138] The right sort often meant wealthy women, such as two Roman "ladies" who turned their small shop into a major venture vending 2,000 pounds of tea in its first year alone. India's planters also helped a German woman open a luxurious tea shop in Leipzigerstrasse in Berlin, in which Indian waiters quietly served "good quality Indian tea."[139] Other branches soon opened in Berlin, Hamburg, and Brussels.[140] Empire, fashionable feminine consumerism, and profits went hand in hand in Germany, Italy, France, and, as we will see in the next chapter, the United States and colonial settings as well.

Afternoon tea became big business, and, by end of the century, there were approximately seven thousand tea shops in London alone.[141] Men patronized these eateries, but "dainty" foods and decor, their physical locale within shopping districts, and the fact that they served tea marked them as a feminine public space. These were also imperial institutions that show us how businesswomen exploited the imperial project and changes in gender and urban space that were already underway. At the same time, tea planters liked tea shops because they allowed them to sell directly to wealthy female consumers, bypassing unenthusiastic buyers, deceptive blenders, and domestic servants. Tea shops also made the empire's tea fashionable. In 1891, a female journalist asked the readers of a woman's paper, "How many of you, I wonder, really like Indian tea, and how many drink it because it is the fashion?"[142] By the 1890s, tea drinkers still may have preferred the taste of Chinese tea, but advertising and dainty tea rooms had improved the reputation of the empire's tea. Planters favored female entrepreneurship because they knew that wealthy women elevated the image of their product and thus produced new markets. Female-owned and managed tea shops succeeded for a variety of reasons but especially because these institutions were part of familial, religious, political, philanthropic, and business communities that provided capital, customers, and stock.

EXHIBITING MODERN TASTES

Like so many other new products and ideas, the backers of the new empire-grown teas also made great use of international and local exhibitions to find buyers and change tastes. The new teas generated much excitement at the International Health Exhibition held in London in 1884 and at the Colonial and Indian Exhibition two years later. At both exhibitions tea growers staged the story of industry and empire for millions of visitors. These two exhibitions helped India and Ceylon teas establish markets, but they also became a source of tension as colonial producers began to compete for buyers at these shows.

An updated version of the early modern fair, late nineteenth- and early twentieth-century exhibitions served many purposes and conveyed multiple meanings about race and nation, economy and modernity.[143] As Walter Benjamin conceived in the 1930s, nineteenth-century exhibitions became "places of pilgrimage to the commodity fetish."[144] Exhibitions emphasized the material promises of colonial possessions and displayed racial hierarchies as a form of entertainment. They turned the world into an emporium.[145] Eating and drinking added to the fantastic exhibition experience, creating what some scholars have described as food nations or national cuisines.[146] But these fantasy worlds were not just for consumers. Business and officialdom also fantasized about new products and markets at these shows. Exhibitions invited buyers and sellers to form relationships around particular goods. They were mass gatherings in which people congregated to think about the nature, appeal, and problems of global capitalism.

Four million attended the Health Exhibition in London in 1884, a strange show that was half fair and half public health conference. Lectures, displays, and refreshments demonstrated improvements in housing, water, dress, temperance, and diet, as well as new "scientific" forms of food production.[147] India's growers were especially excited about this event because they had already been selling their industry as an example of this new hygienic world.[148] There was so much Indian tea at this show that a reporter for the *Home and Colonial Mail* joked, "From the time the visitor goes into the building . . . until he leaves . . . it is his own fault if he fails to be refreshed with occasional cups of the fragrant beverage." Indian tea could be purchased at the ITA's display and tea rooms, the National Training School of Cookery's refreshment rooms, Lockhart's refreshment rooms, Etzenberger's tea and coffee stall, and the Hand's Afternoon tea stall. The Science and Art Department's "very neatly arranged pavilion" served Ceylon's tea and coffee as well. Moreover, "Indian tea in its dry state" was "seen everywhere," in glass receptacles at Carter's seed stall and at "Phillips's, Sabine's, Hand's, Bowden's, Barry's, and the Ceylon Tea Company's stalls." The ITA, however, mounted the most impressive exhibit, which included photographs of the "various processes of manufacture, tea gardens and machinery." The Indian court included a "full-sized Sirocco drying machine" and working models of numerous other tea machines, as well as a large map of India on which tea districts were colored green and tables of statistics of the relative output of each region were prominently featured. Pamphlets taught consumers that India was the true home of the tea plant and exhorted consumers to "ask your tea dealer for pure, *i.e.* unmixed Indian tea." All of these efforts were intended to "popularize Indian tea."[149] Here, Ceylon was simply part of India.[150] Exhibition officials had literally blended the empire's teas.

In a magnificent display directly opposite India's building, the Chinese court countered images of its nation's backwardness by presenting China as a place of refined consumerism. Visitors strolled down a replica of a Chinese shopping street, sampled "Chinese" food in the first Chinese restaurants in Britain, and drank an excellent "Imperial," Chinese tea.[151] One prominent Australian visitor remembered the exhibit's "excellent tea," despite its being served with odd and "uncouth" music.[152] Like so many exhibits, however, the Chinese court was a multinational effort. The British firm Messrs. Holland and Sons built the restaurant using plans prepared by Mr. Purdon Clarke of the Indian Museum in South Kensington. The Chinese chefs worked under the "experienced manager of one of the West End Clubs," English girls served at the tea house, and the proceeds from these endeavors went to the exhibition's general funds.[153] Visitors would not have cared about authenticity, however, and no doubt enjoyed drinking "real" China tea in posh Oriental surroundings.[154] At the Health Exhibition Indian and Chinese teas appeared to be from wholly different nations, but exhibition displays were always multinational efforts and British experts helped mount both displays.

As planning began for the Colonial and Indian Exhibition, however, imperial unity unraveled when Ceylon adamantly refused to have its teas "classed" with those from any other colony or country, especially "its great rival India."[155] Ceylon was a distinct colony, but exhibition displays, advertising, retailing, and linguistic practices often made the island seem to be an extension of the Subcontinent. For example, labels such as "British-grown," "Empire-grown," "imperial," or "colonial," and sometimes just "Indian" were used to connote all teas grown within the formal boundaries of the British Empire. In 1886, however, Ceylon's officials wanted to create a separate brand identity, and this required a tea house "quite distinct and separate from the Indian tea house—or that of any other Colony."[156] The building's architecture and displays tried to identify distinctive elements in Sinhalese culture and promoted the natural beauty of the island colony. From "whatever direction it is approached," the official guidebook explained, Ceylon "unfolds a scene of loveliness and grandeur unsurpassed."[157] At this exhibition, Ceylon became a land of beautiful beaches, fragrant, spicy breezes, and delicious tea.

John Loudan-Shand was a leading author of this vision of Ceylon. Born in Scotland in 1845, J. L. Shand, as he was usually known, ventured to Ceylon to become a coffee planter.[158] After coffee failed, he turned to tea and politics. He chaired the Planters' Association, served as the planters' representative on the Legislative Council, and in 1886 returned to London and with another tea planter, R. C. Haldane, formed Shand, Haldane and Co., tea and rubber estate agents and importers. One of his ten sons, W. E. Loudan-Shand, followed in his father's footsteps and became a planter before returning to London to join the sales side of the business in 1916.[159] J. L. Shand had a gift for publicity and put together a talented team to sell Ceylon in London in 1886. J. G. Smither, former architect to the Government of Ceylon, designed the exhibition buildings, which were erected by Messrs.

Maple and Company, one of the most fashionable and successful West End furnishers. Shand also became a theorist of empire who argued that "the power of producing and consuming is our strongest Imperial bond," but for this show he had been hired to sell Ceylon, not the empire as a whole.[160]

In addition to selling the island as a beautiful destination, Shand emphasized its Buddhist heritage. For example, the Ceylon court had yellow walls and roof to signify the sacred color of Buddhism. The nine-foot-high dado was ornamented with representations of the elephant, lion, bull, horse, and goose, "as they appear sculptured on ruined monuments in the ancient cities" of the island. Above these, a frieze was covered with paintings "depicting some of the more popular birth stories of Buddha." The Ceylon Tea House, a separate building situated between the Ceylon Court and the Old London exhibit and facing the Indian Palace, was built with Sinhalese timber architecture. Its interior included a frieze composed of the leaves and blossoms of the tea plant and lotus flowers. Seven Sinhalese men were "imported" to England to serve tea, and their appearance in their "national dress" and with "combs in their hair" was reported to be a "very striking characteristic of the country."[161] While this ornamentation conveyed Ceylon's ancient Buddhist heritage, viewers were to understand that British technology had harnessed the fruits of paradise. Paintings hung in the court's four interior bays depicted a view of Colombo from its harbor, a tea estate, a factory and bungalow, the weighing of the leaf, and a view of Devon Estate at Dimbula, with its bungalow and picturesque waterfall. At the end of a hall, organizers hung a painting of what became the classic image of the Tamil girl picking leaves. Photographs and pamphlets also emphasized that a modern colonial industry had manufactured Ceylon's tea.[162] The exhibition catalogue also described how British consumers should buy empire products, claiming "the national feeling is daily becoming stronger to consume articles grown in our empire over those of foreign countries."[163] Such statements taught British consumers that this strange and temperate island of magnificent natural vistas belonged to them and was in a sense designed for their pleasure.[164] Yet by labeling all teas from the empire as British or empire-grown official publications undercut such branding.[165] The report of the Colonial and Indian Exhibition, for example, boasted that the British Empire served 47,239 pounds of dry tea and 730,980 cups of brewed colonial teas.[166] As diverse growing regions developed in the empire in the 1880s, imperial unity began to unravel as growers in places such as Ceylon wanted consumers to understand the distinct nature of their product, and they especially didn't want to buyers to think of Ceylon as a region of India.[167] Such tensions were not present in 1884, but by 1886 Ceylon displayed its island and its tea as unique, whether or not visitors recognized the differences between tea-growing colonies.

As popular as they were, not everyone even liked exhibitions. One planter complained that he had given tea away for a week at "an exhibition at the Agricultural Hall, and "every 'dead beat' in the place drank the tea and expressed himself delighted with it, but bought none."[168] The free sample thus did not always result in a sale, especially if the tea did not taste good.[169] Nevertheless, these exhibitions, along with advertising and other publicity, steadily increased the volume and proportion of empire teas in the British market. By 1887 British planters announced that they had finally vanquished the Celestial Empire.

THE JUBILEE OF INDIAN TEA

In 1887 Queen Victoria had reigned for fifty years and the nation celebrated with countless official and commercial publications, displays, and events marking her Diamond Jubilee. Observers naturally reflected upon the changes the country had witnessed in the half century since Victoria ascended to the throne.[170] Many entities also "discovered" that their history coincided with or was in some way connected to the reign of the sovereign. Birthdays were remembered and stories of material progress and success were written. Like so many others, the Indian tea industry caught jubilee fever and announced 1887 as its fiftieth anniversary. "The jubilee of the tea industry in Assam," E. M. Clerke declared in the *Asiatic Quarterly Review*, commemorated 1837 as the year that the first Indian tea reached England and April 1887 as the first moment that imports from India and Ceylon exceeded those from China.[171] These two stories were only partially true. Indian tea was first sold in Britain in 1839, and one needed to measure Indian and Ceylon imports together to declare victory over the Celestial Empire. The tea jubilee also ignored the fact that Irish consumers had switched to Indian varieties some years earlier. Tea's jubilee thus celebrated a Whiggish history that wove together several global tales about people, places, and power but also ignored and obscured others. The jubilee celebration overlooked tensions between buyers and sellers, managers and workers, and different colonies, and presented the nation/empire/colony as a bounded, cohesive territory.[172]

Of course, the Indian tea industry was not born in a single year. The plantation economy was never purely "British," and for most of the nineteenth century it was a risky business. In truth even its much-lauded machinery, which supposedly made better tea than hand methods was rarely used until the end of the century.[173] But in 1887, a seemingly unified imperial tea business celebrated the triumph of British industry, colonialism, and masculinity over Chinese inertia, weakness, and femininity. Many industries also used verbose advertising during the jubilee to espouse material progress as an ideal and an achievement.[174] In an imperial context, however, such language often celebrated white imperial masculinity.

Invariably, the British planter "redeemed" the jungle by transforming it into a useful and profitable Garden of Eden.[175] This history magnified the differences between hand and industrial production, China and India, Asians and Europeans, strong and weak, and past and present.

In May 1887, the Royal Society of Arts formally celebrated tea's jubilee by inviting industry founder J. Berry White to give a lecture on the commodity's past and future. When Sir Roper Lethbridge introduced White he used Indian tea to describe the British as an industrious race. "The tea industry," Lethbridge proposed, "was one of which the British race might be proud. Its history in the past, especially the immediate past, illustrated in a remarkable degree the pluck and industry of the British race, and its prospects for the future."[176] Lethbridge had recently been elected a Tory MP, but he had previously been a professor in the Bengal Education Department, a fellow of Calcutta University, an agent in the Indian Political Department, press commissioner, and editor of the *Calcutta Quarterly Review*.[177] Lethbridge's introduction cultivated economic nationalism and yet also managed to describe Indian tea as a product of free trade and Britain's racial and industrial preeminence.

When White mounted the podium he provided ample historical, commercial, and statistical evidence to back up Lethbridge's propositions. A planter, the medical officer in Assam, and longtime promoter of Indian tea, White developed a clear account of an industrial revolution in the empire and consumer revolution in Britain. Downplaying indigenous ownership, investment, and consumption, White emphasized a British imperial story. He began with Britons discovering indigenous tea in Assam, spreading the plant to other regions, and recovering from the speculation and crash of the 1860s. He documented empire in terms of acreage tilled, capital invested, and pounds produced, exported, and consumed. White then explained how Indian production costs had been reduced via more efficient growing, manufacturing, transport, and storage and other modern innovations. He acknowledged labor abuses and particularly condemned the "vicious system" of labor recruitment that had existed, but he argued that reforms had now created a "happier and more contented" and efficient labor force.[178] Modern business methods, economies of scale, labor reforms, and improved transportation had lowered costs and won over British tastes. While some in the audience questioned White's conclusions, others applauded his mastery of statistics and difficult issues.

In the published version of his lecture, White included a table in which he added together India's and Ceylon's output to compare the consumption of British and Chinese tea and illustrate the connections between Britain's growth and China's decline (see table 5.2). To make the British Empire appear the victor in this battle, White had to combine India's and Ceylon's

TABLE 5.2. PERCENTAGE OF INDIAN AND CHINA
TEA CONSUMED IN THE UK, 1865–86

YEAR	PERCENTAGE OF INDIAN (INCLUDING CEYLON)	PERCENTAGE OF CHINA	TOTAL
1865	3	97	100
1866	4	96	100
1867	6	94	100
1868	7	93	100
1869	10	90	100
1870	11	89	100
1871	13	87	100
1872	15	85	100
1873	16	84	100
1874	17	83	100
1875	19	81	100
1876	23	77	100
1877	22	78	100
1878	28	72	100
1879	22	78	100
1880	28	72	100
1881	30	70	100
1882	31	69	100
1883	34	66	100
1884	37	73	100
1885	39	61	100
1886	41	59	100

Source: J. Berry White, "The Indian Tea Industry: Its Rise,
Progress during Fifty Years, and Prospects Considered from
a Commercial Point of View," *Journal of the Royal Society of
Arts* (10 June 1887): 740.

imports.[179] While the table did not include 1887, the text informed readers that April 1887 was "a truly memorable month in the history of the enterprise" because together India and Ceylon accounted "for 51 per cent of the whole."[180] The Jubilee of Indian tea had thus conveniently marked Britain's triumph over the Celestial Empire.

Official sources gave slightly different numbers, but they told the same story. The Board of Customs and Excise published yearly per capita consumption rates derived from comparing import records with population growth and re-exports, and in 1873 the Board began to distinguish among imports' country of origin.[181] According to these reports, Indian tea accounted for only 2.84 percent of the market in 1864. In 1870 it had reached 9.17 percent and by 1880 it accounted for nearly 22 percent, while Ceylon exported a mere .30 percent. By 1885 India stood at 30.35 percent and Ceylon 2 percent, but by 1888 together India and Ceylon had climbed to over 50 percent of the market.[182] In the 1890s, Ceylon began to make remarkable strides, surpassing Chinese imports and climbing to over 36 percent of the market in the late 1890s. Since one pound of dry leaf converted to about 7 gallons of brewed tea, by 1891 the English populace drank approximately 37 gallons a year, four times as much as in 1821.[183] In their much-cited report of 1889, the commissioners perceptively theorized that "the strong ties of relationship everywhere connecting the planters to the mother country" had changed the British tastes.[184] They also acknowledged the growing role of nationalism in buying decisions and proposed that advertising too had convinced buyers that the empire offered good value for money.[185] These officials assumed that personal connections, nationalism, advertising, and economics had manufactured imperial tastes in all of Great Britain and Ireland.

Most accounts were far more simplistic. As writer Arthur Montefiore enthused in 1888: "China has been forced to yield its monopoly and take a second place, while British pertinacity and vigour have once more asserted their supremacy. In fact, the Caucasian has met the Celestial, and by sheer superiority, driven him step by step from his vantage ground."[186] In the aptly titled "The Revolution in Tea," which appeared in *Chambers's Journal* in 1889, the author argued that machinery and European supervision had produced a better, more modern tea that was wholly different from the old-fashioned filth that China produced. "It is natural and proper," then, the author concluded, "that our sympathies should be with the triumph of our Indian industry."[187] Social analyst C. H. Denyer reported in 1893 that "in Whitechapel and similar districts the demand for a penn'orth of tea and sugar is enormous. The factory girls have the teapot by the fire all day . . . [and] they insist on having the strongest Indian tea."[188] In 1897 retired planter and seller of tea machinery David Crole wrote in his textbook on the industry that it was the "obstinate barbarism" of the Chinese as much

FIGURE 5.5. "Comparative Consumption." Sir James Buckingham, *A Few Facts about Indian Tea and How to Brew It* (London: Indian Tea Association, 1910), 4. (By permission of British Library, shelfmark 07076.f.48.(4.))

as "our [British] civilization and energy" that had produced the "triumph of the West over the Flowery Land."[189] Crole understood market competition in militaristic, nationalistic, historical, and racial terms. This story was represented graphically as well. In the promotional booklet *A Few Facts about Indian Tea and How to Brew It*, the ITA included a striking representation of the battle of the teas. In a cartoon titled "Comparative Consumption," India grows from a tiny to a towering presence over a shrinking China (fig. 5.5).[190]

The Jubilee of Indian tea celebrated in lecture halls, trade journals, and periodicals proclaimed the empire and metropole as a single marketplace in which buyers and sellers could and should help one another. This notion made sense as long as China was India's main rival, and if one were willing to ignore the fact that diverse nationalities were involved in the China, India, and Ceylon tea industries. Coming to terribly simple conclusions, celebrants argued that racial difference explained market shifts. Chinese racial characteristics, for example, had led to their desire to adulterate tea and to their so-called refusal to modernize production, while the British were driven by their "race" to innovate. These explanations, of course, ignored the fact that the Chinese had created the mass market, that the British often adulterated tea, and that many British growers did not use machinery until late in the century. The story nevertheless nationalized consumer culture by teaching consumers to prefer colonial goods.

MAZAWATTEE'S GRANNY AND LIPTON'S BLACK ARMY

Yet the history of industry and empire that planters invented could never entirely dominate public debate. At the end of the century, a few retailers and importers grew into major brands, and in a contradictory fashion they both aided and undermined the planters' story. Lipton, Twinings, Brooke Bond, Mazawattee, the United Kingdom Tea Company, Ridgways, Horniman's, and a few others invested huge sums in press advertising to sell their brands in the 1890s. At times, the new brands seemed to sell the same idea of industry and empire that the planters had promoted, but the concept of the brand inherently suggested that not all teas were the same.

In the early 1890s, the importers Densham and Sons registered Mazawattee brand tea, and its advertising announced it imported direct from the "sweet-scented island of Ceylon."[191] The name "Mazawattee," a mixture of the Hindu word for luscious and Sinhalese word meaning garden or growth, implied little distance from the garden to the pot.[192] Mazawattee advertising asserted that Ceylon and their firm were the sources of healthy tea.[193] Its ads often featured the firm's "scientific" tasting and blending rooms at its headquarters in Tower Hill, for example.[194] Other advertisements were nationalistic in tone, with many referencing current international issues, such as the Venezuela boundary question, the exploration of the North Pole, and the South African crisis. At times, Mazawattee ads read like a commentary on colonial news. One advertisement from 1896, for example, placed Chamberlain in the Transvaal telling Kruger, "You will at least agree with me that affairs can best be discussed over a cup of delicious Mazawattee." In another similar ad John Bull comforts Jameson with this advice: "You've a pretty stiff ordeal to go through Dr. Jim, so take this Cup of Mazawattee to steady your nerves."[195] Another showed black South Africans hauling Mazawattee from the Cape Colony to "the troops engaged in the Matabele War."[196] All of these ads proposed that Ceylon's modern tea both calmed and energized empire builders who were expanding their influence in Southern Africa at the end of the century.

The most famous icon associated with Mazawattee, however, was the bonneted smiling Victorian granny who with her granddaughter sipped a brew that "recalls the Delicious Teas of Thirty Years Ago."[197] Mazawattee's granny evoked a nostalgic, comforting, domestic, rural, and feminine celebration of Britishness (fig. 5.6). By this time, the old lady tea drinker had become something of a stock

FIGURE 5.6. Mazawattee tea advertisement, c. 1892. (Wikimedia)

character in popular culture, advertising, literature, and art.[198] Sitting by a hearth in a timeless cottage, the old lady with her cup of tea removed the commodity from politics, the market, and other modern troubles. The childish tea drinker functioned the same way. Both high art and popular culture began to reproduce sentimental scenes of tea in the nursery, the garden, the parlor, the conservatory, and at the breakfast table.[199] Such images transformed tea drinking into a feminine pastime rooted in a premodern past.[200] If we read these ads together, Mazawattee advertisements from this era suggest that tea was a modern imperial product that sustained British domesticity. The Mazawattee granny may have appealed to consumers who did not want to think about change, but this new brand was also dedicated to selling popular imperialism.

The United Kingdom Tea Company was one of Mazawattee's major competitors. This company's advertising typically featured mandarins and other images of China, but one much-used advertisement from the early 1890s captures the global rather than imperial nature of the late-Victorian tea trade. At the center of the ad the British market is represented as a gigantic, sleeping bourgeois woman who is unaware of the global nature of the contents of her teapot (fig. 5.7). Chinese, Irish, Scottish, and English fairies haul a packet of tea onto the tea table and into the sleeping giantess's teapot, while they mock and play tricks on this unconscious consumer. Referencing the genre of Victorian fairy paintings, Swift's *Gulliver's Travels*, and the popular subject of the sleeping woman, this advertisement inadvertently elicited the fears and fantasies about the foreign

"UNITED KINGDOM TEA COMPANY'S TEAS ARE USED ALL OVER THE WORLD."

FIGURE 5.7. United Kingdom Tea Company advertisement, c. 1892–93.
(From author's collection)

things that fed the British nation. Like so many other images of the tea drinker in this era, however, it figured the middle-class female consumer at the center of global trade, but she is asleep and unaware of the world around her. This, as I have shown, was not an accurate representation of women's relationship to their tea or global capitalism. Nor were bourgeois women tea's most important market; this was something that Thomas Lipton well recognized when he entered the tea business in 1889.

In 1890 Thomas Lipton paraded what he called "a black army" through Glasgow's streets. In a publicity stunt aimed at announcing his entrance into the tea trade, he transformed his large warehouse into a theatrical dressing room, laid out with "a couple hundred Cingalese costumes." He hired dressers to affect what he called a miraculous disguise and turned several hundred working-class Glaswegians into Sinhalese "natives." After donning makeup and costumes, each man was given a sandwich board announcing that "Lipton's Tea is the Finest in the World" and that it was "Direct from the Tea Gardens to the Tea Pot." In an apocryphal tale about the effectiveness of theatrical blackface, Lipton recalled how the incensed wife of a man who worked as a sandwich man shouted: "Ye should be ashamed o'yersels, ye black devels, comin' to Glesca an' daien' honest Scotsmen oot o' their jobs!" Whereupon a nearby policeman reminded her, "These chaps only arrived frae the Indies this mornin' an' canna understaun' a word ye're sayin."[201] That evening, however, the woman learned that she and the policeman had been fooled and that she had in fact berated her own husband. Lipton ensured that this story made its way into the press since he felt it enhanced his reputation as a master of publicity and the carnivalesque. Lipton and other advertisers had already paraded giant hams, cheeses, and other commodities through city streets, but this spectacle and the story of a housewife's racism and the policeman's foolishness emphasize the racial, class, and gender dynamics at the heart of late-Victorian commodity culture. Lipton's black army brought the empire home and positioned the Scottish working classes as white, imperial consumers.

Planters and retailers, like Thomas Lipton, used spectacles and parades, exhibitions and print advertising, tea shops and commodity histories to write an imperial chapter of the British Industrial Revolution. This account of tea's past was intended to denigrate China and thereby to teach the British to prefer the taste of their empire. By the 1890s and especially after the turn of the century, planters should have been satisfied since China had been ousted from the British market. However, as the big brands grew in power, surpluses mounted, prices fell, and the metropolitan government seemed singularly uninterested in supporting tea planters. As we explore in the following chapters, this situation drove planters to explore and conquer colonial and foreign markets and it encouraged them to form political organizations to protect their hard-won markets.

———

Many years ago, Joseph Schumpeter pinpointed Benjamin Disraeli's 1872 Crystal Palace speech and the 1874 general election as the moments when "imperialism became a catch phrase in domestic policy" and began to appear in commercial advertising.[202] Yet as we have seen here, this was not an easy or straightforward development. If we look closely at specific examples of imperialism in consumer and trade advertising, we can see fractures appearing in the foundations of the British Empire. In the 1870s and 1880s, merchants, planters, and advertising professionals argued about whether and how to teach consumers to prefer the British Empire. But by the late 1880s, popular imperialism had won the day; most Britons agreed that colonialism, plantation agriculture, and industrial forms of production guaranteed product safety in a globalizing world. Purity had thus become an industrial and imperial concept. The empire's new tea now had racial, national, moral, and gendered characteristics, and buying and drinking tea became imperial and political gestures.

Edwardian Britons drank almost entirely Indian tea, but they too felt compelled to explain and celebrate this development in terms of race and modernity. In 1912 Edith Browne, author of a series of popular business histories, described a Ceylon tea factory as "One of the Prettiest Sights in the Industrial World," which was nothing like the "old-fashioned" methods used by Chinese "peasant farmers" who made tea in barns, sheds, and outhouses, wearing "very little clothing, and perspir[ing] as freely as though they were taking a Turkish bath."[203] Thus, in the early twentieth century, popular histories still reinforced Britain's modernity and China's reputation as a nation peopled by naked, dirty, sweaty laborers who contaminated Western bodies. The Chinese were well aware of such criticisms. A member of Fujian's provincial assembly complained, for example, how "Westerners apply the principles of nationalism. . . . They employ mechanization to dazzle the eyes and ears. . . . their newspapers slander Chinese tea as unsanitary, and this arouses distaste for it in foreign markets. If they can use nationalism to repress our markets, how is it that we cannot use nationalism to restore our reputation?"[204] A good question and one that would not go away.

Between the 1870s and World War I, the British market was influenced by nationalism, imperialism, and powerful notions of gender, class, and racial difference. While selling their teas, British planters argued that imperialism made global foods acceptable, knowable, safe, and cheap. They also taught buyers, consumers, and governments to prefer technology and uniformity to handmade diversity. This story publicized an *imperial and industrial* vision of tea, Great Britain, and consumer society. And, by the end of the century, a combination of advertising, politics, and personal connections had transformed British tea tastes and London had become the global center of the tea trade. In terms of production, trade, capital investment, and taste, tea thereby wove together the economy and culture of empire.[205] Yet neither growers nor distributors rested upon their laurels, for in truth this concentration of power and money enabled tea to embark on a new kind of expansion that reinforced the British Empire's place in a larger global world.

6

THE PLANTER ABROAD

Building Foreign Markets in the Fin de Siècle

In 1882 the directors of the Assam Company revealed to their shareholders that during the previous year they had joined with other Indian tea growers to form a syndicate "to open direct markets other than in England," notably in the colonies and North America.[1] Not satisfied with peddling their wares only in the British Isles, planters embarked on a global marketing campaign that had few parallels.[2] Such a move was typical for industries facing growing surpluses and falling prices during the economic downturn between the mid-1870s and 1890s. However, just as racial and imperial ideologies shaped business practices, consumer tastes, and public policy in Great Britain, similar factors influenced the geography of market expansion. The key question in these years was where would it be easiest to make or grow markets: the white settler colonies that had small but very eager populations, the United States with its wealthy consumers that seemed "British," or the vast, yet extremely poor Indian populace that would benefit from tea's health-giving and "civilizing" properties. All the while, planters did not want to neglect the working- and middle-class markets within Britain. As we will see, intracolonial competition and transnational relationships, migrations, and misconceptions influenced many decisions and erected the boundaries of a global empire of tea that took shape at the end of the nineteenth century.

As I began to indicate in the previous chapter, by the late 1870s there was a great deal of overlap within the fields of planting and metropolitan, colonial, and foreign sales. Planters designed and paid for consumer and commercial advertising and they engaged in countless face-to-face encounters with distributors and shoppers. Commercial advertising and promotion were especially important when opening new markets and changing tastes since producers had to encourage distributors to source their product rather than other commodities or varieties of tea; basically, they had to demonstrate that their product would sell. Whether dealing with shoppers, small vendors, or big buyers, however, the empire's tea growers believed that people needed to see, taste, and smell products to acquire a taste for goods. This encouraged the development of new institutions such as tea shops, the constant travel to exhibitions, and the growth of a veritable army of paid and unpaid tea experts who lectured audiences, displayed how to brew and drink tea, and offered a great many free samples. Several new and quite powerful planters associations spearheaded such efforts, giving individual growers a great deal of clout when they encountered laborers, buyers, shoppers, publicists, and politicians. These industry-wide bodies became the public and global voice of the planter as they sought to demarcate the contours and characteristics of the empire of tea.

Nearly all tea planters were of Scottish heritage and part of what historians have described as the British World. In general, all Britons were a very mobile community in the nineteenth century, and in this chapter we see how men who often began their careers in planting moved from colony to colony, to the metropole, and to the United States. In consumer markets these figures played up their transnational knowledge and connections as they transformed themselves into distributors and experts on tropical produce and economies.[3] We find them growing and selling tea in Colombo, Calcutta, London, Glasgow, Philadelphia, Charleston, Montreal, Sydney, and Chicago. British India and other parts of the Asian and African empire were also part of this world, and we find members of the transnational Planter Raj shaping commercial and consumer cultures within the Indian, Atlantic, and Pacific Ocean arenas.[4] By listening in on planters' conversations and following them to all these places, we have the unique opportunity to see how the racial, class, and gender attitudes of these peripatetic individuals informed how they understood consumers and markets during the fin de siècle. This mobile Planter Raj attempted to build a global marketplace for what they saw as a British good, but instead of producing a transnational British consumer culture, they often produced diverse national and other local consumer cultures.

Tea's global marketing reveals the tensions but also the collaborations between Europe and the growing U.S. empire. The late nineteenth and early twentieth centuries were the high-water mark of European colonial expansion and the beginning of a new, more intensive form of American global supremacy. American-based multinationals such as the United Fruit Company, Ford Motor Company, and J. Walter Thompson began to transform the land, people, and polities in Europe, Central America, and so many other regions of the globe.[5] At the same time, a handful of European countries "scrambled" to conquer lands in Africa and intensified the exploitation of colonies they already possessed. These conquering impulses were driven by economic and political anxieties and competition and were reactions to changes in the colonies and the metropole. While recent work on global and imperial history has documented the connections among peoples, goods, and capital across vast distances, in this chapter I also examine the significance of animosities, jealousies, stereotypes, and prejudices in shaping this world.[6] Confusion did as well. While British colonial business believed their heritage and racial similarity would make it easier to sell goods in the United States and the white settler colonies, everywhere they went they encountered an opaque landscape in which they struggled to figure out the nature of diverse places, cultures, and economies. To clarify this landscape, business relied on simplistic comparisons and contrasts, reinforcing their belief that race, gender, and nation determined tastes and buying habits. The project of making markets necessarily invited contemplation of the thorny questions of whether or not and to whom the British Empire mattered. Finally, this chapter charts the connections between the social worlds of advertising, publicity, and imperialism; it is no accident that the language of marketing and that of colonialism were virtually identical.

THE BATTLE OF THE TEAS IN "GREATER BRITAIN"

India's and Ceylon's conquest of the British tea market in the 1880s was widely celebrated but did not assuage many planters' growing apprehension that, as one expert put it, "the British people are surfeited with tea, and no material increase of consumption can be expected within the limits of the United Kingdom."[7] The notion that British consumers had reached the limits of their thirst for tea, whether accurate or not, drove planters overseas and ignited antagonisms between India and Ceylon. According to one authority, a new "Battle of the Teas!" had begun. Writing in 1894, this trade journalist announced that competition for markets had shifted from a struggle between East and West to a fight among "the British producers themselves." Using a Social Darwinian framework of struggle and scarcity, this writer warned that it was "no longer in the British market, but in the market of the world, that the struggle must be fought out." He wondered whether Ceylon and India would cooperate or fight each other as they attempted to sell "British" tea "on a great scale outside of the British Empire."[8] Eventually these two colonial industries would cooperate, but between the 1890s and 1910s antagonism was the order of the day.

Ceylon excelled in this combative environment. Though its tea was not so different from that produced in India, as we saw in the previous chapter, in the late 1880s the colony began to brand its teas and indeed the whole of the island as distinct from India.[9] This impulse, for example, complicated the ways in which empire teas were sold at the Colonial and Indian Exhibition in London in 1886. That event was simply the beginning of a longer process that branded Ceylon tea as superior to that produced in India. In the second half of the nineteenth century, Ceylon's planters became some of the world's most adept publicists, a fact well recognized at the time. One planter assumed that it was the unique combination of "Scotch dourness" and "English pluck" that made the colony's planters so determined "not to be beat by anybody or anything."[10] Of course, India's growers were cut from the same cloth, and some liberal-minded businessmen maintained that "the friendly rivalry" between the two colonies would "stimulate rather than weaken the efforts of Indian tea planters."[11] However, by the late 1880s, India looked with trepidation at Ceylon's dramatic successes and scoffed at its penchant to push its wares in an aggressive and unseemly manner. In 1888, a self-declared "OLD FOGEY" wrote how annoyed he was to find that "on every public occasion, Ceylon tea is always advertised and represented, while Indian tea interests are usually nowhere."[12] India had actually started the fight in 1879 when its planters formed a syndicate dedicated to exporting tea to the colonies and America. This was the same body the Assam Company mentioned to its shareholders, and it was also most likely related to the formation of the Indian Tea Districts Association and the publication of the *Home and Colonial Mail* that same year.[13] At that time Ceylon barely produced any tea, but it was not long before its growers also began to plow what A. M. Ferguson, editor of the *Ceylon Observer* and former planter, called "fresh fields as outlets for our produce."[14] This desire to find global markets and the intense competition between these two "tea" colonies produced a variety of export schemes and publicity campaigns that lasted well into the late twentieth century. Global marketing campaigns arose then out of surpluses and falling prices and out of competition between colonies within the British Empire.

Each colony debated where and how to open fresh fields, but a combination of factors brought most of their efforts to Australia, Canada, the United States, and India. Though they had very different political relationships to Great Britain, they were part of a territory known as "Greater Britain." A malleable and powerful idea with widespread currency in these years, Greater Britain could variously connote all the disparate reaches of the formal British Empire, the settlement colonies, and the "English-speaking" or Anglo-Saxon countries, including the United States.[15] The publication of Charles Dilke's *Greater Britain* in 1868 and J. R. Seeley's *The Expansion of England* in 1883 gave the idea coherence. Tea planters believed in and actively sought to strengthen the notion of a Greater Britain. In general, many British businessmen imagined that the United States was a large and hungry British child eager to consume the surplus goods that were churned out of British factories and plantations. Those living in the colonies shared this idea, as did some Americans. So, for example, when the American John Blake published his lengthy *Tea Hints for Retailers* in 1903, he suggested Americans should buy and sell British-grown teas because "the business energy and acumen of the Anglo-Indian tea grower, blender, exporter, and broker we cannot but admire. *We are of his race*, and our business methods are similar to his."[16]

A defining feature of Greater Britain was the way in which boom periods that were often driven by the discovery of gold attracted investments and migrants, particularly young settlers who were determined to make their fortune in new frontiers.[17] Such booms tended to inspire very rapid urbanization, and new cities such as Chicago and Melbourne swelled to become huge metropolitan centers that served vast hinterlands. As James Belich noted, for example, in 1891 Melbourne had grown to almost half a million inhabitants and "ruled Victoria, a colony as populous and rich in 1890 as the American state of California."[18] These boom periods also enticed retailers and distributors of all kinds, and thus Greater Britain developed urban centers with shopping districts and high streets, food markets, grocers, and a mass media and advertising culture.[19] Rural areas too were well served and seem to have particularly liked tea.[20] Precise data varied, but all authorities acknowledged that Australians, New Zealanders, and Tasmanians drank the most tea per head, and Great Britain, the United States, and Russia were the largest national tea markets at the end of the nineteenth century.[21] While Ceylon and India embarked on trade expeditions in Russia and other parts of Europe, they spent most of their resources battling for attention in the English-speaking world. Australia was at the top of their list, which as one official described it in 1910 "is one of the greatest tea-drinking countries in the world."[22]

Commenting on Australia's drink habits in 1883, writer Richard Twopeny declared, "Tea may fairly claim to be the national beverage."[23] "Australia has recently come forward as a large consumer," Indian planter-turned-author George Barker also remarked in 1884.[24] Throughout the nineteenth century, Australians consumed more tea per capita than anywhere in the British World.[25] The reasons for this passion for the hot brew are complex and not fully understood, though it seems a combination of colonial culture, economics, and trade relations shaped this market. The first colonists who arrived in the 1780s were already avid tea drinkers, so they began to experiment with local plants, and in the 1790s military officers began to import Chinese tea.[26] A regular trade developed so that by the 1820s stocks were ample, especially in cities such as Sydney.[27] Rural Australia, though, particularly liked its tea. Workers' and convicts' rations included tea, and temperance tea parties and tea meetings were also very popular.[28] In the 1840s Australians were drinking on average nearly ten pounds per annum, and Queenslanders and Western Australians were the most ardent of these consumers.[29] Tea's thirst-quenching characteristics were no doubt appealing in the sweltering Australian colonies, but climate was only one part of this story.

Some scholars have proposed that the key to this extraordinary market lay in the fact that colonists liked their tea in large cups brewed "strong enough to tan a horse's hide."[30] Obviously, however, consumers had to be able to afford to drink tea in this way. In the late nineteenth century, Australia was urbanizing at a very rapid rate, its colonists had a relatively high standard of living, and it possessed one of the fastest-growing economies in the world.[31] Victorian Australians were thus able to consume more and varied goods, but colonial attitudes and numerous personal, business, military, and other connections around the British World also produced Australian tea conventions.[32] Settlers in societies such as Australia often prized foods and drinks designated as "European," believing that their consumption created distinctions between themselves and the people they were colonizing.[33] Of course, colonized people could also consume the same things, but the desire for racial distinction fed certain consumer patterns. In Australia tea sustained settlers' social and racial identities, even as aborigines were known to drink tea.[34] Importers and retailers eagerly exploited such ideas.[35]

India's and Ceylon's planters used Australians' affinities for the mother country and its empire and their growing fears of Chinese invasion to seize this tea market in much the same way they did in Britain. In the 1880s, the Calcutta Tea Syndicate hired James Inglis to organize a continent-wide advertising campaign and host major displays at two important international exhibitions to be held in Sydney and Melbourne. The nomadic Inglis was a good choice. Born in Scotland in 1845, Inglis moved to New Zealand at the age of nineteen, and then in 1866 he became an indigo planter in India. His health forced him to leave the Subcontinent, but he maintained connections with the colony; among other things, he became a journalist who wrote about Australia as a site of investment for Anglo-Indian capital. A noted lecturer on India and Scotland, he was also, as Sir Charles Dilke called him, "an out-and-out free trader."[36] His drive to sell tea anywhere and everywhere reflected this position, but he could not have succeeded without the resources and official backing of India's colonial government and the Calcutta Tea Syndicate. According to all reports, Inglis put on spectacular displays at Sydney's international exhibition in 1879 and in Melbourne in 1880.[37] These exhibitions were also the center of broader publicity campaigns that included demonstrations, lectures, pamphlets, and newspaper advertising. India's tea planters concluded that advertising paid because exports to Australia and New Zealand increased from 684,327 pounds for the second half of 1881 to 2,246,847 in 1882.[38] In 1887, at the same moment as in England, the "Indian herb" became the largest ingredient in the Australian teapot.[39] By the early 1890s, Australians were consuming virtually half of the twenty million pounds of tea that India and Ceylon sold outside of Great Britain.[40] In 1892 Australia was Ceylon's second-biggest market after Britain.[41] During the twentieth century, Australia's preference for the taste of Ceylon grew, a fact exploited by brand advertising. Bushells, for example, made much of the image of the comely

Ceylon tea picker in its advertising from the early twentieth century, developing what one historian has described as a prestige brand.[42]

How did this happen? One writer noted that it would not be an easy accomplishment for India's planters to entice her Australian "cousin" and "cut out the barbarian." This would take the subtle maneuvers and flirtations of courtship. Australia needed to be patiently wooed, for she "is not to be snatched at discretion from the embrace of China; she is both coy and diffident about changing her lover."[43] British India needed to please, gratify, and court Australia since tea growers did not feel that imperial membership alone would convince committed Chinese tea drinkers to change their tastes.[44] Australian grocers were reluctant to stock the new teas because they were unpopular with consumers.[45] With a hefty dose of anti-Chinese sentiment, India's Australian campaign thus pushed the benefits of empire-grown varieties.[46] Exhibitions and advertising informed Australians that Chinese tea was adulterated and unhealthy, while Indian tea was pure, modern, and machine made.[47] The empire's modern teas were the patriotic, healthy, and economical choice.

Also, as we saw at work elsewhere, tea planters frequently became exhibition experts, retailers, and advertisers. James Inglis, for example, founded his own company that sold a new brand known as Billy Tea, and within a few short years this brand became one of the most successful in the Antipodes.[48] By 1890, 6,000,000 pounds of Billy Tea were sold annually in Australia, New Zealand, and Tasmania.[49] Billy tea, or tea brewed in a tin can over a campsite, was a much-memorialized part of bush life, and emigrant memoirs describe how pioneers drank billy tea literally from daybreak to bedtime.[50] Billy brand tea thus commercialized white frontier masculinity, as ads and packaging featured a bushman smoking tobacco, conversing with a kangaroo, and drinking tea. Inglis thus manufactured some of the key symbols of Australian national identity before and after the period that Australian colonists began to think about themselves as a nation. To be sure, immigration restrictions targeting Chinese workers and the various twists and turns that brought about federation in 1901 signaled the role of race in the formation of Australian identity, but advertising did as well.[51] Billy brand tea exemplifies the global, local, and imperial processes producing national tastes and international commercial cultures. In hindsight, we can also see that mass markets grew quickly in places where a masculine work culture embraced tea, and this was very much the case in Australia.

Anti-Chinese sentiment was strong in Australia, but Chinese entrepreneurial skills also developed the Australian market. One of the most successful and innovative tea merchants was a man by the name of Quong Tart, who had been born in Canton in the 1850s. Tart relied on much the same techniques as Thomas Lipton, Kate Cranston, or James Inglis. He handed out free samples to shoppers in the Sydney Arcade and established a chain of tea rooms, including one in King Street that cost £6,000 to build and decorate.[52] At the same time, China tea importers also denounced India's and Ceylon's "misrepresentations" of their product in the press and advertising, but they were unable to stop the steady growth of empire-grown teas.[53]

Yet, it is striking that at the same time that consumers in Oceania acquired a thirst for the empire's teas, per capita consumption began to decline. Western Australians still drank an enormous 14.6 pounds annually between 1895 and 1899, but this was down from a record 15.7 during the first half of the 1890s. Soon other Australian colonies fell to between 6 and 7 pounds annually, which was just above the averages for the UK at this time.[54] The Australian economy did go through a recession, but the price of tea was very low. The decline in per capita consumption may have had more to do with taste. As we have seen, the new empire-grown teas were darker and stronger than most Chinese varieties, so it is likely that Australians used less tea to brew the same number of cups as they had previously. During this period, however, the tea interests did not consider these issues in great detail and assumed that most market problems could be solved by advertising and publicity. Thus in the Antipodes the growth of Indian and Ceylon tea brought about a decline in per capita consumption and a growth in advertising.

British tea planters also had their eye on Canada, another settler colony with a longstanding taste for tea.[55] In the second half of the nineteenth century, a mass migration of Britons brought tea to the prairies and parlors throughout this huge and diverse land.[56] Retailers, temperance communities, and, by the twentieth century, imperial-oriented women's groups, such as the Imperial Order of the Daughters of the British Empire and the Society of the Overseas Settlement of British Women, promoted tea as an empire product.[57] But here too empire tastes had to be nourished, particularly since, like the United States, Canada held to a strong preference for East Asian green teas. Men with close ties to the planting communities in India and Ceylon moved to Canada to change this situation. Charles Frederick Amery of the Indian Forest Service and father of the famous Conservative and pro-empire British politician Leopold Amery was one such figure. He established an agency for the sale of Indian teas in Montreal, with the conviction that Canada had "a market large enough to absorb the whole Indian output."[58] Amery also told planters to start to develop a good quality green tea, ironically inventing a notion of Canadian national tastes and habits. As in Australia, brand advertising and tea rooms promoted Britishness, imperialism, and Canadian identity at the same time.[59]

Tea growers were also enthralled with the United States and wistfully remembered the days before the American Revolution when colonists loved the beverage. As we have noted, nineteenth-century American merchants rushed to China and temperance activists eagerly hosted massive tea parties throughout the States. However, per capita consumption stagnated and the British tea industry believed that the revolution and recent immigration from continental Europe had turned American consumers off tea. The industry also imagined that the large number of Britons living in the United States could bring this nation back into the empire of tea. During the last third of the century, the U.S. population grew from 40 to 76 million people, far faster than Great Britain, which increased from 31 to 41 million in the same period.[60] Many "Americans" had been born in Ireland, Scotland, England, or British colonies; until the end of the century roughly two-thirds of all British emigrants preferred the United States to colonial destinations.[61] Between the 1860s and 1900, the flow of migration increased in waves, with some 600,000 British migrants coming in the 1860s alone. Another peak came in 1887 and 1888 when about 130,000 Britons settled into many walks of life and were especially attracted to the American West.[62]

These migrants established transnational business relationships and markets for British goods.[63] Approximately 1,500 British companies were founded between the 1860s and 1900 specifically to do business with the trans-Mississippi West, and their employees traveled regularly between the United States and the British Empire.[64] Some, like Thomas Lipton, spent their formative years in this New World acquiring sales expertise and forging personal connections that would help them later build transnational business empires. Others moved between Britain, various colonies, and the States as importers, advertisers, publicists, and exhibition professionals. America's wealth, its enduring role as a market for other British manufactured goods, its general appreciation for new products and tastes, and its presumed British heritage excited tea planters. The American population was not exclusively British and the government was erecting tariffs and other trade barriers, but many planters held fast to their belief in a shared Anglo-American culture and they were sure that British products could and should have an advantage in this "country of big things," including its appetites.[65] At the same moment American theorists were becoming convinced that the U.S. market was not large enough to absorb its surpluses, British tea planters were enthralled by this great land of people with latent Anglo-Saxon tastes, big cities, modern industry, wealthy workers, and a sophisticated advertising industry.

Holding many of the same ideologies and attitudes that also set off the scramble for African colonies in the 1880s and 1890s, tea growers raced to outdo their rivals and conquer American consumers. During the 1880s, the Assam Company, the Indian Tea Districts Association (ITDA, which soon became known just as the Indian Tea Association), and individual businessmen began to collect information about this huge continent of "Anglo-Saxon" consumers.[66]

As in the UK, special agencies dedicated to selling only India's and Ceylon's growths opened around this time.[67] In 1881 the Assam Company reported that it had exported to both the "Colonies and America with marked success." Nevertheless, the firm's directors were cautious and explained that "it is necessary to guard against overstocking new markets."[68] In general, India's largest producers were worried about "speculative movements, such as opening new markets."[69] Such attitudes delayed a full-scale assault and opened the door for Ceylon. One insightful observer later commented that Ceylon was more adventurous because communication was easier in this smaller and less physically scattered industry and because its government took a more active interest in promoting the islands' businesses.[70] The truth is India was having so much success in Great Britain, Australia, and India that some felt the U.S. market was unnecessary. Indian growers were divided about how much money to put into North America. Half-hearted attempts in the early 1880s left some growers later in the decade reflecting that although "American and Canadian markets have to be won[,] at present nothing has been done for Indian teas beyond an endeavor on the part of a few enterprising men to arouse a spirit of 'go' in members of the industry more generally."[71] More was being done than that, but this author was comparing India's efforts to the strides that Ceylon had made in this land.[72]

Ceylon was also working in Australia, but its planters found the wealthy and novelty-seeking consumers in the United States especially attractive.[73] The United States presented unique problems and possibilities, however. In the autumn of 1883, the Ceylon Planters' Association met in Kandy to discuss how to introduce their teas into "foreign" markets. Their conversation quickly turned to America. One of the planters present, H. R. Stimson, enthusiastically discussed the United States and Canada and was excited that several forthcoming exhibitions were being planned for New York, Cincinnati, and Boston. Stimson argued that Americans were especially good at putting on these shows because they were a people open to seeing, buying, and tasting new things. He then passed around engravings of the forthcoming Boston Exposition, calling attention to its large, attractive buildings. In urging that Ceylon should go to Boston, Stimson explained that "our exhibits will go there and be seen by the sort of people interested in them and they will open the eyes of those people to what can be done in Ceylon."[74] The colony's leading tea propagandist and exhibitor, J. L. Loudan-Shand, preferred to work in the United States because as he saw it, "the entire population of Australia is not equal to that of one of the rising American States."[75] In another essay, Shand adopted imperial rhetoric when he wrote, "The United States and Canada are two great countries that have to be conquered for tea." He went on to suggest that both countries were "peopled mainly by Anglo-Saxon and Celtic peoples—by the same people in the main who constitute tea-drinkers in the United Kingdom." He warned, however, that Germans and other coffee-drinking nationalities had chipped away at Anglo-American tastes.[76] Shand, Stimson, and others were drawn to the size of America's population and its seemingly innate desire to consume new things. They were motivated by a powerful fantasy about American business and consumer cultures and hoped to profit from the spectacle of its economic growth in the late nineteenth century. They also imagined North America, both Canada and the United States, as similar Anglo spaces under threat from foreign (that is, non-British) migration.

In truth, exporters faced a bigger problem than coffee-drinking immigrants. When Ceylon first shipped teas to New York, a "Ring" bought the entire shipment and shipped it right back to London. Shand and his close colleague H. K. Rutherford responded to this defiant act by arguing that only "unity of action" and a "defined plan" could defeat the New York Ring and introduce "our teas into America."[77] Another planter recommended avoiding New York and the typical lines of distribution altogether and instead courting consumers directly, especially "householders and housewives in the towns of New England . . . and the Central and Western States."[78] Yet another opined that the surest route to retailers and to the "heads of families" was to lecture to them. "We know of no better means of reaching the American intelligence than by lectures," this author believed.[79] Ceylon then hired Shand to conduct a "judiciously managed lecturing tour through the States and Canada."[80] Such discussions reveal that Ceylon's planters saw Americans as an educated and rational people whose tastes could be conquered through facts. This was, as we will see, very different from how exporters viewed African and Indian consumers.

Shand and his colleagues were learning as well as teaching when they toured North America.[81] Lecture tours were encounters between buyers and sellers in which ideally both sides came away with market knowledge. Shand learned about American habits, but he did not change how he worked to accommodate local tastes. Rather, he was a master of recycling ideas, display, and advertising materials from other exhibitions, and everywhere he habitually condemned China's "inferior teas."[82] He used the same ideas and methods far beyond the United States. In the late 1880s, Shand had hired colonial merchants and planters as agents to publicize Indian tea in Europe, Australia, New Zealand, South Africa, the West Indies, and other British colonies, as well as Argentina, Ireland, Russia, Austria, and the Ottoman Empire.[83] The problem, of course, was how to pay for such efforts and how to hire the right people to sell Ceylon's story.

Several former planters residing in the United States applied for the job. In 1885 James McCombie Murray and his partner, R. E. Pineo, moved to Philadelphia and built up a firm to "energetically" sell *"pure* Ceylon tea" in North America. Murray, who was from a well-connected Aberdeen family, moved to Ceylon to plant coffee instead of pursuing a music career, but he soon tried tea as well. He married an American woman and the couple relocated to Philadelphia.[84] Pineo had also been a coffee and tea planter in the 1870s and no doubt the two became acquainted on the island.[85] Pineo and Murray began their business by distributing free samples of their "Kootee" brand tea to leading Philadelphia families and President Grover Cleveland, who evidently wrote them a nice note saying that he thought their tea tasted "good."Whether truthful or not, the story made good advertising copy and began the work of linking Ceylon and tea drinking with elite social status.[86] Most of this company's advertising, however, explained how Ceylon's phoenix-like tea industry had miraculously grown from the ashes of the devastated coffee plantations. Directly addressing American ladies, this publicity placed the fate of an industry and an island in their teacups but also condemned India's substandard product:

Fair Ladies! All, of every charm possessed,
To you alone, these lines are now addressed,
On you we feel that all our hopes depend,
Through you alone, we hope to gain our end.

We're strangers; Yes! But cannot so remain,
Unless we long do work, and work in vain,
If you, fair ladies, greet us with a smile,
We'll pine no more for Ceylon's Spice Isle . . .

India, our northern neighbors, were zealous,
But soon of our speedy success became jealous;
For strength in the cup they were equal in favor,
But as pure drinking tea we could beat them in flavour.[87]

Pineo and Murray worked hard, but their progress was slow. Pineo explained that despite Murray's "gentleman's vigor and push," the two felt overwhelmed by the size of the United States. They nevertheless learned a great deal from their mistakes, so that when they advised planters how to break into the U.S. market in 1888, they urged them to alter their teas to suit North American tastes, to avoid grocers, retail tea dealers, and jobbers, and to hire instead "A man with push, energy, an abundance of capital, who was thoroughly versed in the art (?) of American advertising."[88] A few months later, Murray reiterated that to be "progressive in this country . . . one must be *aggressive.*"[89] An associate of

Pineo's, the New York entrepreneur S. Elwood May, who had promoted several different new commodities, fit the bill.[90] He promised that if he were named the "Accredited Representative Agent of the Planters' Association of Ceylon," he would advertise extensively, package Ceylon's tea in an "attractive" manner, and distribute it free of charge.[91] Some growers resented this boldness and questioned May's character and motives, but the Dimbula Planters' Association resolved to work with him.[92] The more general Planters' Association rejected May's proposal, however, because he would not buy their teas unless he was named the association's special agent.[93] The rejected but not dejected May then joined forces with R. E. Pineo and John Joseph Grinlinton to start the Ceylon Planters' American Tea Company in 1889.[94] By 1893 he was selling pure Ceylon tea to large distributors in Boston, New York, Chicago, St. Louis, Cleveland, Washington, Philadelphia, and Baltimore. Despite this success, the company folded that year due to credit and banking difficulties and because Thomas Lipton was named Ceylon's tea agent for the Chicago World's Fair.[95] Pineo left the business and became a choirmaster but May went on to sell his own teas. Grinlinton became Ceylon's tea commissioner at Chicago and then had a long career as a lobbyist and publicist for tea.

Many British and colonial-born emigrants sold British tea in the British World in the 1880s and 1890s. For example, Charles Ker Reid was born in Newcastle upon Tyne but moved to Melbourne at the age of eighteen in 1852, where he worked as a specialty dealer for Assam's tea before moving his large family to Philadelphia to found a coffee-roasting and tea-packing firm.[96] Reid became a vocal publicist for Indian tea.[97] He also urged growers to develop products that would appeal to America's palate, and, like Pineo and Murray, he surmised that it would take the efforts of a "missionary . . . to revolutionize the palate" of this country, comparing the task to establishing a new religion.[98] By the late 1880s, long-forgotten businesses and soon-to-be-famous brands also staked claims in the United States.[99] Ridgways introduced "Her Majesty's Blend" in England in 1886, and just two years later they began pushing this tea across the Atlantic, a move that inaugurated the company's overseas growth.[100] Arthur Brooke, founder of Brooke Bond, opened retail outlets in Chicago and New Orleans at the same time, though he eventually became a wholesaler in the United States. Brooke's passion for publicity was ignited on an American sojourn, and several years later the company hired an American-born advertising consultant to inject new vigor into the sales side of the business.[101]

Thomas Lipton was the most notable Briton to make his name in America. In 1890, it will be recalled, he purchased estates in Ceylon, and immediately the island's planters began to call Lipton "The Greatest Advertising Tea Grocer in the World." They anticipated great things as he hinted that he would open new markets in Australia and the United States.[102] In June 1890, Lipton "tiffined," that is, lunched, with Pineo and May to discuss the United States. When the *Ceylon Independent* reported on the meeting it snidely suggested that if he decided to sell tea in the States, Lipton's "bite would be like that of a shark compared with the [Pineo and May's] Company's flea bite."[103] After purchasing the Haputale Estate in Ceylon, Lipton became a member of the Planters' Association and curried favor by donating to their advertising fund.[104] Nevertheless, many resented Lipton's style and pointed out that even before he purchased any estates he was already advertising that his teas were direct from garden to pot. Critics also worried that although he would "boom" Ceylon across America, he would blend Ceylon with India and China teas.[105] The *Ceylon Observer* assured readers, however, that Lipton was "doing more for this Colony in a short space of time than our Tea Fund Committee and the Ceylon American Tea Company could do in a score of years." The paper recommended that Lipton take over all the Tea Fund's promotional work.[106] The growers' association did not give away their entire operation, but they subsidized Lipton and gave his brand pride of place in their display at the Chicago World's Fair. Lipton won this contract because he was already a mercantile celebrity and he convinced Ceylon's planters that he would open hundreds of retail outlets and spend immense sums on advertising Ceylon in America.[107] Lipton was also well connected to other large food processors and claimed that his good friend P. D. Armour of meatpacking fame was one of "his first private customers."[108]

The United States, Thomas Lipton recalled, "was a practically limitless market for an enterprising merchant confident in his wares." He saw the country as rich, open, and ignorant, especially about tea. After spending a day or two giving the American tea trade the "once-over," Lipton remembered being "astonished beyond measure" when he found that "to all intents and purposes there was *no* tea-trade in America." As evidence of this, Lipton recalled how when he had asked for tea in his hotel the waiter looked at him "in blank amazement" as though he had never heard of the drink. Where it was sold, Lipton noted that the commodity was carelessly handled. Dry teas sold in bulk in New York and Chicago were expensive and "terrible," kept in open receptacles, and thus treated as "on the same level as barley, rice, and maize." As was typical in stories of entrepreneurial self-fashioning, Lipton explained how he possessed a unique ability to discover hidden possibilities and overcome ignorance and backwardness. Yet he never opened retail shops, acting instead as a wholesaler selling Lipton's teas through established vendors. He did, however, spend a small fortune on a "Continent-wide advertising campaign" across the United States and Canada.[109] Considering this work a great success, Lipton later boasted that his large sky-sign above his company's Hoboken, New Jersey, headquarters had become a "familiar landmark to New Yorkers and every transatlantic traveler."[110] Lipton's sign rising above the Hudson River was as much a symbol of the age as was the Statue of Liberty. It denoted the growing power of an Anglo-American capitalist empire that stretched from California to Ceylon.[111]

FROM CHICAGO TO ST. LOUIS: DREAMING OF AMERICA AT THE WORLD'S FAIRS

By the summer of 1888, J. L. Loudan-Shand had traveled to so many exhibitions, he wrote that he was "personally . . . sick of them." However, he advised that he could "think of no better way of pushing our teas than an Exhibition" and urged Ceylon not "*to lose the chance of an Exhibition anywhere.*"[112] In the previous decade, he and a handful of colleagues had been to Australia, India, and Great Britain.[113] They had been in Amsterdam in 1883, London in 1884 and 1886, Liverpool in 1887, Glasgow, Brussels, and Melbourne in 1888, and France and New Zealand in 1889, and they would soon go to Chicago in 1893, Russia in 1894, and St. Louis in 1904.[114] Tea displays were also mounted at lesser but nonetheless very important spectacles.[115] But the place where they spent the most time and money was the American Midwest.

In the 1890s, when businessmen around the world thought of the United States, they could not help but think of Chicago. The millions who attended the World's Columbian Exposition in Chicago in 1893 gazed upon a globalizing and spectacular economy and culture.[116] Chicago in the 1890s was a gateway city that connected agricultural to commercial wealth and linked the East Coast and the world to the middle and western parts of the United States.[117] Packaged meat from the stockyards of "porkopolis" shipped throughout the States and across the Atlantic. After the turn of the century, Gordon Selfridge transferred the American-style department store from Chicago to Edwardian London and brought with it a deep and abiding faith in publicity.[118] It was Chicago's plutocrats that Thorstein Veblen observed in the 1890s when he wrote his famous *The Theory of the Leisure Class.*[119] Upton Sinclair too developed his trenchant critique of the modern industrial food system gazing upon Chicago's stockyards.[120] Turn-of-the-century Chicago was thus a capitalist utopia and nightmare. It was also the place to be if one wanted to profit from the ever-expanding American mass market.[121]

Tea planters envisioned the Chicago World's Fair as a once-in-a-lifetime opportunity.[122] This exhibition was to announce America's stature as an industrial and consumer-oriented nation driven by an insatiable urge to buy and sell new things.[123] Chicago confirmed what many tea men already knew: America was the greatest market the world had ever seen, but it also was one of the most difficult and expensive to conquer and control. Marking Columbus's arrival in the Americas, the Chicago World's Fair celebrated the industrial and imperial progress of the New World. But Ceylon's and India's displays in Chicago made Old World imperialism enticing as well. At all such world's fairs of this era, race often advertised goods, especially new foodstuffs. Indeed, the advertising icon "Aunt Jemima" first appeared at Chicago in the person of Nancy Green, a former slave from Kentucky, who served pancakes to fairgoers from inside a booth designed to look like a giant flour barrel.[124] Displays of non-white peoples were everywhere and reappeared in countless cartoons and commentary, but racism operated in multiple and often contradictory ways.[125] Visitors, for example, sampled many versions of Asia. For example, the Japan Central Tea Association constructed an impressive display in Chicago and at many other American and European exhibitions.[126] This organization also mounted extensive advertising campaigns in the early twentieth century.[127] Japan, Ceylon, Formosa, China, and India competed for the American consumer, leaving all but the most sophisticated of buyers confused by the many Asian teas on the market.

The difficulty was not just consumer ignorance, however. Exhibitions as a whole tended to collapse distinctions and create a generic sense that "native" peoples served and entertained the West. Exhibitions framed the East as a general concept or an ideal that gained meaning in contrast to an undifferentiated West. When travelers encountered real Asian spaces they often were disoriented by their strangeness, which seemed so unlike the countless facsimiles of the East on show at exhibitions and cognate enterprises. This propelled Westerners to colonize such chaotic places, that is, to "re-order" the Orient.[128] In this way commodity culture not only reflected but also propelled imperialism. It also made it difficult for consumers to understand and appreciate Asia's diversity. Nations, empires, and colonies thus tended to come together and apart at these fairs. These world events had many lasting ramifications, particularly in the business of global advertising.

Ceylon and India had been advertising in the United States for more than a decade before the Chicago World's Fair, but as the chairman of the joint Indian and Ceylon American Advertising Fund explained in 1906, "The very machinery for the active pushing of India and Ceylon Teas did not exist prior to Chicago."[129] By machinery, he largely meant money and expertise. Prior to Chicago, the money came from voluntary funds and government subsidies, but this simply was not enough for Chicago.[130] In 1892 H. K. Rutherford, a leading figure in Ceylon's planting world, encouraged the colonial government to introduce a compulsory and statutory export levy to pay for the exhibition. The government agreed and in January 1893 Ceylon introduced such a levy, at a rate of 10 cents per 100 pounds of tea. The duty, known as a cess, thus grew as exports expanded. Ceylon abandoned the cess in the early twentieth century but reinstated it in 1932. Following Ceylon's example, India introduced a cess in 1903 to pay for the World's Fair to be held in St. Louis the next year, and it maintained this tax throughout the century. Cess funds paid for industry-wide advertising and political activity that would expand markets. Growers sometimes complained about these taxes, but cesses helped alter distribution systems on a global scale, supported private industry, and subsidized a massive amount of advertising. Cess funds were administered by quasi-governmental agencies, which effectively became the promotional arm of the planter classes. The Indian Tea Cess Committee (ITCC), a subcommittee of the Indian Tea Association, handled India's global advertising until the 1930s, while in Ceylon the Committee of Thirty was the responsible body.[131]

By initiating a cess a decade before India, Ceylon was able to outdo its rival in Chicago. During the first year, the Committee of Thirty spent 80 percent of its budget in Chicago, and it also secured £21,000 from the colonial government, chambers of commerce, and the Planters' Association. J. J. Grinlinton, the island's tea commissioner for Chicago, thus had the funds necessary to spend an entire year in Chicago establishing a good working relationship with exhibition officials. Ceylon's planters were very excited about these developments, but some worried that the "land of big things" had influenced Grinlinton, who far exceeded his proposed budget.[132] Thomas Lipton, who became Ceylon's exclusive tea agent at Chicago, may have also influenced Grinlinton to spend more money. This, in turn, promoted the island's exports and aided Lipton's global expansion.

The Ceylon Court juxtaposed ancient culture and modern art and industry, and established a visual language that consumers would associate with Ceylon for years to come.[133] Much grander than that of previous displays, the main court was built entirely out of native wood, which was carved in a style demonstrating the island's ancient architecture. Both its structure and decorative motifs conveyed Ceylon's religious and artistic history. For example, the cobra-shrouded figures guarding the steps leading to the main court were adaptations from the ruined temples at Anurádhapura and Polonnáruwa, two ancient capitals. These same symbols could also be found guarding shrines throughout Ceylon as they were thought to ward off evil.[134] Pillars, windows, and ceilings were all similarly decorated with elephants, lions, dancers, and other symbols of Sinhalese culture. Sinhalese artists depicted the island's religions with painted scenes from the life of Buddha, and colossal statues of Buddha and Vishnu also flanked the central hall.[135] The spacious tea room in the Woman's Building was chock-full of rugs, fabric, and objects to such a degree that it looked like an Orientalist dream and/or nightmare (fig. 6.1). Grinlinton had convinced the wealthy Mrs. Potter Palmer, who was in charge of the Woman's Building, to provide special space for a Ceylon tea room, and a committee of ladies, headed by Lady Havelock, the wife of Ceylon's

FIGURE 6.1. Ceylon tea room, the Woman's Building, Chicago World's Fair, 1893. *Views of the World's Fair and Midway Plaisance* (Chicago: W. B. Conkey Company, 1894), 108. (Library of Congress/Internet Archive)

governor, put the room together.[136] Grinlinton also secured a special space for the main court and for three mini displays, all of which contained "native" servants serving visitors cups of hot tea. Architecture and the location that Ceylon secured for its building within the fairgrounds presented the island colony as a distinct economy and space rather than part of an imperial system, though it certainly conveyed an Orientalist aura. The court stood between France and Austria and across from Norway. It was a short distance from Ecuador, Guatemala, and Costa Rica. Ceylon was not too far from Great Britain, but it was not all that close either. From a visitor's perspective Ceylon probably looked like a nation rich in history and culture, an exotic island paradise, and not a British dependency.

India responded by hiring famed Chicago architect Henry Ives Cobb to design its pavilion. Cobb's structure was "Oriental in its minutest detail," including mosaic work inlaid with filigree and precious metals.[137] Turbaned Indians using hand-painted crockery "distributed little pots of tea to all comers free of charge."[138] Mr. Richard Blechynden, the Indian tea commissioner, stated in an interview that he would not let India be "outdone by their Ceylon rivals." After serving nearly 6,000 cups of the "fragrant-smelling liquid" a day, he claimed that almost as soon as the brew touched their lips, customers became convinced that black Indian tea was better than the "faintly-coloured beverage" to which they were accustomed.[139] Such hyperbolic statements found their way into newspapers that published articles with titles such as "From Old Bombay," "Looking for New Markets," and "They Wish to Establish Trade with America."[140] Blechynden achieved his aims. Over 1,500 American firms signed agreements in Chicago to stock Indian tea. After the fair closed, Blechynden raised another £7,000 to coordinate a newspaper campaign and pay his "Indian servants" dressed in "picturesque costumes" to move from store to store and city to city to serve tea at "leading American tea firms," department stores, and "food shows" throughout the Midwest.[141] Ceylon remained active as well, and one trade observer maintained in 1897 that everywhere he went he encountered "photographs and scenes in the tea gardens of Ceylon." Many of these emphasized the beauty of the gardens and the virtues of "machine-made tea."[142]

Chicago's afterlife could be felt throughout the United States, India, and Ceylon. Grinlinton packed up the rugs, furniture, and other items from Chicago's tea room and transferred them to a large store he opened on State Street in downtown Chicago. When explaining this project to planters back home, Grinlinton argued that like Oxford Street in London, State Street was the territory of wealthy lady shoppers, who had no other place to "have a cup of tea and sit down for a quarter of an hour or so."[143] The State Street shop closed down, but Grinlinton received a knighthood and Chicago remained an important center for promotion for decades to come.[144] India felt that though it made a good effort, its smaller rival had simply put on a better show. They would be better prepared the next time.

The Louisiana Purchase Exposition held in St. Louis in 1904 had a similar impact on the colonial tea industry. Anticipating the costs associated with this forthcoming show, Indian growers asked Lord Curzon, who was then viceroy, to create a cess. After much discussion, the Indian Tea Cess Act of 1903 (No. 9) became law and created a "fund to be expended for the promotion of the interests of the Indian tea industry."[145] The Act extended the voluntary fund that had been in place since 1893 and was renewed and extended several times before and after Indian Independence.[146] The ITCC managed the fund, hired advertising agencies, subsidized large distributors, and engaged in market and scientific research and product development.[147] Like the Committee of Thirty, it studied population size and wealth, distribution systems, taxes, tariffs, and related policies, and discussed how gender, class, race, religion, and national habits influenced tea tastes and marketing methods.

India and Ceylon spent a great deal in Missouri in 1904.[148] Ceylon was so active that the *Home and Colonial Mail* stated that "the people are full of Ceylon and the Press is also full of her."[149] India matched these efforts and built a dramatic pavilion, which imitated the mosque of Itmad-ul-Dowlah at Agra (fig. 6.2). Tea was served within this mosque, which also housed a huge

FIGURE 6.2. "East Indian Pavilion," Louisiana Purchase Exhibition, 1904. *Louisiana and the Fair: An Exposition of the World, Its People and Their Achievements*, ed. J. W. Buel, 6:2154. (University of California, Library/Internet Archive)

wooden carved reproduction of a Jain temple.[150] In an apocryphal tale about the so-called American invention of iced tea, Richard Blechynden, India's tea commissioner, evidently had trouble giving away hot tea in Missouri's sweltering heat, so he instructed his "natives" to serve iced tea. Iced tea was in fact drunk in England, India, and New York City long before this moment.[151] Cookbooks such as Marion Harland's *Breakfast, Luncheon and Tea* recommended this "delicious summertime beverage" at least as early as 1875, but the myth of iced tea being invented at the St. Louis World's Fair has lasted to this day.[152] We will see why this was the case in chapter 8.

The fair itself was only part of the show. As he had done after Chicago, Blechynden carried out a "systematic" advertising campaign during and after St. Louis closed.[153] He assumed that advertising sold tea, but, just as important, it created friends among the distributing trade and was critical to controlling supply chains.[154] He thus placed ads in the "patent insides," or inside sheets of country newspapers, and in the large colored supplements in midwestern Sunday papers. In the second half of 1904, ads appeared in 669 weekly papers and 11 Sunday supplements, covering Missouri, parts of Illinois, Indiana, and Kansas, reaching an estimated population of 11,250,000.[155] Despite such efforts, Blechynden constantly complained that he did not have enough money.[156] This problem could be solved if Ceylon and India joined forces.[157] Blechynden invited Ceylon to contribute to his campaign, and for a time Blechynden pushed both colonies' teas.[158] Time after time, however, India and Ceylon would break and renew their alliance. This meant that sometimes tea was advertised simply as a generic beverage, while at other times it might be identified as from Ceylon, India, or the British Empire. This no doubt confused retailers and consumers alike.

Nevertheless, Ceylon's Committee of Thirty and the ITCC subsidized the growth of mass marketing and retailing, improved planters' relationships with American merchants, and brought South Asian culture and products into America's heartland. While Ceylon worked closely with Lipton, Richard Blechynden worked with the country's most aggressive chain stores and packet tea firms, such as James Butler in New York, the Great Atlantic and Pacific Tea Company, and the Retail Grocers' Association in Philadelphia, which at that time controlled around 700 stores. Newspaper advertisements declared that Indian tea was available at these chains in New York, Pennsylvania, New Hampshire, Vermont, Alabama, Tennessee, Louisiana, New Jersey, Delaware, Maryland, and elsewhere.[159] In return for free advertising, retailers furnished customer mailing lists, which Blechynden used to distribute thousands of postcards typically featuring the requisite image of a "native" female tea picker.[160] Such advertising, supported by cess funds, convinced American retailers that South Asian teas had "come to stay."[161] American preference for British-grown teas grew and journals such as the *American Grocer* praised Blechynden's "splendid work."[162]

Along with many others, Blechynden, Lipton, and Loudan-Shand began to develop a commercial and consumer culture around tea in the United States. In January 1899, leading U.S. importers founded the American Tea Association, a trade organization that circulated commercial intelligence, became involved in transportation and warehousing issues, and lobbied government, influencing, for example, adulteration legislation and tax policy.[163] In 1901, William Harrison Ukers founded the New York–based *Tea and Coffee Trade Journal* and became arguably the greatest expert on tea and coffee in the twentieth century.[164] This native Philadelphian had no experience with these commodities when he became editor of *The Spice Mill*, then the house organ of the Jabez Burns Company. Burns was a Scot who had made his fortune in coffee-roasting machines. After Burns refused to turn the magazine into a fully-fledged trade publication, Ukers struck out on his own.[165] Eventually *The Spice Mill* did become an important journal as well, but Ukers's many publications provided a massive amount of information about growing, distributing, and selling tea, coffee, and related commodities in Latin America, Africa, Europe, and East and South Asia, among other places. Working with and writing for an international business community, Ukers befriended Thomas Lipton, and in 1906 he became an advisor to the Ceylon tea commissioner and embarked on his first tour of tea-producing countries.[166] Ukers represented America's growing global power, but like Lipton, he was a hybrid figure with a mother from England and many transatlantic and transimperial contacts. When he toured the world to do research for *All about Tea*, Ukers visited every growing region, did research in the British Museum Library, and hired a team of researchers, which included a British woman, a Mrs. Osler, who is identified in one photograph simply as "his British researcher."[167] When the book was published in 1935, Ukers thanked numerous individuals and associations, but he did not acknowledge Mrs. Osler. The two-volume tome relied on international connections and research but identified Ukers as the leading "American" expert on tea.

While men such as Ukers and Lipton became well-known throughout the global tea trade, middle- and upper-class ladies in the United States, as in the UK, also developed America's tea culture and knowledge. Female college graduates and other New Women managed and patronized thousands of tea rooms in major cities, at resorts, and along America's highways.[168] In the South, progressive women congregated in tea rooms to discuss women's rights, temperance, and a host of other issues.[169] "The tea room industry is sweeping America," claimed an advertisement for the Lewis Tea Room Institute, which promised to train women interested in the "tremendous" opportunities as managers, hostesses, table

70743 AFTERNOON TEA AT THE ROYAL POINCIANA, PALM BEACH, FLA.

FIGURE 6.3. Afternoon tea, Hotel Royal Poinciana Gardens, Palm Beach, Florida, 1910. (The Miriam and Ira D. Wallach Division of Art, Prints and Photographs, New York Public Library, shelf locator MFY 95–29)

directors, buyers, and executives in this new and exciting industry.[170] American tea rooms took on many forms, including dark bohemian dens in Greenwich Village, Japanese tea houses, colonial-inspired enterprises, and elegant hotel and department store tea rooms. Even in the humid Florida summer, American ladies dressed up to enjoy afternoon tea under the palm trees (fig. 6.3). Tea culture was feminine and bourgeois but it also could become cosmopolitan. Literary journals and articles such as "Tea Drinking in Japan and China" and "Tea-Drinking in Many Lands" implied that everywhere tea was a sophisticated and cosmopolitan beverage.[171] These articles and Asian-themed tea rooms likely especially appealed to wealthy American humanists who were collecting Japanese art and culture.[172] Men patronized these enterprises, but female ownership, the liberal use of chintz, lace, pink paint, and floral wallpaper, and sweets-laden menus demarcated tea shops as female spaces. This was true in the UK as well, but the chain tea shops in Britain were often far less feminine in their decor and associated with mercantile giants such as Lipton. Women, however, dominated America's tea rooms.

When drinking tea American women could assert an Anglo-Saxon heritage. Advertisers and etiquette writers frequently underlined the Englishness of afternoon tea. Cookbooks such as *Breakfast and Dinner Parties* (1889) taught American housewives how to bake English and Scotch cakes, as well as English pies and puddings.[173] The Boston-based London Tea Company advertised fine

"English decorated" tea and coffee china to the readers of the *Ladies' Home Journal* in the 1890s.[174] Afternoon tea did not always connote Englishness, however. Colonial-themed tea rooms hearkened back to a time before the Revolution had supposedly banished the beverage from colonial homes. In 1905 one expert even recommended the meal as a delightful way to celebrate Washington's birthday, explaining how to set a "Patriotic Tea-Table."[175] It might have shocked General Washington to see that tea was no longer the disloyal commodity it had once been and sit down to a table decorated with American flags and other national iconography.

American tea rooms and afternoon tea culture were never wholly English. They might have served scones and English cakes, but tea rooms also offered American specialties such as waffles, cinnamon toast, fried chicken, biscuits, and iced tea.[176] Recipes, advertising, and consumer practices Americanized tea but did not displace coffee, even on the tea table. Food writers and nutritionists such as Mrs. S. T. Rorer, who worked for the *Ladies' Home Journal* in the 1890s, listed tea among those "Foods that are Enemies," claiming it caused indigestion, headaches, and other health problems.[177] The *Ladies' Home Journal* certainly did not reflect the actual habits and tastes of all American consumers, but it was a very influential publication and contributed to the growth of American consumer culture.[178] But as the perceptive expert on the subject, Agnes Repellier, wrote in 1932: "We cannot think that tea gives to Americans what it gives to the English." Tea rooms had nevertheless seized the American woman's imagination.

> Never since the Revolution have we returned so heartily to tea. . . . Innumerable "Tea-Rooms" dot the New England coast, charming little cottages with surroundings as beautiful as land and sea can make them. They are filled with women eating ices, drinking sugary liquids, cold and delicately coloured, or buying the kind of merchandise labeled "Gifts," and which no purchaser wants to keep, or means to, keep for herself.

Repellier was perhaps correct when she proposed that "the setting" was more important than the quality of the food and drink, scoffing that some tea rooms did not even serve tea.[179]

Tea had found a place in American culture during the turn of the century. The tea industry had grown more organized, thousands of shops stocked teas, and increasingly that tea came from the British Empire, though many Americans liked Japanese teas as well. Thomas Lipton, William Ukers, Richard Blechynden, J. J. Grinlinton, and the countless women who opened charming little cottage-style tea rooms selling "gifts" helped build the empire of tea. Tea did not replace coffee, however, and planters' efforts may have backfired over the long run. The countless Oriental displays that appeared in American shops and entertained visitors in Chicago, St. Louis, and at hundreds of food shows stimulated interest in far-off tropical islands such as Ceylon, but it is unclear whether consumers would have seen such places as part of the British Empire. Men and women from Muncie, Indiana, Joplin, Missouri, and Sioux City, Iowa, encountered South Asia every day as they read their morning paper, opened their mailbox, and shopped for groceries. However, they did not necessarily recognize South Asia as British; rather, it became a sphere for their own desires and adventures.

India's and Ceylon's growers and British retailers had come to the United States in the 1880s believing that they merely had to guide Americans to rediscover their lost Britishness. This project appeared to be working during the turn of the century. Overall American tea consumption averaged 1.36 pounds per head between 1880 and 1897. Thereafter aggregate consumption began to fall, but Americans began to drink proportionately more British-grown tea as a share in the overall market, and as one expert wrote in 1901, "Nothing is so convincing to the Yankee as 'tall talk' in advertisements."[180] This may have been true, but as we will see, in general Americans increasingly considered tea a distasteful reminder of colonial dependency and, worse, a feminine beverage singularly inappropriate for "masculine" American tastes. In the postcolonial United States, British entrepreneurs had not quite relinquished the idea that America was British, but Americans certainly had and their memories of empire contributed to the decline of tea drinking in twentieth-century America. In India, colonial politics also determined the nature and meaning of tea consumption but in more immediate ways than in Chicago and St. Louis.

MAKING AN EMPIRE OF TEA DRINKERS IN COLONIAL INDIA

The author of an article titled "Indian Markets for Indian Tea: How to Reach the Native Consumer," published in 1901 in the new journal *Tea*, asserted, "It is somewhat strange that Indian planters, while waiting for the opening up of foreign markets, should apparently overlook the vast market in India itself, which might swallow up immense quantities of the surplus production." While recognizing that America and the Continent should not be neglected, this author surmised that "the seventy millions of Bengal alone ought to be able to consume the output of the adjacent tea plantations of Assam."[181] Another journalist, writing in the Calcutta journal *Capital*, commented, "It is all very well to spend money in America," but "it would be nothing for India to consume at least four ounces per head per annum, and a new customer taking 50 or 60 million lbs. per year would put tea on its legs at once." The journalist surmised that "tea drinking is an easily acquired habit," requiring only the packaging of tea in small, two-ounce packets, sold at one anna each, and then distributed by shops and itinerant hawkers. With "every coolie and tiller of the soil" drinking tea, India would thus achieve "a commercial revolution."[182] What bound all of these writers together was their faith that India was a vast, underdeveloped market that because it was a colony might be easier to control and certainly cheaper to develop than that of the United States. Such thinking about this colonial market naturalized the idea of India as a national space.[183]

The creation of the Indian market was intertwined with national and colonial politics.[184] At the turn of the century, Lord Curzon, India's viceroy, traveled to the tea districts and proposed to planters that their labor problems could be solved if Indians learned to drink tea. Sir Edwin Arnold, poet, writer, journalist, and one-time editor of the *Daily Telegraph*, sanctioned this idea. Arnold had also been the principal of Government College at Poona and authored *The Light of Asia*, an epic poem on the life and teachings of Buddha published in 1879. Arnold imagined that this social beverage would protect Indians from their dangerous water, nourish their bodies, and create "conversation and family peace." Tea would also be a special boon to "the patient, gentle womenfolk, who have few such pleasures." Arnold admitted, however, that tea would be drunk differently in India than in Europe. He supposed that the "Hindoo housewife" would most likely drink tea "as the Japanese take it, pure and simple, without cumbrous paraphernalia," such as milk and sugar and the "spoons, plates, and cream jugs."[185] Arnold, who lived for a time in Japan and was married to a Japanese woman, believed there might be pan-Asian drink cultures. He certainly considered tea a civilizing force.

At the time Curzon and Arnold were endorsing tea and proposing it would "civilize" Indians, groups such as the Anti-Slavery Society and the Aborigines' Protection Society were publicly questioning the "civility" of Portuguese, Belgian, and British planters who had introduced modern slaveries in Africa and elsewhere.[186] The Edwardian popular press was filled with stories and images of colonial atrocities in the Congo in particular. Sir Henry Cotton, the chief commissioner for Assam, even admitted that his region's tea growers were slave drivers, and in 1903 a notorious court case reinforced such views. W. A. Bain, a young planter, was sentenced to six months' imprisonment for having beaten a coolie to death in Cachar. He had been found guilty of "simple assault," but the judge stated that the European jury had treated the case too lightly so he gave Bain a heavier sentence to "prevent similar punishments of natives."[187] Bain's brother appealed the case, but it appears that Bain served his sentence; he also became an industry leader who led the defense against the charge that tea planters were the "twentieth-century representatives of the slave holders of the Southern States."[188] Planters sold tea in India to make money and dispose of surpluses, but they also saw tea and advertising as a way to improve their public image.

In India, planters often described advertising as akin to spreading the gospel, and, like missionaries, publicists were often unwelcome. For example, the trade paper *Tea* congratulated planters for their "philanthropic efforts to spread the blessings of tea among the heathen who sit in darkness and smoke opium. Tea is what the benighted Indians require for their social elevation, and tea they must take."[189] Some planters also formed an informal "temperance party" that agitated against alcohol and for tea. These advocates repeatedly espoused tea as "the cause of health and temperance" and a cure for fever, dysentery, and other diseases.[190] While we do not know if Indian consumers bought into this civilizing story, the language publicists used to describe their efforts was not the same as in the United States or UK at this time. Basically, planters and distributors promoted the idea that Indians would have to be taught what was good for them.

While both the British and Indian nationalists believed that the tea habit was a creation of colonialism, as we saw in the first chapter, this was not precisely the case.[191] Merchants living in Surat drank Chinese tea in the seventeenth century, and as far as we know the first coffeehouse (which also served tea) opened in Calcutta in 1780.[192] People living in the hills of Assam and other parts of the northeast and traders along the borders with Central Asia also consumed tea. In the early nineteenth century, European and Indian planters began to sell directly off their estates, and we know that Maniram Dewan developed local tea markets in the 1840s and 1850s. The Tea Planters of the Kangra Valley, a body that uniquely included two female growers, claimed to be "pioneers of the introduction of the custom of tea drinking among the native population in India."[193] The growth of plantations inevitably led to the growth of local markets, but it should be noted that Indians, like so many others, were also importing a great deal of Chinese tea. In 1880 over a million and a half pounds of Chinese tea were imported into India, and planters believed that most of this was consumed by "natives."[194]

At the end of the century, merchants and tea planters began to try to wean Indians and British colonists from their taste for Chinese teas and teach those who were ignorant of its pleasures to drink the Indian brew. English- and vernacular-language newspapers included advertisements for Indian-owned shops and brands.[195] The Calcutta tea merchant I. B. Gupta advertised in *The Statesman*, the leading English-language paper, and the Bengali women's magazine, *Antahpur*, in 1899 (if not before).[196] Targeting the wealthy Indian housewife, the British, and the Anglo-Indian community, Gupta advertised his tea as "The Favorite Drink" sold everywhere.[197] Also based in Calcutta, Prankissen Chatterjee advertised his "Pure Indian Tea: Direct from the Garden" in *The Statesman* in 1899.[198] The London-based Kaiser-I-Hind Tea Press Company sold machines that turned fannings and dust into compressed cakes, a convenient and cheap version of "Indian tea" for the poorest consumer.[199] In 1887 some "gentlemen" in the tea industry held a meeting in Calcutta to launch a company that would purchase low-quality teas, package them in very small quantities, and distribute them among native village shopkeepers, asserting, "It is well known that natives of all classes have a great liking for tea."[200] Investors sunk capital into this scheme.[201] Around the same time, the big British-owned companies, George Payne, Brooke Bond, and Lipton's, began to advertise tea to Indian consumers.[202] Working with these big distributors, the Indian Tea Association eagerly took up the task of converting India's "native populations into an empire of tea drinkers."[203]

Although all these merchants were excited about the Indian consumer, they also used simplistic racial, religious, and class stereotypes and described Indians as ignorant souls who needed to be forced to have new wants, not educated rational consumers like the Americans encountered earlier in this chapter. In 1901 one journalist admitted, "The coolie is, for the most part, utterly ignorant of the incalculable benefits to be derived from drinking . . . [tea, but] steps are being taken to awaken him to a sense of his needs." He credited the Indian Tea Association for beginning to convince the coolie that he does indeed need tea: "By the time that coolie has disposed of all those free samples it is hoped that the tea habit will have taken possession of him, and that his annas will contribute to the material salvation of the industry."[204] The passive voice is important here. Indian consumers were often described as passive and ignorant beings in need of a stern education. Such language suggests that this writer felt distant from and likely confused by Indian culture, particularly with its myriad caste and religious traditions shaping dietary habits. It also implies a certain discomfort that a great British industry needed colonial consumers for its survival. Other colonial subjects were also described in the same derogatory manner, particularly those in Africa and the Middle East. For example, when commenting on a business trip to Egypt, Mr. Henry Bois told the "Tea Tattler" that he might "be able to convince the Fellaheen that they only want British-grown tea to complete the benefits that are supposed to have showered upon them through British occupation of their country."[205]

Such condescension shaped business and advertising practices. Though it is unlikely that tea planters read Thorstein Veblen, they certainly shared his assumptions about the sociology of consumption when they argued that tastes trickled down the social scale from "ruling chiefs," especially those who had visited Europe, to government servants and village landlords.[206] While Veblen saw consumption as a kind of religion, tea experts worried that Indian religions might hinder market growth. Some believed that orthodox Hindus were prejudiced "against tea," but most felt there were no true dietary restrictions on tea as such and in fact religious laws could benefit tea: "Tea ought to prove a veritable godsend to the coolie, whose religious and caste prejudices oblige him to be very fastidious in the choice of his liquid refreshments. Alcohol is tabooed by the Mohammedan, but neither his creed, nor that of the Hindu, so far as I am aware, contains any condemnation against tea."[207] Race and religion inflected business decisions as experts denied diversity by effectively lumping all of India's populace into two categories, Muslim or Hindu. And both were of course "Oriental" in their tastes. In a similar way that the tea trade believed that Americans' British heritage shaped their tastes, they also held that Indians' "Oriental" nature made them natural tea drinkers. One author, for example, was convinced that Muslims in the Punjab, Sind, and Baluchistan "will readily take to tea-drinking for it is the universal beverage in the big towns of Afghanistan and Central Asia, and at every important halting-place of caravans."[208] The author thus hoped India's Muslim population would share the predilections of those who, because they lived near the Silk/Tea Road, had enjoyed tea for centuries.

The irony here is that though tea promoters spent much time describing India's ancient cultural traditions, when the ITA launched a widespread and long-lasting publicity campaign, its efforts differed little from those used in the United States, Australia, and Great Britain. The organization took tea to public gatherings, demonstrated how and where tea was grown, and showed consumers how to "properly" brew and drink the beverage. ITA tea stalls were erected in railway stations, in post offices, at large workplaces, at leisure events, and at religious and other festivals. The organization also encouraged the growth of tea shops and built tea pavilions at numerous exhibitions.[209] Finally, they subsidized and enabled the growth of large-scale British-owned retailing.

Immediately after Curzon mentioned the civilizing effects of drinking tea, Messrs. Yule and Co. agreed to distribute tea to the "native population" without remuneration for three years. The ITA and most of the large agency houses contributed three quarters of a million pounds to finance this effort.[210] They also funded Messrs. Parry and Co., Lipton's, and Brooke Bond. In 1903, these companies and the ITCC literally divided India into distinct territories in order, as a Brooke Bond executive explained, "to prevent any clashing or overlapping." The ITA also provided Brooke Bond with a £500 per annum subsidy to help them expand Indian consumption.[211] It hired Lipton's to display Indian tea at the United Provinces Exhibition in 1910 and other exhibitions as well. As they did elsewhere, exhibition goers drank free cups of tea, read pamphlets, and saw pictures extolling the modernity of India's tea gardens.[212]

Generally speaking, Hindu orthodoxy did not discount tea but it did frown upon public dining because of questions of purity and food preparation, but also because eating in public was said to "leave the diner vulnerable to evil influences."[213] Nevertheless, a public dining culture did emerge in major cities. Parsees from Persia opened tea shops, for example, in Bombay, Delhi, and other regions of urban India. Typically near large labor yards, these shops catered to diverse religious and caste backgrounds, serving aerated water, tea, and coffee. The tea, known as "Irani" tea, was initially from China, however.[214] The Irani cafés grew into full restaurants serving a distinctive Parsi cuisine in a setting of marble tabletops, mirrors, and bentwood chairs and became known as the "poor man's parlor," though some offered facilities for families and "special accommodation for ladies." They also sold canned goods, biscuits, and other "Westernized items." In 1909 Bombay reportedly had 494 tea and coffeehouses, encouraging the taste for both of these new beverages.[215] Everywhere, tea shops contributed to market growth, but in India these began as masculine institutions.

European, mixed-race, and indigenous employees distributed a great many free samples. Often these agents were already involved in selling tea. For example, the ITA hired a German naval officer who had been distributing tea on the frontier with Persia, in western Persia, and in Turkestan.[216] This agent also catered to the Indian army because he felt that soldiers did not possess the natives' "inherent suspicion of European articles of consumption."[217] According to one report, such efforts had made headway "amongst the men of the native army, on the railways, at the exhibitions, in the theaters," as well as among miners and mica and jute workers.[218] Such public venues were especially useful in India because, in general, tea promoters felt barred from the private household, despite the fact that they sponsored Indian-only essay contests on such topics as "How to bring Indian tea to Indian Homes."[219] One of the ITA's employees, a "smart Dacca-born Indian assistant," even began to segment this market when he evidently told Hindus "that tea is a vegetarian's drink" and Indians in general that tea was a "product of their Mother Country."[220]

Of course, most Indians could barely feed themselves, let alone spend money on tea. The ITA understood this and produced a variant of Chinese brick tea, a very cheap commodity that could be kept for long periods of time without becoming stale. They also tried to sell iced tea, and several years before the exhibition in St. Louis, a tea agency in India sold this "refreshing draught" at railway stations, markets, jetties, and football matches in Lahore and Calcutta.[221] Richard Blechynden was no doubt well aware of such efforts before he introduced the drink in St. Louis. This history has remained hidden in the archives, however, rather than boomed in advertising for more than a century. Often marketing in India was quite simple, but the ITA also dove headfirst into the most modern forms of advertising as well. Just before the war, the ITA hired the well-known French firm Messrs. Pathé Frères to make a film to teach "natives" how tea was manufactured and thereby presumably encourage them to identify the drink as a native production.[222] Such efforts tried to adjust the commodity to fit the market and began to rebrand a "European" commodity as an indigenous good.

While busily publicizing the merits of their imperial product in India, the United States, Australia, Canada, and elsewhere, planters also became involved in British politics for they recognized that making markets took more than advertising, lectures, and free samples. Growers understood that fiscal and trade policies influenced prices and sales even in well-established markets. While there is no doubt that tea planters wielded significant political power in the colonies, this was not the case at home. In fact, while they learned the skills of political lobbying and influence, many regarded themselves as politically weak outsiders who lacked a voice in the metropole. This sense of being outsiders was particularly strong during and after the turn of the century, when the metropolitan government relied on their nation's remarkable tea habit to pay for war.

TAXING TEA AND PLANTERS' POLITICS IN EDWARDIAN ENGLAND

During the South African War (1899–1902), Britain's Conservative government raised the tea duty to offset the costs of this imperial conflict. This decision led to a short-lived but interesting episode in planter activism that demonstrates how planters influenced metropolitan politics to protect their markets at home and in so doing contributed to the transformation of liberalism in Edwardian Britain. In this period, most planters were free-trade liberals, but they nevertheless began to develop arguments that the Tory Party would put forth after World War I.[223] As planters fought against the new tax on tea, they relied on and promoted older understandings of tea as a sober and healthy beverage, echoing the liberal critique of the East India Company's monopoly nearly a century earlier. The methods of liberal politics had changed considerably, however. Using their sizable resources built up from the tea cess in both Ceylon and India, planters financed their politics with the same funds they were using to popularize their teas elsewhere. What is also striking about this political moment is that tea growers hoped to forge an alliance with working-class women, whom they regarded as consumer citizens. The fight to lower the new tax also drew India and Ceylon together in ways that helped them confront new problems and rivals in the twentieth century.

The South African War was longer and more difficult than had been expected. It served to highlight the weakness of the imperial state and the poor physical health of the working classes, and it resurrected the question of whether and how impoverished consumers should pay for war. The Conservative government believed that they should. In 1900 Chancellor of the Exchequer Sir Michael Hicks Beach raised the tea duty from 4 to 6d. a pound. Along with hefty military spending, the rising costs of government and social reform had increased state expenditures to a level that threatened the liberal underpinnings of the Victorian fiscal state.[224] Hicks Beach also raised the duty on coffee, cocoa, beer, spirits, and tobacco, and reinstated that on sugar, but tea planters' associations, importers, and distributors pointed out that while coffee and cocoa were "chiefly imported from foreign countries," tea was "grown by British subjects and . . . British capital."[225] Because Britons no longer drank Chinese teas, Hicks Beach had unwittingly raised a new question—namely, did a tax that purported to be for imperial defense unfairly penalize a British imperial industry?

The higher tax was not removed after hostilities ended, and in 1904 Austen Chamberlain raised the duty to 8d. per pound. The additional 2d. was removed in 1905, but the "war tax" remained so India's and Ceylon's growers formed the Anti-Tea-Duty League (ATDL) to fight against "The Injustice of the High Duty."[226] A non-partisan lobbying body whose sole aim was to pressure government to lower the tea tax, the ATDL united growers from diverse colonies and articulated a new vision of working-class consumers as imperial citizens. This group's agitation thus sheds light on the political and economic contexts that propelled the use of imperial rhetoric and imagery in early twentieth-century commodity culture.[227]

The ATDL's main significance lay in how they used new media and propaganda techniques to create an *imagined* alliance between the colonial planter and the working-class consumer. League propaganda described planters as selflessly toiling in the jungle to satisfy and indeed comfort the poor, beleaguered, typically female tea drinker. The ATDL employed the latest advertising techniques, which it paid for with the tea cess, which coincidently had just finished financing the Louisiana Purchase Exhibition. ATDL rhetoric and tactics took much from the free-trade movement of this era, and thus it gained sympathy among leading Liberals.[228] Yet its popular imperialism resembled that of the Tariff Reform League (TRL), which had just been founded by Joseph Chamberlain in 1903. The TRL sought to erect preferential imperial tariffs in order to develop empire markets, stimulate the domestic economy, solve unemployment, and help pay for much-needed social reforms. Free traders contended instead that tariff reform would raise the cost of food and thereby hurt the poor consumer.[229] At this point, the ATDL placed their bet with the Liberals and helped achieve their famous landslide victory in 1906, but as we will see in the next chapter, after the war these same planters would abandon free trade and increasingly push for imperial preferences. At this point, however, their efforts supported the Liberal Party and drove it to think about the British Empire.

The ATDL was founded in January 1905 at a joint meeting of the Indian Tea Association, the Ceylon Planters' Association, large distributors, and colonial politicians. F. A. Roberts, chairman of the ITA and an executive with the Jorehaut and Darjeeling tea companies, was elected chairman. Sir West Ridgeway, who had been governor of Ceylon, became president. The Executive Committee also included Ceylon's most famous planter-publicists, H. K. Rutherford, J. L. Loudan-Shand, and Sir John Grinlinton. Grinlinton, it will be recalled, had been Ceylon's tea commissioner for the 1904 Louisiana Purchase Exhibition, and he became president of the Ceylon Association in 1912 and a planting member in the Ceylon Legislative Council. Arthur Brooke, the owner of Brooke, Bond and Co., and A. G. Stanton, Britain's premier expert on tea statistics and economics and founder of the tea brokers Gow, Wilson and Stanton, Ltd., represented distribution on the ATDL board.[230] Sir Roper Lethbridge, whom we met introducing J. Berry White in 1887, developed many of the movement's economic arguments.[231]

The ATDL's day-to-day operations were almost entirely the handiwork of Herbert Compton, a retired planter, popular writer, and well-known political propagandist. Compton had been one of the Tariff Reform League's leading publicists, and so the tea industry asked him to "do for tea what the agitation of the 'Forties' did for corn."[232] This request referred to the free-trade publication *The Hungry Forties*. Published in 1904 by Cobden's granddaughter Jane Cobden Unwin and her husband, this book was a collection of letters from elderly Britons who recalled their personal suffering caused by the high cost of food before the corn laws were repealed in the 1840s. *The Hungry Forties*, as Frank Trentmann has argued, helped create a popular memory or history for free trade.[233] This was the case, but Compton thought the book was a poor example of propaganda. He nevertheless agreed: "the taxation of food does, and ever will, and rightly, stink like an exhumed corpse in the nostrils of the living people of this country."[234] Compton believed he could make cheap tea as symbolically important as the cheap loaf.

Compton feverishly wrote press releases and letters to the editors of a wide variety of papers, and he launched a new journal, the *Monthly Message of the Anti-Tea-Duty League*. He published a book called *Come to Tea with Us* and a collection of letters and articles titled *What Started the League?*[235] He was also fond of posters, and in the summer of 1905, 8,000 ATDL posters were plastered on hoardings throughout Britain and reproduced in newspapers, periodicals, and the trade press. Within a few months, Compton had also placed 50 cartoons and approximately 3,000 letters and articles in the press, which he then sent to politicians in Britain, India, and Ceylon, to agency houses, wholesale firms, grocers, caterers, shipping companies, temperance and philanthropic agencies, and public libraries. The league's London office also became a permanent "tea display" designed to educate government and industry. Finally, the league lobbied sitting and prospective politicians and canvassed for those (typically but not always Liberal) candidates who endorsed their cause.[236]

League publicity had to find a place on the hoarding alongside free trade, tariff reform, Irish Home Rule, women's suffrage, and a score of other issues, so posters used bright colors, repetition, humor, simple designs, and the powerful argument that the poor paid a higher tax for their tea than did the rich.[237] In *Come to Tea with Us*, Compton essentially revived the same sort of arguments that liberals had used before when he wrote: "Tea is warmth, is comfort, is solace to our narrow lives. Tea leads us not into temptation, supports us in sobriety, strengthens us in industry, and stimulates us to labour in long hours. Tea is as bread in our mouths, and in our women's mouths, and in our children's mouths. Tea must be free!"[238] None of these ideas was new, and in this period battles over free trade and tariff reform had especially politicized the spectacle of the hungry and suffering woman and child.[239]

ATDL letters, posters, and cartoons visually and rhetorically claimed, however, that it was the tea planter who was fighting for the poor female consumer. A "Tea Planter on Furlough" wondered, for example, whether the duty was so high because "a woman's drink" did not incite male voters, as would a tax on beer. A self-declared "Assamite" maintained that "Tea is an absolute necessity of our daily diet. . . . It is the one comfort of the very poor, especially women and children, and it is a notable factor in promoting temperance."[240] While many posters characterized the poor woman as in need of protection, others illustrated women as political actors—a radical act during a time when women's suffrage was gaining momentum and threatening the very definition of politics as a male preserve. This is not to say that the league supported women's suffrage, a cause they avoided, but Compton did hire female canvassers and league artwork illustrated the collective power of female consumer citizens. A "Deputation of Charwomen to Parliamentary Candidate," for example, recalled the march of French market women to Versailles in October 1789 (fig. 6.4). Just as market women attacked the authority of the French monarchy and pointed out its failure to feed the people, these charwomen challenged this parliamentary candidate's assertion that "revenue must be raised."[241] Though positioned below the politician on the dais, these female consumers appear to be virtuous defenders of free trade and low taxes. To be sure, female consumers had for centuries enforced the moral economy. The difference here is that colonial businessmen used the female consumer to achieve their own political goals.

League publicity also validated the political power of the workingman (fig. 6.5). In the poster "It Don't Seem Right to Me" a worker versified:

There's a question which touches us every one,
And touches us twice a day;
Whenever we drink a cup of tea

FIGURE 6.4. "Deputation of Charwomen to Parliamentary Candidate," *Monthly Message of the Anti-Tea-Duty League*, 31 December 1905. (By permission of the British Library, shelf mark LOU.LON 963 [1905])

Do you know what we've got to pay?
A tax as much as the tea is worth!
Which makes it plain to see
We've got to pay a penn'orth of tax
For drinking a penn'orth of tea![242]

A photograph of this poster republished in the *Monthly Message* focused on the political power of the masses and visual power of the poster by showing crowds of men reading the poster in Birmingham, Manchester, London, and Liverpool. As we can see from this illustration, the Edwardian hoarding necessarily conflated buying and drinking brand-name cheap goods with the rights of citizenship. Yet at this point, tea planters were asking workingmen to use their vote to defend imperial business.

ATDL pamphlets, such as *Tea: The Injustice of the High Duty*, drew evidence from poverty and budget studies, government blue books, Adam Smith, and other political economists to argue that taxing tea threatened the nation and liberalism itself. Compton argued, "We who are Free Traders, tax a British grown product without mercy and fling our free food views to the winds when it comes to dealing for revenue purposes with a staple article of the people's diet."[243] League

FIGURE 6.5. "It Don't Seem Right to Me," *Monthly Message of the Anti-Tea-Duty League*, 31 January 1906. (By permission of the British Library, shelf mark Asia Pacific & Africa SV 790)

publicity even appropriated the Boston Tea Party as a symbol of all colonists' right to protest arbitrary and despotic metropolitan power. This move made their trade-based politics appear to be a chapter in a larger story about imperial governance and democratization. In *Come to Tea with Us*, Compton praised the American revolutionaries who had so vociferously declared in 1773 that "tea should not be taxed."[244] The colonial story appealed to planters who identified with the call against taxation without representation and used it to present themselves as politically voiceless. The American Revolution also played into another key rhetorical turn, fashioning the planter as a political and social outsider.

League rhetoric thus stressed the unity of colony and metropole, planters and consumers. Letters from supportive planters made much of their so-called victimization. "One who has suffered" wrote in a letter to the editor of the *Leeds Mercury* how he had "spent the best years of his life in the frontier jungles of India, and found himself none the richer for it."[245] Another writer proposed, "The British tea-planter is 10,000 miles away and has no vote, and so can be mulcted with impunity."[246] "Ten Years in the Jungle" recalled a harrowing tale in which planters were "bravely holding on to their estates . . . at a dead loss, unable to have their children properly educated . . . all because of this cruel, merciless tax on tea."[247] In a long letter Compton sent to the *Pall Mall Gazette* in January 1905, he observed how "it is not often any one hears anything about the tea planter. He is an inarticulate and unheeded unit of Empire, for all practical and demonstrative purposes buried, like his own tea bushes, in the jungle." Rather than living a life of luxury, the planter was enfeebled by "an enervating climate . . . fever, cholera, dysentery." On top of all these inconveniences, this hardworking British subject "has no time to write to the papers . . . [and] he has no political vote" and thus must call upon "the consumer" to "make his power felt, and extort pledges from his Parliamentary representatives."[248] Throughout all its propaganda, the ATDL repeatedly stated: "the consumer is the only person who can remedy this state of affairs."[249] Though they toiled in the jungle, planters asserted that they were no less British than a Yorkshire woolen manufacturer, suggested one writer.[250] Tea coming from India and Ceylon is "British grown in British territory, with British capital, under the direct superintendence of British planters, and with labour of British colonial subjects . . . the producer, let it never be forgotten, is not a foreigner, but of our own race."[251] Planters, and by extension the Empire, made "a universal article of diet . . . a National drink." "Chinese tea was the luxury of the rich, but now Indian tea is the comfort of the poor" became an oft-repeated league mantra.[252]

Planters were of course spending countless hours writing to the papers and cultivating a pathetic self-portrait to shape policy.[253] When Austen Chamberlain lowered the tea duty in 1905 he acknowledged the ATDL and repeated the argument that "our present supplies of this article come almost entirely from British dependencies and Colonies."[254] Numerous Liberal candidates made similar arguments in the run-up to the 1906 election.[255] The league then claimed that their agitation had secured the Liberal victory. Compton explained the £3,000 he spent on over two million leaflets, sixty thousand posters, and contributions to election funds had helped 163 league-backed candidates win their seats.[256]

Yet, just after the Liberal landslide, the ATDL abruptly dismissed Herbert Compton, probably because he had started criticizing the large distributors who had also supported his cause. After he was fired, Compton formed the Free Tea League and lashed out at the Tea Buyers' Association, a body he argued represented "the capitalist monopolist." It was, as he put it, "Capital on the one side and the People and Planters on the other; the Monopolist *versus* the Consumer and Colonist."[257] Compton accurately saw how the buying side of the industry was gaining power. In 1906 approximately twenty firms controlled the sale of tea in Britain, and the higher duty had encouraged amalgamation since only larger firms could afford to pay the tax.[258] Compton's animus was an updated expression of the tensions we saw shape the blending debate in the 1880s. He believed buyers cared little about the empire, and to a certain degree he was right.

Compton's career was cut short, however, when he met an untimely death from drowning after having fallen overboard on a voyage to Madeira in 1906. It is not clear whether this was an accident, murder, or suicide since Compton had been suffering from a nervous breakdown brought on by his political frustrations and years of struggling with malaria.[259] His ideas and his methods nevertheless became especially popular and widely accepted in the 1920s and 1930s.

Rivalries between India and Ceylon and China and Japan encouraged numerous agencies to seek export markets and develop American, colonial, and what came to be understood as "native" or local markets in India. Planters had acquired a tremendous faith in publicity and they were convinced that with enough money, drive, and local knowledge, propaganda could make markets anywhere. The Ceylon and Indian tea associations believed their efforts were slowly switching North Americans from East Asian green to South Asian black teas after the Chicago World's Fair.[260] They also noted the same shift in Australia and the rest of Oceania, and they downplayed the fact that per capita consumption began to decline in the early twentieth century. As we have seen, print advertising was but a small part of a much bigger effort. Personal contacts and relationships were also very important, as they were in shaping the UK market. The planters who became retailers, exhibition experts, journalists, buyers, and advertisers maintained close relations with their friends, families, and colleagues on the plantation, and this transnational community helped fashion an imperial consumer culture that on the surface looked the same across the empire and the United States but at the same time began to also reflect growing nationalism. Thomas Lipton was a well-known member of this community; so too were Herbert Compton, J. L. Loudan-Shand, Richard Blechynden, J. J. Grinlinton, William Ukers, and the unnamed but "smart Dacca-born Indian assistant" who sought to teach the "blessings" of tea to indigenous populations. Further research on the social history of consumption within India and other markets will need to explore the way local cultures shaped the meaning of tea in each context. Here, however, I have emphasized how a transnational commercial community forged in newspapers and trade journals, at exhibitions, in meetings, and at home recognized differences in consumers' ability and desire to consume but believed that tastes could be cultivated the same way around the world.

Wherever they traveled, planters conceived of the creation of markets as akin to the process of colonization, and racial and nationalistic thinking determined many of their assumptions. They held a missionary-like belief that despite diversity all people had the potential to like and want the same things. They invented an ideal of a global consumer, of a being willing if not able to consume virtually anything. This idea was central to nineteenth- and early twentieth-century forms of globalization. It was especially visible in the tea industry because tea had become such an inexpensive product. However, this version of globalization was not a democratizing or equalizing notion and it did not create a homogeneous global consumer culture. When discussing North Americans and Australians, for example, planters imagined that they were bringing civilized drinks to sophisticated "British" consumers. When they worked in India, planters held they were carrying the gospel of consumerism to people they regarded as untouched by the market. Preexisting ideas, local economies and politics, and consumer and retail practices shaped the meaning and uses surrounding the commodity. Tea planters and their publicists saw the world in both global and local terms, and they struggled to balance their faith in the unifying nature of consumerism with racial and national ideologies that promoted difference. During and after World War I, this quandary became increasingly politicized as governments and citizens began to express new understandings of the relationship between the economy, consumption, and the state.

7

"EVERY KITCHEN AN
EMPIRE KITCHEN"

The Politics of Imperial Consumerism

On a June evening in 1923, nearly three hundred politicians and businessmen gathered at the annual Assam Dinner in Great Queen Street, London. This was a lavish and lighthearted but not apolitical meeting of imperial and metropolitan power brokers. Most in attendance had spent their careers managing plantations and working for export, import, and retail firms. Others were involved in shipping and insurance companies, banks, and agency houses. Viscount Peel, secretary of state for India, D. M. Dalal, India's high commissioner, and Viscount Inchcape, who would soon become the 1st Earl of Inchcape, also dined together that evening.[1] These were some of the most influential architects of the global economy in the 1920s. Inchcape, for example, had been born James Mackay and was the son of a wealthy shipmaster, but by 1923 he reigned over a commercial empire that included the largest shipping group in the world, controlling lines between Britain, Asia, and Australia. With interests in coal, jute, cotton, wool, coffee, and tea, among other commodities, Mackay's reach could be felt in South and Southeast Asia, the Far East and Persian Gulf, and West Africa.[2]

In his welcoming address, the chairman of the Indian Tea Association, none other than the convicted murderer W. A. Bain, described the dinner as a chance to "renew old friendships, to revive old memories, and to recall the good old times that have passed; to discuss, and possibly, grouse over, the problems and perplexities which surround the present, and to conjure up rosy pictures of the future." Those perplexities included the dislocations of total war, revolution in Russia, rapidly shifting commodity prices, and labor unrest and nationalism in the tea gardens and throughout the Subcontinent. In painting a "rosy picture" of the future, Bain assured his audience that worker protests had quieted and manufacturing had improved. He also jested that the recent discovery that tea was rich in vitamin B implied that the "tea gardens of Assam" could now claim, along with the "playing fields of Eton," a share in the "victories of the Empire." When Viscount Peel mounted the podium he too was anxious, but he turned his worries into a joke about women's suffrage: "Nowadays, when women have votes—and they are your great clientele—I suppose that the consumption of tea occupies a position in the political arena such as it never attained before." Women's vote had changed the rules of the game, but it was more than female suffrage that had politicized the tea business. As Peel himself explained, the planters had cleverly deployed the "whole machinery of Governments, military and public offices . . . as machinery for your own advertisements." Here he was referring to India and describing how the tea associations had garnered government backing for their relentless pursuit of Indian consumers during the previous two decades.[3] These speeches may have been delivered in a breezy style, but they captured the anxieties of imperial business during the interwar era. Wartime shortages, the growth of socialism and organized labor movements, the expansion of "indigenous" capitalism, and constitutional changes in India and elsewhere in the empire, not to mention the near collapse of world trade with the onset of the Great Depression, politicized imperial commodities and consumers in ways that had not occurred since the Boston Tea Party.

On that June evening in 1923, tea was in a somewhat unique position compared to other commodities because the British Empire virtually monopolized this global trade, along with its ancillary businesses. Tea "is largely a concern of the British Empire," explained an Imperial Economic Committee report in 1931; it had reached 1 percent of the value of the total merchandise entering world trade. The report continued:

> Over 70 per cent of the tea exported is produced in the Empire, and nearly 70 per cent is consumed by the Empire. Over two-thirds of the entire capital engaged in tea production is provided by the Empire. All the machinery employed in India and Ceylon is of Empire origin, and over 60 per cent of the chests used for the transport of tea are imported from Empire countries.[4]

This monopoly was never absolute, however, and Dutch East Indian teas were making headway in major markets, while the Chinese began to export and advertise in Australia as well.[5] The planting industry met such problems by creating powerful new corporate bodies, affiliating themselves with popular political movements, and mobilizing the political and cultural power of shareholders, shopkeepers, and consumers. Viscount Peel had joked about female suffrage and tea planters' habit of using the "machinery of government" to create markets, but what he was really talking about was a near worldwide abandonment of the idea that politics and economy, and indeed public and private, should be separate spheres. After World War I, nearly all liberal, fascist, socialist, and nationalist states and parties lost confidence in free trade. Yet this crisis of faith in liberalism endowed consumers with the power to make or break nations and empires.[6] The nationalization of consumption legitimized, expanded, and in a counterintuitive fashion globalized the advertising and culture industries.

The economic nationalism of the interwar years altered what it meant to be a consumer and the meaning of imperial commodities such as tea in nearly every national setting, but its impact varied considerably.[7] In Britain, tea jumped on a powerful "Buy British" bandwagon and gained support from quasi-governmental agencies such as the Empire Marketing Board, conservative ideologues, politicians, and journalists, and especially from conservative women.[8] Together these groups promoted the consumption of British-grown tea as an imperial duty, rather than a form of personal pleasure, an expression of individualism, or even a democratic right. In the United States, high levels of consumerism came to be identified as a defining feature of national identity, a way of life, "a right and entitlement."[9] Government policies shaped and created this ideology and justified the export of American power abroad. The belief that consumption was a national practice hurt the tea market, however, because consumers spent money on new, more exciting "American" drinks, and tea came to be seen as an old-fashioned, un-American, and feminine brew. In India, colonial administrators and the tea interests proposed that drinking tea would pacify labor and nationalist unrest, but nationalists turned this story on its head and rejected tea advertising and the Planter Raj as a form of European imperialism. Unlike Revolutionary America, however, nationalist calls to boycott British brands had no perceptible impact on per capita consumption and the Indian market continued to expand. Everywhere, however, men and women across the class and political spectrum agreed on one thing: consumerism was a powerful political force that could sustain or topple empires and nations. This licensed women, the working classes, and non-white colonial consumers to emerge as both the allies and enemies of global businesses. Though they were just beginning to be invited to the table, these troubling subjects were whispering in the background at the Assam Dinner in London in 1923. The power brokers who dined together that night soon began to squabble with one another as well. Ultimately, consumers became imperial citizens, but not in the ways that the men at the Assam Dinner anticipated.

AFTERNOON TEA IN WAR AND PEACE

In July 1917, John Maitland, who worked for Ridgways, a firm that had been exporting to the United States since the 1880s, explained to one of his American agents, "I need hardly tell you that we are having a very difficult time. . . . The export business from this country is entirely stopped, and we have to arrange supplies direct from the East to America."[10] Maitland's comments reflected a dramatic shift in the global political economy. World War I brought to a close an expansive phase in global capitalism and ushered in a time when Europe's and especially Britain's share of world trade declined.[11] Labor and material shortages, transportation difficulties, and the shift to military production transformed the manufacture and movement of commodities around the globe. The colonial tea industry shifted directions as well. Of course, trade with Germany and Austria ceased, cess collections diminished with the decline in exports, and advertising in the United States terminated. In England, and most likely elsewhere, the need for the government to limit consumption called into question the morality of the most luxurious versions of afternoon tea. Tea for soldiers, factory workers, and colonial consumers was an altogether different matter, however. Despite numerous problems and a general tendency for demand to outstrip supply, planters and exporters continued to advertise, explore new markets, and defend tea's place in the wartime diet.

War politicized food and provisioning among all belligerents. Blockades and the use of fats and fertilizers to produce weapons rather than food produced hunger and mass starvation on the home front, especially in Russia and Germany. Food riots erupted and consumers protested not only absolute want but also the legitimacy of governments that could not feed their people.[12] State intervention became the norm even in Britain, which had gone to war believing that it could hold on to "normal" laissez-faire principles.[13] Although it imported nearly 60 percent of its food supplies, Britain did not face the extreme shortages of other nations. Civilians certainly felt deprived, but higher earnings, smaller families, and an adjustment in family expenditures helped maintain and at times improve the working-class diet.[14] Nevertheless, the rising prices for basic foodstuffs and long shopping queues politicized consumers, particularly working-class housewives. New consumer councils and feminist and labor organizations created the conditions for the consumer to speak and act in the public sphere.[15] Consumption had become political, a fact well recognized by one working-class mother who, in describing wartime shortages, spoke out: "I was always a bit of a Socialist but I am a rank one now and I've a vote at the next General Election. And I've a tongue and when I am waiting in mobs it is not quiet. Nothing will make my tongue wag more than want of a cup of tea."[16] The tea industry appropriated rather than suppressed this expression of consumer rights, while the government responded haphazardly to consumer demands.

By the middle of the war, food shortages and consumer and labor unrest pushed the British government to shed its commitment to free trade. In 1916 the Ministry of Food was established, and within a year its 40,000-person staff was charged with reorganizing the entire food provision system. This body was ambivalent about how to treat tea. Some measures labeled tea a foreign luxury that should be heavily taxed. Early in the war, Liberal Chancellor of the Exchequer Reginald McKenna raised the duty on tea, coffee, and cocoa by 50 percent. The Indian Tea Association protested to little effect.[17] The tea industry was, however, in fairly good shape early in the war. Large growers and investors had already diversified into rubber and other commodities useful to the war effort.[18] Good harvests in 1915 and 1916 helped production keep pace with consumption, and, in general, growers were receiving high prices for their tea. The military, an important and large market, made sure that soldiers had ample supplies. However, in 1916 stocks began to fall and the cost of ocean shipment increased, leading retail prices in Britain to rise to nearly double those of 1914.[19] Tea that had averaged at about 1s. 6d. climbed toward 3s. a pound. Consumer protests soon forced the government to consider tea's importance to the war effort. In 1916 the food controller, Lord Devonport, instituted price controls decreeing that 40 percent of all tea had to be retailed at not more than 2s. 4d. Price maintenance implied that tea was a necessity, but at the same time it remained on the Imports Restrictions List of luxury foodstuffs and drinks. This situation reduced imports and created shortages that led to consumer protests.[20] In the autumn of 1917, shoppers waited for hours in long lines to buy limited supplies.[21] By late November, women in Sheffield and elsewhere threatened to raid stores, and by winter crowds were similarly rushing shops and stalls demanding tea and other basic foods.[22] The government contracted for more supplies and instituted new price controls on 90 percent of all tea. In February 1918 rationing was introduced and consumers had to register with their grocer or other dealer in order to receive 2 ounces a week of National Control Tea, for which they paid 2s. 8d. per pound.

Shortages, consumer and industry protests, and government responses all turned upon the question of tea's status as a luxury or necessity. Government authorities and food scientists insisted that "the value of tea from the point of view of food is negligible."[23] Nutritional science did not pay much attention to the drink.[24] These new experts believed that cereals and animal protein were foods and that tea was a luxury.[25] As food shortages and transportation difficulties increased, some in the government attacked afternoon tea, defining it as a wasteful social ritual engaged in by wealthy women with nothing better to do than stuff themselves with sweets.[26] In November 1916, Burton Chadwick, the director of Munitions Overseas Transport, led the attack. "Afternoon tea is not a meal; it is a habit," Chadwick wrote in a letter to *The Times*. Prohibiting this "well-to-do-habit" would level class distinctions and teach all civilians about the "self-sacrifice" needed to achieve victory.[27] Male and female consumers and the lower-middle-class proprietors who served them challenged Chadwick's assessment and effectively invented the notion that tea was a wartime necessity.

Lower-middle-class tea shop and restaurant proprietors and patrons asserted that afternoon tea was a democratic meal enjoyed by men and women of all classes, and that as such it aided the war effort.[28] It was a simple pleasure that helped one deal with shortages, hunger, and long work hours. One officer captured this sentiment well when he wrote, "Men would put up with almost any deprivation as long as they had their tea."[29] A "Worker in South London" also defended the right of women who worked twelve-hour shifts in munitions factories to enjoy the meal.[30] Caterers and their customers insisted that this democratic, temperate, and healthful beverage, and the foods that accompanied tea, maintained a productive and satisfied labor and fighting force.

Despite such protests, afternoon tea did become a victim of wartime shortages when on 18 April 1917 Lord Devonport instituted "The Cake and Pastry Order." The order suppressed the "manufacture and sale of fancy pastries" and virtually abolished "muffins, crumpets, and teacakes." Only bread, sugarless scones, and other creations that did not include more than 30 percent of wheaten flour or 15 percent of sugar were allowed.[31] Opinion and policy had thus turned against the sweetest incarnation of afternoon tea. Women who sipped tea and ate pastries at tea shops, hotels, and other places of public resort had become shirkers, while poor housewives, munitions workers, and soldiers who were serving the nation had earned their right to a hot cup of tea. Crumpets and muffins became suspect pleasures, but tea was protected as a weapon of war and tea importers and growers gained a greater role in government. For example, Richard Piggott, a senior partner in a firm of importers, packers, and wholesale dealers, became chairman of the Tea Control Committee and then director of tea supplies at the Ministry of Food.[32]

In India, tea flowed liberally during the war, and, as Peel had admitted at the Assam Dinner in 1923, planters continued to deploy the "whole machinery of Governments, military and public offices" as "machinery for [their] own advertisements."[33] Whereas tea shops had come under scrutiny in the UK, a Brooke Bond executive commented favorably on the thousands of tea shops that had popped up "over the length and breadth of India," selling affordable tea at prices even the "the poorest natives" could afford.[34] The war also ensured that the Indian army was well supplied. H. W. Newby, who had been Lipton's Calcutta manager and was now the Indian Tea Cess Committee's commissioner in India, convinced over two hundred commanding officers to open tea rooms for their units and mine and factory owners to serve tea in their wartime canteens.[35] The 1917 report of the Indian Tea Cess Committee explained: "The quantity consumed in the mill or factory is not the ultimate object. It is expected that the employee, having learnt to drink tea at his work, will take the habit with him into his home, and so accustom his family and friends to tea."[36] Thus the workplace was in effect an avenue to the household and a critical place to promote new tastes.

Between 1917 and 1920, Newby and his employees also canvassed grocers, demonstrated how to brew tea in countless village bazaars, and set up tea services on the railways and inland steamship lines in the Punjab, the United Provinces, Bengal, Calcutta, and southern India.[37] They painted pro-tea and anti-coffee impressions on city walls. Gramophones, bioscopes, games, music, prizes, and other circus-like attractions flooded public spaces in wartime India and stimulated mass interest in drinking tea.[38] Such tactics seemed to work. Whereas in 1910 India's population had consumed only 13 million pounds of tea per year, by 1920 the country consumed 60 million pounds.[39] Per capita consumption was still low, but India was becoming an important consumer market. The ITCC believed that its colonization of the army and other public spaces had had a dramatic impact.

Whether or not consumption increased or decreased, World War I politicized tea's consumer cultures. In the UK, tea came to be controlled and protected as a wartime necessity, but crumpets, muffins, and pastries were condemned as wasteful drains on the nation's resources. While the metropolitan government sought to restrain consumption and rationed tea, the colonial government worked with industry to ensure that soldiers, workers, and even society's poorest consumers were warmed by a hot cup of tea. People living in or near producing regions drank the tea that could not make it to wartime Europe or the United States. In the empire, the planter class had far more power than they did at home and they were able to shape public policy and inundate the public sphere with tea. This ironically led to the growth of the huge number of what came to be known as *chai wallahs*, or small-scale tea sellers that brew up the drink virtually across the length and breadth of the Subcontinent. In the UK, small-scale tea dealers found it an increasingly difficult environment, while large-scale catering companies were better positioned to ride out the difficulties of this period. During the war, marketers acknowledged the importance of working-class and colonial consumers, but immediately after the war they once again returned to the United States, where a booming economy, the wartime alliance, and Prohibition seemed to offer a world of opportunity.

YOU CAN LEAD A HORSE TO WATER; OR, THE FRUSTRATIONS
OF SELLING AN OLD LADY'S DRINK IN JAZZ-AGE AMERICA

During the 1920s, British business began to think in terms of a kind of "dual mandate" in which they would learn new "American-style" sales strategies and in turn bring British "refinement" to the American consumer. What American methods actually were was not always clear, but in general experts understood them to include market research, professional advertising agencies, and ads that used simple, repetitive phrases and well-drawn images, as well as a liberal use of new media, especially cinema and radio.[40] Though such methods were becoming common in the UK and other countries, they were touted as uniquely American and the key to the growth of its economy in these years. When the British tea industry half-heartedly tried such methods in the United States, they utterly failed to dissuade Americans from their belief that hot tea was feminine, fussy, and weak. While the tea trade could not improve tea's image in the United States, they did develop lasting friendships and partnerships. The colonial tea industry would not have developed its global sales force in the way that it did had its growers not spent so much time selling to reluctant American consumers.

In the early 1920s, British tea growers and exporters hoped that the voracious appetites of the wealthy "Anglo-Saxon" United States could preserve the British Empire. But to harness those appetites, growers needed to spend money and hire professionals. In 1921 the US Tea Association urged their colleagues in India to recognize that "more and more the American people are being swayed by advertising in making their purchases. The feeling is gaining ground that the worthwhile things are advertised."[41] There certainly were critics such as the *Financial Times*, which opined that for the tea trade to spend money in America was equivalent to throwing it down the sink, but the Indian government and planters disagreed and pointed to the fact that Americans were switching from East Asian green teas to South Asian black teas. Pound for pound tea cost twice as much as coffee, but the onset of Prohibition and the fact that both Formosa and Japan were embarking on major campaigns encouraged the ITA to begin a new, vigorous campaign.[42] During these years Ceylon did not have a tea cess, but the Indian government raised the rate of their cess and in 1924 the ITA hired one of Britain's foremost advertisers, Sir Charles Higham, to direct a massive five-year, multimillion-dollar advertising campaign.[43]

Dubbed "an Advertising King" and "super-propagandist" by the *Planters' Chronicle*, Sir Charles Higham was one of two agency heads who dominated Britain's interwar advertising profession.[44] Higham's career was remarkably similar to that of his friend Sir Thomas Lipton. Born in England, Higham moved to the United States as a teen where he tried out many jobs, including working as a reporter for a Brooklyn newspaper. After a stint in the U.S. Army fighting against Spain, Higham turned to advertising. Debating whether to move to Los Angeles or London, Higham let a coin toss decide his fate and he returned home to gain prominence working on wartime campaigns recruiting soldiers and selling war bonds. In 1918 Higham became Director of Publicity for the Coalition in the 1918 general election, and he also represented South

Islington in Parliament until 1922.[45] Thereafter, Higham became a missionary devoted to fostering the cultural, political, and economic connections between the UK and the United States. During a trip Higham took to the United States in 1922, the *New York Times* lauded his achievements but also pointed out that he was "partly an American product" who had learned the art of publicity in the United States.[46] Higham had come to America, however, to promote British business. Lord Northcliffe, the British newspaper mogul, had sent Higham west to invite the American members of the Associated Advertising Clubs of the World to attend the group's annual convention that was to be held in London in 1924. He was also there to encourage trade, explaining in countless speeches and broadcasts how "America's opportunity in England is a great one . . . for the English eat and drink American products and wear American clothes."[47] Higham believed that both nations would profit from the expansion of Anglo-American consumer culture.

So when the ITA sought to change the "Customs of a Continent," as one headline described it, they hired Higham, who was "equally versed in the psychology of England and America."[48] He was also chosen because he was especially known for his enthusiastic use of "collective" advertising. Higham believed that rather than brand names fighting for market share, successful advertising "collectively" promoted the taste for a product or service.[49] The U.S. fruit industry had already used this method to sell pineapples, lemons, prunes, and walnuts.[50] British advertisers also relied on such methods to sell cars, potatoes, fish, fruit, and many other commodities and services.[51] Higham elevated such practices to a theory: "Group publicity," he contended, "is wonderfully useful for creating markets, maintaining markets, stimulating the desire for the more costly amenities of life and educating the public taste."[52] For generic advertising to work, however, Higham knew he had to secure the goodwill of the media and retail. He thus met with groups such as the Boston-based Pilgrims' Publicity Association, a group that represented advertisers, wholesale grocers, and tea merchants. He visited with the Advertising Club and the Sphinx Club, and other associations of publishers, advertisers, and agency figures. Louis Wiley, the publisher of the *New York Times*, announced that he was behind the tea campaign; so too was the Six Point League, an organization that represented nearly all the newspapers in the country. Lipton's, Tetley, Ridgways, Salada, and the American Chain Stores Organization also backed Higham and his effort to sell Indian tea to American consumers.[53]

Higham's speeches were broadcast on the radio and published in countless journals and newspapers, generating much reflection on the Anglo-American relationship.[54] Some supportive journalists described the Indian tea campaign as an example of British vitality and the beginning of a "general advertising movement on behalf of British industries throughout the world."[55] Back in England, Higham revealed a slight disdain for American consumers. In a lecture titled "The United States Today" which he gave at the Old Colony Club, he jested that Americans were willing to pay "half as much again for a British article as for an American."[56] At a luncheon given by the Self-Supporting Empire League, Sir Charles countered prevailing concerns about Americanization. It "oftentimes appeared as though America had surpassed Britain as master salesmen," but, in fact, "India has gotten the United States beaten . . . [since it was] the only country in the world that, at the suggestion of the growers or manufacturers of a product, has gotten the government by act of Parliament to collect a cess and use it to promote the sale of the product in question." Higham thus proposed that the British Empire rivaled America in the modernity of its salesmanship.[57]

With India's money, Higham's campaign stressed the emotional and social experiences of consumption rather than the benefits of consuming modern British-grown tea.[58] Ads also deliberately tried to shift the gender identity of tea by calling it "A Man's Drink."[59] One typical ad explained: "I have been told that many American men consider tea drinking effeminate! But what was said of the man who smoked cigarettes 20 years ago, or the man who wore a wristwatch before 1914? No—there is nothing a real man does, that he liked to do, that makes him less of a man."[60] Such advertising challenged, as the *Tea and Coffee Trade Journal* put it, the notion that tea was "a mollycoddle's drink."[61] "Mollycoddle" was a known euphemism for a homosexual man, and thus this reference tells us that business feared the worst, that tea jeopardized American manhood, heterosexuality, and nationality. Yet ads that reminded readers that real men did not drink tea unintentionally reinforced such ideas. Higham did not, however, present tea as consistently masculine or American. Trying to appeal to middle-class American women, many ads reinforced the Englishness of afternoon tea. A typical example from 1925 explained how in England "every cottage and mansion" and "office and workshop" served afternoon tea. Another emphasized how American women could learn to serve tea "in the English way."[62] Illustrations of modern fashionable women sitting around a tea table presented Great Britain as quaint, dainty, and feminine. It was not particularly modern and it did not include "real" men.

Reflecting on the impact of Higham's work, one advertising specialist asserted, "In less than a year a whole continent is rapidly acquiring a habit which took more than a century to inculcate in Britain."[63] By the end of 1927, Higham announced that advertising had turned the United States into a "tea-drinking" nation that consumed one-sixth of the world's supplies. The *Home and Colonial Mail* also insisted that "true to the instincts of an English-speaking race, the United States of America is beginning at last to rise to the occasion" and drink tea.[64] Yet skeptics questioned such conclusions. In 1925 the president of a New York ad agency had commented that the campaign had not "found itself." It "lacked pith and pep" and "an inspiring objective." They were "just ads."[65] A merchandising expert opined that most customers still thought of tea "in a class with the herb drink of our grandmothers." Of course, this expert recommended more advertising to build up tea as "a he-man's drink" or "a vogue" that would be followed by fashionable women.[66] A few months later another advertiser argued that, in contrast to coffee advertising, the India tea campaign did not feel "American."[67] Market surveys began to segment the United States into a country of regional and microregional tastes, shaped largely by migration patterns.[68] Higham, however, ignored ethnic or regional differences and the research that proposed that there was no such thing as a national American consumer culture.[69]

Statistics showed that the American market was static and even declining, leading one of Higham's critics to remark, "A horse may be taken to water but he cannot be forced to drink. So it is with the Americans."[70] In December 1927, the ITA fired Higham and hired Leopold Beling in his stead. Born in Ceylon in 1869, Beling had served as secretary to J. J. Grinlinton, Ceylon's tea commissioner during the Chicago World's Fair and one of the founders of the Anti-Tea-Duty League. Beling had worked for the British firm Peek Bros. & Winch's American operations, and in 1927 he had been in charge of the tea department of a New York import firm.[71] Whereas Higham was an advertising specialist who had sold many products, Beling was a tea man schooled in late Victorian colonial business.

Beling renamed his operations the India Tea Bureau, moved to impressive new offices in the Singer building, one New York's most famous skyscrapers, and hired the New York–based advertising agency Paris & Peart to conduct a campaign more explicitly "directed at the American housewife."[72] Supported by a healthy and growing tea cess fund, ads appeared in 150 newspapers, including America's three leading family and women's magazines, the *Saturday Evening Post*, the *Ladies' Home Journal*, and *Good Housekeeping*. The campaign adopted a new emblem, a silhouette of the map of India with the words "India tea" in stark black lettering, which appeared on all packaging and display materials of brands that contained "an adequate percentage" of Indian tea.[73] The percentage remained vague. Nevertheless, for a full year, "122,000,000 magazine messages" reminded 40 million consumers that they should look for the map of India if they wanted to be assured they were getting the world's best tea.[74] Consumers need not think about why this was the case. Indeed, the India tea emblem, much like *Good Housekeeping*'s seal of approval, told consumers they did not need to think about their choice. An article titled "American Women Shown How to Choose a Good Tea" explained that the emblem "led [women] out of the wilderness of brand and blend confusion."[75] The emblem simplified buying and appealed to the consumer through its "eye-compelling" design. In fact, the emblem was small and uninspired when compared to other ads in these major papers.[76] And rather than try to disabuse Americans of their belief that tea was feminine, Beling's campaign emphasized tea's femininity and assumed that its buyers and drinkers were women.

Beling marketed to girls and housewives in schools, restaurants, and female-oriented stores. In 1929 the Tea Bureau worked with the Home Makers Educational Service to create lesson plans for schoolgirls in domestic science classes that would, as a memo from the Tea Bureau explained, create a "tie up between the coming generation of housewives."[77] In one year over a million women and girls had attended tea demonstrations at cooking schools in their high school domestic science class.[78] The Bureau also created lessons for grown women. In 1930 two and a half million "housewives" had attended Bureau demonstrations and three-quarters of a billion advertisements broadcast India tea "messages" in the cinema, on the radio, in newspapers, trade journals, and booklets; one hundred and twenty brands bore the India tea emblem, 46 percent of which claimed to be pure India teas.[79] Tea was by no means the only industry turning the school into a commercial space, and the United States was only one part of a broader global culture emerging in the 1920s, but the scale of the U.S. campaign was enormous and effectively furthered the belief that tea was a feminine brew.

A market survey done in 1934 found that tea was still viewed as "a woman's drink, unfit for and unworthy of a man unless he is a sissy." Young people considered the drink "not the thing" and explained how they preferred the newer soft drinks.[80] The survey could not explain why Americans persisted in such beliefs, but several factors were at work. Formosa and Japan were spending nearly as much as India did on tea advertising. Japan had retained the services of J. Walter Thompson, and, though sophisticated, these ads tended to reinforce the foreign and feminine image of tea. As we saw in the previous chapter, America's tea rooms were awfully feminine. Prohibition of the sale and use of all alcohol from 1920 until repeal in 1933 may have helped tea in some areas, but it also likely secured tea's reputation as a killjoy. Finally, Indian planters did not have the support of the American army or industrialists, and the lack of these male markets may have in the end made the difference. Rather than giving up on the United States, however, planters and the U.S. tea trade continued to pour money into the effort, trying all the latest advertising and marketing tools that the country could offer. While tea retained a negative image in the United States, during the 1920s, the ITA did succeed in shifting American tastes to a degree. By 1931, the Imperial Economic Committee estimated that together India and Ceylon accounted for half the tea consumed in the United States.[81] We will return to this relentless drive in later chapters, because although it never succeeded, the tea industry tried "American" modes of advertising elsewhere and experienced much more success than it had in the United States.

"EVERY KITCHEN AN EMPIRE KITCHEN": CONSERVATIVES SHOP FOR THE EMPIRE

In Britain during the 1920s, conservative politicians, journalists, and private industry adopted Higham's and Beling's methods to attempt to shift the Conservative Party from free trade to protectionism, or what was euphemistically known as Empire Free Trade. The Russian Revolution, the return to the gold standard in 1925, and mounting tariffs abroad made it difficult for manufacturing to hold on to traditional markets. Many conservatives decided that the time was ripe to adopt protectionism, but one way they did this was by exploiting and transforming the idea of a citizen consumer, which liberals had essentially invented. As noted historian of the popular and political culture of free trade Frank Trentmann has explained so pithily, in the 1920s British "Conservatives took the civic consumer from its liberal parents and gave it a conservative pedigree."[82] Conservatives were divided about how and when to abandon free trade, but all agreed they needed to stimulate imperial shopping habits. This notion was one factor in explaining tea planters' collective decision to push for voluntary *and* formal imperial preferences and generally speaking to shift from the Liberal to the Tory Party. The idea of empire shopping also united the planting interests and effectively ended the sectional disputes that had defined the Battle of the Teas of the 1890s.

Most British protectionists did not advocate national tariffs; rather they desired an economic free-trade union surrounding the entire British Empire. Building on Joseph Chamberlain's Edwardian Tariff Reform League, they believed that differential tariffs and duties could solve domestic and imperial economic problems and create closer ties between the disparate entities that made up the empire.[83] Differences surrounding whether and how to institute imperial preference nevertheless rocked the Conservative Party.[84] During the early 1920s, most Tories did not as yet support tariffs, but they hoped that voluntary preference or imperial consumerism would solve economic stagnation and appeal to the newly important female electorate. Especially after the defeat of the short-lived Labour government in 1924 and in the wake of growing and radicalizing imperial and domestic labor movements, Tory politicians and popular conservative organizations and private industry reached out to shopkeepers, shareholders, housewives, and children. Professional marketers and advertisers delivered this message through many routes, but they were especially interested in enlisting the purchasing and political power of women. Unlike the situation in the United States, these maneuvers gave afternoon tea political legitimacy. In the 1920s and 1930s, tea became something of a poster child for the entire empire shopping movement.

Scholars of the empire shopping movement have begun to explore how it represented shifting electoral strategies within the Tory Party, but most of the work has focused on the successes and failures of the Empire Marketing Board (EMB). The EMB was a government-funded agency that from 1926 to 1933 was charged to create a "National Movement with a view to spreading and fostering [the idea] that Empire purchasing creates an increased demand for the manufactured products of the United Kingdom and therefore stimulates employment at home."[85] Under the direction of the talented propagandist Stephen Tallents, the EMB advocated a materialistic understanding of the British Empire through publicity, education, funding scientific and economic research, and marketing schemes.[86] Although generally underfunded and relatively short-lived, the board became a school for the budding field of public relations—a place where numerous men and women learned how to sell commodities, industries, services, nations, and empires. Its publicity committee, for example, included William Crawford, founder and head of one of Britain's most important advertising agencies and Sir Charles Higham's main competitor; Frank McDougall, the son of the chairman of the London County Council who had grown fruit in Australia and had returned to London as a representative of the Australian Dried Fruits Board; Frank Pick, the managing director of the London Underground, known for its striking and artistic publicity posters; Lord Burnham, the owner of the *Daily Telegraph*; and Sir Woodman Burbidge, the chairman of Harrods department store.[87] The EMB was also uniquely, as an early report explained, an "inter-Imperial body" that had members from India and the dominions and that consulted with colonial governments and encouraged financial contributions from them as well.[88] Although officially the EMB was a non-party group, its work dovetailed perfectly with the conservative drive to develop imperial buying habits.

Another leader of the empire shopping movement was the Canadian-born Lord Beaverbrook. A quintessential representative of the British World and an example of the growing merger of business and politics, Beaverbrook, born Max Aitkin, had relatively humble beginnings. Beaverbrook's father had been a Scottish Presbyterian minister who had moved to Ontario, Canada, where he and his wife raised a large family. Their son Max was born in 1879, and by the time he turned thirty he had made a fortune investing in a wide variety of trades, including engineering and power companies, cement, and newspapers. After moving to Britain in 1910, Aitkin joined the Unionist Party and won a seat in the House, and in 1911 George V knighted Aitkin. Thereafter, he became a publicist of the first order, gaining a controlling interest in the *Daily Express* and creating the Canadian War Records Office in London, which employed the latest propaganda techniques to sell the story of Canada's contribution to the war effort, was appointed president of the Board of Trade, and in 1917 received a peerage, taking the Canadian-sounding title of "Beaverbrook." At the end of the war, he became the first minister of information, handling propaganda in Allied and neutral countries. He expanded his newspaper empire, but Labour's victory and Beaverbrook's frustrations with Conservative leader Stanley Baldwin encouraged him to support independent Conservatives and launch what he called an "Empire Crusade" in 1929.[89] The Empire Crusade pressured Baldwin and Tory leadership to adopt protectionism. Imperial preference, Beaverbrook explained, would allow the "British people," including those in the colonies, "to insulate themselves from the economic follies and miseries of the world."[90] Beaverbrook even went so far as to create a separate, though short-lived, political party of Empire crusaders.[91]

In 1931, the Tory-dominated newly elected National Government did not as yet adopt protectionism, but it did initiate a massive Buy British Campaign. One of the largest government propaganda campaigns ever conducted in peacetime, the Buy British Campaign tried to use persuasion, not tariffs, to solve Britain's mounting trade deficit, unemployment, and declining profits.[92] The movement defined British products as those grown and produced in the British Isles and secondarily those grown or manufactured in the empire. The EMB enlisted support from some of the most significant agencies in the UK, including the Ministry of Agriculture, Board of Trade, Post Office, Co-operative Society, BBC, Boy Scouts, Federation of British Industries, railway companies, football clubs, and countless others. Together these agencies asked Britons to think about the imperial nation every time they made a purchase or sat down to the dinner table.

Both the EMB's and Beaverbrook's approaches were theoretically class and gender neutral, but in practice they assumed that women, especially housewives, did the lion's share of the nation's purchasing and were moved by pocketbook issues.[93] Commenting on Baldwin's reluctance to adopt protectionism, Lord Beaverbrook, for example, exhorted "the women of England . . . to give comfort to the faltering politicians and show them the way to greater faith in Britain and the Empire."[94] The British Empire Producers' Organization, a trade group representing many imperial and domestic industries, also targeted women and employed a great deal of propaganda to teach the average housewife that her shopping basket and her kitchen were imperial spaces.[95] Many conservative women took up the cause. The large and powerful Primrose League, for example, defined women's shopping as a way to unite "Home, Nation, and Empire."[96]

The pro-empire women's group the Forum Club hosted Buy British luncheons and meetings at which businessmen informed women that "as shoppers" they were "employing British Labour and helping to build up the British Empire overseas."[97] The Duchess of York pronounced that only "Empire Products" should be used in royal kitchens, and the League of Empire Housewives' motto became "Every Kitchen an Empire Kitchen." Their manifesto explained: "Our existence as a nation depends on buying as much as possible from producers at home and in the Empire."[98] In addition, the Empire Day Medal Association instructed children that the prosperity of the "Overseas Dominions is indissolubly linked with the prosperity of the working classes of the Home Country."[99]

This nationalistic shopping movement was most prevalent between the International Exhibition held at Wembley in 1924 and Britain's adoption of imperial protectionism at Ottawa in 1932. Such ideas were not new, but they gained urgency as the colonies were pushing for greater political autonomy and the United States was moving into what had been thought of as British markets. The stock market crash of 1929 and near collapse in global markets thereafter, nationalism in India, and the passage of the Statute of Westminster, which granted self-governance to the dominions in December 1931, only intensified the project. These activists did not assume that consumers naturally preferred the empire, but they did believe they could be educated to do so.[100] They resolutely maintained that educated consumers could *preserve* the British Empire. Consumer education rather than social welfare thus became a prominent solution to the domestic and international challenges of the 1920s and 1930s. It is within this politicized moment that the tea industry turned to the consumer as an ally in its battles with the government, large producers, and workers.

THE FIGHT FOR AN IMPERIAL LABEL

Though rocked by global recession and other problems in 1920 and early 1921, tea production and consumption expanded steadily during the 1920s.[101] Indian output doubled from 201 million pounds in 1901 to 404 million in 1928, with Assam still the single greatest producer at 174 million pounds annually. Ceylon grew from 144 to 251 million pounds, and production began in Nyasaland, Kenya, and Tanganyika.[102] Between 1920 and 1930, acreage under cultivation in Java and Sumatra doubled, and exports increased from 35,000 tons in 1921 to 72,000 in 1929.[103] During that year Dutch-grown teas accounted for 16.1 percent of UK imports, up from 11.4 percent in 1925.[104] Consumption kept pace with growing supplies until the end of the decade. In the United Kingdom, gross imports had doubled and per capita consumption had climbed from 6.06 pounds in 1901 to 9.56 in 1931, a figure that excluded the Irish Free State so that

TABLE 7.1. PER CAPITA CONSUMPTION OF TEA
IN THE UK, 1871–1937 (IN POUNDS)

YEAR	PER CAPITA CONSUMPTION	ADJUSTED
1871	3.88	4.89
1881	4.67	5.87
1891	5.28	6.56
1901	6.06	7.45
1911	6.47	7.88
1921	8.43	10.81
1931	9.56	11.24
1937	9.37	10.91

Source: Gervas Huxley, Confidential Circular "The Price of Tea,"
16 November 1951, ITA Mss Eur F174/2074, British Library.

Note: The adjusted amount factors for variations in age of population
and is based on the rate of the adult population, which increased in
proportion to the whole population in these years.

consumption was likely even higher than these numbers suggest (table 7.1).[105] If adjusted for the adult population, per capita consumption in 1931 reached 11.24 pounds.[106] Despite shortages, rationing at the end of the war, and a lack of pastries, average growth rates were fastest during the decade between 1911 and 1921 (table 7.2). These numbers included the tea sent to soldiers, and it is likely that this accounts for the unusual surge in consumption. Nevertheless, for the entire period between the 1870s and the early 1930s, only tobacco experienced faster growth, and throughout this time prices remained low, especially relative to the cost of living so that tea absorbed a smaller portion of the working-class budget (tables 7.3 and 7.4).[107]

Several of the retailers that had sold tea at the end of the nineteenth century were now retail behemoths. The English and Scottish Wholesale Co-operative Society was the single largest distributor of tea in the country. In 1927 it sold 60,000,000 pounds annually, about one-tenth of the world's tea production. By the early 1930s, it was handling some 127,000,000 pounds, or what amounted to about one-fifth of the nation's tea supply.[108] At the same time, tea shops grew into big business.[109] J. Lyons, which had opened its first tea shop in Piccadilly

TABLE 7.2. ANNUAL RATE OF INCREASE IN PER CAPITA
TEA CONSUMPTION IN THE UK (ADJUSTED), 1871–1937

PERIOD	% INCREASE
1871–81	2.0
1881–91	1.2
1891–1901	1.4
1901–11	0.6
1911–21	3.7
1921–31	0.4
1931–37	–0.5

Source: Gervas Huxley, Confidential Circular "The Price of Tea,"
16 November 1951, ITA Mss Eur F174/2074, British Library.

TABLE 7.3. RATE OF INCREASE OF TEA, TOBACCO, SUGAR, MEAT, AND
WHEAT PER CAPITA CONSUMPTION IN THE UK, 1870S–1930S

COMMODITY	% INCREASE
Tea	+135
Tobacco	+160
Sugar	+100
Meat	+35
Wheat	+11

Source: Gervas Huxley, Confidential Circular "The Price of Tea,"
16 November 1951, ITA Mss Eur F174/2074, British Library.

TABLE 7.4. CHANGES IN RETAIL TEA PRICES IN RELATION
TO THE COST OF LIVING IN THE UK, 1870–1938

PERIOD	RETAIL PRICE	COST OF LIVING
1870–1914	−49%	−9%
1914–20	+85%	+148%
1920–29	−24%	−34%
1929–33	−16%	−15%
1933–38	+28%	+11%

Source: Gervas Huxley, Confidential Circular "The Price of Tea,"
16 November 1951, ITA Mss Eur F174/2074, British Library.

in London in 1894, served approximately 10,000,000 customers a week in their tea shops and restaurants and sold approximately 1,000,000 packets of dry tea a day in 1927. Nearly seventy different blends of Lyons tea were packed in the company's new factory in Greenford, Middlesex.[110] Built in 1921, this was the world's largest facility of its kind and it helped ensure J. Lyons's tight grip on an ever-growing working-class market. Exerting ever more power over tea's supply chain, Brooke Bond, Lyons, and the Co-op bought up smaller importers, purchased plantations in South Asia and Africa, and increasingly invested in and sourced tea from the Dutch East Indies, effectively preserving their right to buy in a global marketplace during a time when imperial protectionism was gaining ground.[111]

Imperial protectionism had actually started before the war. As mentioned in the last chapter, Chamberlain and the Tariff Reform League had advocated such ideas, but it was in the dominions that empire-grown tea first enjoyed differential tariffs. Canada introduced an imperial preference for the empire's teas in 1897, and during the war Australia briefly excluded all non-empire teas.[112] New Zealand also instituted such a preference, while Southern Rhodesia and Newfoundland had one for Ceylon's teas.[113] In the UK, the Finance Act of 1919 granted tea, cocoa, coffee, sugar, dried fruits, and several other commodities a modest imperial preference, which meant that for the next decade British-grown teas were taxed at only five-sixths of the full duty. Yet the differential price the Finance Act introduced was too small to stop the flow of Dutch teas into Britain. British manufacturing increasingly relied on empire markets. Whereas in 1913 empire markets absorbed 22 percent of British manufactured goods, by 1938 the empire purchased 47 percent.[114] Virtually all overseas investment also went to the colonies and dominions in this era, but industries such as tea still did not feel that their market, either at home or in the colonies, was secure. The tea industry recognized that what historians have called the "empire effect" was as much a product of policy as emotions.[115] They worked then on both fronts.

Ceylon's and India's planters wanted to create a voluntary preference for empire teas, but consumer and retailer education was key to this policy. They maintained that buyers had the right to know where their tea originated. Referring to the India emblem that was in use in the United States, tea planters insisted that tea needed an imperial label at home. The government had passed the Merchandise Marks Act of 1926, which required many items to carry a country-of-origin label at the point of importation and sale. Tea, however, did not make it on the initial list of protected goods so the ITA, Ceylon Association, and newly formed South Indian Association applied for tea's inclusion in the scheme after the fact. The Board of Trade (BOT) agreed to set up a committee to assess this application in 1928, but after gathering much evidence, the board rejected their request.[116]

Buyers who insisted on their British right to purchase teas from anywhere were thus victorious. Tea was not legally required to carry a country-of-origin label. In this case, free trade trumped economic nationalism.

When considering these issues, the BOT explored whether consumers had a right to know what was in their food. As we see in today's debates on food labeling laws, large food companies tend to oppose such actions. So it was in the 1920s. The BOT inquiry shows us, however, that in 1928, politicians and planters were unsure about the uses of nationalism in the market and metropolitan authorities stumbled their way through the issue. As they did in the tea blending debate in the 1880s, India's and Ceylon's planters declared themselves the watchdogs of consumer protection and market transparency.[117] In a wonderfully colorful exchange, Mr. Willink, who represented the British planters, explained, "Once they get beyond Mincing Lane, the Java and Sumatra plant is a very shy creature, and it does not disclose its identity in any way so far as we are aware."[118] To prevent such deception, India and Ceylon asserted that an official empire mark would "put it within the consumer's power to identify Empire tea."[119]

In the late nineteenth century, such arguments helped push Chinese teas out of the British and other markets, but now they didn't work so well because tea growers came up against the well-organized power of the distributor. The Tea Buyers' Association, the Federation of Grocers' Associations of the United Kingdom, the Scottish Federation of Grocers' and Provision Merchants Associations, the Scottish Wholesale Tea Trade Association, the Co-operative movement, and a group representing the British tea industry in Java and Sumatra argued that an imperial label would not stop foreign dumping, working-class consumers did not care about the empire, and as a blended product tea could not in truth have a national appellation.[120] Distributors' refrain was simple: "Tea is bought by the public, not because of its country of origin, but solely and exclusively because of its being a recognized blend indicative of a standard quality."[121] A representative of the Co-operative Society contended, "The large body of consumers in this country owing to their economic conditions are not concerned whether the supply is of Empire or Foreign origin."[122] A Lyons employee confirmed that the working classes, who were "the largest consumers of tea," were not interested in imperial buying.[123] The president of the Tea Buyers' Association and director of Messrs. Horniman and Company, John Douglas Garrett, stated that people walked into a shop and asked for brands and did not inquire about country of origin.[124] Trade experts concurred that the average consumer did not want to know about production. The author of *Salesmanship for the Grocer and Provision Dealer* opined that "unless in special cases the salesman need not make a parade of such names as 'Darjeeling,' 'Kintuck,' 'Travancore,' 'Assam'—they may mean very little to the customer, however much they may mean to the grocer." He warned, "Some people may even suspect that a string of technical terms is in the nature of 'camouflage' and may inwardly resent it."[125] The big distributors defended their right to purchase foreign goods by claiming that brand- and price-conscious working-class customers would not shop for the empire.

But why then, asked several members of the BOT committee, did distributors use Oriental and imperial imagery and names on packaging and in advertising?[126] Sellers came up with a range of different explanations, except admitting that they wanted to harness or cultivate patriotism. The director of the Home and Colonial Stores, William Saunders, insisted that despite his company's name, its regular participation in empire shopping weeks, and its Asian-style advertising, imperialism was irrelevant in the marketplace. "Whenever there is an Empire week, or when British goods are being put forward we always endeavour to take our share by putting forward our tea," Saunders admitted, but then he followed up by saying, "I cannot say that we have ever got any additional sale of that which is Empire grown." When directly asked whether "Home and Colonial Nizam Tea, with a picture of something that looks very much like an Indian temple on it suggests Indian tea," Saunders answered, "I do not think there is any tea grown in the Nizam's dominions, in which case it is foreign tea, I suppose. The picture is the Taj Mahal. I had the privilege of seeing that on a trip to India when I was getting out this label and I wanted something pretty."[127] The embarrassed committee member had not recognized the Taj Mahal. It is no wonder that experts felt consumers were ignorant. Yet this curious exchange illuminates how the tea trade was both saturated with and wished to eschew imperial culture in the 1920s. Large distributors may have truly believed that the masses were not patriotic, but they made this argument because they operated in a global not imperial marketplace.

An imperial label would have created the fiction that tea had "national" characteristics in a global age.[128] British nationals worked for and had considerable capital invested in Dutch tea.[129] Along with indigenous entrepreneurs, Chinese, and other foreign nationals, the British managed and owned estates in Java and Sumatra.[130] "In Batavia," noted one author in 1925, "the tea trade is practically in the hands of the few local British firms," foremost among them W. P. Phipps and Co., which was the first British firm to arrive in 1910.[131] British steamships earned money importing these teas, and British manufacturers sold machinery and other supplies to Dutch companies.[132] Thus, a representative of the British in the Dutch East Indies opposed a merchandise mark because he argued it confusingly told consumers, "An article which is largely produced by Britishers is non-British."[133] Finally, sellers simply claimed it would be a logistical nightmare to alter packaging. Lyons, for example, had approximately seventy blends, none of which was a pure empire blend, and there was basically "no description at all" on their packaging other than price and brand name.[134] Lipton's used imperial imagery in its advertising, but the company sourced from all major producers and like Lyons and other big brands it too fought empire marking.[135]

This story is not only about free traders versus protectionists or producers versus sellers. Distributors were looking for new sources of supply outside of South Asia in the early 1920s in part because they were nervous that anti-colonial nationalism and social and economic instability in the producing areas in India were causing shortages, higher prices, and other difficulties.[136] Things were especially tense in Assam in 1920 and 1921. Garden workers were rioting, striking, attacking European and Indian managerial staff, and simply leaving the gardens in a mass exodus. Planters blamed Gandhi and concluded that the strikes were caused by "politics not economics."[137] The assistant secretary to the ITA in the district wrote to his London colleagues that "Mr. Gandhi's supporters" had created "disaffection," and these so-called outsiders had "worked on the religious emotions" of workers and persuaded them to leave the gardens.[138] *The Statesman* similarly impugned Gandhi and "certain Indian-owned newspapers" for encouraging laborers to "no longer work for European employers" and telling them "the British Raj is over."[139] Labor was protesting low wages, the system of indenture, and a range of other economic and social problems, and nationalists were placing economics within a wider framework about colonialism.[140] But the problems visible on the tea estates had been there for nearly a century. Nationalism had simply reframed these issues. Distributors nevertheless grew fearful and purchased Dutch teas in part to diffuse Indian workers' power. Rather than admit their political motives, distributors who wanted to continue to purchase Dutch teas fought the empire label by invoking consumer apathy, technical difficulties, and the costs of packaging. The Board of Trade conceded to the large food companies and refused to mandate tea carry an imperial label.[141]

Planters had hoped to bring the commercial and political boundaries of the imperial nation into alignment but found that the globalizing food industry wreaked havoc with the idea of imperial consumerism. Labor and nationalist unrest in India scared buyers who hoped that sourcing from the Dutch Empire and buying plantations in Africa would protect their vast and growing businesses. Those businesses dedicated to South Asian teas, however, did not have the power in the 1920s to protect their monopoly in the UK consumer market. Planter activism continued after the Labour government came to power in the summer of 1929. However, it was not until the simultaneous collapse in commodity prices and the election of the new National Government in 1931 that colonial growers felt the time was ripe for a huge propaganda campaign to encourage consumers to vote for imperial preference in the shop and the polling booth.

THE DRINK EMPIRE TEA CAMPAIGN

In 1930 and 1931, the world economy was in a steep downward spiral and Britain faced political as well as economic crises at home and in the empire.[142] "For the moment the world suffers from a glut of materials and products. There is too much tea, too much silver, too much rubber, too much tin, too much cotton," a panic-stricken journalist wrote in *The Statesman* in 1930.[143] The *Home and Colonial Mail* similarly printed this dire statement in early summer 1931: "Last year, and it looks as if this year also, will go down in the annals as the most disastrous in the history of the tea plantation industry."[144] In September 1931, prices had tumbled to all-time lows.[145] The ITA sent a panicky telegram to the Chancellor of the Exchequer explaining: "Indian Tea Trade almost paralyzed— many gardens closed—thousands of labourers unemployed." The telegram urged the chancellor to reimpose a six-pence import duty with a four-pence rebate on empire produce.[146] Though in the past British-grown teas had enjoyed an imperial preference, Winston Churchill as Chancellor of the Exchequer abolished this modest imperial preference in 1929. His successor, the socialist free trader Philip Snowden, did not change course and he too refused to concede to planters' wishes and introduce a protective tariff.[147]

Feeling desperate in the way they had during the days of the Anti-Tea-Duty League, planters initiated a massive public relations campaign to teach consumers to prefer teas from India, Ceylon, and British East Africa to those from the Netherlands East Indies. The Drink Empire Tea campaign piggybacked on the Buy British movement, which peaked during the early 1930s. In the autumn of 1931, Labour prime minister Ramsay MacDonald stood at the helm of the Tory-dominated National government. Chamberlain at the Exchequer and protectionist Sir Philip Cunliffe-Lister as secretary of state for the colonies also shaped imperial trade policy. These men addressed the alarming trade deficit, high unemployment, and the virtual collapse of the global economy through austerity measures and by taking Britain off the gold standard, but they were reluctant to adopt protectionism, however, because they feared higher food prices and trade retaliations.

The tea crisis was thus a part of a broader collapse in the British free-trade global system. Tea producers curtailed output, fired workers, asked for tariff protection, and launched the Drink Empire Tea Campaign.[148] This campaign hoped to entice consumers to shop for the empire, buyers to source from the empire, and politicians to protect the empire. The ITA and Ceylon Association, with the help of the Indian Trade Commissioner and the Empire Marketing Board, asked shoppers to use a variety of means to push the government to institute formal imperial preferences.[149] This campaign is important for a number of reasons. Like the Chicago World's Fair in 1893, it encouraged Ceylon to revive the cess, which it did in 1932, and join India to pay for politics and publicity.[150] It is also important for what it tells us about the growing power of women in imperial and consumer politics. Many women's associations believed they could reform shopping habits to support imperial unity and global security and fight socialism, anticolonial movements, and the Great Depression.[151]

The Drink Empire Tea Campaign highlights how the same institutions that advertised tea also politicized consumers. For example, John Harpur, who had worked for the ITA developing Indian markets, directed the Drink Empire Tea Campaign. Gervas Huxley, who worked for the EMB, became Harpur's main advisor and acted as liaison between the EMB and the Indian Tea Cess Committee.[152] A member of one of Britain's most famous families that straddled the worlds of science, imperial administration, fiction, and publicity, Gervas Huxley was the grandson of evolutionary scientist Thomas Huxley, cousin of both Julian Huxley, the evolutionary biologist, and the writer Aldous Huxley. Gervas had recently met and would soon marry Elspeth Grant, who under her married name became a very popular writer, especially known for her autobiographical novel, *The Flame Trees of Thika* (1959), which described her memories of growing up on a coffee farm in Kenya. Before she took to writing, Elspeth Huxley gained a degree in agriculture from the University of Reading and also studied at Cornell University in New York. She served as the assistant press officer to the EMB and at around the same time was made honorary treasurer of the Women's Institute, a huge and growing non-sectarian movement that had begun in Canada in 1915 but quickly spread to the metropole. By 1927 there were 4,000 branches of the WI, as it endearingly came to be known, with 250,000 members and a hugely popular journal, *Home and Country*.[153] Its members were precisely the sort of women the Buy British movement appealed to, and it is likely that Elspeth pushed Gervas and Harpur to see the marketing potential in such groups.

Gervas Huxley would become the most important tea propagandist in the twentieth century, working for several agencies, but especially for the Ceylon Tea Propaganda Board and related bodies between the early 1930s and late 1960s. We will track his career during depression, war, austerity, and affluence. As we will see in the next chapter, both Huxleys befriended and worked with Americans who were at the forefront of the emerging profession of market research and public relations.[154] This transatlantic community envisioned selling as occurring in the store, advertisement, trade journal, and newspaper, as well as in myriad other settings in ways that the public would not recognize as selling at all. They began to develop such techniques at the EMB and while working on the Drink Empire Tea Campaign.

This campaign used the same materials that had long sold tea, including shop displays, trade and consumer advertising, posters, radio talks, movies, and public lectures given to consumers, retailers, local authorities, mass caterers, and workers at large industrial concerns. It influenced lessons in schools and asked government agencies to serve only empire teas.[155] The campaign disseminated numerous pamphlets, the most important of which was *Empire Grown Tea*, a popular version of the Imperial Economic Committee's 1931 *Report on Tea*, which instructed tens of thousands of retailers, shareholders, politicians, and consumers about how free trade was destroying an imperial industry built on British energy, enthusiasm, and knowledge. It then pleaded with consumers to "create a demand for 'EMPIRE TEA'" and to "obtain protection for such teas in the home market," give their "active help" to support "Empire tea" by purchasing it when possible, asking for it at the shop, and recommending it to friends.[156] Sir Charles Campbell McLeod emphasized the same themes in a speech he first gave at the Royal Empire Society in November 1931, which was then published and widely distributed. McLeod, who had served as chairman of the National Bank of India, the Imperial Tea Company, and the Royal Colonial Institute, saw politics and economics as deeply intertwined. He explained to consumers that their buying habits could save their own and a million tea garden workers' jobs by drinking British tea.[157]

Challenging the big buyers' lack of interest in promoting empire buying, the Drink Empire Tea Campaign explained to struggling retailers: "The public want empire goods . . . it is good business to cater for what they want."[158] Trade experts elaborated that imperial imagery elevated the mundane by placing everyday commodities into compelling narratives. Scenes of exotic tropical lands and empire production—which had been used to denigrate Chinese production—now became a means to engage consumers in the human story behind the product and provoke them to fantasize about the exotic travels of food and household items. Empire made the everyday special. While we know a great deal more about empire displays at the great international world's fairs of this era, the same sort of displays could be found at humdrum trade shows and food fairs, grocers' shops, and department stores. Commenting on an imperial display erected in Lewis's Manchester department store, one journalist exclaimed that now visitors would see the "East" as "an annex of Manchester." Known to serve a working-class clientele, Lewis's mock India allowed working-class customers to feel, taste, and listen to a highly attractive, romanticized, and consumer-oriented Raj as "a tourist would like to see it." Visitors sipped Indian tea and listened to music played by a native orchestra brought over from India for the Wembley Exhibition while gazing at paintings depicting staged scenes of "old Benares" and the Taj Mahal. According to the enthusiastic journalist, "Many people took the opportunity to-day of escaping from Manchester's misty streets to a fragrant atmosphere of the colourful East, where a warm sun shone permanently on tea plantations and dark-skinned men and women."[159] A few days later, Lewis's moved this spectacle to their Liverpool store, where it too received a good deal of free newspaper publicity. According to the firm's sales figures, customers had purchased 20 percent more tea since Lewis's had erected their "show" in Manchester.[160] Shopkeepers thus indulged planters' wishes when they assembled these commercial and sanitized versions of India.

Films such as *Empire-Grown Tea* and the famous *The Song of Ceylon* (1934) and beautifully designed posters replicated the themes presented in such exhibitions.[161] For example, a pair of posters by H. S. Williamson placed a white wealthy and fashionable female consumer and a non-white tea picker both in the tea garden (figs. 7.1 and 7.2). Color, layout, setting, gender, and text highlighted global connections even as race and fashion mapped differences between consumer and producer. This portrayal of tea's commodity chain purported to make production and consumption visible. Yet this common but anachronistic image of the West consuming the East hid men's activities and the importance of non-white colonial consumers to the global economy. It obscured as much as it revealed, and this was just what empire activists wanted.

Williamson's posters, like those of the EMB in general, have been well kept in archives and museums, but most of the material from the Buy British and the Drink Empire Tea campaigns involved face-to-face exchanges and ephemera that have simply wound up in the rubbish bin. However, the trade associations that were footing the bill for the tea campaign kept careful records from which we can glean a sense of just how much advertising material was created and disseminated. In one month alone, November 1931, the campaign distributed 52,459 window bills and 118,224 leaflets to retailers in 806 towns. By December, 40,000 grocers were displaying these materials and Lipton's, Home and Colonial Stores, Maypole Dairy, the Co-operative Wholesale Society, and the International Tea Stores had brought out one or more empire brands and empire labels were affixed to myriad smaller brands.[162] Some companies brought out stationery that demanded that customers "HELP THE EMPIRE all *you* can by Developing Empire Trade. There are many ways! A very important one is to insist on Ridgways EMPIRE GROWN TEA."[163] If nothing else the Drink Empire Tea Campaign had convinced retailers to sell imperialism. Of course it is not possible to know how these advertisements compared to the wider field of popular culture, but in the early 1930s many businesses used the empire to add value to an ordinary product and to activate consumers' interest in protectionism. Businesses such as Ridgways objected to a Merchandise Marks label as a requirement but slapped an empire label on their products when they thought it would boost sales and because they knew the label had no legal significance.

FIGURE 7.1. "Drinking Empire-Grown Tea," H. S. Williamson, 1931.
(By permission of the National Archives, CO 956/442)

A pressing question for advertisers at the time, and for historians today, is: How did consumers react to such messages? This was the question that motivated businesses to begin to pay for rudimentary forms of market research. The tea trade, for example, began to hire women to lecture and "sell" tea because they might understand and communicate better than men with female shoppers. Like Elspeth Huxley, who worked with her husband, most of the planters' female employees were college educated; some were married to colonial officials or politicians, while others were single women with a mission. For example, Mrs. C. Romanne-James, a former suffragist and author

FIGURE 7.2. "Picking Empire-Grown Tea," H. S. Williamson, 1931.
(By permission of the National Archives, CO 956/440)

who had lived in India and had frequently given "travel talks" for the BBC, began to work for the ITA in these years.[164] F. M. Imandt, a journalist who had worked for the *Daily Telegraph* and the *Glasgow Herald* and who had just returned from two years traveling "the world," also lectured for the ITA.[165] One of the most active of these saleswomen, however, was Mrs. Lidderdale, the secretary of the Women's Guild of Empire, who in the employ of the tea campaign addressed women's groups all over the country. Lidderdale's detailed reports to the ITCC in Calcutta explain where she held lectures, how many attended, and what type of reception she received.[166] They provide an unusually rich window into the class, gender, and political dynamics that shaped her work and the role of "lecturing" as a form of marketing and market research. At her lectures, Lidderdale learned about consumers, but she also learned that though they slapped empire labels on their products, the big companies were still resistant to the empire shopping movement.

In the summer of 1932, Lidderdale began speaking at meetings of the Women's Institute and the women's sections of the British Legion, the Conservative Party, and similar organizations.[167] In July she delivered twelve lectures at the Women's Conservative and Unionist Association, the Women's Guild of Empire, the Conservative Women's Society, the Central Mission in Tottenham Court Road, and the Young Women's Christian Association. Audiences, whom Lidderdale characterized as ignorant but receptive, were typically composed of forty to eighty women and a few male vicars, tea planters, reporters, and grocers. She described her audience at the Women's Conservative and Unionist Association in Kent, for example, as "women in good circumstances but many of them not very intelligent—it was necessary to repeat the same point again and again . . . from a different angle." They were "attentive" and very much liked the postcards that she handed out, however. Even worse were the poorer, less educated women Lidderdale met, since she asserted they knew nearly nothing about where their tea came from and essentially believed that because they "bought tea in a local shop it must be British."[168] Lidderdale also spoke to "middle class women who do not go much to political and philanthropic meetings" at libraries and rotary clubs. She organized mixed-class meetings as well, believing that society women could influence the shopping habits of their social inferiors.[169]

Lidderdale learned much, in fact, from her supposedly ignorant audiences. Officially, large companies were pushing empire teas, but she discovered and reported to planters that these firms' agents did not even necessarily know what this meant. While Lyons had been showing its factory workers "a most interesting entertainment with a lantern, showing the processes of tea making," the female owner of a small general shop revealed that the Lyons traveler who came to her store had never heard of Empire Grown Tea.[170] The "owner of a very nice teashop in Dorking" told the same story about a Brooke Bond traveler.[171] We can imagine how frustrated a woman like Lidderdale must have been when she labored to teach women to shop for the empire and companies did not make this possible. Lidderdale's reports gave her employers a clear sense of who their allies at home really were, and their most reliable friends apparently were older conservative women.

About a month after the Drink Empire Tea and Buy British campaigns began, a market research survey concluded that "the movement is definitely swinging the country over to buying British in everything from coffee to collar studs."

The survey quoted shopkeepers such as a London grocer who estimated that 90 percent of his customers were asking for empire goods and a Wolverhampton shopkeeper who reported a 60 percent increase in the demand for such goods. However, the survey found that public interest varied by region, gender, age, commodity, and socioeconomic status. Shopkeepers claimed men were more patriotic than women and that "younger girls" preferred "foreign" goods, no doubt because they were considered more stylish. Husbands sometimes returned foreign goods, no doubt inspiring marital conflict. Regional differences emerged as well, with the Midlands leading the call to engage in empire, buying. Everywhere older conservative ladies were especially enthusiastic.[172] The nation's poorest customers demonstrated no imperial preference, presumably because they had to stretch their meager incomes to feed their families.[173] Virtually all Britons drank tea, but they did not all universally accept the values and logic of imperial consumer culture.

Though we seem to have rich information on how shopkeepers, large companies, and consumers responded to the movement, in truth, this "research" is quite suspect. It is highly unlikely that in a depressed economy sales would increase so rapidly, and if Lidderdale's reports are to be believed empire goods were not always even on the shelf. This early market research did encourage sellers to believe that imperial sentiment added value, but it is clear that this was a highly debated issue at the time. It is very likely that age, gender, region, class, politics, and profession shaped the "market" for such ideas as well as empire goods. These reports give us a rare glimpse into how promotions worked on the ground and how dogged women like Mrs. Lidderdale went from meeting to meeting to build up markets and generate imperial enthusiasm.

It is difficult nevertheless to measure the impact of the Drink Empire Tea Campaign on buying habits for a number of reasons. In April 1932, the government reinstated a differential tea duty as part of a broader program of imperial preference known as the Ottawa Agreements. British-grown teas were imported with a nominal duty of 2d. per pound, while foreign teas were charged 4d. The duty was, relatively speaking, quite low and though it pleased the planters who had long wanted this policy, this move and other major changes in global currencies and international financial arrangements vastly complicate our ability to measure the degree to which consumers and distributors were moved by nationalistic buying campaigns.

We cannot know then whether shoppers saw empire buying as a way to solve the problem of unemployment, stimulate trade, and maintain Britain's imperial power. We can conclude that a great many men and women in both the colonies and Britain hoped they could manufacture imperial sentiment for commercial and political ends. Resistance nevertheless came in many forms.

Economic constraints, habits, tastes, and politics determined whether Britons willingly turned their shopping basket and their kitchen into an imperial space. Large importers and retailers may have affixed imperial labels in the early 1930s, but they subtly and overtly rejected regulations that would have forced them to source from the empire. Resistance was not the end but rather the beginning of a new chapter in tea's globalization. The uneven and contradictory nature of government policies and the globalizing tendencies of large food companies worked against the nationalization of British consumer culture. The most articulate and fully developed defiance to Indian tea producers and sellers, however, appeared in India.

"UNTRUTHFUL ADVERTISEMENTS": TEA AND ITS DISCONTENTS IN INTERWAR INDIA

In August 1935, Mahatma Gandhi penned a brief but ardent article titled "Untruthful Advertisements," which uncovered what he contended were the falsehoods of the "very vigorous propaganda . . . going on in Bengal and probably in other provinces in favor of drinking Indian tea." Written just as the ITCC was launching its most extensive campaign yet, this essay called attention to the moral, physical, and psychological dangers of advertising and the immoderate drinking of strong tea. Gandhi's essay was a cautionary tale that used the outrageous claims of tea advertising as a lesson in temperance and in the necessity of reading critically. In order to teach naïve Indians not to "treat the printed word in a book or a newspaper as gospel truth," Gandhi quoted a recent advertisement in a Bengali newspaper that had proposed that "tea helps retain a youthful look and energy." The ad told the story of Shiriyut Nepal Chandra Bhattacharya, who, though forty-eight years old, looked a mere thirty-four because since he was fourteen years old he had drunk nearly thirty cups of tea daily. This ad, which looked like "a report from the paper's own correspondent," provided a clear example of what Gandhi presented as the fictional world of commodity culture.[174] Such advertising was dangerous on two fronts: it broke a kind of contract between reader and text by mimicking the style of the news sections of the paper, and it invited consumers to commit self-violence through unnecessary and even harmful consumer behaviors. With its state support and wide reach, the tea campaign stood out as a particularly egregious example of commodity culture's colonialism. "Strong tea," like the British Empire, was quite simply "poison."[175]

Gandhi wrote "Untruthful Advertisements" at a critical moment in India's history and in the history of cultural theory. Brand-name capitalism was making headway in late colonial India, and, if slow and uneven, advertisements sought to sell the urban middle classes a range of new commodities from lightbulbs and toiletries to medicines and packaged foods. In India, as elsewhere, such commodities and the advertising and print culture that promoted them invented new ideals of youth culture, beauty and hygiene, family, and bourgeois notions of domesticity.[176] This was also the moment that Walter Benjamin and other theorists had begun to interrogate the historical, aesthetic, and political implications of the commodity spectacle.[177] Like Benjamin, Gandhi worried about the blurring of the line between the real and the fictional, but he also saw the advertisement as a tool of colonization.[178] There were, however, several meanings that Indian consumers could and did ascribe to the consumption of so-called Western goods, forms of leisure, and ideals of beauty and health.

Gandhi had long called on Indians to boycott European products and support indigenous goods known as *swadeshi*. This appeal did not lead to a culture of pure abstinence, however, but instead middle-class supporters invented a "nationalist" style as they adorned their bodies and their homes with *khadi*, that is, homespun cotton cloth, and other "swadeshi" products.[179] Especially in the 1930s, *swadeshi* proponents gave up the distinction between handmade and industrial goods and instead simply emphasized Indian-made products. Nationalists used exhibitions, magic lantern shows, catalogues, newspaper advertising, posters, radio, and cinema to sell such goods and help expel the British government and British products from the Subcontinent.[180] These were the same methods that business and pro-empire ideologues were using at this time. In truth, both anticolonial nationalists and British conservatives believed that empire buying sustained the British imperial nation. Though they had a very different vision of the ideal relationship between India and Britain, the proponents and the critics of empire were calling on consumers to shape the fate of their nation. These were not merely parallel movements since Gandhi and other nationalists were rejecting Beaverbrook's protectionism, which saw India as subordinate within the imperial nation, and advertisers' attempts to incorporate Indians into the empire of consumers. In the end, however, this anticolonial and anticommercial movement further commercialized India by defining buying as a form of nation-building. This is not what Gandhi had wanted, but it is what happened.

In interwar India, politicians, planters, publicists, consumers, and workers argued about the boundaries of "India," the British Empire, the political potential of the consumer, and the politics of tea in Liverpool and Bombay. While tea never achieved the same significance in the nationalist movement as cotton, it was one of the most heavily publicized commodities in India. During the interwar years, private firms and ITA advertising often identified tea in India with modernity, elite social status, health, and a new sense of Indian nationality.[181] Indian nationalists responded in a variety of ways to what they saw as this dangerous and unhealthy development. Gandhi expressed his disquiet first in his 1917 essay, "Third Class in Indian Railways." In this essay, he illustrated the poor treatment of the Indian masses by describing how the tea service on the railways served up a particularly unhealthy product, calling it "tannin water with filthy sugar and a whitish looking liquid mis-called milk which gave this water a muddy appearance."[182] While the ITA quantified modernity and success in terms of the growth of tea stalls, Gandhi looked into the teacup and saw colonial exploitation.

After the war, nationalists who attacked the labor politics of the ITA also condemned its marketing to Indians. In 1921, the Bengali newspaper *Basumati* issued a scathing response to the ITCC's efforts "to introduce tea in every hearth and home in India" and pointed out that "to introduce tea among people who can ill afford two meals a day is to ruin them absolutely."[183] The beverage was an unnecessary luxury that channeled funds away from food and other necessities. It also was a drug. The author contended that Calcutta's tea stall owners mixed small amounts of opium into the tea to add "flavor," producing "an exhilarating effect upon the consumer." No doubt such laced tea was exhilarating, but this author believed it was turning the sons of the city's new middle classes into opium addicts.[184] Opium was a "homegrown" stimulant that the non-cooperation movement had urged Indians to give up, along with alcohol, ganja, cigarettes, and other drugs.[185] In addition to doing physical harm, opium was a taxed commodity that supported the colonial regime.

These attacks on tea described the colonialism of consumerism but they also stemmed from an understanding of the conditions of tea garden labor. During the 1920s, the labor movement had contended that for an Indian to drink tea was to become a colonizer who profited from the unfair treatment of the poor worker toiling in the gardens. Such protests came in waves, however, just as did the non-cooperative movement in general. One groundswell of anti-tea protests came in the spring of 1921, shortly after Gandhi had visited Assam. *Young India*, a paper that Gandhi edited, often reported on tensions between planters and the *swadeshi* movement during this period. For example, in 1921 the paper stated that in Jorhat a "European" planter entered a shop and became angered that it was selling *khadi* cloth. He used his stick to remove the *khadi* caps the storekeepers were wearing and encouraged the authorities to turn them out of their shop. Similarly, a European manager of a tea estate was so incensed that the estate's cobbler was "committing the crime of wearing *khadi*" that he "got him stripped naked before sending him away."[186] So much for free trade. The planters recognized the power of a politicized marketplace and thus felt they needed to punish what might appear to be small gestures but signified an allegiance to a growing movement to oust the British from the Subcontinent.

While tea planters tried to stop their workers from becoming political consumers and wearing homespun clothing, crowds of peasants also made the connection between their consumer choices and the life of tea workers. They interrupted tea lectures, refused free tea, closed tea shops, and shouted statements such as "I will never drink tea as it would be drinking the blood of my brothers."[187] Everywhere there was anti-European and anti-government feeling, such as in the Punjab, the Tea Committee ran into opposition. Shopkeepers who were committed to non-cooperation especially resented ITA inspections of their shops. In southern India, Muslim vendors were reluctant to do anything that was perceived as overtly connected with the colonial state, so tea sellers and ITA employees avoided mentioning the government and instead explained how drinking tea would "assist" their "own people."[188] In other words, retailers recognized that the ITA was an arm of the government, but ITA employees responded by arguing that tea was good for Indians and an Indian good.

The tea industry felt compelled to shift gears if it hoped to maintain control of plantations and markets in India. The ITCC thus tried to appease nationalists by adding Indians to their organizations and committees. In 1923, A. C. Sen became the first Indian national to serve on the ITCC. The body also worked harder to convince industrialists and government representatives that more—not less—tea would solve India's economic and political problems. For example, in 1922 the Reed Committee, appointed by the government of Bombay to investigate labor problems and provide ways to settle disputes, proposed that "in an exhausting climate like that of Bombay, where the day's work takes a heavy toll on the individual, nature demands some mild stimulant and the best and most innocuous is tea." Moreover, "the man or the woman, who can obtain a cup of tea in clean and cheerful surroundings, is less likely to dissipate his or her substance in the grog shop." The report then recommended the expansion of industrial canteens, along the lines of wartime Britain, because bright, clean, cheerful tea shops were an "emblem of what home can be."[189] Here were all the same tropes that we saw operating in early industrial and in contemporary Britain. A temperate brew that if taken in the right way and the correct places would combat dissipation, labor unrest, and provide a cheerful example of European-style domesticity. Employers and nationalists did not always accept such ideas, however, and by the 1930s the debate grew more heated.

In the early 1930s, non-cooperation gained momentum, Indians were increasingly in positions of political and economic power, and anti-tea protests grew more organized. In the Central Provinces, for example, Indians boycotted Brooke Bond teas, claiming, as one "Congress man" put it, it was a "Blighty company" that was trying to "oust the good Swadeshi teas, such as Savant, Primrose and Elias" from the Indian market.[190] Nationalists thus began to support Indian-owned or identified companies, a process that was very common in other industries as well. The ITCC reacted by asserting that all teas were "swadeshi," that is, an indigenous Indian product. The two camps faced off in many places, including *swadeshi* exhibitions, where both the ITCC and "swadeshi" brands set up tea stalls.[191] Ironically, these exhibitions effectively became trade shows in which countless businesses promoted "Indian" products.[192] However, the pursuit of the Indian consumer increased nationalists' opposition to the tea industry, the ITA, and advertising even though many Indians, including nationalists, grew, sold, and were invested in tea. In fact, a prominent member in the underground terrorist movement, Narendra Nath Bhattacharya, who would later assume the name Manabendra Nath Roy while living in Palo Alto, California, had funded his studies by running a tea stall on Clive Street in Calcutta.[193]

The debate about tea in India intensified in 1935 when the Government of India Act increased Indian legislative representation and the tea trade asked this body to raise the tea cess and approve the creation of the International Tea Market Expansion Board, a body whose international tea promotions we will explore in the next chapter. This debate provided a moment for nationalists in the legislature to protest the ubiquitous place that both tea and advertising had gained in India. At the same time, other Indian politicians argued that tea was deeply embedded in Indian culture and society, and its growth and consumption developed healthy bodies and a modern political economy. Indian and European politicians argued about whether tea was a European commodity, whether it was beneficial to India's impoverished masses, and whether advertising was a wasteful or corrupt practice. The deliberations were rife with irony, humor, and moral outrage, but this debate shows just how far tea was helping this colony work out the meaning of capitalism and consumerism in Indian society.

In 1935, when the Tea Cess Act came up for renewal, several Indian representatives spoke passionately against its extension; some even pushed for repeal. Sri Prakasa, the non-Muslim rural representative for the Allahabad and Jhansi divisions, ignited the debate when he offered personal, medical, and political evidence against tea drinking. He began by admitting that for some twenty-five years or more he had been a "victim of the tea habit." He felt his addiction most keenly, however, when he had been deprived of his "usual supply of morning and afternoon tea" during his imprisonment by the government. This torture, he claimed, had enabled him to realize tea's addictive and hence immoral properties. Prakasa then joked that he was "in favor of dear old drinks like *sharbat*, *thandai*, or perhaps even *bhang*," and surmised that "if, instead of this new tea drinking habit we go back to the old habits, I believe the Government also will be happier because if Members on this side of the house took *bhang*, they would not be able to give so much trouble to the Government. In fact, if one takes tea, the brain is stimulated and one gets in the mood to be troublesome to Government."[194] In other words, Sri Prakasa jested that unlike sedatives such as *bhang*, a cannabis-based drink, as a stimulant tea made one radical. Cannabis still had an important place in Ayurvedic medicine and was integral to Hindu religious practice. However, the British increasingly associated cannabis with insanity, criminality, and dangerous Eastern drugs, and in 1928 it had officially become illegal to possess or supply the drug in Britain.[195] Thus, Sri Prakasa was asserting the value of indigenous pleasures and consumer practices that were embedded in "traditional" medical and religious cultures. Tea, he argued, was "modern" and "Western," but his joke about *bhang* was meant to be ironic and was making fun of nationalists' tendency to worship the "traditional."[196] Others picked up on Sri Prakasa's tone and meaning. So, for example, when Ghanshyam Singh Gupta, the Hindu representative for the Central Provinces, raised concerns about the efficacy of tea propaganda, he began by asserting that he was neither a "tea taker, nor a *bhang* taker." He then repeated, "I never take tea and have never taken tea, almost never," a claim that left the others in the room laughing at his obvious white lie.[197] The commodity's supporters enjoyed pointing out that some of the beverage's loudest critics were inveterate tea drinkers. Kuladhar Chaliha, who was the non-Muslim representative for the Assam Valley and nationalist leader, was in favor of extending the cess though he hoped that there would be a great deal more Indian representation and oversight of the ITCC.[198] Chaliha wryly commented during the debate that tea's biggest detractor, his honorable friend Pandit Nilakantha Das, had frequently offered him tea when he visited his home and they had daily drunk tea when they had lived together.

Pandit Nilakantha Das, the architect of the modern state of Orissa, was a Hindu nationalist, writer, educator, and legislator who worked closely with Gandhi, Nehru, and Chandra Bose. He served as a member of the Central Legislative Assembly for a decade before independence and in the Orissa Legislative Assembly after independence. Orissa, a small and poor agricultural coastal state on the Bay of Bengal, below West Bengal, officially came into existence in 1936, though the region had been under British rule since 1803.[199] Das took a stand against the tea cess just as the region was developing a distinctive political identity. His district had long been a source of tea garden labor and thus its people had been much exploited by the industry. Like Gandhi, Das believed that the immoderate use of tea was a dangerous indulgence and that the tea campaign was the worst example of modern capitalism's manipulation of India's masses.

Das admitted that it was true that he, like others who had developed "Anglicized and Europeanised habits in cities like Delhi and Calcutta," had learned to drink tea, spend money, and live in an "occidental urban state of civilization." What especially worried him, however, was how the European vice was being pushed among the rural poor, whom he wanted to protect from the onslaughts of imperial modernity.[200] To build his argument, Das emphasized that tea was not a food, "like rice, wheat or *dal*," but a luxury that "our agriculturalists" could not afford. He worried about how buses and motorcars carried the beverage and tea's "official propaganda" into the "remotest parts of districts," where only the very lowest-quality tea was on sale. He was also furious that the Education Department in the United Provinces had approved the introduction of tea lessons in children's textbooks. Holding up a children's picture book that quoted Victorian Sidney Smith's quip, "Thank God for Tea," Das bemoaned how children were being controlled "from the school house."[201] He did not ask the government to outlaw the drink altogether, but he did call for the expansion and enforcement of anti-adulteration laws and the protection of India's most vulnerable consumers, children. A representative from Lucknow agreed and stated that if tea lessons were allowed, why not allow coffee or Ovaltine to similarly turn schoolbooks into advertisements?[202]

Other politicians were concerned about the illegal or at least immoral behavior of the "gentlemen of the Tea Cess Committee." One resented how committee employees had painted all over the municipal building that housed the Committee of Drugs in his district, "'Take Tea, Take Tea', and all that sort of thing."[203] Kuladhar Chaliha, who had poked such fun at Das's tea habit, complained that the committee had primarily employed Indians as "menials," and he wanted greater Indian presence on the ITCC and related agencies so they might "acquaint themselves with the world" and thus become ready for Independence.[204] The Muslim representative from Assam, Abdul Matin Chaudhury, agreed but he strongly supported the activities of the Tea Cess Committee because, as he put it, "the welfare and happiness of thousands of people in my province are closely bound up with the prosperity of this industry."[205]

As in Britain, Indian tea politics did not fall neatly along religious, regional, or other sectarian lines. Not surprisingly, supporters were often closely connected to the tea industry and related businesses or, as in the case of the recently knighted Sir Muhammed Zafrullah Khan, were working to achieve greater equality and status for Indians within the parameters of the British Empire.[206] Khan did not have a major part in the tea debate but he did tease Das for being a "tea addict" and asserted that he drank far less tea in a day than did the Honorable Member (Das) who so opposed the drink.[207] At the time Khan spoke out in favor of the tea industry, he was already a jurist and statesman who had served on the Punjab Legislative Council and had participated in the Round Table conferences held in London. He was president of the Muslim League, served as the Muslim representative on the viceroy's Executive Council, and had just become India's first railway minister. The author of the Pakistan Resolution, Khan would become Pakistan's first foreign minister, represent Pakistan at the United Nations, and later serve as president of the United Nations General Assembly and the International Court of Justice. He supported the cess and tea as a means to build up the Indian economy before Partition. Others pointed to the benefits of this "nourishing substance" and talked of tea as "the cup that cheers but does not inebriate."[208] Amarendra Nath Chattopadhyaya emphasized the fact that 20 percent of the industry was now in Indian hands and therefore it was not surprising that tea was "gradually becoming India's own national beverage." In wealthier urban districts consumption had reached more than 4 pounds per head, a rate on par with that of Canada.[209] Khan Bahadur Nawab Musharaff Hussain, one of the founders of the Indian Tea Planters' Association in Jalpaiguri in 1919, an all-Indian planters' organization that worked closely with the Indian Tea Association, also claimed tea was an Indian concern.[210]

Angered by such assertions, Ram Narayan Singh from Chota Nagpur exclaimed, "The whole of the tea industry is in the hands of Europeans. Not more than 15% of it is in Indian hands . . . [and] the European concerns in this country are the agents of British imperialism."[211] As time went on even former supporters of the tea cess such as Kuladhar Chaliha became apprehensive about the ITA after one of the fund's assistant superintendents, Mr. Powell, also known "Mr. Blood," was convicted of embezzlement in 1938.[212] In 1942, in the midst of the Quit India movement and wartime rationing, the famed educator and mathematician Ziauddin Ahmed introduced a bill to repeal the Indian Tea Cess Act of 1903 because he believed the ITCC was a fraudulent organization that symbolized British racism and moral bankruptcy. He illustrated this point by explaining how while traveling from Dacca to Calcutta via boat, Ahmed encountered "an Anglo-Indian who was in service of the Tea Cess Committee who, dead drunk . . . came in and began to make water on my blanket."[213] The ITCC, he proposed, was literally and figuratively stealing from and pissing on India.

Rather than backing down in the face of such attacks, the ITA intensified its work and at every public gathering encouraged Indians to drink Indian tea with countless ads and posters such as one that explained how "This Man and his Brothers Always Drink Tea" (figs. 7.3 and 7.4). In 1937, for example, the Tea Board inserted ads in 110 publications in nine different languages. Because newspapers were passed from hand to hand and often read aloud, the board believed that in one year it had effectively issued 120 million "messages." The ITCC sent a pamphlet titled "How to Prepare Tea" to high school students, teachers, medical practitioners, housewives, the heads of village *panchayats*, and local assemblies.[214] They also grew more intrusive and began to regulate how tea was sold and consumed. Not only did they inspect tea stalls for cleanliness

FIGURE 7.3. Indian Tea Cess Committee stall, Indian Industrial Exhibition, Delhi, c. 1935.
Tea Tells the World (London: International Tea Market Expansion Board, 1937), 41.
(By permission of UC Davis Special Collections)

FIGURE 7.4. "This Man and his Brothers Always Drink Tea." Advertising poster, India.
Tea Tells the World (London: International Tea Market Expansion Board, 1937), 39.
(By permission of UC Davis Special Collections)

and adulteration, the ITCC defined the practice of merchants selling tea "highly flavored with spices" as a form of adulteration.[215] Instead of seeing the spiced, milky, sweet tea—or what is sold today at so many Western cafés as chai—as a creative way that Indians made tea more familiar and affordable, promoters worried that this "spiced tea" would not contain enough actual tea and thus lead to diminished demand for their product. They made efforts therefore to try to teach people how to brew, sell, and drink tea as the British drank it. The ITCC's use of nationalism to sell tea was thus quite superficial, since they advertised tea as Indian but wanted Indians to shop, sell, and drink tea like the British.

The ITCC recognized that nationalism was a powerful force, so they did not mention that tea with milk and sugar served in dainty cups in the home was British; they simply featured Indian housewives making tea in this way and commissioned Indian artists to depict this "Universal Beverage" as "100% Swadeshi."[216] As historian Gautram Bhadra contends, the posters that Indian commercial artists used in the late 1930s deployed literary and visual categories that placed the consumption of tea into the category of high art.[217] Countless ads, however, also concentrated on tea's cheapness and "refreshing and stimulating properties."[218]

Tea was not a universal drink, but its consumption did begin to alter gender, class, regional, religious, and other identities. For example, the tea campaign increasingly sought out female consumers and tried to develop the type of middle-class female public culture that was emerging elsewhere.[219] It erected all-female enclosures in public spaces, hired "women's parties" to work in the *zenanas*, and set up women's pavilions at exhibitions.[220] The ITCC also built separate Hindu and Muslim tea stalls. Tea was also beginning to mark class identities, which differed by region. In Bengal in the 1930s, for example, tea was widespread and middle-class writers who began to grow nostalgic for the "authentic," healthy diet of the villages bemoaned how "tea and biscuits" had replaced "milk and yogurt" and had led to diabetes and dyspepsia.[221] "I do not like this tea-drinking life," wrote Hemantabala Debi, who went on to lament the loss of simplicity and the presumed restraint of the diet of the past. "Having 'foreign' foods like bread, eggs, and cake insult Indian culture," and thus Debi continued, "[we] forget our God and cheat ourselves."[222] In Tamilnadu in southern India, however, coffee signified middle-class status and tea became a working-class habit. Both beverages nevertheless were often condemned as a problematic product of colonialism that undid "traditional" diets and bodies.[223]

When Gandhi condemned tea advertising in 1935, he was participating in a very intense and widespread debate about the place of tea and consumer culture in global, national, and domestic economies. In India, the scale of

FIGURE 7.5. Breakfast meeting, Mahatma Gandhi and Lord Mountbatten at Government House, 1947. (Dinodia Photos/Alamy)

labor exploitation, the long-lasting drive to turn India into a nation of tea drinkers, and Gandhi's and other nationalists' sense that consumerism was an insidious form of colonization inspired a debate that echoed reactions to tea's introduction and taxation in early modern Britain and North America. Indians nevertheless did not reject tea, but they made it their own. Nothing captures the complex place of tea in India better than the photograph of the viceroy and Gandhi breakfasting together in 1947. Mountbatten, no doubt, needed to calm his nerves with a cup of tea while discussing the future of a postcolonial India with Gandhi (fig. 7.5).

———

During World War I and the 1920s and 1930s, Lord Beaverbrook, Mrs. Lidderdale, Sir Charles Higham, and Mahatma Gandhi understood that consumers had a political role to play. In Great Britain, protectionists, like Beaverbrook, argued that the mass consumption of empire-made goods would solve unemployment and bind together a fragile British Empire. The empire's tea growers took great advantage of such ideas, as they moved to the right and suggested that protectionism and consumerism, not liberalism and free trade, would save the empire. They harnessed grassroots conservatism to make the case that British consumers and buyers needed to purchase empire goods and urge their government to support protectionism, though it took some time before they achieved these aims, and they were never able to halt the globalization of production and markets in these years. Despite the fact that tea was becoming a global rather than an imperial good, the early 1930s was the high-water mark of the British empire of tea.

Tea's association with Britishness in these years led to very different consequences outside of the UK. American consumers resented this so-called British product, perhaps because of some leftover associations with colonial-era dependency but, more likely, because advertising often presented the ideal tea drinker as a middle-class, vaguely "British" woman. Some ads admitted that tea was a "he-man's drink," and planters spent a great deal in the States, but they came away feeling that this consumer-oriented nation simply would not be swayed. In India, planters and colonial officials still claimed, as they had in the prewar years, that consumption was a civilizing force that could quiet class conflict and nationalist protests. Some Indian nationalists discouraged consumption precisely because they rejected such views and wanted to limit tea's place in India's political economy. Instead of a cheerful beverage, they saw a deleterious force colonizing Indian consumers and laborers. Such protests were widespread and took many forms, but, in the end, they encouraged Indian-owned businesses and tea supporters to rebrand tea as an Indian product. The nationalization of Indian tea grew stronger after Independence, but in the late-colonial period politicians and Gandhi himself were deeply uncomfortable with tea, even as they admitted their own addiction to the drink.

British and American business experts, colonial officials, conservative activists, and Indian nationalists disagreed about the virtues of empire, but they all saw consumption as a social, political, and global act. All of these players broadened the idea of the consumer by highlighting the political and global implications of shopping. In Britain, this vision enfranchised women as imperial actors, but it did not question the class and racial dimensions of consumer culture. This critique did emerge in India. While nationalists did not stop Indians from drinking tea, they exposed how such a global trade that purported to be healthy could, as Gandhi claimed, also be poisonous. Just as today's consumer activists remind purchasers that their buying habits can have ramifications for workers and suppliers around the globe, the empire buying movement and anticolonial nationalism disclosed the global history of the commodity.

8

"TEA REVIVES THE WORLD"

Selling Vitality during the Depression

Duduring the 1920s and early 1930s, conservative politicians and activists had been enchanted with an empire that resembled a department store. Instead of appealing to the senses and individual desires, however, this store traded in duty and patriotism. State policy underwrote this mart, but it did so inconsistently and not all goods received the same space on the shelf. The meaning of empire and its products was inevitably complicated by intracolonial rivalries, party politics, tensions along and within the commodity chain, and the nature of local consumer and commercial cultures. With the adoption of imperial preferences in 1932, British and colonial governments appeared to have endorsed the logic of the empire buying movement. Yet the empire did not become a private emporium.[1] Something surprising happened instead.

The empire shopping ideal lost much of its vigor. In its place new international alliances and rhetorical strategies came to the foreground. Whether a similar turn occurred in other industries is not clear, but tea discarded imperialism as its primary advertising approach in the mid-1930s.[2] Remnants endured as trademarks and brand names, and the industry as a whole was still very much an imperial system, but planters and their publicists officially decolonized advertising and publicity. With a few notable exceptions, they stopped using and/or significantly altered the meaning of terms such as "empire grown" in promotions and replaced the ubiquitous pictures of plantations, tea factories, machinery, and sari-clad tea pickers with a small, round, jovial, talking teapot, aptly named Mr. T. Pott (fig. 8.1). Afrikaners called him Mr. T. Potje; in the

FIGURE 8.1. Mr. T. Pott and the Cuplets on a bus banner, *Tea Tells the World* (London: International Tea Market Expansion Board, 1937), 23. (By permission of UC Davis Special Collections)

United States, he often appeared as Mr. Ice Cube, but British popular culture, American advertising techniques, and internationalist-oriented modern graphic artists designed this advertising icon to represent and sell empire-grown teas from the 1930s until the 1950s. Developed by an organization of British and Dutch colonial tea growers known as the International Tea Market Expansion Board (ITMEB), Mr. T. Pott represented tea's first coordinated global advertising campaign. This forgotten but amusing character demonstrates how new European collaborations, commodity control schemes, protectionism, and the collective, emotional consequences of a depressed economy transformed both tea and advertising.

Instead of imperialism, Mr. T. Pott offered tea and sympathy. Uttering the mantra, "Tea Revives You," Mr. T. Pott characterized tea as a comfort, a pick-me-up, a friend, and a solace in hard times. Such ideas had been around for centuries, but they had been drowned out by the anti-Chinese rhetoric of the late nineteenth century and the bombast of the empire shopping movement of the early twentieth century. By the mid-1930s, however, the psychological experiences of living during the Depression, transformations in the global political economy of tea, and changes in consumer markets and the advertising profession made patriotism and specifically the empire pitch a hard sell and set the stage for Mr. T. Pott. The Tea Revives You Campaign proposed to cure the emotional and psychological consequences of unemployment, hunger, racial and class conflict, and imperial and other international crises.[3] Advertisers had always promised salvation, but during the Depression they relied on psychological and social sciences to understand consumer behaviors and emphasized themes of trauma and recovery. In the United States, for example, ads often advised confused and demoralized consumers on how to navigate the problems of modernity. Advertisers, speaking through products, promised to "console, befriend, and reassure the public as well as stimulate and guide it."[4] Outside of the United States, the therapeutic language of consumption was equally common but did not necessarily convey democracy, and democracy did not always mean unlimited access to goods as it did in America.[5] For example, as we will see in the last part of this chapter, the colonial state, missionaries, educational authorities, and business used therapeutic language to create a mass market in the decidedly undemocratic society of South Africa.[6] The appearance of Mr. T. Pott in 1934 and his travels thereafter suggest that many of the core characteristics of post–World War II consumer society began to develop in boardrooms, on drafting tables, and in offices in London, Calcutta, New York, and Durban in the 1930s.

REGULATING PRODUCTION AND FOSTERING CONSUMPTION:
THE ORIGINS OF THE INTERNATIONAL TEA MARKET
EXPANSION BOARD

As humble as he seemed, Mr. T. Pott personified shifts in imperial politics and global economic realities during the Depression. It is not surprising that he appeared when he did because, as one historian has written, "by 1933 the world economy was dead in the water." This was a period of "economic warfare" in which "war debts were repudiated, trade wars declared, competitive devaluations and exchange controls celebrated, and reparations denied."[7] Nevertheless, devalued currencies began to revive wages and living standards improved as retail prices declined. On the Continent, particularly in central and southern Europe, fascist economies rejected an older version of free trade and erected economic borders around the nation-state.[8] Britain instead put up borders around its empire, but this did not negate the formation of international corporatist arrangements.

In 1933 Dutch and British tea growers abandoned their longstanding commercial rivalry and signed an agreement to restrict the production of tea. A number of factors drove these empires together to sign what was known as the International Tea Agreement. After the British adopted protectionism in Ottawa in 1932, Dutch tea interests became concerned that they would lose the market share they had been gaining during the previous decade.[9] Hitler's appointment as chancellor in Germany and Mussolini's growing power in Italy also drew the British and Dutch together, but the immediate push for British tea growers was the realization that imperial preference had not stopped distributors from sourcing Dutch colonial teas. It had certainly not made up for the comparative price benefits that Dutch teas enjoyed after the British had abandoned the gold standard in September 1931 and British sterling had devalued against the Dutch guilder. Rather than continue to drive down prices, the Dutch and British put aside differences and formed an international cartel.[10] The institutions they created were designed to protect their imperial industries, but the Tea Agreement was also a step toward European economic integration.

Production formally came under control on 1 April 1933, when the Indian Tea Association, South Indian Association, Ceylon Association, Vereniging voor de Thee-Cultuur in Nederlandsch Indië (Amsterdam), and the Nederlandsch Indische Vereniging voor de Thee-Cultuur in Nederlandsch Indië (Batavia) entered into a legally binding agreement to regulate exports for a period of five years, subject to renewal thereafter. Since tea supplies vary by the extent of plucking—fine plucking is taking two leaves and a bud, while coarse plucking involves taking more leaves—outputs are difficult to control, so the plan that went into effect was based on the restriction of exports. The International Tea

Agreement set reduced export quotas based on a percentage of the maximum volume in the best of the three years between 1929 and 1931. India's quota was initially fixed at 382,594,779 pounds, Ceylon at 251,522,617, and the Netherlands East Indies (NEI) at 173,597,000.[11] The agreement also limited the export of seed, colonial governments' power to sell or lease further land for cultivation, and growers' ability to convert lands used for other crops into tea estates. In 1934 Nyasaland (Malawi), Kenya, Uganda, and Tanganyika were brought into the scheme. Southern Rhodesia and British Malaya did not join but they did limit the expansion of production.[12]

The International Tea Agreement strengthened the bonds between British, Dutch, and "native" producers, while widening the gulf between those in the agreement and other growing nations and regions. China, Japan, Formosa, Portuguese East Africa, and French Indochina did not sign on to the agreement, though China did voluntarily restrict exports to try to revive the tea market. Most of these areas did not produce or export enough to affect prices, however.[13] As time went on quotas were renegotiated and by 1937 prices returned to levels not seen since the late 1920s. As a result, the agreement was renegotiated in 1938. Tea control also, however, maintained British hegemony in this industry. The International Tea Committee, the new administrative body that oversaw production and its regulation, was based in London and membership was calculated in relation to export quotas, giving India 38 votes, Ceylon 25, and the NEI 17. Together Ceylon and India could influence decisions, but since it required a unanimous vote to make major changes, British producers could not totally dominate. The committee included indigenous membership even as many European businesses resisted "indigenization" and the constitutional reforms that were incorporating colonized people into colonial governments at the same time.[14]

Historians are still debating whether indigenization was a conscious means to plan for or stave off decolonization.[15] After the fact, many saw this process simply as a power play to retain markets with or without formal political controls. In an interview given long after Independence, a former employee of Imperial Tobacco concluded that he and other Indians were being hired by British firms in the 1930s because these businesses "realized that one day they would have to go and they knew once the Empire was gone they couldn't afford to lose their commercial interests."[16] Moreover, trade association reports and other business documents are so quiet and so uniform during a time of intense nationalist fervor that we should see them as a public relations effort that sought to present corporate bodies as a united front, with Europeans and non-Europeans working together to fight the Depression.[17] We know from the Indian legislative debates discussed in the last chapter that racial and political tensions existed and that tea's propagandists often misbehaved, embezzled funds, painted graffiti on walls, and pissed on the belongings of Indian politicians. Yet the rhetoric surrounding the International Tea Agreement emphasized collaboration, inclusion, and international friendship in ways that suppressed opposition and bolstered the status quo. Advertising did as well.

A little-recognized but very important aspect of the International Tea Agreement was a clause requiring member governments to levy cesses to support global propaganda. The idea of the cess, it will be remembered, first developed in Ceylon in the early 1890s to secure funds to put on a really big show in Chicago and produce a distinctive "brand" identity for their tea and their island. Using this same kind of tax, the International Tea Agreement created the International Tea Market Expansion Board (ITMEB) in July 1935, a body whose sole purpose was to promote global consumption of British and Dutch colonial teas. With an initial annual budget of £250,000, collected from governments and planters' associations in India, Ceylon, and the NEI, and smaller amounts from British Africa, the ITMEB publicized the merits of tea drinking in the United Kingdom and other major markets.[18] Its territorial reach and remit were similar to the ad hoc arrangements that had worked since the 1880s, yet there is some evidence to suggest that the Tea Board, as it came to be known, was also influenced by the new market landscape created by the Sterling bloc, a group of countries that since 1931 had fixed their currencies to sterling and did most of their trading in that currency.[19] The ITMEB's territory kept old markets alive but also added new territories from within the Sterling bloc. The ITMEB initially chose to market tea in the UK, the United States, Canada, Australia, Holland, Belgium, Sweden, South Africa, Egypt, India, Ceylon, and the NEI. In a sense, then we see another international trade relationship emerging and overlapping with but not replacing the British World and the British Empire.

Territories would be gained and lost, but the ITMEB lasted through depression, war, postwar austerity, and the early years of South Asian decolonization. It became the basis for later efforts at market expansion and remains the key model for producer marketing of generic products, especially foods and agricultural commodities. The Tea Board expanded markets during the surpluses of the 1930s and preserved tea's consumer culture during wartime rationing and the shortages of the 1940s and early 1950s. In addition to selling tea, this body created and sustained transnational business relationships, espoused the ideals of international cooperation, and measured, described, and advertised to "national" markets. Lest we forget, when we are interrogating its advertising, the ITMEB was a colonial institution paid for by the sweat of laborers who cleared land, weeded, fertilized, picked, sorted, and manufactured tea.

At the first meeting of the ITMEB, the chairman of the International Tea Committee, the body that regulated production, Sir Robert Graham, explained the ITMEB's raison d'être: "It is only through an expansion in the consumption of tea that we are likely to bring about a complete recovery of the industry."[20] Though in the past he had often pushed Indian tea in preference to alternatives, Graham now proposed that advertising should be generic since "propaganda directed towards the appropriation of one country's market by another country's does not help to increase consumption of the industry's combined output."[21] Sir Charles Higham had argued this point in the United States a decade earlier and Gervas Huxley had already begun to make the same argument when he asserted that to advertise one colony's tea over that of another was a waste of resources that merely diverted "trade from one producer to another."[22] Tea growers from the major producing colonies came to the same conclusion.[23] The ITMEB made this view their policy and advertised tea as simply tea. Moreover, it couched its efforts in language reminiscent of the Spirit of Locarno, the 1925 treaty that admitted Germany into the League of Nations. As the European peace settlement was quickly unraveling, however, the ITMEB offered tea as a symbol of internationalism that would preserve the British Empire and its liberal allies—a heavy burden, indeed.

The ITMEB was, in fact, a parent organization for several similar regional promotional bodies. The Indian Tea Cess Committee, for example, became the Indian Tea Market Expansion Board in 1937.[24] In 1932, Ceylon reimposed the cess and set up the Ceylon Tea Propaganda Board, which Gervas Huxley directed for the next thirty-five years, along with his work for the ITMEB.[25] In 1933, the Dutch colonial government established the Batavia-based Crisis-Tea-Central Bureau, which beginning in 1936 was funded by a tea cess.[26] These bodies also worked closely with the Indian Tea Association, the Ceylon Association, and the Association for Tea Culture in the Netherlands East Indies (Vereniging Voor de Thee-Cultuur in Nederlandsh-Indië). The bodies shared personnel, market information, and strategies, but the International Tea Market Expansion Board ruled as the global center for international tea marketing through the war and for more than a decade after these colonies gained independence.

All of these organizations were racially mixed. For example, a third of the Indian Tea Market Expansion Board and its executive committee were designated for "Indian" representation, who were nominated by the Bengal, Madras, South Indian, and Associated Chambers of Commerce, the Federation of Indian Chambers of Commerce and Industry, and the Indian Tea Association.[27] Huxley recalled in his memoir how he determined that half of Ceylon's board should be of Tamil, Sinhalese, Sinhalese-Portuguese, and Sinhalese-Dutch descent.[28] This was written much later, but nevertheless these bodies included local businessmen, who often rose to leadership positions after independence. Despite this development, European businessmen and virtually all the major tea-producing companies led and were well represented on these boards.

Sir Robert Graham, for example, had been a planter in Assam and a partner in the firm of P. R. Buchanan and Company; he occupied the chairmanship of James Finlay and Co., and at various times served as chairman of the Indian Tea Association, the Indian Tea Cess Committee, and related bodies. He was a member of the Assam Legislative Council and represented the province on the Simon Commission in 1930, among numerous other jobs.[29] The ITMEB's first chairman, Sir Alfred D. Pickford, had worked with Graham in Assam and served as chairman of Begg, Dunlop and Co. in 1915–16. Pickford was also a leading figure in the Boy Scout movement and was as much an empire enthusiast as was the movement's founder, Sir Baden-Powell.[30] The ITMEB's three "technical" members, Gervas Huxley (Ceylon), J. A. Milligan (India), and Dirk Lageman (NEI), handled the ITMEB's global advertising. While Gervas Huxley had cut his teeth working for the Empire Marketing Board, J. A. Milligan came from Graham and Pickford's world. He was the representative of the Bengal European Constituency in the Legislative Assembly and one of the most determined advocates for the continuation of the tea cess in 1935. He also had been chairman of the Indian Tea Cess Committee in Calcutta and was an industry advisor especially well versed in African and Middle Eastern markets.[31] Lageman had worked for the Dutch firm George Wehry and Co., which had managed large tea, coffee, and rubber estates in Java and was also a major importer of Manchester goods, hardware, general provisions, and several brand-name alcoholic and nonalcoholic beverages. By the 1920s, the firm had offices throughout Southeast Asia and in Manchester, Amsterdam, and Paris.[32] As these men's biographies indicate, the ITMEB consisted of globetrotting merchants, planters, and propagandists who were convinced that global mass markets would preserve the interests and needs of the British and Dutch empires.

Based in London, the ITMEB was also closely connected with metropolitan ad men and women and was a venue for colonial business and officialdom to meet American and British advertising experts. At its meetings planters learned about publicity and advertisers studied global markets and consumer cultures. While the ITMEB's message was very different from that of the Empire Marketing Board and it produced far less famous advertising and posters, this now forgotten entity took over many of the functions and even the staff of the EMB. Between 1935 and 1952, the ITMEB coordinated and funded advertising and publicity campaigns that targeted and in a sense constituted a global mass market, appealing to working-class and non-white as well as middle- and upper-class consumers on several continents at once. While brand advertising tried to create differences among similar products, the ITMEB's advertising homogenized and standardized tea. The ITMEB did this by inventing simple slogans and emblems that could easily travel across regions, borders, classes, races, and genders. The institution was sensitive to cultural differences, but its primary philosophy was that the same cup of tea could satisfy all consumers. The ITMEB's leadership imagined that all consumers were essentially the same, at least in their desires if not their capacities to consume. Yet they also reached consumers by insinuating tea into local understandings of the nation, the psyche, and the body. This standardization of the product and advertising was critical to tea's globalization, but as cultural theorist Arjun Appadurai has explained, advertising also "repatriated" global goods within "heterogeneous" ideals of national sovereignty.[33] Mr. T. Pott helps us see how this process unfolded.

MR. T. POTT, GRACIE FIELDS, AND THE THERAPEUTIC VALUE OF TEA AND SYMPATHY

In 1935 a teacher at a secondary school in North Finchley, London, asked students between the ages of twelve and fifteen to develop an advertisement for any J. Lyons and Company product. The students invented several catchy and sophisticated jingles that echoed themes already present in the firm's advertising. Barbara Yates, for example, suggested that "If you feel Weary, A Cup of Lyons Tea Will Buck you Up." Another student labeled Lyons tea "The Genie of Strength."[34] This school project originated in Lyons's corporate headquarters, the results were published in an advertising trade journal, and the students' finished work was stored in the company's archive. Lyons's brands would have been very familiar to the children. Its tea shops, corner houses, restaurants, and catering department had fed and entertained millions since the late nineteenth century. Its branded foods and drinks were staples in most British larders, and its huge tea-packing plant, then the largest in the world, was but a few miles away from the children's homes.[35] This school assignment is a snippet in a larger account about the invention of the child consumer and the commercialization of the schoolroom.[36] However, this assignment also uncovers how advertising began to obscure the imperial origins of the commodity. None of the boys and girls wrote about the history, geography, or imperial provenance of tea despite decades of propaganda that had explicitly tried to make Britons recognize its colonial history. What then does the absence of national and imperial stories suggest? One might assume that British youth knew and cared little about the empire or the labor that manufactured their way of life, or that they had somehow missed the object lessons that had for so long demonstrated the value of empire shopping.[37] I argue, however, that, far from being inattentive, these children were savvy readers of popular culture with a clear awareness of the most up-to-date advertising trends. Whereas Victorian and Edwardian advertising had almost obsessively sought to nationalize the commodity by focusing on the mode of production, interwar advertising increasingly attributed national characteristics to consumers.[38] These were never mutually exclusive, but during the Depression advertisers increasingly described how drinking tea benefited economically and psychologically depressed consumers, a notion that easily crossed political borders. Though British business did not invest as much in mass marketing as U.S. corporations did, the ITMEB and related bodies did embrace market research, indicating that an older colonial business welcomed "modern" publicity methods associated with U.S. business, and indeed Americans worked for the ITMEB in a variety of capacities but most often as consultants.[39] British advertising was thus a transnational institution well before the postwar era of affluence and prosperity, and in the 1930s this international business found new tools to describe and produce national consumer cultures.[40]

Like so much of interwar mass culture, ITMEB's advertising tried to strike a balance between the wants and needs of diverse audiences.[41] Humor was one way to do this since it often played upon and assumed a sense of commonality and camaraderie, and lightheartedly challenged class and gender hierarchies. Mass culture in the 1930s, was especially preoccupied with what one study of humor in advertising described as "playful confusion and contrasts."[42] This was Walt Disney's approach. In the late 1920s and early 1930s, he invented a menagerie of energetic and intelligent animals, talking objects, and surreal fantasy worlds that broke with the strict divisions of Victorian culture and sensibilities.[43] To be sure, Victorian advertisers liked humor and spectacle, but Disney used humor to build a new kind of global empire of leisure, fantasy, and consumerism.[44] Disney's humor, and that of the 1930s in general, was in a sense understood as modern because of the way it played with and undermined Victorian separate spheres.[45]

Advertising in the 1930s also broke down what had been the separate spheres of the comic strip and the traditional advertisement. Advertisements began to impersonate the style of the comic strip by creating a series of discrete panels advancing a narrative about a product and its users, and these ads often appeared within the comic pages of major newspapers. In the United States, it appears that General Foods' "Suburban Joe" Grape-Nuts cereal ads from 1931 launched a wave of similar attempts from the likes of Jell-O, Ovaltine, Listerine, and many other brands.[46] Other ads drew from the style of comics, for example, using word balloons, alliterative language, cartoon characters, and memorable punch lines.[47] Whether they were copying Disney or merely responding to the same contexts, advertisers also created an array of cartoon-like product "characters" and anthropomorphic animals to represent brands. This sort of advertising transformed the things themselves into entertainers whose antics amused consumers of all ages.

Perhaps no form of advertising better fits what Marx had called commodity fetishism. In his much-cited passage in *Capital* that introduced the idea, Marx wrote, "A commodity appears, at first sight, a very trivial thing, and easily understood. Its analysis shows that it is, in reality a very queer thing, abounding in metaphysical subtleties and theological niceties."[48] For Marx, the magical or mysterious quality of things came from the way in which they represented without revealing the sum total of the labor that produced them. As he explained, commodities were "social things whose qualities are at the same time perceptible and imperceptible by the senses."[49] While late Victorian and Edwardian tea advertising commodified the laborer, the factory, and the machine, and the empire shopping movement introduced the notion of a shared community of consumers, 1930s advertisers proposed that the consumer too could be revived or brought to life through consumption of the lively and cheerful commodity.[50]

S. H. Benson, one of Britain's leading advertising agencies, handled the ITMEB's British campaign.[51] Samuel Herbert Benson had originally worked as an advertising agent to handle the Bovril account in 1893, but within a decade his firm was in charge of many brands.[52] In the interwar years, Benson's Guinness, Bovril, and Coleman Mustard campaigns were so well-known that the advertising executive David Ogilvy later remarked they "were part of the warp and woof of English life."[53] Dorothy L. Sayers worked at Benson's as a copywriter and she helped invent such memorable catchphrases as "Guinness for Strength" and "My Goodness, My Guinness."[54] Sayers also worked closely with illustrator John Gilroy to develop Guinness's amusing zoo animals, and especially its famous toucan. The ads and objects that accompanied Benson's Guinness campaign turned an Irish product that had been around since the eighteenth century into one of the most successful beverage brands in the world.[55]

Benson's Tea Board campaign, much of which was drawn by Gilroy, was similar to and likely derivative of the Guinness campaign. Instead of strength, however, tea gave vitality, though it too featured anthropomorphic animals and objects. Mr. T. Pott had actually been developed in the autumn of 1934 for Indian and Ceylon planters' UK advertising just before the formation of the ITMEB. In 1935, however, he became an international icon that globalized then prevalent notions of British character. Mr. T. Pott was fundamentally working class, jovial, domestic, and far removed from plantations and empires. Mr. T. Pott was not a fancy china import but modeled after the famous Brown Betty. Invented in the late Georgian period, the so-called Brown Betty was a terracotta clay pot covered with a brown Rockingham glaze and was treasured not as a work of art but as a utilitarian object that because it retained heat well made good tea. The Brown Betty was and remains a democratic symbol in Britain, treasured by rich and poor alike.[56]

In imitating the round shape of John Bull, Mr. T. Pott also echoed other expressions of Britishness popular in the 1930s and reflected the "Anglocentric" turn in interwar culture.[57] Novelists, historians, social scientists, politicians, and popular culture became obsessed with uncovering the essence of "English national character."[58] Though Britishness and Englishness were often used interchangeably at home and in the empire, increasingly John Bull shifted from the expansionist empire builder of Kipling's day to what Harold Nicholson described as "small, kindly, bewildered, modest, obstinate and very lovable."[59] This inward-looking, island-oriented Englishness recast women and especially men as domestic, "nice, decent, essentially private people . . . self-effacing and without bombast."[60] This humble, working-class Englishness also contrasted with violent, fascist expressions of national identity that were becoming prevalent on the Continent.[61] It was also a means to conveniently displace the realities of the colonial world, which certainly were not nice, decent, or kind.

Mr. T. Pott's personality projected the new island-centered, domestic national identity, but in experts' eyes he also exemplified thoroughly modern advertising. The planters' journal *Home and Colonial Mail* predicted that Mr. T. Pott, a "brilliantly designed and entirely new advertising figure," would become as well-known and important as "Johnny Walker," but he would tell the British and the world all they needed was "a good cup of tea."[62] Johnny Walker Whisky introduced the Striding Man logo in 1908, and though it was altered from time to time over the course of the last century, the Striding Man has remained one of the most famous advertising icons in the world. Like the Striding Man, Mr. T. Pott could appear in virtually any type or form of advertisement, but unlike him he lacked elegance and in a way that was the point. Mr. T. Pott and his sidekicks the Cuplets were ordinary and accompanied the British working classes especially to work and even on vacation, appearing, for example, on the side of tea trolleys at Butlin's holiday camp in Skegness (fig. 8.2).[63] This "advertising celebrity" was said to be leading a "crusade against the droops" in London and the Home Counties, the Midlands, Lancashire and Yorkshire, Scotland, and Ireland.[64] The slogan "Down the Droops with Tea" was soon replaced by the pithy phrase "Tea Revives You," but the sentiment was the same. Tea would revive a depressed United Kingdom.

The Tea Board also employed real celebrities, such as the British film star Gracie Fields, to sell tea. "Our Gracie," as she often was called, was known as the "Lancashire Lass" whose humor and northern working-class background represented the new domestic, self-effacing, anti-heroic Britishness.[65] Of all

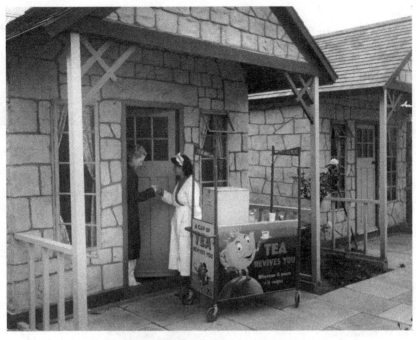

FIGURE 8.2. A tea lady at a Butlin's holiday camp in Skegness, c. 1930s.
(Hulton Getty/Getty Images)

British film stars in this period, Gracie Fields personified national consensus and a never-give-up attitude. *World Film News* described Fields as the "clown member of the family who can be relied on to chase away the blues. The mill girl . . . made good."[66] Fields was a symbol of social mobility and, as one scholar has suggested, an anti-American form of film celebrity who preferred "a hot pot straight off the hob" to American "waffles and corn on the cob."[67] Fields especially spoke to the working class and unemployed who went to the movies and lingered daily over a cheap pot of tea in a neighborhood café.[68] But she also symbolized the new forms of working-class leisure that emerged during these years. Fields, for example, entertained Butlin's holiday campers at Skegness in the summer of 1938. Along with Mr. T. Pott, and the holiday camps' many entertainments, Fields revived Britain's weary working classes, particularly its tired housewives.[69] "Our Gracie" and Mr. T. Pott thus gave an old and cheap commodity a kind of everyday celebrity that fit the vision of the island nation that J. B. Priestly and others were inventing in the 1930s and through the war years.[70] Still, the real person who would be cheered by such ads was the shopkeeper; as an ITMEB display explained to tea dealers and grocers, "Miss Gracie Fields' smile in your window means more business in your shop" (fig. 8.3).[71]

I. THREE-PIECE PELMET

Designed, like the 'proscenium' of a theatre, to be an attractive display in itself and to carry the full advertising message. Centre strip 12¼″ × 60″; side pieces 13¼″ × 17¼″ each; full width 86¼″. Side pieces can be closed in to fit exact size of smaller window.

2. CENTRE-PIECE

Chief attention-getter for window display. Carrying full advertising message. Especially designed to be useful inside the shop, after window display. Takes a number of packets. Size 24″ × 21″.

3 and 3A. STICKERS

Size 17″ × 7″. These stress "Tea Occasions" featured in press advertising, i.e., Early Morning and Mid-Morning Tea. A third, featuring Mid-Evening Tea, is available (3B).

4 and 4A. CARDS

Size 12″ × 9″. Attractive for window or interior use; both stressing "Good Tea."

5 and 5A. CUT-OUTS

Two companion cut-outs, each holding a packet and both selling "Good Tea." Size 14½″ × 12½″. Splendid for window, counter or shelf.

MISS GRACIE FIELDS' SN

FIGURE 8.3. Gracie Fields store display, ITMEB, c. 1935.
(Courtesy of Mike Brain/The Brain Family, Leeds, England)

ITMEB publicity also transformed the factory worker into a celebrity. John Gilroy drew one of the campaign's most memorable posters that featured a middle-aged assembly line worker smiling as he smells a hot cup of tea coming down the line (fig. 8.4).[72] This poster sold tea as a necessary tool of modern industry, and it continued the nearly century-long effort to introduce tea breaks and services at work. The poster proposed that doing so would create a productive, content, and "modern" working class. The new automobile factory that was featured here was no coincidence, since the auto industry was among the segments of the economy that were leading Britain out of the Depression. This poster fit a theme in this period: tea was said to energize tired factory and office workers, housewives and agricultural laborers, university students and schoolchildren. Tea made everyone feel "vital" and "refreshed." It was in effect a panacea suitable for everyone living in a pressured modern world.

Tea was not sexy and it would not make one more beautiful or attractive, as other products claimed. Rather it made one feel less pain, listlessness, and nervous energy. During the Depression, an array of nerve tonics, vitamins, mouthwashes, and other products also promised to make one less sluggish. Some scholars have proposed that this phenomenon was a resurgence of the quack medicine puffery that was common in the eighteenth century.[73] However, these products and therapeutic-type advertising echoed the new psychosocial language of expertise that was becoming popular at this time and seems to have also seeped into consumers' vocabulary and self-perceptions.[74] Such advertising also furthered new ideals of health and physical fitness that emerged as a reaction to the devastating physical experience of dismember-ment and disease brought by the Great War.[75] Gilroy's happy and healthy worker was a stark contrast to common representations of unemployed fathers

FIGURE 8.4. "Tea Revives You." Poster by John Gilroy, ITMEB, c. 1935.
(Courtesy of Gilroy Family Estate)

and husbands in the 1930s. The figure in Gilroy's Tea Board poster was a fantasy for so many, but the poster also implied that at least a cup of tea was an attainable desire.

In addition to cartoonish characters and posters, film was becoming a mainstay of modern propaganda. The Conservative Party, Empire Marketing Board, General Post Office, Colonial Office, and many other entities, for example, developed film units to educate people at home and in the colonies about the logic of imperial protectionism. A new screening culture also emerged, which included mainstream movie theaters but also included mobile vans, schools, museums, and a host of other seemingly noncommercial spheres.[76] The Tea Board, too, hired well-known filmmakers and created long and short films, which it distributed to all of its major markets. Some films closely fit the Tea Revives You theme and presented tea as engendering good humor and a sense of comfort. For example, *Tea Town*, an "amusing" cartoon, opened with a parade of "merry Teapot gnomes" who scurry "into the world to make it a more cheerful place to live in." The gnomes encounter and ultimately cheer up the gloomy "Ancient Order of the Droops."[77] In this film, the teapot is a kind, happy, and harmless creature whose aim is to lead consumers out of their personal and national depression. However, other films updated the type of imperial advertising that was so popular during the end of the previous century. *Monsoon Island*, *The Villages of Lanka*, and *Negombo Coast*, and the much more famous full-length documentary produced by Basil Wright for the Ceylon Tea Propaganda Board, *The Song of Ceylon* (1934), distributed by the ITMEB, were ethnographic documentaries typical of much late imperial filmmaking.[78] Purporting to be realistic, these documentaries commodified indigenous laborers as spectacle and celebrated the way that colonialism had brought modern "Western" technology to develop the colonies. These films explained how tea was made, where it grew, and how it traveled to the world to reach an imagined Western consumer. They romanticized tea gardens as Oriental spaces, eroticized the bodies of female tea pickers, and celebrated the modernity of industrial colonial agriculture. Young and old viewers at home and in the colonies watched both kinds of films together, thus making the point that the empire ultimately made them healthy and cheerful.

These films and ITMEB advertising revealed a perceptible and growing tension then between nostalgia and modernity, and different versions of both ideologies. Nostalgia was itself a reaction to and product of modernity.[79] The heritage industry was a cultural response to the perception that Britain, particularly its industrial economy, was in decline, but it also was one of the most dynamic sectors of the British economy and one that the tea industry seized upon.[80] To give just one example, the 1930s tea shop invented a version of its own and Britain's past that was never reality but made tea part of the interwar heritage industry. The Victorian tea shop had been a global, modern retail and marketing institution, but owners and designers of such institutions tried to make it seem as though they had been a feature of village life since at least the early Victorian days. Commenting on this trend, one expert suspiciously suggested that tea shops' efforts to advertise "wholesome home-made cakes" with their "old-fashioned goodness" were merely a ploy to counter housewives' suspicion (sometimes with good reason) "that mass-produced cakes have faked chemical flavors."[81] Tea shops of this era mastered the Old World style that was a ubiquitous feature of the modern tourist industry in Great Britain. The Thistle Tea Rooms in the Haymarket, for example, were decorated with paintings "of typical Scottish scenes," the waitresses wore tartan uniforms, and the menu created "an all important part of national atmosphere." Scotch broth with plenty of barley and shortbread conveyed a rural and old-fashioned Scotland to the English, foreign tourists, and Scots who missed the taste of home.[82] In this era, tea shops that had been furnished with Oriental decor were often redecorated with mock Tudor furniture, chintz, and memorabilia of village life. Tea thus became part of the heritage industry dedicated to selling nostalgia. This environment reinforced the story that tea was calming and quintessentially British—and, depending on the context, Scottish, Welsh, Irish, or English.

Quaint tea rooms, Mr. T. Pott, and Gracie Fields nationalized tea in a way that made it difficult for consumers to look beyond the British Isles and see how they were participating in supporting an aggressive imperial industry. Promises of health and recovery, humor, heritage, insular nationalism, and celebrations of the common people and social harmony encouraged a country of tea drinkers to buy and drink even more of their favorite beverage, but these ideologies severed the stories of production and consumption that Victorian tea interests and later empire enthusiasts had so diligently manufactured. Neither style of advertising was particularly truthful, but they reflect different understandings of the British nation that were common in each era. The 1930s had many leftovers of old-style imperial propaganda, but consumers who ventured into the Thistle Tea Rooms, the grocer who put Gracie Fields's smile in his shop window, and the working-class housewife who opened the door of her holiday camp bungalow to find Mr. T. Pott bringing her a morning cuppa would have had to work very hard indeed to discover the part they played in violent and repressive forms of colonial rule and globalization. When Barbara Yates devised the slogan "If you feel Weary, A Cup of Lyons Tea Will Buck you Up," she was not demonstrating her innate ignorance of the fruits of the British Empire. She was showing just how clearly she understood the grammar of advertising during the Depression.

THE GLOBAL TRAVELS OF MR. T. POTT

As we have seen, the iconography associated with the ITMEB's Tea Revives You Campaign echoed the shifting ideas of nation and the growing professionalization of global advertising. But this was not merely a British campaign, for, at the same time the ITMEB advertised throughout the British Isles, it also worked in a number of foreign markets, where it confronted consumers and merchants with a bewildering array of habits and tastes. The ITMEB thus felt that they needed to gather quantitative and qualitative data to help them adjust their message to local conditions. Based on this research, the board typically altered the image of the consumer, but not the commodity, and only slightly adjusted their ad campaign's underlying message. Generally speaking, the board researched what they viewed were "national" markets and they sought to adopt Mr. T. Pott's look to fit "national" tastes. Similar processes were at work elsewhere as international businesses, trade, and migration created and exported national cultures, cuisines, and foodways. Italian immigrants in the United States, for example, largely produced and internationalized the key elements of what we now recognize as Italian cuisine. French chefs introduced techniques and flavors that became identified as French but they also helped shape Mexican and other food traditions. Cookbook authors and food writers critically codified and standardized this process and defined food nations.[83] The ITMEB's history demonstrates how colonial business and the advertising world did so as well, inserting tea into multiple food nations at once.

Like any business, the ITMEB could not sell on a truly global scale. In order to determine where to invest their energies, the board's technical members, Huxley, Milligan, and Lageman, went on frequent investigative business trips and began to develop the basic tools of modern market research. According to one leading scholar on the subject, modern marketing involved "deciding marketing objectives in relation to a firm's products and then integrating research, production, advertising, selling and distribution into a policy and program designed to secure these objectives."[84] Huxley, Milligan, and Lageman did just that as they gathered information about population size and income, tariffs, duties and other taxes, distribution systems, established drink habits, cultural prejudices, and desires.[85] They then decided where and how to sell their goods based on this information. They initially chose the United States, Canada, Australia, Holland, Belgium, Sweden, South Africa, and Egypt—a familiar yet also new geography held together by transnational, imperial, and personal relationships, and the new trade dynamics established by the Sterling bloc. Britain, India, Ceylon, and the Netherlands East Indies were also important markets, so much so that work in these territories was officially left to local boards that reported to the ITMEB.

The ITMEB and local boards engaged in quantitative and qualitative forms of research. Research began with a series of meetings and conversations and ended with reports, correspondence, phone calls, and more meetings. There were two key periods when economic conditions generated a great deal of market research. One was in the mid-1930s, just after the ITMEB formed, and the other was in the early 1950s, when the ITMEB broke up into separate market expansion boards and when a free trade in tea production and consumption returned after more than a decade of rationing and controls. In addition to the studies done by the ITMEB, the Indian and Ceylon boards also hired market research agencies even during the war, and in the 1950s the South African branch of the ITMEB conducted some of the most sophisticated analyses of all. Such research became the basis for massive advertising and merchandising promotions that explained how tea was cheap, healthy, and "reviving."

In the 1930s, market researchers tended to assume that national "character" determined and was shaped by drink habits. Some countries, such as France, were wine-imbibing nations, while others enjoyed beer, coffee, or other beverages. However, researchers were not so naïve as to think that this meant that people only liked products that their nation produced and consumed. Indeed, by this era the ITMEB's experts understood that nationalism could operate in complex and often unforeseen ways. Lageman, for example, theorized that nations could adopt the tastes and habits of other nations. In his reports on northern Europe, Lageman frequently ruminated on such questions. For example, after visiting Norway, Lageman concluded that Norwegians would learn to like tea because "the population is very anglophile and therefore *loves to take over English habits.*" Although Lageman concluded that Norwegians were by nature conservative, he also acknowledged that their "social democratic" views made them open to cooperative advertising campaigns.[86] By this he meant that Norwegians would like the generic, seemingly classless sort of advertising that was being used in the UK at the time. Similarly, in his study of Belgium, he announced: "Everything English is very popular in Belgium."[87] Belgium was a tiny market with a population of eight million in 1936 and per capita tea consumption at just over one and a third the Tea Board believed that cultural factors were more significant than numbers, and it wrestled with such questions in every market.[88]

While venturing tentatively into new markets, the ITMEB tended to repeat many past efforts, recycling the type of advertising that planters' associations had used for decades. In this respect, the body reflected the cyclical and I would argue repetitive nature of capitalist culture. Capitalism, as Joyce Appleby tells us, is a "relentless revolution," but while it produced ongoing change in the sphere of production, this was not always the case in the realm of advertising, with its endless repetition with subtle variations.[89] One of these repetitions was the tea industry's desire to "tap [the] enormous potentialities" of the United States, but *not* because experts still looked on it as an Anglophile nation.[90] Huxley asserted he was very "familiar with the American way of life" and thus could confidently say that contrary to popular opinion Americans did not "behave like Englishmen" and did not "look at the world through English eyes." He wrote in his memoir that Englishmen "tended to forget how much of the population of the United States was of non-British stock, and that such people had no common historical ties with us, or, like the Irish, had good reason to dislike us." Huxley further pointed out that one need only visit a midwestern town like Wichita, Kansas, to "understand how remote Europe and its problems must seem to its inhabitants."[91]

Huxley thus declared that it was necessary to cook up a distinctive American tea culture, but he shared many of the same assumptions as his predecessors. To "Americanize" tea, Huxley hired Bill Esty, a former top executive with J. Walter Thompson, to use his "cynical, no-nonsense" and "purely American approach" and work "right away" to minimize the "prevalent notion that tea was just an English beverage."[92] In an ironic episode, however, that underscores the "Englishness" of U.S. tea cultures, Huxley asked Helen Rogers Reid, Ogden Reid's wife, who became publisher of the *New York Herald Tribune* after his death in 1947, to host an elegant "English tea" in her Park Avenue mansion to convince Lageman and Milligan to hire Esty. Born in Appleton, Wisconsin, in 1882, Helen Rogers began her career in journalism as the social secretary to Elizabeth Mills Reid, who was married to the owner of the *New York Tribune*. Helen married the couple's son Ogden but it was she, as the person in charge of advertising, who became responsible for transforming the newspaper into a successful venture. She instituted various editorial features to attract suburban and female readers, such as hiring a food writer and introducing a Sunday literary section, and she lured such journalistic luminaries as Walter Lippmann and Dorothy Thompson to become regular columnists at the paper. Helen Reid was a suffragist who also, along with her husband, became deeply involved in Republican politics.[93] Reid was thus a major force in American politics and publishing. When she spoke highly of Bill Esty, Milligan and Lageman listened.[94]

At a feminine, upper-class, English-style tea party, Helen Reid explained how Esty would help them Americanize tea. In addition to Esty, the ITMEB turned to other key figures in the emerging world of American market research. Esty was part of a team that included Elmo Roper, one of the masterminds of modern polling techniques, and Earl Newsom, a founder of modern public relations. Esty, Roper, and Newsom were a dream team of American advertising, marketing, and polling expertise.[95] Earl Newsom's Company (ENCO) would later represent the Ford Motor Company, General Motors, Standard Oil, CBS, and Republican politicians Dwight D. Eisenhower and Richard Nixon. Newsom and his wife became especially close with the Huxleys, and for decades the couples carried on a regular correspondence, discussing family, politics, art, literature, and sales strategies. Along with George Gallup, Elmo Roper was one of the founders of American opinion polling in the 1930s. Roper, a Nebraskan native, had first developed survey and statistical techniques that he would soon apply to political campaigns working for a jewelry company, and in 1935 he became the director of *Fortune* magazine's quarterly survey.[96] His methods drew the attention of Richardson Wood, who worked at J. Walter Thompson, and Paul Cherington, a professor at Harvard's School of Business. Roper, Wood, and Cherington set up a firm in New York City and soon attracted a host of corporate clients, including Time, Inc., the National Broadcasting Company, and the American Meat Institute.[97] As one historian has written, "Pollsters and their allies in the field of market research claimed to uncover what the American public wanted," but for the tea industry, they studied what the public didn't want.[98] Using surveys and interviews, gathering and interpreting statistical data, these men measured and thus also created consumers, commodities, and the economy itself.[99] They had an especially capacious understanding of selling, often defining it as a form of public education. They gathered knowledge about people and sold information about goods at the same time and in the same places.

An example of the overlapping nature of acquiring and selling knowledge was what the ITMEB called Tea Bureaus. These were both branch offices and information centers where people in the trade and consumers could gain knowledge about tea, its production, distribution, history, and consumption. Earl Newsom, who came up with the idea, opened the first Tea Bureau in New York City in 1936, though the term itself had been used earlier.[100] Thereafter, the ITMEB and related bodies opened tea bureaus in each key market, which after the war they came to be known as Tea Centres. While Newsom set up New York's Tea Bureau, Roper went to work gathering information about American consumers by conducting a national market survey in 1937.[101] Referring to this research, Newsom recalled how "for the first time we have had a really intelligent and thorough reconnaissance into the enemy's territory."[102] With military-like precision, these men felt that they finally understood how the "enemy," that is, the coffee-drinking American, ticked. Newsom analyzed Roper's findings and used them to outline a new plan for tea. The most important problem in the United States, both men believed, was that Americans did not know how to brew tea properly. Roper had compiled many statistics and conducted many interviews and found that Americans at home and in public did not use enough tea in the pot, they did not let it brew long enough, and they did not add milk and sugar. They thus concocted a weak, watery drink that could not stand up to coffee. Roper found that 84.1 percent of those he had interviewed had drunk tea on some occasion, but only about a third of them made tea properly. He also learned that nearly 60 percent of Americans did not like the taste of this poorly made drink and that was why they regarded it as a "'sissy' drink."[103] Lageman, who was also in the United States at the time, believed that class prejudices were at work as well because he noted how the middle-class "American hostess" thought it was "vulgar" to add milk and sugar to tea.[104] Lageman and his colleagues disparaged such ideas rather than investigating where they might have originated. For all their expertise, these tea experts did not ask such questions.

Esty, Newsom, and their colleagues at the ITMEB developed an American version of the Tea Revives You Campaign that, based on their research, worked with and against what they saw as American prejudices. Instead of telling Americans that "Tea Revives You," Mr. T. Pott and other celebrities explained that "vital" people such as male workers and athletes were turning to tea.[105] Evoking energy and modernity, many ads used little text and much humor, looking quite a bit like comic strips. Recognizable "American" types, such as football players, then ordered the public to "Turn to Tea Today," while housewives asserted that they had followed this directive (fig. 8.5). Such an approach was not unique since many products, particularly those directed at men, were selling "Vim, Vigor and Vitality," demonstrating how diet, exercise, and the right products could produce strength and energy.[106] The American mass press and advertising business were particularly concerned with defining new notions of athletic masculinity as older Victorian ideals of patriarchal masculinity were being undermined by the growth of corporate capitalism and the changing roles of women and family structures.[107] Especially during the Depression, when so many men were out of work, the idea of the healthy American man who consumed the right things became paramount and hence generated much advertising revenue. And yet, as though they could not help themselves or perhaps they did not want to desert their most reliable customers, much brand and producer advertising still used Englishness to sell tea to middle-class white women.[108] While the Tea Revives You Campaign emphasized modern men and women in energetic activities, other advertising presented tea as a part of a feminine English culture that American bourgeois women were thought to enjoy.[109]

If hot tea retained its feminine and English identity in the United States, iced tea was another matter entirely. Americans had drunk iced tea since at least the 1870s, but in the twentieth century tea growers, working with ice, sugar, and fruit companies, commercialized and nationalized this summertime drink. As we saw in chapter 6, Richard Blechynden claimed to have invented iced tea at the St. Louis World's Fair in 1904, but iced tea could not have become a widespread everyday beverage without a cheap and ready supply of ice and refrigeration.

FIGURE 8.5. "Turn to Tea Today." *Tea Tells the World* (London: International Tea Market Expansion Board, 1937), 7. (By permission of UC Davis Special Collections)

The ancient Chinese and Romans knew how to harvest and store ice, but in the United States the first icebox, essentially a metal-lined tub, was patented in 1803.[110] Already by the 1850s, Americans consumed so much ice that it became something of "an American institution."[111] Ice companies were big business and ice was a widely marketed product, but home refrigeration did not take off until the 1930s after General Electric came out with the Monitor Top refrigerator.[112] By that time, the majority of urban households had electricity and the New Deal's rural electrification program was slowly but surely bringing rural America onto the grid. The older ice companies and refrigerator manufacturers battled one another for some time, but whether delivered or produced at home, ice came to be seen almost as an American right.

The addition of ice, lemons, and sugar made tea into an American beverage. This invention had a long history, but, in the early twentieth century, the Indian Tea Market Expansion Board, Domino sugar, and Sunkist embarked on a decades-long joint promotion that branded the drink as a healthy, refreshing American summertime treat. If hot tea was British and for old ladies, iced tea became a thoroughly American drink that did not carry any particular gender or class associations. Sunkist was a trademark of the California Fruit Growers Exchange (CFGE), a cooperative of California citrus growers formed in 1893. While there was already an established orange and lemon industry in California, the CFGE built a veritable "Orange Empire" in Southern California. Like the empire of tea I have described here, the CFGE had "spheres of influence" over land, labor, and consumers, "colonizing public and private spaces across the country with alluring advertisements."[113] Sunkist marketed California as a Garden of Eden and invented new drinks, including orange juice, lemonade, and iced tea. Corporate cookbooks, for example, taught American women how to make and serve iced tea with lots of sugar and with a fresh lemon slice decoratively poised on the rim of a tall, ice-filled glass.[114] Sunkist thus also helped nationalize tea by providing a new cluster of homegrown associations and dietary and material culture. It also popularized the new religion that a modern healthy diet and life-style contained fruit, defined as a mixture of vitamins and sunshine.[115] Of course, probably no amount of vitamin C could compensate for the large amount of sugar that was often added to iced tea. That taste was also the product of widespread and enduring advertising, much of which was associated with Domino brand sugar, brought out by New York–based sugar refiners Havemeyers & Elder in 1898. With a big-budget ad campaign that proposed sugar cubes were modern, clean, and unadulterated, Domino became identified as "A Triumph in Sugar Making!"[116] In 1929, the company then introduced superfine loose table sugar, designed and advertised to dissolve completely in cold drinks such as iced tea.

So, by the time that the ITMEB advertised iced tea in the 1930s, all the ingredients were in place and the Tea Board's iced tea campaigns contributed to the sale of all these commodities. In 1936 some twenty million consumers in thirty-six different cities read ads telling them that iced tea *"keeps* you cool."[117] The campaign, like that for hot tea, didn't tackle the whole country but engaged in intensive regional efforts, particularly in the South and the West. Advertising, often included American flags and other nationalistic imagery and explicitly stated that iced tea was "America's Own Discovery" (fig 8.6). Clear glassware, as opposed to a teapot and cup, also demarcated iced tea's distinctive identity, and Mr. Ice Cube, rather than Mr. T. Pott, reminded consumers that tea keeps

FIGURE 8.6. "America's Own Discovery." Advertisement,
ITMEB, c. 1930s. (From author's private collection)

FIGURE 8.7. Mr. Ice Cube, detail from "America's Own Discovery."
Advertisement, ITMEB, c. 1930s. (From author's private collection)

up your "vitality" (fig. 8.7). Hot tourists strolling down the Atlantic City boardwalk in the summer of 1939 could thus look up at a billboard and thirst for a
tall, cool glass of iced tea and the curvy, glamorous pinup that proposed, "Tea

FIGURE 8.8. "Tea Peps You Up." Billboard, Atlantic City Boardwalk, ITMEB, July 1939.
(By permission of R. C. Maxwell Company Outdoor Advertising, John W. Hartman
Center for Sales, Advertising and Marketing History, Duke University)

Peps You Up" (fig. 8.8).[118] Such ads were so ubiquitous that the public came to
believe that Americans had invented iced tea. In the 1950s, a Sunkist executive
remarked that the decades-long joint campaign had transformed the lemon
from an unpopular "sour little fruit which was useful in scouring brass and
copper" to an important ingredient in the popular "American" beverage.[119] Iced
tea was a modern drink. Long-distance trade, new household and transportation
technologies, and the efforts and capital of the sugar, citrus, and tea industries
stretching from California to Calcutta and beyond invented the beverage and the
leisured lifestyle that it represented. Over time regionalism produced distinctive
versions of this American drink, with the most famous being the South's "sweet
tea."[120] At this time, however, marketers seemed indifferent to or unaware of
regional tastes and instead consistently worked within a national framework.
The tea cess nevertheless helped pay for the campaign that ensured that iced
tea was present at so many American picnics and barbeques.

   While the tea industry was inventing new drinks in the United States, in
that and other markets new cold drinks came to be seen as tea's enemy. For
example, when trying to explain why per capita tea consumption had declined

so dramatically in Australia, the ITMEB suggested that coffee, fruit juices, and milk-based drinks had become attractive to young consumers. This would be the exact same theory used to explain postwar shifts in British drink habits. In 1930s, Australia and the ITMEB tried to counter such developments but they did not see changing tastes as a sign that Australia might be developing distinctive food and drink cultures. In Australia and Canada, the ITMEB's campaign deployed the same stock slogans and characters that they were using in Britain. In Canada, for example, comic strip–style ads at the bottom of the funny papers featured Mr. T. Pott, who explained how Tea "chased away the Work-Day droops."[121] In a 1939 ad from the *Winnipeg Free Press*, a housewife tells her tired husband that what he needs after a bad day at the office is "a good cup of tea." Other advertising tried to fortify distinctive national identities.[122] In Australia, ITMEB advertising frequently invoked the idea that hot tea was the country's "National Beverage."[123] The campaign also promoted iced tea, but, as one market report explained, this had mixed results, with Sydney taking to the brew and Melbourne, with its shorter "heat spells," indifferent to the cooling pleasures of the beverage.[124] In Australia and Canada, the ITMEB campaigns simultaneously publicized both British and new national—that is, postcolonial—identities.

Britishness could be sold outside the empire as well. The northern European campaign, for example, emphasized tea's Britishness because Lageman believed that Norwegians and Belgians loved English culture. Yet he also sought to appeal to distinct national fashions and proposed that Mr. T. Pott should be dressed in a way that would give him a Belgian look.[125] Northern European publicity targeted men and women but in different spaces and ways. Bourgeois women encountered tea propaganda at clubs and while out shopping, while working-class girls learned about tea in domestic science classes. Virtually all publicity, however, featured tea as a pick-me-up that revived one at the low point in the middle of the afternoon. Painted on the side of a lorry, Mr. T. Pott traveled through European cities announcing tea's reviving properties.[126] The ITMEB erected a tea stall at the Brussels World Exhibition held in 1935, in department stores, and in demonstration tea stores, and everywhere demonstrators distributed information, advertising material, and brewed tea (fig. 8.9).[127] On Belgian radio, men and women from "all walks of life" testified how they had "realized" tea's good qualities. Mr. T. Pott asked Belgian consumers, "Pourquoi Pas Un Thé?" Swedish ads featured athletes, businessmen, and housewives who all explained how the beverage helped them get through "the dead point" in their day. Secretaries, manual laborers, and athletes, in this case, skiers, professed that tea stimulated and revived their tired bodies and minds.[128] As one report maintained, the "1936 campaign in Sweden was adapted to Swedish customs

FIGURE 8.9. Mr. T. Pott display, department store, Belgium, ITMEB. *Tea Tells the World* (London: International Tea Market Expansion Board, 1937), 11. (By permission of UC Davis Special Collections)

and consisted mainly of printed paper serviettes for restaurants, hanging cards, streamers, display cards, tea-pot transparencies, folders and tea measures for the public."[129] Very similar techniques were carried out in the Netherlands. Domestic science classes and housewives associations formed the backbone of this campaign, and tens of thousands of women were taught to make tea the English way. Many received free gifts such as calendars, pictures for the nursery, and Mr. T. Pott scarf pins.[130]

Nearly everywhere a version of the slogan "Tea Revives You" accompanied some version of the cheerful Mr. T. Pott. These themes were dressed up differently to fit men and women or speak to local cultures, and we can also detect an emerging rhetoric of internationalism in this campaign. However, if we look at how the ITMEB advertised in South Africa, we can see some of the underlying racial anxieties and stereotypes that still acted as the foundation of the empire of tea, despite the banishment of overt imperial language and imagery.

TEA AND THE "LONG CONVERSATION" IN SOUTHERN AFRICA

In the nineteenth and twentieth centuries, European-based corporations came to Africa to peddle cheap goods such as tea, soap and other toiletries, mass entertainments, and new identities.[131] They typically did not acknowledge, forgot about, or simply were unaware of the history of African local, regional, and long-distance trading systems that stretched across the Atlantic and Indian Ocean worlds.[132] This willful forgetting was central to the process of colonization, since Europeans imagined they were inviting Africans into the empire of Christendom and commerce. The colonial marketplace in Africa as in British India became both the site of racialization and a space in which Africans constructed their own ideas of modernity, sociability, beauty, and pleasure.[133] For example, African women who purchased and wore cosmetics, fashions, and other beauty products were often challenging stereotypes about race and beauty. Inspired by the African American press and the ideas of W. E. B. Du Bois, Marcus Garvey, and Booker T. Washington, South African journalists also saw revolutionary potential in African entrepreneurship and argued that even establishing the idea that African women were beautiful in itself contributed to the "project of racial uplift."[134] Buying the right goods for the home or body could demonstrate that Africans were like everyone else and thus should have access to political and civil rights. For Africans living in colonial regimes, the consumption of mass-market goods could also displace and/or support empires and corporate power, and at the same time manifest new social and cultural hierarchies and power relations.[135] In this section, I propose that while many Africans began to drink tea for a variety of reasons, many saw the drink as a form of European colonialism that was waging an assault on African leisure practices and gender identities.

After World War I, the tea industry was especially interested in growing and selling tea in Africa, and it began to do market studies of Tunisia, Algeria, Morocco, the Sudan, Northern Rhodesia, Kenya, Uganda, Ghana, and Nigeria. Gervas Huxley was particularly enthusiastic about Africa's potential, and we can surmise that some of his ideas likely came from conversations both with his wife and his cousin the evolutionary biologist Julian Huxley, who in 1929 had been hired by the Colonial Advisory Committee on Native Education to study how East Africans responded to educational films. Julian Huxley's ideas were somewhat at variance with those of other leading figures in that he imagined a more sophisticated African film viewer. He went on to become a leading internationalist as the first director of UNESCO in 1946 and established the World Wildlife Fund, an achievement for which he was knighted. While both Huxleys saw themselves as humanitarians, they also believed wholeheartedly in the power of propaganda to remake African cultures and identities.[136] Gervas was equally influenced by Elspeth, who in the mid-1930s was writing a biography of Lord Delamere, a leading advocate of white settlement in Kenya.[137] In South Africa and throughout much of Africa, however, the Huxleys found numerous allies, including colonial officials, missionaries, educators, and industrialists. Together, these communities gave tea a great deal of political and cultural power.

While planters often imagined that Africans did not drink tea until the twentieth century, this was not the case as it had been a popular drink in much of North and sub-Saharan Africa for centuries. The Dutch East India Company and settlers who arrived in the seventeenth and eighteenth centuries had brought tea, coffee, and sugar with them when they came to the Cape colony, and it appears that tea occupied a similar place as it had in Australia, Canada, and other settler colonies.[138] When the British took over the Cape Colony in 1795, drinking tea helped settlers project their sense of whiteness and respectability on the frontier.[139] It was also considered a healthy brew; farm families drank weak tea without milk and sugar, from morning until night, and one author explained that this was especially true in places that had brackish water.[140] But tea shifted from being a sign of whiteness only to a symbol of Christianity when, as discussed in chapter 2, European missionaries began to serve tea to help convert non-white South Africans to the faith. Seeing conversion as a spiritual and material experience, missionaries preached the gospel of sobriety and rational consumption.[141] They also believed that tea would transform Africans into industrious workers and rational consumers who accepted the logic of a wage-based capitalist economy. Mission stores were thus generally well stocked with cheap consumables such as coffee, tea, and sugar.[142] Lady missionaries often served tea and other English foods to inculcate Christian behaviors and teach African girls about domesticity. In one instance in the 1930s Belgian Congo, a British woman described an intimate tea party as separating the African participants from their "savage" past and instructing girls "about etiquette and, catering to company."[143] In the twentieth century, African Christians hosted tea parties, often with the support of white religious bodies, such as the Wesleyan Church, to raise funds for charitable and social concerns and to demonstrate their middle-class social status.[144] Although they buttressed the ideologies of missionaries and capitalists, tea parties were not always what they appeared, as Africans refashioned the meaning of temperance, tea, and other consumer practices. Temperance had long been an avenue of respectability in Southern Africa, as it had been for working-class Britons and African Americans.[145] Tea was thus part of what John and Jean Comaroff have described as the "long conversation" that had taken place between missionaries, businessmen, colonial authorities, and colonized subjects since at least the early nineteenth century.[146] It was still part of this conversation in the 1930s.

The ITMEB chose to work in South Africa in the 1930s because they understood this to be an industrializing and urbanizing society in which missionaries and the colonial state had already begun their work. The ITMEB sold tea to Dutch and English South Africans, as well as the numerous ethnic groups that colonial authorities described interchangeably as Bantu, Native, or Black.

Assuming English settlers already drank tea, the ITMEB targeted the Bantu and the Boer, or Dutch Afrikaners, but in slightly different ways. Mr. T. Potje told Afrikaners that tea was their national beverage and that it would revive them. Mr. and Mrs. Tea Drinker explained to "Bantu" consumers, however, that tea was good for them by representing how tea drinkers were modern, Christian, and upwardly mobile, totally unlike the disparaged and criminalized masculine drink cultures that had developed in Southern Africa. Mr. and Mrs. Tea Drinker demonstrated that the good African man was a hard worker, an attentive husband, and a church-goer, and the good African woman was a housewife who kept a tidy home, served delicious foods, and created a sacred, separate sphere that encouraged her husband and children to find their pleasures at home.

In addition to the same sorts of merchandising and face-to-face promotions that it did elsewhere, the ITMEB relied heavily on newspaper advertising to reach the Boer and the Bantu. One of the key papers it chose for the Afrikaner campaign was *Die Burger*, which was associated with D. F. Malan's Gesuiwerde (purified) National Party. Formed in 1934, the party appealed to Afrikaner farmers, civil servants, teachers, workers, and poor whites.[147] This campaign adopted many of the themes that we saw in play in other white settler communities, and especially proposed that tea was part of an imagined frontier past. In *Die Burger* Mr. T. Potje explained how tea had always been South Africa's national drink. A notable advertisement from 1937, for example, provided a lengthy history of how tea had been in the land since "the time of Van Riebeeck, when a stately East Indiamen sailed into Table Bay, the section of her cargo most eagerly awaited was tea from the East." It continued the tale with a description of how "the people in the outlying districts would hitch up their oxen and prepare for the long journey to Cape Town for fresh supplies of their precious tea." Thus from the time of the first settlers "tea has been South Africa's National drink up to the present day."[148] This ad simply inserted tea into the vision of a white Dutch South Africa that nationalists dreamed about.

Other advertisements presented tea as masculine and modern, a source of energy for the sedentary office worker or manual laborer. Tea energized tired men. "I don't know what is wrong. It is just before noon and I feel really tired right now," one man explains to his coworker. The second man responds by describing an article he had read about how "tea restores energy" and will make you feel better if you always have tea at eleven o'clock. Well, of course the first man tried tea, felt revived, and enjoyed the delicious drink.[149] As in the United States, these ads sought to masculinize a drink no doubt linked with Englishness and femininity. Some advertising even tried to teach women to make tea in a slightly different way for men. One ad proposed that when men "come home after a day of tiring work or an afternoon of strenuous exercise," they will need fresh tea to quench their "strong thirst." The article advised that men like their tea stronger than women do and that they should try "two tested recipes" for raisin cake and nutmeg bread that "will be delicious at a man's tea party" since men "do not like rich and creamy cake." They like manly sandwiches filled with a mixture of sardines, mayonnaise, lemon juice and Worcestershire sauce, and salt and pepper, topped off with either gherkins or onions.[150] In other words, real men don't like sweets with their strong tea. They eat manly, savory sandwiches.

Advertisements also instructed Afrikaners on how to make and serve tea like the British: warm a clean teapot, add a teaspoon of tea for every cup and one extra for the pot, use boiling water, and brew for five minutes.[151] This reviving drink was good for children, the elderly, those who work with their hands, and those who work with their brains.[152] Tea was for everyone. Though drinking tea was typically presented as a white South African habit, a few ads also invited Afrikaners into a cosmopolitan, global consumer society, explaining that tea was "the world's most popular drink," enjoyed by hockey stars in Canada, soldiers in the United States, hikers in the Alps, and Tibetans and Russians.[153] This approach captured the underlying internationalist theme of the Tea Revives You Campaign, which often sold the drink as both a national and global good.

In many respects the Bantu campaign looked similar to the Afrikaner, but the context was very different because in Southern Africa the state had criminalized and racially segregated alcohol consumption. Tea helped this process and became a tool to combat "illegal" forms of alcohol consumption and leisure that were identified with black African working-class men. The ITMEB demonized drink when it delineated what appropriate recreation should look like in its long-running advertising campaign in the *Bantu World*. By comparing the depictions of African consumer culture in the tea campaign in *Bantu World* with that in the white nationalist *Die Burger*, we can see how advertisers erected, negotiated, and at times contested the racial divide that was growing in sub-Saharan Africa.

Unintentionally, this campaign helped support the first national newspaper directed at a growing middle-class black readership in the Union of South Africa. In 1932, an ex-farmer and advertising salesman, Bertram F. G. Paver, founded Bantu Press and the newspaper *Bantu World*. As Paver explained it, this newspaper would "provide the Native people with a platform for fair comment and the presentation of their needs and aspirations."[154] Much of the paper was in English, but it uniquely also had significant portions in Zulu, Xhosa, Sotho, and Tswana. A white liberal, Paver attracted black African investors and hired Richard V. Selope Thema as editor, a job he kept for the next two decades.[155] Thema was an African nationalist who fought against attempts to limit the Cape's African voters. He and his staff enjoyed quite a bit of editorial freedom. The paper included many articles and opinion pieces criticizing police brutality, job reservation for whites, pass laws, slum conditions, and the plight of the unemployed, but the paper's views generally conformed to those of the white liberals who helped launch it.[156] Argus Printing and Publishing, the largest press monopoly in Africa with direct ties to the mining industry, acquired the paper, and by 1945 the company published ten weekly papers and handled the printing, advertising, and distribution for another dozen publications in eleven different languages. With far-reaching interests throughout southern and southwest Africa, *Bantu World* became a model for postwar commercial newspapers, but in the interwar period it had little competition. In 1938, *Bantu World* had a circulation of 24,000, and estimates suggest that at least five adults read each issue.[157] Only 12.4 percent of South African adults were literate in 1931, but as in other similar societies, newspapers were read aloud and thus reached a wide audience.[158] The paper's target audience was the small but influential group of mission-educated, middle-class Christians who worked as clerks, teachers, nurses, and clergy who were seeking respectability and struggling to oppose the loss of political and civil rights during a time of increasing racial segregation. These men and women, like South Africans in general, were also experiencing rapidly changing gender and family roles that came with industrialization and urbanization.[159] *Bantu World* proposed that while state-sanctioned racism proscribed behaviors, temperate forms of consumerism could be an avenue to social respectability and mobility.

In *Bantu World*, ads, editorial content, and letters to the editor demonstrated how new products, standards of beauty, taste, and leisure activities could lead to success or failure in a variety of spheres. In the accurate words of one historian, the paper was "saturated" with the cultural and social concerns of the petty bourgeoisie, chronicling "dances, beauty contests and other competitions, fund-raisers, farewells and reunions, exhibitions, teas and dinners, parties, receptions, concerns, speeches and meetings."[160] Ads, which filled approximately a third of the space, covered a wide range of health and body care products, household items, and services, but the Tea Board was one of the most consistent advertisers, providing a crucial source of revenue then for the early black press in South Africa.[161] Because of the prohibition placed on the consumption of European alcoholic beverages, the paper only promoted nonalcoholic drinks, such as tea, Ovaltine, and eventually Coca-Cola.[162] Between the 1930s and 1950s, however, tea was queen in the *Bantu World*.

Every week, the paper featured large, cartoon-like advertisements indicating that tea drinking led to rising social status and respectability. Many ads implied that tea was reviving, but the slogan most commonly used was simply "Tea is Good for You."[163] In dozens of variations, "Mr. and Mrs. Tea Drinker" gazed in a didactic fashion directly at readers/consumers, urging them to "always drink tea," morning and night, for "work or play."[164] They explained that good-quality tea was "pleasant to drink," easy to make, and refreshing.[165] Soon joined by their children, Mr. and Mrs. Tea Drinker were paternalistic authority figures whose dress and demeanor represented the bourgeois Christian African family that missionaries had long fantasized about. Tea was domestic and a wholesome social pleasure, enjoyed at home and work, while studying, dancing, or playing tennis, football, or any other sport.

Some ads implicitly proposed that by drinking tea, Africans shared in European culture. African achievements were equated with European milestones. For example, an advertisement from December 1936 proposed that mountain climbers in the Swiss Alps and Bantu Football clubs trained on tea. Another told of how tea had helped Commodore Perry reach the North Pole, and, featuring black athletes, it also noted how tea was an "essential part of a cricket match."[166] One ad explained that "at one time only Kings and very rich people could afford to Drink tea," but "now tea is plentiful and Everyone can Enjoy this most refreshing drink." Tea thus became a thread that linked Africans to a British past and a democratic present (fig. 8.10). A somewhat unusual version proposed that tea brought relief to sweltering white and black colonial consumers in Australia, Burma, India, and South Africa.[167] At precisely the same moment that South Africans were confronting new forms of racial and class segregation, advertisers were constructing a vision of racial equality achieved by participating in a respectable, middle-class consumer culture. This is not to say that consumer culture created equality—far from it. Market experts did not see Africans as equal to Europeans, but the print ads they created implied that it was through consumption that African men and women could rise in social status and in effect think of themselves as partaking in European heritage.

ITMEB advertising also tried to instill new gender- and age-related habits that mirrored key aspects of European society. Whereas other ads and articles created a South African version of the "modern girl," who bobbed her hair, wore cosmetics, and enjoyed leisure pursuits, the tea ads demonstrated the modern African housewife who cooked, cleaned, shopped, and gossiped, who dressed in European fashions, ate European-style foods, and drank European-style beverages while sitting in European-style homes.[168] This housewife was fully articulated in a weekly column on the Women's Page of the *Bantu World* titled "Over the Tea Cups." This column described many types of consumption, but tea drinking became a symbol of and gateway to a Europeanized, feminine, middle-class consumer culture. Specifically, "Over the Tea Cups" featured two Westernized African women named Arabele and Isabel who spent their afternoons gossiping about shopping, cooking, and other consumer "problems" over many cups of tea.[169] Tea set the stage for talking and thinking about other

FIGURE 8.10. "Tea is Good for You." Advertisement, *Bantu World,* January 1936. (By permission of the Historical Newspaper Research Archive, University of Witwatersrand)

forms of female consumerism. Consumerism became naturalized as feminine practice in ways that approximated European and American conceptions of femininity and economy.

The South African Tea Board, as the local branch of the ITMEB came to be known, was equally if not more committed to turning children into Western-style consumers. In 1936 the *Bantu World* began publishing a weekly children's supplement that was entirely devoted to tea. The supplement featured humorous stories, historical articles, songs, games, and crossword puzzles about tea. The children's supplement steeped tea in European history and culture, explaining through a variety of lessons how Europeans brought tea from the east to the west and, by extension, to South Africa. Through such methods, the new "European" diet that revolved around tea, sugar, wheat, and dairy became respectable, a source of energy, and good for work, study, and leisure. Such ideals gained force through the steady and ever-present contrast with alcohol and other forms of rebellious leisure most feared by officials, missionaries, and white settlers. Marketers constructed tea as a new modern pleasure for all South Africans, but it had been and continued to be a tool of racial and colonial politics.

Advertising in the *Bantu World* was part of a broader contest over race, alcohol, and the dangers and pleasures of leisure. The ITMEB's South African office was in Durban, a port city with many immigrant Indians and known to be a "model for urban 'native administration.'"[170] The Durban Town Council monopolized the sale of sorghum beer (*utshwala*) and made a tidy profit from the town's municipal beer halls, which then funded the Native Administration Department and built homes and more beer halls for workers. Thus monopolized, "legal" beer promoted and funded the reproduction of the migrant, male workforce. In the Union of South Africa, the passage in 1928 of the Liquor Act consolidated previous laws and prohibited the sale of all European liquor to blacks, with the exception of a few educated men who were granted special permits.[171] In part as a response to this situation, between the 1920s and 1950s, the number of *shebeens* (illicit, masculine drinking spots) grew, particularly in urban areas, and became sites of male camaraderie, though women, who made homemade brews, or *skokiaan*, usually ran the *shebeens*.[172] Leisure and drink became a way in which subaltern Africans rejected missionary and colonial ideals, as historian Mhoze Chikowero and others have proposed.[173] Beer boycotts, for example, opposed the state monopoly of the legal beer halls, with leaders championing Africans', particularly women's, "national right" to brew their own beer.[174] And the fight over drink gave rise to a politicized music culture. In the 1940s, the Zimbabwean musician August Machona Musarurwa composed an instrumental version of the song "Skokiaan," which was subsequently transformed in dozens of versions both in the West and regionally.[175] As Chikowero notes, the song became a metaphor for African urban life, and Louis Armstrong, Herb Alpert, Hugh Masekela, and many others performed versions, with its meaning changing with different styles, lyrics, and contexts.[176] The ITMEB, however, battled *skokiaan* and *shebeen* culture, endeavoring to sell tea by suppressing African cultural expressions and political and domestic economies.

The local tea commissioner A. J. Bouchier thought of himself as a progressive, who believed that hiring blacks and whites to work together contributed to Africa's development. In truth, white employees managed a black staff, hardly a modern arrangement. Together, however, the Tea Board employees drove a "fleet of motor vans" in the Transvaal and Transkeian territories and in Zululand. Each van distributed materials to schools and stores and at village gatherings. They showed films and gave demonstrations on how to brew and drink tea. Though these methods were used elsewhere, in Africa the motor vehicle and film were touted as modern technologies able to penetrate vast interior spaces and the unknown reaches of the minds of illiterate African consumers.[177] After World War II, the American firm 20th Century Fox helped widen distribution when it signed a deal to distribute Tea Board films in South Africa, North and South Rhodesia, British East Africa, the Belgian Congo, Mozambique, Réunion, Mauritius, and Madagascar. In Nigeria, the African Railway Institute also screened these shows, while in Kenya the Government Mobile Cinema Units did as well.[178] In South Africa, the Union government's Department of Native Affairs showed ITMEB films along with government films on "agriculture, hygiene and other educational subjects."[179] The colonial state thus supported corporate capitalism and vice versa.[180]

Assuming that African viewers often read film overly literally, African educational films often had simple plots delineating stark differences between good and evil.[181] ITMEB films thus invariably contrasted temperate, respectable, and upwardly mobile tea drinkers with criminal alcoholics. The 1949 film *Mr. Tea and Mr. Skokiaan*, for example, juxtaposed good and bad consumer cultures by articulating the normative class, gender, and racial ideologies of the new apartheid state. In this film, a well-dressed and temperate "Mr. Tea" enjoys success at work and "the advantages of healthy leisure" with his girlfriend, Miss Sugar. The tattered Mr. Skokiaan "spends his leisure breathing smoke after imbibing *skokiaan*," which the film describes in exceedingly derogatory terms as "a bootleg concoction made from yeast, carbide, methylated spirits, sugar and the like."[182] The film has a happy ending, however, because Mr. Tea and Miss Sugar convert and hence redeem the rebel consumer. In a similar, "semi-documentary" film titled *Njuma* we again see the divergent fates of an upstanding tea worker/consumer and his "wayward brother" who persists in drinking *skokiaan*.[183] Retelling a story that missionaries and the temperance movement had clung to since the 1820s, these films harnessed tea to the African state's endless battle to control and rationalize African economies, commodities, leisure, and food practices.

Before, during, and after the war, the ITMEB urged employers to see tea as a means to improve productivity, stamina, health, punctuality, and respect for employers. However, the onset of apartheid in South Africa further cemented together labor, leisure, and alimentary and racial politics. The South African Tea Bureau thus focused on promoting tea in the thousands of "industrial concerns" in Johannesburg, Cape Town, Port Elizabeth, East London, and Durban.[184] Targeting workers was not new or especially unique, but in South Africa during these years the ITMEB emphasized how tea inculcated labor discipline.[185] An African version of *Tea: The Worker's Drink*, a British publication, explained how tea speeds "the wheels of South African Industry."[186] By no means criticizing apartheid, the pamphlet implied that tea was especially reviving for the "non-European worker" who had "poor home facilities" for food preparation and had to travel long distances for work. In other words, the ITMEB exploited the fact that racial segregation had produced the need for food and drink at work.[187] In truth, this document sought to convince employers to serve tea at work. The back cover of this pamphlet placed the phrase "Just see how Tea Revives Them" above an illustration of a male miner drinking tea. Note the difference in emphasis: from "Tea Revives You" to "Tea Revives Them." Tea was being sold to employers as the fuel of industry and as a means to settle racial and class tensions.

In much of late colonial Africa, tea became a tool of development, a means to transform Africans into self-controlled workers who didn't drink, didn't fall ill, showed up for work on time, and had the energy to work hard with low pay. Many plantations, for example, distributed free tea to increase "output" and to prevent waterborne intestinal infections.[188] The Kenya Tea Company offered a free mug of hot tea as part of their "incentive system," handing out the beverage only after pickers "turned in a set quantity of leaf."[189] Similarly, a cement factory outside of Cairo gave a free cup of tea to employees who showed up for work on time.[190] As in Victorian Britain, tea became a means to entice workers to behave themselves and was also used to quash labor and nationalist demands.

In the 1950s, many Africans drank tea but they did not necessarily accept its racial and class logic. By this time, many Africans were boycotting European goods and engaging in armed struggle against European settlers and the colonial state. Market research, as well as tea, became popular in this context in part because it was thought to be a means to understand, and hopefully control, unruly Africans. Marketing experts preached what Timothy Burke has called a new religion, claiming as one researcher did in 1960 that "the only African markets that do exist are those that have been created, those that have been made through the efforts, conscious or otherwise, of manufactures and marketer."[191] With such views in mind, professors and graduate students at Natal University, Pretoria, and Rhodes University, as well as the South African Institute of Race Relations, categorized, studied, and compared bodily and other daily habits. The ITMEB was very eager to use these new tools, but in South Africa their research confounded racial stereotypes by revealing that black South Africans drank much more tea than Afrikaners did. A 1953 study interviewed 2,700 black and white South Africans about when they drank tea, their knowledge of comparative beverage prices and brewing methods, and their reactions to current promotions. This was a national study that included people from different income levels, genders, races, ethnicities, and marital statuses. The findings, however, were reported in three main categories: rural Afrikaans-speaking families, urban European families (both English and Afrikaans speaking), and urban "Bantu" families. Both the rural and urban Afrikaans-speaking populations drank equivalent amounts of coffee and tea, while the urban English-speaking and Bantu population drank far more tea than coffee. Researchers were struck by the fact that so-called Bantu consumers also used far more dry leaf to brew their tea. Thus, while the English South African drank more tea than everyone at an average of 4.49 cups daily, the "urban Bantu" used more tea to brew his or her 2.85 cups a day.[192] While national averages were also studied, consumption was nevertheless now measured with a great deal more nuance.[193] The study implied that language, culture, and lifestyle trumped race and class, and this was something that made white South African society extremely uncomfortable.[194] However, for all their nuance, researchers did not ask about religion or migration patterns, and they ignored historical precedents. If they had done so, they might have considered the impact of earlier promotions, brand advertising, temperance movements, and the relentless push to serve tea in factories, mines, schools, and other public arenas. They might have wondered about Indian migration and its impact on South Africa's commercial culture. Marketers did not study or acknowledge this long history.

––––––––––

Just before war broke out, the ITMEB celebrated its global accomplishments when it commissioned MacDonald "Max" Gill, a noted decorative mapmaker, mural painter, and architect, to produce a map, which he titled "Tea Revives the World" (fig. 8.11). Gill had been known for his colorful, recognizable posters and cartoon-like maps that evoked the graphic map design of the early modern period and the modern yet gothic look of the Arts and Crafts movement. Gill had already worked for the Ceylon tea industry when in 1933 he drew a whimsical map showing the lush green island as a land of tea. Gill's "Tea Revives the

FIGURE 8.11. "Tea Revives the World." Decorative map by MacDonald Gill, ITMEB, 1940. (Courtesy of the Estate of Macdonald Gill)

World" map depicted the entire global history of tea on a twenty-by-ten-foot canvas.[195] On this map, camels, clipper ships, steamers, railways, dog teams, and airplanes transport crops grown in Uganda, Nyasaland, Nilgiris in southern India, Assam and Darjeeling in the north, and Ceylon, Sumatra, and Java. Tea is portrayed as a global drink, enjoyed by the Dutch, or "original settlers in south Africa," and "it is the favorite beverage of the Bantu," prized by sheep shearers in Australia and New Zealand and the Fellaheen "working on their farms in the ancient way" in Egypt. It was drunk in Russia, Lapland, and France, and, of course, "The peoples of the British Isles are the world's greatest tea drinkers."

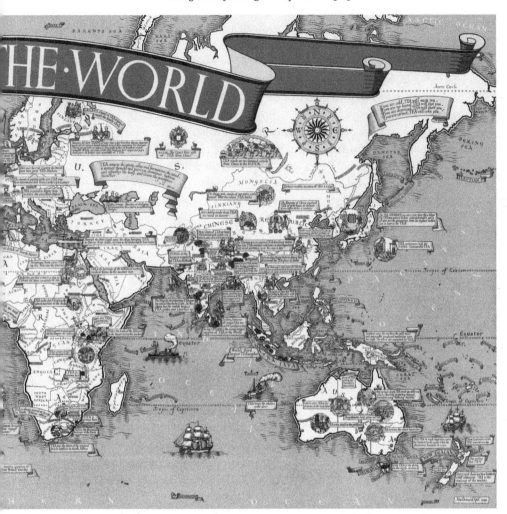

"Hollywood stars, directors, and writers keep going on Tea"; skiers, mountain climbers, and lumberjacks also indulged. Iced tea was "America's Own Discovery" enjoyed year-round in the South. Everywhere people seemingly ascribed to the Victorian liberal prime minister William Gladstone's ode: "If you are cold, TEA will warm you. If you are too heated, TEA will cool you. If you are depressed, TEA will cheer you. If you are excited Tea will calm you." Gill's map tells a global story that ignores and distorts as much as it reveals. Mexico and South America are virtually blank spaces. China's and Japan's tea cultures are depicted but Formosa is simply a blank island off the coast of China. The whole of the Indian Subcontinent is far too small and there is no indication of South Asian consumers. African production and consumption, however, occupy the very center of this empire of tea. This is likely because the ITMEB, which paid for the map, was so absorbed with African markets and teas at this time.

Gill's map had its own global history, but it was especially prevalent in Africa where it showed up on countless hoardings and became the backdrop for white male demonstrators and African assistants to instruct consumers, many of whom were children, about this empire of tea during the 1940s and 1950s.[196] With each stop in their travels, "mobile tea units" unpacked the great tea map and used it as a kind of wall in an outdoor classroom in which children and adults sat attentively looking at posters and listening to a tea kettle's hiss, watching films in which tea always represented right over wrong. The map thus helped convey how Western capitalism enveloped Africans into a new global culture of consumption. The map appeared in India and Ceylon too, and a poster of the original still hangs in the entrance to the Happy Valley Tea Estate, the first tea plantation opened in Darjeeling in 1854. The Abootia tea group, which now owns the estate, produces high-quality organic teas that are sold at Harrods department store in London. Happy Valley and Harrods are in many respects contemporary participants in the empire of tea.[197] The following chapters will examine how war, decolonization, and the cultural and social upheavals of the postwar world altered but did not entirely destroy the empire that Gill depicted in 1940.

Gill's map, Mr. T. Pott, Mr. Ice Cube, and Mr. and Mrs. Tea Drinker did not explicitly promote tea as a colonial commodity, but they were nevertheless imperial icons. The presence or absence of explicit imperial references or Oriental imagery should not be the measure of whether or not imperialism influenced metropolitan or colonial consumer cultures. In the 1930s, changes in the advertising industry, the desire to develop colonial and working-class markets, and industry collaboration across empires and between and along commodity chains shifted the iconography and narrative of tea advertising in ways that highlighted the consumer and not the producer. Oversupply and precipitously falling prices led British and Dutch planters to collude to save their ailing industry and to rely on advertising agencies and marketing boards. The rise of economic nationalism in fascist countries and anticolonial nationalism in producing regions also made overt references to the British Empire slightly distasteful. In other words, by the later 1930s, it was no longer clear that empire added value. Instead, health and bodily renewal became watchwords of the day, shaping advertising and many other facets of European culture. The simple idea that drinking tea would make you feel better, or as Barbara Yates put it, would "Buck you Up," was then a sign of an imperial industry attempting to keep up with the times.

9

"HOT DRINKS MEAN MUCH IN THE JUNGLE"

Tea in the Service of War

During World War II, everyday life was under siege, lending routine and small things great power. In Great Britain a hot cup of tea was one of those small things. The beverage had already become so embedded in the sensual and social understandings of normalcy that government officials, business, and consumers all assumed that its absence would be psychologically devastating and a sign of the collapse of civilization. Such ideas had been centuries in the making, but war provided a new context for an old habit. Stories about tea's ability to lift morale and calm one's nerves entered into the mythology of the war. Soldiers brewed tea in empty metal drums in the North African desert, sailors drank tea on destroyers and submarines, neighbors shared with those who lost their homes in the Blitz, women volunteers served a hot cuppa in shelters and from mobile canteens, and the tea break became firmly fixed in work culture in factories and offices.[1] Countless memoirs and diaries, photographs, and films captured the moment of service as a symbol of calm and shared sacrifice in a chaotic and frightening world.[2] Seemingly drunk by everyone on the home front and in the fields of war, tea became shorthand for the People's War, the widely held belief that more than at any other time in history average Britons were united as a common community.[3]

George Orwell famously contributed to this vision of the war, tea, and Englishness in a 1941 essay in which he proclaimed:

> We are a nation of flower-lovers, but also a nation of stamp-collectors, pigeon fanciers, amateur carpenters, coupon-snippers, darts-players, crossword-puzzle fanciers. All the culture that is most truly native centres round things which even when they are communal are not official—the pub, the football match, the back garden, the fireside and the "nice cup of tea."[4]

Orwell's flower-loving, tea-sipping, stamp-collecting Britons enjoyed their simple pleasures at home, in their gardens, and in their local pub. Such a contrast with fascist organized leisure and American-style mass culture, or was it? Orwell's nativism reflected a broader reworking of ideals of Britishness that had begun in the interwar period and lasted into the 1950s. Orwell was trying to deny the impact of mass culture on British society, but many aspects of his Great Britain were creations of the mass market and empire. By 1941, the idea that tea would allow one to keep calm and carry on seemed so natural that its origins have not been questioned. However, government officials, colonial tea producers, and the advertising experts we met in the last chapter orchestrated tea's wartime mythology.

PUT THE KETTLE ON

Like its precursor, World War II was a food fight. A pervasive anxiety that shrinking agricultural sectors could not feed growing urban populations partly determined Germany's, Italy's, and Japan's expansionist policies and wartime decisions. Military authorities and national governments redirected food from conquered territories and mass starvation became a deliberate weapon designed to weaken civilians and soldiers. Allied governments also recognized the pressing need to feed their citizenry, fearing the specter of social revolution that came with hunger at the end of the Great War. In Britain government planning, an extensive system of rationing and controls, improved agricultural productivity, the institution of Lend-Lease in 1941, and intensive exploitation of imperial resources and labor kept its population relatively well fed.[5] Food scientists such as Jack Drummond, who headed the scientific advice division of the Ministry of Food, even optimistically saw an opportunity to improve the nutritional condition of the people.[6] Ultimately, the wartime diet was monotonous, but impoverished Britons did experience modest nutritional gains, while colonial subjects, especially Bengalis, faced hunger and starvation on an unheard-of scale.[7]

Everywhere hunger loomed, but in Britain wartime rhetoric emphasized "fair shares" and the importance of the kitchen front. Canteens, British Restaurants, and other forms of collective feeding, coupled with growing working-class purchasing power, lessened the gross nutritional inequalities among the social classes. Britons became what one scholar has described as a "'food-based community', a nation defined in part by its shared consumption patterns and rituals."[8] Government policies and a make-do attitude instigated new national tastes, routines, and spaces for shopping, cooking, and eating. One of the greatest changes in Great Britain, however, was the government's near total control of the importation, distribution, and sale of basic foods, including tea. Rather than absolute scarcity, a mixture of politics, economic theory, and social thought set the timing and nature of food control.[9]

Rationing established a new social democratic compact between government and the population, but, in truth, it did not end social tensions.[10] People complained about how the wealthy could afford unrationed delicacies, eat "off the ration" in restaurants and clubs, and purchase black market foods.[11] Those living in the countryside earned money selling extra fruits and vegetables they had grown in their "victory" gardens.[12] Men and women also experienced rationing differently. Despite these failures to live up to the ideology of equality, food controls did prevent inflation and helped maintain prewar levels of consumption and expenditure. People accepted austerity during the war, but in peacetime the continuation of rationing unraveled support for the Labour Party and helped secure Conservative electoral victories in the early 1950s.[13]

In a general sense, this war shored up the British Empire's dominance of the world tea trade. Liberal ideals about the primacy of market freedom and the ubiquitous belief that Britons and their allies simply could not fight a war without their tea shaped tea control policies. Tea was considered so important that the government developed plans to protect the nation's tea several years before the onset of hostilities.[14] Tea control did not begin with rationing, however. The International Tea Agreement, which had brought production under control in 1935, was still in effect.[15] On 5 September 1939, the government assumed control of imports and the Director of Tea under the Ministry of Food became responsible for contracting directly with producers. Domestic wholesale and resale prices were fixed, and the London auctions immediately shut down. Storage, blending, and packing facilities were decentralized, and by 1942 most of the nation's tea was dispersed to more than five hundred warehouses throughout the country. Tea was still lost to enemy action when Mincing Lane suffered during the Blitz, but government measures preserved the nation's supplies.[16] In 1942 the Director of Tea at the Ministry of Food and the Combined Food Board in Washington became the sole purchaser of tea for the Allies and certain neutral countries.[17] The auctions in Colombo and Calcutta could supply their internal markets, but all exports other than those under the Ministry of Food were officially stopped.[18] The government also gave generous bonuses to growers, and controls guaranteed stable markets. Tea shares rose, and most estates made considerable profits early in the war.[19]

Just as the government protected supplies, it also began to reinforce tea's special place in the British imagination. As soon as war broke out, the Home Publicity Division of the Ministry of Information considered how tea could reduce the panic expected with air raids. One member, Lady Grigg, explained to her colleagues that "the most comforting thing—at least where women were concerned—was to have a cup of tea and get together to talk things over." The committee agreed and appealed "to householders to supply tea to anyone in their neighborhood who needed it during or after an air-raid."[20] Perhaps tea was given such prominence because Gervas Huxley sat on this body. Huxley soon resigned in frustration, however, claiming that he simply did not know what this agency was supposed to accomplish.[21] In 1942 he returned to the Ministry of Information as the person in charge of creating "good relations" between British civilians and Americans. He also directed the ministry's Empire Division, which was assigned the task of improving empire publicity and communications between the Colonial Office and the British media.[22] Huxley's connections with governmental and nongovernmental agencies enabled him to carve out a special place for tea in the fight against fascism and present tea as a form of social welfare and public good.

Lord Woolton, minister of food between 1940 and 1943, shared many of these beliefs and was very reluctant to ration tea at all. When it did prove necessary, he protected consumers' right to purchase their favorite brands.[23] By this time, only four companies, the English and Scottish Wholesale Co-operative Society, Lyons, Brooke Bond, and Allied Suppliers, which bought for Unilever retail chains, controlled virtually the entire importation and distribution of tea in the UK, though they offered dozens of different brands.[24] In the middle of the war when transport issues became dire, Woolton faced pressure to pool all teas into a national control tea, as had been done at the end of World War I. He refused to do so, acknowledging that the "public *does* like the tea it likes and I want to preserve this amenity for as long as possible. . . . Politically . . . I am always warned against interfering with the people's Tea."[25] Woolton's desire to maintain brands may have partly come from political pressure from these four powerful corporations, but his experience as managing director of Lewis's department store in Liverpool may also have shaped his beliefs. "If we had given up during the war the blending of tea, [and] the use of brands, if we had decided on this dull level of equality, we should have lost something in our national life," Woolton later explained. Furthermore, he continued, "taste, individual taste, is worth preserving . . . it adds to the joy of living and flavours existence."[26] Woolton was not equally committed to preserving brand names for margarine, soft drinks, and other products, but as we saw in the 1920s and 1930s, the government had frequently defended the rights of the big brand teas.[27] For Woolton brand-name teas in the shop signified the market-based freedoms that were central to British identity.

Nevertheless, the closing of the Mediterranean had put extreme pressure on shipping, and on 9 July 1940 rationing began. Consumers were restricted to two ounces of tea per week, but as Woolton had wanted, they were allowed to buy brand-name tea from any shop, not just at the one where they were registered.[28] The amount of the ration varied until it finally ended in October 1952, but for the most part it remained at around two ounces per person, roughly two-thirds of prewar averages. In the summer of 1942 when Japan conquered Burma and it looked as though Britain might lose the tea gardens of Assam, and Ceylon too seemed threatened, the government curtailed the ration for very young children.[29] At this time, however, Britain still ruled the empire of tea.

Rationing, food control, and scarcity ignited multiple conversations surrounding diet and health, inevitably prompting people to think and talk about the consumer culture they inhabited.[30] Food talk was everywhere; and, as opposed to what they had done during earlier conflicts, market and social researchers tried to listen. Surveying, interviewing, and observing consumers became a major preoccupation of governmental and commercial agencies.[31] Drawing from the quantitative and qualitative methods of sociology, anthropology, and psychology, business and the state tried to comprehend and channel individual and national consumer habits and tastes. For example, the social research agency Mass Observation, founded in 1937, has left us with a huge archive of diaries, surveys, and interviews conducted by hundreds of paid and unpaid volunteers. Investigators asked questions on many different topics, but one of their key preoccupations was documenting individuals' relationship to their material world.[32]

Mass Observation (M-O) spent much time gauging people's attitudes toward rationing; it found that although people became resigned to it, the tea ration was an unpopular measure that seemed to come without warning at a time when the country appeared to have ample supplies at hand. Rationing, M-O discovered, seemed to differentially punish poor women who subsisted on tea. During the first days of rationing, M-O investigators interviewed poor men and women in Stepney in the East End of London and the wealthier residents of the village of Bourne End in Buckinghamshire. Nearly everyone was unhappy. "Sugar, it was bad; butter—it's terrible. But tea—it's worst of the lot," complained a middle-aged tailor whose wife was a grocer.[33] One thirty-five-year-old Stepney woman captured the feeling of many when she bemoaned:

> Isn't it terrible. We've just got used to going without sugar, and then they start rationing tea. . . . I'd sooner they rationed clothes, and let us have our necessities. I know we're asked to make sacrifices, but it's pretty hard, our tea. I think some of us women live for our cup of tea.[34]

A sixty-year-old man also responded: "It hits my old missus. She likes her cup of tea."[35] A wealthier self-identified coffee drinker from Bourne End sympathized that "it's sad for the working classes—they live on tea poor things."[36] A young woman also from Bourne End remarked how she had ordered more coffee but she too thought the ration would be "terrible for the poor people."[37] Tea may have been drunk by people from all walks of life, but in their support and criticisms of government policy many consumers described how the hot brew especially helped poor women cope with the stresses of life. M-O found that Britons placed tea in a special category, more important than sugar, butter, and clothing. All Britons recognized that tea had come to occupy a singular place in the female working-class diet.

The Ministry of Food thus had a difficult job when it tried to restrain the tea habit through various forms of propaganda. The ministry encouraged housewives to try cocoa and other alternative beverages and brew weaker tea in the interests of the nation.[38] Revising the classic recipe of one teaspoon per person and one for the pot, a Ministry of Food jingle, for example, exhorted:

One spoon each and none for the pot,
When you make tea you mustn't use a lot,
Just one spoon each and none for the pot.[39]

People did use less sugar, milk, and tea, and they tried other drinks. One woman, for example, explained that she "got in some Horlicks. . . . Expensive isn't it? But I thought, I'm not going to be left without a drink altogether."[40] Another middle-aged woman despondently exclaimed, "We'll have to start drinking coffee, I can see."[41] The wealthier respondents living in Bourne End were more familiar with coffee than were the poor, and they admitted that they would simply order more of that beverage.[42] During the war, the United Kingdom was the only European country able to increase coffee imports.[43] Coffee was relatively expensive, however, averaging 32d. a pound in 1942.[44] Prices rose with shipping shortages that were especially severe during the Battle of the Atlantic, as the bulk of African and Dutch East Indian sources were cut off by enemy action. Nevertheless, many people who had never tried coffee or other drinks first did so during the more than twelve years of tea rationing.[45]

All of these changes worried tea planters, who wanted to keep tea in the public eye and to protect markets without appearing as though they were opposing government efforts.[46] To do this, tea had to be used efficiently and had to maintain its identity as a necessity or wartime weapon, a tool in the service of war. Basically tea had to become a public good. The tea industry recognized and promoted this idea in several ways, including making sure that tea flowed liberally in all public settings. During the war, people were increasingly taking their meals in public rather than at home. Restaurants, cafés, tea shops, public houses, fish and chip shops, factory canteens, and street food, not to mention school meals and army and workhouse rations, had long been a part of British urban and rural cultures, but the war transformed the meaning of eating and drinking tea in public.[47]

DINING OUT IN WARTIME

The war years witnessed a dramatic growth in public dining at commercial, voluntary, and state-run catering facilities.[48] Collective feeding at schools and the workplace originated in the nineteenth century as a form of welfare that sought to improve both the health and the behavior of the working classes. World War I and the growth of new ideas about food and workers' morale and productivity made the canteen and school lunch more widespread phenomena.[49] The move of women into wartime production, shifts in population caused by evacuation and enemy bombing, and the general belief that hot food boosted morale led to a vast expansion of public eating during World War II.

The Ministry of Food undertook a variety of mass-feeding schemes; one of the most significant centered on the state-run British Restaurants. Like rationing, the British Restaurants became a means to improve the public's health and preserve civilian morale. Countering concerns that they would compete with the private sector, the minister of food explained:

> The development of Community Feeding is settled Government policy, the object of which is to ensure that people who find difficulty for any reason in obtaining nutritious food should, as far as possible, have the opportunity of getting at least one hot meal each day. For a variety of reasons, e.g., the rise of the cost of living, the evacuation of womenfolk, the transference of male labour, and the expansion of female labour in industry, real difficulties are being experienced and it is of paramount importance in the interests of public morale and as part of the war effort that everything possible should be done by the Government to meet this problem.[50]

In 1943 there were two thousand British Restaurants and countless similar institutions set up by voluntary agencies such as the YWCA, Women's Voluntary Services (WVS), the Red Cross, and local authorities.[51] The movement peaked in September when there were 2,160 restaurants serving 630,000 meals a day.[52] Patrons often complained about cold or even spoiled food, vile coffee, and weak tea. However, the food and drink were not invariably terrible. Middle-class diarist Vere Hodgson recalled how, when she dined at "the Lord Woolton Restaurant" in Notting Hill Gate in 1941, the menu offered "steamed Fish, or Rabbit with Parsley Sauce, and two vegetables. All this only 11d. Really good. I sat down at an oilcloth-covered table and ate my stew. Not the last time I shall go."[53]

Tea was always available in these public settings. The domestic tea ration had been set at two-thirds of the prewar averages to make sure the military, government bodies, charities, and the workplace had enough tea. Politicians and factory owners had accepted the idea, over a century in the making, that tea increased workers' productivity. Minister of Labour Ernest Bevin personally encouraged large firms to give their employees tea breaks. In a speech before the Works Management Association in London in September 1940, Bevin claimed the director of one large firm stated he would never abolish the tea break because it had increased worker productivity.[54] The Factory (Canteens) Order of 1940 required the establishment of a canteen in all firms employing over 250 workers involved in munitions or government production.

In some places, restaurants and other eateries experienced a wartime boom. Glasgow's famous tea shops fed wealthy American soldiers and the men and women who came to work in the city's shipyards and munitions factories. At times, as one historian has remarked, this spectacle of abundance could be quite unsettling to visitors; one journalist wrote in 1941 about seeing ovens filled with "large fowls and plump turkeys" that were "sizzling and richly browning."[55] Businesses hard hit by enemy action such as those in central London saw a falling off in trade, but as the records of one midsize chain, Kardomah Ltd., reveal, many recovered quickly. Known for its high-quality specialty coffees, Kardomah made record profits during the war. The company began in 1845 as a Liverpool grocery shop. In 1868 it became incorporated under the name Liverpool China and India Tea Co., Ltd., and by the end of the century it issued its own proprietary packet tea. The company developed a thriving van sales division that served retailers in Merseyside, Manchester, Birmingham, and South Wales. In 1893 it opened what it called an Exhibition café in Church Street, Liverpool, largely as an advertising strategy, but it was such a success that by 1939 the company had thirty-five outlets, including one in Paris. Kardomah cafés acquired a bohemian reputation. The most famous, in Castle Street, Swansea, became the hangout of the "Kardomah gang," a group of poets, artists, and writers that included Dylan Thomas. The aroma of brewed coffee and modern decor helped create the right environment for 1930s bohemia.[56] The early cafés had a "William Morris" type design, while some later cafés included smoking rooms done up in a "pseudo Jacobean style." In 1936 the company hired Misha Black to update the image of the cafés. Black was a modernist who would later become famous for his bold graphics and clean lines, but for the Kardomah he incorporated a good deal of teak and mahogany panelling and an Indian Pavilion motif in order to evoke an "atmosphere of the east."[57] This design was more in keeping with earlier tea shop Orientalism, but at the Kardomah the "Eastern atmosphere" became associated with bohemianism, a style that crystallized in the postwar coffeehouse.

The war did present ongoing problems, however. Counter sales were affected by the loss of display in barricaded windows. The restaurant side of the business suffered from shorter operating hours as customers and staff rushed home early each night because of the blackout. Transportation difficulties and gas shortages were serious problems as was the general evacuation of London and other hard-hit areas.[58] Kardomah lost a large London café in the bombing in September 1940, two others were damaged in Birmingham, and only three out of the seven Manchester cafés remained open in December 1940.[59] High taxes and severe labor and food shortages affected all the cafés, and 1941 was an especially difficult year. Food stocks were so scarce that some cafés had to close or drastically reduce their menus. The cafés were nevertheless busy because of a growing "tendency on the part of the public to feed 'off the domestic ration.'"[60] Owing to severe staff shortages in 1942, Kardomah, like Lyons and other major chains, introduced cafeteria-style self-service. Kardomah's directors marveled at how the change allowed them to serve nearly a million more customers a year.[61] They did not abandon all their waitress service, however, since many customers still preferred being waited upon. In 1943 the ability to cater to more people and the increase in the average amount per ticket, which was largely due to price increases, meant that turnover from the café section increased by 25 percent in 1944.

The tea trade eagerly exploited this growing restaurant culture and wartime market. For a small charge tea was always available in shelters, restaurants, cafés, canteens, and other eateries.[62] A food control official noted this when he jested that during the war, "people could not run a village dance, raise money for Spitfire funds, get married, make steel, or maintain *morale* during air raids, without tea."[63] The armed services especially were awash in tea.[64] Civil defense workers and countless others deemed necessary to the war effort also received extra supplies.[65] Such policies increased consumption outside of the home and identified the worker, soldier, and "needy" as especially deserving; these were precisely the same communities that would be targeted by postwar social programs.[66] Much like the temperance tea party or the exhibition in the nineteenth century, wartime catering served a captive mass market.

FROM CANADA TO CAPE TOWN: THE EMPIRE APPEAL

In May 1940, while Germany was invading France, Frederick Ernest Gourlay, the International Tea Market Expansion Board's assistant director of propaganda, traveled from Canada to Cape Town to survey the board's overseas operations. During the next six months, Gourlay visited Kenya, Rhodesia, Nyasaland, and Australia before returning home to Canada.[67] Travel might have been difficult, but on this trip he laid the groundwork for wartime propaganda and postwar global consumer society. Gourlay had been born in Scotland in 1900, served in the RAF during the war, and then went out to Ceylon to plant tea. By the 1940s, he had been working for the Tea Board in Canada and was friends with J. A. Milligan, Gervas Huxley, Earl Newsom, and Bill Esty. These men were deeply troubled by the war and rationing, but they also saw new opportunities and used wartime conditions to advance the field of public relations. While private industries and local governments had begun to hire PR experts in the early 1930s, during the war public bodies and corporations developed a fuller understanding of the value of PR, and tea was at the forefront of these developments. PR helped the tea industry not only achieve a central role in wartime memories and business but also ride out the years of austerity and decolonization after the war ended. Indeed, wartime controls pushed industry to recognize just how much their public image mattered.

To be sure, advertising personnel, newsprint, and paper were scarce. Yet the drive to organize public opinion, maintain morale, convey information, and alter society's consumer habits provided a wide field of operation for advertisers. Thirty-four government departments spent £9,500,000 on advertising during the war, with the Ministry of Food being allocated £2,000,000 of that budget.[68] Propaganda, as Siân Nicholas has argued in relation to the BBC, involved "covert attempts to influence hearts and minds." It also had a more neutral definition of simply disseminating information.[69] Business used the term for advertising that existed outside conventional media channels.

Despite reduced budgets, staff shortages, restrictions on advertising, particularly in dollar areas, the loss of European markets, and increased costs due to rising taxation and shortages on labor, supplies, and shipping, the ITMEB carried on its tea propaganda in the United States, Canada, Australia, Egypt, Ceylon, India, South Africa, and Britain. In the UK, the ITMEB began calling itself the Empire Tea Bureau, and after 1948 it became simply the Tea Bureau. Sir Alfred D. Pickford was still chairman and Gervas Huxley remained the director of propaganda, but in name only did the bureau still represent the Dutch. Dr. G. H. C. Hart, head of the Economics Section of the Netherlands Ministry for the Colonies (London), represented the Dutch after communications from Amsterdam were silenced following the German invasion.[70] This coalition was deeply symbolic, especially after the Japanese occupied the NEI in early 1942. The Tea Cess Board of Kenya and the Nyasaland Tea Association contributed small amounts to the budget throughout this period. After a bomb damaged temporary offices in Wimbledon, a scaled-down ITMEB moved nearly a hundred miles further west to Cirencester in Gloucestershire and it redefined its purpose as maintaining tea's place in the public consciousness of the nation.

Gervas Huxley took the opportunity to experiment with "modern" publicity methods now known as public relations, which he defined as "the relations of an organization, whether a business, or a Government Department, or, as in the case of tea, a whole industry, with all the 'publics' with which it came into contact, employees, shareholders, local communities, customers, as well as the public at large."[71] In other words, public relations sold a public entity to multiple publics. During the Depression Huxley had already begun to think in these terms as he worked with Newsom, Esty, and Roper.[72] American corporations and the federal government were using public relations to portray consumption as "the American Way of Life."[73] The ITMEB used similar methods to declare that the right to drink tea defined the British way of life, and the industry, whether at home or in the colonies, that manufactured this good was engaged in a form of national service.

In his enthusiasm for PR Huxley should not be seen as a mere conduit of Americanization. Rather, he invented public relations with colleagues across the Atlantic and in the British Empire.[74] Many British market researchers such as Mark Abrams and the founders of M-O were on the political Left and believed in what Stefan Schwarzkopf has characterized as a "necessary balance between . . . exports and imports, public and private consumption."[75] Huxley was a liberal imperialist who would vote Tory after the war, but he too shared the vision of society most famously associated with the Beveridge Report, which came out in 1942. The apex of faith in the government's ability to end Ignorance, Idleness, Want, Squalor, and Disease, the report outlined a plan for postwar reconstruction in which increased public spending on health care, social insurance, education, and similar policies would free individuals to spend more on themselves, their families, their homes, and their communities.[76] Working together, labor, the state, and private enterprise preached a new view of welfare and consumerism, but so too did large companies and producer organizations. The ITMEB extolled public-private partnerships as it sold to the new "publics" in the canteens, factories, and front lines that were at war with fascism.

But for all their public-spirited language, in their private correspondence, Huxley and his colleagues admitted that they were using wartime anxieties to manufacture popular imperialism. In 1941, Huxley wrote to Gourlay, who was then based in Canada, that "the public mind is very ripe indeed" for nationalistic advertising and that the Empire Tea Bureau should manipulate this "strong emotional attitude" in support of the British imperial nation.[77] Even more telling was the next paragraph in which Huxley urged:

Let us, above all else, try and publicise a belief that all patriotic people in Canada *are already* [emphasis in the original] drinking tea as their exclusive beverage in order to help the Empire, so that—were this true of only one or two individuals or not—the mass of the public might believe this and jump on the bandwagon on which they must hurry to jump.[78]

Here, tucked away in an archive in Madison, Wisconsin, is a very revealing letter in which this group of businessmen admitted that they were trying to stoke imperial sentiment. These were the same men who had abandoned that technique in the mid-1930s, but in 1941, when the empire was on the brink of defeat, Huxley and Gourlay confessed a desire to exploit Canadians' sense of service to the empire. At the time, Earl Newsom's firm was conducting the Canadian campaign, and Gourlay urged him to work even harder to "get this Empire story over even more often and forcibly in the future than you have in the past."[79] This exchange reveals a level of cynicism that perhaps had not existed in the past and yet likely indicates how advertisers and colonial business hoped to profit from wartime conditions. Responding to Gourlay's advice, the Canadian Tea Board stoked popular imperialism by adding "illustrations of soldiers, airmen, etc.," to its advertising, and also stressing "the Empire origin of the tea used in Canada and the importance of Empire buying as an aid to winning the war."[80] By 1942, however, shipping pressures and dollar restrictions drastically limited the scope of this campaign.

Other regions, such as Australia, South Africa, and of course Britain, also began to appeal to consumers' sense of imperial duty, but mainly this meant depicting soldiers with a cup of tea in hand. For example, in one ad, a private explains how after "handling those hefty tanks" a cup of tea from the canteen "snaps" him back to normal.[81] Making a joke out of the 1930s campaign, one ITMEB postcard produced in Australia depicted a soldier offering tea to his mate, who is thoroughly ensnared in barbed wire, with a caption that read: "Tea *Revives* You!"[82] Similar themes also were used in South Africa during the war, especially since tea was not rationed, though distribution came under government control.[83] During this time, the children's supplement in the *Bantu World* included many imperial and militaristic themes.[84] A 1944 Tea Board poster featured King George VI on board a battleship, accompanied by seven scenes of Africans fighting for the motherland as stretcher-bearers, medics, gunners, firefighters, and lorry drivers (fig. 9.1). Mr. and Mrs. Tea Drinker and their children, with cups in hand, reminded consumers that to win the war they should "Always Drink Tea" because "Tea Is Good for Us!" King and colonist, black and white, civilian and soldier would save the empire together. Such messages made it appear as though the consumer marketplace was not racially segregated, when, of course, it was no less segregated than any other part of South African society.

His Majesty King George VI on board a British battleship.

HOW TO BUY TEA

Always buy a good-quality tea. It tastes better and goes farther. Buy your tea in quarter-pound packets or larger. You get better value that way, and save paper.

1944 ALMANAC

IT IS VERY EASY TO MAKE TEA

1. Warm the teapot thoroughly with hot water.
2. Then put in one teaspoonful of tea for each person you wish to serve, and one extra for the pot.
3. Immediately the water boils, pour it into the pot.
4. Allow teapot to stand for four to five minutes before pouring the tea into cups.

JANUARY					
Sunday		2	9	16	23 30
Monday		3	10	17	24 31
Tuesday		4	11	18	25
Wednesday		5	12	19	26
Thursday		6	13	20	27
Friday		7	14	21	28
Saturday	1	8	15	22	29

FEBRUARY					
Sunday		6	13	20	27
Monday		7	14	21	28
Tuesday	1	8	15	22	29
Wednesday	2	9	16	23	
Thursday	3	10	17	24	
Friday	4	11	18	25	
Saturday	5	12	19	26	

MARCH					
Sunday		5	12	19	26
Monday		6	13	20	27
Tuesday		7	14	21	28
Wednesday	1	8	15	22	29
Thursday	2	9	16	23	30
Friday	3	10	17	24	31
Saturday	4	11	18	25	

APRIL					
Sunday		2	9	16	23 30
Monday		3	10	17	24
Tuesday		4	11	18	25
Wednesday		5	12	19	26
Thursday		6	13	20	27
Friday		7	14	21	28
Saturday	1	8	15	22	29

MAY					
Sunday		7	14	21	28
Monday	1	8	15	22	29
Tuesday	2	9	16	23	30
Wednesday	3	10	17	24	31
Thursday	4	11	18	25	
Friday	5	12	19	26	
Saturday	6	13	20	27	

JUNE					
Sunday		4	11	18	25
Monday		5	12	19	26
Tuesday		6	13	20	27
Wednesday		7	14	21	28
Thursday	1	8	15	22	29
Friday	2	9	16	23	30
Saturday	3	10	17	24	

JULY					
Sunday		2	9	16	23 30
Monday		3	10	17	24 31
Tuesday		4	11	18	25
Wednesday		5	12	19	26
Thursday		6	13	20	27
Friday		7	14	21	28
Saturday	1	8	15	22	29

AUGUST					
Sunday		6	13	20	27
Monday		7	14	21	28
Tuesday	1	8	15	22	29
Wednesday	2	9	16	23	30
Thursday	3	10	17	24	31
Friday	4	11	18	25	
Saturday	5	12	19	26	

SEPTEMBER					
Sunday		3	10	17	24
Monday		4	11	18	25
Tuesday		5	12	19	26
Wednesday		6	13	20	27
Thursday		7	14	21	28
Friday	1	8	15	22	29
Saturday	2	9	16	23	30

OCTOBER					
Sunday	1	8	15	22	29
Monday	2	9	16	23	30
Tuesday	3	10	17	24	31
Wednesday	4	11	18	25	
Thursday	5	12	19	26	
Friday	6	13	20	27	
Saturday	7	14	21	28	

NOVEMBER					
Sunday		5	12	19	26
Monday		6	13	20	27
Tuesday		7	14	21	28
Wednesday	1	8	15	22	29
Thursday	2	9	16	23	30
Friday	3	10	17	24	
Saturday	4	11	18	25	

DECEMBER					
Sunday		3	10	17	24 31
Monday		4	11	18	25
Tuesday		5	12	19	26
Wednesday		6	13	20	27
Thursday		7	14	21	28
Friday	1	8	15	22	29
Saturday	2	9	16	23	30

A demonstration of fire-fighting drill by African troops.

An African lorry driver attached to the Royal Army Service Corps.

An African soldier rests beside a 13-pounder gun after a spell of duty.

First-aid dressing in the field. Tea is often given in cases of shock.

African soldiers help with tank maintenance and are here seen at work.

African army stretcher-bearers stand proudly to attention for inspection.

A demonstration of life-saving given by African fire-fighters.

Mr. and Mrs. **TEA-DRINKER** and their family say:

"ALWAYS DRINK TEA"

TEA is good for us!

COPYRIGHT BY THE TEA MARKET EXPANSION BUREAU P.O. BOX 1027 DURBAN

FIGURE 9.1. "Always Drink Tea," 1944 Almanac, South Africa, ITMEB. (British National Archives, INF 2/4 (100), 1944)

THE SERVICE APPEAL

While rousing nationalistic buying habits and selling tea as a weapon of war, the ITMEB and the big distributors also engaged in a parallel campaign, which they loosely defined as the Service Appeal. This propaganda defined tea as a form of welfare that people deserved as a social right. This approach was very strong in the UK, but it also was common in India and Ceylon, two places where tea was plentiful and could be presented as a form of aid to the poor and hungry. Tea as welfare and relief targeted consumer markets that had been created by the war: workers, soldiers, refugees, and other victims of the conflict.

Although tea was tightly rationed, consumers were able to choose the brand they preferred. Brand advertising therefore continued, as firms carefully encouraged sales even in this regulated economy. This was a difficult task because advertisers had to avoid appearing to condone overconsumption or any form of indulgence that could appear to direct money or energy away from the war effort. To do this, brand advertising, like that of the ITMEB, sought to maintain public goodwill and promote collective forms of consumption directed toward the common good. Patriotic appeals sold many products in many nations during this war, but the tea industry developed a powerful new argument: tea, the industry claimed, was a form of social welfare and therefore a public good.[85]

It should not be surprising that the Co-operative Society, which still championed working-class collectivity and social ownership, made tea's service to the public a central theme in their wartime consumer advertising. When rationing was introduced, 28 percent of the population, or thirteen and a half million people, registered to do their shopping at the Co-op. With representation on local councils and in Parliament, an annual turnover of £272 million, a quarter of a million employees on the retail side, and another hundred thousand in production and distribution, the Co-op was a significant economic and political power.[86] Its wartime advertising thus left a deep imprint on the nation and its sense of the place of consumerism in British culture.

In many respects, the Co-op's wartime ads were very similar to government-sponsored public service campaigns and reflected the ideas that the International Tea Market Expansion Board had been promoting since the mid-1930s. Co-op ads continued to use their prewar slogan that it was filling "The Nation's Tea Pot," and most of its ads advanced the People's War ideology. When Britons read their local newspaper they encountered air wardens, fireguards, truck drivers, policemen, and soldiers fighting the war on the Co-op's tea. For example, an ad featuring two air wardens sharing a midnight cuppa stated: "On duty all night, how eagerly a man looks forward to the heartening refreshment of a piping hot cup of really flavoursome tea!"[87] Another campaign that revolved around the slogan "This Is a Good Cup of Tea!" reminded shoppers that all of the Co-op's blends were a good value and good quality.[88] This campaign validated and normalized masculine forms of hospitality and even domesticity in the army or wartime workplace.[89] In one ad two policemen enjoy the tea in their canteen, while sharing consumer knowledge gleaned from a woman. One tells the other how to buy tea, explaining that "the [canteen] Manageress told me how it's done. 'There's an art in buying everything.'"[90] Another depicted two fireguards in an intimate scene, with one sleeping while the other reads a book and enjoys "the drink to keep you on the alert." The ads preserved traditional gender norms, however, by acknowledging that female knowledge was ultimately responsible for producing masculine domesticity. The tea-drinking fireguard explains, "I pick the book and the wife sees to the tea . . . and she buys from a Co-operative Society."[91]

Same-sex hospitality could be feminine as well, as in an ad featuring female factory workers enjoying a tea break in their canteen. The copy affirmed: "A good cup of tea is a blessing when you're working long hours in a factory. And we DO get a good cup here."[92] No doubt responding to the weak, poor quality tea served in canteens, shelters, and British Restaurants, advertising assured consumers that the Co-op brand was always tasty. One ad thus featured a grandmotherly Mrs. Throwle, "an experienced canteen worker," who "caters for thirty" and uses only Co-op tea so she has "no grumbles" about weak tea.[93] Not surprisingly, the idea that "Co-op tea makes the ration go further" became a mainstay of wartime advertising. Other companies made the same point. The canteen manageress became a surrogate wife or mother and a new food expert who brewed good tea while upholding austerity measures.

Good service and hospitality were equally prominent themes in ITMEB wartime advertising, but the agency of tea planters went further than the Co-op did to develop the notion of tea as service. In Britain, Australia, and Canada, Huxley and his colleagues forged very profitable relationships with other businesses, government, and the catering trade by selling the ITMEB as a catering advisory service. At the end of 1940, the ITMEB hired C. G. Gardiner, a man with years of catering experience, to head its new division called the National Catering Service. The service worked under the Canteen Catering Department of the Ministry of Supply to establish a mid-shift tea service to half a million workers in over fifty ordnance factories. It also assisted tea and food catering in the Navy, Army and Air Force Institutes (NAAFI), the Ministry of Agriculture and Fisheries, the Ministry of Food, the Admiralty, the Board of Education and Ministry of Works, and over six hundred private firms.[94] By 1943, the remit of the National Catering Service expanded when it began to advise the National

Service Hostels, pit-head canteens, British Restaurants, Port of London Authority, Manchester Ship Canal, South Africa House, and even the Polish government.[95] In 1944 it worked with 3,000 private firms and distributed some 37,000 copies of its wartime publications.[96]

The National Catering Service established good tea as a worker's right. It educated employers about how to build an industrial kitchen that included up-to-date equipment, recipes, and decor, as well as how to increase productivity and create a sense of comfort and community in the factory. Gardiner published several works on all of these subjects, including *Canteens at Work*, which was published by Oxford University Press in 1941, *Tea for the Workers*, *Tea at Work*, *The Small Canteen*, and *Feeding the Young Worker*, as well as other textbooks and histories, many of which have become standard sources for tea and food historians.[97] The ITMEB's National Catering Service continued to publish after the war, and many well-known books about tea, including Osbert Lancaster's *The Story of Tea*, James Laver's *Eating Out*, and R. D. Morrison's *Tea—Its Production and Marketing*, all originated from the catering service and ultimately were paid for by tea planters in the empire. Of course, there were other entities pushing for industrial catering, but colonial planters were also a powerful but unrecognized voice that created a new notion of social welfare and workplace conditions within the UK, a right that workers would later fight to maintain. The modern factory, the National Catering Service proposed, served food and drink, especially tea. "The canteen," Gardiner wrote, had "turned the ill-lit factory of fifty-years ago into a place as healthy as a home." And the heart or center of every canteen was tea, a drink science now "proved" not only checked "flagging energy but also led to *higher output* figures."[98] This was especially true for women, who needed, Gardiner believed, more frequent breaks than men. The National Catering Service thus created many of the ideas around the worker's tea and industrial relations, and shaped how tea was served and remembered in wartime and postwar Britain.[99]

After the war ended, the ITMEB "Tea for the Workers Campaign" stuck to this same idea that tea was a social service, a form of welfare, and added the notion that tea was a tool of postwar reconstruction.[100] In 1946–47, the ITMEB placed advertisements in journals such as *Automobile Engineer*, *Engineering*, *The Builder*, *Shipbuilding*, *Architect's Journal*, and *Pottery Gazette*, informing employers that tea would revive their tired workforce and would help keep up production levels. Such ads referred to the lessons learned in wartime when "tea for the workers did much to assist tired bodies, jaded minds and strong nerves." "That is why," one ad continued, "in preparation for peacetime production, so many managements are ensuring that tea services in factories continue or are put in place."[101]

The social welfare appeal was also tried in wartime India, but it unfolded in a different way than in the UK. The Indian Tea Board was very active during the war and it invaded the Indian household like a military strike force. The board divided each target town into areas, numbered each house, and set up a "demonstration" table in each street, mapping and collecting information on entire towns in this fashion.[102] Although he expected resistance, W. H. Mills, the Tea Board's commissioner, noted happily that the board's "lady supervisors" had managed to enter even the most "orthodox and conservative places" and been able to demonstrate how to brew tea "right inside the house."[103] As Gandhi and others had predicted, the Tea Board had become a part of the colonial state with the power to inspect and reform private cooking methods and public facilities. In 1942 and 1943, the retail price of tea rose to three times the normal price, but despite this consumption grew, especially where the propagandists had worked most intensively.[104] Colony-wide consumption almost doubled from 96 million pounds a year in 1939 to 165 million by the end of the war.[105] The Tea Board felt confident that advertising worked even in the most difficult circumstances, but they nevertheless ran into stumbling blocks.

In 1943 and 1944, approximately three million Bengalis died of starvation. Environmental and economic factors contributed to the geography and severity of the famine, but most scholars nevertheless agree with Amartya Sen, who emphasized that political decisions had made food unattainable and unaffordable for key groups and regions within Bengal.[106] Colonial economic policies during the Depression and the war contributed to a credit crisis, skyrocketing inflation, falling real wages, and shifts in the supply of food to urban areas.[107] Though regional in nature, the Bengal famine demonstrated the huge discrepancy between metropolitan and colonial government approaches to food. British food controls have been remembered as one of the key successes of wartime planning, creating a notion of social equality and fair shares for all. In Bengal, government policy contributed to starvation and furnished nationalists with further evidence of the failures of the Raj.

The Tea Board, however, actually exploited the famine and wartime shortages when it launched a new "Problems Appeal" advertising campaign, which stressed that tea was "an unfailing comforter in these times of stress and worry."[108] Similarly, Ceylon Tea Board employees served thousands of cups of tea to flood victims in north Colombo in 1941.[109] However, despite this actual act of charity, many large employers refused to give their workers concessions—even a cup of tea—claiming that they did not want to interfere with "the established routine of factories."[110] In southern India, for example, industrialists complained that "economic conditions did not permit the expense involved."[111] Workers nevertheless refreshed themselves at the many liquid tea shops in the vicinity of workplaces.[112] The reasons for owners' reluctance to serve tea are complex. Unlike in Britain, outside contractors were often in charge of tea and food service in the cotton factories in Bombay and Gujarat. They paid heavy rents to owners and thus were a source of income that mill owners did not want to dispense with.[113] At the same time, workers could not afford to take tea breaks, since they were paid by the piece. However, it is likely that British-owned companies did not want to invest anything in their businesses and labor force because many felt they would soon be kicked out of India. In summarizing some of the difficulties he had encountered in Cawnpore, the Indian tea commissioner wrote: "Personally, I feel that it is not economic conditions alone that have caused this failure. I think that there is a general hardening of opinion in regard to the provision of amenities to a labour force which has already had a number of concessions."[114] In other words, class struggles and political conflicts in India's textile factories had reached a point where owners were uninterested in the physical welfare of their workers.[115] While in the 1920s owners were starting to believe that tea would satisfy workers, by the 1940s many were unwilling to buy into this idea.

In response to such problems, the Indian Tea Board established a Cooperative Canteen System that was less expensive than hiring outside contractors.[116] The Indian Tea Association also pressured the powerful Bombay Mill Owners Association and the government to establish the canteen system.[117] By 1944 food shortages and inflation meant that industrial work gained importance and advertisements relentlessly promoted the idea that tea breaks led to "maximum industrial efficiency."[118] Although they were established, industrial canteens did not feed into the same mythologies of fair shares, democratization, or imperial consumerism that were visible in England at the time. Tea was a fuel of the modern industrial factory worker, but in India owners were not committed to this notion and the workplace did not inevitably become a sphere of consumerism in the same way that occurred elsewhere.

The National Catering Service defined the tea break as a right for manual laborers and office staff in Britain, South Africa, Canada, Australia, and New Zealand and tried to do so in India and other colonies or former parts of the empire.[119] The ITMEB's catering service extolled public-private partnerships, a defining feature of the postwar economy, transformed the nature of public eating, and offered employers and government agencies a way to streamline collective feeding. It did not guarantee that the food served was particularly tasty. However, it did ensure that the tea was hot and strong across the British Empire and it helped tea acquire a powerful and special place in the national imagination in Great Britain especially. When politicians and employers sought to reduce the time dedicated to workplace tea breaks, or to shift them from communal affairs to drinking on the job, workers in all of these regions went on strike to defend their right to drink tea. Outside observers often saw these tea-break strikes as silly or frivolous, when in fact they reveal the degree to which workers had embraced the idea that drinking tea at work was a social right.

WOMEN BREWING THE PEOPLE'S TEA

In the heat of battle, families who had lost their homes in the Blitz, neighbors who sheltered together in the Underground during Hitler's nightly raids, land girls who plowed farms to grow the people's food, and soldiers who were stranded on the beaches of Dunkirk or battled in the deserts of northern Africa all drank tea to cope with everyday life during war. This is the mythology of tea at war, and though people certainly served each other the hot brew as they faced untold dangers and hardships, this tea story did not just appear out of thin air. The Co-operative Society and other brand advertising, the National Catering Service, and the ITMEB determined that tea was a central part of the wartime experience and memories. Tens of thousands of women who volunteered for the YMCA, Red Cross, and especially the WVS brewed up countless cups of tea and shaped the experience and memory of the war. This army of women and the photographers and journalists who documented and published their stories manufactured the mythology of the People's Tea.

Gervas Huxley, who seemed to be behind so many of these efforts, authored the basic plot line, which others then elaborated upon.[120] Huxley understood that he had to keep tea in the public eye on a shoestring budget. He thus came up with the idea of what came to be known as tea cars, or "mobile canteens," to reach consumers who were displaced by war, working in isolated shops, victims of bombing, or simply soldiers in the field. Mobile canteens had been used in World War I, but Huxley claimed that he came up with the idea at the beginning of World War II.[121] His real innovation was to make sure journalists, photographers, and filmmakers documented this story.

At the beginning of the war, Huxley and Pickford approached the YMCA, the largest voluntary organization that provided canteen services to the military, and offered them use of four tea cars as a prototype. The agency accepted the plan and the first tea car opened for business at the YMCA center at Plaistow in the East End of London. In addition to tea, the cars were stocked with books and writing paper, snacks, sweets, and cigarettes. Charging only 1d. for a cup for tea, the cars even managed to make a small profit.[122] The YMCA, Salvation Army, Church Army, and WVS raised the funds for and operated about five hundred mobile tea cars and hundreds more were in production.[123] Throughout the war, these mobile units served tea to civilians and soldiers in Britain, Canada,

Iceland, Egypt, East Africa, South Africa, India, Burma, and many other home and battlefronts.[124] They boosted morale while securing the global expansion of the tea habit.[125]

In many ways the tea cars were simply continuing the demonstration work that the ITMEB had done before, and in fact the first cars were redesigned versions of the mobile tea vans that had driven around Britain, India, Ceylon, Egypt, Southern Africa, and northern Europe in the 1930s. They even used the very same equipment that the Tea Board had set up in the 1930s to run an early morning tea service at holiday camps. At these popular centers of working-class leisure, the board had devised the insulated urns known as "multipots."[126] As R. L. Barnes, the board's commissioner, later explained:

> Our recipe was: Take one or two multipots from a holiday camp trolley and place on a re-painted secondhand van; add mugs, milk, sugar, chocolate, biscuits, cake, razor blades, postage stamps, etc., mix well together. Result—one mobile canteen or *Tea Car.*[127]

The bright-red tea car fleet quickly became an international institution paid for by subscriptions from businesses, voluntary agencies, and private individuals in the United States and empire.[128] A list of gifts to the National YMCA War Service Fund in 1940 reveals this wide support. Not surprisingly, tea planters gave a great deal to the effort. Over £9,700 came from a group designated as the "Tea Trade." In addition, the Joklai (Assam) Tea Co., Ltd., Alex Lawrie and Co., and importers and retailers such as the East India and China Tea Company donated considerable sums.[129] In 1941 the Gyro Clubs of Canada; the employees of T. Eaton and Company in Hamilton (the famous chain of department stores); the Friday Club of Jewish Women (Toronto); the United Empire Loyalists of Toronto; the Patriotic Salvage Committee of Winnipeg; Mr. and Mrs. Elmer Davis of Kingston; "The Twenty-Four of Us"; and the Bowling Owners Association of Hamilton raised funds for eight tea cars, costing $2,500 apiece. Endorsing this groundswell of wartime activism, the *Montreal Gazette* outlined the degree to which Canadians had helped shape this movement.[130] Canadians who had been driving the vehicles in Britain incorporated their ideas into a new design that went into production in Toronto in 1941. These new Canadian tea cars, which had "Everything" for troops' comfort, served soup, other hot foods, and gallons of tea and dispensed "all sorts of little odds and ends that soldiers really need such as boot laces, tooth paste, shoe polish, cigarettes and magazines . . . and sports equipment."[131] Religious and labor organizations, groups of employees, and leisure clubs all chipped in. The South African Women's Auxiliary Service (SAWAS), South African Tea Board, and Kenya Welfare Fund, as well as the

FIGURE 9.2. The Iron Duke at Duke University during World War II.
(By permission of Rubenstein Library/ Duke University)

Civil Servants of Kenya, also raised so much money for tea cars that in April 1941 the military asked the YMCA and SAWAS to start outfitting cinema vans to entertain and comfort soldiers.[132]

While money came from people all over the world, the vehicles also traveled across the Atlantic. In 1941, the most famous such vehicle, a battered tea car christened "The Iron Duke," began a North American tour under the auspices of the British War Relief Society. Named after the Duke of Wellington and the HMS *Iron Duke*, the ship that had led the British fleet in the Battle of Jutland in World War I and was placed out of commission during World War II after a German air attack, the Tea Board's Iron Duke was a self-conscious attempt to make tea into a British war hero and to push U.S. public opinion to support going to war. "Everywhere it went," the Ceylon Tea Propaganda Board Report noted, the Iron Duke "became the subject of much newspaper and radio publicity, in which Tea, of course, played a prominent part."[133] Duke University, though it had nothing to do with the name of the vehicle, was one stop on this tour, and as we can see in figure 9.2, a group of young, attractive "Duke Girls" helped draw attention to tea and the war effort.

In Britain the plucky and courageous vehicles became icons of the People's War. This story first emerged after reports came home that the cars had served tea to the British Expeditionary Force in France and Flanders. This fleet was in Dunkirk at the time of the retreat, and it shared in the symbolic heroism of the flotilla of fishing boats and other small ships that evacuated the army. Under the direction of the Tea Bureau's public relations officer, Hereward Phillips, the cars famously served the troops on the beaches until they were all rescued and the final car was heroically destroyed by a bomb. After the event the undersecretary of war wrote that the service "rendered to the Army by Institutes and Mobile Canteens has done more than any single factor to maintain the morale of the Forces and to keep the Troops happy."[134]

By obscuring its role in creating and funding the tea cars, the ITMEB appeared as a philanthropic, not commercial, institution. The media underscored this vision by proposing that tea was serving the nation. Most public commentary featured the bravery and generosity of the girls of the "Blitz Canteens," explaining how these heroines encountered and overcame myriad dangers to attend to the nation. A *Picture Post* photo essay of twenty-six images, "A Day in the Life: Girls of the Blitz Canteen," introduced readers to two intrepid "society" girls, eighteen-year-old Patience "Boo" Brand and Rachel Bingham, two members of the WVS who cheerfully, and with their hair done and lipstick applied, scrubbed floors, lifted heavy tea urns, heated meat pies, carried heavy trays of buns, and served countless cups of tea to civilians in shelters, men of the Royal Engineer Corps, and others in need. Boo and Rachel were young, beautiful, energetic, strong, and selfless. They were also cheerful, and like the tea they served their optimism revived a nation under extreme duress. This photo essay thus romanticized wartime struggles. In one photo (fig. 9.3), Boo and a

FIGURE 9.3. "Girl with the Urn," *Picture Post*, 1941. (© IWM D2173)

Royal Engineer are shown draining hot water together, with Boo carrying the urn and the engineer simply turning the spigot, while the other men look on and smile, suggesting a hint of romance between these young heroes. This is PR at its best; tea became slightly sexy, and it earned a place in the national imagination.[135] Men and women, rich and poor, American and British, public and private forces come together to revive the wartime nation, the empire, and the Allies with a hot cup of tea.

The mass media and transnational agencies such as the YMCA and the Salvation Army spread news of the mobile canteens around the empire.[136] Tea in the desert and the jungle made especially good war stories. South African children read about the exploits of the tea cars in the *Bantu World*.[137] Australians were told much the same story in their newspapers. For example, an article titled "Hot Drinks Mean Much in the Jungle," published in the *Cairns Post*, related how tea accompanied the troops as they battled the Japanese in the jungles of New Guinea. In the words of the YMCA officer in charge of these operations, the infantryman who was in constant danger, who had to sleep in water and mud, "needs comforts most and we try to give him hot drinks and help as far forward as possible . . . the slogan 'Tea Revives You' certainly means something up there."[138]

This story moved from the media into memoirs, and the tea cars drove through rubble into the mythology of the Battle of Britain. A police inspector's memory of one night during the Blitz is illuminating:

> Fires were burning fiercely, and the whole sky to the northward, the east and the south was an orange-red glow. The dome of St. Paul's stood out, boldly silhouetted against the flame-red skies which, reflected in the river, made old Father Thames look quite beautiful, when the city was in anguish. . . . Just then a mobile canteen came lumbering over the bridge. It stopped abreast my car and in it were three WVS canteen workers going about their abnormal duty as unconcerned and unafraid as though they were going shopping. One of the women kindly shouted out, "Will you have a cup of tea, police-inspector?"[139]

Tea, St. Paul's, the Thames, and the women of the WVS symbolized a stalwart nation living through its "darkest hour." The tea car brought hot food and other comforts but also signified normalcy, captured in this description of the WVS volunteers acting as though they were merely "going shopping." Tea and hot food were a real comfort, but such memoirs and other accounts did not just emerge out of a kind of collective British spirit.

The wartime propaganda machine, with its photographers, filmmakers, and journalists, helped the Tea Board sell this story.[140] Newsreels, for example,

FIGURE 9.4. Homeless and orphaned children depicted as happily enjoying a meal and
a cup of tea at an air-raid shelter at the John Keble Church, Mill Hill, London, 1940.
Ministry of Information Photo Division, Imperial War Museum Ministry
of Information, Second World War Collection. (© IWM D1442)

documented the king and queen inspecting the fleet of tea cars setting off to join the British Expeditionary Force in France.[141] London's Lord Mayor and his wife also drank tea from these canteens, with the event captured in a newsreel titled "Tea for Tommy Atkins."[142] Gracie Fields accompanied a tea car that visited an army barracks in France and personally served the troops, handing out hundreds of mugs of tea, spooning in sugar, and throwing buns to the hordes of soldiers before sitting down and entertaining them with a song.[143] Like this working-class celebrity doing her bit, those who funded, drove, and read about the tea cars, as well as those who watched them in action, felt they were also helping the war effort by serving tea. The ITMEB even produced a documentary sound film about the tea cars, called *Tea for Heroes*. When this film depicting the activities of a "Tea Car during a 'blitz' in London" was shown in the United States, Wendell Willkie, who was the Republican nominee for president in 1940, added a prologue endorsing the tea car's war work.[144]

Wartime photography similarly immortalized tea as an evocative symbol of communities forged under stress. The Ministry of Information Photo Division, Army Photography units, and the famous British fashion photographer Cecil Beaton produced countless images of tea served to the homeless, to evacuees, to wounded soldiers, to land girls, to munitions workers, and to victims who had experienced untold suffering. Tea appeared after defeat in battle and in the most unlikely and alien places. It seemed as though the war was not yet lost as long as one could still serve and be served a cup of tea. Often these photos isolated an individual being served a hot cuppa, but it was especially common for groups to be photographed taking tea together in shelters, deserts, and jungles (fig. 9.4). Taken together these wartime images implied that civilians and soldiers were allied in the fight against fascism. Even in the hardest moments, Britons could smile when they had their cup of tea.

At the beginning of the war, tea helped soldiers cope with defeat. By the end of the war, stories circulated about how tea cars had invigorated the Allies and helped them in their drive to stop the Axis powers. Tea thus traveled with "the Army of the Nile in its victorious advance into Libya."[145] In 1943 tea went with the British forces that journeyed "From Alamein to Tunis, crossed into Sicily," and would eventually fight to liberate Italy.[146] In 1944, 37 tea cars were serving 21½ million cups of tea to troops all over India, and five had famously traveled into Burma where military authorities and the press gave them a great deal of free publicity.[147]

Some photos of soldiers focused on multiracial masculine communities. For example, a number of photos depicted European and South Asian troops drinking together in the scorching frontiers of the North African desert. Figure 9.5 is one such illustration of an imagined multiethnic empire at war and at leisure.[148]

FIGURE 9.5. A mobile tea canteen in North Africa, 31 July 1942. (© IWM E15079)

FIGURE 9.6. Troops queue for a mug of tea at an Egyptian port,
12 July 1943. (© IWM E25711)

While most of these photos arranged subjects in groups to highlight equality
and camaraderie, others unwittingly reinforced racial difference.[149] Service
could imply racial, class, and gender hierarchies, as in the case of an image of an
Egyptian man serving British troops before they board ships for Sicily in July
1943 (fig. 9.6). It was true that soldiers drank tea from metal drums in the desert,
but who really was doing the work to serve this tea and were diverse people really
coming together at the tea table as many official photographs implied? How did
such images paper over very real tensions within the armed services and between
soldiers and civilians? In these portraits of men making tea not war, the viewer
forgets the violent purpose of war and the way in which World War II unleashed
both intimate and official forms of violence upon civilians.[150] The ITMEB and
the Co-operative Society's wartime advertising had depicted groups of men cooking and eating together and in other ways taking part in a masculine consumer
culture. As we have seen, there was nothing new about advertisers stressing tea's
masculinity. However, with so many men at war and so many fronts to be served,
total war offered myriad opportunities for the industry to sell tea to men. With
the slogan "The Soldiers' Drink—Tea" painted prominently on their side, the tea
cars constituted a new kind of male consumer culture. Armies had always been
markets, but the modern mass media commodified soldiers' bodies in new and
decidedly modern ways.

FIGURE 9.7. A British soldier drinking tea next to a mobile tea canteen at the Calcutta airport, 1944. Photograph by Cecil Beaton. (© IWM IB 1882)

The best example of this process can be found in a striking photograph that Cecil Beaton took at the Calcutta airport in 1944 (fig. 9.7). Commissioned by the Ministry of Information to capture the everyday experience of war, Britain's most well-known fashion photographer used his skilled eye to reproduce wartime mythologies. Beaton made the soldier drinking tea literally beautiful. The muscular, blond soldier in profile is framed so that the viewer is drawn to the bare arm that lifts a mug of tea to this soldier's lips. The strong vertical lines of the mobile tea car and contrasting bright light and shadow add drama to an everyday experience, glamorizing the soldier and tea. The image is not about cheerfulness or community; it focuses on the soldier's fit and beautiful body. Although Beaton took the photo, this image implied that tea, served by the Indian Tea Expansion Board, produced this strong male body. Together this agency and Cecil Beaton sexualized the consuming soldier, but in a way that recalled the racial and gender politics of colonialism.[151] This tea-drinking soldier casts his gaze outward in a position reminiscent of a colonial planter or administrator surveying the land over which he rules. If war had made the empire and the male body vulnerable, the soldier's pose and the fact that he is drinking tea implied that white men still ruled the empire, a story that in 1944 did not yet have a neat conclusion.

In 1946 George Orwell wrote an entire essay on the pleasures of a good cup of tea, a fantasy written as rationing unexpectedly tightened during a bleak year of postwar austerity. Conjuring up memories and anticipating the future, Orwell used tea to describe British liberties, or one might say, eccentricities. He playfully described how Britons were engaged in a "violent dispute" about the strength of the brew, the amount of sugar and milk added, the shape of the pot and cup, and the timing and nature of the meal that accompanied one's tea. The one thing that all tea drinkers agreed upon, however, was that good tea was always "Indian or Ceylonese." "China tea has virtues," Orwell confessed, but "there is not much stimulation in it. One does not feel wiser, braver or more optimistic after drinking it." Reiterating his point, Orwell concluded that "anyone who uses the phrase, 'a nice cup of tea,' invariably means Indian tea."[152] George Orwell, an intense critic of propaganda, had unwittingly absorbed decades of advertising that had highlighted the strength and healthiness of India over the effeminacy of China. His essay shows just how well the empire's advertising and propaganda had worked.

While it seems so natural to think of tea as a comfort in wartime, the tea industry guaranteed that this idea was widely available even when tea itself was not. The industry was very worried that rationing and Ministry of Food propaganda would alter tastes over the long run and threaten the collapse of their primary markets. Hiding behind what looked like public service agencies, such as the National Catering Service and the tea cars, the industry successfully transformed tea into a weapon of war, a social service, a form of relief, and a worker's right. Tea aided workers, soldiers, refugees, and homeless civilians across the People's Empire. In a literal sense, the global tea trade was "imperial" during the war. The Japanese occupation of Java and Sumatra in 1942 and wartime policies had left Britain in control of the entire Allied trade. The war produced numerous difficulties for growers, distributors, and retailers, but it also presented a number of new marketing and propaganda opportunities. Capturing the contradictory nature of the war years, the ITMEB's report for 1940 indicated "how war conditions, while imposing restrictions on normal propaganda activities in some theatres, have in others created opportunities for new and fruitful lines of work which the Board have been quick to seize and exploit for the present and future benefit of the tea producing industry."[153] Governments, voluntary agencies, and business served tea in the battlefield, at work, in canteens, and in other communal settings. The public-private compact and the reverential place of tea in wartime Britain did not protect the postwar industry from the political, social, and cultural upheavals of the postwar era, however. While tea became a national icon during World War II, this conflagration also set off a series of events that led to the collapse of both the British Empire and the empire of tea.

PART III

Aftertastes

10

LEFTOVERS

An Imperial Industry at the End of Empire

F ormer tea planter Philip Witham could not contain his bitter feelings over the loss of the British Empire when he spoke about the tea trade on the BBC Home Service in April 1954. Although he admitted that British companies still held a significant stake in tea, he dismissed these interests as the scraps rather than the fruits of empire. As he explained to his listeners: "The main producing countries of India, Pakistan, and Ceylon are all independent states in the Commonwealth and so they can all call the tune regardless of the fact that practically all capital of these tea companies comes from Britain."[1] More than a loss of earnings bothered Witham. He resented how decolonization had shattered the dream of living a comfortable life as a planter sahib overseeing acres of green bushes from the veranda of one's bungalow.[2] He was not alone, but, as one trade expert remarked curtly in 1951, growers who "felt their freedom curtailed" in South Asia simply made the "pilgrimage" to British East Africa.[3] As these men well understood, empires do not die on a single day, and Witham wondered whether the fact that together British and Irish consumers drank half of the world's output could perhaps still impact "the economies of these new nations."[4] In other words, he queried whether consuming countries, those nations with the largest markets, could harness their power and reproduce the political dynamics of colonialism. Witham sensed without fully articulating how tea shaped postcolonial political economies. In 1954 neither producers nor consumers could have foreseen how the tea industry would bind together Britain and its former empire/commonwealth for decades to come. The unanswered question for everyone, however, was: Who would accrue the profits and prestige that the imperial tea industry had for so long afforded white Britons?

Witham's lament captures the psychological experience of decolonization for many white men who were working in or governing the empire in the late 1940s and early 1950s.[5] The tea industry was not entirely in white hands, but it nevertheless had been a place where white men could make a good living and wield enormous authority. Thus, as the Indian Subcontinent gained its independence in 1947 and African colonies began to do so a decade later, the empire's businessmen felt adrift. Many regained their composure and adjusted to postcolonial conditions, but in the immediate postwar period panic was the order of the day. Planters like Witham blamed decolonization for their woes, when in truth they were fighting much broader shifts underway in the mid-twentieth century. The growing scale and transformations of corporate capitalism and the emergence of viable communist and socialist economies in Europe and throughout what then began to be called the developing or Third World made it impossible for British planters to maintain the status quo.

Decolonization necessarily revived questions about what truly constituted an empire and whether economic relationships were exploitive or profitable and for whom. It also profoundly altered the relationship between empires and globalization. For centuries, the British Empire had been an agent of globalization, transferring capital, crops, labor, technologies, ideologies, and tastes throughout much of the world. After World War II, this relationship reversed itself and a new phase of global capitalism and transnational independence movements chipped away at the British imperial system and ideologies. Yet for many nationalists in Africa and South Asia the end of empire did not happen fast enough, and they frustratingly denounced this uneven process in which economics, culture, and politics did not follow the same timeline.[6] European business proved remarkably difficult to dislodge.[7] Exploring this problem, theorists have debated the relative power of metropolitan versus colonial actors, the role of "gentlemanly capitalism" or financial institutions, and the ubiquitous and dramatic spread of the multinational.[8] Attention has also focused on the influence of the United States, the Soviet Union, the United Nations, and NGOs.[9] All of these approaches have explicitly or implicitly documented the vitality and/or weakness of British economic and political institutions in a rapidly changing global climate. A compelling question for those living through this era and for scholars and activists today is: How did Western capital and ideologies carry on after Independence? Examining the postcolonial tea industry allows us to begin to answer this question.

The concluding two chapters of this book trace what happened to tea after empire. We begin by considering how tea planters wrote about their experience of decolonization, then outline the structural changes that occurred between the 1940s and 1970s before considering how planters in what were now diverse nations understood and carried on the production of consumption in key markets, particularly South Africa, Egypt, India, and the United States. The final chapter will then return to Great Britain and examine how tea's consumer culture became a site in which businesses and consumers battled over the very meaning of their postcolonial nation. The concluding chapters of this book thus use tea to explore how Britain and its former colonies and allies understood their economic relationship after empire; how advertising and publicity managed decolonization;

and how business and consumers debated the balance between imports and exports, economies of restraint, and promises of material abundance. I argue that, between the 1940s and 1970s, advertisers and propaganda boards played a neocolonial role and tried to hold together an empire that no longer existed in reality. The spread of production, trade, and consumption well beyond tea's former empire, the growing global influence of American capital and consumer culture, and new Cold War and postcolonial international relationships eventually ended Britain's and India's dominance of this industry, but this process took nearly five decades and is still unfinished business.[10]

DODGING THE SICKLE BLOW

During the most intense years of decolonization, many British and some indigenous planters and managers feared they were about to be thrown into an abyss.[11] The tea industry in the northeast was most affected by Partition, or the division of the Subcontinent into Pakistan and India, a process that began in August 1947 but took years to play out. Partition's new borders cut through older polities and irreparably damaged cultures, the environment, and especially the political economy of the northeast.[12] Historians are still interpreting how communities, families, and individuals rebuilt their worlds and created new identities in the wake of the violent confusion and sense of displacement of Partition.[13] Here, however, I am interested in recording just a few of the ways in which the planting community narrated its own Independence and Partition stories. Turning our attention to a group of people who had for so long victimized others might seem at first glance frivolous or perhaps a means to water down the terrors of Partition. However, we have to study how colonial officials and businesses understood and explained what they thought was occurring in order to illuminate how their fear, racism, memories of past revolts, and individual experiences shaped responses to emerging postcolonial economies and cultures.

Private letters and memos in the colonial business archive exude a penetrating sense of injury and pervasive fear of losing control. Frightened by disturbances in manufacturing and transport and by the belief that communists and socialists were leading riots, attacking managers, and starting strikes and work stoppages in the gardens and at the docks in London, Colombo, and Calcutta, planters felt physically and financially defenseless. They worried about higher taxes, wage rises, and welfare legislation and dreaded indigenization policies and moves to nationalize "European" industries. Buyers ruminated as well about high prices, an apparent decline in quality, and the return of widespread adulteration and contamination. The industry also viewed Coke and coffee as foreign invaders conquering their former "subjects." Far from being silent about the impact of decolonization, the business archive is a veritable warehouse packed with information about how decolonization and the growing influence of both Soviet and American power unhinged the British colonial businesses classes. These records are replete with men writing about their sense of impotence and foreboding.

In a lengthy private summary sent to Sir Percival Griffiths and his colleagues in London in the summer of 1948, J. L. Llewellyn, deputy chairman of the Indian Tea Association, composed one such Partition story. Focusing on Assam, Cachar, Sylhet, and nearby areas, Llewellyn described the flight of Hindus, border skirmishes, countless searches and inspections, delayed mail, and confused procedures in Calcutta.[14] Rather than talk about how Indians were hurting and killing each other, Llewellyn instead described what he believed was politically motivated, class-based, racial violence on the tea estates and in surrounding communities. Violence had erupted between garden workers and management, but it is quite telling that Llewellyn described these desperate days as a chaotic world in which planters' wives defended and saved their husbands' lives from "natives." Llewellyn wrote at length, for example, about how a Mrs. Forest had saved her husband's life after a "sickle blow" had "almost severed Forest's jugular vein." He then praised a Mrs. Dewar for dragging her "unconscious husband" to a "neighbouring bungalow" after rioters had assaulted him, smashed their furniture, and wrecked their car. She had evidently "tried to barricade the doors as the mob rushed onto the landing, and it was her courageous address at the top of the stairs which saved her husband's life."[15]

Such tales of women protecting their men from dangerous, rioting "natives" showed just how much Llewellyn felt he was living in an unstable and incomprehensible world. Planters were unconscious and lying half dead with their throats cut in damaged households, factories, and offices. Many men simply fled the scene. The European superintendent of police in Jalpaiguri, for example, resigned with "dreams" of going to Abyssinia. Most of the European staff at the Indian Tea Association's Research Station at Tocklai also renounced their posts.[16] And things only worsened after Gandhi's murder, an event Llewellyn believed destroyed "the emotional and political center or glue" keeping India together.[17] Like Witham's radio broadcast, Llewellyn's report intertwined the public and personal. His desperate tone and lengthy descriptions of these confused days were similar to the way Britons narrated and remembered the 1857 Mutiny. The story of the brave memsahib, a common trope in Mutiny narratives, reappeared here to emphasize Indian savagery unleashed by the loosening of (masculine) Western authority. When white women had to protect white men, something was very wrong indeed.

Llewellyn feared for his and others' safety, but his anxieties were also inspired by the economic consequences of the Partition of the country into

India, West Pakistan, and East Pakistan. The tea industry literally was severed into two as Sylhet, Tripura, and surroundings became part of the Dominion of Pakistan (and after 1971 Bangladesh), while Assam, Cachar, the Dooars, Terai, and Darjeeling remained in India.[18] Age-old trade routes between Assam and Calcutta and Chittagong were thus destroyed, with road, rail, and river routes blocked off or made insecure.[19] Disrupted supply chains added to severe shortages of coal, food, fuel, fertilizers, seed, and tea chests. In 1948 Anthony Tasker, the assistant organizing director of the ITMEB, tried to calm importers by claiming in a rather detached way that "there is nothing in this complication which cannot be solved by mutual agreement."[20] He was wrong. Border violence, labor unrest, and a series of natural disasters meant that supplies were still not secure in the early 1950s. Investors were especially wary of a region that was so unstable. The situation was exceptionally chaotic in 1962 when China invaded and briefly occupied Assam and during the wars between India and Pakistan in 1947, 1965, and 1971.[21] "Our frontiers are still beset with dangers," announced K. L. Khaitan, chairman of the Cachar branch of the Indian Tea Association, in 1965 when he spoke about the danger posed by China's recent testing of an atomic bomb.[22] Investors and capital dried up, and even the new state government's development funds tended "to bypassed the border areas," leading one scholar to describe Partition as "the political assassination of this regional economy."[23]

Ceylon's transition to an independent dominion in the Commonwealth in February 1948 was initially much smoother, and the British held up this transfer of power as a symbol of the triumph of liberal secular democracy and a demonstration of the feasibility of a multiracial Commonwealth.[24] However, here too planters and capitalists were deeply worried. In 1948, power was handed to Don Stephen Senanayake. Senanayake came from a well-established, middle-class Buddhist family that had thrived under the colonial state. Don Stephen's father, Don Spater, had made his money in graphite mining, but he also had interests in coconut and rubber, and like many in this class he accrued wealth from the arrack business. Arrack is distilled liquor, which in Sri Lanka was made entirely from the fermentation of the sap of the unopened flower of a coconut palm. Don Stephen also worked on his father's rubber plantations and rose in the colonial government, becoming a member of the Legislative Council in 1924 and serving in the State Council from 1931 to 1947 before becoming prime minister in 1948.[25] He was one of the founding members of the United National Party, a pro-Sinhalese coalition that excluded the far Left, and his supposedly moderate government quickly passed several citizenship laws that made the plantation Tamils stateless, thereby laying the groundwork for the civil war that subsequently plagued the island.[26] Even before ethnic and religious tensions erupted in full force as they would later on, class struggles were widespread.

After World War II ended, rapidly falling tea and rubber prices brought about unemployment and massive labor struggles and created a fertile ground for communist organizing.[27] Edgy importers such as Kardomah Ltd. assumed that "Russian influence" had instigated a series of garden worker strikes and contributed to violent attacks on British managers, resulting in at least one death.[28] As they had in Calcutta and London, dockworkers in Colombo also went on strike, creating further shortages and rising costs and leading to a reduction of the tea ration in the UK in 1947. British consumers complained about high prices without knowing the degree to which the tea ration had been influenced by the disruptions of decolonization.

Accusations flew in many directions. The shift from wartime to peacetime economies, decolonization, and the return to free markets brought wildly fluctuating prices. The year 1954 came to be known as the Great Tea Scramble as prices rose to double the average price since the end of rationing. Housewives and major buyers went on "strike," curtailing consumption until the bottom fell out of the market on 16 February 1955, known as "Wild Wednesday" in the trade.[29] Consumer organizations pressured the government to investigate this spike in prices.[30] The British press debated whether wages and tax hikes in India and Ceylon, profiteering of the British agency houses, floods in Assam, or dockworker strikes in Calcutta, Colombo, and London were to blame.[31] On a visit to England, Sir John Kotelawala, who was close to Senanayake and served as Ceylon's prime minister between 1953 and 1956, accused blenders of rigging markets, while sellers blamed the "independence of producers." Kardomah's directors expressed concern that producing nations were artificially raising prices and simply could not be governed as they had in the past. In 1955 they began to bemoan the fact that "the tea market was being controlled by two producer governments [Indian and Ceylon] who would not co-operate; their sole object was to raise the price of tea one way or other."[32] Cooperation then was a key desire for an industry that had been broken into diverse nations and interests. Tensions between growers and buyers were nothing new, but decolonization resurrected differences between and within these communities.

Things came to a head again in 1956, when a more aggressively anti-British socialist government came to power in Ceylon. Soloman Bandaranaike and his new Sri Lankan Freedom Party had campaigned on promises to nationalize key industries, tea included. Before he accomplished this task, Bandaranaike was assassinated and a year of instability followed with both major parties briefly in power. In July 1960, Soloman's wife, Sirimavo, became prime minister; as a committed socialist she began to move her country away from Britain and toward China and the Soviet Union. She formed a coalition with the Marxist Lanka Sama Samaja Party and pressed forward with the nationalization of foreign business. This scared private investors and led to a considerable sterling disinvestment and a drop in tea share estate prices; as one observer put it a few years later, "Some clergymen's widows realized with a shock that the 40% they had come to expect on their Ceylon tea shares was not as safe as they imagined."[33] British companies responded to the situation by engaging in a good deal of behind-the-scenes deal making and propaganda.[34] The Ceylon Association, which still represented several hundred private members and about a hundred planting, shipping, banking, and insurance companies, lobbied the British and Ceylon governments, protesting, for example, the nationalization of the Port of Colombo and Road Transport System and the expected nationalization of tea.[35] As they did in India, companies divested their colonial holdings, shifted operations to British Africa, and diversified into new industries.[36] They also hired public relations experts to protect British business during the turbulent years of decolonization.

In February 1959, a special committee of the Ceylon Association hired a conservative public relations expert, E. D. "Toby" O'Brien, to try to prevent the nationalization of plantation industries. O'Brien had already turned the British public against the idea of the nationalization of sugar in the UK with a clever "Mr. Cube" publicity campaign, and he had also lobbied on behalf of the Ashanti Goldfields Company in Ghana.[37] In 1959, before Sirimavo Bandaranaike came to power, O'Brien traveled to Ceylon to try to prevent her election and stated nationalization policies. Upon meeting planters and other businessmen, politicians, advisors, journalists, and acquaintances, O'Brien concluded that in all parties "corrupt" politicians were pushing nationalization merely as a way to enhance their personal reputations.[38] He was, however, equally dismissive of the left-leaning naïve British politicians, whom he called "starry-eyed believers in the possibility of turning Colonial politicians, overnight, into Liberal 19th century British M.P.s, educated at the right public schools and having been brought up with the right British traditions of political and commercial morality." O'Brien told his employers that with the exception of Don Stephen's son Dudley Senanayake, none of Ceylon's leaders could be trusted.[39] With contempt for both the British Left and new postcolonial politicians, O'Brien turned to underhanded methods. Political influence was an "expensive business," he advised the Ceylon Association, explaining that they should make "a contribution to Dudley's election fund" as a "useful hedging bet." He also encouraged British business to befriend educated "Tamil" clerks in the Colombo offices, men who could be "persuaded that their island's future prosperity lay in maintaining the European content" in tea, rubber, and coconut.[40] To help with this project,

O'Brien recommended that the association hire Cedric Salter, a war hero and journalist. As a noncombatant war correspondent on his way to Singapore in January 1941, Salter had personally downed a Japanese fighter plane when the tail gunner in Salter's plane had been killed. After the war, under the employ of O'Brien, Salter worked for the Spanish State Tourist Department selling Franco's Spain through a series of travel books and producing sequels on Portugal and Turkey.[41] In Ceylon, Salter was to again pose as a travel writer but in truth this was supposed to be the cover he needed for writing pieces for the press, radio, and film designed to stimulate opposition to nationalization.

Such covert efforts intensified racial, religious, ethnic, and political conflicts that have plagued Sri Lanka since Independence. Men like O'Brien allied themselves with indigenous capitalists and middle-level managers and clerks, and created distance between these groups and what O'Brien identified as the enemies of European capitalism: Buddhist priests, town laborers, "harbor coolies," office workers, students, young graduates, low-country Sinhalese villagers, labor union members, shopkeepers, publicans in towns, and especially "The Communists."[42] O'Brien's memos and proposals to the Ceylon Association were peppered with racial and political resentments, as he repeatedly insulted both the British Labour Party and the newly powerful "indigenous" politicians. It is not clear how much influence men like O'Brien actually wielded, but Ceylon's government did not nationalize the gardens until 1975. Even more striking, British companies prospered and the government enthusiastically endorsed advertising, public relations, and other capitalist tools to sell its tea.

THE CENTRIFUGAL FORCES OF DECOLONIZATION

Although Philip Witham and J. L. Llewellyn thought their world was collapsing in the late 1940s and early 1950s, from a longer perspective we can see that tea was arguably one of the slowest industries to shed the racial, class, gender, and labor hierarchies born in the colonial era.[43] Already in the 1950s, British and South Asian observers on the Left and the Right singled out tea as a particularly clear example of the persistence of empire. This came out in many ways. Pushing for the end of rationing in 1950, for example, the conservative *Sunday Times* anticipated that this move would not, as the Left had contended, increase "the cruel exploitation of the people of India, Ceylon, and Assam." Mocking anticolonialism as weak thinking, the author asserted: "Don't start on that argument or you'll get the worst of it. Those people are now free to tear up all the tea bushes, and root out the accursed trade with the West. I'll bet you they don't."[44] With an angry, hateful tone directed at the British Labour Party and the new ruling class in South Asia, this *Times* correspondent predicted that for all their talk about the oppressive nature of colonial capitalism, South Asians would maintain what had been a highly profitable business. Ironically, nationalists often made the same argument.

In South Asia and elsewhere, nationalists, socialists, and communists understood that imperialism had planted itself deep within colonial societies and political independence was only a first step toward its eradication. Indian Marxist S. A. Dange made this point in 1954 when he criticized a recent wage cut for plantation workers. He felt that in agreeing to the cut, the Indian government had bent to the wishes of an "international cartel" of tea interests. Dange also pointed to a shocking episode in which a British planter had recently shot and wounded eight female workers in West Bengal. Retelling this story, he exclaimed, "And this happened in 1954 and not in the last century!"[45] While Dange bemoaned the vestiges of colonialism, Indian businessman Smo Das, who entered the tea industry in the 1970s, proudly acknowledged that as a "brown sahib" he maintained a system the British had created.[46] Likewise, the tea broker Appan Nair recalled how much he had initially enjoyed white privileges such as being among the first Indians to attend the weekly Scottish Highland dance held at the Cochin Club in the 1960s, but as time went on he became disturbed by his complicity in what he concluded was a corrupt system.[47] These men recognized that empire was not merely a political entity; nor was it only manifested in the continued presence of foreign capital.

Despite their political differences, Witham, Das, Nair, and Dange agreed that in the early 1950s power and profits primarily flowed to European owners and managers rather than to Indian workers.[48] However, over the next several decades the tea industry underwent massive restructuring. Local capital, expertise, and ownership increased, as did state control over many facets of the industry, but so too did the power and reach of European-based multinational corporations. Commodity chains increasingly bypassed London, but, for all these changes, older imperial structures and ideas were very difficult to displace even as tea slowly shifted from being an imperial to a global industry.

Both the Labour and Tory governments that came to power in Britain after the war contributed to this history. In 1945 the Labour Party oversaw South Asian Independence, but their major focus was on building a social democratic society in the UK during a time of massive debt, weakened sterling, continued food, housing, and other shortages, and pressing financial burdens.[49] The government partially paid for this new world by encouraging production for export, by restraining consumption at home and in the colonies, and by intensifying land and labor exploitation in colonial Africa and Southeast Asia. For example, the 1945 Colonial Development and Welfare Act provided £120 million to be spent in the colonies over ten years. The money, however, primarily subsidized the cultivation and sale of dollar-earning export commodities, including East African tea and Malayan tin and rubber, dispossessing local farmers and contributing to particularly violent independence struggles in those regions.[50]

The Conservatives in power from 1951 until 1964 sought to protect imperial business interests, and many had close personal and economic connections with expatriate business.[51] Yet the costs of the Korean War, the repression of colonial insurgencies in Malaya and Kenya, the Suez crisis, and other foreign policy "expenses" seriously weakened Britain's ability to hold on to its empire. It was thus under Tory governments that many of the African colonies achieved independence. In Southern and East Africa, a large and growing number of white settlers (many of whom were involved in planting and export industries) made decolonization more protracted, which led to ruthless attempts to maintain white control.[52] In Kenya, the colonial government killed, imprisoned, and tortured hundreds of thousands of Kikuyu during the Mau Mau Crisis (1952–55) to protect white settlers and the corporations that were invested in the region's plantation economy.[53] Ultimately, however, Kenya achieved independence in 1963. This development and the rising tide of anticolonial nationalism elsewhere in Africa inflamed white nationalism in Southern Africa, and in the 1960s both South Africa and Southern Rhodesia declared a complete break with the Commonwealth in order to ensure white supremacist rule.

Political independence, however, did not sever economic ties.[54] For decades left-leaning Asian and African political parties and governments strove to end dependency through a multitude of new tax, wage, and welfare legislation, import substitution, trade and monetary restrictions, and nationalization and indigenization policies.[55] Pursuing a general policy of economic nationalism, governments sought greater control over marketing and advertising of commodities, diversified overseas markets, and developed domestic consumption. By the early 1970s, this process was at its apex, with India imposing some of the most severe restrictions on foreign companies and it investments of any postcolonial nation. The Amendment to the Foreign Exchange Regulation Act (FERA) passed by Indira Gandhi's government in 1973 vastly restricted foreign direct investment. Among other things, it required that all firms become rupee companies and it required majority Indian ownership. It nevertheless took decades for India to "dislodge," as one scholar has put it, European influence.[56] Instead of uprooting the tea industry, India, Ceylon, and other former colonies employed it as a tool of modernization, hoping it would provide employment for rural populations, diversify agrarian economies, and bring much-needed foreign exchange earnings.[57]

As a result of these and other developments, the geography of tea production, distribution, and consumption broke out of the former imperial boundaries. Cultivation, for example, spread around and beyond the Indian Ocean.[58] The

Soviet Union intensified production and Argentina, Brazil, Peru, and Ecuador also began to grow tea.[59] In many regions new production methods and thriving young plants produced high yields and garnered good prices at auction. Together with the reemergence of China as an exporter, the world's tea supply nearly doubled between 1950 and 1964.[60] The most extraordinary growth took place in British East Africa. Colonial and postcolonial governments, development initiatives and ideologies, and multinationals set the trajectories of African tea. African colonies offered low labor and production costs, higher prices at auction, and the class and racial privileges that planters had formerly enjoyed in the Raj. Kenya, Uganda, Tanzania, Southern Rhodesia, and Malawi (Nyasaland prior to 1964) became the most important producers, but Mozambique, Zaire, Rwanda, Burundi, and Cameroon also tried to develop the crop.[61] Nyasaland was initially the most important African tea colony. A gardener at the Church of Scotland Mission in Blantyre first grew tea in the mission garden in 1878, but the industry really began when Henry Brown, a planter from Ceylon, introduced the mission's seeds on his estate in the Mulanje district of the Shire Highlands.[62] Nyasaland's industry was never entirely British, however. With a diploma in agriculture, extensive experience in tobacco, and a network of compatriots to help him, Italian Ignacio Confozi became a very successful grower in this region.[63] In truth, though, multinationals were really behind the industry. Lyons, for example, purchased its first estate in Nyasaland in 1926.[64] By 1948 it employed 44,000 men and women and possessed 21,201 cultivated acres.[65]

In Kenya, production began with a few experimental gardens and a slipshod, government effort to settle World War I veterans as tea farmers. After they failed, private companies scooped up land at bargain basement prices. The colonial state offered a variety of incentives, including a prohibition denying Africans the opportunity to grow tea. Brooke Bond purchased a small piece of land at Limuru in 1924 and a larger estate near Lake Victoria at Kericho soon after.[66] James Finlay and Company acquired 23,000 acres in 1926, importing seed and managerial expertise from India.[67] In the early 1950s, the colonial government relaxed prohibitions against African growers in order to try to quell the Mau Mau rebellion.[68] Kenya soon displaced Nyasaland as Africa's major producer.[69] The absolute and relative value of tea in the Kenyan economy increased, and by 1957 tea accounted for 10.8 percent of the value of the country's agricultural exports.[70] In 1963 tea was Kenya's third most important export after coffee and sisal. The new government encouraged smallholder production (typically 50 acres or under), which grew from about 6 to 20 percent of the market between 1964 and 1970.[71] By 1983 tea exports paid for half of Kenya's oil imports, with the country producing 11 percent of the world's tea exports.[72]

Foreign companies maintained control in Ceylon, which became the world's largest exporter in 1964–65.[73] During the 1970s, however, Sri Lanka (renamed as such in 1972) pushed to reduce its reliance on Western capital. The Land Reform Law of 1972 and its amendment in 1975 nationalized the tea gardens, and the government worked to expand sales to the Soviet Union and Soviet bloc countries, to Africa (including South Africa), and to the Middle East.[74] In 1975 Pakistan became Sri Lanka's biggest market, for example.[75] Sri Lanka's government also encouraged the development of smallholdings, and by 1978 just over 20 percent of the island's tea was grown on estates of 50 acres or less.[76] However, between the 1970s and 1990s Sri Lanka's global market share declined. Yields and profitability fell and a general decline by 67 percent in the real prices for tea between 1970 and 1995 meant that Sri Lanka's export earnings shrank dramatically.[77] Cold War trade agreements and new alliances among the postcolonial world reconfigured commodity chains and opened new markets, but ultimately Sri Lanka's tea economy deteriorated. In 1993 the United National Party reprivatized estates and welcomed back British and other foreign companies, further tethering Sri Lanka's economy to tea.[78]

As perhaps can already be guessed, India slowly lost its dominance of the global tea trade, even as it grew into a formidable consuming nation in this period.[79] In 1951 tea accounted for 13.3 percent of India's export trade; after jute and cotton, tea was the country's most important foreign exchange earner. In the 1950s and 1960s, India's global market share fell, however, from 40 to 33 percent.[80] Although policies have varied, the Indian state believed that developing the internal or domestic market would protect the nation from the upheavals of global capitalism. Indian consumers have responded, and the tea market has increased by about 5–6 percent a year, even as per capita consumption has remained low in many areas.[81] Nevertheless, by the early 1970s, India surpassed the UK as the greatest market for its tea.[82] But tea was already among the least profitable of the major industries in India.[83]

War, occupation, and independence abruptly halted the growth of Indonesia's tea industry.[84] The Japanese uprooted many acres to replant with food crops, and the independence struggle that lasted from 1945 to 1949 meant that estates were not rehabilitated until well into the 1950s. All European-owned estates were nationalized in 1957, but, as one scholar has noted, high inflation, an overvalued currency, a substantial profit tax, and a depressed market left the industry with "little incentive" or means to revitalize the estates.[85] In 1969, Indonesia had the worst year on record, with its tea prices declining three times faster than those for India and Sri Lanka.[86] During the same period, China began to export again.[87] Chinese output increased by over 7 percent per annum during the 1970s.[88] Exports grew rapidly, and by 1990 China was once again the second-largest tea exporter, with its primary markets being the Soviet Union, Morocco,

Hong Kong, Poland, Japan, France, the United States, Mauritania, Tunisia, and Libya, in that order.[89] The virtue of this export drive has been questioned, however, given the decline in average world prices.

These structural realignments reverberated in the metropole. Mincing Lane, that "great market for tea, sugar, spices and colonial produce," as it was described in 1891, slowly lost its hold as the epicenter of the global tea trade.[90] War, decolonization, labor struggles, the mechanization of warehousing and packing facilities, and the expansion of corporate capitalism decentralized the buying and selling of many colonial commodities, tea included.[91] London's docklands were rebuilt after the war; for a short time tea was once again landing at Tilbury. Soon, however, dockworker and tally clerk strikes shifted tea to alternative ports in the west of England, particularly Avonmouth in Bristol and Liverpool.[92] In 1962, 76 percent of all teas that came through Britain still landed in London, but less than a decade later this figure was down to 39 percent, with Avonmouth rapidly growing from about 5 percent to nearly 32 percent during the same period.[93] In 1965 nearly 30 percent of the world's tea was auctioned in London. By 1975 this was down to 15 percent, and by 1982 only 8 percent of the world's teas came through the metropolis.[94] This shift negatively impacted invisible earnings from agents' commissions and freight charges (about half of the tea shipped to London in 1977 was on British ships).[95] Still, London set global prices as the only mart to sell tea from all over the world.

Mincing Lane's losses were not simply a by-product of globalization. Independent governments tried to reroute earnings and power away from London by encouraging the development of local packing, warehousing, and auctioning facilities.[96] Local auctions had been established long before the postwar era, but with independence each major producing nation wanted to become a leading marketplace. Calcutta's auction had first opened in 1861, but in 1949 India sought to develop Calcutta into "a World Tea Market" and Pakistan expanded facilities in Chittagong.[97] In 1958, Kenya's colonial government set up Nairobi as a pan-African tea market, but other auctions also opened in Mombasa in 1969 and Limbe the year after.[98] Colombo, which had first opened in 1883, grew into the world's single largest tea auction center in the mid-1960s, a position it held for the next decade.[99] British firms and brokers initially opposed such moves, but they soon opened modern and highly mechanized local facilities for packing and warehousing, often spotlighting these efforts as a sign of their commitment to African or South Asian development.[100]

Perhaps nothing encapsulates the impact of decolonization on Mincing Lane more than the fate of the tea auction room in Plantation House. One of the largest office buildings in its day, the neoclassical exterior and rich interior was an impressive work of public relations that used architecture to project British global power at a particularly crisis-ridden moment. At the opening ceremony of the new tea auction room in January 1937, Lord Selsdon, chairman of the board of Plantation House, described this office building as "the home of the 'plantation trades,'" which he hoped would be "a worthy Empire center for the Empire's outposts."[101] The building fulfilled this mission for decades. The markets for rubber, coffee, cocoa, sugar, copra, vegetable oils, pepper, and spices operated in the building, and firms and banks associated with such trade resided there, as did the International Tea Market Expansion Board.[102] In 1966 a lack of business forced the tea auction room to be cut in half only to close entirely five years later. In 1971 high rents in Mincing Lane drove the trade to a much smaller, forty-five-seat room in Sir John Lyon House in Upper Thames Street.[103] The new building was still close to the river and housed the International Tea Committee and many brokers, traders, and buyers. The auction room became a new space for the global tea trade, but its value and volume had waned.

By the 1970s, theorists illuminated the colonial underpinnings of economic underdevelopment, with tea being a prime example of the long-term consequences of colonialism. One study, aptly named *Tea: The Colonial Legacy*, conducted by the Cambridge World Development Action Group in 1975, argued, "Tea growing in India and Sri Lanka (Ceylon) has become a 'lame-duck' industry," in which tea was often grown at a loss. But instead of taking responsibility for the situation that they had created, British firms "turn a blind eye to the starvation that occurs when Third World suppliers of our raw materials face collapse." These firms were "keen to sell up and get out of Asia" and in effect were "leaving a sinking ship."[104] The report then went on to deliver a scathing account of how British firms engaged in a host of underhanded practices that extracted wealth and resources from their former South Asian colonies. At the same time as they were undermining profits and fair wages in Sri Lanka, Pakistan, and India, these companies moved to Africa where they re-created the "colonial conditions of low taxation and low wages" and thus increased profitability compared to South Asian producers.[105] While in Africa the colonial state offered tea firms encouragement "through the allocation of crown lands, financial credits and through local price stabilisation measures," the South Asian governments were attempting to assert greater control over foreign business.[106] Underscoring the point that it is "colonial history" that underlies contemporary "facts and figures," the author of the pamphlet could not have been clearer: "The ultimate responsibility for the state of the world tea industry rests with Britain, however conscious or unconscious have been her actions in the past."[107]

To summarize, between the late 1940s and the 1970s, the political ramifications of the winding up of the British and Dutch empires, the rise of socialist and communist forms of state control, and development funds that encouraged dollar-earning export crops like tea globalized cultivation, sales, and consumption well beyond former imperial boundaries. Some areas such as Sri Lanka and Kenya challenged the plantation model by aiding the growth of the smallholder sector, new producers emerged, and China reasserted its presence in global markets. These trade patterns had colonial origins, but they were no longer wholly controlled by or contained within European empires. Acreage and yields expanded, prices fluctuated, and long-term downward trends left many workers with starvation wages and horrible living and working conditions. The uneven nature of the global economy has meant that over the long run tea, like so many other tropical commodities, has rarely lived up to its promises in the postwar world.[108]

COCA-COLA COMES TO AFRICA

In October 1947, longtime employee of the International Tea Market Expansion Board Ernest Gourlay announced the beginning of a new, vigorous propaganda campaign with yet another lengthy research trip, this time across Africa.[109] Covering thousands of miles from the Cape to Cairo, Gourlay was pleased to find that tea supplies were steady, distribution networks in place, and prices good. Unlike England, South Africa had "plentiful supplies"; and, according to one person Gourlay talked to, "the Bantu were buying freely and often three or four pounds at a time, which was unheard of before the war."[110] Things were apparently so good there that Gourlay was certain that "nowhere else do I know of a better potential market than in South Africa."[111] Gourlay was clearly shocked then when he encountered the American Coca-Cola Company colonizing this market. His report is worth quoting at length because it reveals how Gourlay imagined decolonization as Great Britain's inability to control former markets, tastes, and consumer habits. Gourlay told his colleagues:

> I was alarmed at the obvious inroads competitive beverages are making into tea's natural market, I refer especially to the Coca Cola Company of America. From time to time I have reported on the activities of this Company and how they affect this Board's work, but never have I been so distressed as during this tour, not only in South Africa but Egypt. . . . The Company are said to be spending in the region of fifty thousand pounds per year on advertising and work in the merchandising field, which includes the public service of the beverage. I went out to the opening day of the first horse race meeting ever to be held in the Orange Free State, where I was told the Bureau had been responsible for the introduction of a number of Thermos urns. I regret to say that the Bureau's efforts were completely

and utterly swamped by those of the aforementioned bottled beverage, which was readily available everywhere, from the most expensive stand to the free enclosures. It was quite a common sight to see an extremely smartly dressed woman in a 50-guinea gown sucking a Coca Cola from a bottle through a straw. At one stage I saw two five-ton trucks fully laden with this beverage arrive. I saw them depart shortly afterwards empty.[112]

Gourlay had worked closely with Americans for decades, yet he was "alarmed" and "distressed" to find the "Coca Cola Company of America" in tea's "natural market." Coke's five-ton trucks and the spectacle of an "extremely smartly dressed woman in a 50-guinea gown sucking a Coca Cola from a bottle through a straw" symbolized the growing power of American corporate capitalism and its new forms of imperialism. Gourlay's sexualization of the consumer, whom he described as sucking on a straw and cradling a phallic Coke bottle (though this was the common way people drank sodas at the time), conjured up the feelings of a husband coming home to find a new lover seducing his wife. And this was a very wealthy and clever lover indeed. Gourlay found in Egypt:

> Every small village or group of houses seems to have the Coca Cola ice-box, in the most conspicuous place, backing them up are all wall signs and other point of purchase advertising, all cleverly placed. In the bigger towns they have built cigarette kiosks, which virtually look like a Coca Cola fountain. All their advertising is done in two vivid colours so that it catches the eye of every passing potential consumer, not that this is necessary, for the volume is so large that it overshadows everything else.[113]

In Port Said, Gourlay "noticed a small native boy with a box containing 12 bottles of the beverage slung round his neck. On top of the whole was a large lump of ice." When Gourlay inquired about how many bottles he had sold that day, the boy claimed that he was starting his fourth dozen. "It was then only ten o'clock in the morning and a reasonably cool day for Egypt . . . this was only one of the many small boys doing the same job," Gourlay worriedly wrote.[114] Coke had not only transformed tastes but turned the Egyptian boy's body into an advertisement and cog in a vast distribution machine. The boy was also an informant of sorts, but his information would not have helped the tea industry at this moment. In 1947, Egypt left the Sterling bloc and rumors circulated that all tea imports would be curtailed.[115]

John Harpur, who had run the Buy Empire Tea Campaign in Britain in 1931–32 and who was now ITMEB tea commissioner in Egypt, told exactly the same story. He bemoaned: "Everywhere I go in Egypt . . . Advertisements appeared . . . in the press, on hoardings and on the form of containers of a particularly glaring shade of red with the words 'Coca Cola' superimposed in white in Arabic characters." Harpur had "no doubt that the taste for the drink is growing among the public, very largely due to the publicity that has been devoted to the product."[116] It was not just publicity, however, that made the difference. By 1950 Coke had six Egyptian bottling plants capable of manufacturing 350 million drinks annually. Company skits performed for bottling plant employees even featured talking Coke bottles proclaiming: "I am Coca-Cola, vigorous with life and more than a mere shape . . . I am . . . the object of your strivings."[117] Coke had created a new kind of franchise-based colonialism, which incorporated local capital and energies into its empire in a way that tea had not done. Like tea, however, Coke used the factory as a promotional space, but whereas tea had emphasized how it made good workers, Coke recognized African workers' desires and strivings for a better life.

As is well known, Coke followed the American military during World War II to penetrate swiftly into Africa, South Asia, and the Middle East.[118] Coke did not just serve the army; the military served the company with army personnel and prisoners of war building, maintaining, and working in its bottling plants.[119] Tea had also used the war to expand into new territories, but Coke did not sell itself as a form of aid or relief but as a pleasurable taste for modern times. For tea's salesmen in Africa, however, Coke embodied the shift from a British- to an American-dominated world system. This shift happened first in the empire because Coke and other brand-name sodas were banned in the UK until sugar rationing was lifted in 1952.[120] Also, in the UK sodas were primarily associated with children and summer outings, picnics, and beach parties but were not an everyday part of the adult diet in these years.[121] As late as 1970, soft drinks accounted for only 6.4 percent of all drinks consumed (except tap water) by individuals over the age of ten. This doubled by 1985, and by 1995 over half the people responding to a major survey stated that they drank soft drinks on a daily basis.[122] The soft drinks revolution certainly influenced British drink habits, but it came late and was never as threatening as it was in empire markets.

Coke nevertheless was symbolic of wider changes, namely American corporate expansionism. In 1948, the new journal *Tea Times of Africa* (the mouthpiece of Ceylon's tea growers) stated in no uncertain terms: "Among the manifestations of the American way of life which is to-day spreading across the African continent in the train of expanding American trade, can be numbered such tokens as juke-boxes, bubble gum, superman comics, Spike Jones and soft drinks." Clearly worried but also trying to sound upbeat, the author quoted the *South African Hotel Review*, which joked, "The cheerful pot of tea has triumphantly withstood the onslaught of all the cocktails and colas devised by this generation, and it will no doubt withstand all the atomic drinks of the next."[123] Coca-Cola, whether manufactured in the United States or not, was read as a token of American mass culture.[124] While Ernest Gourlay and John Harpur regretted the growth of American corporate power they were also writing a story about decolonization. They too felt the impotence that Philip Witham expressed in his BBC broadcast, for even in Africa British colonial power could not keep American business at bay. Africans did drink more tea, but British business realized that they were now doing battle with their former ally, the American market empire.[125] U.S. corporations had a great deal of money, but they were also engaging a dramatically weakened foe.

"THE NATIONAL SHOP WINDOW OF THE TEA TRADE"

When Gourlay, Harpur, Gervas Huxley, and their colleagues thought about selling tea after the war, they were not sure whom they worked for, what they were selling, how to go about promotion, or whether they would be paid. Independence, Partition, Coca-Cola, communism, austerity, and the continuation of rationing in Britain challenged an industry that had devolved into rival nations with unclear borders. The end of empire made bodies such as the International Tea Market Expansion Board anachronistic or, worse, a holdover from the imperial past. Thus it might be surprising to learn that this body and its successors did not immediately disband at independence. India, Ceylon, Pakistan, and other producing nations actually continued to work together to sell tea in key markets, employed the same sort of methods they had used in the past, and even more strangely the same men who had been running the show since before the war found new and sometimes better jobs during this turbulent time. To put it simply, while producing areas became separate nations, trade associations, large companies, and international agencies, such as the ITMEB, acted as though they were working in the same world that had existed in the 1930s.

The ITMEB's postwar history tells us a bit about how the tea industry (and its imperial nature) rode out one of the most dramatic periods of upheaval in world history. This chameleon agency dropped imperial rhetoric and presented itself wholly as "a service organization" that provided "information and service to those who sell, distribute or consume tea." Or, as Gervas Huxley explained, his job and that of the ITMEB was "to maintain and expand a climate of public opinion favorable to tea consumption."[126] This involved selling itself as an "international" agency that could foster "frequent personal interchanges" between producers and consumers in Britain and its former colonies.[127] The Tea Buyers' Association called the ITMEB a "producer organization," "the national shop window of the Tea Trade," and a "press liaison service," disseminating, documenting, and shaping media information about the commodity.[128] This idea dated back at least to 1936 when Earl Newsom had first set up New York's Tea Bureau, but now the service idea was more relevant than ever.[129] Throughout the postwar years, Huxley and his colleagues tried to maintain the status quo—with British companies and institutions still at the helm of this decolonizing industry. But eventually the centrifugal forces of decolonization, trade liberalization, and economic nationalism in producing regions limited the ITMEB's ability to withstand its own internal conflicts and it disbanded in 1952. In 1955, the International Tea Agreement ended as well, and thereafter prices and yields fluctuated, and this along with exchange problems made tea production a difficult industry and encouraged large companies to diversify their holdings further, which, as we will look at more directly in the next chapter, actually contributed to the decline of tea consumption in key markets.[130] But it took a decade for things to fall apart, and even after the ITMEB disbanded regional Tea Boards functioned as neocolonial institutions in which European and non-European businessmen and officials reinforced their shared belief that industrialization, plantation agriculture, and global consumerism would benefit new nations and old colonies.

During the first years after South Asia gained independence, India, Ceylon, Indonesia, Pakistan, Nyasaland, Southern Rhodesia, and the East African colonies retained membership in the ITMEB and reaffirmed their commitments to the expansion of global consumerism, much to the surprise and dismay of socialists and nationalists in these countries.[131] Their faith in exporting, global marketing, and the ITMEB was not a foregone conclusion. The African members were still under British control, but in 1947 India and Pakistan went to war over Kashmir, relations between Ceylon and India deteriorated, and everywhere there were nationalists who wanted to kick out Western capital and influence. It was in this confusing climate that India, Pakistan, and Ceylon held independent conferences and formed committees to consider tea's place in their new nations. Pakistan, for example, held a major conference in Sylhet in January 1949, leading to the government signing on to the International Tea Agreement.[132] It also joined the ITMEB and agreed to collect a cess at a rate of Rs. 1.37 for every hundred pounds of tea produced. However, it soon transferred these funds to the new Pakistan Tea Board that was created in 1950.[133] In 1949 India set up the Chettur Ad Hoc Committee, under the chairmanship of K. K. Chettur, secretary to the Government of India in the Ministry of Commerce, to study the impact of the war and independence on the industry and determine its future relationship to the ITMEB.[134] Nearly all the managers, planters, and buyers who responded to the committee's many queries advised India to preserve Mincing Lane as tea's global marketplace and support the ITMEB and its cooperative global advertising.[135] One of their main arguments was that the tea industry needed a united front to combat the onslaught of coffee, milk drinks, carbonated beverages, and fruit drinks.[136] India could not rebuild its industry, find new markets, and fight Coca-Cola and coffee on its own. India agreed and stayed in the ITMEB.

Based in London, the ITMEB served the same masters as it had in the past, and for a time business proceeded as usual. India contributed just over 50 percent of the budget, Ceylon put up just over 36 percent, Indonesia and Pakistan sent about 5 percent each, and African producers provided smaller amounts.[137] Officials representing producing nations, such as M. J. Desai, commercial advisor to the high commissioner for India, and C. E. P. Jayasuriya, Ceylon's trade commissioner in London, joined the board's leadership in 1949.[138] The Central Tea Board of India, a statutory body under the Ministry of Commerce, absorbed and expanded the functions of the Indian Tea Market Expansion Board. Although now an Indian government agency chaired by S. K. Sinha, the Central Tea Board preserved its connection with the International Tea Market Expansion Board and upheld its "integrated scheme of propaganda for promoting the consumption of tea in all parts of the world."[139] At the same time, India's Central Tea Board decided to spend half its revenue developing Indian consumption and promoting "labour welfare" and scientific "research."[140] In other words, India split its efforts between domestic and overseas markets. Another key change was the presence of organized labor at the table, but all of the tea associations and the largest companies, including Andrew Yule, Lipton's, Brooke Bond, and James Finlay, had seats on the Central Tea Board of India. Even J. L. Llewellyn, who had been in a state of panic during Partition, was one of four regional representatives for Assam. Similar compromises occurred in Ceylon, Pakistan, and other producing nations, and throughout these years Gervas Huxley remained in charge of tea promotion at the ITMEB and the Ceylon Tea Propaganda Board.

Working with tighter budgets, unpredictable supplies, and a range of different controls on global trade, the postwar ITMEB pursued a cautious program in which it changed neither its tactics nor its imagined geography. In 1949 it began to reopen offices, known as Tea Bureaus, in large commercial cities, including Amsterdam, Brussels, Zürich, Copenhagen, Nairobi, Baghdad, Ibadan, Salisbury, Johannesburg, Cairo, Sydney, Wellington, Toronto, London, and New York City.[141] In 1951, out of a total budget of £748,960, nearly half (£357,140) was allocated to the United States, £113,820 to Canada, £95,000 to the UK and Ireland, £55,000 to Africa and the Middle East, and £50,000 to continental Europe.[142] Each bureau had a local staff and engaged in some in-house advertising and they publicity, but normally they commissioned professional advertising, market research, and public relations firms. Together these agencies authored pamphlets, books, radio scripts, and educational and feature-length films, and they produced a number of new trade journals, including *Tea Promotion: News from Campaigns of the International Tea Market Expansion Board*; *Tea Times*;

and the South African *Tea Times of Africa*, which later became the *Tea Times of Africa Quarterly*. They circulated very similar information, or as one planter put it, "Everyone is busy writing on tea these days . . . [and] everyone else is busy copying what everyone writes."[143] Sharing with and copying each other, these journals produced a new transnational promotional culture that easily crossed old and new political borders.

The ITMEB built one new lasting institution during the postwar years, which they called Tea Centres.[144] The first opened on lower Regent Street in London in 1946, but soon others were built in major cities in the UK, United States, Africa, Asia, Oceana, the Middle East, and Europe. Each Tea Centre had a library, tea lounge, equipment showroom, and exhibition and lecture space.[145] Catering to the trade and the public, these institutions gathered and circulated market information, displayed knowledge about production, distribution, and consumption, and dispensed a lot of hot tea in ultramodern surroundings. Schoolchildren and business people, caterers, grocers, planters, advertisers, tourists, shoppers, and government officials came to drink tea, watch films, listen to lectures, read literature, look at the latest catering equipment, and wander through exhibitions. A progeny of the exhibition, museum, tea shop, library, mechanic's institute, trade association, and trade paper, Tea Centres served as international venues that promoted nationalism and cosmopolitanism, innovation and nostalgia. They modified or one could say modernized what had been colonial-era ideas, institutions, and experiences.

Tea Centres were nearly always in shopping and entertainment neighborhoods, not older financial districts. Regent Street, for example, was the physical center of West End consumer and leisure cultures.[146] Americans, Australians, Canadians, Italians, Greeks, and other foreigners owned and patronized the area's businesses, which included strip clubs, sex shops, brothels, coffeehouses, and queer commercial spaces.[147] Yet the Tea Centre was also adjacent to a more traditional elite masculine consumer culture of clubs and exclusive men's shops in Piccadilly, Jermyn Street, and Bond Street. Like the district surrounding it, the Tea Centre combined many worlds. The heritage industry, leftover remnants of imperial culture and business, and London's cosmopolitan artistic and commercial communities designed these institutions in ways that updated tea's past for an uncertain future. Misha Black, one of Europe's "most experienced exhibition designers," headed a team of industrial designers and architects who worked on the Regent Street Centre (fig. 10.1).[148] Black, who had redesigned Kardomah's cafés in 1936, was now a leading modernist who believed in what Milner Gray called "propaganda in three dimensions."[149] Black worked for numerous private and public entities, was exhibition officer for the Ministry of Information during the war, and served on the Executive Committee for the 1951 Festival of Britain.[150] Huxley claimed he hired Black to "give Tea the most modern setting for its display to

FIGURE 10.1. Ceylon Tea Centre, reception hall, Lower Regent Street, London.
(1951, RIBA 58592)

the world."[151] Like the Festival of Britain's sprawling buildings on the South Bank, the Tea Centre's clean lines, bold colors, and new materials demonstrated a forward-looking "scientific" industry. Black even designed stainless steel tea sets and cast aluminum frame tables with "stain and burn resistant" tops of plastic "impregnated veneer."[152]

In 1952, after India pulled out of the ITMEB, Ceylon took over and gave the newly named Ceylon Tea Centre and its branches a new look with specific motifs from Sinhalese culture. Increasingly, these became tourist centers that helped design Ceylon's national "look." Melbourne's Ceylon Tea Centre, for example, blended modernist design and depictions of a spicy island with ancient culture. A large mural decorated one wall of its tea room, while a set of Kandyan masks was featured opposite, and tiny sari-clad tea picker statues decorated each table (fig. 10.2). The furniture, fixtures, and table decor thus demonstrated a new tropical modern aesthetic, but it was not all that different from the Ceylon tea room at the Chicago World's Fair. Recycling and upgrading older motifs, these centers sharpened the distinctive nature of Ceylon, India, and other producing regions for postcolonial visitors. They maintained, however, some of the basic sensual traditions that had emerged during the late nineteenth century. As though they were visiting a Ceylon display at a world's fair in the 1880s, visitors sipped hot

FIGURE 10.2. Ceylon Tea Centre, basement, Melbourne, Australia, 1960. (By permission of the State Library of Victoria, Wolfgang Sievers, Photographer, #H98.30/239)

tea, gazed upon aspects of tea production, distribution, and consumption, and fantasized about exotic far-off lands with lovely dark-skinned women.

Some visitors just came in for a rest and a cup of tea, but others spent hours reading pamphlets and histories in well-stocked business libraries.[153] Some perhaps researched the history of organizations such as the International Tea Committee, the Tea Boards, and the grocery trade and catering business.[154] Tea Centre literature, exhibits, courses, and "tea evenings" sometimes reminded audiences that tea was "a great Empire product" with "therapeutic and psychological value."[155] Schoolchildren came on field trips to learn about the geography, economics, history, and home economics of the empire of tea.[156] Elegantly attired Sinhalese receptionists answered questions and directed visitors to the lounge for tea and scones.[157] Tea Centres were also exhibition spaces. In 1949 and 1950, Regent Street hosted an exhibit titled *Tea: A Progressive Industry*. This exhibit and its accompanying booklet told visitors a great deal about where tea was grown, how it was made, and how it was transported to primary markets, but in doing so it also ignored the violence and problems the tea trade was experiencing. This exhibit and others like it primarily emphasized how technology sped tea's travels from seed to cup. Just as things were literally falling apart in producing areas, the exhibit demonstrated that "modern tea production fully earns its place in the vanguard of the world's progressive industries."[158]

Tea Centres thus began to advance "soft power," or the idea that state- and industry-sponsored cultural exchanges would create and maintain bonds between diverse nations. In 1951, during the Festival of Britain, architects Maxwell Fry and Jane Drew enlarged and improved Regent Street's Tea Centre to make it a worthy attraction for international visitors. The Council of Industrial Design, which was also working on the festival, then staged several exhibitions at the Tea Centre, including "Hospitality at Home," "The Traveller Refreshed," and "Scandinavia at Table," an exhibit that stimulated the current rage for Scandinavian design.[159] Propaganda claiming that tea and the tea industry brought disparate races, classes, nations, and genders together found its way into schools and other institutions.[160] In these years, the ITMEB and its progeny especially liked to make the point that tea was a global commodity by depicting diverse people around the world drinking tea (often this act of consumption took place in London however). In 1949, for example, the Nigerian Touring Football team, a trade journalist pointed out, was the "most recent and picturesque" example of consumer internationalism and reassuringly opined that these Nigerian athletes were "enchanted with the Tea Centre" and would surely serve tea the "English Way" when they returned home.[161] Such articles promoted new ideas of the Commonwealth as a collection of diverse races and nations, while others on American celebrities and dignitaries such as film star Jayne Mansfield evoked the Anglo-American "special relationship." Manchester United, Queen Elizabeth, and even Churchill also came to the Tea Centre in Regent Street in the 1950s and 1960s.[162]

At the same time it promoted ideas of international collaboration and harmony, the Regent Street Tea Centre also conveyed a nostalgic, insular popular history of tea and Great Britain and its empire. An exhibit titled "The Romance of Tea" coproduced with Harrods department store, for example, traced tea's place in British culture since the seventeenth century. Displaying reproductions of sketches from Rowlandson and other artists as well as antique furniture, tea caddies, and tea sets from the time of Charles II through the early Victorians, the exhibit used material culture to relate what had become a hackneyed story of tea as the Nation's Drink. A panorama of photographs also followed tea from plantation to packet, implying that the Nation's Drink was still an imperial product.[163] The Tea Centre's modern decor did not discount Britain's imperial past; it embedded imperialism and tea in modern British culture.[164] It reminded Britons that tea was central to their identity, culture, and economy despite the loss of the Raj.

Tea Centres functioned in similar ways in other locales. In Ibadan, Nigeria, in 1949, the ITMEB opened a second center. Nigerians did not as yet drink much tea (approximately .02 pounds per year), but half a million people lived in the city and the Tea Centre was built in a busy commercial area between the railway station and the Rex Cinema, placed to attract shoppers, pleasure seekers, workers, and those interested in the tea trade. Ibadan's Tea Centre also consisted of a tea lounge, an equipment showroom, an information section, and facilities for showing films.[165] The *Crown Colonist* called the center a modern cross-class rendezvous for both "Europeans and Africans alike." It hoped to teach Nigerians how to properly make tea, including the "necessity of warming the pot before putting in the tea."[166] The Tea Centre and a sympathetic English-language press thus emphasized the modernity of British eating and drinking practices. Tea commissioner Pat Bichard, a "young man, full of enthusiasm and bright ideas," insisted on employing an all-African staff.[167] Bichard believed he was working in the interest of racial uplift and African development, but he also desperately hoped that Africans would appreciate British, rather than American, commercial and consumer culture.

All seemed to be going well until 1952, when India abruptly announced it was pulling out of the International Tea Market Expansion Board. Tea Board chairman J. S. Graham had insisted that "cooperative" approaches to global advertising, market research, and publicity had helped a "progressive" industry ride out "the new economic phase, which is following upon the dislocation of war."[168] However, as free trade returned, the ITMEB buckled under the pressures of decolonization and the geopolitical realignments that came in its wake. It felt like "a bolt fell from the blue," Huxley recalled, when he heard of India's decision, and he surmised that the growing "friction" between the Indian and Ceylon governments over the rights of the Indian Tamils, who made up the majority of the tea estate labor force in Ceylon, was the source of the trouble.[169] India officially stated that the 1952 slump hit it harder than other nations and its government felt that "the advantages reaped" by cooperative advertising were "doubtful."[170] Pakistan pulled out at the same time, leaving Ceylon anxious that "All 'Drink more Tea' propaganda throughout the world is in danger of being abandoned. . . . This would mean the collapse of the whole tea propaganda effort built up over the last twenty years."[171]

Ceylon acquired all of the ITMEB's property, including offices, tea bureaus, and centers. Huxley's former assistant became the board's organizing director and Huxley became vice chairman, and thereafter moved into a fee-paid but advisory position, which he held until 1967.[172] Huxley and his colleagues recovered quickly from the breakup of the ITMEB, and almost immediately, they began selling postcolonial Ceylon to thirsty Britons, opening new Ceylon

Tea Centres in Leicester (1957),[173] Manchester (1960),[174] Glasgow (1961),[175] Birmingham and Exeter (1963),[176] and Leeds (1964).[177] Demonstrating global ambitions, Ceylon then opened a Tea Centre on the Via Sardegna in Rome and another in Johannesburg in 1959.[178] Copenhagen followed in 1961.[179] These Tea Centres played up the role of tea as cultural ambassador and Ceylon as a nation and tourist destination. So, for example, in 1958 Kalaguru Gunaya and his famous Kandyan dancers performed at the Tea Centre in Regent Street following a successful international tour.[180] Dancers and drummers, sari-clad tea pickers, fragrant flowers, elephants, masks, and the logo of a golden lion became emblems of this new nation. These symbols appeared in shop windows and at trade shows all over the UK and in foreign markets, and they were imprinted on tea caddies, packaging, tea towels, and other gifts.[181] "Sinhalese" ladies demonstrated how to serve good tea at the center and in shops all over the country. Dressed in saris, a Mrs. Sinnadurai and M. De Alvis answered questions about Ceylon in a shop in Harrogate in 1958.[182] A Miss Ray Blaze gave a talk titled "Ceylon's People and Homes" as part of UNESCO's East-West Project.[183] Female demonstrators taught Bristol's women, who notably also wore saris, how to cook a Ceylon rice and curry dish.[184] Housewives also learned "to recognize Ceylon teas by the 'Lion of Ceylon,'" explained one article on a 1966 promotional campaign.[185] Or so it was claimed. When surveyed in 1965 about visiting the Tea Centre, one young woman said, "I get a kick out of going to the Tea Centre. . . . It's very popular."[186]

As might be expected, India opened a rival Tea Centre in Oxford Street in London and then others in Dublin, Edinburgh, Cairo, and after 1955 in urban India as well.[187] On 5 June 1956, Shri T. T. Krishnamachari, India's minister of commerce, inaugurated a new Tea Centre in a prominent building in the Churchgate area of Bombay. According to the Central Tea Board, the object of the center was threefold: "to serve a pot of good Tea in pleasant surroundings, to tell consumers how Tea should be prepared through daily demonstration, to tell consumers the part which tea plays in advancing the wealth of the Country." Visitors were also supposed to develop a sophisticated palate able to taste and differentiate among teas grown in Darjeeling, Dooars, Assam, Nilgiris, and Travancore, and to taste green teas, sample iced tea, and eat tea-infused ice cream and other snacks.[188] Whether in Manchester, Rome, or Bombay, Tea Centres were the shop window of the tea trade, which sought to dazzle, feed, and entertain visitors rather than have them think about the realities of an industry that was radically changing. We will now examine more closely how these stories played out in two major markets: India and the United States.

A BREADWINNER FOR THE NATION:
ADVERTISING TEA IN POSTCOLONIAL INDIA

India's postwar tea culture was an extension of that of the colonial era, a locus of cultural and business innovation and conflict, and one site of a wider global formation. Old and new collaborations emerged and dissolved as India redefined its relationships with Great Britain, the United States, Soviet bloc countries, Africa, and other nations in Asia as well. We have a great deal more to learn about the politics of Indian consumer culture in general and postwar tea cultures in particular, but here I focus on the more limited task of examining how, despite the reorientation of the balance between domestic and global markets and the shifting nature of those global markets, India's government and private industry continued to deploy many colonial-era ideas and strategies in the manufacture and marketing of tea.

After Independence, most plantations remained largely in the hands of British firms, though state control grew and many Indians condemned both the industry and the drink. Imperial legacies were not completely obliterated, even as corporate advertising and the Indian state sought to turn tea from "an imperial product to a national drink."[189] We could say that while the government did not nationalize production, it did succeed in nationalizing tea's consumer culture. Brand and Indian Tea Board advertising promised health and efficiency, but it especially championed "tea as India's National Beverage," a drink that purportedly unified "diverse religious, linguistic, and caste groups."[190] Over time, the power and meaning of nationalism changed and the interpretation and nature of print ads and other forms of publicity varied in this heterogeneous nation, but nationalism was a very powerful theme in postcolonial advertising.

In April 1954, the new Central Tea Board stepped back to scrutinize the nature of Indian and overseas markets, as well as the failures and successes of colonial-era propaganda. Indian tea was losing global market share, but some of the board's executives believed this was fine since home markets were the key to economic sovereignty. Studying the Indian market in 1955, the Central Tea Board's propaganda committee opined that if India did not want to be "dictated by the requirements of the overseas market," it was necessary to "develop the internal market."[191] They then went on to complain, however, that this was hard to do because they lacked market research and centralized statistics. It was not that the work had not been done; it had, but the data that been collected were literally "buried individually under a pile of loose papers" and the Indian Tea Market Expansion Board had left behind only "one solitary working report form relating to canteen work, and even this is now outdated."[192] One wonders if the Indian Tea Board was just messy and disorganized, whether it destroyed its work on its way out, or whether the data was only stored in London at the offices of the International Tea Market Expansion Board, though that is unlikely since there are very few reports on the Indian market done from this period currently in the ITMEB's archive. Whatever happened, when the Central Tea Board tried to figure out the best way to sell India's tea, it literally had to start from scratch. In South Africa, Great Britain, the United States, and other major markets, promoters had a wealth of market data. India did not. In 1952 when India pulled out of the International Tea Market Expansion Board, it lost access to decades of knowledge about the Indian consumer.

Despite, or perhaps because of, this lack of continuity and information, the Central Tea Board did not markedly change the style or message of tea promotions. Keeping with the theme of nationalism that had been first used to combat the nationalists' contention that tea was a foreign good, the Central Tea Board promoted an ideal of a modern, liberal nation, in which a thriving consumer market and agricultural development worked hand in hand. The board sold this story in advertising but also through a tactical assault on the Indian home. The board selected towns with populations of twenty to thirty thousand people and claimed that they went into every other household to teach families "the *right way of making tea* . . . [and discourage] any *prejudice against tea*."[193] This assault spread to big cities and villages, and in addition to engaging in face-to-face promotions, the board also produced booklets, leaflets, and print ads in which tea explained: "I am Indian Tea—The World's Most Popular Tea" and "I am Tea—The Wealth of India."[194] Show cards, print advertising, and posters and film all told versions of the same story, which became embodied in a new national icon, known as the "Tea Man." An Indianized version of Mr. T. Pott, the Tea Man represented tea as Indian but also revealed economic debates within India over the value of domestic versus foreign markets to economic development. For example, a typical advertisement from the 1960s demonstrates how the same icons could serve different ends. In this ad Mr. Tea Man announces the launch of a new export drive for Indian tea (fig. 10.3). The detailed text gives facts and figures about the global tea market to substantiate the idea that Indian tea has "become a way of life with many peoples of many countries . . . [and] serving tea has become a traditional form of hospitality." This ad appeared in several languages, but it was directed at an educated, middle-class Indian readership, asking them, "Aren't you proud of me—Indian Tea—being regarded as the bridge of friendship amongst millions of people all over the world."

FIGURE 10.3. "I am Tea . . ." Central Tea Board advertisement, c. mid-1960s.
(CL 00036, Mounted Tea Advertisement from the collection of CSSSC
archives, courtesy Parimal Ray, Kolkata, India)

Also during this period, the industry began to write easy-to-digest histories that highlighted Indians' role in making this industry, but often the images used were the same as they had been in the colonial era. For example, a small, illustrated booklet titled *Indian Tea* depicted photographs of lovely young girls sowing seeds and nourishing young plants, misty mountain landscapes, and men driving tea to the factory via tractors, while the factory is identified as a marvel of modern architecture and industrial design. Indian and European men sit together in the auction room and try samples in the tasting room. As they had long been, women are presented as Nature, the sower and the picker, while men are Modernity, engaged in the technical side of the business. Together this new India of nature and modernity manufactured a universal pleasure, "drunk in some form or other practically throughout the world." This booklet tells us, "Tea drinking, in fact, is part of man's cultural heritage—an expression of social living; a habit that gently stimulates but does not inebriate."[195] Chinese ideologies had worked their way through Europe, where they had been altered by evangelicalism and liberalism and returned to Asia to become Indian.[196] By selling such ideas, however, now India became the source and origin of universalism and global harmony.

While carrying on and promulgating ideologies and an older visual tradition for selling tea, this booklet also represented a dramatic shift in economic policy. Just as consumption was growing steadily if unevenly in India, the government chose to privilege export markets as the key method to developing Indian agriculture, tea included.[197] In 1960–61, India initiated its Third Five-Year Plan, and this one prioritized agricultural development. The poor performance in this sector, coupled with a growing population, threatened India's food supply and intensified the country's mounting and considerable balance of payment problem.[198] Exports were offered as the answer.[199] In 1960 the Central Tea Board thus began a major campaign in Great Britain that sought to "create a modern, exciting and sophisticated image for tea."[200] In 1964, the Indian government even gave financial assistance to forty-four export houses upon the condition that they organize advertising campaigns and sponsor market research. In other words, the Indian government pushed the globalization of Indian tea via private industry, helping both Indian and British-based sterling companies, and presumably the Indian economy as a whole.[201]

The Indian government had a heavy stake in teaching the world to drink its tea in the 1960s. We will examine this campaign in the UK in the next chapter, but it is important to note here that not all foreign markets were the same. During this time, India developed new global relationships by creating markets in the Soviet Union, in the Middle East, and in regions then becoming known as "the developing world." Trade reflected the growth of new South-South relationships as India sent trade missions to Moscow, Cairo, Khartoum, Nairobi, Kabul, Manila, Tokyo, Hong Kong, Madagascar, Kuala Lumpur, and Tehran.[202] The Central Tea Board also put on exhibitions in New York City, Paris, Seattle, Padua, and Stockholm, but thousands of pounds of tea and display materials also went to Poland, Damascus, Beijing, Shanghai, and even the coffee strongholds of Buenos Aires and Santiago.[203] This geography reflected politicians' and business men's desire to end their dependency on Great Britain and the rest of the capitalist West.

Despite the Tea Board's reorientation toward export, Indian consumption grew at phenomenal rates during the 1960s and 1970s. B. K. Goswami, the chairman of the Central Tea Board, wrote with optimism in 1979 that "the country today is the leading consumer of tea in the world," absorbing about 60 percent of its own production.[204] Measured as a nation, India had surpassed the UK as the greatest tea market, but nationally per capita consumption remained low.[205] Tea had come to occupy a central place in India's diet and culture, but people drank tea differently in Assam, Bengal, the Punjab, Bihar, and the Himalayas, even as "chai" became "synonymous with being Indian," as one journalist wrote in 2002.[206] We need far more work on postcolonial developments, which would consider how tea reinforced and/or altered gender, caste, class, regional, and religious and other identities, and we also need to know more about how Indian nationals and corporations made tea India's national drink, but this would merit another book-length study. This chapter instead follows Indian business, capital, and tea to the United States: a place where producers and sellers had always looked for consumers and where they encountered new ideas, and this was especially true in the first decades after the war.

FROM MINCING LANE TO MADISON AVENUE

African and Asian producers and governments needed American tea drinkers more than ever, but capturing this wealthy and elusive market was a more expensive and difficult enterprise than it had been in the past. Postwar Americans were bombarded with advertising and merchandising for foods and drinks and all manner of household products. The growth of television provided access to national markets for those who could handle the high sticker price for commercials. In the 1950s and 1960s, producing nations, however, wanted to learn American-style publicity techniques and they nurtured and maintained industry-wide connections in the vast American hinterland. We must return to America once again and specifically examine the formation and work of the U.S. Tea Council, because this development reveals how the remnants of the British Empire encountered the growing power of the American market empire.

In May 1950, India, Ceylon, Indonesia, and U.S. importers and retailers formed the U.S. Tea Council, a body charged with teaching Americans to like tea.[207] C. O. Coorey, secretary of the Ceylon Tea Propaganda Board, positively described the agency as "the biggest effort ever made to pump more tea into the potentially big American market." If successful, the author noted, producing nations would earn much-desired dollars and secure long-term price stabilization.[208] The origins of this body lay in the devaluation of the pound in 1949. Gervas Huxley met with Robert Smallwood, the head of Lipton's U.S. and chairman of the U.S. Tea Association, and explained how the extra money available from a devalued pound should be spent on promoting "the tea habit." Smallwood agreed and the idea of a joint Tea Council representing producers and distributors took shape.[209] An article on the council defined it as "a non-profit organization established to wage tea's competitive fight for increased U.S. sales and consumption. It is a corporation without precedent in this country; an international partnership jointly owned by the Governments of India, Ceylon, Indonesia and the Tea Association of the USA."[210] Half of the Board of Directors were preserved for members of the U.S. tea trade, while the other half came from producing countries. Anthony Hyde, as executive director, was responsible for research, advertising, merchandising, sales promotion, and publicity.

Yet another transatlantic figure, Hyde was born in England in 1907, but he received his BA in economics at Yale in 1929, worked as a reporter for the *Washington Times*, as a director of promotion for the *Washington Herald*, as a copywriter for Young and Rubicam, and then moved to Lord & Thomas.

During the war, he was the campaign coordinator for the Office of War Information and worked on several other boards in charge of mobilization and economics. In 1948 he was named president and managing director of the U.S. Tea Bureau before serving as executive director of the U.S. Tea Council from 1953 to 1955. Hyde was in all respects a transatlantic figure comfortable in the world of advertising and politics and the public and private sectors.[211] Hyde believed that American ad agencies knew how to sell in the United States, so the council retained the Chicago-based firm Leo Burnett, with the notion that this agency had an army of successful and experienced "copywriters, *media* experts, television producers and directors, research specialists, artists and production personnel."[212] Burnett had also handled major food and tobacco firms such as Pillsbury, Kellogg's, and Philip Morris, and Chicago of course had long been an important center for tea marketing in the United States.

Businessmen from India and Ceylon who served on or worked with the U.S. Tea Council believed that they would learn about advertising, business, and mass markets in America, not Great Britain. For example, in 1953, S. C. Datta, who would become an authority on exporting, visited the Tea Council's headquarters on the fifty-third floor of the Empire State Building and met with Anthony Hyde and Fred Rosen, who was then in charge of the council's public relations.[213] Writing an article on his visit for the tea trade, Datta described how he was awestruck by New York's skyscrapers and the American standard of living. He was impressed with the lifestyle of workers whose "homes have such things as big cars, good furniture, television sets, washing machines, refrigerators, electric kitchens and many other electrical conveniences." He was amazed as well by the nation's factories, such as Lipton's Hoboken plant that packed 2,500,000 tea bags a day. In upstate New York, Datta also enthusiastically described dairy cows that "provided 40 to 50 pounds of milk a day."[214] Such scenes of material abundance convinced Datta that India should spend its advertising budget in this wealthy, productive, and fruitful land.

Cold War politics were also at play here. Anthony Hyde believed consumerism would defeat communism, and this shaped how he viewed international economic relationships. At the yearly meeting of the entire trade, the U.S. Tea Association's annual convention which in 1954 met at Bretton Woods, New Hampshire, Hyde acknowledged the Cold War's bifurcation of the world but affirmed:

> We *do* live in One World. . . . What happens in Russia, England and France is our concern. What happens in the United States is very much their concern. As time goes on, it will become clear that the welfare and happiness of the people in India, Ceylon and Indonesia affect us—our

peace and prosperity—just as surely as what happens to the people in Arkansas, Utah, or California.[215]

The U.S. Tea Council, Hyde asserted, secured direct relationships between the United States and India, and Ceylon and other producing nations as well, implying that London was no longer the arbitrator between these nations. The new Tea Council, the Bretton Woods convention, and Hyde's speech all announced America as the center of global trade in a new era of open markets and political struggles between East and West. Bretton Woods was an especially symbolic venue in 1954. This was the ten-year anniversary of the famous Bretton Woods Convention, in which 730 delegates from 44 allied nations established the key structures and ideas for the postwar global economy. Initiating the World Bank, currency convertibility, the International Monetary Fund, and the International Trade Agreement, Bretton Woods laid the foundation of an American-dominated, "free trade" global economy.[216] Once again, we see the chameleon tea industry change its skin depending on its environment. Tea represented economic nationalism in India, but, in the United States in the mid-1950s, it donned the garb of the new American-led, free-trade driven economic order.

Plantation expert, business leader, former colonial politician, and the author of the most authoritative history of Indian tea, Sir Percival Griffiths attended the tea convention with ITA vice chairman H. K. Stringfellow, G. C. Ghose, Central Tea Board member, and P. K. Barooah, who was also a member of the Assam Tea Planters' Association. Sir Percival Griffiths is most remembered for his monumental *History of the Indian Tea Industry* (1967), but he had long been involved in tea and colonial governance.[217] His historical writing reinforced his public relations efforts to ensure the long-term success of British business in what was now the Commonwealth. Though very academic in comparison to other studies done at the time, Griffiths's history implied that tea, Britain, and India had been inextricably linked and that this bond had survived and would continue to survive decolonization. Griffiths had been a member of the Indian Civil Service and the leader of the Europe group in the Indian Legislative Assembly between 1937 and 1947.[218] During the war, he became publicity advisor to Lord Linlithgow's government in British India and was a critic of both the Muslim League and Congress Party. After Independence he served as the director of numerous companies, president of the India, Pakistan and Burma Association, and political advisor to the Indian Tea Association, the Pakistan Tea Association, and the International Tea Market Expansion Board.[219] Like his counterparts in earlier generations, this planter turned politician and publicist also saw America as a market and business school.

Griffiths and his fellow colleagues from India attended the U.S. Tea Convention in 1954 as one stop on a North American tour. They started in Toronto before visiting Montreal, New York, Washington, D.C., Baltimore, and Ottawa. Griffiths went back to England at this point but the rest went on to Chicago, San Francisco, and Los Angeles. In addition to visiting the big packers and distributors such as Salada, Lipton, and Tetley, they met with Safeway Stores, visited the Supermarket Institute, and paid a visit to the Independent Grocers Alliance. They called on the new U.S. Tea Council and visited a second council that had just formed in Canada. They spent time at Leo Burnett's Chicago office before continuing on to Los Angeles, where they visited 20th Century Fox Film Studios. They even watched how television shows were produced at the Hal Roach studios and at CBS's "Television City."[220] Griffiths, a product of the Raj, was now studying American consumer culture with Indian colleagues in order to build a new kind of global consumer culture that would improve Indian economic development and help British companies as well.

After this American sojourn, Griffiths was a bit despondent, however, because after so many years of advertising, Americans still disliked tea. Between the 1820s and 1870s, per capita consumption had paralleled British trends, growing gradually until peaking at around 2.5 pounds annually in the 1890s, whereupon it began a steady descent. British and Dutch-grown black teas had displaced green and scented East Asia varieties, but all tea had fallen to just over 0.6 pounds per person by the time of Indian Independence.[221] Griffiths blamed coffee: "the orientation of American business interests towards South America in this period may have been a factor in the great development of the coffee drinking habit to the detriment of tea."[222] Historian Steven Topik has made the same argument. Tea had also failed, Griffiths argued, to stand up to the "great advertising pressure exerted by the manufacturers of fruit juices and other soft drinks."[223] Tea's advertising budget had simply not been robust enough. The "USA today is advertising mad," Griffiths told his colleagues. He backed this up with cold hard facts. In 1939, $1.9 billion were spent on all U.S. advertising; in 1953 the number had climbed to $7.8 billion, with food advertising climbing faster than that of other commodities. Television had contributed to these changes; already in 1953, the "average American family had radio and television sets turned on for 5½ hours a day."[224] Consumer society had become an expensive pursuit in the States.

Americans had the highest standard of living in the world. Whether measured by per capita income, Gross National Product, or some other standard, the average U.S. citizen was relatively wealthy. Americans also spent more on food, particularly branded and processed foods, than other nations did, and the U.S. food industry spent more on advertising than its rivals did.[225] Food advertising was also powerfully gendered. Manufacturers relentlessly preached to women that planning, purchasing, and preparing food was solely their responsibility, an expression of their femininity and their love for their families. Supermarkets became the new "Housewife's Paradise."[226]

The tea industry wanted to compete, however, so they hired the same sorts of market experts that the rest of the food industry had turned to in these years. In the 1950s, they retained European-born Jewish social scientists Hans Zeisel and Ernest Dichter to figure out why Americans hated tea. Both had fled the Nazis and began to introduce a new psychological approach to selling goods in the United States. Zeisel, the Tea Council's first director of market research, had been born in Czechoslovakia and grew up in Vienna, where he earned doctorates in law and political science at the University of Vienna. In the United States, Zeisel became a pioneering social scientist, expert on the American legal system, consultant for government and private industry, and professor at Rutgers, Columbia, and the University of Chicago.[227] He was on the Chicago faculty when the Tea Council retained him. Griffiths met with Zeisel in 1954 and initially felt somewhat confused by his methods, remarking that "to assess the accuracy of Dr. Zeisel's conclusions would take many months and would demand knowledge we do not possess, but it is clear that Dr. Zeisel has brought a good analytical mind to bear on these problems [and] he inspires us with confidence." Whether it was good or not, Griffiths was resigned to the fact that "much of American advertising is founded on research of this kind."[228] Though they could not make heads or tails of Zeisel's appraisal, Griffiths and his colleagues accepted the need for such complex and scientific market research.

The Tea Council and several major brands also availed themselves of the Austrian-born émigré and student of Freudian psychoanalysis Ernest Dichter. As a teenager, Dichter had worked at his uncle's department store in Vienna. He studied humanistic psychology with Charlotte Bühler, an approach that emphasized "self-realization, personal fulfillment, and a motivation-based theory of personality."[229] He also studied with Paul Lazarsfeld at the Psychoeconomic Institute in Vienna in 1936. After having been jailed and interrogated by the Nazis, Dichter fled Austria and arrived in New York in 1938, where he would develop what came to be known as motivational research.[230] He used in-depth, non-directive interviews and projective tests to discover consumers' deep, subconscious attitudes toward goods and services. Dichter became a champion of America's consumer culture, believing that consumption allowed people to "grow in self-awareness and self-esteem" and that high levels of consumer spending led to the stability of democracy.[231] As Dichter saw it, buying was "an expression of creativity," and the market researcher's job was to search for "the soul, the meaning of objects."[232] He theorized that buying decisions were driven by consumers' psychology, an amalgam of passions, desires, prejudices, and disgusts.

While he worked for many firms in the beverage and food industries, tea producers desperately hoped that Dichter could uncover the real source behind American anti-tea prejudices. Dichter conducted several studies of hot and iced tea, coffee, and a number of different brands in the early 1950s, but already in a 1951 phone conversation with Henry Starr, the research director at Leo Burnett, Dichter insisted that tea's fundamental problem was that it was "considered a 'sissy drink,'" literally and symbolically weak.[233] He elaborated on this idea in a speech he gave to the U.S. Tea Association at their annual convention in 1955, which met that year in White Sulphur Springs, Virginia. The title of his talk was "Can We Build a New 'Tea Culture' in the United States?" While he touched on many issues, at base Dichter contended that in some countries, "tea has become a cultural center of life . . . surrounded with rituals, associations, and history." America did not have a tea culture, but even worse the beverage was perceived as an "English habit," and this, he believed, was the psychological "obstacle" that prevented market growth in the United States.[234] While he did not come right out and call England a country of "sissies," that was of course the implication.

"From his earliest formative years," Dichter proposed, "the American youth is imbued with what may be called an 'anti-tea' attitude. When the dramatic story of the Boston Tea Party is told to him, [he] pictures Sam Adams in Indian costume, along with his disguised Bostonian friends, tossing tea into the water from the deck of a British ship." The retellings of the Revolution create "a negative attitude to tea itself," and this explained why "tea" was a slang word for cocaine (it was also slang for marijuana) and why it inspired associations with "effeminacy."[235] A jump to be sure, but this odd leap from the Revolution to cocaine and effeminacy suggests that for Dichter colonial oppression was an effeminizing condition. Americans' growing distaste for British-style imperialism in the 1950s may have made things even worse for tea—Dichter assumed that Americans disliked tea because it represented their colonial past, which they especially wanted to forget.

Dichter had to interpret data creatively to support this argument. His reports and proposals quoted liberally from hundreds of in-depth interviews designed to expose unconscious desires and prejudices, but it is interesting how he interpreted his evidence. Dichter conducted his first market study for the U.S. Tea Bureau in 1951. Dichter and his team did fifty "psychological depth interviews" with respondents alleged to represent a cross section of the population, married and single, male and female, young and old, coffee and tea drinkers. The entire sample actually came from New York, the youngest was twenty, only three were over fifty, and most were married middle-class women. While he would later do larger national studies, Dichter extrapolated a great deal from this northeastern middle-class female sample. Dichter listened to responses and closely read people's language, which he saw as individual "texts." Some of his reports also included quantitative data, but Dichter claimed interviews brought fresh evidence to the table. Nevertheless, he ignored quite a bit of what his respondents told him so that their answers would support his preconceived notions.

Many interviewees referred to drink cultures as expressions of national heritage and their understanding of Britishness. For example, one respondent stated, "I think Americans don't drink more tea because they are a wholesome people who like to call an ace an ace and a spade a spade." By contrast, this respondent continued, "There is always an undercurrent with these people [the English and Americans who ape their culture] who have a habit of drinking tea and giving tea parties—it is just not wholesome, that's all I can say. I've been invited to tea parties and I never like it. Nobody was natural and everybody was putting on an act. I don't like it."[236] A self-professed American Anglophile, who came from a German coffee-drinking background, explained that she (or he, it isn't clear) had learned to like tea while at college after drinking it in the afternoon with "an English couple."[237] Another interviewee said, "I was born in Ireland, so I drink tea all the time, and I have drunk it all my life." Similarly another mentioned, "At home we used to have a lot of tea. I was brought up on it. I am Canadian and you know in Canada just like the English they have much more tea."[238] One person admitted that he/she acquired "a mental landscape of tea . . . from books, the movies, and plays. Yes, they [tea drinkers] would have ever so slight a British accent."[239] Dichter quoted all these individuals to make many points, but he did not propose that "Americans" were using tea either to identify with their English, Irish, or Canadian heritage or to distance themselves from those cultures. This is odd given Dichter's basic belief that tea represented Americans' British past that they wanted to forget. This contradiction may have stemmed from the fact that he believed nationalism was in general a false identity associated with fascist and Nazi propaganda. His respondents, however, did think in these terms, describing their drink habits as part of their ethnicity and national traditions, though as we can see from the first respondent quoted above, nationality was also a way for Americans to discuss social class.

Dichter's respondents also talked about gender. In 1951, Dichter found that 72 percent of his sample believed tea was for women. His interviews supported this idea. "I like tea but my husband likes coffee," stated one interviewee.[240] America's body and diet culture reinforced such views. "My mother drinks tea when she is dieting and she is always dieting," sarcastically explained one respondent. Another launched into her own weight troubles and said, "I am on a diet again and I even drink black coffee for breakfast but I hate that. I've got to lose some weight. Summer is coming and I want to get into my clothes from last year. I gained about eight pounds this winter . . . I think it is easier to drink tea without sugar or milk than to drink coffee like that."[241] Some men Dichter interviewed reinforced the researcher's theories about gender and the unconscious. One of the first men he talked to was very blunt: "No, I don't drink tea . . . I detest the thing. I told you I want something that peps me up and gives me lift and not something that tastes like hot water, and reminds me of urine."[242] This American consumer had simply been unmoved by decades of ITMEB advertising, which had claimed that tea was masculine, that it peps you up, and that it tasted good.

After he completed his research, however, Dichter returned to his earlier theories and argued that tea needed to eradicate its associations with England, Empire, and Women. Instead, all advertising should feature tea as playing "a lusty, masculine part—in the life of the American frontier."[243] The 1952 U.S. Tea Council ad campaign, Take Tea and See, tried to make tea masculine but did not follow all of Dichter's advice. A diminutive Charles Atlas–style weight lifter holding up a teapot and exhorting consumers to try tea on the "hefty side" appeared in many ads, but others, particularly those on television, described an economical, thirst-quenching, non-filling, and non-fattening beverage, implying it was for women. The industry also relied on hokey regional publicity drives known as hot and iced tea weeks. In 1952 the Tea Council chose Stamford, Connecticut, a supposedly "typical New England town," to be the center of the Tea Council's national campaign. The Tea Council "enlisted the enthusiastic support of the Mayor and his Civic Development Committee," the chamber of commerce, other business associations, the Rotary Club and Boy Scouts, grocers, caterers, packers, and teachers. A beauty contest picked a tea queen, who presided over a parade through Stamford's principal streets at the end of the week. The parade symbolized the new alliance of American civic and business culture and businessmen from India and Ceylon. The mayor and one of Connecticut's senators led the parade, followed by "bands and military colour guards carrying the flags of India, Ceylon, Pakistan, and Indonesia." "Cowboys on horses" and decorated floats illustrating "scenes of tea production and different aspects of tea consumption" completed the spectacle. According to Stamford's chief of police, never before in his "40 years' experience [had] so many Stamford citizens turned out to watch a parade."[244] This promotion and so many others across the nation encouraged consumers to think about the rest of the world as a marketplace, and in this sense it promoted the expansion of the American market empire. Cowboys and Indians (from South Asia) paraded through small-town America, selling themes that had been present since the exhibitions and advertising of the 1890s. However, none of this did much to shift American tastes or drink cultures.

When the U.S. Tea Council was restructured in 1953, it abandoned the Take Tea and See Campaign and hired the Bureau of Applied Social Research at Columbia University[245] and Gallup and Robinson, Inc.[246] In 1956 Ceylon injected more funds into the Tea Council budget, which then grew by 40 percent, enough to enable television advertising in the West, Midwest, and Northeast.[247] Despite all his money and expertise, when Dichter studied the tea market for J. Lyons and Company in 1958, he conceded that things had gotten worse. Social changes that had occurred since the war had meant that many "traditional" habits had come to be seen as "inappropriate for contemporary living." In general, he noted how "the younger generation is tending to reject a number of traditional products."[248] Even before he conducted his research, Dichter concluded, "We believe it is necessary to modernize the whole concept of tea."[249]

He was unable to do this, however, because some of the packers withdrew their support from the Tea Council. These companies sold competitive beverages and they decided to divert their advertising budgets to brand promotion. The Tea Council cut its budget from $1,708,700 in 1961 to $500,000 in 1962 and eliminated direct consumer advertising for the future. It continued to pay for public relations work, but as the Indian representatives from the Central Tea Board explained it in 1962, "media advertising was prohibitively expensive."[250] The industry estimated that it was outspent $40 to $1 by other beverages. In a 1963 article George Witt, president of the Tea Association, lamented: "Just think about the fight for the beverage business. Have you ever before been so much a target for beer, wine, whisky, milk, colas, fruit and vegetable drinks—not to mention coffee?"[251] By 1962 the massive increase in the use of tea bags, which accounted for 70 percent of the market in the United States, and the growing use of quick brew Assam CTC (cut-tear-curl) tea meant that Americans were using less tea to make more cups than in the past.[252] Average annual imports increased modestly, but Ceylon's market share grew at India's expense.[253] In the 1960s, Americans tended to drink mass-produced tea in the form of tea bags and often used instant tea to make iced tea. Most thought of tea as a summertime treat, not a symbol of the masculine frontier as Dichter and the companies who hired him had hoped.

———

Between the 1940s and 1970s, the global tea industry burst out of its former imperial boundaries and production spread around the world, even to South America.

New producing nations tried to harness tea to serve their economic needs. At times this meant forging new trade agreements and attempting to develop markets and business relations in the Soviet Union or the Middle East, the United States, and other former colonies. Throughout the 1950s, India believed that growing consumption at home would end colonial dependency, but by the mid-1960s a number of factors shifted attention back to exports, where Ceylon had been doing so well. This led to a bifurcated situation in which India and Ceylon worked together in the United States and competed in the UK and other markets.

The fate of the Tea Centres demonstrates many of these tensions. Initially they represented all tea producers, but by 1952, when the International Tea Market Board collapsed, Tea Boards began to invent new histories for distinct nations and branded tea with national characteristics. Yet as we saw, this was a difficult task and no amount of modern architecture and design could shake the imperial nostalgia that pervaded postwar British culture. The tensions between nostalgia and modernity reverberated in advertising, propaganda, and the shape of consumer markets throughout the 1950s and 1960s. In the final chapter, we will examine how these ideas worked themselves out specifically in postwar Britain as a means to carry on the argument that I have made throughout this book, namely that consumerism and imperialism were intertwined phenomena. Postwar British consumer society struggled to accommodate and then erase the place of empire in British culture, but ultimately it was quite often the same people and companies that had been selling tea and empire since the 1930s that fought Coke in Africa, nationalized tea in India, sought to Americanize and masculinize tea in the United States, and manufactured a nostalgic *and* cosmopolitan tea culture in postwar Britain.

11

"JOIN THE TEA SET"

Youth, Modernity, and the Legacies of Empire

during the Swinging Sixties

The Home and Colonial is not so baronial
Now the old Empire has flopped.
We shall soon see—"Commonwealth tea."
The tasty tea flavour we'll soon start to savour
Like "café espresso" or "Coke."

This ditty published in *The Grocer* in 1962 was inspired by a shift in corporate identity. In 1960, the huge Victorian retail chain the Home and Colonial stores restructured and began trading under the name Allied Suppliers.[1] Reporting this news, the author of this witty poem condensed many of the same issues that Philip Witham's BBC broadcast had pondered, namely, how did the end of the British Empire impact commercial and consumer cultures in the metropole? For precisely a century, *The Grocer* had navigated the global marketplace and it was still fulfilling this function. In this case, the journal was considering how broader international and cultural realignments taking place in the postwar years impacted their business. Decolonization, American economic and cultural influence, and rebellious young consumers had rejected or altered many cherished traditions. In 1965, the broadcast journalist William Hardcastle interpreted such changing tastes as national decline when he asked listeners of the BBC's morning current affairs program, *Today*:

> How much more can you take? You've smiled bravely at the dissolution of the British Empire; you've suffered the cult of the teenager, the weakening of the British Navy, the end of the 9 o'clock news. How much, I ask, can this nation stand? I ask it this morning for I have news of a threat to yet another great British institution. The cup of tea.[2]

Hardcastle was commenting on a recent report on the rise of coffee and decline of tea, which he saw as symptomatic of the decline of Britain. "Tea drinkers of Britain," he asked, "could we have braved the blitz with instant coffee? Can you imagine the great British working-man going on strike over his instant coffee break?" His answer was obvious, for, as he concluded, the ability to make a good cup of tea was "in the very fabric of the British heritage," which explains why, he proposed, "in no land untouched by the gentle brush of British Imperialism, is it possible to get a decent cup of tea."[3] There was of course nothing "gentle" about imperialism, but Hardcastle's strident position illuminates how tea's history enabled Britons to see, or one should say taste and talk about, the intimate history of the empire and its demise. *The Grocer*'s poet and William Hardcastle were part of a very vocal and impassioned conversation that took place in the media and within business settings, households, and shops about the place of tea in postcolonial British society and culture. Whether they liked it or not, most Britons believed that the decline of tea and the growth of coffee and Coke was a fundamental social and cultural revolution.

It is striking that at the same moment the Suez crisis illuminated the imperial nation's diminished global power, Britons began to drink less tea. In 1956–57, Britain, France, and Israel invaded Egypt to try to oust President Nasser and reassert European power in the region, only to be forced to back down by American president Dwight D. Eisenhower. Suez had many consequences, but I am not suggesting it was responsible for long-term shifts in British demand for tea.[4] Rather, I am arguing that British commentators implicitly understood that Britain's enormous thirst for tea was a product of its possession of a vast overseas empire, and like the Suez crisis the decline of tea symbolized waning power on the global stage. After a brief surge in 1959, UK per capita consumption of tea began a steady decline in the 1960s that continued throughout the second half of the twentieth century.[5] If measured per head, rather than as a national aggregate, as many analysts liked to do, then Britons were losing their taste for tea. Britons still drink a great deal of tea, but they also enjoy coffee. In 1993, for example, Britons on average drank 3.5 cups of tea a day and 1.7 cups of coffee.[6] In 2015, Turkish people drank the most tea in the world, at 6.961 pounds per head, followed by Ireland at 4.831, and the UK at 4.281. India is still comparatively low at 0.715, but U.S. consumption is tiny at 0.0503.[7] In the twenty-first century British drink habits look more like they did in the early nineteenth century when coffee and tea were both popular.[8] Canada, Australia, and New Zealand have experienced similar changes, while consumption has increased by leaps and bounds in many areas of the Middle East, Africa, and South Asia.[9]

There are many reasons for this global reorientation. Newly independent producing nations had desired such a reconfiguration, but as tea drinking declined in the

UK and white dominion markets, India and other major producers grew alarmed and agreed to collaborate with each other and even work with the big corporate buyers to halt changing tastes. Ironically, the globalization, that is, diversification, of British drink cultures in the late 1950s and 1960s scared producing nations to such a degree that they returned to their old imperial habits and formed an updated version of the International Tea Market Expansion Board, which they called the UK Tea Council. Working with the multinational ad agency Ogilvy and Mather, this new international promotional body wanted to preserve the place of tea in British culture. To do this, they initiated a major rebranding effort, which tried to transform an old habit into a modern, hip, youthful, and cosmopolitan pleasure. At the same time, other sellers continued to sell a nostalgic, imperial, and traditional brew. Consumers received then a mixed message that reflected older worries and jealousies within the tea industry and a more general confusion about the nature of postcolonial British culture and identities.[10]

FREE TRADE AND THE RETURN OF MAZAWATTEE'S GRANNY

Seeking to reverse weakening markets, the tea industry in the 1950s and 1960s promoted at least three versions of Great Britain: an insular island nation, a new multinational Commonwealth, and a young, hip, cosmopolitan country that looked to both Europe and the United States. This was a schizophrenic project in which multinational corporations and other international institutions were simultaneously advancing oppositional understandings of British national identity. In many ways, they were responding to a general fear that the United Kingdom simply was not the nation it had been. The industry looked both backward and forward as it sought to return to business as usual, but as we saw in the last chapter, nothing seemed the same in the postwar decades.

At a dinner dance celebrating his firm's 125th birthday in 1951, the chairman of Horniman's urged the end of rationing with the simple assertion: "It's not roast beef that has made England great—it's the tea. Look at men like the Elder and Younger Pitt or Samuel Johnson—they drank anything from 40 to 70 cups a day."[11] By proposing that excessive tea drinking had made Britain a world power, postwar rationing could be seen as a source of national degeneration. So in October 1952 when the Ministry of Food finally ended rationing, journalists announced the revival of liberalism, British pride, and "normal" gender relations, or as one pundit expressed it, this day revived the liberty of the freeborn British housewife.[12] A Tea Bureau ad announced: "Tea Cheers More Tea for Everyone!"[13] The American newspaper the *Newark Sunday News* took note of "free" tea's significance with a headline that read: "Atomic Test Plus Tea Renews British Pride."[14] Britain did test their first nuclear weapon on the same day that tea was derationed so it is not surprising that the media played up the global significance with witty headlines such as "Britain again enjoys the freedom of the teas!"[15] The Central Tea Board of India jumped on board and it too claimed tea as a source of British power in an ad stating: "This is what the Everest Conquerors say about Indian Tea. During our ascent of Mt. Everest, Indian tea constantly gave us cheer and vigour."[16] The end of the tea ration could not in truth compare to the acquisition of the bomb, but along with the conquest of Everest, Queen Elizabeth's coronation, and the Festival of Britain, a free trade in tea signified the dawn of a new Elizabethan age.[17] This celebration of the freedom of the teas aroused a wistful longing for the good old days when Victoria was on the throne and Britannia ruled the waves.

With the return to free trade, the various tea boards and companies engaged in a great deal of market research. Journalist Eric Wainwright joked about this phenomenon in 1952 when he wrote that the Tea Bureau was about to conduct a "nation-wide snoop into your tea habits."[18] What this study discovered was worrying, however. Although per capita consumption returned to prewar levels as soon as rationing ended, Britons brewed their tea differently. Dudley Barker wrote in the *Daily Herald* that shockingly, "most households in this country no longer pay attention to the sacred, time-honoured rules for making tea; and that a whole English generation has grown up that has never tasted a cup of decent tea in its life." Wondering whether "the English have lost the art of making tea," Barker then patronizingly concluded: "Back to the rule ladies. One for each person and one for the pot."[19] This recipe was so central to high consumption rates that when TV chef Philip Harben called it an "old-wives' tale," the Tea Bureau took him to task.[20] A second survey done in 1953 quieted fears by revealing that all adult Britons and nearly 84 percent of "infants," or children under the age of four, drank some tea and that annual consumption had climbed again to prewar levels at just over ten pounds per year.[21] Perhaps Britons were inspired by popular actress and singer Petula Clark's hit single "Anytime Is Tea Time Now," which the Tea Bureau had sponsored and released in 1952. To an upbeat tune, Clark celebrated how Britons could now "have a cup of the cup that cheers," morning, noon, and night. Though Clark was already a big star and by no means considered old-fashioned, the lyrics evoke the 1930s when Clark sings that over a cup of tea, "you'll make good friends and you don't need wealth."[22]

Such nostalgia was also common in brand advertising of the early 1950s.[23] Either because they could not afford to pay for new slogans or because companies wanted to re-create the good old days when Britons were awash in tea, revivalism dominated corporate advertising.[24] The Co-operative Society, for example, reminded Britons that it was still "Filling the Nation's Tea Pot."[25] Ridgways repeated it had been "preferred since 1836 through six reigns."[26] Mazawattee recycled its famous Victorian granny and Horniman's reproduced Victorian ads, such as one from 1888 featuring Prince Albert drinking tea.[27] Even as late as 1966, Horniman's founder, "honest John," reminded Britons that Horniman's had been selling unadulterated tea since 1826.[28] Twinings highlighted the company's long history with the slogan "Modern as the minute for 255 years."[29] Updating the temperance tea party, Lyons began hosting what the company called "housewives tea parties." These were mass marketing events that took place in public halls in provincial towns all over the UK. Rather than listen to former drunkards preach the virtues of sobriety, television and radio personalities, such as Derek Roy, hosted variety programs that included music, comedy, fashion shows, and beauty competitions. "Housewives this is your show," one advertisement for these tea parties explained.[30] Like other consumer advertising targeting housewives in the 1950s, Lyons's tea parties nevertheless reaffirmed older gender and domestic norms at a time when those ideals and family structures were changing.

The transformation of the clipper ship the *Cutty Sark* into a tourist site is another example of the neo-Victorian commercialism of this era. In 1954, the *Cutty Sark* found its permanent home as a refurbished tourist site on the Thames in Greenwich (fig. 11.1). Although the ship was originally built in 1869 and was only used after the opening of the Suez Canal made the clippers unnecessary, the ship became a museum that demonstrated a time when Britain

FIGURE 11.1. The *Cutty Sark*. Greenwich. Photographed by John Gay, 1955–65. (Heritage Image Partnership Ltd./Alamy)

ruled the empire of tea. International tourists and British visitors can still almost smell the crates of tea as they wander the ship's hull and learn about the technological prowess of the swift clippers. Many forces and groups were behind this preservationist episode, but a list of contributors to the refurbishment fund is revealing. The big tea companies and tea associations that paid for the tea cars during the Blitz and the postwar Tea Centre in Regent Street brought the *Cutty Sark* to Greenwich. Export taxes on tea and government subsidies from India, Ceylon, and Africa underwrote this romanticized vision of the British maritime and tea-drinking past.[31]

For all this looking back, Britons did not drink the same beverage that their grandparents or even their parents had enjoyed. African, South American, and Chinese leaf, for example, were increasingly blended with South Asian varieties, and the biggest change of all was the growing use of CTC teas and tea bags. CTC (cut-tear-curl) manufacturing was invented in 1931 but was not commonly used in Britain until after the war. CTC manufacturing was similar to orthodox methods, but the rolling process was more "severe," reducing leaf size and rupturing nearly all the leaf's cells. These leaves fermented faster and steeped more quickly, and the "thicker" liquid produced a higher yield per cup.[32] Because they looked and tasted different than orthodox teas, CTC teas tended to be used in tea bags and marketed as "quick brews." This was yet another turning point in which the commodity changed, and blending, marketing, and packaging sometimes hid these changes or offered them up as the most modern, best way to enjoy an old habit.

Tetley introduced the tea bag before the war, but the company relaunched the product with a wave of advertising in the UK in 1953. These ads informed the public that tea bags were an "American innovation" that was good for those "who drop the tea caddy, lose the scoop and make a mess of old leaves" and for "busy people."[33] If sloppy men might have been one target market, the harried housewife was another. Ads explained, for example, how tea bags were "convenient for the early morning cup of tea or the occasional cup which the housewife often wishes to make for herself."[34] These ads made a virtue of convenience and efficiency.[35] Tea bags were "The Modern Way to Make Delicious Tea."[36] But very old Britons often sold modernity. An elderly man dressed in a tweed vest laughed as he drank Lyons Quick Brew in a 1963 advertisement.[37] Consumers were also likely unaware of the fact that in 1964 Tetley belonged to the conglomerate Beech-Nut Life Savers Group. The company kept the Tetley name and invested £250,000 a year to promote tea bags.[38] This American-based multinational sold both nostalgia and modernity in 1960s Great Britain.

Commercial television was launched in the UK in 1955, dramatically raising the costs of selling products.[39] Television ownership increased quickly, with licenses growing from three to nearly six million between 1954 and 1956. Advertising expenditure in general rose from £123 to £176 million a year.[40] Press advertising was still extremely important, however, with Britain's most read evening paper, the *London Evening News*, selling 1.5 million copies daily. Aggregate circulation figures were high at nearly 17 million papers purchased daily, and press advertising budgets growing at a very healthy pace.[41] The large tea companies with money on hand quickly figured out how to make the most of TV advertising. For example, Brooke Bond introduced its famous anthropomorphic chimps to advertise P.G. Tips in 1956, and for decades these celebrities starred in countless commercials, were featured on tea cards, became collectible figurines, and appeared at many public promotions. This idea probably came from photos of chimps at Regent's Park Zoo having a tea party that had been displayed at the Festival of Britain in 1951, but it is striking the degree to which Brooke Bond's chimps impersonated the comforting working-class, humorous Britishness of Mr. T. Pott and Gracie Fields.[42] While at times they appeared to impersonate posh types, in general the chimps adopted the mannerisms and lifestyle of the working and lower-middle classes who did such things as vacation at a Butlin's holiday camp or "emigrate" to a zoo in New Zealand.[43] Tetley's Tea Folk, which first appeared in 1973, had similar characteristics. The working-class Tea Folk have recently returned and now they encounter aliens and even have their own Facebook page, but in general they evoke nostalgia for a working-class culture that was devoted to tea.[44] New promotional formats thus have provided a wider arena for reliving the past.

COFFEE OR TEA? HOUSEWIVES, TEENS, AND OTHER REBELLIOUS CONSUMERS

However cute the chimps may have been, slowly but perceptibly Britons' love affair with tea began to lose its intensity.[45] The British taste for tea grew and declined in fits and starts, but consumption that had followed the flag, so to speak, began to fall as the empire contracted. There is some debate about when the slide began, but, during and after 1956 and 1957 and, certainly, by the 1960s, tea consumption steadily and relentlessly declined. Of course, national aggregates do not tell the whole story, but the confluence of shrinking per capita consumption, the end of the empire, and the rise of global youth cultures and corporate capitalism—represented by coffee and Coke—gave the tea industry and social commentators much to think about.

A great deal was at stake here. A retail journalist reminded the industry that "the tea trade has helped build political empires, [and] commercial empires have been founded on tea, in brief, it is big business."[46] In India tea employed over a million workers, and by the mid-1960s it also accounted for 15 percent of all foreign earnings. So when "India's biggest customer" began "taking less Indian tea, and paying less for it," the Indian government and tea industry were deeply concerned.[47] Even a slight change in habits posed a threat to a very large industry, and this is not taking into account other key markets, such as Australia, where similar shifts were underway. Restricting production would reduce fiscal stability in new nations, so once again the expansion of consumption seemed to be the only viable solution.

Private memos and studies blamed the "influence of the big [tea] packers," the "apathy of the British catering companies," and the "unintelligence of the British grocer." These "market manipulators," as one study called them, pushed cheap mass-market teas, refused good-quality brands, and in the long run destroyed the taste for tea.[48] In public, however, journalists and trade experts refocused attention not on the companies that were introducing cheap teas and new and more exciting foods, drinks, and eateries, but on consumers and social and cultural change. They framed the issue as a battle between beverages, as though coffee and Coke were autonomous forces beguiling consumers. Coke was conquering Africa, and it and coffee threatened to colonize other tea strongholds as well.

In Canada and Australia, the legacies of wartime rationing and changing demographics, trade relationships, and lifestyles gave coffee a growing share of the beverage market. In Canada, for example, coffee drinking expanded during and since the war; it was becoming a "breakfast drink" and was very popular with the young.[49] Some believed this change was due to advertising, and it is the case that both the coffee and soft drink industries had launched huge ad campaigns in Canada in the late 1940s.[50] Immigration and closer ties to the United States were making Canada less British, experts believed. When Sir Percival Griffiths studied the Canadian market in 1954, he saw many factors at work: he noted how the "growth of American influence on social habits," a decline in the "British element in the population," intensive advertising, and Canadians' tendency toward "labour saving and convenience" had made coffee and especially instant coffee popular.[51] Precisely the same situation seemed to be developing in Australia.[52] Between 1948 and 1968, per capita coffee consumption rose from 0.9 to 2.6 pounds per annum.[53] A 1970 study pointed to immigration "of people from non tea-drinking countries," effective marketing, and the "trend toward greater coffee consumption by younger age groups" as responsible for shifting tastes.[54] Tea held its place as the "traditional beverage of Australia," but instant coffee and immigrant-owned espresso bars, the report proposed, "contributed to the popularity of coffee drinking" and coffee had become the "dining out" beverage that the young enjoyed.[55]

All of these experts ascribed the decline of tea and growth of coffee to several factors: the attraction of American lifestyles and products, the power of large advertising campaigns, the influence of immigration, the rebellious nature of teens who preferred spending their time in foreign, immigrant-owned coffee bars rather than at home drinking tea with their families, and finally housewives who valued convenience over quality. Among all of these factors, however, market researchers directed their microscope at two groups in particular: teenagers and housewives.[56] A business journalist explained the porous borders between these two categories when he noted:

> The 14-year old girl, at this moment swooning and screaming over The Beatles or whoever else happens to be topping the charts just now, is the same girl who, in a few years' time, will be married, looking after a home and family, and probably complain about the teenagers of the day. She will also do the family shopping, for she will be that very important person, the housewife. This housewife (who is an ex-teenager) will buy something for the family to drink. What will she buy?[57]

The postwar housewife, business proposed, was a tool of modernization and economic reconstruction, an agent of change or tradition, and, through her consumer choices, a nation-builder.[58] In Britain, the decline of domestic service and the growth of new forms of food retailing such as self-service supermarkets added food shopping and cooking to the housewife's domain and thus she became the target of much postwar advertising. Market research therefore spent most of its energy identifying her wants and needs.

Marketers also "discovered" another potent agent of change: youth. An amorphous term, "youth" primarily referred to men and women between ages fifteen and twenty-five. Historians have long debated when this consumer type first appeared and whether young people or advertisers or some sort of combination lay behind its invention. But most agree that the essence of youth culture was the idea that young people created their identities and sense of community through the use of distinctive consumer goods, leisure spaces, entertainments, and styles.[59] We have already seen many examples of the tea business appealing to and using young consumers; however, as Harry Hopkins wrote in 1963, "Never had 'Youth' with a capital 'Y'—been so earnestly discussed, so frequently surveyed, so extensively seen *and* heard."[60] "Youth," like class, gender, and race, came to be defined in relationship or contrast to an identified Other, which at this time was primarily the prewar generation. Postwar youth culture was also affluent. In Britain, for example, teenage real incomes were reported to be 50 percent higher than before the war and increasing at a rate double that of adults.[61] Young men earned significantly more than women and thus they became identified as a key market. Hopkins estimated that the teenage market amounted to £900 million a year and many industries wanted a part of this pie. Girls were not neglected, however.[62] With a shorter workweek, later school leaving age, and higher incomes, this first wave of the baby boom generation was a market to be reckoned with. They were also a social phenomenon to study and control. The tea industry was worried that this was not an easy prospect and they were convinced, as were many forces of tradition, that youthful rebellion, expressed by the consumption of espresso and other new pleasures in urban coffee bars, represented the decline of England. In reality, young consumers benefited coffee growers but hurt tea producers, and this especially threatened the stability of Ceylon's economy, which was so totally dependent on the export of this crop. If anything, shifting tastes hurt postcolonial nations far more than the metropole.

Young and affluent consumers were spending a good deal of time if not much money in the new bohemian coffee bars that sprouted in metropolitan centers on both sides of the Atlantic and throughout the Commonwealth in the 1950s and 1960s. Often, but not always started by Italian or other immigrants, coffee bars typically featured a gleaming Gaggia espresso machine, jukeboxes, and a young clientele who made the spaces their own.[63] They first appeared in the early 1950s and by 1960 London had nearly 500 coffee bars and there were 2,000 countrywide.[64] In London, these "revolutionary" institutions became a nursery for rock 'n' roll and a conduit for other new European and American forms of mass culture. Soho coffee bars, and particularly the 2i's opened by Freddie and Sammy Irani at 59 Old Compton Street, Soho, in 1955, sold many new foreign pleasures. The brothers left the coffee bar in 1956 to an Australian wrestler, Paul "Dr. Death" Lincoln, and promoter Ray "Rebel" Hunter. Former doorman and judo instructor Tom Littlewood became manager in 1958. Audiences packed the small dark cellar under the café to listen to the Vipers, Terry Dean, Vince Taylor and the Playboys, Cliff Richard, the Beatles, and the coffee bar's most famous "discovery," Tommy Steele.[65] Music, energy, young crowds, caffeine, and drugs created a palpable sexual energy. Ian Samwell, the bassist for Cliff Richard and the Drifters, played at the 2i's in 1958 and he later recalled:

> The 2 i's was packed. The 2 i's was hot. The 2 i's was rockin'! It was also very, very small.
>
> Even from the street you could tell that there was something going on, something special in the air that night. Maybe it was the muffled beat of rock 'n' roll booming up from the basement. Maybe it was the energy of the teenagers hanging around outside.

Samwell's memories capture the intensity of the new consumer culture that appeared to be colonizing the metropole. He mentioned, for example, how "a large emblem resembling a Pepsi Cola bottle cap" was hung on the front and inside, "through the glass door past the American jukebox," and there was a "serving counter with its coffee machine, orange juice dispenser and sandwich display case on the left, and a long formica shelf on which to place your tiny glass espresso coffee cup and saucer to the right." Mocking the commercialism of its owner, Samwell joked, "And there, there at the end of the room by the entrance to the narrow stairway that led down to the world famous basement of the world famous 2i's stood the one and only, world famous Tom Littlewood, manager of the 2i's, God rest his avaricious soul."[66] Pepsi, Coke, orange juice, Formica, espresso, music, and drugs created a new kind of bodily and sensual consumer culture that was hot, loud, energetic, steamy, and sexy.

In many respects coffee bars were tea shops' Other, fighting Victorianism by selling "modern" American and European beverages and music and by reviving a carnivalesque British past. The coffee bar's ambiance was totally unlike that of the sedate, dainty, and chintzy tea room. The coffee bar was a space for a new kind of performance in which identities could be put on and taken off like a costume. For example, in September 1960, the prankster performer known as Screaming Lord Sutch performed with the Elvis-like singer Vince Taylor at the 2i's (fig. 11.2). Both performers mixed American and British culture to invent new personas. Sutch especially parodied the British class system and

FIGURE 11.2. Screaming Lord Sutch performs with Vince Taylor at the 2i's Coffee Bar, London, 24 September 1960. (Trinity Mirror/Mirrorpix/Alamy)

Victorian gothic melodrama and named himself after the African American singer Screamin' Jay Hawkings and an imaginary peer, the 3rd Earl of Harrow. Sutch often dressed as Jack the Ripper and released a song by that name in 1963.[67] Here he satirized the Victorians, transforming fears into commodities, no doubt deliberately disturbing an older generation who cherished different memories of the British past.

It should not be surprising then that British cultural studies, the intellectual movement that engaged seriously with the notion that people express their identity through fashion, music, and other forms of consumption, owed its origins in part to coffee bars as well.[68] The *New Left Review*, founded in 1960 by Stuart Hall, occupied the floor above a coffee bar in Carlisle Street in London.[69] Not all on the Left appreciated the coffee bars, however. Literary critic Richard Hoggart famously criticized these institutions, jukeboxes, and mass culture in his 1957 *Uses of Literacy*. Hoggart saw the coffee bars as a corrosive American form of capitalist influence destroying indigenous "British" working-class culture, particularly of its young men. These "Juke-Box Boys," as Hoggart called them, had grown accustomed to a "regular, increasing, and almost entirely unvaried diet of sensation . . . [that would] render its consumers less capable of responding openly and responsibly to life."[70] Thus Hoggart condemned mass culture as a foreign import that would inevitably produce apathetic, apolitical consumers. While coming from a very different political position than William Hardcastle, Hoggart nevertheless contributed to the argument that coffee bars and mass culture were not British and were colonizing the metropole. Such critiques also reinforced the sense that tea represented an older and more authentic working-class culture. Hoggart's protégé, Ray Gosling, shared Hoggart's interpretation that a powerful new culture had arrived in modern Britain, but he very much enjoyed this America.

Gosling, a well-known television broadcaster, filmmaker, and gay rights activist, remembered how as a child he had enjoyed the weekly treat of going out for afternoon tea with his working-class family,

> . . . if we were lucky, and if we'd been good. We'd be shown in by the manageress and sat at a table laid for four, and waited on by waitresses in trim black skirts, pleated white blouses with little black caps and white pinnies. Sometimes my mother knew the waitress from the bus or church or our street. We'd have to keep our hands off the tablecloth and a fidget would prompt: "Don't you dare put your elbows on the table." We were allowed one cake from the cake stand. We never ate out for a meal. Proper tea [meaning a meal] was cooked at home.[71]

Going out to tea was an experience, but one Gosling also associated with a re-strained, puritanical, working-class culture in which one couldn't fidget and only one cake was allowed. This was the traditional world of leisure that his generation rejected. They did not discard consumerism, however. Indeed, whether they were teddy boys, mods, or rockers, they used clothing, fashion, and consumer behaviors in a more self-conscious and deliberate way than their predecessors had.

Gosling was born in Northampton in 1939 and was part of the generation of artists, designers, writers, musicians, and filmmakers that produced, consumed, and exported Britain's rebellious youth culture.[72] He became a talented writer who met and was mentored by Hoggart in the early 1960s. Like Hoggart, he was fascinated with youth culture. Unlike Hoggart, he also enjoyed it and loved the affluent, attractive, and sexy American men stationed at an airfield near his home. Gosling wrote: "The Americans were something else . . . their bodies seemed different—bigger and broader-beamed, and they walked with a swagger. . . . [They] had affluence: a roll of banknote readies stuffed in the back pocket . . . they *looked* good." Around age fourteen or fifteen he recalled how he loved following and looking at these men and thus his sexuality shaped his sense of the world and of the United States in particular. As he wrote: "The most exciting thing about being alive was looking at Americans. America was the dream, to go to America. Be like them."[73] Gosling realized this dream by starting his own coffee bar. In contrast to the "Wedgwood tea-shop or the Durngate bus station café, [where] you had to hold the cup with your little finger up, drink quietly. . . . [and] you felt you were a prisoner," Gosling remembered:

> When we were out on our own, drinking coffee, we could do what we wanted, hold a cup with our elbows on the table. We wanted a new world, where you weren't hidebound by class and etiquette and by having to follow your betters and where you could respond to basic instincts and have some fun and be free like the Americans were. We wanted to kick the old world of afternoon tea and school dinners and having to sit upright. . . . And we did.[74]

The bodily and sexual freedom that became the mantra of the 1960s generation simply did not go with afternoon tea and school dinners. Tea represented class and etiquette and bodily restraint. However, Gosling's self-conscious reconstruction of the history of the coffee bar does not reveal the whole story.

When Gosling was eighteen, he and his friends established their own youth club and coffee bar in Leicester that was funded by a Quaker charity. This charity included university teachers and Quaker businessmen and women, and a sympathetic Hoggart even served as chairman![75] This was not really a contradiction since though it had a jukebox and served new foods and drinks, this coffee bar was not a product of the mass market, but rather it sought to provide an attractive alternative to the mass market.[76] Gosling and his friends did not think of what they were doing in the same way as the adult backers did, however; indeed, he conveniently failed to mention them at all when he later claimed: "We were successful—ran a coffee bar by ourselves with no adult help. Real espresso. Genuine Coca-Cola. Best hamburgers. . . . We sold a lot of hamburgers, cheeseburgers too."[77] Ironically, social experiments such as this coffee bar in Leicester promoted new tastes and habits that mass-market companies then profited from. These retrospective statements have to be read carefully, but they do reveal how postwar youth were attracted to the idea of foreign cultures and rejected what they believed to be the English past. Gosling, and no doubt many other young people, used mass culture to destroy Victorian conceptions of the body, the self, the community, the nation, and the marketplace, but they probably had no idea about the global consequences of their global tastes.

While Gosling believed he and his friends were building an alternative politics and culture, they were becoming a new "market" that big corporations could study and profit from. For example, J. Lyons, one of the first companies to introduce the mass-market chain tea shop, also contributed to its death when in 1953 it converted its Coventry Street Corner House into a Wimpy Bar, thus pioneering the fast food hamburger in Britain. This American hamburger chain, named after J. Wellington Wimpy, the character who downed countless burgers in the Popeye cartoons, had first opened in Indiana in the 1930s. In 1953, Lyons expanded the franchise under a subsidiary known as Pleasure Foods, Inc. By the late 1960s, there were 460 Wimpy Bars in the UK and others in Germany, Italy, Holland, Luxembourg, Lebanon, Cyprus, Libya, Tanzania, and Uganda, among other places.[78] Wimpy's served tea and coffee, but this chain challenged tea far more than Gosling and the founders of the 2i's coffee shop could ever have done. Companies that had stimulated the world's thirst for imperial teas now aroused new globalized tastes for coffee, Coke, hamburgers, and other foods and drinks that directly competed with tea. And yet businesses perpetually blamed consumers for the source of change!

The same companies that were selling rival beverages and introducing new foods paid for market research to discover why consumers were no longer excited by tea. In 1962 J. Lyons, for example, hired Ernest Dichter to study the coffee and tea market in the UK. Dichter conducted in-depth interviews, and, as in the United States, respondents invariably contrasted coffee and tea.

Whether or not they actually liked coffee, they described coffee bars and the drink as European or Middle Eastern, exotic, special, and an important part of nightlife and dating culture. "When I think of espresso bars," one person explained, "I associate them with various types of black-jeans and motorcycles. Pretty daring sort of thing you know. They are usually dark, intimate . . . and one feels bold somehow sitting in one, sort of doing something special."[79] Even those past their teen years felt the same way. "When I go out with my husband to an espresso bar I always take espresso coffee and listen to all that music," recalled one young housewife, but then she added, "at home we have tea mostly."[80] Dichter concluded that coffee "is seen as more 'fun' and [a] pleasure drink than is tea by comparison. The image of coffee is identified with *young people*—with excitement and has a gay flair. Though coffee is a foreign drink, it is not foreign in a negative way but is identified with *worldliness*. Because of its more *libertine* image, and partly because of inherent conservatism, older people are less inclined to consume coffee."[81] He further explained that while the "coffee bar provides a sense of excitement and a feeling that it is the 'smart thing to do,' . . . among older conservative groups it is sometimes identified with 'beatniks,' 'teddy boys' and other unconventional types."[82] Unconventional sensuality was exactly what Ray Gosling enjoyed but others found distasteful. As one person put it, "When I think of espresso bars I think of bars, and horrible juke boxes, and beatniks in it. I tend to avoid those places, and if I have to go in it is only by force."[83]

In 1964 the advertising agency Ogilvy and Mather prepared a market report for the Tea Board and it too introduced the idea that the two brews occupied different consumer worlds:

> Since the beginning of the last war many thousands of refugees, immigrants, students and businessmen have entered the U.K. from countries where the coffee habit is widespread, and their influence is making itself increasingly felt. Again, coffee machines have spawned thousands of coffee bars out-dating the tea-shops almost overnight, and the young have flocked to these coffee bars where they could relax in an atmosphere of modernity.[84]

"Modernity" was an amorphous and flexible term that in this context implied a new and relaxed atmosphere. According to Ogilvy and Mather, young people were setting these new trends.[85] As we saw in discussions of Canada and Australia, market researchers also proposed that refugees and immigrants from "countries where the coffee habit is widespread" were bringing their "coffee machines" and making the tea shop an outmoded institution.

Despite the allure of the coffee bar, tea's real competitor was instant coffee. The Swiss-owned firm Nestlè and the American company Maxwell House controlled 90 percent of the instant coffee market in Britain in 1959, and both conglomerates spent a huge amount on advertising.[86] It became quite clear to those in the industry that, while espresso and cappuccino might have endowed coffee with a new European identity, in fact, instant coffee was a much bigger threat to tea. In 1964 the British housewife's average weekly expenditure on tea was down by 10 percent, about 5d. a week, while the average amount spent on coffee was up by 3d. a week. Commenting on this discovery, a caption in *The Grocer* simply stated: "Tea Sales *Down*. Coffee Sales *Up*."[87] *The Times, Manchester Guardian,* and *Financial Times* agreed with the *Sun*, which stated: "The biggest threat to Britain's 'Nation of Tea Drinkers' today is instant coffee."[88] *The Times* put these shifts in a wider context, explaining how housewives were increasingly buying the "labour-saving products" produced by the new "food technology—freezing, powdering, and new forms of canning."[89] This coffee did not taste good, but it seemed ever so modern and convenient.

During the 1960s, British market researchers conducted a number of surveys that asked thousands of Britons about their "attitudes" toward beverages, brands, and the consumer cultures that surrounded commodities.[90] Market researchers probed domestic economies and health issues, but they were most interested in how consumers perceived drinks as reflective of their "lifestyle" and "aspirations." They encouraged consumers to *explain* how their prejudices and desires affected their shopping habits, and this in turn encouraged people to think of themselves as consumers whose identities were shaped by what they bought, wore, and ate. These surveys also assumed, as Dichter had proposed in the 1950s, that commodities had personalities. Summarizing their findings of a "tea attitude survey," Ogilvy and Mather reported that although "tea is very well liked" and was "an all-class" beverage, it lacked glamour. Tea was "traditional, and that was a bad thing in 1965."[91] This study sampled housewives and a small number of "unmarried persons" between ages sixteen and twenty-four. Both groups were asked to compare tea, coffee, milk, cocoa, and soft drinks in terms of where, when, and how these drinks fit their lifestyle. Although Ogilvy and Mather were unaware of this, respondents' comments demonstrate the success of previous Tea Board and brand advertising. Housewives, for example, told researchers that they liked tea because

> "It bucks you up, it refreshes you . . . it gives you that much strength that you can carry on."

> "Tea gives you a lift, more energy—a new lease on life."

"When you've got worries it takes your mind off them and helps you think and relaxes you."

"It's more like a friend really because the first thing you fly to is a cup of tea."

"If I wasn't offered tea at a friend's house, I wouldn't feel welcome."[92]

Decades of advertising had described tea as reviving, comforting, and relaxing during stressful periods, and in a sense this is how tea's consumer culture had developed in the twentieth century. It was not fun, exotic, or even vaguely foreign. When asked about Chinese teas, the housewives invariably revealed insular attitudes with comments such as:

"People say China tea's weak and scented and if it is scented I wouldn't like it."

"I didn't like it. It had a scenty taste to it and a scented smell as well."

"I didn't know the Chinese liked tea."

"The Chinese couldn't know how to make good tea."[93]

Here we see the type of anti-Chinese rhetoric of the early and mid-nineteenth-century adulteration scare and much subsequent Indian and Ceylon tea advertising. British tea was black, unscented, and straightforward. Consumers did not have the same knowledge about the product that their mothers and grandmothers had possessed, but in a sense they had inherited some of their prejudices. Ogilvy and Mather delved further and found that most British consumers also

had not heard of *Darjeeling* tea and only two or three had tried it. One quarter of the sample only thought it would be Indian tea. It was expected that it would be an expensive, better quality tea a little stronger than normal probably. It was thought it would be a bit "posh". Our informants did not think that they would like it and evinced no desire to try it. It was thought that it might be scented which was seen as a disadvantage.[94]

Along the same lines, "Informants had only very vague and confused notions about the growing, blending and packing of tea." While some knew it came from China, India, and Ceylon, "most did not know where their own tea came from and did not appear to regard this as important." Several respondents denied "having heard of India or Ceylon tea."[95] Some revealed a muddled geography shaped by television commercials. One respondent "conjured up a vision of an Indian teashop where the girl from the Turkish Delight commercial served black tea."[96]

Such consumer ignorance was a product of a long history in which the big brands had won the battle over the meaning of the commodity. The major importers had blended teas since the late nineteenth century and had generally resisted country-of-origin labeling. At key points, such as during the late 1920s and early 1930s, again during the war, in the Tea Centre, at school, and on the deck of the *Cutty Sark*, planters' associations cultivated knowledge about tea as a product of the empire, but they had also presented tea as a pick-me-up, a working-class right, a form of relief or social welfare, particularly for poor working women. Thus, it is not surprising that most young housewives, many of whom were born during or just after the war, did not think of the empire when they brewed their tea. This does not mean that imperialism was not shaping metropolitan society and culture. The planting industries were paying experts for such surveys. They had simply been so successful in selling tea as a friendly, mild, and innocent pleasure, a solace in hard times, and the drink that got one through the war, that now it lacked the glamour of "European" espresso, the convenience of instant coffee, the novelty of Coca-Cola, or the exoticism of empire.

The key problem, Ogilvy and Mather explained to their clients, was that tea had been around too long. Tea shops, for example, had "a desirable olde world image of a clean, homely place in the country which serves homemade cakes and scones" or "a less desirable town teashop where the tea is stewed, lukewarm and served in thick cups in scruffy surroundings."[97] Most such places "[help] downgrade the image of tea in a fashionable sense—particularly with young people who spend a great deal of their leisure time in social pursuits outside the home."[98] Moreover, the drink of austerity no longer fit "these days of an affluent and expanding economy. People with money to spend now wanted new things and new foods. Young, fashionable people have already decimated the traditional English breakfast in favour of cereals and toast," warned an agency report, and thus "unless protective action is taken coffee could invade the home for a meal that has long been a most important traditional tea drinking occasion." The agency recommended that tea embark on a major "generic campaign to protect and increase the size of the overall market . . . [to] provide a bigger cake for all to share."[99] The diverse tea industry had to put aside its differences so that "tea" could better fight coffee and Coke.[100] The proliferation of new drink cultures need not have displaced tea, but this is how market experts understood and responded to the decline of the hot brew.

"JOIN THE TEA SET": REBRANDING TEA IN THE
SWINGING SIXTIES

"The coffee-bar generation is apt to think of tea-drinking as what Mum and Dad did during the air raids," explained one trade expert in 1965.[101] Everyone in the industry assumed tea had an image problem. Experts were not dismayed, however, for if espresso machines and instant coffee had rebranded coffee, why couldn't tea change as well? Virtually all brands sought to make over tea, but the UK Tea Council led the way when in 1965 it launched a massive campaign that asked "hip" young Britons to "Join the Tea Set." The chairman of the Tea Trade Committee, an organization that represented buyers, first raised the idea in 1963, stating it was time for "all sides of the industry" to "get together and raise a large sum of money to promote a 'DRINK MORE TEA' campaign in the U.K."[102] Ceylon and India considered whether doing so would undermine their efforts to brand their nation's tea.[103] However, the growing fear of rival beverages convinced them to once again join hands.[104] They continued to promote their own produce as well but agreed to fund and join the new UK Tea Council.[105] Based in London, the council was modeled on the International Tea Market Expansion Board, the U.S. Tea Council, and the Pan American Coffee Bureau.[106] But in fact tea had, as we have seen, repeatedly done this sort of thing.

The tea trade hired Mather and Crowther (soon to be Ogilvy and Mather) as their advertising agency to develop tea's exciting new image. A medium-sized agency that had been around since 1850, it was known for its famous generic advertising for Milk, Eggs, Fish, Fruit, Gas, Electricity, and Tea.[107] As we have seen, tea had engaged in generic advertising since the late nineteenth century, but in the 1950s, experts believed these kinds of campaigns were primarily intended to "arrest long-term sales declines: declines, unite competitors who in happier times would not dream of cooperating."[108] At the end of 1964, Mather and Crowther merged with New York–based Ogilvy, Benson and Mather to become Ogilvy and Mather International, a multinational giant, with billings of nearly £50 million a year and accounts in seven countries in North America and Europe.[109] This Anglo-American conglomerate produced the Join the Tea Set campaign, but the same old hands that sold tea since the 1930s ran the UK Tea Council.

Gervas Huxley served as the first chairman of the UK Tea Council's technical committee, resigning in 1967 only after the council was well established. The Tea Council's acting secretary was J. L. Llewellyn, the former planter who we saw had become unhinged during Partition. J. Lyons and Brooke Bond executives were members, as was advertising expert Fred Oppè.[110] In 1966 Ray Culverhouse, chairman and managing director of Ridgways, Ltd., became chairman; he had much experience representing the buying side of the business as former president of the Tea Buyers' Association and vice chairman of the Tea Trade Committee.[111] The "Sixties" generation of publicists included young, exciting ad men and women, but if we look at the Tea Council we find the same people who had sold tea since the 1930s trying to reestablish the type of relationships they had during the empire days; in fact, the UK Tea Council was in many respects simply a new version of the ITMEB.

Old rivalries and jealousies also materialized with this new effort. Before the Tea Council came into being, Ogilvy and Mather conducted market research, drew up plans, and presented proposals, but the various players involved could not even agree on what to call the "nonprofit" body. Distributors disliked the term "council," seeing it as old-fashioned and associated with "parish councils, local church councils, council schools, and the like: It is in fact not 'with it.'"[112] Producing nations, however, already sat on similar councils elsewhere and associated the term with up-to-date public relations. Responding to concerns, Mather and Crowther sampled reactions to possible alternatives, proposing Tea Expansion Association or Tea Expansion Alliance (both of which could be shortened to TEA). Evidently they found the term "council" wasn't so bad after all, and the UK Tea Council acquired the name it held for over half a century.

In addition to the squabbling over the body's name, financial tensions among producing nations threatened the whole operation. Mather and Crowther had planned a major campaign designed to dwarf competitors' ad campaigns, assuming that India and Ceylon would foot the bill. However, Ceylon only agreed to a small sum—Rs. 15 lakhs annually (£112,500). India offered Rs. 25 lakhs or £187,500 for only one year. Other producers agreed "in principle to contribute," but as late as August 1965—a month before the scheduled launch of the campaign—they would not specify an actual amount.[113] Insecure financing forced Mather and Crowther to scale back and cut the budget by more than half from £1,500,000 to £600,000 a year.[114] This was of course only a fraction of the overall budget spent to promote tea in the UK, but industry estimates showed that both brand and trade advertising spent on tea was far below that of beer, wine, and other beverages, whether measured as a gross total or proportion of overall sales.[115] In the end, India and Ceylon did commit nearly half the funding, and distributors gave the other half, while in 1966 Kenya, Tanzania, Uganda, Malawi, and Portuguese East Africa also donated to these efforts.[116] This was not an auspicious beginning.

The source of the problem was not just money. Producing nations were also reticent to join forces because they had been working since independence to establish "uninational" brands and they were interested in creating several new markets rather than just reviving old ones. India had been directing its energies at home, in Eastern Europe, and in the Middle East and was unsure about how to proceed in the UK, where Ceylon had been in charge of most of the industry-level advertising.[117] All producers were also casting a new eye at Western Europe since the European Economic Community, which came into being in 1957, had abolished tea duties in 1964.[118] Producers had also independently begun to rebrand tea as youthful before the UK Tea Council came into being. For example, picking up on the new image of India as a site of youthful transgression and liberation, the Indian Tea Centre in Oxford Street specifically appealed to this rebellious market. One promotion, for example, featured the image of a "hip" young South Asian woman serving tea to nineteen-year-old "Welshman" Mike Jones during a tea-drinking contest. Jones won by downing eighty-seven cups in fifteen hours (fig. 11.3). India was thus renovating its own image to encourage young people to see tea as an Indian, not an imperial, product, and the India they hoped to sell was as exotic and sexy as a Soho coffee bar, or so they hoped.

FIGURE 11.3. Nineteen-year-old Welshman Mike Jones drinks eighty-seven cups of tea in fifteen hours at the Indian Tea Centre. (Trinity Mirror/Mirrorpix/Alamy)

While producing governments were cautious about the UK Tea Council, the advertising industry, packers, brokers, and large retailers were generally enthusiastic about the new body and its proposed ad campaign.[119] Great Britain should not be lost without a fight, offered Arthur Parker, a leading tea broker. At the Annual Tea Trade Dinner in London in 1964, he urged: "We should turn at once to the problems on our very doorstep . . . [and] encourage the younger generation to drink tea."[120] J. R. Sumner, Ty-Phoo's chairman, was also strongly behind the Tea Council, believing that "from a long term point of view," the industry had to capture the "younger generation."[121] Sumner backed up this belief with cash, providing £200,000 to the campaign for the first year, approximately a third of its annual budget. Brooke Bond was equally motivated.[122]

Finally in 1965, after two years of planning, the Tea Council launched the multiyear campaign that asked young Britons to "Join the Tea Set." This was a pun on the meaning of "set" as both an "in" group and a term for tea ware. It also referred to marijuana consumption, which is probably why Pink Floyd was first known as the Tea Set in 1964.[123] A Dutch rock group also performed under this name.[124] Whether the Tea Council was aware of it or not, the slogan had prior meanings associated with rock 'n' roll, drugs, and youth culture. They tamed such meanings, however, when they defined the "tea set" as young, heterosexual, and playful consumers. The campaign nevertheless celebrated Britain's supposedly classless and multiethnic postwar society. The new tea drinker was not just peppy but exciting, unrestrained, and cosmopolitan. Essentially the campaign sought to appropriate the sexy coffee bar culture, but instead it watered down youth culture's edginess.

A "tea teach-in" held at the Savoy Hotel on 21 September 1965 announced the objectives of the Join the Tea Set Campaign. The "teach-in" was in fact a press conference designed to spread the word that an old beverage was about to get a "more fashionable, more exciting and more modern image." British and foreign news agencies such as American magazines *Newsweek* and *Business Week*, the BBC, ITV, and the Central Office of Information attended the event. Dignitaries, celebrities, and the leading importers, packers, brokers, and tea associations were there as well. Gunapala Piyasena Malalasekera, Ceylon's high commissioner for Canada and his country's permanent representative to the U.N., K. S. Raghupathi, minister of economics for India, and Mr. Dennis Phombeah, administrative attaché for Tanzania who was also the secretary-general of the Committee of African Organizations in London, and other politicians listened to speeches by J. R. Vernede, then chairman of the Tea Council, and Ray Culverhouse. They looked at mock-ups of advertisements, previewed television commercials, and enjoyed the music of two current pop sensations, Unit 4 + 2 and the Ivy League, who were also going to perform in the Tea Council's commercials.[125]

This "teach-in" exemplifies tea's strategy in the 1960s and 1970s. The industry ran after the new, trying to learn and replicate what they thought young people enjoyed. Businessmen and women, the international media, and African and Asian trade ministers were celebrating a new face of tea while listening to pop bands. Although largely forgotten today, Unit 4 + 2's single "Concrete and Clay" hit number 1 on the charts in April 1965, pushing out the Rolling Stones' "The Last Time," which had held onto the position for three weeks. Unit 4 + 2 thus briefly joined the likes of Elvis Presley, the Beatles, the Hollies, the Byrds, Tom Jones, the Kinks, the Moody Blues, and several other performers who were at the top of the charts at this time.[126] The Ivy League's moment of glory was briefer than that of Unit 4 + 2. The vocal trio formed in 1964, first performed as background vocalists for The Who's single "I Can't Explain" and then recorded several hits that made the top ten and one album, *This Is the Ivy League*, in 1965.[127] Both bands were short-lived sensations, achieving just enough notoriety for the UK Tea Council to hire them.

Paul Jones and the band to which he belonged at the time, Manfred Mann, also sang for their tea. Television commercials featured these musicians holding simple black display cards printed with words and phrases such as "refreshing," "delicious," "reviving," and "thirst quenching" and performed a jingle asking people to "Join the Tea Set."[128] Mimicking the satirical humor of the Beatles, in one commercial the band pretends to be a firing squad whose victim's last request is a cup of tea, while Paul Jones sings, "Deny me . . . decry me but babe don't deprive me of my rightful cup of tea."[129] The council, like many companies, also manufactured celebrities. In 1967 the Tea Council announced a competition in which pop groups could get their "big chance" and appear on TV—all they had to do was compose a song titled "Join the Tea Set." The winning song could not resemble jingles already on television and the only catch was the band would thereafter have to be known as "The Tea Set."[130] The winners won a TV audition, a recording session with a major label, and the publication of the song titled "The Tea Set." The winning group, five men and one woman, thus became a "living advertisement for tea."[131]

"The objective of the advertising is to up-date Tea with a more fashionable, more exciting and more modern image, and with an appeal to youth," explained *Tea Campaign News*, the Tea Council's trade publication.[132] In addition to television featuring (or creating) pop stars, the campaign tried to make tea youthful by, for example, inventing recipes for nonalcoholic cocktails, or "mar-tea-nees," and sponsoring dance contests and pirate radio programs.[133] The UK Tea Council's sister bodies in other countries produced a similar commercialized form of youth culture. The Tea Council of Australia even managed to hire the Beatles to drink tea on one of its television commercials.[134] The New Zealand Tea Council

FIGURE 11.4. "Surf'N Tea." Advertisement brochure, New Zealand Tea Council, c. 1965. (New Zealand Tea Council/Hocken Collections/Uare Taoka o Hakena/ University of Otago)

promoted tea as part of surf culture and recommended recipes that went well with sand, sun, and fun (fig. 11.4). In commenting on the use of popular music to sell tea, one ad executive explained in 1966, "Endorsement from stars such as these carries great weight with the public."[135] This stiff explanation reveals the anxious dance in which business, performers, and other tastemakers vied for teenagers' attention. All of these dancers assumed that music, media, and marketing could harness youthful desires.

Posters and print and TV ads presented tea drinkers as a cohort of hip young people with long hair, dressed in black, and sporting turtlenecks, "tea shirts," miniskirts, jeans, and other new fashions. Claiming to be jazz and folk musicians, bohemian intellectuals, and fashion designers, Britain's artistic youth joined the Tea Set (fig. 11.5). In one very frequently used advertisement, four girls who were trying to break into the fashion industry exclaim: "We're in fashion, so is tea!"[136] Another set of commercials featured the working-class actor from Liverpool, Tony Booth, remembered for playing the left-wing Mike Rawlins on the sitcom *Till Death Us Do Part* (1965–75) and notable as the father of Cherie Booth, wife of

FIGURE 11.5. "Join the Tea Set." UK Tea Council, advertising, 1965–66. (By permission of the British Library shelf mark, ITA Mss Eur F174/805 and UK Tea Council)

Prime Minister Tony Blair. Somehow or other tea managed to never stray very far from politics and popular culture. At the time, however, Booth and the other young hipsters in the Tea Set commercials presented consumer culture as a shared social practice and a form of play, demonstrating belonging in a tea-drinking yet youthful subculture. Tea Council ads photographed subjects in motion, with bodies seemingly free of constraints. Often they were literally nowhere. Stylistically the ads imitated poses and motifs of high fashion photography and rock music.

The Tea Council also engaged in numerous promotions and produced a large number of kitschy collectibles. Silly puns and campaign slogans written in psychedelic graphics appeared on "tea shirts," hats, buttons, and bumper stickers. One set of buttons from 1966–67 played on the famous World War I recruiting poster but had Lord Kitchener tell the public to "Make Tea Not War." It is not clear when this phrase first appeared. Monty Python's Flying Circus satirized the phrase in a skit featuring a gang of "Hell's grannies" spraying "Make Tea Not Love" on a wall behind an innocent bobby. Wherever it came from, "Make Tea Not War" is still a fixture in the antiwar lexicon to this day. Slogans, collectibles, and psychedelic graphics arrogated left-leaning politics and student rebellions, but such appropriations can and did move back into political culture. All over Britain, the Tea Council hosted beauty contests, battles of the bands, dance and singing contests in such places as the Rank Ballrooms and at Pontin's holiday camps, sporting events, and even rock and folk music festivals.[137] In 1966 a Tea Set Tea Bar was opened in Slough. Though Slough's Tea Bar had a jukebox and "mod" decor, it was unlikely that young people would see this as an improvement on an espresso bar or even the Tea Board's Tea Centres.[138] Slough, that much-disparaged symbol of postindustrial Britain most recently satirized as home to the paper company in the BBC's comedy series *The Office*, nevertheless was perhaps a perfect location for the cultural battles between young and old, coffee and tea, urban and rural.

Disk jockeys and television personalities, Emperor Rosko, Paul Burnett, and quite unfortunately Jimmy Savile also asked Britons to Join the Tea Set. In the 1960s and 1970s, this prankster celebrity was involved in numerous charities and hosted *Top of the Pops* and several television series. Savile also became one of the most well-known spokespersons for tea. Sporting long white hair, a big cigar, large sunglasses, and track suits, Savile appeared at hundreds of promotional events. In 1973, for example, with Murray Kash, Savile hosted promotions known as "Tea Goes Pop around the Country." The two men visited Sunderland, Hemel Hempstead, Leeds, and other towns, meeting local dignitaries, judging beauty contests, and meeting throngs of teens.[139] Savile inserted puff pieces about tea in his weekly column in the *Sunday People* (13 million readers), on his BBC TV series (audience of 18 million), and on his weekly radio program, *Savile's Travels* (audience of 5 million). He went to youth clubs and charity and sporting events in a large bus that displayed various Tea Council slogans. Wearing a "Tea-rific T-shirt," he led 30,000 people on a charity walk in Southampton.[140] Since his death in 2011, investigations have revealed that Savile committed literally hundreds of acts of sexual abuse, revelations that paint a very different picture of Savile's pied-piper charms.[141] The tea industry wanted a rakish, intemperate, and ill-behaved image. Sadly they got much more than they bargained for.

Not all Tea Council advertising starred the young, however. Worried about losing older committed tea drinkers, Tea Council ads also included brass bands and middle-aged businessmen. Irish comic Dermot Kelly, for example, played an aging, working-class, self-deprecating tea drinker in several ads.[142] These ads may have been a direct response to consumers such as one "lady" who worriedly asked, "But you will let the older ones, also, drink tea, won't you?" To which the Tea Council responded: "Younger ones, older ones—everyone can Join the Tea Set!"[143] Ads also appeared in traditional women's magazines and mainstream journals, which created an updated and youthful domesticity. In 1966 the Tea Council began a drive to get Britons to drink tea at night while they watched television. A set of ads thus portrayed happy young families snuggled on the couch in front of the telly. But the Tea Council was far more interested in creating new consumers because older folks did not require much attention.

Finally, the Tea Council also urged caterers to "Join the Tea Set" by updating their decor and brewing better tea.[144] Booklets and trade advertising pushed new tea-making paraphernalia and quality tea and encouraged caterers to use more leaf when brewing for the masses.[145] A 1968 ad showed a man pouring his tea into an aspidistra, and the copy asked: "Do you give them the kind of tea that would kill an aspidistra? Lots of caterers do."[146] The Caterers' Tea Advisory Service, the public relations arm of the Tea Council, could provide help. This was thus simply a revised version of the ITMEB's National Catering Service, and hence for all its apparent novelty, the Tea Council was very similar to the types of organizations we have traced in this book.

The Tea Council's efforts slowed but did not halt shifting drink habits. Experts tend to agree that for generic campaigns to work they need to be extremely well funded and long lasting.[147] In its first three years, the Tea Council spent £2.6 million, but this was relatively modest in comparison to what was spent on advertising other foods and beverages. In late 1968 an independent survey urged that the campaign continue for another five years, but two of the larger firms pulled out and with them the campaign lost 30 percent of its budget. In 1969 Brooke Bond Liebig, Ltd., Ty-Phoo, and India, Ceylon, and Kenya funded a very limited "holding" campaign with a tiny budget of £185,000 for 1969–70.[148] Scholars have seen the pruning of this campaign as an example of the eroding relationship between the UK and India during these years, but in fact the Tea Council's fate was shaped by older tensions within the global tea industry.[149] After a full decade of cooperative advertising, Indian producers were frustrated and complained that rival beverages were better advertised and promoted.[150] India wanted more imaginative advertising and quicker and more accurate feedback from "consuming countries." At times producers professed a desire to return to the type of cooperative promotions seen in the days of the International Tea Market Expansion Board, without losing their distinctive brand identity at home or in foreign markets. Indian producers complained that the government had followed a confused and ambivalent marketing policy particularly in the UK; as a result, "the traditional habit of tea drinking is facing a gradual erosion as the age group accustomed to it is slowly disappearing."[151] Growers still believed in advertising, but the Join the Tea Set Campaign and related promotions outside of the UK had simply failed to compete. Producing nations, and not British corporations, suffered the most, from tea's inexorable losses.

North Americans, Britons, South Asians, and Africans had jointly created the UK Tea Council and the Join the Tea Set Campaign to brand tea as a symbol of a new postcolonial, swinging Britain. They harnessed the energy and excitement of youth culture, but the Tea Council, like earlier entities, was also the child of Victorian tea parties, exhibitions, and trade associations, though the fiction of a united industry with its empire of tea was getting harder and harder to sustain. Massive social change and shifting global political economies in the 1960s and 1970s left the tea industry in a relatively weak position to compete with new beverages and lifestyles. While many major industries similarly characterized their products as modern and youthful, this effort by the tea industry has allowed us to see how multinational firms, marketing experts, and postcolonial governments contributed to the making of modern Britain. India and England still had a shared history, though now it was the Indian government and Indian planters who sought to modernize and update the metropole. They did not do this on their own, however, and South Asia found it necessary to employ American methods and firms to sell to Britons. Together, American and British ad men, European-turned-American market researchers, celebrities, and media personalities manufactured new images of the tea consumer to replace Mazawattee's granny, the Edwardian lady of leisure, and even the YMCA volunteers who served tea to Indian soldiers during the war.

The Join the Tea Set Campaign and UK Tea Council were not able to stave off decline but were able to keep tea in Britain's national culture despite shrinking markets. We should not interpret the decline in tea drinking as a failure of advertising per se or even a reflection of the decline of Britain, however. Coke, espresso, and instant coffee arrived just as the tea industry was undergoing the most painful period of decolonization and postwar rebuilding. Tea was not in a very good position to compete and, even more important, may not have wanted to. Indian producers and the Indian government were wary of being dependent on the British market and they successfully built other trade relations and a vibrant domestic market for tea. Pakistan (and later Bangladesh) for obvious reasons refused to work with India, and mounting tensions between India and Ceylon did not help matters. Ceylon/Sri Lanka continued advertising but only had a slim budget to combat sliding markets. Moreover, I would argue that a huge but often unacknowledged problem was the fact that the big companies were fickle in their support, sold other beverages, and introduced new diets and lifestyles that made tea seem old-fashioned.

Beyond these structural realignments, however, tea did have a very pronounced image as a temperate and moral brew in many markets. This understanding was imported from China in the seventeenth century and was taken up by liberals, evangelicals, Quaker merchants, colonial politicians and businessmen, and consumers. Nomadic planters added the notion of imperial duty and the benefits of machine production and plantations. In the 1930s and during the war, tea became a friend and comfort, the drink that allowed one to stay calm and carry on. All of these ideas had been repeated over a long period of time, over and over again. Perhaps the best evidence that they had taken hold is that in the 1950s and 1960s, Britons who were asked described tea as a cheerful pick-me-up. Advertising worked, but sobriety, domesticity, and empire had gone out of fashion. Tea's image had not changed, but the world around it had.

Tea's history allows us then to think of postwar consumer society a bit differently. Instead of focusing on expanding markets, new commodities and forms of leisure, and the cultivation of profitable global youth markets, we should perhaps think in terms of restructuring, in which older pastimes, foods and drinks, and fashions were abandoned, markets shrank, and businesses failed. Capitalism is of course just as much about destroying the old as it is about producing the new. Looked at this way, we might also need to revise our sense of the 1960s and 1970s and see this as the moment when a particular phase of an imperial and industrial-based consumer society declined to make way for new global commodities, companies, and cultural influences. Some British industries, particularly fashion and music, prospered in this new consumer revolution, but tea fared rather badly.

While it is beyond the scope of this book to write this history, it is very important to point out that tea did not decline everywhere. In South Asia, Africa, and the Middle East, and even among certain consumers in the United States, tea did become part of postcolonial, postwar consumer revolutions. While young Britons, Canadians, Australians, and New Zealanders defined themselves against their parents' generation by rejecting tea, young people in Africa and South and Southeast Asia may have picked up a taste for the brew for the same reasons, but perhaps for other reasons as well. Further research that looks at both consumer cultures and political economies in postcolonial nations will likely reveal the degree to which tea's trade and consumption forged new identities and global relationships, even as its production has retained some of the inequalities of the age of empire. Decline as a framework only fits tea's history in the British metropole and a handful of former settler colonies; a truly global perspective that investigates the late twentieth century may look quite different.

AFTERTASTES

FIGURE 11.6. Frank Sinatra drinks tea at the Royal Albert Hall. UK Tea Council Annual Report, 1975. (By permission of the British Library shelf mark ITA Mss Eur F174/804 and UK Tea Council)

A photograph of Frank Sinatra drinking the "cup that cheers" onstage in the Royal Albert Hall appeared on the cover of the UK Tea Council's annual report in 1975 (fig. 11.6). The report was tucked away in the huge archive of the Indian Tea Association housed in what used to be known as the Oriental and India Office Collections in the British Library. Discovering this compelling image of an aging American celebrity situated in the midst of an imperial business archive in the center of London inspired me to write this book. I had been exploring the Tea Association's archive in order to investigate the imperial dimensions of British consumer culture, but I had not intended to write a whole book on tea. I assumed that we already knew a great deal about the commodity and its place in British culture and global commerce. Sinatra's perplexing portrait intrigued me, however, for it dislodged my sense that I understood this history or even what constituted British history. My first thought was: Why were the records of the UK Tea Council housed in this colonial business archive? I also wondered whether those who read the council's annual report would have considered, as I did, Frank Sinatra a peculiar icon to sell tea in 1975. To my mind, Sinatra was a cocktail-drinking Italian American celebrity from Hoboken, New Jersey, who spent more time in Las Vegas than London. Granted, in 1975 Sinatra was not quite the rebel he had been, but the crooner still projected a sexy bad-boy masculinity that seemed to have nothing whatsoever to do with tea, and so I laughed a bit as I read William Cowper's famous, albeit misquoted, phrase, "the cup that cheers," positioned above Sinatra's portrait. At that moment, I felt driven to uncover the world that could encompass an eighteenth-century evangelical poet and a twentieth-century American entertainer. I wanted to unearth the history that made the pairing of Sinatra and tea so strange and the phrase "the cup that cheers" so familiar.

As I would learn, the UK Tea Council was yet another iteration of the transnational corporate bodies whose histories I have chronicled in this book; and thus its records belonged with those of the Indian Tea Cess Committee, the Ceylon Tea Propaganda Board, the U.S. Tea Council, and the International Tea Market Expansion Board. An international ad agency, multinational food corporations, South Asian and African governments, and of course the indomitable Gervas Huxley had created this promotional body. Far smaller and much less impressive than East India House, Plantation House, or the Chicago World's Fair, the UK Tea Council was nevertheless constructed out of the same materials and desires as these earlier marketplaces.

And yet why Sinatra? In 1975 he could still fill the Royal Albert Hall, but both Sinatra and tea were staging a comeback in London. However, the real question is why we think it odd that tea was paired with an American celebrity who was known to imbibe "harder" beverages, as though one could not enjoy both cocktails and tea. As we have seen, many cultures have long proposed this opposition and a great deal of advertising has also made us think in these terms. Additionally, we are so used to images of tea as a feminine and British drink, it is simply hard to imagine the American producers and consumers who have played an important role in creating the empire of tea. Concepts such as Americanization simply do not capture the long-lived transnational exchanges that made tea one of the most popular drinks in the world, and for some one of the most distasteful brews as well. Frank Sinatra's portrait, like Mr. T. Pott, Gracie Fields, and even Jimmy Savile, was a legacy of empire and an attempt to erase knowledge of that past.

In 1970s Great Britain, no amount of advertising could remove tea's slightly bitter aftertaste. While many Britons seem to have forgotten the imperial origins of their national drink, the decline of tea in the postwar world was a remnant of a time when so many had worked to sell this commodity as a moral, sobering, industrious, and imperial good. Those associations were hard to shake in part because 1950s corporate advertising had often placed tea in scenes from the British past. This, along with long-term structural problems in the tea trade and numerous changes in family, gender, and national identities, made tea unpalatable to many consumers by 1975.

The postcolonial tea industry exudes what Paul Gilroy has detected as a melancholic disorientation that came with the loss of colonial certainties.[152] After World War II and during decolonization, planters and distributors first tried to reassert certainties by updating the methods and style of advertising they had relied on for centuries. This produced nostalgic expressions of neo-Victorianism and a revival of working-class popular comic culture. By the mid-1960s, nostalgia had itself become problematic, and the Tea Council wholeheartedly went for a streamlined, efficient, sexy, youth-oriented culture of modernity. None of these developments determined how much tea was bought and drunk, but they did help people remember *and* forget about Great Britain's imperial past. Sinatra's image, like that of the Indian soldiers on the front cover of this book, exemplifies the multifaceted global history of modern Britain, the deep-rooted history of contemporary global consumer society, and the everyday and almost imperceptible ways in which we live in a world shaped by an imperial past.

In *A Thirst for Empire*, I have thus revisited questions that Sidney Mintz raised over thirty years ago when he asked how a commodity such as sugar could be a source both of delight and pleasure and of exploitation and unhappiness, often for the same person at the same time.[153] Like Mintz, I have demonstrated some of Great Britain's particular contributions to the making and unmaking of global capitalism and consumer society. Looking at these questions from the vantage point of the twenty-first century, however, during a time when nationalism, fundamentalism, and racism have resurfaced as defensive responses to the inequities of globalization, I have been particularly concerned with how global capitalism has produced both ideologies of internationalism and multiple articulations of nationalism and racism. Mintz highlighted the racism inherent in Atlantic slavery and the unequal class system that emerged during England's industrial revolution. I have amended the relationship between culture and capitalism that he proposed by arguing that class, gender, and race produced the very structures and ideologies of global capitalism and consumer cultures. I have also argued that there was not a linear commodity chain carrying goods produced in the Global South to consumers in the Global North. Production and consumption happened at the same time in many places. Distribution was a constantly shifting, highly contentious arena in which different companies, colonies, nations, and individuals fought for power and profits, all the while claiming to civilize consumers, laborers, and nations. Yet pushing temperance and cheerfulness had very different outcomes in colonial India, the 1890s United States, apartheid-era South Africa, and 1960s Great Britain.

When I began writing this book, I did not foresee the way that tea would uncannily show up as a protagonist in key events, movements, and turning points in Britain's domestic and international history. Of course, I knew the role it had played in the American Revolution and the creation of bourgeois domesticity and gender identities, and I also knew that it had stimulated tired industrial workers, but I had not been aware of how early modern Britons and North American colonists incorporated Chinese ideals and culture as they imported their tea, even as they condemned mercantilism and Chinese and British monopolies. Beset by war, disease, and revolution, early modern Britons and nineteenth-century evangelicals, liberals, and working-class consumers desired health, sobriety, and a calming influence on their society. Ironically, this desire shaped the geography and timing of colonial conquest, altered power relations in Asia, and created new sources of inequality, wealth, and poverty. Tea was often said to belong in the "domestic" and feminine realm, and yet women often championed tea and imperialism in the public sphere. The industry was moreover perpetually trying to expand markets through creating masculine tea cultures in the workplace and army and through advertising images of men, such as Frank Sinatra, drinking tea. Tea also showed up during the heady days of Edwardian liberal politics and helped the interwar Conservative Party redefine itself. It calmed Britons as they faced the terrors of war, survived the bleak years of postwar austerity, and manufactured the youth culture of the Swinging Sixties. This history thus has demonstrated how everyday habits reveal "the outside that is inside British history."[154]

Additionally, tea illuminates the "outside" that is in South Asian, African, and American history, histories that I have only begun to outline in this book. Here I have sought to show how tea tightly bound together the United Kingdom with its empire, former colonies, and trading partners through daily habits and bodily desires, through myriad financial and commercial relations, and through a global network of salesmen and women who managed tea's image as an industry, a commodity, and a beverage. This has enabled me to uncover multiple points of contention and conflict among colonies and former colonies, growers and retailers, the industry and the state, labor and managers, buyers and sellers. Tea's history has thus allowed us to see the empire as a set of relationships between producers and consumers, as a taste and a habit, as an everyday encounter, and a slogan in which repetition augmented but also downplayed its significance. We must remember, however, that imperial culture did not always take an obvious, measurable, or detectable form and that it can be felt far beyond formal imperial boundaries.[155]

An apparently simple thing such as a cup of tea is in truth a constellation of ideas, communities, territories, and physical and psychological experiences. It is an empire created by the relentless movement of ideas, material, money, and people across vast territories and long time periods. I have used "a thirst for empire" not because this is a catchy turn of phrase but because tea's commercial empire exerted political power. It inevitably encountered resistance from rival empires, from small- and large-scale insurgencies, and from communities and individuals. As I have intimated, there is not just one empire of tea but several interconnected domains from which power emanated from different centers. The Chinese, Japanese, Russians, Dutch, and more recently Indians, Sri Lankans, and Kenyans also built empires surrounding this commodity, but this book has focused on the rise and fall of the British Empire of tea.

I invite others to revise this narrative by studying these other empires and the local and transnational cultures they have produced. The fact is we do not know as much as we think we do about tea. We could know a great deal more about the history of its consumption in colonial markets and how colonialism produced new desires and distastes. We could also ask how it has been possible for a handful of large European-based multinationals to still control tea's commodity chain.[156] For example, in the 1990s, Unilever held about 35 percent of the world trade in tea through acquiring Lipton (USA), Brooke Bond (UK), Salada (Canada), Bushells (Australia), and Quality Packers (New Zealand), among other firms.[157] The last decade or so indicates another reorientation as neoliberalism in India has inspired a rapid growth of Indian multinationals. In 1983, for example, Tata Tea took over James Finlay's tea estates, a highly symbolic gesture given that this was one of the first companies to set out plantations in India. Tata Global Beverages also owns the U.S. brands Eight O'Clock Coffee and Good Earth Tea, and in 2012 it entered into a partnership with Starbucks to introduce that chain into India.[158] We need to know a great deal more about how these companies influenced national and international policies, production, and global markets. We also must explore further the connections between the globalization and diversification of tea companies and decolonization. The essential characteristic of the multinational, of course, is to dispense with regional and national distinctions as it sources, manufactures, and sells multiple products. Thus, we require more historical analysis on how multinationals destroy as well as make markets, habits, tastes, and identities.

Finally, we should also admit that the discipline of history is implicated in the production of markets, consumer cultures, and capitalism. The tea industry, as I have shown, repeatedly employed historical methodologies and narratives to shape its markets, and this continues today. For example, the ubiquitous image of the Asian female tea picker gracing so much packaging and display material nevertheless continues to evoke a nostalgic and incredibly one-dimensional image of tea's past history and present conditions. Histories and cookbooks, menus and tea shops, museums, hotels, department stores, and websites also serve up equally sentimental neo-Victorian versions of afternoon tea throughout the world.[159] At the same time, tea promotions do not always conjure up the past but can also sell health, modernity, and cosmopolitanism. For example, hoping to recuperate its British and international reputation, and recapture a mass market that sold to men as well as women, India engaged in a major promotion of its tea at the London Olympics in 2012.[160] For a few short weeks, London once again became the center of an international empire of tea.

Thus, we could say that the tea party has never been, strictly speaking, a private affair. Rather, its history exemplifies the pervasive manner in which the contemporary world market has come into being, is challenged, and is reinforced. This global market did not incorporate the entire world—far from it. Nor did it always dispense with preexisting and alternative economies and cultural systems. It did not inevitably homogenize production or consumption. It did not create equality or inevitably bring democracy, but it was a historical invention that we can trace through the study of the women and men who produced and exchanged the "cup that cheers." Tea is still a product of empire, even though it is no longer an imperial product.

NOTES

INTRODUCTION: A SOLDIERS' TEA PARTY IN SURREY

1. There are countless studies of this commodity, but the academic histories that I am most indebted to include Piya Chatterjee, *A Time for Tea: Women: Labor and Post/Colonial Politics on an Indian Plantation* (Durham: Duke University Press, 2001); Jayeeta Sharma, *Empire's Garden: Assam and the Making of India* (Durham: Duke University Press, 2011); Julie E. Fromer, *A Necessary Luxury: Tea in Victorian England* (Athens: Ohio University Press, 2008); James A. Benn, *Tea in China: A Religious and Cultural History* (Honolulu: University of Hawai'i Press, 2016); Suzanne Daly, *The Empire Inside: Indian Commodities in Victorian Domestic Novels* (Ann Arbor: University of Michigan Press, 2011), chap. 4; Rudi Matthee, *The Pursuit of Pleasure: Drugs and Stimulants in Iranian History, 1500–1900* (Princeton: Princeton University Press, 2005), 237–91; Audra Jo Yoder, "Myth and Memory in Russian Tea Culture," *Studies in Slavic Cultures* 8 (2009): 65–89; and Martha Avery, *The Tea Road: China and Russia Meet across the Steppe* (Beijing: China International Press, 2003). There are many studies on tea in Japan, but an important recent work is Kristin Surak, *Making Tea, Making Japan: Cultural Nationalism in Practice* (Stanford: Stanford University Press, 2013).
2. J. R. Whiteman and S. E. Whiteman, *Victorian Woking: Being a Short Account of the Development of the Town and Parish in the Victorian Era* (Guilford: Surrey Archaeological Society, 1970), 49–52; K. Humayun Ansari, "The Woking Mosque: A Case Study of Muslim Engagement with British Society since 1889," *Immigrants & Minorities* 21, no. 3 (November 2002): 1–24; Jeffrey M. Diamond, "The Orientalist-Literati Relationship in the Northwest: G. W. Leitner, Muhammad Hussain Azad and the Rhetoric of Neo-Orientalism in Colonial Lahore," *South Asia Research* 31, no. (2011): 25–43; Mark Crinson, "The Mosque and the Metropolis," in *Orientalism's Interlocutors: Painting, Architecture, Photography*, ed. Jill Beaulieu and Mary Roberts (Durham: Duke University Press, 2002), 82–83.
3. Quoted in the introduction to *Tea on Service* (London: The Tea Centre, 1947), 14.
4. Ibid., 25.
5. *Report of the Work of the Ceylon Tea Propaganda Board* (hereafter *CTPB Report*), 1941, 21, Indian Tea Association Archive (hereafter ITA), Oriental and India Office Records, British Library, Mss Eur F174/793.
6. Ibid.
7. Yasmin Khan, *India at War: The Subcontinent and the Second World War* (Oxford: Oxford University Press, 2015), 158–62.
8. *CTPB Report*, 1942, 6.
9. H. Lu et al., "Earliest Tea as Evidence for One Branch of the Silk Road across the Tibetan Plateau," *Scientific Reports* 6 (January 2016), no. 18955; doi: 10.1038/srep18955.
10. Bennett Alan Weinberg and Bonnie K. Bealer, *The World of Caffeine: The Science and Culture of the World's Most Popular Drug* (New York: Routledge, 2002).
11. See, for example, *Materia Medica of Curative Foodstuff*, quoted in Benn, *Tea in China*, 7.

12. Susan M. Zieger, *Inventing the Addict: Drugs, Race, and Sexuality in Nineteenth-Century British and American Literature* (Amherst: University of Massachusetts Press, 2008); David T. Courtwright, *Forces of Habit: Drugs and the Making of the Modern World* (Cambridge, MA: Harvard University Press, 2001); Jordan Goodman, Paul Lovejoy, and Andrew Sherratt, eds., *Consuming Habits: Drugs in History and Anthropology* (London: Routledge, 1995).

13. Two excellent models for this sort of cultural appropriation are Brian Cowan, *The Social Life of Coffee: The Emergence of the British Coffeehouse* (New Haven: Yale University Press, 2005) and Marcy Norton, *Sacred Gifts, Profane Pleasures: A History of Tobacco and Chocolate in the Atlantic World* (Ithaca: Cornell University Press, 2008).

14. For a classic discussion of the ideas about commerce and civilization, see Albert O. Hirschman, *The Passions and the Interests: Political Arguments for Capitalism before Its Triumph* (Princeton: Princeton University Press, 1977). Also see Joyce Appleby, "Consumption in Early Modern Social Thought," in *Consumption and the World of Goods*, ed. John Brewer and Roy Porter (London: Routledge, 1993), 162–73.

15. T. J. Jackson Lears explored such apparent contradictions in *Fables of Abundance: A Cultural History of Advertising in America* (New York: Basic Books, 1994). For further discussions, see chapter 2.

16. There are a large number of general focus works on British food history. For an excellent assessment of some of the key debates and a bibliography of specialized studies and articles, see Christopher Otter, "The British Nutrition Transition and Its Histories," *History Compass* 10, no. 11 (2012): 812–25, doi: 10.1111/hic3.12001. Some of the classic general works include Arnold Palmer, *Movable Feasts: A Reconnaissance of the Origins and Consequences of Fluctuations in Meal Times with special attention to the Introduction of Luncheon and Afternoon Tea* (London: Oxford University Press, 1952); John Burnett, *Plenty and Want: A Social History of Diet in England from 1815 to the Present Day*, rev. ed. (London: Scolar Press, 1979); Jack C. Drummond and Anne Wilbraham, *The Englishman's Food: A History of Five Centuries of English Diet*, rev. Dorothy Hollingsworth (1940; London: Pimlico, 1991); Stephen Mennell, *All Manners of Food: Eating and Taste in England and France from the Middle Ages to the Present*, 2nd ed. (Urbana: University of Illinois Press, 1996); Christopher Driver, *The British at Table, 1940–1980* (London: Hogarth Press, 1983); John Walton, *Fish and Chips and the British Working Class, 1870–1940* (Leicester: Leicester University Press, 1992); Christina Hardyment, *Slice of Life: The British Way of Eating since 1945* (London: BBC Books, 1995); Ben Rogers, *Beef and Liberty: Roast Beef, John Bull and the English Nation* (London: Vintage, 2003); Derek J. Oddy, *From Plain Fare to Fusion Food: British Diet from the 1890s to the 1990s* (Suffolk: Boydell Press, 2003); C. Anne Wilson, ed., *Eating with the Victorians* (Gloucestershire: Sutton, 2004); Colin Spencer, *British Food: An Extraordinary Thousand Years of History* (New York: Columbia University Press, 2002); Laura Mason, *Food Culture in Great Britain* (Westport, CT: Greenwood Press, 2004); and Panikos Panayi, *Spicing Up Britain: The Multicultural History of British Food* (London: Reaktion, 2008). Scholars are beginning to also consider the impact of the empire and the creation of colonial foodways and practices. See, for example, Cecilia Leong-Salobir, *Food Culture in Colonial Asia: A Taste of Empire* (London: Routledge, 2011) and Lizzie Collingham, *Curry: A Tale of Cooks and Conquerors* (Oxford: Oxford University Press, 2006). On the transnational and colonial construction of South Asian food cultures, see Anita

Mannur, *Culinary Fictions: Food in South Asian Diasporic Culture* (Philadelphia: Temple University Press, 2010); Krishnendu Ray and Tulasi Srinivas, eds., *Curried Cultures: Globalization, Food and South Asia* (Berkeley: University of California Press, 2012); and Utsa Ray, *Culinary Culture in Colonial India: A Cosmopolitan Platter and the Middle Class* (Cambridge: Cambridge University Press, 2015).

17. *Tea and the Tea Trade: Parts First and Second,* with a postscript by Gideon Nye Jr. of Canton (New York: Geo. W. Wood, 1850), 5, first published in *Hunt's Merchants Magazine* (January and February 1850).

18. Okakura Kakuzo, *The Book of Tea* (1906; Boston, Charles E. Tuttle, 1956), 4.

19. "Prospectus," *The Quiver* (September 1861): 550.

20. A. E. Duchesne, "Tea and Temperance," *The Quiver* 49, no. 12 (October 1914): 1153.

21. Ibid., 1154.

22. Ibid., 1154–55.

23. On the "bottom-up" approach to writing world/global history, see Lynn Hunt, *Writing History in the Global Era* (New York: W. W. Norton, 2014), 63–70.

24. The archive of the Indian Tea Association includes 2,344 items covering the period 1879–1982 and incorporates materials from many other important trade organizations. Its core archive is housed in the British Library, Oriental and India Office Collections, reference number Mss Eur F174. I have visited many other business and personal archives and have made extensive use of newspapers and trade journals. Throughout this book I have interrogated how archives tell and suppress stories and viewpoints. For this approach, see Ann Laura Stoler, *Along the Archival Grain: Epistemic Anxieties and Colonial Common Sense* (Princeton: Princeton University Press, 2009); Antoinette Burton, ed., *Archive Stories: Facts, Fictions and the Writing of History* (Durham: Duke University Press, 2006); and Carolyn Kay Steedman, *Dust: The Archive and Cultural History* (Manchester: Manchester University Press, 2002).

25. Two important new books that in different ways complicate this history are Jonathan Eacott, *Selling Empire: India in the Making of Britain and America, 1600–1830* (Chapel Hill: University of North Carolina Press, 2016) and Richard J. Grace, *Opium and Empire: The Lives and Careers of William Jardine and James Matheson* (Montreal: McGill-Queen's University Press, 2014). Also, work such as Claude Markovits, *The Global World of Indian Merchants, 1750–1947: Traders of Sind from Bukhara to Panama* (Cambridge: Cambridge University Press, 2000) and other studies on trade diasporas are very useful. For the continuities and discontinuities between these phases of global capitalism, see Geoffrey Jones, *Merchants to Multinationals: British Trading Companies in the Nineteenth and Twentieth Centuries* (Oxford: Oxford University Press, 2000) and his *Multinationals and Global Capitalism from the Nineteenth to the Twenty-First Century* (Oxford: Oxford University Press, 2005); and Alfred D. Chandler Jr. and Bruce Mazlish, eds., *Leviathans: Multinational Corporations and the New Global History* (Cambridge: Cambridge University Press, 2005). A very thorough study of an individual firm is D. K. Fieldhouse, *Unilever Overseas: The Anatomy of a Multinational, 1895–1965* (London: Croom Helm, 1978).

26. I am building on work that has demonstrated the porous and decentered nature of the nation, empire, and transnational relationships. See Antoinette Burton, "Introduction: On the Inadequacy and the Indispensability of the Nation," in *After the Imperial*

Turn: Thinking with and through the Nation, ed. Antoinette Burton (Durham: Duke University Press, 2003), 1–23; Durba Ghosh and Dane Kennedy, eds., *Decentering Empire: Britain, India and the Transcolonial World* (Hyderabad: Orient Longman, 2006); Kevin Grant, Philippa Levine, and Frank Trentmann, eds., *Beyond Sovereignty: Britain, Empire and Transnationalism, c. 1860–1950* (Houndmills, Basingstoke: Palgrave Macmillan, 2007); Gary B. Magee and Andrew S. Thompson, *Empire and Globalisation: Networks of People, Goods and Capital in the British World, c. 1850–1914* (Cambridge: Cambridge University Press, 2010); James Belich, *Replenishing the Earth: The Settler Revolution and the Rise of the Anglo-World, 1783–1939* (Oxford: Oxford University Press, 2009); and the monumental P. J. Cain and A. G. Hopkins, *British Imperialism, 1688–2000*, 2nd ed. (Harlow, Essex: Longman, 2002).

27. Raymond K. Renford, *The Non-Official British in India to 1920* (Delhi: Oxford University Press, 1987), 15, 29.

28. For a general portrait of indigenous enterprise in Ceylon, see Kumari Jayawardena, *Nobodies to Somebodies: The Rise of the Colonial Bourgeoisie in Sri Lanka* (London: Zed Books, 2002).

29. There is a large body of work on gender, family, and empire. See, for example, Durba Ghosh, *Sex and the Family in Colonial India: The Making of Empire* (Cambridge: Cambridge University Press, 2006); Ann Laura Stoler, *Carnal Knowledge and Imperial Power: Race and the Intimate in Colonial Rule* (Berkeley: University of California Press, 2002); Catherine Hall, *Civilizing Subjects: Colony and Metropole in the English Imagination, 1830–1867* (Chicago: University of Chicago Press, 2002); Elizabeth Buettner, *Empire Families: Britons and Late Imperial India* (New York: Oxford University Press, 2004); and Mary A. Procida, *Married to the Empire: Gender, Politics and Imperialism in India, 1883–1947* (Manchester: Manchester University Press, 2002).

30. On the "global" nineteenth century, see Sven Beckert, *Empire of Cotton: A Global History* (New York: Knopf, 2014); Emily S. Rosenberg, *Transnational Currents in a Shrinking World, 1870–1945* (Cambridge, MA: Belknap Press of Harvard University Press, 2012); Steven C. Topik and Allen Wells, *Global Markets Transformed, 1870–1945* (Cambridge, MA: Belknap Press of Harvard University Press, 2012); Tony Ballantyne and Antoinette Burton, *Empires and the Reach of the Global, 1870–1945* (Cambridge, MA: Belknap Press of Harvard University Press, 2012); and Jürgen Osterhammel, *The Transformation of the World: A Global History of the Nineteenth Century* (Princeton: Princeton University Press, 2009).

31. The field of gender and consumer culture has grown a great deal since the publication of Victoria de Grazia and Ellen Furlough, eds., *The Sex of Things: Gender and Consumption in Historical Perspective* (Berkeley: University of California Press, 1996), but the history of global capitalism and commodity studies have tended to ignore questions pertaining to gender or women's history. A notable exception is Sarah Abrevaya Stein, *Plumes: Ostrich Feathers, Jews, and a Lost World of Global Commerce* (New Haven: Yale University Press, 2008).

32. Edward Smith, MD, *Foods* (New York: D. Appleton and Company, 1874), 331.

33. For example, the American editor of the *Tea and Coffee Trade Journal* and industry consultant William H. Ukers wrote the massive two-volume *All about Tea* (New York: Tea and Coffee Trade Journal, 1935). Colonial businessman and politician Sir

Percival Griffiths wrote *The History of the Indian Tea Industry* (London: Weidenfeld and Nicolson, 1967). His son, John Griffiths, published *Tea: The Drink That Changed the World* (London: Andre Deutsch, 2007). Gervas Huxley, the leading figure in the global marketing of tea from the 1930s through the 1960s, wrote *Talking of Tea: Here Is the Whole Fascinating Story of Tea* (Ivylan, PA: John Wagner and Sons, 1956). Denys Forrest, an associate of Huxley's, published *A Hundred Years of Ceylon Tea, 1867–1967* (London: Chatto and Windus, 1967) and *Tea for the British: The Social and Economic History of a Famous Trade* (London: Chatto and Windus, 1973). Edward Bramah, who wrote *Tea and Coffee: A Modern View of Three Hundred Years of Tradition* (London: Hutchinson, 1972), worked in different parts of the tea and coffee industry. Jane Pettigrew, an industry consultant, has written *A Social History of Tea* (London: The National Trust, 2001).

34. A recent exception is Markman Ellis, Richard Coulton, and Matthew Mauger, *Empire of Tea: The Asian Leaf That Conquered the World* (London: Reaktion, 2015). More general studies include Arup Kumar Dutta, *Cha Garam! The Tea Story* (Guwahati, Assam: Paloma Publications, 1992); Alan Macfarlane and Iris Macfarlane, *Green Gold: The Empire of Tea: A Remarkable History of the Plant That Took Over the World* (London: Ebury Press, 2003); Roy Moxham, *Tea: Addiction, Exploitation, and Empire* (New York: Carroll and Graff, 2003); Beatrice Hohenegger, *Liquid Jade: The Story of Tea from East to West* (New York: St. Martin's Press, 2006); Victor H. Mair and Erling Hoh, *The True History of Tea* (London: Thames and Hudson, 2009); and Laura C. Martin, *Tea: The Drink That Changed the World* (Tokyo: Tuttle Publishing, 2007).

35. Woodruff D. Smith, *Consumption and the Making of Respectability, 1600–1800* (New York: Routledge, 2002), chap. 6; Elizabeth Kowaleski-Wallace, *Consuming Subjects: Women, Shopping, and Business in the Eighteenth Century* (New York: Columbia University Press, 1997), 19–36; James Walvin, *Fruits of Empire: Exotic Produce and British Taste, 1688–1800* (Houndmills, Basingstoke: Macmillan, 1997), chap. 2; Wolfgang Schivelbusch, *Tastes of Paradise: A Social History of Spices, Stimulants, and Intoxicants* (New York: Vintage, 1993), 79–85; Ina Baghdiantz McCabe, *A History of Global Consumption, 1500–1800* (London: Routledge, 2015); Hoh-Cheung Mui and Lorna H. Mui, *The Management of Monopoly: A Study of the East India Company's Conduct of Its Tea Trade, 1784–1833* (Vancouver: University of British Columbia Press, 1984); Liu Yong, *The Dutch East India Company's Trade with China, 1757–1781* (Leiden: Brill, 2007); Chris Nierstrasz, *Rivalry for Trade in Tea and Textiles: The English and Dutch East India Companies, 1700–1800* (Houndmills, Basingstoke: Palgrave Macmillan, 2015); Hanna Hodacs, *Silk and Tea in the North: Scandinavian Trade and the Market for Asian Goods in Eighteenth Century Europe* (Houndmills, Basingstoke: Palgrave Macmillan, 2016); part 5 of Philip Lawson, *A Taste for Empire and Glory: Studies in British Overseas Expansion, 1660–1800* (Aldershot: Variorum, 1997) is also still very useful.

36. Sidney Mintz, *Sweetness and Power: The Place of Sugar in Modern History* (New York: Penguin, 1985); Jan de Vries, *The Industrious Revolution: Consumer Behavior and the Household Economy, 1650 to the Present* (Cambridge: Cambridge University Press, 2008); Jon Stobart, *Sugar and Spice: Grocers and Groceries in Provincial England, 1650–1830* (Oxford: Oxford University Press, 2013); Cowan, *Social Life of Coffee*; Jordan Goodman, "Excitantia, or, How Enlightenment Europe Took to Soft Drugs,"

in *Consuming Habits: Drugs in History and Anthropology*, ed. Jordan Goodman, Paul Lovejoy, and Andrew Sherratt (London: Routledge, 1995), 126–47; Carole Shammas, *The Pre-industrial Consumer in England and America* (Oxford: Oxford University Press, 1990); Lorna Weatherill, *Consumer Behaviour and Material Culture in Britain, 1660–1760* (London: Routledge, 1988). For two very different approaches to the intersection of enlightened ideals and spaces and the early modern economy, see Simon Gikandi, *Slavery and the Culture of Taste* (Princeton: Princeton University Press, 2011) and Joel Mokyr, *The Enlightened Economy: An Economic History of Britain, 1700–1850* (New Haven: Yale University Press, 2009).

37. For a Chinese-centered study of capitalism, see Kenneth Pomeranz, *The Great Divergence: China, Europe and the Making of the Modern World Economy* (Princeton: Princeton University Press, 2000).

38. Frank Trentmann, *Empire of Things: How We Became a World of Consumers, from the Fifteenth Century to the Twenty-First* (New York: Harper Collins, 2016); Frank Trentmann, ed., *The Oxford Handbook of the History of Consumption* (Oxford: Oxford University Press, 2012). A very brief treatment is Peter N. Stearns, *Consumerism in World History: The Global Transformation of Desire* (London: Routledge, 2001). For challenges to this view, see Jeremy Prestholdt, *Domesticating the World: African Consumerism and the Genealogies of Globalization* (Berkeley: University of California Press, 2008); Timothy Burke, *Lifebuoy Men, Lux Women: Commodification, Consumption, and Cleanliness in Modern Zimbabwe* (Durham: Duke University Press 1996); Jean Allman, ed., *Fashioning Africa: Power and the Politics of Dress* (Bloomington: Indiana University Press, 2004); Brenda Chalfin, *Shea Butter Republic: State Power, Global Markets, and the Making of an Indigenous Commodity* (New York: Routledge, 2004); Craig Clunas, *Superfluous Things: Material Culture and Social Status in Early Modern China*, 2nd ed. (Honolulu: University of Hawai'i Press, 2007); Michelle Maskiell, "Consuming Kashmir: Shawls and Empires, 1500–2000," *Journal of World History* 13, no. 1 (2002): 27–65; Donald Quataert, ed., *Consumption Studies and the History of the Ottoman Empire, 1550–1922: An Introduction* (New York: State University of New York Press, 2000); and Giorgio Riello and Tirthankar Roy, eds., *How India Clothed the World: The World of South Asian Textiles* (Leiden: Brill, 2009).

39. Chatterjee, *A Time for Tea*; Sharma, *Empire's Garden*; Sarah Rose, *For All the Tea in China: How England Stole the World's Favorite Drink and Changed History* (New York: Penguin, 2009).

40. There are many studies of plantation labor; for some important works, see Rana P. Behal, *One Hundred Years of Servitude: Political Economy of Tea Plantations in Colonial Assam* (Delhi: Tulika Books, 2014); Ravi Raman, *Global Capital and Peripheral Labour: The History and Political Economy of Plantation Workers in India* (London: Routledge, 2010); and Patrick Peebles, *The Plantation Tamils of Ceylon* (London: Leicester University Press, 2001). For a study of the contemporary situation, see Sarah Besky, *The Darjeeling Distinction: Labor and Justice on Fair-Trade Tea Plantations* (Berkeley: University of California Press, 2014). On the political economy of the environment and agriculture of tea, see Gunnel Cederlöf, *Founding an Empire on India's North-Eastern Frontiers, 1790–1840: Climate, Commerce, Polity* (Oxford: Oxford University Press, 2014).

41. Beckert, *Empire of Cotton*, 38.

42. Joyce Appleby, *The Relentless Revolution: A History of Capitalism* (New York: W. W. Norton, 2010), 21–22.

43. Victoria de Grazia, *Irresistible Empire: America's Advance through 20th Century Europe* (Cambridge, MA: Belknap Press of Harvard University Press, 2005).

44. There has been very little work on distribution and consumption in colonial contexts, but this is changing. On Indian tea consumption, see Gautam Bhadra, *From an Imperial Product to a National Drink: The Culture of Tea Consumption in Modern India* (Calcutta: Centre for Studies in Social Sciences and the Tea Board of India, 2005); Philip Lutgendorf, "Making Tea in India: Chai, Capitalism, Culture," *Thesis Eleven* 113, no. 1 (December 2012): 11–31; Collingham, *Curry*, 187–214; A. R. Venkatachalapathy, "'In those days there was no coffee': Coffee-Drinking and Middle-Class Culture in Colonial Tamilnadu," *Indian Economic and Social History Review* 39 (2002): 301–16; and K. T. Achaya, *The Food Industries of British India* (Delhi: Oxford University Press, 1994), 178–79.

45. Thomas Metcalf, *Imperial Connections: India in the Indian Ocean Arena, 1860–1920* (Berkeley: University of California Press, 2007); Sugata Bose, *A Hundred Horizons: The Indian Ocean in the Age of Global Empire* (Cambridge, MA: Harvard University Press, 2006).

46. Arjun Appadurai, ed., *The Social Life of Things: Commodities in Cultural Perspective* (Cambridge: Cambridge University Press, 1986), 5.

47. Ibid., 9.

48. This is a very large literature. In addition to those already mentioned, books I have found especially useful include Susanne Freidberg, *French Beans and Food Scares: Culture and Commerce in an Anxious Age* (Oxford: Oxford University Press, 2004); Timothy Brook and Bob Tadashi Wakabayashi, eds., *Opium Regimes: China, Britain, and Japan, 1839–1952* (Berkeley: University of California Press, 2000); Deborah Valenze, *Milk: A Global and Local History* (New Haven: Yale University Press, 2011); Douglas Cazaux Sackman, *Orange Empire: California and the Fruits of Eden* (Berkeley: University of California Press, 2005); Giorgio Riello, *Cotton: The Fabric That Made the Modern World* (Cambridge: Cambridge University Press, 2013); and Bernhard Rieger, *The People's Car: A Global History of the Volkswagen Beetle* (Cambridge, MA: Harvard University Press, 2013).

49. See Erika Rappaport, "Consumption," in *The Ashgate Research Companion to Modern Imperial Histories*, ed. Philippa Levine and John Marriott (Farnham, Surrey: Ashgate, 2012), 343–58. Also see Rappaport, "Imperial Possessions, Cultural Histories, and the Material Turn," *Victorian Studies* 50, no. 2 (Winter 1008): 289–96.

50. Jennifer Bair, ed., *Frontiers of Commodity Chain Research* (Stanford: Stanford University Press, 2009); Warren Belasco and Roger Horowitz, ed., *Food Chains: From Farmyard to Shopping Cart* (Philadelphia: University of Pennsylvania Press, 2009); William Gervase Clarence-Smith and Steven Topik, eds., *The Global Coffee Economy in Africa, Asia, and Latin America, 1500–1989* (Cambridge: Cambridge University Press, 2003); Steven Topik, Carlos Marichal, and Zephyr Frank, eds., *From Silver to Cocaine: Latin American Commodity Chains and the Building of the World Economy, 1500–2000* (Durham: Duke University Press, 2006).

51. Alexander Nützenadel and Frank Trentmann, eds., *Food and Globalization: Consumption, Markets and Politics in the Modern World* (New York: Berg, 2008); Raymond Grew,

ed., *Food in Global History* (Boulder, CO: Westview, 1999); David Inglis and Debra Gimlin, eds., *The Globalization of Food* (Oxford: Berg, 2009); Warren Belasco and Philip Scranton, eds., *Food Nations: Selling Taste in Consumer Societies* (New York: Routledge, 2002); Kyri W. Claflin and Peter Scholliers, *Writing Food History: A Global Perspective* (London: Berg, 2012).

52. See, for example, Alys Eve Weinbaum, Lynn M. Thomas, Priti Ramamurthy, Uta G. Poiger, Madeleine Yue Dong, and Tani E. Barlow, eds., *The Modern Girl around the World: Consumption, Modernity and Globalization* (Durham: Duke University Press, 2008); Anandi Ramamurthy, *Imperial Persuaders: Images of Africa and Asia in British Advertising* (Manchester: Manchester University Press, 2003); Peter H. Hoffenberg, *An Empire on Display: English, Indian, and Australian Exhibitions from the Crystal Palace to the Great War* (Berkeley: University of California Press, 2001); and several of the key articles in Carol A. Breckenridge, ed., *Consuming Modernity: Public Culture in a South Asian World* (Minneapolis: University of Minnesota Press, 1995).

53. Kaison Chang, *World Tea Production and Trade: Current and Future Development* (Rome: Food and Agricultural Organization of the United Nations, 2015).

54. Sir Charles Higham, *Advertising: Its Use and Abuse* (London: Williams and Norgate, 1925), 146–47.

55. Frederick Cooper, *Colonialism in Question: Theory, Knowledge, History* (Berkeley: University of California Press, 2005), 10, 91.

56. Here I am building James Vernon's argument in *Hunger: A Modern History* (Cambridge, MA: Belknap Press of Harvard University Press, 2007). Taste has an intellectual and social component, of course, as well. See Pierre Bourdieu, *Distinction: A Social Critique of the Judgment of Taste*, trans. Richard Nice (Cambridge, MA: Harvard University Press, 1984).

57. Andrew Sherratt, "Alcohol and Its Alternatives: Symbol and Substance in Pre-Industrial Cultures," in *Consuming Habits*, ed. Goodman, Lovejoy, and Sherratt, 13.

58. For nationalism, war, and drink in the United States, see Lisa Jacobson, "Beer Goes to War: The Politics of Beer Promotion and Production in the Second World War," *Food, Culture and Society* 12 (September 2009): 275–312, and her forthcoming study, tentatively titled *Fashioning New Cultures of Drink: Alcohol's Quest for Legitimacy after Prohibition.*

59. For an excellent exploration of some of these issues, see Radhika Mohanram, *Imperial White: Race, Diaspora, and the British Empire* (Minneapolis: University of Minnesota Press, 2007).

60. Manu Goswami, *Producing India: From Colonial Economy to National Space* (Chicago: University of Chicago Press, 2004); Sherene Seikaly, *Men of Capital: Scarcity and Economy in Mandate Palestine* (Stanford: Stanford University Press, 2016).

61. Stuart Hall, "Old and New Identities, Old and New Ethnicities," in *Culture, Globalization and the World System: Contemporary Conditions for the Representation of Identity*, ed. Anthony D. King (Minneapolis: University of Minnesota Press, 1997), 48–49.

62. There are many scholars who have theorized about the intimate experience of colonialism. See, for example, Ashis Nandy, *The Intimate Enemy: Loss and Recovery of Self under Colonialism* (New Delhi: Oxford University Press, 1983).

CHAPTER I. "A CHINA DRINK APPROVED BY ALL PHYSICIANS"

1. Samuel Pepys, *The Diary of Samuel Pepys*, vol. 2 (1667; Berkeley: University of California Press, 1970), 277.
2. Samuel Pepys, *The Diary of Samuel Pepys*, vol. 1 (1667; Berkeley: University of California Press, 1970), 49.
3. This is a huge literature. See, for example, Ina Baghdiantz McCabe, *A History of Global Consumption, 1500–1800* (London: Routledge, 2012); Maxine Berg with Felicia Gottmann, Hanna Hodacs, and Chris Nierstrasz, eds., *Goods from the East, 1600–1800: Trading Eurasia* (Houndmills: Palgrave Macmillan, 2015); and Frank Trentmann, *Empire of Things: How We Became a World of Consumers, from the Fifteenth Century to the Twenty-First* (New York: Harper Collins, 2016).
4. Brian Cowan, *The Social Life of Coffee: The Emergence of the British Coffeehouse* (New Haven: Yale University Press, 2005); Marcy Norton, *Sacred Gifts, Profane Pleasures: A History of Tobacco and Chocolate in the Atlantic World* (Ithaca: Cornell University Press, 2008).
5. Robert K. Batchelor, *London: The Seldon Map and the Making of a Global City, 1549–1689* (Chicago: University of Chicago Press, 2014); David Porter, *Ideographia: The Chinese Cipher in Early Modern Europe* (Stanford: Stanford University Press, 2001); Debra Johanyak and Walter S. H. Lim, eds., *The English Renaissance, Orientalism, and the Idea of Asia* (Basingstoke: Palgrave Macmillan, 2010); Robert Markley, *The Far East and the English Imagination, 1600–1730* (Cambridge: Cambridge University Press, 2006); Michael North, ed., *Artistic and Cultural Exchanges between Europe and Asia, 1400–1900* (Surrey: Ashgate, 2010). On economic interactions, see John E. Wills and J. L. Cranmer-Byng, *China and Maritime Europe, 1500–1800: Trade, Settlement, Diplomacy and Missions* (New York: Cambridge University Press, 2010) and Denys Lombard and Jean Aubin, eds., *Asian Merchants and Businessmen in the Indian Ocean and the China Sea* (Oxford: Oxford University Press, 2000).
6. Maxine Berg, *Luxury and Pleasure in Eighteenth-Century Britain* (Oxford: Oxford University Press, 2005).
7. Sidney W. Mintz, *Sweetness and Power: The Place of Sugar in Modern History* (New York: Penguin, 1985); Susan Dwyer Amussen, *Caribbean Exchanges: Slavery and the Transformation of English Society, 1640–1700* (Chapel Hill: University of North Carolina Press, 2007); Simon Gikandi, *Slavery and the Culture of Taste* (Princeton: Princeton University Press, 2011).
8. Judith A. Carney, *Black Rice: The African Origins of Rice Cultivation in the Americas* (Cambridge, MA: Harvard University Press, 2002).
9. Cowan, *Social Life of Coffee*. On cosmopolitanism, see Margaret C. Jacob, *Strangers Nowhere in the World: The Rise of Cosmopolitanism in Early Modern Europe* (Philadelphia: University of Pennsylvania Press, 2006) and Miles Ogborn, *Spaces of Modernity: London's Geographies, 1680–1780* (New York: Guildford Press, 1998).
10. See, for example, O. R. Impey, *Chinoiserie: The Impact of Oriental Styles on Western Art and Decoration* (Oxford: Oxford University Press, 1977); David Porter, *The Chinese Taste in Eighteenth-Century England* (Cambridge: Cambridge University Press, 2010); Stacey Sloboda, *Chinoiserie: Commerce and Critical Ornament in Eighteenth-Century Britain* (Manchester: Manchester University Press, 2014); and Christopher M. S.

Johns, *China and the Church: Chinoiserie in Global Contexts* (Berkeley: University of California Press, 2016).

11. Porter, *Chinese Taste*; Sloboda, *Chinoiserie*; Elizabeth Kowaleski-Wallace, *Consuming Subjects: Women, Shopping, and Business in the Eighteenth Century* (New York: Columbia University Press, 1997).

12. Woodruff D. Smith, *Consumption and the Making of Respectability, 1600–1800* (New York: Routledge, 2002), 75.

13. Wolfgang Schivelbusch, *Tastes of Paradise: A Social History of Spices, Stimulants, and Intoxicants* (New York: Vintage, 1993); Jordan Goodman, "Exitantia: Or, How Enlightenment Europe Took to Soft Drugs," in *Consuming Habits: Drugs in History and Anthropology*, ed. Jordan Goodman, Paul E. Lovejoy, and Andrew Sherratt (London and New York: Routledge, 1995), 126–47; James Walvin, *Fruits of Empire: Exotic Produce and British Taste, 1660–1800* (Houndmills: Macmillan, 1997); W. G. Clarence-Smith, "The Global Consumption of Hot Beverages, c. 1500–c. 1900," in *Food and Globalization: Consumption, Markets and Politics in the Modern World*, ed. Alexander Nützenadel and Frank Trentmann(New York: Berg, 2008), 37–55.

14. Paul Freedman, *Out of the East: Spices and the Medieval Imagination* (New Haven: Yale University Press, 2008), 172–73.

15. Ibid., 72.

16. Ken Albala, *Eating Right in the Renaissance* (Berkeley: University of California Press, 2002), 5, 30–36.

17. Here I rely primarily on the excellent new study by James A. Benn, *Tea in China: A Religious and Cultural History* (Honolulu: University of Hawaii Press, 2014).

18. Ling Wang, *Tea and Chinese Culture* (San Francisco: Long River Press, 2005), 2–3.

19. Benn, *Tea in China*, 7–8.

20. Robert Gardella, *Harvesting Mountains: Fujian and the China Tea Trade, 1757–1937* (Berkeley: University of California Press, 1994), 29–30.

21. Hoh-Cheung and Lorna H. Mui, *The Management of Monopoly: A Study of the East India Company's Conduct of its Tea Trade, 1784–1833* (Vancouver: University of British Columbia Press, 1984), 4.

22. Gardella, *Harvesting Mountains*, 45–46.

23. Mui and Mui, *Management of Monopoly*, 5–6.

24. Ibid., 9.

25. Ibid., 8.

26. Ibid., 12.

27. Benn, *Tea in China*, 43.

28. Ibid., 82, 85.

29. Ibid., 70.

30. Wang, *Tea and Chinese Culture*, 23.

31. Ibid., 12–16.

32. Quoted in Gardella, *Harvesting Mountains*, 25.

33. Benn, *Tea in China*, 120.

34. Paul J. Smith, *Taxing Heaven's Storehouse: Horses, Bureaucrats, and the Destruction of the Sichuan Tea Industry, 1074–1224* (Cambridge, MA: Council on East Asian Studies, Harvard University, 1991), 308–9.

35. Victor H. Mair and Erling Hoh, *The True History of Tea* (London: Thames and Hudson, 2009), 78.

36. Benn, *Tea in China*, 122.
37. Ibid., 173–74.
38. Craig Clunas, *Superfluous Things: Material Culture and Social Status in Early Modern China* (Urbana: University of Illinois Press, 1991), 8.
39. Quoted in Gardella, *Harvesting Mountains*, 21.
40. Benn, *Tea in China*, chap. 3; Murai Yasuhiko, trans. Paul Varley, "The Development of *Chanoyu:* Before Rikyū," in *Tea in Japan: Essays on the History of Chanoyu*, ed. H. Paul Varley and Isao Kamakuro (Honolulu: University of Hawaii Press, 1989), 8–9.
41. Benn, *Tea in China*, 157.
42. Ibid., 146.
43. Yasuhiko, "The Development of *Chanoyu*," 29–30. Also see Surak, *Making Tea, Making Japan.*
44. Michael Cooper, "The Early Europeans and Tea," in *Tea in Japan*, ed. Varley and Kamakuroi, 121.
45. William Ukers, *All about Tea* (New York: New York Tea and Coffee Trade Journal, 1935), 1:25.
46. Chris Nierstrasz, *Rivalry for Trade in Tea and Textiles: The English and Dutch East India Companies (1700–1800)* (London: Palgrave Macmillan, 2015), 75.
47. Ronald Findlay and Kevin H. O'Rourke, *Power and Plenty: Trade, War, and the World Economy in the Second Millennium* (Princeton: Princeton University Press, 2007), 45.
48. Roy Moxham, *Tea: Addiction, Exploitation, and Empire* (New York: Carroll and Graf, 2003), 16–17.
49. Ukers, *All about Tea*, 1:23; Rudi Matthee, *The Pursuit of Pleasure: Drugs and Stimulants in Iranian History, 1500–1900* (Princeton: Princeton University Press, 2005), 238.
50. Ralph S. Hattox, *Coffee and Coffee Houses: The Origins of a Social Beverage in the Medieval Near East* (Seattle: University of Washington Press, 1985), 3.
51. Matthee, *Pursuit of Pleasure*, 238.
52. Adam Olearius, *Voyages and Travels of the Ambassadors from the Duke of Holstein to the Great Duke of Muscovy, and the King of Persia*, trans. John Davies (London: Thomas Dring, 1662), 323.
53. *Mandelslo's Travels to the Indies, the Fifth Book* (London: John Starkey, 1669), 13.
54. John Phipps, *A Practical Treatise on the China and Eastern Trade* (Calcutta: Thacker and Co., 1835), 75.
55. Philip J. Stern, *The Company-State: Corporate Sovereignty and the Early Modern Foundations of the British Empire in India* (Oxford: Oxford University Press, 2011), chap. 5.
56. John Ovington, *A Voyage to Suratt in the Year 1689*, ed. H. G. Rawlinson (1696; London: Oxford University Press, 1929), 180.
57. Farhat Hasan, "The Mughal Port Cities of Surat and Hugli," in *Ports, Towns, Cities: A Historical Tour of the Indian Littoral*, ed. Lakshmi Subramanian (Mumbai: Marg Publications, 2008), 80; Ruby Maloni, *Surat: Port of the Mughal Empire* (Mumbai: Himalaya Publishing House, 2003), xvi; Balkrishna Govind Gokhale, *Surat in the Seventeenth Century: A Study in the Urban History of Pre-modern India* (London and Malmö: Scandinavian Institute of Asian Studies, 1979).
58. Cowan, *Social Life of Coffee*, 61.
59. Hasan, "The Mughal Port Cities," 84.
60. Ovington, *A Voyage to Surat*, 131.

61. Tea is not a key commodity in works on Indian Ocean commerce. See, for example, Om Prakash, *Bullion for Goods: European and Indian Merchants in the Indian Ocean Trade, 1500–1800* (New Delhi: Manohar, 2004).

62. Tea was a part of elite and merchant cultures in western India, but this topic has yet to find its historian.

63. Ashin Das Gupta, *Indian Merchants and the Decline of Surat, c. 1700–1750* (Wiesbaden: Franz Steiner Verlag, 1979).

64. Yong Liu, *The Dutch East India Company's Tea Trade with China, 1757–1781* (Leiden: Brill, 2007), 2.

65. Quoted in Denys Mostyn Forrest, *Tea for the British: The Social and Economic History of a Famous Trade* (London: Chatto and Windus, 1973), 21. On France, see Daniel Roche, *A History of Everyday Things: The Birth of Consumption in France, 1600–1800* (Cambridge: Cambridge University Press, 2000), 244.

66. Quoted in Schivelbusch, *Tastes of Paradise*, 23.

67. Robert S. DuPlessis, *The Material Atlantic: Clothing, Commerce and Colonization in the Atlantic World, 1650–1800* (Cambridge: Cambridge University Press, 2015).

68. John Ovington, *An Essay upon the Nature and Qualities of Tea* (London: R. Roberts, 1699), dedication.

69. Ibid., 2–3.

70. The English aristocracy had adopted continental foods in the early part of the century. Colin Spencer, *British Food: An Extraordinary Thousand Years of History* (New York: Columbia, 2002), 134.

71. Ukers, *All about Tea*, 1:44, Linda Levy Peck, *Consuming Splendor: Society and Culture in Seventeenth Century England* (Cambridge: Cambridge University Press, 2005), 243.

72. Stern, *Company-State*, 255.

73. Edmund Waller, "On Tea, Commended by her Majesty," ed. Robert Bell, *Poetical Works of Edmund Waller* (1663; London: Charles Griffin, 1871), 211.

74. Kowaleski-Wallace, *Consuming Subjects*, 22–23.

75. Agnes Strickland, *Lives of the Queens of England, From the Norman Conquest*, 4th ed., vol. 5 (London: H. Colburn, 1854). For versions of this story, see Ukers, *All about Tea*, 2:43–44; Arnold Palmer, *Movable Feasts* (London: Oxford University Press, 1952), 97; and Gertrude Z. Thomas, *Richer than Spices: How a Royal Bride's Dowry Introduced Cane, Lacquer, Cottons, Tea, and Porcelain to England, and So Revolutionized Taste, Manners, Craftsmanship, and History in Both England and America* (New York: Knopf, 1965).

76. Strickland, *Lives of the Queens of England*, 521.

77. Bombay was ceded to the Crown in full sovereignty but the Crown leased the settlement to the East India Company in 1668. Holden Furber, *Rival Empires of Trade in the Orient, 1600–1800: Europe and the World in the Age of Expansion* (Minneapolis: University of Minnesota Press, 1976), 2:90, 92.

78. Ukers, *All about Tea*, 1:46.

79. Andrew Mackillop, "A North Europe World of Tea: Scotland and the Tea Trade, c. 1690–c. 1790," in *Goods from the East*, ed. Berg, 294–308.

80. Jürgen Habermas, *The Structural Transformation of the Public Sphere: An Inquiry into a Category of Bourgeois Society* (Cambridge, MA: MIT Press, 1989).

81. Gikandi, *Slavery and the Culture of Taste*, 60.

82. Ibid., and Cowan, *Social Life of Coffee*.

83. Arjun Appadurai and Carol A. Breckenridge, "Why Public Culture?" *Public Culture Bulletin* 1, no. 1 (Fall 1988): 6.

84. Jan de Vries, *The Industrious Revolution: Consumer Behavior and the Household Economy, 1650 to the Present* (Cambridge: Cambridge University Press, 2008).

85. Cowan, *Social Life of Coffee*, 11.

86. Peck, *Consuming Splendor*, 314.

87. Barbara C. Morison, "Povey, Thomas (b. 1613/14 d. in or before 1705)," *Oxford Dictionary of National Biography*, online ed., January 2008.

88. Ukers, *All about Tea*, 1:39–40.

89. Samuel Price, "The Virtues of Coffee, Chocolette, and Thee or Tea" (London, 1690).

90. Philippe Sylvestre Dufour, *The Manner of Making Coffee, Tea, and Chocolate, As it is used in Most parts of Europe, Asia, Africa and America with their Vertues*, trans. John Chamberlayne (1671; London: William Crook, 1685). The British Library's edition of this text belonged to Joseph Banks, the famous naturalist, who encouraged the establishment of tea culture in India.

91. John Chamberlayne, *The Natural History of Coffee, Thee, Chocolate and Tobacco* (London: Christopher Wilkinson, 1682), 11; Reavley Gair, "Chamberlayne, John (1668/9–1723)," *Oxford Dictionary of National Biography*, online ed., October 2009.

92. Chamberlayne, *The Natural History*, 9–11.

93. Cowan, *Social Life of Coffee*, 25.

94. Steve Pincus, "'Coffee Politicians Does Create': Coffeehouses and Restoration Political Culture," *Journal of Modern History* 67, no. 4 (December 1995): 807–34.

95. Ukers, *All about Tea*, 1:45. After the Glorious Revolution critics again condemned what they now saw as Whig institutions. Pincus, "'Coffee Politicians,'" 824.

96. Ukers, *All about Tea*, 1:42–43.

97. Forrest, *Tea for the British*, 33–34.

98. Ukers, *All about Tea*, 1:42–43.

99. Thomas Garway, "An Exact Description of the Growth, Quality and Vertues of the Leaf Tea" (London, 1660). "Garway" was also spelled Garraway and Garaway.

100. Susanna Centlivre, *A Bold Stroke for a Wife: A Comedy*, ed. Thalia Stathas (1717; Lincoln: University of Nebraska Press, 1968), 54.

101. Ogborn, *Spaces of Modernity*, 123.

102. Hannah Greig, *The Beau Monde: Fashionable Society in Georgian London* (Oxford: Oxford University Press, 2013), 75.

103. Peter Borsay, *The English Urban Renaissance: Culture and Society in the Provincial Town, 1660–1770* (Oxford: Clarendon, 1989), chap. 6.

104. Ukers, *All about Tea*, 1:49–48.

105. Rodris Roth, *Tea Drinking in 18th Century America: Its Etiquette and Equipage* (Washington, DC: Smithsonian Institution, 1961), 6.

106. Many scholars have charted the growth of wealth, consumption, and commerce during the eighteenth century, increasingly seeing this as a transnational process that had multiple centers and peripheries. Carole Shammas, "The Revolutionary Impact of European Demand for Tropical Goods," in *The Early Modern Atlantic Economy*, ed. John J. McCusker and Kenneth Morgan (Cambridge: Cambridge University Press, 2000), 165; Jonathan Eacott, "The Cultural History of

Commerce in the Atlantic World," in *The Atlantic World*, ed. D'Maris Coffman, Adrian Leonard, and William O'Reilly (London: Routledge, 2015), 546–72; McKendrick, Brewer, and Plumb, *Birth of a Consumer Society*; Mintz, *Sweetness and Power*; John Brewer and Roy Porter, eds., *Consumption and the World of Goods* (London: Routledge, 1994); Ann Bermingham and John Brewer, eds., *The Consumption of Culture, 1600–1800: Image, Object, Text* (London: Routledge, 1995); Kowaleski-Wallace, *Consuming Subjects*; Maxine Berg and Helen Clifford, eds., *Consumers and Luxury: Consumer Culture in Europe, 1650–1850* (Manchester: Manchester University Press, 1999); Mark Overton, Jane Whittle, Darron Dean, and Andrew Hann, eds., *Production and Consumption in English Households, 1600–1750* (London: Routledge, 2004); John Styles, *The Dress of the People: Everyday Fashion in Eighteenth-Century England* (New Haven: Yale University Press, 2007).

107. Nierstrasz, *Rivalry for Trade*. Also Jan Parmentier, *Tea Time in Flanders: The Maritime Trade between the Southern Netherlands and China in the 18th Century* (Bruge: Ludion Press, 1996), 63.
108. Liu, *Dutch East India Company's Tea Trade*, 126.
109. Ibid., 120.
110. Ibid., 135.
111. Cited in Liu, *Dutch East India Company's Tea Trade*, 139.
112. Nierstrasz, *Rivalry for Trade*, 36.
113. Ibid., 56.
114. Furber, *Rival Empires of Trade*, 126.
115. Philip Lawson, "Tea, Vice, and the English State, 1660–1784," in Philip Lawson, *A Taste for Empire and Glory: Studies in British Overseas Expansion* (Aldershot: Variorum, 1997), 2.
116. Nierstrasz, *Rivalry for Trade*, 60.
117. Quoted in Gardella, *Harvesting Mountains*, 33.
118. Nierstrasz, *Rivalry for Trade*, 161. The Chinese deliberately encouraged European competition so that they could get the best price for their teas.
119. Lawson, "Tea, Vice, and the English State," 3.
120. Stern, *Company-State*, 6–7.
121. H. V. Bowen, *The Business of Empire: The East India Company and Imperial Britain, 1756–1833* (Cambridge: Cambridge University Press, 2006), 30; John Brewer, *The Sinews of Power: War, Money and the English State, 1688–1783* (New York: Knopf, 1989).
122. Emily Erikson, *Between Monopoly and Free Trade: The English East India Company, 1600–1757* (Oxford: Oxford University Press, 2014).
123. P. J. Cain and A. G. Hopkins, *British Imperialism: 1688–2000*, 2nd ed. (Harlow: Longman, 2002), chap. 2. For an assessment of the debate on this idea, see Anthony Webster, *The Twilight of the East India Company: The Evolution of Anglo-Asian Commerce and Politics, 1790–1860* (Suffolk: Boydell Press, 2009).
124. Bowen, *The Business of Empire*, 32, 106–7.
125. Ibid., 95. Also see his more general analysis of EIC investors on pages 84–117.
126. Quoted in Bowen, *The Business of Empire*, 64–66.
127. Ibid., 112–13, 116.

128. Nierstrasz, *Rivalry for Trade*, 103.
129. H. V. Bowen, John McAleer, and Robert J. Blyth, *Monsoon Traders: The Maritime World of the East India Company* (London: Scala, 2011), 96–7.
130. Mui and Mui, *Management of Monopoly*, 115.
131. Nierstrasz, *Rivalry for Trade*, chap. 3.
132. Hoh-Cheung Mui and Lorna H. Mui, "Smuggling and the British Tea Trade before 1784," *American Historical Review* 74, no. 1 (October 1968): 44–73.
133. Agnes Repplier, *To Think of Tea!* (Boston: Houghton Mifflin, 1932), 42–43.
134. Mui and Mui, "Smuggling," 48.
135. Cal Winslow, "Sussex Smugglers," in *Albion's Fatal Tree: Crime and Society in Eighteenth-Century England*, ed. Douglas Hay, Peter Linebaugh, John G. Rule, E. P. Thompson, and Cal Winslow (New York: Pantheon, 1975), 126–27.
136. Winslow, "Sussex Smugglers," 124.
137. Mui and Mui, "Smuggling," 56–59.
138. Ibid., 51.
139. Winslow, "Sussex Smugglers," 156–57.
140. Shammas, *Pre-industrial Consumer*, 86.
141. Mui and Mui, *Management of Monopoly*, 12–13.
142. Shammas, *Pre-Industrial Consumer*, 86. One estimate places the rise of consumption in Britain between 1784 and 1795 at an astonishing 350 percent. *Tea and the Tea Trade*.
143. Mui and Mui, "Smuggling," 53.
144. John Benson and Laura Ugolini, eds., *A Nation of Shopkeepers: Five Centuries of British Retailing* (London: I. B. Tauris, 2003); Stobart, *Sugar and Spice*; Jon Stobart, Andrew Hann, and Victoria Morgan, *Spaces of Consumption: Leisure and Shopping the English Town, c. 1680–1830* (London: Routledge, 2007); Ian Mitchell, *Tradition and Innovation in English Retailing, 1700–1850: Narratives of Consumption* (Farnham: Ashgate, 2014); Jan Hein Furnée and Clé Lesger, eds., *The Landscape of Consumption: Shopping Streets and Cultures in Western Europe, 1600–1900* (Houndmills, Basingstoke: Palgrave Macmillan, 2014).
145. R. Campbell, *The London Tradesman: Being a Compendious View of all the Trades, Professions, Arts, both Liberal and Mechanic, now Practiced in Cities of London and Minster* (London: T. Gardner, 1747), 188.
146. *Daily Courant*, 5 November 1720, 2.
147. Ukers, *All about Tea*, 2:159–60.
148. Ibid., 2:157.
149. Richard Twining, *Remarks on the Report of the East India Directors, Respecting the Sale and Prices of Tea* (London: T. Cadell, 1784), 37.
150. Stobart, *Sugar and Spice*. For tea in particular, see chapters 8 and 9. Nancy C. Cox, *The Complete Tradesman: A Study of Retailing, 1550–1820* (Aldershot: Ashgate, 2000), 204–5.
151. Campbell, *The London Tradesman*, 188.
152. Ibid.
153. Thomas Boot advertisement (London, c. 1790), Bodleian Library, Oxford, Document #CW3306463157, *Eighteenth Century Collections Online*, Gale Group.
154. Cox, *Complete Tradesman*, 134, 138.
155. Shammas, *Pre-Industrial Consumer*, 268.

156. Rhys Isaac, *The Transformation of Virginia, 1740–1790*, rev. ed. (Chapel Hill: University of North Carolina Press, published for the Omohundro Institute of Early American History and Culture, 1999), 45.

157. De Vries, *Industrious Revolution*, chap. 4 assesses much of this literature. The vague nature of the term "mass" has plagued scholars working in a period of inaccurate and missing record keeping. I have adopted the definition of noted scholar Carole Shammas, who defined a mass commodity simply as an item purchased on a regular basis by people at varying income levels. Shammas, *Pre-industrial Consumer*, 78. Also Overton et al., *Production and Consumption*, 13–32.

158. Weatherill, *Consumer Behavior and Material Culture in Britain*, 185.

159. Overton et al., *Production and Consumption*, 11; Cox, *Complete Tradesman*, 3.

160. London already had a population of 575,000 in 1700. Keith Wrightson, *Earthly Necessities: Economic Lives in Early Modern Britain* (New Haven: Yale University Press, 2000), 235.

161. Weatherill, *Consumer Behavior and Material Culture in Britain*, 31.

162. Overton et al., *Production and Consumption*, 106–7.

163. Ibid., 58–59.

164. De Vries, *Industrious Revolution*, 151–54; Shammas, *Pre-industrial Consumer*, 183–86; Anne E. C. McCants, "Exotic Goods, Popular Consumption, and the Standard of Living: Thinking about Globalization in the Early Modern World," *Journal of World History* 18, no. 4 (December 2007): 433-62.

165. Wrightson, *Earthly Necessities*, 230.

166. W. D. Smith, "Accounting for Taste: British Coffee Consumption in Historical Perspective," *Journal of Interdisciplinary History* 27, no. 2 (Autumn 1996): 184–86.

167. Steven Topik, "The Integration of the World Coffee Market," in *Global Coffee Economy*, ed. Clarence-Smith and Topik, 28–29.

168. Cowan, *Social Life of Coffee*, 77.

169. Henry Martin, "An Essay Towards Finding the Ballance of our Whole Trade" (c. 1720), quoted in Smith, "Accounting for Taste," 196.

170. Smith, "Accounting for Taste."

171. De Vries, *Industrious Revolution*, 159–60.

172. Styles, *Dress of the People*, 19.

173. Eric Jay Dolin, *When America First Met China: An Exotic History of Tea, Drugs, and Money in the Age of Sail* (New York: W. W. Norton, 2012), 57.

174. Peter Kalm, *Travels into North America*, trans. John Reinhold Forester (London: T. Lowndes, 1771), 2:267.

175. Ibid., 2:179.

176. Ibid., 35.

177. Lawson, "Tea, Vice and the English State," 9.

178. Jean Gelman Taylor, *The Social World of Batavia: European and Eurasian in Dutch Asia* (Madison: University of Wisconsin Press, 1983), 59, 69.

179. Sir Frederick Morton Eden, *The State of the Poor, or, An History of the Labouring classes in England, from the Conquest to the Present Period* (London: J. Davis, 1797), 1:535.

180. Joseph A. Dearden, *A Brief History of Ancient and Modern Tee-Totalism* (Preston: J. Livesey, 1840), 4–5; Ian Levitt and Christopher Smout, *The State of the Scottish Working-Class in 1843: A Statistical and Spatial Enquiry Based on the Data from the Poor Law Commission Report of 1844* (Edinburgh: Scottish Academic Press, 1979), 25–35.

181. Jane Gray, "Gender and Plebian Culture in Ulster," *Journal of Interdisciplinary History* 24, no. 2 (Autumn 1993): 251–70; Patricia Lysaght, "'When I makes Tea, I makes Tea . . .': Innovation in Food—The Case of Tea in Ireland," *Ulster Folklife* 33 (1987): 44–71; E. Margaret Crawford, "Aspects of the Irish Diet" (PhD thesis, London School of Economics, 1985), 146.

182. P. Daryl, *Ireland's Disease* (London, 1888), 147, quoted in Crawford, "Aspects of the Irish Diet," 146.

183. D. A. Chart, "Unskilled Labour in Dublin: Its Housing and Living Conditions," *Journal of the Statistical and Social Inquiry Society of Ireland* 13, part 44 (1913/14): 169–70.

184. John Burnett, *Liquid Pleasures: A Social History of Drinks in Modern Britain* (London: Routledge, 1999), 57.

185. John Waldron, *A Satyr against Tea, or, Ovington's Essay upon the Nature and Qualities of Tea, &c, Dissected and Burlesqued* (Dublin: Sylvanus Pepyae, 1733), 9.

186. Leonore Davidoff and Catherine Hall, *Family Fortunes: Men and Women of the English Middle Class, 1780–1850* (Chicago: University of Chicago Press, 1987).

187. Scottish Captain Alexander Hamilton doubted Ovington's knowledge about production, not consumption. Captain Alexander Hamilton, *A New Account of the East Indies* (Edinburgh, 1727), cited in introduction to Ovington, *A Voyage to Suratt*, xvi.

188. Thomas Short, MD, *A Dissertation Upon Tea, Explaining its Nature and Properties* (London: W. Bowyer, 1730), 2.

189. "Thomas Short, M.D.: An Eighteenth Century Medical Practitioner in Sheffield," *British Medical Journal* (14 April 1934): 680.

190. Short, *A Dissertation Upon Tea*, 3.

191. Ibid., 22.

192. Ibid., 61–63.

193. Waldron, *A Satyr against Tea*, 5, 12.

194. James Stephen Taylor, "Philanthropy and Empire: Jonas Hanway and the Infant Poor of London," *Eighteenth-Century Studies* 12, no. 3 (Spring 1979): 288.

195. Jonas Hanway, *An Essay on Tea: Considered as Pernicious to Health; Obstructing Industry; and Impoverishing the Nation* (London: H. Woodfall, 1756), 213.

196. Ibid., 216.

197. Ibid., 223–24.

198. Ibid., 235.

199. Ibid., 244.

200. Ibid., 299.

201. Timothy H. Breen, *The Marketplace of Revolution: How Consumer Politics Shaped American Independence* (Oxford: Oxford University Press, 2004), 298.

202. Ibid., 301.

203. Ibid., 305.

204. Ibid., 306.

205. Ibid., 308.

206. Ibid., 317.

207. Dolin, *When America First Met China*, 84.

208. Ibid., 90.

209. De Vries, *Industrious Revolution*, 31.

CHAPTER 2. THE TEMPERANCE TEA PARTY

1. Leonore Davidoff and Catherine Hall, *Family Fortunes: Men and Women of the English Middle Class, 1780–1850* (Chicago: University of Chicago Press, 1987); Deborah Cohen, *Household Gods: The British and Their Possessions* (New Haven: Yale University Press, 2006). Also on the cultural influence of evangelicalism, see Ian C. Bradley, *The Call to Seriousness: The Evangelical Impact on the Victorians* (London: J. Cape, 1976), 100–102 and Boyd Hilton, *The Age of Atonement: The Influence of Evangelicalism on Social and Economic Thought, 1795–1865* (Oxford: Oxford University Press, 1988).
2. A few important works include Peter Bailey, *Leisure and Class in Victorian England: Rational Recreation and the Contest for Control, 1830–1885* (London: Routledge and Kegan Paul, 1978); Hugh Cunningham, *Leisure in the Industrial Revolution, c. 1780–1880* (London: Croom Helm, 1980); and Hugh Cunningham, *Time, Work and Leisure: Life Changes in England since 1700* (Manchester: Manchester University Press, 2014).
3. Sven Beckert, *Empire of Cotton: A Global History* (New York: Knopf, 2014) and Giorgio Riello, *Cotton: The Fabric That Made the Modern World* (Cambridge: Cambridge University Press, 2013).
4. Sidney W. Mintz, *Sweetness and Power: The Place of Sugar in Modern History* (New York: Penguin, 1985).
5. Ibid. Also see Anson Rabinbach, *The Human Motor: Energy, Fatigue, and the Origins of Modernity* (Berkeley: University of California Press, 1990).
6. Martin Daunton, *Trusting Leviathan: The Politics of Taxation in Britain, 1799–1914* (Cambridge: Cambridge University Press, 2001), 54–57.
7. Quoted in E. P. Thompson, *The Making of the English Working Class* (New York: Vintage, 1966), 740.
8. Quoted in Anna Clark, *The Struggle for the Breeches: Gender and the Making of the British Working Class* (Berkeley: University of California Press, 1995), 160.
9. William Cobbett, *Cottage Economy* (1822; London: Peter Davies, 1926), 15–19.
10. Leonora Nattrass, *William Cobbett: The Politics of Style* (Cambridge: Cambridge University Press, 1995), 152–56.
11. Esther Copley, *Cottage Comforts*, 12th ed. (1825; London: Simpkin and Marshall, 1834), 1.
12. Ibid., 37, 65–66.
13. Craig Muldrew, *Food, Energy and the Creation of Industriousness: Work and Material Culture in Agrarian England, 1550–1780* (Cambridge: Cambridge University Press, 2011).
14. William Rathbone Greg, *An Enquiry into the State of the Manufacturing Population, and the Causes and Cures of the Evils Therein Existing* (London: James Ridgway, 1831), 10.
15. James Phillips Kay-Shuttleworth, MD, *The Moral and Physical Condition of the Working Classes Employed in the Cotton Manufacture in Manchester* (London: James Ridgway, 1832), 9; Peter Gaskell, *The Manufacturing Population of England: Its Moral, Social, and Physical Conditions, and the Changes which have Arisen from the Use of Steam Machinery* (London: Baldwin and Cradock, 1833), 107–10; Friedrich Engels, *The Condition of the Working Class in England* (1845; Harmondsworth: Penguin, 1987), 106.
16. William A. Alcott, *Tea and Coffee* (Boston: G. W. Light, 1839), 17–18. Also see J. A. Chartres, "Spirits in the North-East? Gin and Other Vices in the Long Eighteenth Century," in *Creating and Consuming Culture in North-East England, 1660–1830*, ed. Helen Berry and Jeremy Gregory (Aldershot: Ashgate, 2004), 38, 51–52.

17. John Bowes, *Temperance as it is Opposed to Strong Drinks, Tobacco and Snuff, Tea and Coffee* (Aberdeen: MacKay and Davidson, 1836), 12.
18. Thompson, *Making of the English Working Class*, 318. For an alternative view, see Paul Clayton and Judith Rowbotham, "An Unsuitable and Degraded Diet? Part Two: Realities of the Mid-Victorian Diet," *Journal of the Royal Society of Medicine* 101 (2008): 350–57.
19. John Wesley, *A Letter to a Friend Concerning Tea*, 2nd ed. (London: W. Strahan, 1748). For other examples of Methodism's support, see Samuel Woolmer, "On the Tea Plant," *Methodist Magazine* 23 (1811): 45–49.
20. William Cowper, *The Task: A Poem. In Six Books* (1785; London: C. & C. Whittingham, 1817), book IV, 131.
21. Brian Harrison, *Drink and the Victorians: The Temperance Question in England, 1815–1872* (Pittsburgh: University of Pittsburgh Press, 1971). Also see Lilian Lewis Shiman, *Crusade against Drink in Victorian England* (Hampshire: Macmillan, 1988); Mariana Valverde, *Diseases of the Will: Alcohol and the Dilemmas of Freedom* (Cambridge: Cambridge University Press, 1998); John R. Greenaway, *Drink and British Politics since 1830: A Study in Policy-Making* (New York: Palgrave Macmillan, 2003); James Nicholls, *The Politics of Alcohol: A History of the Drink Question in England* (Manchester: Manchester University Press, 2009); and Elizabeth Malcolm, *"Ireland Sober, Ireland Free": Drink and Temperance in Nineteenth-Century Ireland* (Dublin: Gill and Macmillan, 1986).
22. Davidoff and Hall, *Family Fortunes*; John Tosh, *A Man's Place: Masculinity and the Middle-Class Home in Victorian England* (New Haven: Yale University Press, 2007).
23. For an example of the pro-EIC argument, see *Cui bono? Or the Prospects of a Free Trade in Tea: A Dialogue between an Antimonopolist and a Proprietor of East India Stock* (London: J. Hatchard, 1833).
24. For a careful treatment of the specific social and economic groups that challenged the EIC's tea monopoly, see Yukihisa Kumagai, *Breaking into the Monopoly: Provincial Merchants and Manufacturers' Campaigns for Access to the Asian Market, 1790–1833* (Leiden: Brill, 2013).
25. Michael Greenberg, *British Trade and the Opening of China, 1800–1842* (Cambridge: Cambridge University Press, 1951), 175–95; *First Report from the Select Committee on the Affairs of the East India Company (China Trade)* (London: Parbury, Allen and Co., 1830); *Report from the Select Committee of the House of Lords appointed to Enquire into the Present State of the Affairs of the East-India Company and into the Trade between Great Britain, the East-Indies and China* (London: J. L. Cox, 1830); D. A. Farnie, *The English Cotton Industry and the World Market, 1815–1896* (Oxford: Clarendon, 1979), 86.
26. *Letters on the East India Monopoly*, originally published in the *Glasgow Chronicle* 1 (1812): 106.
27. *James Finlay & Company Limited: Manufacturers and East India Merchants, 1750–1950* (Glasgow: Jackson and Co., 1951), 7.
28. For a snapshot of the company today, http://www.finlays.net.
29. Beckert, *Empire of Cotton*, 88; John Ramsey McCulloch, *Observations on the Influence of the East India Company's Monopoly on the Price and Supply of Tea; and on the Commerce with India, China, etc. . . .* (London, 1831), 5; *Corrected Report of the Speeches of Sir George Staunton on the China Trade in the House of Commons, June 4 and June 14th, 1833* (London: Simpkin and Marshall, 1833).
30. Finlays already owned many tea plantations in India in the 1890s. See Stanley Chapman, "British Free-Standing Companies and Investment Groups in India and the Far East,"

in *The Free Standing Company in the World Economy, 1830–1996,* ed. Mira Wilkins and Harm G. Schröter (New York: Oxford University Press, 1998), 212–13.

31. Hoh-cheung and Lorna H. Mui, *The Management of Monopoly: A Study of the English East India Company's Conduct of its Tea Trade, 1784–1833* (Vancouver: University of British Columbia Press, 1984).

32. Greenberg, *British Trade and the Opening of China,* 175.

33. Robert Gardella, *Harvesting Mountains: Fujian and the China Tea Trade, 1757–1937* (Berkeley: University of California Press, 1994).

34. See, for example, Charles Marjoribanks, Esq., MP, *Letter to the Right Hon. Charles Grant, President of the Board of Controul, on the present state of British Intercourse with China* (London: Hatchard and Son, 1833).

35. Ralph E. Turner, *James Silk Buckingham, 1786–1855: A Social Biography* (New York: Whittlesey House, McGraw Hill, 1934), 43.

36. Ibid., 51.

37. Ibid., 66.

38. On his travels in these years, see ibid., chap. 2.

39. Ibid., 129–30.

40. Ibid., 295.

41. James Silk Buckingham, "Speech of Mr. Buckingham on the Extent, Causes, and Effects of Drunkenness," delivered in the House of Commons on Tuesday, 3 June 1834, *Parliamentary Review* (7 June 1834): 742.

42. P. T. Winskill, *The Temperance Movement and Its Workers: A Record of Social, Moral, Religious and Political Progress* (London: Blackie, 1891), 1:11.

43. Turner, *James Silk Buckingham,* 275.

44. Ibid., 411.

45. "Report on Tea Duties," ordered by the House of Commons, printed 25 July 1834, *Westminster Review* 22, no. 44 (April 1835): 373.

46. John Phipps, *A Practical Treatise on the China and Eastern Trade* (Calcutta: Thacker, 1835), 106–7.

47. *Preston Temperance Advocate* (January 1836): 7.

48. Robert S. Sephton, *The Oxford of J. J. Faulkner, 1798–1857: Grocer, Chartist and Temperance Advocate* (Oxford: R. S. Sephton, 2001), 37. Also see John Ramsey McCulloch's position in "Commutation of Taxes," *Edinburgh Review* (April 1833): 2.

49. *Report of the Proceedings of the Public Meeting on the Tea Duties* (Liverpool, 1846), v.

50. Ibid., 3, 5.

51. Edward Brodribb, speech on taxation before the Financial Reform Association, *Liverpool Times* (22 November 1849), also published in *Hunt's Merchants Magazine* (January and February 1850): 35.

52. See, for example, Charles Knight, "Illustrations of Cheapness: Tea," *Household Words* (8 June 1850): 256.

53. *Report of the Joint Committee of the Legislative Council and House of Assembly of Upper Canada on the Subject of the Importation of Tea, 15 January 1824* (York: John Carey, 1824).

54. David Hancock, *Oceans of Wine: Madeira and the Emergence of American Trade and Taste* (New Haven: Yale University Press, 2009), especially part 3.

55. For a similar earlier argument, see Jessica Warner, "Faith in Numbers: Quantifying Gin and Sin in Eighteenth-Century England," *Journal of British Studies* 50, no. 1 (January 2011): 76–99.

56. Quoted in Harrison, *Drink and the Victorians,* 62.

57. Ibid., 61.
58. Dearden, *A Brief History of Ancient and Modern Tee-Totalism* (Preston: J. Livesey, 1840), 21.
59. The Cloth Hall could accommodate about six hundred persons. "The Conditions of our Towns: Preston, Cotton Factory Town," *The Builder* (7 December 1861), reprinted in David John Hindle, *Life in Victorian Preston* (Gloucestershire: Amberley, 2014), 22. Also see Charles Hardwick, *History of the Borough of Preston and Its Environs in the County of Lancaster* (Preston: Worthington and Company, 1857), 393–94.
60. "Temperance Cause in Preston," *Moral Reformer, and Protestor against Vices, Abuses, and Corruptions of the Age* 2, no. 8 (1 August 1832): 246.
61. On temperance and consumer culture, see Donica Belisle's forthcoming study, *Contesting Consumption: Women and the Rise of Canadian Consumer Modernity*, chap. 2. I want to thank Donica for sharing this manuscript with me before publication.
62. "Tea Parties," *Poor Man's Guardian* (18 March 1831): 7. Also see 12 March 1831, 8 and 23 April 1831, 8. Clark, *Struggle for the Breeches*; James Vernon, *Politics and the People: A Study in English Political Culture, c. 1815–1867* (Cambridge: Cambridge University Press, 1993), 207–50; James Epstein, "Some Organizational and Cultural Aspects of the Chartist Movement in Nottingham," in *The Chartist Experience: Studies in Working Class Radicalism and Culture, 1830–1860*, ed. James Epstein and Dorothy Thompson (London: Macmillan, 1982), 221–68.
63. Barbara Taylor, *Eve and the New Jerusalem: Socialism and Feminism in the Nineteenth Century* (New York: Pantheon, 1983), 222.
64. *Poor Man's Guardian* (18 March 1831): 7.
65. "Female Opposition to the New Poor Law," *Cleave's Weekly Police Gazette* (9 April 1836): n.p.; James Vernon, *Hunger: A Modern History* (Cambridge, MA: Belknap Press of Harvard University Press, 2007), 18–20.
66. Taylor, *Eve and the New Jerusalem*, 222.
67. Nicholls, *Politics of Alcohol*, 98; Harrison, *Drink and the Victorians*, 103–6; Winskill, *Temperance Movement*, 5.
68. Harrison, *Drink and the Victorians*, 130.
69. Nicholls, *Politics of Alcohol*, 89.
70. Vernon, *Politics and the People*; Nicholls, *The Politics of Alcohol*, 81.
71. Hindle, *Life in Victorian Preston*, 29.
72. John K. Walton, *Lancashire: A Social History, 1558–1939* (Manchester: Manchester University Press, 1987), 251.
73. Weavers, spinners, shoemakers, mechanics, cabinetmakers, and shopkeepers were the first to sign the pledge. Winskill, *Temperance Movement*, 107; James Ellison, *Dawn of Teetotalism: Being the Story of the Origin of the Total Abstinence Pledge signed by the "Seven Men of Preston," and the Introduction of Teetotalism* (Preston: J. Ellison, 1932); Ian Levitt, ed., *Joseph Livesey of Preston: Business, Temperance and Moral Reform* (Lancashire: University of Central Lancashire, 1996); E. C. Urwin, *A Weaver at the Loom of Time: A Sketch of the Life of Joseph Livesey the Early Temperance Reformer* (London: Sunday School Union, 1923); Harrison, *Drink and the Victorians*, 117–18; Shiman, *Crusade against Drink*, 18.
74. Harrison, *Drink and the Victorians*, 95.
75. Anthony Howe, *The Cotton Masters, 1830–1860* (Oxford: Oxford University Press 1984), 273; For the social and cultural history of this community, see Brian Lewis: *The Middlemost and the Milltowns: Bourgeois Culture and Politics in Early Industrial*

England (Stanford: Stanford University Press, 2002); Bailey, *Leisure and Class in Victorian England*; Simon Gunn, *The Public Culture of the Victorian Middle Class: Ritual and Authority in the English Industrial City, 1840–1914* (Manchester: Manchester University Press, 2000); Rachel Rich, *Bourgeois Consumption: Food, Space and Identity in London and Paris, 1850–1914* (Manchester: Manchester University Press, 2011); Amy Woodson-Boulton, *Transformative Beauty: Art Museums in Industrial Britain* (Stanford: Stanford University Press, 2012).

76. Derek Antrobus, *A Guiltless Feast: The Salford Bible Christian Church and the Rise of the Modern Vegetarian Movement* (Salford: City of Salford, Education and Leisure, 1997), 59. On the particular denominations, see Louis Billington, "Popular Religion and Social Reform: A Study of Revivalism and Teetotalism, 1830–1850," *Journal of Religious History* 10, no. 3 (June 1979): 266–93. On Christian food ideals, see David Grumett and Rachel Muers, *Theology on the Menu: Asceticism, Meat, and the Christian Diet* (London: Routledge, 2010).

77. Billington, "Popular Religion and Social Reform."

78. Harrison, *Drink and the Victorians*, 117–18.

79. Ken Williams, *The Story of Ty-phoo and the Birmingham Tea Industry* (London: Quiller, 1990), 11–13; Shiman, *Crusade against Drink*, 64; Harrison, *Drink and the Victorians*, 179–95.

80. "Bolton Tea Party," *Moral Reformer, and Protestor Against the Vices, Abuses, and Corruptions of the Age* 3, no. 11 (November 1833): 353.

81. "Female Abstinence Society," *Teetotal Times and General Advertiser* 1, no. 1 (15 December 1838): n.p.

82. Tara Moore, "National Identity and Victorian Christmas Foods," in *Consuming Culture in the Long Nineteenth Century: Narratives of Consumption, 1700–1900*, ed. Tamara S. Wagner and Narin Hassan (Lanham, MD: Lexington Books, 2007), 141–54.

83. "Splendid Tea Party," *Preston Temperance Advocate* (January 1834): 1.

84. "Preston Temperance Tea Party," *Preston Temperance Advocate* (February 1836): 12–13.

85. In the 1820s Preston was a thriving cotton and market town. *A Topographical, Statistical, and Historical Account of the Borough of Preston* (Preston, 1821), 118. Ten years later its weavers were utterly destitute. *Poor Man's Guardian* (4 February 1831): 1; Howe, *The Cotton Masters*, 164.

86. *Preston Temperance Advocate* (May 1836): 39.

87. For a related discussion, see Peter J. Gurney, "'Rejoicing in Potatoes': The Politics of Consumption in England during the 'Hungry Forties,'" *Past and Present* 203 (May 2009): 133.

88. "Temperance Society of Congress," *Spirit of the Age and Journal of Humanity* 1, no. 42 (6 March 1834): 2; *Trumpet and Universalist Magazine* 6, no. 42 (8 March 1834): 147.

89. "Tea Parties," *Livesey's Moral Reformer* 2 (January 1838): 10.

90. Winskill, *Temperance Movement*, 105.

91. "Tea Party," *Preston Temperance Advocate* (January 1834): 7.

92. Letter to the editor, *Preston Temperance Advocate* (January 1834): 11.

93. The other key leader of the Anti-Corn Law League, Richard Cobden also subscribed to the British Association for the Promotion of Temperance when it formed in Manchester in 1835. *Preston Temperance Advocate* (November 1835): 94.

94. *Preston Temperance Advocate* (September 1836), quoted in Winskill, *Temperance Movement*, 150.

95. Winskill, *Temperance Movement*, 2.

96. Samuel Couling, *A History of the Temperance Movement in Great Britain and Ireland* (London: W. Tweedie, 1862), 65.

97. Harrison, *Drink and the Victorians*, 109.

98. "Tea Festival at Kendal" *Preston Temperance Advocate* (February 1836): 12; "London Tea Party," *Preston Temperance Advocate* (March 1836): 20.

99. "Tea Parties," *Livesey's Moral Reformer* 2 (January 1838): 10.

100. Dearden, *A Brief History of Ancient and Modern Tee-Totalism*, 21.

101. Winskill, *Temperance Movement*, 117.

102. Thomas Richards, *The Commodity Culture of Victorian England: Advertising and Spectacle, 1851–1914* (Stanford: Stanford University Press, 1990), 48–49.

103. John Burnett, *Plenty and Want: A Social History of Diet in England from 1815 to the Present Day* (London: Scolar Press, 1979), 48–73.

104. *The Temperance Movement*, pamphlet, c. 1845, 17.

105. "Coffee Shops in London," *Penny Magazine* 9, no. 558 (12 December 1840): 488; Burnett, *Plenty and Want*, 83; John Burnett, *England Eats Out: A Social History of Eating Out in England from 1830 to the Present* (Harlow: Pearson Longman, 2004), 46–50; *Preston Temperance Advocate* (January 1834): 14; Nathaniel Whittock, *The Complete Book of Trades, or, the Parent's Guide and Youth's Instructor: Forming a Popular Encyclopedia of Trades, Manufactures, and Commerce* (London: T. Tegg, 1842), 159.

106. Dearden, *A Brief History of Ancient and Modern Tee-Totalism*, 21.

107. Mintz, *Sweetness and Power*, 143.

108. *Domestic Life, or, Hints for Daily Use* (London, 1841).

109. "Female Abstinence Festival."

110. Quoted in William Cooke Taylor, *Factories and the Factory System: From Parliamentary Documents and Personal Examination* (London: Jeremiah How, 1844), 53.

111. Catherine Marsh, *English Hearts and English Hands, or, The Railway and the Trenches* (New York: R. Carter, 1858), 16, 353.

112. On this populist discourse, see Patrick Joyce, *Visions of the People: Industrial England and the Question of Class, 1848–1914* (Cambridge: Cambridge University Press, 1991) and *Democratic Subjects: The Self and the Social in Nineteenth-Century England* (Cambridge: Cambridge University Press, 1994).

113. John Styles, *The Dress of the People: Everyday Fashion in Eighteenth-Century England* (New Haven: Yale University Press, 2007).

114. "Annual Christmas Tea Party of the Preston Temperance Society," *Teetotal Times and General Advertiser* 1, no. 4 (5 January 1839): n.p.

115. Clark, *Struggle for the Breeches*, 79–82.

116. "Wigan Temperance Tea Party," *Teetotal Times and General Advertiser* 1, no. 3 (29 December 1838): n.p.

117. Albert O. Hirschman, *The Passions and the Interests: Political Arguments for Capitalism before Its Triumph* (Princeton: Princeton University Press, 1977).

118. Harrison, *Drink and the Victorians*, 95.

119. Rev. James Birmingham, *A Memoir of the Very Rev. Theobald Matthew* (Dublin: Milliken and Son, 1840), 69.

120. Quoted in Harrison, *Drink and the Victorians*, 97.

121. Ibid., 119. Also see Arthur W. Silver, *Manchester Men and Indian Cotton, 1847–1872* (New York: Barnes and Noble, 1966), 31. The midcentury cotton industry was particularly export oriented, however, and between 1834 and 1873, exports grew three times faster than the home market. See Farnie, *The English Cotton Industry and the World Market*, 86.

122. On the liberal consumer, see Frank Trentmann, *Free Trade Nation: Commerce, Consumption, and Civil Society in Modern Britain* (Oxford: Oxford University Press, 2008).

123. Harrison, *Drink and the Victorians*, 101.

124. Winskill, *Temperance Movement*, 5.

125. For other aspects of this transnational community, see Carl Bridge and Kent Fedorowich, eds., *The British World: Diaspora, Culture and Identity* (London: Frank Cass, 2003); James Belich, *Replenishing the Earth: The Settler Revolution and the Rise of the Anglo-World, 1783–1939* (Oxford: Oxford University Press, 2009).

126. Winskill, *Temperance Movement*, 58, 63, 75–76.

127. Ibid., 60.

128. *The American Missionary Register for the Year 1825* 6 (December 1825): 375.

129. Elizabeth Elbourne, *Blood Ground: Colonialism, Missions, and the Contest for Christianity in the Cape Colony and Britain, 1799–1853* (Montreal: McGill-Queen's University Press, 2002), 234–43.

130. Ibid., 241–43.

131. Rev. John Campbell, *Travels in South Africa, undertaken at the request of the London Missionary Society; being an account of a Second Journey in the Interior of the Cape* (London: Francis Westley, 1822), 1:164.

132. Quoted in John L. Comaroff and Jean Comaroff, *Of Revelation and Revolution: The Dialectics of Modernity on a South African Frontier* (Chicago: University of Chicago Press, 1997), 2:236.

133. Ibid.

134. As quoted in *The American Missionary Register for the Year 1825, Vol. VI* (New York: United Foreign Missionary Society, 1825).

135. "Baptist Tea Meeting," *The Liberator* 25, no. 55 (31 August 1855): 140, American Periodicals, Proquest.

136. T. Brooks, "Temperance in India," *Livesey's Moral Reformer* 22 (January 1839): 213.

137. John Sharpe, letter to *Primitive Methodist Magazine*, 24 January 1852, 3rd ser., 10 (1852): 368–71, republished in William E. Van Vugt, ed., *British Immigration to the United States, 1776–1914* (London: Pickering and Chatto, 2009), 3:293–94.

138. *Evangelist* 2, no. 10 (October 1851): 151, republished in *British Immigration to the United States*, 3:298.

139. "Tea Parties," *Friends' Review: A Religious, Literary and Miscellaneous Journal* (29 December 1849): 282.

140. *Report of the Executive Committee of the American Union, 1844* (New York, 1844), 14.

141. "Brooklyn Methodists Take Tea," *Christian Advocate* (7 April 1887): 224; *Religious, Literary and Miscellaneous Journal* (29 December 1849): 282.

142. "The Tea Saloon," *Public Opinion* 26, no. 25 (June 1899): 782.

143. Peter Gurney, *Co-Operative Culture and the Politics of Consumption in England, 1870–1930* (Manchester: Manchester University Press, 1996); Paul A. Pickering

and Alex Tyrrell, *The People's Bread: A History of the Anti-Corn Law League* (London: Leicester University Press, 2000), 134.

144. *Report of the Conservative Tea Party* (Birmingham, 1836), 49.
145. Quoted in Bradley, *Call to Seriousness*, 47.
146. Carol Kennedy, *Business Pioneers: Family, Fortune, and Philanthropy: Cadbury, Sainsbury and John Lewis* (London: Random House, 2000), 15–25.
147. Williams, *Story of Ty-Phoo*, 12; Charles Dellheim, "The Creation of a Company Culture: Cadburys, 1861–1931," *American Historical Review* 92 (February 1987): 13–44.
148. G. Holden Pike, *John Cassell* (London: Cassell and Company, 1894), 18.
149. *Journal of the New British and Foreign Temperance Society* 1, no. 28 (13 July 1839): 255; 1, no. 37 (23 November 1839): 403; 2, no. 8 (15 August 1840): 100. John Bright was vice president of the society at this time.
150. *The Story of the House of Cassell* (London: Cassell and Company, 1922), 13.
151. Ibid., 12–15.
152. *The Metropolitan: The Ladies Newspaper* (19 October 1850): 212.
153. *The Temperance Record* (25 January 1873): 47. By the 1880s, a specialized journal, the *Temperance Caterer*, served this socially-minded catering trade.
154. Harrison, *Drink and the Victorians*, 37.
155. Arnold Palmer, *Movable Feasts: A Reconnaissance of the Origins and Consequences of Fluctuations in Meal Times with special attention to the Introduction of Luncheon and Afternoon Tea* (London: Oxford University Press, 1952), 59; Laura Mason, "Everything Stops for Tea," in *Eating with the Victorians*, ed. C. Anne Wilson (London, 1994), 68–85; Andrea Broomfield, *Food and Cooking in Victorian England: A History* (Westport, CT: Praeger, 2007), 58–77.
156. Jean Rey, *The Whole Art of Dining* (London: Carmona and Baker, 1921), 50–51.
157. Ivan Day, "Teatime," in *Eat, Drink and Be Merry: The British at Table, 1600–2000*, ed. Ivan Day (London: P. Wilson, 2000), 107–30. There is also some evidence that in the 1830s working-class women began to drink tea at 4:00, while their husbands drank beer. See Zachariah Allen, *The Practical Tourist: Sketches of Useful Arts, and of Society, Scenery, etc. . . . in Great Britain, France, and Holland* (Providence: A. S. Beckwith), I:210.
158. Arjun Appadurai, "Disjuncture and Difference in the Global Cultural Economy," in *Modernity at Large: Cultural Dimensions of Globalization*, ed. Arjun Appadurai (Minneapolis: University of Minnesota Press, 1996), 42. Also see, Daniel Miller, "Coca-Cola: A Black Sweet Drink from Trinidad," in *Material Cultures: Why Some Things Matter*, ed. Daniel Miller (Chicago: University of Chicago Press, 1998), 170.
159. Harrison, *Drink and the Victorians*, 119–20.

CHAPTER 3. A LITTLE OPIUM, SWEET WORDS, AND CHEAP GUNS

1. Charles A. Murray in reply to Mr. Gordon's Circular, December 1838, "Correspondence Relating to Assam Tea, 1838," BL Add. Mss. 22717.
2. Lady Alicia Gordon, in the name of Princess Sophia Matilda, December 1838, in reply to Mr. Gordon's Circular, BL Add. Mss. 22717.

436 Notes to Pages 85–86

3. Andrew Melrose to the Provost of Edinburgh, December 1838, BL Add. Mss. 22717. For more on this business, see Hoh-Cheung and Lorna H. Mui, eds., *William Melrose in China, 1845–1945: The Letters of a Scottish Tea Merchant* (Edinburgh: T. and A. Constable, 1973).

4. Lord Richard Wellesley, "Correspondence Relating to Assam Tea, 1840," BL Add. Mss. 22717.

5. Provost Milne, Aberdeen, 12 December 1838, in reply to Mr. Gordon's Circular, BL Add. Mss. 22717.

6. There are several very important studies on this and related topics. See Piya Chatterjee, *A Time for Tea: Women, Labor and Post/Colonial Politics on an Indian Plantation* (Durham: Duke University Press, 2001); Jayeeta Sharma, *Empire's Garden: Assam and the Making of India* (Durham: Duke University Press, 2011); Gunnel Cederlöf, *Founding an Empire on India's North-Eastern Frontiers, 1790-1840: Climate, Commerce, Polity* (Oxford: Oxford University Press, 2014); Rana P. Behal, *One Hundred Years of Servitude: Political Economy of Tea Plantations in Colonial Assam* (New Delhi: Tulika Books, 2014); Rajen Saikia, *The Social and Economic History of Assam, 1853–1921* (New Delhi: Manohar, 2000); Amalenda Guha, "Colonisation of Assam: Second Phase, 1840–1859," *Indian Economic and Social History Review* 4, no. 4 (1967): 289–317; Sanghamitra Misra, *Becoming a Borderland: The Politics of Space and Identity in Colonial Northeastern India* (London: Routledge, 2011); Andrew B. Liu, "The Birth of a Noble Tea Country: On the Geography of Colonial Capital and the Origins of Indian Tea," *Journal of Historical Sociology* 23, no. 1 (March 2010): 73–100; and Asim Chaudhuri, *Enclaves in a Peasant Society: Political Economy of Tea in Western Dooars in Northern Bengal* (New Delhi: People's Publishing House, 1995). Older accounts include Sir Percival Griffiths, *The History of the Indian Tea Industry* (London: Weidenfeld and Nicolson, 1967); H. A. Antrobus, *A History of the Assam Company, 1839–1953* (Edinburgh: T. and A. Constable, Ltd., 1957); and his *A History of the Jorehaut Tea Company Ltd., 1859–1946* (London: Tea and Rubber Mail, 1948).

7. For studies of the political economy of northern India, see Sudipta Sen, *Empire of Free Trade: The East India Company and the Making of the Colonial Marketplace* (Philadelphia: University of Pennsylvania Press, 1998); Christopher A. Bayly, *Rulers, Townsmen and Bazaars: Northern Indian Society in the Age of British Expansion, 1770–1870* (Cambridge: Cambridge University Press, 1988); and his "The Age of Hiatus: The North Indian Economy and Society, 1830–1850," in *Trade and Finance in Colonial India, 1750–1860*, ed. Asiya Siddiqi (Delhi: Oxford University Press, 1995), 218–49.

8. The Tea Committee acknowledged the "discovery" somewhat earlier, but a letter of 24 December made it official. Nathaniel Wallich to W. H. Macnaghten, in *The Correspondence of Lord William Cavendish Bentinck: Governor-General of India, 1828–1835*, ed. C. H. Philips (Oxford: Oxford University Press, 1977), 2:1389–90.

9. On indigenous capital and Indian capitalism, see Christopher A. Bayly, *Indian Society and the Making of the British Empire* (Cambridge: Cambridge University Press, 1988), especially chap. 2; Dwijendra Tripathi, *The Oxford History of Indian Business* (Oxford: Oxford University Press, 2004), 44–72.

10. William Robinson, *A Descriptive Account of Asam: With a Sketch of the Local Geography, and a Concise History of the Tea Plant of Asam* (1841; Delhi: Sanskaran Prakashak, 1975), 141.

11. "Proceedings of the Committee appointed by the Government for the Introduction of the Tea Plant into the Company's Territories," 13 February 1834, in *Copy of Papers Received from India Relating to the Measures Adopted for Introducing the Cultivation of the Tea Plant within the British Possessions in India* (London: HMSO, 1839), 18–20 (hereafter I have referred to this collection as Papers on the Cultivation of the Tea Plant).

12. The agency houses were private companies with interests that stretched from Europe to India and the Far East. See Tony Webster, "An Early Global Business in a Colonial Context: The Strategies, Management, and Failure of John Palmer and Company of Calcutta, 1780–1830," *Enterprise and Society* 6, no. 1 (March 2005): 98–133; Michael Greenberg, *British Trade and the Opening of China, 1800–1842* (Cambridge: Cambridge University Press, 1951); S. B. Singh, *European Agency Houses in Bengal, 1783–1833* (Calcutta: Firma K. L. Mukhopadhyay, 1966); and Amales Tripathi, *Trade and Finance in the Bengal Presidency, 1793–1833* (Calcutta: Oxford University Press, 1979).

13. K. N. Chaudhuri, ed., *The Economic Development of India under the East India Company, 1814–58: A Selection of Contemporary Writings* (Cambridge: Cambridge University Press, 1971), 18. Bentinck has been especially associated with the era of utilitarian reforms in India. John Rosselli, *Lord William Bentinck: The Making of a Liberal Imperialist* (Berkeley: University of California Press, 1974). Also see Eric Stokes, *The English Utilitarians and India* (Oxford: Clarendon, 1959); Uday Singh Mehta, *Liberalism and Empire: A Study in Nineteenth-Century British Liberal Thought* (Chicago: University of Chicago Press, 1999); and Jennifer Pitts, *A Turn to Empire: The Rise of Imperial Liberalism in Britain and France* (Princeton: Princeton University Press, 2005), 103.

14. Rosselli, *Bentinck*, 24, 56–65.

15. William H. Ukers, *All About Tea* (New York: The Tea and Coffee Trade Journal Company, 1935), 1:109–15.

16. Ibid., 115–18.

17. D. M. Etherington, "The Indonesian Tea Industry," *Bulletin of Indonesian Economic Studies* 10, no. 2 (July 1974): 85.

18. Ibid., 85–86.

19. Minute by the Governor-General, Lord William Bentinck, 24 January 1834, 5, Papers on the Cultivation of the Tea Plant.

20. Griffiths, *History of the Indian Tea Industry*, 33–35. On Banks, see John Gasgoigne, *Science in the Service of Empire: Joseph Banks, the British State and the Uses of Science in the Age of Revolution* (Cambridge: Cambridge University Press, 1998).

21. Nathaniel Wallich, "Observations on the Cultivation of the Tea Plant for Commercial Purposes, in the Mountainous parts of Hindostan," 14, Papers on the Cultivation of the Tea Plant.

22. Ukers, *All about Tea*, 1:135.

23. Adam Smith had recognized that China's internal trade was so large as to make foreign trade unnecessary, but most businesses did not consider this view. See Robert Paul Gardella, *Harvesting Mountains: Fujian and the China Tea Trade, 1757–1937* (Berkeley: University of California Press, 1994), 1.

24. There is a very large body of work on this topic, but for a revisionist perspective that downplays economics, see Glenn Melancon, *Britain's China Policy and the Opium Crisis: Balancing Drugs, Violence and National Honour, 1833–1840* (Aldershot: Ashgate, 2003). For a thorough overview, see Peter Ward Fay, *The Opium War, 1840–1842* (Chapel Hill: University of North Carolina Press, 1975).

25. *Canton Register and Price Current* 1, no. 22 (31 May 1828): 88.
26. Ibid., 1, no. 28 (19 July 1828): 109.
27. Ibid., 4, no. 14 (4 July 1831): 62.
28. For a fuller analysis of how such arguments developed, see Frank Trentmann, *Free Trade Nation: Commerce, Consumption, and Civil Society in Modern Britain* (Oxford: Oxford University Press, 2008).
29. Minute by the Governor-General, Lord William Bentinck, 24 January 1834, 5, Papers on the Cultivation of the Tea Plant.
30. See discussion of the memo, for example, in "Our Own History of Tea Cultivation in India," *The Grocer* (27 October 1866): 302.
31. John Walker, "Proposition to the Honourable Directors of the East India Company to Cultivate Tea upon the Nepaul hills, and such other parts of the Territories of the East India Company as May be Suitable to its Growth," extract from India Revenue Consultations, reprinted 1 February 1834, 12, 6, Papers on the Cultivation of the Tea Plant.
32. Ibid., 6–7.
33. Ibid., 7.
34. "A Concise Statement Relative to the Cultivation and Manufacture of Tea in Upper Assam," 12 February 1839, meeting of London Board of Assam Company, Ltd., London Board Minute Book, 12 February 1839–17 December 1845, Assam Company Archives, CLS/B/123/MS09924/001. These records have moved from the Guildhall Library, London, to the London Metropolitan Archives (LMA) and are part of the Inchape Group Collection. I have used the new reference numbers throughout.
35. Walker, "Proposition," 11.
36. Members of the Tea Committee to W. H. Macnaghten, Esq., Secretary to the Government in the Revenue Department, 24 December 1834, 32, Papers on the Cultivation of the Tea Plant.
37. Amalendu Guha, *Planter-Raj to Swaraj: Freedom Struggle and Electoral Politics in Assam, 1826–1947* (New Delhi: Indian Council of Historical Research, 1977) and Nitin Anant Gokhale, *The Hot Brew: The Assam Tea Industry's Most Turbulent Decade, 1987–1997* (Guwahati: Spectrum Publications, 1998).
38. See, for example, Henry Hobhouse, *Seeds of Change: Five Plants That Transformed Mankind* (New York: Harper and Row, 1985), 95–137.
39. Guha, "Colonisation of Assam."
40. Saikia, *History of Assam*, 145. Other studies emphasize economics but downplay the role of tea. See, for example, S. K. Bhuyan, *Anglo-Assamese Relations, 1771–1826*, 2nd ed. (1949; Gauhati, Assam: Lawyer's Book Stall, 1979); Rebati Mohan Lahiri, *The Annexation of Assam (1824–1854)* (Calcutta: General Printers and Publishers, 1954).
41. W. Nassau Lees, *Tea Cultivation, Cotton and Other Agricultural Experiments in India* (London: Wm. H. Allen, 1863).
42. Chatterjee, *A Time for Tea* and Sharma, *Empire's Garden*.
43. Cederlöf, *Founding an Empire*, 5, 10.
44. E. A. Gait, *A History of Assam* (Calcutta: Thacker, Spink and Co., 1906); B. B. Hazarika, *Political Life in Assam during the Nineteenth Century* (Shakti Nagar, Delhi: Gian Publishing House, 1987); Saikia, *History of Assam*; Bhuyan, *Anglo-Assamese Relations*;

Lahiri, *The Annexation of Assam*; Suhas Chatterjee, *A Socio Economic History of South Assam* (Jaipur: Printwell Publishers, 2000).

45. Cederlöf provides a good overview of this history and how it influenced the nature of colonization in *Founding an Empire*, 83.

46. Bhuyan, *Anglo-Assamese Relations*, 55.

47. Quoted in ibid., 54.

48. Ibid., 301, 361.

49. See the discussion of Pitt's 1784 India Act and the policy of nonintervention in Assam in Hazarika, *Political Life in Assam during the Nineteenth Century*, 132–33.

50. Ibid.; Lahiri, *Annexation of Assam*; Bhuyan, *Anglo-Assamese Relations*; Gait, *History of Assam*.

51. Misra, *Becoming a Borderland*; Michael Baud and William Van Schendel, "Towards a Comparative History of Borderlands," *Journal of World History* 8, no. 2 (Fall 1997): 211–42. For the contemporary period, see Willem van Schendel, *The Bengal Borderland: Beyond State and Nation in South Asia* (London: Anthem, 2005); Nandana Dutta, *Questions of Identity in Assam: Location, Migration, Hybridity* (Los Angeles: Sage, 2012); and Sanjoy Hazarika, *Rites of Passage: Border Crossings, Imagined Homelands, India's East and Bangladesh* (London: Penguin Books India, 2000).

52. Bhuyan, *Anglo-Assamese Relations*, 516–17.

53. Quoted in ibid., 524.

54. Ibid., 524–25.

55. Ibid., 552. Bhuyan claims he was the first to record this ballad in 1924 and that it had circulated before that for a hundred years.

56. Hazarika, *Political Life in Assam during the Nineteenth Century*, 122.

57. Quoted in ibid., 126.

58. For a comparison, see Michael Adas, "Imperialist Rhetoric and Modern Historiography: The Case of Lower Burma before and after Conquest," *Journal of Southeast Asian Studies* 3, no. 2 (September 1972): 175–92.

59. Major John Butler, *Travels and Adventures in the Province of Assam: During a Residence of Fourteen Years* (1855; Delhi: Vivek, 1978), 247, 249.

60. Ibid., 250.

61. *Assam: Sketch of its History, Soil, and Productions; with the discovery of the Tea-Plant, and of the Countries Adjoining Assam* (London: Smith Elder and Co., 1839), 8.

62. Bhuyan, *Anglo-Assamese Relations*, 542–43.

63. Scott died before the situation in Assam was resolved. Nirode K. Barooah, *David Scott in North-East India, 1802–1831: A Study in British Paternalism* (New Delhi: Munshiram Manoharlal, 1970), 88–156.

64. Lahiri, *Annexation of Assam*.

65. Bhuyan, *Anglo-Assamese Relations*, 563.

66. Lahiri, *Annexation of Assam*, 192–93.

67. Lieutenant Charlton to Captain Jenkins, 17 May 1834, 35, Papers on the Cultivation of the Tea Plant.

68. Ajit Kumar Dutta, *Maniram Dewan and the Contemporary Assamese Society* (Guwahati, Assam: Anupoma Dutta, 1990), 90.

69. Gait, *History of Assam*, 226.

70. Ukers, *All about Tea*, 1:135–37.

71. James Scott, *The Tea Story* (London: Heinemann, 1964), 66.

72. N. Wallich, MD, on Deputation, to Captain F. Jenkins, Agent to the Governor-general North-east Frontier, 15 March 1836, Papers on the Cultivation of the Tea Plant, 71.

73. Chatterjee, *A Time for Tea*, 86–92; Sharma, *Empire's Garden*.

74. C. A. Bruce to Captain F. Jenkins, 20 September 1836, Papers on the Cultivation of the Tea Plant.

75. N. Wallich to J. W. Grant, Bagoam in the Muttock Country, 19 February 1836, Papers on the Cultivation of the Tea Plant.

76. William Griffith, *Journals of Travels in Assam, Burma, Bootan, Affghanistan and the Neighbouring Countries* (Calcutta: Bishop's College Press, 1847), 16.

77. *Assam: Sketch of its History, Soil, and Productions*, 13.

78. For an analysis, see David Arnold, *The Tropics and the Traveling Gaze: India, Landscape and Science, 1800–1856* (Seattle: University of Washington Press, 2006).

79. Butler, *Travels*, 55, 59.

80. Chatterjee, *A Time for Tea*, 52–53.

81. C. A. Bruce, Esq., Commanding Gun Boats, to Lieutenant J. Millar, Commanding at Suddeya, 14 April 1836, 71, Papers on the Cultivation of the Tea Plant.

82. Major A. White, Political Agent, Upper Assam, to Captain F. Jenkins, Agent to the Governor-general, Assam, 30 May 1836, 69, Papers on the Cultivation of the Tea Plant.

83. C. A. Bruce to Jenkins, 1 October 1836, 84–85, Papers on the Cultivation of the Tea Plant.

84. Captain F. Jenkins, Governor-general's Agent, to G. J. Gordon, Esq., Secretary to the Tea Committee, Fort William, 18 October 1836, Papers on the Cultivation of the Tea Plant.

85. Bruce to Jenkins, 85, Papers on the Cultivation of the Tea Plant.

86. The Tea Committee to W. H. Macnaghten, Esq., Secretary to Governor-General, 6 August 1836, 76–79, Papers on the Cultivation of the Tea Plant.

87. Jenkins to Wallich, 5 May 1836, 71, Papers on the Cultivation of the Tea Plant.

88. Quoted in Dutta, *Dewan*, 95.

89. Major A. White to Wallich, 25 December 1835, 52, Papers on the Cultivation of the Tea Plant.

90. Jenkins to N. Wallich, Esq., MD, 5 May 1836, 72, Papers on the Cultivation of the Tea Plant.

91. Dutta, *Dewan*, 5.

92. Ibid.

93. Ibid., 98–101.

94. Quoted in Antrobus, *Assam Company*, 343–44.

95. Dutta, *Cha Garam*, 62–63.

96. Dutta, *Dewan*, 108–9.

97. Chatterjee, *A Time for Tea*, 87, 97, 99–101; Tripathi, *Oxford History of Indian Business*, 66.

98. See Das Gupta's summary of Sibsankar Mukherjee, "Emergence of Bengali Entrepreneurship in Tea Plantations in Jalpaiguri Duars, 1879–1933" (PhD thesis, N.B.U., 1978), quoted in *Labour in Tea Gardens*, 12–19.

99. Quoted in Griffiths, *History of the Indian Tea Industry*, 53, 110–11.

100. Behal, *One Hundred Years of Servitude*, 34.

101. "A Concise Statement Relative to the Cultivation and Manufacture of Tea in Upper Assam," 12 February 1839, meeting of London Board of Assam Company,

Ltd., London Board Minute Book, 12 February 1839–17 December 1845, Assam Company Archives, CLS/B/123/MS09924/001.

102. For a comparison with the Dutch, see Jan Breman, *Taming the Coolie Beast: Plantation Society and the Colonial Order in Southeast Asia* (Delhi: Oxford University Press, 1989).

103. Hazarika, *Political Life in Assam during the Nineteenth Century*, 8; Birendra Chandra Chakravorty, *British Relations with the Hill Tribes of Assam since 1858* (Calcutta: Firma K. L. Mukhopadhya, 1964).

104. See Ukers, *All about Tea*, vol. 1, chap. 15 for a good description of the overall process.

105. A good example of this impulse to gather knowledge from China is G. J. Gordon, "Journal of an Attempted Ascent of the River Min, to visit the Tea Plantations of the Fuh-kin Province of China," *Journal of the Asiatic Society of Bengal* 4 (1835): 553–64. For a broader narrative account, see Sarah Rose, *For All the Tea in China: How England Stole the World's Favorite Drink and Changed History* (New York: Penguin, 2011).

106. Roy Moxham, *Tea: Addiction, Exploitation, and Empire (London: Carroll and Graf, 2003)*, 127.

107. Arup Kumar Dutta, *Cha Garam! The Tea Story (Guwahati: Paloma Publications, 1992)*, 125–33.

108. One estimate suggested that there were 799,519 people in 1837. Behal, *One Hundred Years of Servitude*, 13.

109. C. A. Bruce, *Report on the Manufacture of Tea, and on the Extent and Produce of the Tea Plantations in Assam*, presented by the Tea Committee and read at a Meeting of the Agricultural and Horticulture Society of India, 14 August 1839, in *Transactions of the Agricultural and Horticultural Society of India* 7 (Calcutta, 1840): 8.

110. Bruce to Jenkins, 10 February 1837, 2, Papers on the Cultivation of the Tea Plant.

111. Bruce, *Report on the Manufacture of Tea*, 1.

112. Ibid., 37.

113. Hazarika, *Political Life in Assam during the Nineteenth Century*, 268–70.

114. Francis Bonynge, *Future Wealth of America: Being a Glance at the Resources of the United States . . . with a Review of the China Trade* (New York: Published by the Author, 1852), 87–96.

115. For a full discussion of this process, see Sharma, *Empire's Garden*; Chatterjee, *A Time for Tea*; Navinder K. Singh, *Role of Women Workers in the Tea Industry of North East India* (New Delhi: Classical Publishing, 2001); Pranab Kumar Das Gupta and Iar Ali Khan, *Impact of Tea Plantation Industry on the Life of Tribal Labourers* (Calcutta: Government of India, 1983); Manas Das Gupta, *Labour in Tea Gardens* (Delhi: Gyan Sagar Publications, 1999); Rana P. Behal and Prabhu P. Mohapatra, "'Tea and Money versus Human Life': The Rise and Fall of the Indenture System in the Assam Tea Plantations, 1840–1908," in *Plantations, Proletarians and Peasants in Colonial Asia*, ed. E. Valentine Daniel, Henry Bernstein, and Tom Brass (London: Frank Cass, 1992), 142–73; and most recently, Behal, *One Hundred Years of Servitude*.

116. Behal, *One Hundred Years of Servitude*, 4.

117. *Report of the Local Directors made to the Shareholders at a General Meeting held at Calcutta*, 11 August 1841 (Calcutta: Bishop's College Press, 1841), Assam Company Archives, CLC/B/123/MS27047.

118. *Report of the Provisional Committee made to the Shareholders at a General Meeting*, 7 May 1841, 18, Assam Company Archives, CLC/B/123/MS27,052/1.

119. Bruce, *Report on the Manufacture of Tea*, 21.
120. Saikia, *History of Assam,* 214.
121. There is some debate about how much opium was cultivated in Assam; see Saikia, *History of Assam*, 213 and Robinson, *A Descriptive Account of Asam*, 24.
122. Bruce, *Report on the Manufacture of Tea*, 34. Also see Butler, *Travels*, 70.
123. Butler, *Travels*, 243, 244–46.
124. "Annual Report of the Provisional Committee to the Shareholders of the Assam Company," 1 May 1857, 4, Assam Company Archives, CLC/B/123/MS27,052/2.
125. Ibid. The 1858 Annual Report is cut out of the volume and the description of events in 1857 ends in midsentence.
126. David T. Courtwright, *Forces of Habit: Drugs and the Making of the Modern World* (Cambridge, MA: Harvard University Press, 2009), 136–37.
127. Sharma, *Empire's Garden*, 65.
128. Antrobus, *Assam Company*, 67.
129. Bruce, *Report on the Manufacture of Tea.*
130. Griffiths, *History of the Indian Tea Industry*, 65–66; Antrobus, *Assam Company*, 49.
131. "Report of the Provisional Committee, made to Shareholders at the General Meeting," 5 May 1843, 15, Assam Company Archives, CLC/B/123/MS27,0521/1; Kalyan K. Sircar, "A Tale of Two Boards: Some Early Management Problems of the Assam Company Ltd., 1839–1864," *Economic and Political Weekly* 21, nos. 10–11 (8–15 March 1986).
132. Antrobus, *Assam Company*, 85.
133. "Indian Teas and Chinese Travellers," *Fraser's Magazine* 47 (January 1853): 97. Robert Fortune stimulated interest as well. His *A Journey to the Tea Countries of China* made exciting reading. For one such review, see "The Tea Countries of China," *Chambers's Edinburgh Journal* 17, no. 442 (19 June 1852): 395–97. On Fortune's career, see Rose, *For All the Tea in China.*
134. Griffiths, *History of the Indian Tea Industry*, 69–70; W. Kenneth Warren, *Tea Tales of Assam* (London: Liss Printers, 1975).
135. Antrobus, *Jorehaut Tea Company*, 39. For a romanticized view of these early planters, see John Weatherstone, *The Pioneers, 1825–1900: The Early British Tea and Coffee Planters and Their Way of Life* (London: Quiller Press, 1986).
136. Griffiths, *History of the Indian Tea Industry*, 71–72.
137. Behal, *One Hundred Years of Servitude*, 36.
138. Ibid., 42–43.
139. Ibid., 55.
140. Cited in Singh, *Women Workers*, 18.
141. Singh, *Women Workers*, 20. For a comparative example, see Madhavi Kale, *Fragments of Empire: Capital, Slavery, and Indian Indentured Labor in the British Caribbean* (Philadelphia: University of Pennsylvania Press, 1998).
142. Ibid., 75.
143. Quoted in Behal, *One Hundred Years of Servitude,* 76.
144. Ibid., 79.
145. Moxham, *Tea*, 134–35.
146. "Dr. Reid's Report on the Causes of Mortality amongst Imported Coolies," 28 February 1866, Ms. 8799: Abstracts of Agents' Reports, 1862–67, Assam Company Archives, CLC/B/123/8799.

147. Behal, *One Hundred Years of Servitude*, 58.
148. Singh, *Women Workers*, chap. 2; Behal, *One Hundred Years of Servitude*; Sharma, *Empire's Garden*; and Chatterjee, *A Time for Tea* all definitively show this to be the case.
149. "Report of the Provisional Committee, made to the Shareholders at a General Meeting," 1 May 1857, Assam Company Archives.
150. Report cited in the Report of the Directors, June 1867, 4, Assam Company Archives, CLC/B/123/MS8801.
151. Tarasankar Banerjee, *Internal Market of India, 1834–1900* (Calcutta: Academic Publishers, 1966).
152. Ritu Birla, *Stages of Capital: Law, Culture, and Market Governance in Late Colonial India* (Durham: Duke University Press, 2009), 3.
153. Prakash Narain Agarwala, *The History of Indian Business: A Complete Account of Trade Exchanges from 3000 B.C. to the Present Day* (New Delhi: Vikas, 1985), 117–23.
154. Parimal Ray, *India's Foreign Trade since 1870* (London: George Routledge and Sons, 1934); Claude Markovits, *The Global World of Indian Merchants, 1750–1947* (Cambridge: Cambridge University Press, 2000); Giovanni Federico, *Feeding the World: An Economic History of Agriculture, 1800–2000* (Princeton: Princeton University Press, 2005) and Arthur Lewis, "The Rate of Growth of World Trade, 1830–1973," in *The World Economic Order: Past and Prospects*, ed. Sven Grassman and Erik Lundberg (New York: St. Martin's Press, 1981), 1–81.
155. A. G. Hopkins, "The History of Globalization—and the Globalization of History?" in *Globalization in World History*, ed. A. G. Hopkins (New York: Norton, 2002), 35.
156. J. Berry White, "The Indian Tea Industry: Its Rise, Progress during Fifty Years, and Prospects Considered from a Commercial Point of View," *Journal of the Royal Society of Arts*, 35 (10 June 1887): 738; J. W. Edgar, "Mr. Edgar's Report on Tea Cultivation," 1873, 1, 3, ITA Mss Eur F174/847.
157. Griffiths, *History of the Indian Tea Industry*, 88.
158. Ibid., 82; "Tea Cultivation in Assam," *Board of Trade Journal* 9 (1890): 106–8.
159. "Tea Cultivation in Assam," 115–16.
160. White, "The Indian Tea Industry," 737.
161. Leonard Wray, "Tea, and Its Production in Various Countries," *Journal of the Society of Arts* 9 (25 January 1861): 145 and "India, Tea Crop at Darjeeling," *Journal of the Society of Arts* 20 (17 November 1872): 94.
162. Robert Fortune, *Report upon the Present Condition and Future Prospects of Tea Cultivation in the North-Western Provinces and in the Punjab* (Calcutta: F. F. Wyman, 1860), 12–13.
163. "Tea Cultivation in Assam," *The Grocer* 8 (14 October 1865): 277.
164. Lees, *Tea Cultivation*, 1; Charles Henry Fielder, "On the Rise, Progress, and Future Prospects of Tea Cultivation in British India," *Journal of the Statistical Society of London* 32 (March 1869): 30.
165. Edgar, "Report on Tea Cultivation," 32–33.
166. "Tea-Planting in Assam," *Chambers's Journal* 57 (July 1880): 471.
167. Edward Money, *The Cultivation and Manufacture of Tea*, 4th ed. (London: W. B. Whittingham, 1883), 2.
168. Ibid., 178–79.
169. Gardella, *Harvesting Mountains*, 62, 74.

170. Quoted in ibid., 102.

171. Ukers, *All about Tea*, 2:230; Gardella, *Harvesting Mountains*, 63–69.

172. Money, *Tea*, 188.

173. Ibid., 184–93. Also see *HCM* (30 May 1879): i; (13 June 1879) iii; and (6 March 1889): iii.

174. *The Grocer* (25 August 1866): 132.

175. *Augusta Sentinel* republished in Bonynge, *Future Wealth of America*, 87.

176. "Tea: Its Consumption and Culture," *Merchant's Magazine and Commercial Review* (February 1863): 117.

177. Quoted in E. Leroy Pond, *Junius Smith: A Biography of the Father of the Atlantic Liner* (1927; New York: Books of the Library Press, 1971), 235.

178. Quoted in ibid., 235–36.

179. Quoted in ibid., 255.

180. Ibid., 241.

181. Erika Rappaport, "'The Bombay Debt': Letter Writing, Domestic Economies and Family Conflict in Colonial India," *Gender and History* 16, no. 2 (August 2004): 233–60.

182. There is a growing body of work looking at how U.S. citizens worked in and profited from the British Empire. See, for example, David Baillargeon, "'A Burmese Wonderland': British World Mining, Finance, and Governmentality in Colonial Burma, 1879–1935" (PhD diss., University of California, Santa Barbara, expected completion spring 2017).

183. Letter dated 14 June 1848, quoted in Pond, *Junius Smith*, 247.

184. "Tea," *Cyclopedia of Commerce and Commercial Navigation*, ed. J. Isaac Homans and J. Isaac Homans Jr. (New York: Harper Brothers, 1860), 1820–21. On plantations in the United States, also see Money, *Tea*, 184; C. Nordhoff, "Tea, Culture in the United States," *Harper's New Monthly Magazine* 19 (1859): 762; La Fayette I. Parks, "Dr. Charles U. Shepard's Tea Plantation near Summerville—Successful Tea-Growing in America," *Cosmopolitan* 24 (April 1898): 534, 584; and R. H. True, "Tea Culture in the United States," *Review of Reviews* 34 (1906): 327.

185. *Colonial Empire and Star of India* 1, no. 1 (7 June 1878): 10. This journal began including a planters' supplement in 1879, when it also changed its name to the *Home and Colonial Mail*.

186. *The Grocer* (23 July 1864): 69.

187. *Pittsburg Commercial* cited in *The Grocer* (15 April 1871): 335. On Hollister, see *The Grocer* (3 February 1872): 121.

188. "Tea: Its Consumption and Culture," 117.

189. *HCM* (20 August 1880): 324.

190. Money, *Tea*, 190.

191. In 1880 the country imported between fifty and sixty million pounds of tea. *HCM* (16 July 1880): 3.

192. *Tea and the Tea Trade*, 11. Also see "Tea Consumption in the United States," *Merchant's Magazine and Commercial Review* (December 1859): 734 and "Tea Drinking in the United States," *HCM* (4 January 1895): v.

193. Roland Wenzlhuemer, *From Coffee to Tea Cultivation in Ceylon, 1880–1900: An Economic and Social History* (Leiden: Brill, 2008); K. M. de Silva, *A History of Sri Lanka* (London: C. Hurst and University of California Press, 1981); Michael Roberts and L. A. Wickremeratne, "Export Agriculture in the Nineteenth Century

Economy," in *University of Ceylon: History of Ceylon*, vol. 3, ed. K. M. Silva (Peradeniya: University of Ceylon, 1973), 89–118. On Sri Lanka's plantation labor force, see Patrick Peebles, *The Plantation Tamils of Ceylon* (London: Leicester University Press, 2001) and Rachel Kurian, "Labor, Race, and Gender on the Coffee Plantations in Ceylon (Sri Lanka), 1834–1880," in *The Global Coffee Economy in Africa, Asia, and Latin America, 1500–1989*, ed. William Gervase Clarence-Smith and Steven Topik (Cambridge: Cambridge University Press, 2003), 173–90.

194. De Silva, *Sri Lanka*, 268–74.
195. Wenzlhuemer, *From Coffee to Tea*; D.M. Forrest, *A Hundred Years of Ceylon Tea 1867–1967* (London: Chatto & Windus, 1967); Maxwell Fernando, *The Story of Ceylon Tea* (Colombo: Mlesna, 2000).
196. Forrest, *Hundred Years of Ceylon Tea*, 50–51.
197. De Silva, *Sri Lanka*, 289–90.
198. *Planters' Gazette* 15 (30 April 1878): 94.
199. "Ceylon Tea," *HCM* (19 June 1885): iii.
200. Money, *Tea*, 184.
201. There is a large body of work on imperial families, but here I am relying on Durba Ghosh, *Sex and the Family in Colonial India: The Making of Empire* (Cambridge: Cambridge University Press 2006) and Elizabeth Buettner, *Empire Families: Britons and Late Imperial India* (Oxford: Oxford University Press, 2004).

CHAPTER 4. PACKAGING CHINA

1. William H. Ukers, *All About Tea* (New York: The Tea and Coffee Trade Journal, 1935): II:132. For the United States, see Susan Strasser, *Satisfaction Guaranteed: The Making of the American Mass Market* (Washington: Smithsonian Institution Press, 1989), 252–85.
2. Harmke Kamminga and Andrew Cunningham, eds., *The Science and Culture of Nutrition, 1840–1940* (Amsterdam: Rodopi, 1995); John Burnett and Derek J. Oddy, eds., *The Origins and Development of Food Policies in Europe* (London: Leicester University Press, 1994); Adel P. den Hartog, ed., *Food Technology, Science and Marketing: European Diet in the Twentieth Century* (East Lothian, Scotland: Tuckwell Press, 1995); Geoffrey Jones and Nicholas J. Morgan, eds., *Adding Value: Brands and Marketing in Food and Drink* (London: Routledge, 1994).
3. There is a large and growing literature on British-Chinese relations in this period. See, for example, Wang Gungwu, *Anglo-Chinese Encounters since 1800: War, Trade, Science and Governance* (Cambridge: Cambridge University Press, 2003). On the place of China in the making of Victorian culture, see Elizabeth Hope Chang, *Britain's Chinese Eye: Literature, Empire and Aesthetics in Nineteenth-Century Britain* (Stanford: Stanford University Press, 2010) and Ross Forman, *China and the Victorian Imagination: Empires Entwined* (Cambridge: Cambridge University Press, 2013). Other studies include James L. Hevia, *Cherishing Men from Afar: Qing Guest Ritual and the Macartney Embassy of 1793* (Durham: Duke University Press, 1995) and *English Lessons: The Pedagogy of Imperialism in Nineteenth-Century China* (Durham: Duke University Press, 2003); Nicholas J. Clifford, *"A Truthful Impression of the Country": British and American Travel Writing in China, 1880–1949* (Ann Arbor: University of Michigan Press, 2001); Robert Bickers, *Britain in China: Community,*

Culture and Colonialism, 1900–1949 (Manchester: Manchester University Press, 1999); and Ulrike Hillemann, *Asian Empire and British Knowledge: China and the Networks of British Imperial Expansion* (Basingstoke: Palgrave Macmillan, 2009).

4. Ingeborg Paulus, *The Search for Pure Food: A Sociology of Legislation in Britain* (London: Martin Robertson, 1974); Michael French and Jim Phillips, *Cheated Not Poisoned? Food Regulation in the United Kingdom, 1875–1938* (Manchester: Manchester University Press, 2000); Derek J. Oddy, "Food Quality in London and the Rise of the Public Analyst, 1870-1939," in *Food and the City in Europe since 1800*, ed. Peter J. Atkins, Peter Lummel, and Derek J. Oddy (Aldershot: Ashgate, 2007), 91–104; Susan Morton, "A Little of What You Fancy Does You . . . Harm!!" in *Criminal Conversations: Victorian Crimes, Social Panic, and Moral Outrage*, ed. Judith Rowbotham and Kim Stevenson (Columbus: Ohio University Press, 2005), 157–76; Hans J. Teuteberg, "Food Adulteration and the Beginnings of Uniform Food Legislation in Late Nineteenth-Century Germany," in *The Origins and Development of Food Policies in Europe*, ed. Burnett and Oddy. For the United States, see Upton Sinclair, *The Jungle* (1906; New York: Penguin, 1985); Lorine Swainston Goodwin, *The Pure Food, Drink, and Drug Crusaders, 1879–1914* (Jefferson, NC: McFarland, 1999); James Harvey Young, *Pure Food: Securing the Federal Food and Drugs Act of 1906* (Princeton: Princeton University Press, 1989); Mitchell Okun, *Fair Play in the Marketplace: The First Battle for Pure Foods and Drugs* (DeKalb: Northern Illinois University Press, 1986) and Harvey A. Levenstein, *Revolution at the Table: The Transformation of the American Diet* (New York: Oxford University Press, 1988).

5. A. D. Beardsworth, "Trans-Science and Moral Panics: Understanding Food Scares," *British Food Journal* 92, no. 5 (1990): 11–16.

6. See especially Michael Pollan, *The Omnivore's Dilemma: A Natural History of Four Meals* (New York: Penguin, 2006); Eric Schlosser, *Fast Food Nation: The Dark Side of the All-American Meal* (Boston: Houghton Mifflin, 2001); and Marion Nestle, *Safe Food: The Politics of Food Safety* (Berkeley: University of California Press, 2010).

7. For similar issues, see K. Waddington, "The Dangerous Sausage: Diet, Meat and Disease in Victorian and Edwardian Britain," *Cultural and Social History* 8, no. 1 (2011): 51–71 and Benjamin R. Cohen, "Analysis as Border Patrol: Chemists along the Boundary between Pure Food and Real Adulteration," *Endeavour* 35, no. 2–3 (September 2011): 66–73.

8. Mary Douglas, *Purity and Danger: An Analysis of the Concepts of Pollution and Taboo* (London: Ark, 1966).

9. Deborah Lupton, *Food, the Body and the Self* (London: Sage, 1996), 112.

10. John Prescott and Beverly J. Tepper, eds., *Genetic Variation in Taste Sensitivity* (New York: Marcel Dekker, 2005).

11. John Burnett, "The History of Food Adulteration in Great Britain in the Nineteenth Century, with Special Reference to Bread, Tea and Beer" (PhD thesis, London University, 1958); Susanne Freidberg, *French Beans and Food Scares: Culture and Commerce in an Anxious Age* (Oxford: Oxford University Press, 2004), 38–39; Francis B. Smith, *The People's Health, 1830–1910* (New York: Holmes and Meier, 1979), 203–14.

12. Dr. Edward Smith, *Foods* (New York: D. Appleton and Co. 1874), 5.

13. Christopher Hamlin, *Cholera: The Biography* (Oxford: Oxford University Press, 2009).

14. Pamela K. Gilbert, *Cholera and Nation: Doctoring the Social Body in Victorian England* (New York: State University of New York Press, 2008), 2–5; Christopher Hamlin, *Public Health and Social Justice in the Age of Chadwick: Britain, 1800–1854* (Cambridge: Cambridge University Press, 1998) and his *A Science of Impurity: Water Analysis in Nineteenth-Century Britain* (Bristol: Adam Hilger, 1990). Other key works include, see Mary Poovey, *Making a Social Body: British Cultural Formation, 1830–1864* (Chicago: University of Chicago Press, 1995) and Michel Foucault, "Governmentality," in *The Foucault Effect: Studies in Governmentality*, ed. Graham Burchell, Colin Gordon, and Peter Miller (Chicago: University of Chicago Press, 1991). For the empire, see David Arnold, *Colonizing the Body: State Medicine and Epidemic Disease in Nineteenth-Century India* (Berkeley: University of California Press, 1993).

15. Thomas Herbert, *The Law on Adulteration* (London: Knight and Co., 1884), 7–12.

16. Oliver MacDonagh, *Early Victorian Government, 1830–1870* (London: Weidenfeld and Nicolson, 1977), 159.

17. Chris Otter, *The Victorian Eye: A Political History of Light and Vision in Britain, 1800–1910* (Chicago: University of Chicago Press, 2008), 107–8; Christopher Hamlin, "The City as a Chemical System? The Chemist as Urban Environmental Professional in France and Britain, 1780–1880," *Journal of Urban History* 33, no. 5 (2007): 702–28.

18. Friedrich Christian Accum, *A Treatise on Adulterations of Food and Culinary Poisons* (Philadelphia: Ab'M Small, 1820), 14; Burnett, "History of Food Adulteration," 11, 43.

19. *The Domestic Chemist: Comprising Instructions for the Detection of Adulteration in Numerous Articles* (London: Bumpus and Griffin, 1831); J. Stevenson, *Advice Medical, and Economical, Relative to the Purchase and Consumption of Tea, Coffee, and Chocolate; Wines and Malt Liquors: Including Tests to Detect Adulteration, Also Remarks on Water with directions to Purify it for Domestic Use* (London: F. C. Westley, 1830), 10.

20. *The Family Manual and Servants' Guide* (London: S. D. Ewins, 1859), 32.

21. William Rathbone Greg, *An Enquiry into the State of the Manufacturing Population, and the Causes and the Cures of the Evils Therein Existing* (London: James Ridgway, 1831), 10; Manchester and Salford Sanitary Association, *Report of the Sub-Committee upon the Adulteration of Food* (Manchester: Powlson and Sons, 1863).

22. *Deadly Adulteration and Slow Poisoning Unmasked, or, Disease and Death in the Pot and the Bottle* (London: Sherwood, Gilbert and Piper, 1839), vi.

23. James Dawson Burn, *The Language of the Walls: And a Voice from the Shop Windows, or, The Mirror of Commercial Roguery* (Manchester: Abel Heywood, 1855).

24. "Frauds: Necessity for taking some steps to Protect the Poor Against Short Weight, Short Measure, and Adulteration," NA: HO 45/5338.

25. Peter Gurney, *Co-Operative Culture and the Politics of Consumption in England, 1870–1930* (Manchester: Manchester University Press, 205–6; Central Co-operative Agency, *Catalogue of Teas, Coffees, Colonial and Italian Produce, and Wines with Prefatory Remarks on Adulteration, Arising from Competition* (London: Central Co-operative Agency, 1852).

26. Edwy Godwin Clayton, *Arthur Hill Hassall: Physician and Sanitary Reformer* (London: Baillière, Tindall, and Cox, 1908), xiii; Ernest A. Gray, *By Candlelight: The Life of Dr. Arthur Hill Hassall, 1817–94* (London: Robert Hale, 1983).

27. William Alexander, MD, *The Adulteration of Food and Drinks* (London: Longman, 1856), 6.

28. Hassall founded *Food, Water, and Air* in 1874 and help establish the Society of Public Analysts that same year. Clayton, *Hassall*, 33.

29. *First Report from the Select Committee on Adulteration of Food, &C; with Minutes of Evidence, and Appendix, 1855* (Great Britain: House of Commons, 1856).

30. Arthur Hill Hassall, MD, *Food and Its Adulterations; Comprising the Reports of the Analytical Sanitary Commission of "The Lancet" for the years 1851 to 1854, revised and extended* (London: Longman, Brown, Green and Longmans, 1855). Also see his *Adulterations Detected, or, Plain Instructions for the Discovery of Frauds in Food and Medicine* (London: Longman, Brown, Green, Longmans, and Roberts, 1857); and his significantly revised *Food: Its Adulterations, and the Methods for Their Detection* (London: Longmans, Green, and Co., 1876).

31. Hassall, *Adulterations Detected*, vii.

32. Ibid., 8–10, 17–18.

33. Ibid., 410–11.

34. Ibid., 33.

35. Ibid., 17.

36. Frederick Stroud and Elsie May Wheeler, *The Judicial Dictionary* (London: Sweet and Maxwell, 1931), quoted in Frederick Arthur Filby, *A History of Food Adulteration and Analysis* (London: George Allen and Unwin, 1934), 16. For a full analysis of the evolving law, see Paulus, *Search for Pure Food.*

37. George Dodd, *The Food of London* (London: Longmans, Green and Longmans, 1856), 16.

38. *Poisoning and Pilfering; Wholesale and Retail*, rev. ed. (London: Longmans, Green and Co., 1871), 7.

39. Hillel Schwartz, *The Culture of the Copy: Striking Likenesses, Unreasonable Facsimiles* (New York: Zone, 1996).

40. Karl Marx, *Capital: A Critique of Political Economy*, ed. Frederick Engels, revised from fourth German edition (New York: Modern Library, 1906), 274.

41. Walter Benjamin, "The Work of Art in the Age of Mechanical Reproduction," in *Illuminations: Essays and Reflections*, edited with introduction by Hannah Arendt, trans. Harry Zohn (New York: Harcourt Brace Jovanovich, 1968), 217–52.

42. Charles Estcourt, "Adulteration of Food," in *Manchester and Salford Sanitary Association: Health Lectures for the People* (Manchester: Simpkin, Marshall, 1878), 166; Burn, *The Language of the Walls*, 231.

43. *Deadly Adulteration*, 83.

44. Wentworth Lascelles Scott, "On Food: Its Adulterations, and the Methods of Detecting Them," *Journal of the Society of Arts* 9, no. 428 (1 February 1861): 159.

45. John Gallagher and Ronald Robinson, "The Imperialism of Free Trade," *Economic History Review*, 2nd ser., 6 (1953): 1–15; C. M. Turnbull, "Formal and Informal Empire in East Asia," in *Historiography: The Oxford History of the British Empire*, ed. Robin Winks (Oxford: Oxford University Press, 1999), 379–402.

46. Burnett, "History of Food Adulteration," 226.
47. Quoted in Michael Greenberg, *British Trade and the Opening of China, 1800–1842* (1951; Cambridge: Cambridge University Press, 1969), 186.
48. John Reeves blamed the "free traders" and a segment of the American trade for importing adulterated teas. See the evidence he gave before the Select Committee on the Tea Duties (1834), (Great Britain: House of Commons, 1834), 36.
49. Burnett, "History of Food Adulteration," 210.
50. Evidence given by Mr. John Reeves before the Select Committee on the Tea Duties (1834), 36.
51. "Tea Consumption in the United States," *Merchant's Magazine and Commercial Review* 40, no. 6 (June 1859): 734. Also see "Tea, Its Consumption and Culture," *Merchant's Magazine and Commercial Review* (February 1863): 119.
52. "The Tea Culture," *Merchant's Magazine and Commercial Review* (December 1855): 759.
53. *Illustrated London News*, 3 December 1842, 469, quoted in Susan Schoenbauer Thurin, *Victorian Travelers and the Opening of China, 1842–1907* (Athens: Ohio University Press, 1999), 28.
54. J. Y. Wong, *Deadly Dreams: Opium, Imperialism, and the Arrow War (1856–1860) in China* (Cambridge: Cambridge University Press, 1998), 346.
55. Ibid., 339, 335.
56. Ibid., 351.
57. *The Times*, 31 July 1858, quoted in Wong, *Deadly Dreams*, 359; Hevia, *English Lessons*, 31–48.
58. Wong, *Deadly Dreams*, 216–17, chap. 7.
59. *Morning Post*, 3 March 1857, quoted in ibid., 226.
60. S. Osborn, *The Past and Future of British Relations in China* (Edinburgh: Blackwood, 1860), 10, quoted in Wong, *Deadly Dreams*, 450.
61. "The Shanghai Tea-Gardens," *Leisure Hour* 14 (1865): 711.
62. "Tea Consumption in the United States," *Merchant's Magazine and Commercial Review* (December 1859): 759–60; Frederic E. Wakeman, *Strangers at the Gate: Social Disorder in Southern China, 1839–1861* (Berkeley: University of California Press, 1966).
63. Robert Gardella, *Harvesting Mountains: Fujian and the China Tea Trade, 1757–1937* (Berkeley: University of California Press, 1994), 93–98.
64. "The Extension of Tea Culture," *The Grocer*, 15 November 1862, 380.
65. Gardella, *Harvesting Mountains*, 52–53. American cotton was competing with British sources in Chinese markets. See Greenberg, *British Trade and the Opening of China*, 186.
66. David Roy MacGregor, *The Tea Clippers: Their History and Development, 1833–1875* (1952; London: Conway Maritime Press and Lloyd's of London Press, 1983).
67. Beatrice Hohenegger, *Liquid Jade: The Story of Tea from East to West* (New York: St. Martin's Press, 2006), 172; William Ukers, *All About Tea* (New York: Tea and Coffee Trade Journal, 1935), 1:87–108.
68. "The Great Tea-Ship Race," *The Grocer*, 8 September 1866, 169.
69. Quoted in Accum, *A Treatise on Adulterations of Food*, 167.

70. *Poisonous Tea! The Trial of Edward Palmer, Grocer,* 2nd ed. (London: John Fairburn, 1818); Burnett, "History of Food Adulteration," 237–38.

71. Hassall, *Food and Its Adulterations,* 273.

72. Quoted in ibid., 278.

73. Ibid., 283–83.

74. Henry Mayhew, *Mayhew's London,* ed. Peter Quennell (1861; London: Bracken Books, 1984), 191.

75. *Anti-Adulteration Review: Dedicated to Amending and Enforcing the Law Against Adulteration and to Ensuring Purity in Food and Drink* 1, no. 2 (December 1871): 20 and 1, no. 4 (February 1872): 55.

76. Mrs. Cobden Unwin, *The Hungry Forties: Life under the Bread Tax* (London: F. T. Unwin, 1904), 161, 72.

77. Frank Trentmann, *Free Trade Nation: Commerce, Consumption, and Civil Society in Modern Britain* (Oxford: Oxford University Press, 2008), 39–45.

78. Robert Warrington, "Observations on the Green Teas of Commerce," extract from "The Memoirs of the Chemical Society," part 8, published in the appendix to *First Report from the Select Committee on Adulteration of Food,* 129–32.

79. Robert Warrington, "Observations on the Teas of Commerce," *Edinburgh New Philosophical Society* 51 (April–October 1851): 248.

80. Hassall, *Food and Its Adulterations,* 296.

81. Ibid., 297.

82. Robert Fortune, *Three Years' Wanderings in the Northern Provinces of China* (London: John Murray, 1847), 218–19. For an account of Fortune's adventures, see Rose, *For All the Tea in China.*

83. Samuel Ball, *An Account of the Cultivation and Manufacture of Tea in China* (London: Longman, Brown, Green and Longmans, 1848), 243.

84. Robert Fortune, *Two Visits to the Tea Countries of China and the British Tea Plantation in the Himalaya,* 3rd ed. (London: John Murray, 1853), 2:70.

85. Stevenson, *Advice Medical,* 6.

86. G.G. Sigmond, *Tea: Its Effects Medicinal and Moral* (London: Longman, Orme, Brown, Green and Longmans, 1839), 7, 9.

87. Jonathon Pereira, *A Treatise on Food and Diet with Observations on the Dietetical Regimen suited for the Disordered States of the Digestive Organs* (New York: Fowler and Wells, 1843), 189.

88. Ibid., 192; Edward Smith, "On the Uses of Tea in the Healthy System," *Journal of the Royal Society of the Arts* 9 (1861): 190.

89. Sigmond, *Tea,* 124.

90. "Green Tea," *Monthly Religious Magazine* (Boston) 28 (1862): 198–99.

91. Elizabeth Gaskell, *Cranford* (1853; Oxford: Oxford University Press, 1972), 146.

92. "Green Tea: A Case Reported by Martin Hesselius, the German Physician," *All the Year Round* 22 (1869): 549. Also see the version republished in J. Sheridan Le Fanu, *In a Glass Darkly* (London: R. Bentley and Son, 1872). Barry Milligan, *Pleasures and Pains: Opium and the Orient in Nineteenth-Century British Culture* (Charlottesville: University of Virginia Press, 1995). For an excellent study of these issues, see Susan Marjorie Zieger, *Inventing the Addict: Drugs, Race, and Sexuality in Nineteenth-Century British and American Literature* (Amherst: University of Massachusetts Press, 2008).

93. Mrs. Nancy Smith, "Confessions of a Green-Tea Drinker," *Monthly Religious Magazine* (May 1861): 317, 326.

94. John C. Draper, "Tea and Its Adulterations," *The Galaxy* 7 (March 1869): 411.

95. "Chinese Method of Colouring Tea," *Hogg's Instructor* (Edinburgh, 1850): 91.

96. Zheng Yangwen, *The Social Life of Opium in China* (Cambridge: Cambridge University Press, 2005).

97. This incident was related in a series of letters in "The Adulteration of Tea," *Journal of the Society of Arts* 9, no. 430 (February 1861): 199–202.

98. Gardella, *Harvesting Mountains*, 99–100.

99. On advertising, race, imperialism, and identities, see John MacKenzie, ed., *Imperialism and Popular Culture* (Manchester: Manchester University Press, 1986) and his *Propaganda and Empire: The Manipulation of British Public Opinion, 1880–1960* (Manchester: Manchester University Press, 1984); Thomas Richards, *The Commodity Culture of Victorian England: Advertising and Spectacle, 1851–1914* (Stanford: Stanford University Press, 1990); Anne McClintock, *Imperial Leather: Race, Gender and Sexuality in the Colonial Contest* (New York: Routledge, 1995); Timothy Burke, *Lifebuoy Men; Lux Women: Commodification, Consumption and Cleanliness in Modern Zimbabwe* (Durham: Duke University Press, 1996); Piya Chatterjee, *A Time for Tea: Women, Labor, and Post/Colonial Politics on an Indian Plantation* (Durham: Duke University Press, 2001); and Anandi Ramamurthy, *Imperial Persuaders: Images of Africa and Asia in British Advertising* (Manchester: Manchester University Press, 2003).

100. Benedict Anderson, *Imagined Communities: Reflections on the Origin and Spread of Nationalism* (New York: Random House, 1983).

101. T. R. Nevett, *Advertising in Britain: A History* (London: Heinemann, 1982), chap. 6.

102. "The Late Mr. Horniman," *Anti-Slavery Reporter and Aborigines' Friend* 13, no. 4 (July 1893): 231.

103. "Famous Tea Houses, No. IV: Horniman's in Wormwood Street," *Tea: A Monthly Journal for Tea Planters, Merchants and Brokers* 1, no. 6 (September 1901): 164–66.

104. Ibid., 166.

105. "History: Hornimans of Forrest Hill," In house history, Horniman Museum, London; Ken Teague, *Mr. Horniman and the Tea Trade: A Permanent Display in the South Hall Gallery of the Horniman Museum* (London: Horniman Museum and Gardens, 1993); Nicky Levell, *Oriental Visions: Exhibitions, Travel and Collecting in the Victorian Age* (London: Horniman Museum and Gardens, 2000); Sheila Gooddie, *Annie Horniman: A Pioneer in the Theater* (London: Methuen, 1990).

106. The earliest example in the Tetley Group Archive, which houses the Horniman archive, is from 1849. The John Johnson Collection of Printed Ephemera also has examples from the 1860s. See Tea and Coffee Advertisements, Boxes 1 and 3, John Johnson Collection, Bodleian Library, Oxford (hereafter John Johnson).

107. S. Baring-Gould, "The 9:30 Up-Train," *Once a Week* (29 August 1863): 253–57. Also see "From Bradford to Brindisi in Two Flights," *All the Year Round* (11 February 1871): 252–56; *Saint Paul's Magazine* 8 (June 1871): 272; and "The Village Shop," *Chambers's Journal of Popular Literature* 398 (17 August 1861): 97. A comic journal asked, "Why is a thief with his hand in an empty pocket like a packet of Horniman's tea? Because he is tin-foiled." *Fun* 3 (7 July 1866): 167.

108. Nevett, *Advertising in Britain*, 25–31.

109. Horniman's advertising appeared in the very first issue of the *Methodist Recorder* in 1861 and continued to appear there into the 1950s. See, for example, 24 September

1953, 5, Acc#4364/01/006, Tetley Group Archive (hereafter TGA), London Metropolitan Archives (hereafter LMA).

110. For a selection of Horniman's advertisements, see *Temperance Recorder* (19 November 1870): 563; *Ragged School Union Magazine* 15, no. 169 (January 1863): n.p.; *Golden Hours: An Illustrated Monthly Magazine for Family and General Reading* (January 1872): 83; *Saturday Review of Politics, Literature, Science and Art* 14, no. 366 (1 November 1862): 552; *National Review* 30 (October 1862): 431; *The Critic* 17, no. 406 (1 March 1858): 118 and 25, no. 632 (January 1863): 221; *The Athenaeum*, no. 1853 (2 May 1863): 599; *England Wine Magazine* (September 1856); and *The Times*, 20 February 1868.

111. *Saturday Review* 14, no. 366 (1 November 1862): 552.

112. Handbill dated 10 March 1854, Acc#4364/01/001, TGA.

113. Advertisement, *England Wine Magazine* (September 1856), Acc #4364/01/002, TGA.

114. Advertisement for H. Ellis Jones, Family and Dispensing Chemist in Swansea, undated, Acc# 436/01/002, TGA.

115. See, for example, the ads in *Temperance Record*, 19 November 1870, 563 and 25 January 1873, 47.

116. *The Grocer*, 5 April 1873, 305.

117. Handbill dated 10 March 1854, Acc#4364/01/001, TGA.

118. "Grocers' Advertisements," *The Grocer*, 14 January 1871, 335.

119. Advertisement, 1883, Evanion Collection, #6218, British Library.

120. Shop card, c. 1860s, Acc#4364/01/001, TGA.

121. Handbill, c. 1860, Acc# 4364/01/001, TGA.

122. Advertisement, c. 1860, Acc# 4364/01/001, TGA. Also see *The Critic*, 26, no. 632 (January 1863): 221.

123. *National Review* 30 (October 1862): 431.

124. For other manufacturers that had similar ads, see Hassall, *Food and Its Adulterations*, 1876.

125. Handbill, c. 1849, Acc#4364/01/001, TGA.

126. Handbill, c. 1860, Acc#4364/01/001, TGA.

127. Ibid.

128. A frequently used illustration, for example, showed the "Chinese at the Drying Pans Colouring tea." Handbill, c. 1860, Acc#4364/01/001, TGA.

129. Advertisement, c. 1875, Acc#4364/01/002, TGA.

130. Advertisement, c. 1865, Acc#4364/01/002, TGA.

131. See, for example, a booklet on how the Chinese prepare tea for export, c. 1860, Acc#4364/01/001, TGA.

132. Advertisement, c. 1875, Acc#4364/01/002, TGA.

133. Hevia, *English Lessons*, 74–118; Catherine Pagani, "Chinese Material Culture and British Perceptions of China in the Mid-Nineteenth Century," in *Colonialism and the Object: Empire, Material Culture and the Museum*, ed. Timothy J. Barringer and Tom Flynn (London: Routledge, 1998), 28; Lara Kriegel, "The Pudding and the Palace: Labor, Print Culture and Imperial Britain in 1851," in *After the Imperial Turn: Thinking with and through the Nation*, ed. Antoinette Burton (Durham: Duke University Press, 2003), 239–40.

134. Advertisement for Peek, Brothers & Co., 6 December 1839, Tea and Coffee, Box 2, John Johnson.

135. Advertisement for T. Sheard, Grocer and Tea Dealer, 21 High Street Oxford, Tea and Grocery, Box 1, John Johnson.

136. Advertisement for A. Evans's Tea & Coffee Warehouse, no. 1, Church Row, Wandsworth, 1857, Tea and Coffee, Box 1, John Johnson.

137. See the advertising, for example, in Tea and Grocery, Box 1, John Johnson. See especially the advertisement for W. M. Henszell's Tea Establishment, Newcastle upon Tyne.

138. *The Grocer*, 1 January 1870.

139. Leonard Wray, "Tea and Its Production in Various Countries," *Journal of the Society of Arts* 9 (January 1861): 148; Burnett, "History of Food Adulteration," 172; *Report on the Production of Tea in Japan* 66 (London: HSMO, 1873); "The Tea Culture," *Merchant's Magazine and Commercial Review* 33 (December 1855): 759–60; John C. Draper, "Tea and Its Adulterations," *The Galaxy* 7 (March 1869): 405–12.

140. Dr. Charles Cameron, evidence given before the *Report from the Select Committee on Adulteration of Food Act (1872) Together with the Proceedings of the Committee, Minutes of Evidence and Appendix* (London: n.p., 1874), 230.

141. Evidence read before the *Select Committee on Adulteration of Food Act (1872)*, 8; *The Art of Tea Blending: A Handbook for the Trade* (London: W. B. Whittingham and Company, 1882), 33.

142. Evidence read before the *Select Committee on Adulteration of Food Act (1872)*, 21.

143. Ibid., 27.

144. Ibid., 78.

145. Ibid., 77.

146. Ibid., 255.

147. Ibid., 177.

148. Ibid., 317.

149. Hassall, *Adulterations Detected*, 2.

150. *Select Committee on Adulteration of Food Act (1872)*, viii.

151. *Report on the Commissioners of Inland Revenue on the Duties Under their Management, for the years 1856–1869 Inclusive* (1870) NA: CUST 44/5, notes that adulteration had declined.

152. Okun, *Fair Play in the Marketplace*, 290.

153. See Thomas Taylor, MD, *Food Product: Tea and Its Adulteration* (Buffalo: Bigelow Printing, 1889), 51–52.

154. Erika Lee, *At America's Gates: Chinese Immigration during the Exclusion Era, 1882–1943* (Chapel Hill: University of North Carolina Press, 2003).

CHAPTER 5. INDUSTRY AND EMPIRE

1. "Popularizing Indian Tea," *HCM*, 10 June 1881, iii.

2. See Piya Chatterjee, *A Time for Tea: Women, Labor, and Post/Colonial Politics on an Indian Plantation* (Durham: Duke University Press, 2001), chap. 4; Anandi Ramamurthy, *Imperial Persuaders: Images of Africa and Asia in British Advertising* (Manchester: Manchester University Press, 2003), chap. 4; Peter H. Hoffenberg, *An Empire on Display: English, Indian, and Australian Exhibitions from the Crystal*

Palace to the Great War (Berkeley: University of California Press, 2001); and Julie E. Fromer, *A Necessary Luxury: Tea in Victorian England* (Athens: Ohio University Press, 2008), chap. 1.

3. "Tea-Planting in Assam," *Chambers's Journal of Popular Literature* 57 (July 1880): 471.

4. For the role of the trade press, see Chris Hosgood, "'The Shopkeeper's Friend': The Retail Trade Press in Late-Victorian and Edwardian Britain," *Victorian Periodicals Review* 25, no. 4 (Winter 1992): 164–72; John J. McCusker, "The Demise of Distance: The Business Press and the Origins of the Information Revolution in the Early Modern Atlantic World," *American Historical Review* 110, no. 2 (April 2005): 295–321. Also see Simon J. Potter, *News and the British World: The Emergence of an Imperial Press System, 1876–1922* (Oxford: Clarendon, 2003).

5. Arnold Toynbee, *Lectures on the Industrial Revolution in England* (London: Rivington's, 1884).

6. Sir Percival Griffiths, *The History of the Indian Tea Industry* (London: Weidenfeld and Nicolson, 1967), 124; Peter Mathias, "The British Tea Trade in the Nineteenth Century," in *The Making of the Modern British Diet*, ed. Derek J. Oddy and Derek S. Miller (London: Croom Helm, 1976), 91–100; Robert Gardella, *Harvesting Mountains: Fujian and the China Tea Trade, 1757–1937* (Berkeley: University of California Press, 1994), 110–60.

7. On shifting company law and structures, see Michael Aldous, "Avoiding Negligence and Profusion: The Failure of the Joint-Stock Form in the Anglo-Indian Tea Trade, 1840–1870," *Enterprise and Society* 16, no. 3 (September 2015): 648–85. For general studies of changes in food retailing, see David Alexander, *Retailing in England during the Industrial Revolution* (London: University of London, Athlone Press, 1970); Peter Mathias, *Retailing Revolution: A History of Multiple Retailing in the Food Trades Based upon the Allied Suppliers Group of Companies* (London: Longmans, 1967); James B. Jefferys, *Retail Trading in Britain, 1850–1950* (Cambridge: Cambridge University Press, 1954) and Geoffrey Jones and Nicholas J. Morgan, ed. *Adding Value: Brands and Marketing in Food and Drink* (London: Routledge, 1994). On the gendered and urban dimensions of these changes, see Erika Diane Rappaport, *Shopping for Pleasure: Women in the Making of London's West End* (Princeton: Princeton University Press, 2000).

8. Alexander Nützenadel and Frank Trentmann, eds., *Food and Globalization: Consumption, Markets and Politics in the Modern World* (Oxford: Berg, 2008), 5; G. Federico, *Feeding the World: An Economic History of Agriculture, 1800–2000* (Princeton: Princeton University Press, 2005); C. A. Bayly, *The Birth of the Modern World, 1780–1914: Global Connections and Comparisons* (Oxford: Blackwell, 2004), chaps. 4 and 5; Emily S. Rosenberg, *A World Connecting, 1870–1945* (Cambridge, MA: Belknap Press of Harvard University Press, 2012).

9. Oddy and Miller, eds., *Making of the Modern British Diet;* Derek J. Oddy, *From Plain Fare to Fusion Food: British Diet from the 1890s to the 1990s* (Suffolk: Boydell, 2003); John Burnett, *Plenty and Want: A Social History of Food in England from 1815 to the Present*, rev. ed. (London: Scolar Press, 1979).

10. Edward Bramah, *Tea and Coffee: A Modern View of Three Hundred Years of Tradition* (London: Hutchinson, 1972), 87; Martha Avery, *The Tea Road: China and Russia Meet Across the Steppe* (Beijing: China Intercontinental Press, 2003).

11. Denys Forrest, *Tea for the British: The Social and Economic History of a Famous Trade* (London: Chatto and Windus, 1973), 148; William H. Ukers, *All about Tea* (New York: Tea and Coffee Trade Journal Company, 1935), 2:38.
12. Forrest, *Tea for the British*, 135.
13. Fiona Rule, *London's Docklands: A History of the Lost Quarter* (Hersham, Surrey: Ian Allen, 2009), 177–78.
14. Forrest, *Tea for the British*, 143.
15. Board of Customs and Excise: Annual Reports on the Customs (1872), 35, NA CUST 44/6.
16. Forrest, *Tea for the British*, 151.
17. Percy Redfern, *The Story of the Co-Operative Wholesale Society: Being the Jubilee History of the Co-Operative Wholesale Society Limited, 1863–1913* (Manchester: Co-Operative Wholesale Society, 1913), 214–19; T. W. Mercer, *Towards the Cooperative Commonwealth* (Manchester: Co-operative Press Limited, 1936), 121.
18. Peter Gurney, *Co-operative Culture and the Politics of Consumption in England, 1870–1930* (Manchester: Manchester University Press, 1996); Lawrence Black and Nicole Robertson, eds., *Consumerism and the Co-operative Movement in Modern British History: Taking Stock* (Manchester: Manchester University Press, 2009).
19. Mathias, *Retailing Revolution*, 40–42.
20. Asa Briggs, *Friends of the People: The Centenary History of Lewis's* (London: B. T. Batsford, 1955), 122–28; Carol Kennedy, *Business Pioneers: Family, Fortune and Philanthropy: Cadbury, Sainsbury and John Lewis* (London: Random House, 2000).
21. Mathias, *Retailing Revolution*, 85.
22. Ibid., 53.
23. Ibid., 126–28.
24. *The Grocer*, 15 March 1879, xxvii and 29 March 1879, xxiii. Also see "Enterprise amongst Tea Retailers," *HCM*, 5 September 1879, 1 and Advertisement for Victoria Tea Company, Lambeth, London, 1883. Evan. 6606, Evanion Collection, British Library.
25. *Daily Telegraph* quoted in *HCM*, 26 January 1883, ii and 17 April 1885, iii.
26. Mathias, *Retailing Revolution*, 96–97.
27. Rappaport, *Shopping for Pleasure*, chap. 1.
28. Sir Thomas Lipton, *Lipton's Autobiography* (New York: Duffield and Green, 1932), 174–78.
29. Ramamurthy, *Imperial Persuaders*, 93, 102–17. Biographies include Captain John J. Hickey, *The Life and Times of the Late Sir Thomas J. Lipton from the Cradle to the Grave: International Sportsman and Dean of the Yachting World* (New York: Hickey Publishing Company, 1932) and James A. Mackay, *The Man Who Invented Himself: A Life of Sir Thomas Lipton* (Edinburgh: Mainstream Publishing, 1998).
30. W. Hamish Fraser, *The Coming of the Mass Market, 1850–1914* (London: Macmillan, 1981), part 1; John Benson, *The Rise of Consumer Society in Britain, 1880–1980* (Harlow, Essex: Longman, 1994), chap. 1.
31. Fraser, *Mass Market*, 3.
32. Ellen Ross, *Love and Toil: Motherhood in Outcast London, 1870–1914* (Oxford: Oxford University Press, 1993), chap. 2; Paul A. Johnson, *Saving and Spending: The Working-Class Economy in Britain, 1870–1939* (Oxford: Clarendon, 1985). For an

overview of this debate, see George R. Boyer, "Living Standards, 1860–1939," in *The Cambridge Economic History of Modern Britain*, vol. 2, *Economic Maturity, 1860–1939*, ed. Roderick Floud and Paul Johnson (Cambridge: Cambridge University Press, 2014), 280–313.

33. Forrest, *Tea for the British*, 150; *Board of Customs and Excise: Annual Reports on the Customs* (1864), 13, NA CUST 44/4; "Consumption of Tea and Sugar," *Journal of the Royal Society of Arts* 14 (13 July 1866): 574.

34. *Board of Customs and Excise: Annual Reports on the Customs* (1869), 12, NA CUST 44/6.

35. *The Grocer*, 25 July 1863, 57.

36. See, for example, "Tea and Coffee Consumption," *Current Literature* 30, no. 3 (March 1901): 298.

37. For an intellectual history of the concept of markets, see Mark Bevir and Frank Trentmann, eds., *Markets in Historical Contexts: Ideas and Politics in the Modern World* (Cambridge: Cambridge University Press, 2004).

38. Laura Mason, "Everything Stops for Tea," in *Eating with the Victorians*, ed. C. Anne Wilson (London: Sutton Publishing, 1994), 68–385; Andrea Broomfield, *Food and Cooking in Victorian England: A History* (Westport, CT: Praeger, 2007), 58–377; Ivan Day, "Teatime," in *Eat, Drink and Be Merry: The British at Table, 1600–2000*, ed. Ivan Day (London: P. Wilson, 2000), 107–330.

39. Pierre Bourdieu, *Distinction: A Social Critique of the Judgement of Taste*, trans. Richard Nice (Cambridge, MA: Harvard University Press, 1984).

40. *The Manners of the Aristocracy* (London: Ward and Lock, 1882), 57.

41. *Manners and Tone of Good Society* (London: Frederick Warne and Co., 1879), 115.

42. *Manners of the Aristocracy*, 51–53; Lady Gertrude Elizabeth Campbell, *Etiquette of Good Society* (London: Cassell, 1893), 156.

43. *Lady's World* (January 1887): 104.

44. Campbell, *Etiquette*, 156–58.

45. *Etiquette for Ladies and Gentlemen* (London: Frederick Warne and Co., 1876), 24.

46. Campbell, *Etiquette*, 155.

47. Ibid., 156.

48. "Tea and Chatter," *Beauty and Fashion* 2, no. 1 (6 December 1890): 34.

49. *Manners and Tone of Good Society*, 111

50. Campbell, *Etiquette*, 155.

51. "Tea and Chatter," 34.

52. *Afternoon Tea* (London: Hopwood and Crew, 1895).

53. *Manners of the Aristocracy*, 55.

54. Mary Farrah and C. Hutchins Lewis, *Afternoon Tea and Other Action Songs for Schools* (London: J. Curwen and Sons, 1907).

55. *Lady's World* (May 1887): 237.

56. "In the Kitchen: An Exhibition Tea," *Ladies Home* (28 May 1898): 72.

57. "Het Excellenste Kruyd Tea," *Saturday Review* (October 1883): 498.

58. "Tea-Drinking and Women's Rights," *Woman's Herald* (13 July 1893): 326.

59. "A Tea-Drinking Lion-Hunter," *Woman's Herald* (9 March 1893): 42.

60. E. H. Skrine and George Brownen, *The Tea We Drink: A Demand for Safeguards in the Interest of the Public and the Producer* (London: Simpkin, Marshall, Hamilton, Kent, 1901), 9.

61. "The London Tea Trade," *Illustrated London News* 65 (12 December 1874): 567.
62. Messrs. J. C. Sillar and Co., circular, quoted in "India v. China," *Planters' Gazette*, 28 February 1878, 40; "Creamy Indian Teas," *The Grocer* 3 (18 December 1880): 683.
63. *The Grocer*, 2 January 1869, 17.
64. *HCM*, 10 March 1880, 3.
65. "An Interview with an Indian Tea Retailer," *HCM*, 26 February 1880, iii.
66. Lieut.-Colonel Edward Money, *The Cultivation and Manufacture of Tea*, 4th ed. (London: W. B. Whittingham and Co., 1883), 174.
67. "The London Tea Trade," *Illustrated London News* 65 (12 December 1874): 567; Lewis and Company, *Tea and Tea Blending*, 4th ed. (London: Eden Fisher and Co., 1894); *The Grocer*, 5 January 1867, 10; "Tea Tasting and Blending," *Chambers's Journal* 5 (February 1902): 113.
68. "Tea and How to Mix It," *The Grocer*, 5 January 1867, 10; "The Packet Tea Trade," *The Grocer*, 13 March 1891, iv; Evidence of Frederick Horniman, *Report from the Select Committee on Adulteration of Food Act (1872)* (London: HMSO, 1874), 301.
69. Evidence of Frederick Goulburn in *Select Committee on Adulteration Report*, 83.
70. Advertisement for William Stewart, tea dealer, *Newcastle Courant*, 12 July 1872.
71. Dr. A. Campbell, "Indian Teas, and the Importance of Extending their Adoption in the Home Market," *Journal of the Society of Arts* 22 (30 January 1873): 173.
72. *HCM*, 10 March 1880, iii.
73. *HCM*, 9 July 1880, iii.
74. *HCM*, 30 April 1880, iii.
75. *The Grocer*, 29 November 1873, 462.
76. "Tea Cultivation in India," *Daily News*, 8 April 1882, 3.
77. "Grocers and Packet Teas," *HCM*, 13 January 1893, iii. For a similar critique, see "Grocers and Packet Teas," *HCM*, 15 May 1891, iii.
78. "The Position of Indian Tea," *HCM*, 16 July 1880, iii.
79. *The Grocer*, 4 January 1862, 8.
80. Ibid., 5 April 1873, 305; 8 December 1883, 804; 14 May 1887, 892.
81. Ibid., 14 June 1862, 421 and 2 January 1869, 17.
82. Ibid., 25 November 1865, 379.
83. Ibid., 19 November 1864, 357; 8 August 1863, 98; 10 October 1863, 246; 30 January 1864, 69; 16 July 1864, 44.
84. Ibid., 19 November 1864, 357.
85. Ibid., 3 December 1864, 402.
86. Ibid., 4 August 1866, 76. Also see "Tea-Planting in Assam," *Chambers's Journal of Popular Literature* 57 (July 1880): 471.
87. Charles Henry Fielder, "On the Rise, Progress and Future Prospects of Tea Cultivation in British India," *Journal of the Statistical Society* 32 (March 1869): 37.
88. Roland Wenzlhuemer, *From Coffee to Tea Cultivation in Ceylon, 1880–1900: An Economic and Social History* (Leiden: Brill, 2008), 64–65.
89. "The Material Progress of Ceylon," *Calcutta Review* 77, no. 153 (July 1883): 7.
90. A. G. Stanton, *A Report on British Grown Tea* (London: William Clowes, 1887), 11.
91. Advertisement for *HCM* in David Crole, *Tea: A Text Book of Tea Planting and Manufacture* (London: Crosby Lockwood and Son, 1897), xxiv and "The Position of Indian Tea," *HCM*, 16 July 1880, iii.

92. "Jubilee Week," *HCM*, 30 May 1929, 1.
93. "The Position of Indian Tea," *HCM*, 16 July 1880, iii.
94. Gary B. Magee and Andrew S. Thompson, *Empire and Globalisation: Networks of People, Goods and Capital in the British World, c. 1850–1914* (Cambridge: Cambridge University Press, 2010), 137.
95. The Javanese Tea Association was founded in 1881. Ukers, *All about Tea,* 1:122. The Japanese Central Tea Association began in 1883. C. R. Harler, *The Culture and Marketing of Tea* (London: Oxford University Press, 1933), 175.
96. Raymond K. Renford, *The Non-Official British in India to 1920* (Delhi: Oxford University Press, 1987), 59–77.
97. *The Planters' Association of Ceylon, 1854–1954* (Colombo: Times of Ceylon, 1954); Wenzlhuemer, *From Coffee to Tea*, 82.
98. "Ceylon Association in London," *HCM*, 24 November 1905, 9.
99. The ITA also had regional branches. See, for example, *Assam Branch: Indian Tea Association, 1889–1989, Centenary Souvenir* (Guwahati, Assam: Indian Tea Association, 1989).
100. Quoted in Ukers, *All about Tea*, 2:198. For a prospectus and list of men who joined the provisional committee, see *Planter's Supplement to the HCM*, 18 July 1879, iii, and for further discussion, see 25 July 1879, iii.
101. Renford, *Non-Official British*, 59; Indian Tea Districts Association Charter (February 1880), ITA Mss Eur F174/1.
102. Ukers, *All about Tea*, 2:199; Konganda T. Achaya, *The Food Industries of British India* (Delhi: Oxford University Press, 1994), 173.
103. Ukers, *All about Tea*, 2:199.
104. Renford, *Non-Official British*, 59–77.
105. Ibid., 210; Mrinalini Sinha, *Colonial Masculinity: The "Manly Englishman" and the "Effeminate Bengali" in the Late Nineteenth Century* (Manchester: Manchester University Press, 1995), chap. 1.
106. I have laid out key aspects of this debate in "Imperial Possessions, Cultural Histories and the Material Turn: Response," *Victorian Studies* 50, no. 2 (Winter 2008): 289–96. Important works on this topic include Thomas Richards, *The Commodity Culture of Victorian England: Advertising and Spectacle, 1851–1914* (Stanford: Stanford University Press, 1990); Anne McClintock, *Imperial Leather: Race, Gender and Sexuality in the Colonial Contest* (New York: Routledge, 1995); John Mackenzie, ed., *Imperialism and Popular Culture* (Manchester: Manchester University Press, 1985) and his *Propaganda and Empire: The Manipulation of Public Opinion, 1880–1960* (Manchester: Manchester University Press, 1984).
107. One of the earliest examples is in the *Daily News*, 27 February 1856, 1.
108. Advertisement for William Smeal and Son, Tea Merchants, *Glasgow Herald*, 2 October 1873, 2. Also see other ads in *The Grocer*, 3 July 1880, 9 and 3 February 1883, 161.
109. *HCM*, 22 October 1880, iii; 7 January 1881, iv; 29 January 1882, iii.
110. *HCM*, 28 January 1881, iii.
111. See, for example, Foster Green & Co.'s advertisement in *Belfast News-Letter*, 15 January 1874, 1 and the Indian Tea Company's in *Belfast News-Letter*, 11 February 1886, 4.

112. Lieut.-Colonel Edward Money, *The Tea Controversy: Indian versus Chinese Teas. Which Are Adulterated? Which Are Better?* 2nd ed. (London: W. B. Whittingham, 1884), 5, 8–9.

113. "Indian Tea in Belfast," *HCM*, 12 March 1886, iii–iv.

114. "Sirocco Tea," *HCM*, 30 November 1888, iii; Ukers, *All about Tea*, 1:159–60.

115. "Indian v. Chinese Methods," *HCM*, 11 October 1889, iii.

116. "Retailing Indian Tea," *HCM*, 25 March 1881, iv. Also see *HCM*, 7 January 1881, iv; 19 November 1880, iii; and 27 August 1880, ii.

117. "The Indian Tea Agency Limited," *HCM*, 31 August 1878, 204.

118. "The Home Trade in Indian Tea," *HCM*, 2 September 1881, iii.

119. *HCM*, 18 November 1881, iii.

120. *HCM*, 29 January 1882, iii; 22 October 1880, iii; and 7 January 1881, iv; *Ninth Annual Report of the Indian Tea Districts Association* (February 1888), ITA Mss Eur F174/1.

121. *HCM*, 14 April 1882, iii, 14; 21 January 1881, iii; and 10 June 1881, iii; "Indian Tea," *Farm and Home* 17 (24 June 1888): 204.

122. "Popularizing Indian Tea," *HCM*, 10 June 1881, iii.

123. "The Home Trade in Indian Tea," *HCM*, 2 September 1881, iii.

124. "Indian Tea in Ireland," *HCM*, 20 May 1881, iii.

125. *HCM*, 18 October 1901, iii.

126. "An Interview with an Indian Tea Retailer," *HCM*, 26 February 1886, iii.

127. *Women's Penny Paper*, 28 June 1890, 428.

128. Perilla Kinchin, *Tea and Taste: The Glasgow Tea Rooms, 1875–1975* (Oxford: White Cockade, 1991), 17–18, 32–36.

129. Cited in ibid., 81.

130. *HCM*, 4 July 1879, 1; Rappaport, *Shopping for Pleasure*, 102–3; "An Enterprising Tea Merchant," *The Grocer*, 5 October 1889, 591; "A Run through Dublin Shops," *Today's Woman: A Weekly Home and Fashion Journal*, 28 August 1896, 6; "Tea Shop and Indian Tea," *HCM*, 31 August 1883, iii.

131. "Ladies and Colonial Tea in the West End," *HCM*, 5 March 1886, iii.

132. "Lady's Tea-Shops in London," *Lady's Realm* 7 (1899–1900): 737.

133. Ladies' Own Tea Association, Statement of Nominal Capital and Memorandum of Articles of Association, 24 February 1892, Board of Trade, Companies Registration Office: Files of Dissolved Companies, NA BT 31/35863.

134. *Lady's Realm* 1 (1897): 215–16.

135. "How to Popularize Indian Tea," *HCM*, 13 June 1879, i. On tea shops and temperance, see *Tea: A Monthly Journal for Planters, Merchants and Brokers* 2, no. 14 (May 1902): 418.

136. "Indian Tea in Continental Europe," *Preliminary Report of the Executive Committee, Indian Tea Cess Committee* (1 June to 31 December 1903), 27, ITA Mss Eur F174/922.

137. *Tea* 1, no. 4 (July 1901): 103; "Five O'Clock Tea," *Tea* 2, no. 14 (May 1902): 418.

138. Indian Tea in Continental Europe, *Preliminary Report*, 29–30.

139. ITCC, *5th Annual Report of the Executive Committee* (1 June to 31 December 1908), 4–7, ITA Mss Eur F174/922.

140. ITCC, *6th Annual Report of the Executive Committee* (1 June to 31 December 1909), 4, ITA Mss Eur F174/922.

141. *HCM*, 20 October 1905, 9.

142. *Hearth and Home* (30 July 1891): 356.
143. Carol A. Breckenridge, "The Aesthetics and Politics of Colonial Collecting: India at World's Fairs," *Comparative Studies in Society and History* 31, no. 2 (April 1989): 195–216; Hoffenberg, *An Empire on Display*; Paul Greenhalgh, *Ephemeral Vistas: The Expositions Universelles: Great Exhibitions and World's Fairs, 1851–1939* (Manchester: Manchester University Press, 1988); Louise Purbrick, ed., *The Great Exhibition of 1851: New Interdisciplinary Essays* (Manchester: Manchester University Press, 2001); Lara Kriegel, *Grand Designs: Labor, Empire, and the Museum in Victorian Culture* (Durham: Duke University Press, 2007); Tim Barringer and Tom Flynn, eds., *Colonialism and the Object: Empire, Material Culture and the Museum* (London: Routledge, 1998); Jeffrey A. Auerbach, *The Great Exhibition of 1851: A Nation on Display* (New Haven: Yale University Press, 1999); Timothy Mitchell, *Colonising Egypt* (Berkeley: University of California Press, 1991); Zeynep Celik, *Displaying the Orient: Architecture of Islam at Nineteenth-Century World's Fairs* (Berkeley: University of California Press, 1992).
144. Walter Benjamin, "Paris, Capital of the Nineteenth Century," in *The Arcades Project*, trans. Howard Eiland and Kevin McLaughlin (Cambridge, MA: Belknap Press of Harvard University, 1999), 7. Also see Richards, *Commodity Culture*, 7–72.
145. Tony Bennett, "The Exhibitionary Complex," *New Formations* 4 (Spring 1988): 73–102 and *The Birth of the Museum: History, Theory, Politics* (London: Routledge, 1995).
146. Nelleke Teughels and Peter Scholliers, eds., *A Taste of Progress: Food at International and World Exhibitions in the Nineteenth and Twentieth Centuries* (Farnham, Surrey: Ashgate, 2015); Adele Wessell, "Between Alimentary Products and the Art of Cooking: The Industrialisation of Eating at the World Fairs—1888/1893," in *Consuming Culture in the Long Nineteenth Century: Narratives of Consumption, 1700–1900*, ed. Tamara S. Wagner and Narin Hassan (Lanham, MD: Rowman and Littlefield, 2007), 107–23.
147. A conference on food adulteration was held in conjunction with the exhibition. *The Adulteration of Food: Conferences by the Institute of Chemistry, 14 and 15 July 1884* (London: William Clowes and Sons, 1884).
148. *Fourth Annual Report of the Indian Tea Districts Association* (February 1884) and *Fifth Annual Report of the Indian Tea Districts Association* (February 1885), ITA Mss Eur F174/1.
149. "Tea at the Health Exhibition," *HCM*, 30 May 1884, iii.
150. *The Sanitary Record Bird's-Eye Guide and Handbook to the International Health Exhibition* (London: Smith, Elder and Co., 1884), 6.
151. *Illustrated Catalogue of the Chinese Collection of Exhibits for the International Health Exhibition, London 1884* (London: William Clowes and Sons, 1884), 136; Karl Gerth, *China Made: Consumer Culture and the Creation of the Nation* (Cambridge, MA: Harvard University Asia Center, 2003), 220.
152. Quoted in Hoffenberg, *An Empire on Display*, xix.
153. *Illustrated Catalogue of the Chinese Collection*, 134.
154. "The Deterioration of Chinese Teas," *HCM*, 30 April 1886, iii; "Chinese Response to Competition," *HCM*, 20 July 1888, iii; "The Ruined Tea Men of China," *HCM*, 13 December 1889, iii; "China as a Competitor," *HCM*, 15 January 1897, v and 22 January 1897, iii. Also see "Chinese Lack of Development," *HCM*, 7 July 1905, 9 and Gardella, *Harvesting Mountains*, 110–60.

155. "Ceylon Teas at the Exhibition," *Ceylon Observer*, 5 January 1886, 9.
156. *Ceylon Observer*, 13 January 1886, 35.
157. *Official Handbook and Catalogue of the Ceylon Court: Colonial and Indian Exhibition, London, 1886*, 2nd ed. (London: William Clowes, 1886), xiv. On Ceylon's appearance at the Crystal Palace, see Lara Kriegel, "The Pudding and the Palace: Labor, Print Culture, and Imperial Britain in 1851," in *After the Imperial Turn: Thinking with and through the Nation*, ed. Antoinette Burton (Durham: Duke University Press, 2003), 237.
158. Ukers, *All about Tea*, 2:186.
159. J. L. Shand, "The Tea, Coffee, and Cocoa Industries of Ceylon," *Journal of the Society of Arts* 38 (24 January 1890): 180, 184; Wenzlhuemer, *From Coffee to Tea*, chap. 5.
160. Shand, "Tea, Coffee," 188.
161. *Catalogue of the Ceylon Court*, x–xii.
162. *Ceylon Tea* (Colombo: Planters Association of Ceylon, 1886), 1.
163. *Catalogue of the Ceylon Court*, 21.
164. *Ceylon Observer*, 27 May 1886, 486; J. L. Shand, "The Increased Consumption of British-Colonial Teas," *Chambers's Journal of Popular Literature, Science and Art* 3 (30 October 1886): 704. Also see "The Colonial and Indian Exhibition," *Westminster Review* 126 (July 1886): 29–59 and "Ceylon Redividus," *All the Year Round* (4 August 1888): 101.
165. *The Grocer*, 5 September 1885, 33.
166. A. G. Stanton, *Report on British-Grown Tea* (London: William Clowes and Sons, 1887), 3–4.
167. J. L. Shand, "British Grown Tea," *HCM*, 18 June 1886, iii. For a reaction, see "Ceylon Tea," *Financial Times*, 16 January 1888, 3.
168. "An Interview with an Indian Tea Retailer," *HCM*, 26 February 1886, iii.
169. "Indian Tea at the London Exhibitions," *HCM*, 22 May 1885, iii.
170. Richards, *Commodity Culture*, 106–7; David Cannadine, "The Context, Performance and Meaning of Ritual: The British Monarchy and the 'Invention of Tradition' c. 1820–1977," in *The Invention of Tradition*, ed. Eric Hobsbawm and Terence Ranger (Cambridge: Cambridge University Press, 1983), 137–38.
171. E. M. Clerke, "Assam and the Indian Tea Trade," *Asiatic Quarterly Review* 5 (January–April 1888): 362.
172. Manu Goswami, *Producing India: From Colonial Economy to National Space* (Chicago: University of Chicago Press, 2004), 42–59.
173. George M. Barker, *A Tea Planter's Life in Assam* (Calcutta: Thacker, Spink and Co., 1884), 142. Also see A. J. Wallis-Tayler, *Tea Machinery and Tea Factories* (London: Crosby Lockwood and Son, 1900).
174. Pamela Walker Laird, *Advertising Progress: American Business and the Rise of Consumer Marketing* (Baltimore: Johns Hopkins University Press, 1998), 102–3.
175. Chatterjee, *A Time for Tea*, 52–53; Sharma, *Empire's Garden*, 25–26.
176. Sir Roper Lethbridge introduction to J. Berry White, "The Indian Tea Industry: Its Rise, Progress during Fifty Years, and Prospects Considered from a Commercial Point of View," *Journal of the Royal Society of Arts*, 35 (10 June 1887): 734.
177. Robert Henry Mair, ed., *Debrett's Illustrated House of Commons and the Judicial Bench* (London: Dean and Son, 1886), 95.
178. White, "The Indian Tea Industry," 742.
179. Gardella, *Harvesting Mountains*, 48–83.

180. White, "The Indian Tea Industry," 740.
181. *Board of Customs and Excise: Annual Report* (1873), 35–36, NA CUST 44/6.
182. *Board of Customs and Excise: Annual Report* (1890), 8, NA CUST 44/11. Between 1854 and 1866 the export of Indian tea increased tenfold. *Imperial Economic Committee Report on Tea* (1931), 2, NA CO 323/1142/18.
183. C. H. Denyer, "The Consumption of Tea and Other Staple Drinks," *Economic Journal* 3, no. 9 (March 1893): 33, 41.
184. *Board of Customs and Excise: Annual Report* (1889), 9, NA CUST 44/9.
185. Ibid.
186. Arthur Montefiore, "Tea Planting in Assam," *Argosy* 46 (September 1888): 183.
187. "The Revolution in Tea," *Chambers's Journal of Popular Literature, Science, and Art* 6 (August 1889): 504.
188. Denyer, "Consumption of Tea," 38.
189. Crole, *Tea*, 42.
190. Sir James Buckingham, *A Few Facts about Indian Tea and How to Brew It* (London: ITA, 1910), 4.
191. Mazawattee tea card, c. 1892, Advertising Association Archive, AA/1/4, History of Advertising Trust (hereafter HAT), Norwich. This phrase also appeared on tea boxes; see, for example, *Graphic*, 25 November 1893, 670. Packaging also included phrases such as "Golden Tips from Gartmore Estate, Ceylon." Advertisement for T. Roberts Family Grocer, 1891, Evan. 6275, Evanion Collection, British Library.
192. Diana James, *The Story of Mazawattee Tea* (Edinburgh: Pentland Press, 1996), 1–14, 20–21.
193. *HCM*, 30 April 1886, iii.
194. For examples, see James, *Mazawattee Tea*, 6–10, 18. The United Kingdom Tea Company also occasionally showed images of its tasting room and other modern departments. "Something about Tea," *Illustrated London News*, 6 May 1893, 557.
195. Mazawattee ads and trade cards from the 1890s, HAT, AA/1/4, History of Advertising Trust, Norwich.
196. *Illustrated London News*, 12 May 1894, 599.
197. This advertisement appeared in many forms. See, for example, *Graphic*, 26 May 1894, 636.
198. Clara de Chatelain, *Cottage Life, or, Tales at Dame Barbara's Tea Table* (London: Addey and Co., 1853), 1; M. E. Frances, "Tea Time in the Village," *Blackwood's Edinburgh Magazine* (October 1896): 520–25.
199. Tania M. Buckrell Pos, *Tea and Taste: The Visual Language of Tea* (Atglen, PA: Schiffer, 2004), 160–63.
200. "A Cup of Tea," *Graphic Summer Number*, 1893, 18. Edward Fahey's "The Favourite" depicted a young girl enjoying tea with dogs. William Powell Frith's "Five O'Clock Tea" offered a social yet domestic example of the tea party. *Illustrated London News*, 5 May 1894, 55; 12 May 1894, 580; 19 May 1894, 619.
201. Lipton, *Autobiography*, 132–34.
202. Joseph A. Schumpeter, *Imperialism and Social Classes* (New York: Augustus M. Kelley, 1951), 12.
203. Edith Browne, *Peeps at Industries: Tea* (London: Adam and Charles Black, 1912), 35.
204. Quoted in Gardella, *Harvesting Mountains*, 111.
205. H. Venkatasubbiah, *Foreign Trade of India, 1900–1940: A Statistical Analysis* (Bombay: Oxford University Press, 1946), 29.

CHAPTER 6. THE PLANTER ABROAD

1. Assam Company, *Report of the Directors and Auditors made to the Shareholders at the General Meeting*, 19 December 1882, Ms. CLC/B/123/27, 052/4, Assam Company Archives, London Metropolitan Archives. Also see H. A. Antrobus, *A History of the Assam Company, 1839–1953* (Edinburgh: T. and A. Constable, 1957).

2. Other inexpensive "drugs" went through a similar process around the same time. See, for example, Howard Cox, *The Global Cigarette: Origins and Evolution of British American Tobacco, 1880–1945* (Oxford: Oxford University Press, 2000) and Mark Pendergrast, *Uncommon Grounds: The History of Coffee and How It Transformed Our World* (New York: Basic Books, 1999).

3. James Belich, *Replenishing the Earth: The Settler Revolution and the Rise of the Anglo-World, 1789–1939* (Oxford: Oxford University Press, 2009). My work reinforces many of Belich's key arguments. Also see Gary B. Magee and Andrew S. Thompson, *Empire and Globalisation: Networks of People, Goods, and Capital in the British World, c. 1850–1914* (Cambridge: Cambridge University Press, 2010).

4. See, for example, Sugata Bose, *A Hundred Horizons: The Indian Ocean in the Age of Global Empire* (Cambridge, MA: Harvard University Press, 2006), chap. 3; Thomas R. Metcalf, *Imperial Connections: India in the Indian Ocean Arena, 1860–1920* (Berkeley: University of California Press, 2007).

5. Victoria de Grazia, *Irresistible Empire: America's Advance through Twentieth-Century Europe* (Cambridge, MA: Belknap Press of Harvard University Press, 2005). This is a huge literature, but important studies include Julie Greene, *The Canal Builders: Making America's Empire at the Panama Canal* (New York: Penguin, 2009); Greg Grandin, *Fordlandia: The Rise and Fall of Henry Ford's Forgotten Jungle City* (New York: Metropolitan Books, 2009); and Jason M. Colby, *The Business of Empire: United Fruit, Race, and U.S. Expansion in Central America* (Ithaca: Cornell University Press, 2011). For a cultural approach, see Mona Domosh, *American Commodities in an Age of Empire* (New York: Routledge, 2006) and Robert W. Rydell and Rob Kroes, *Buffalo Bill in Bologna: The Americanization of the World, 1869–1922* (Chicago: University of Chicago Press, 2005). Americans were also building the British Empire; see David Baillargeon, "A Burmese Wonderland: Race, Empire, and the Burma Corporation, 1907–1935," in *Global Raciality: Empire, Postcoloniality, and Decoloniality*, ed. Paola Bacchetta and Sunaina Maira (London: Routledge, 2017).

6. Emily S. Rosenberg, *A World Connecting, 1870–1945* (Cambridge, MA: Belknap Press of Harvard University Press, 2012). Also see Jürgen Osterhammel, *The Transformation of the World: A Global History of the Nineteenth Century*, trans. Patrick Camiller (Princeton: Princeton University Press, 2009).

7. "The Tea Surplus and How to Diminish It," *Tea* 1, no. 6 (September 1901): 161.

8. "The Battle of the Teas!" *Tea Trader and Grocers' Review* 2, no. 5 (September 1894): 74.

9. Thomas Lipton ran with this idea. Edward D. Melillo, "Empire in a Cup: Imagining Colonial Geographies through British Tea Consumption," in *Eco-Cultural Networks and the British Empire: New Views on Environmental History*, ed. James Beattie, Edward Melillo, and Emily O'Gorman (London: Bloomsbury, 2015), 68–91.

10. *Overland Ceylon Observer*, 24 February 1886, 191.

11. "The Rise of the Tea Industry in Ceylon," *HCM*, 16 April 1886, iv.

12. "Pushing Ceylon in America," *HCM*, 5 October 1888, iii–iv. Also see the other responses on 26 October, 8 and 16 November 1888.
13. It is not clear whether the term "syndicate" is actually referring to the ITA, but I suspect these were separate entities.
14. *Ceylon Observer*, 18 May 1886, 455.
15. Belich, *Replenishing the Earth*; also see Duncan Bell, *The Idea of Greater Britain: Empire and the Future of World Order, 1860–1900* (Princeton: Princeton University Press, 2007), 4–10, 108–13; Theodore Koditschek, *Liberalism, Imperialism, and the Historical Imagination: Nineteenth-Century Visions of a Greater Britain* (Cambridge: Cambridge University Press, 2011); Carl Bridge and Kent Fedorowich, eds., *The British World: Diaspora, Culture and Identity* (London: Frank Cass, 2003); and Lindsay J. Proudfoot and Michael M. Roche, eds., *(Dis)Placing Empire: Renegotiating British Colonial Geographies* (Aldershot: Ashgate, 2005).
16. John H. Blake, *Tea Hints for Retailers* (Denver: Williamson-Haffner Engraving Co., 1903), 33.
17. Belich, *Replenishing the Earth*, chap. 9.
18. Ibid., 357.
19. Some key works include Gail Reekie, *Temptations: Sex, Selling and the Department Store* (St. Leonards, NSW: Allen and Unwin, 1993); Donica Belisle, *Retail Nation: Department Stores and the Making of Modern Canada* (Vancouver: University of British Columbia Press, 2011); David Monod, *Store Wars: Shopkeepers and the Culture of Mass Marketing, 1890–1939* (Toronto: University of Toronto Press, 1996); Robert Crawford, *But Wait There Is More: A History of Australian Advertising, 1900–2000* (Carlton: Melbourne University Press, 2008); Robert Crawford, Judith Smart, and Kim Humphery, eds., *Consumer Australia: Historical Perspectives* (Newcastle upon Tyne: Cambridge Scholars, 2010); Cheryl Krasnick Warsh and Dan Malleck, eds., *Consuming Modernity: Gendered Behaviours and Consumerism before the Baby Boom* (Vancouver: University of British Columbia Press, 2013); and Edwin Barnard, *Emporium: Selling the Dream in Colonial Australia* (Canberra: National Library of Australia, 2015). For an overview, see Donica Belisle, "Toward a Canadian Consumer History," *Labour/Le Travail* 52 (2003): 181–206.
20. Douglas McCalla, *Consumers in the Bush: Shopping in Rural Upper Canada* (Montreal: McGill-Queen's University Press, 2015).
21. Frederick Cane and R. S. McIndoe, *A Sketch of the Growth and History of Tea and Science of Blending particularly adapted to the Canadian Trade* (Toronto: Mail Job Printing, 1891), 24–26.
22. G. H. Knibbs, *Official Yearbook of the Commonwealth of Australia, 1901–1909* (Melbourne: McCarron, Bird, and Co., 1910), 901.
23. Richard Twopeny, *Town Life in Australia* (London: Eliot Stock, 1883), 64. For a discussion, see Michael Symons, *One Continuous Picnic: A Gastronomic History of Australia*, 2nd ed. (Melbourne: Melbourne University Press, 2007), 73.
24. George M. Barker, *A Tea Planter's Life in Assam* (Calcutta: Thacker, Spink and Co., 1884), 239.
25. Peter Griggs, "Black Poison or Beneficial Beverage? Tea Consumption in Colonial Australia," *Journal of Australian Colonial History* 17 (July 2015): 23–44. Also see Susie Khamis, "Class in a Tea Cup: The Bushells Brand, 1895–1920," in *Consumer*

Australia, ed. Crawford, Smart, and Humphery, 13–26 and Jessica Knight, "'A Poisonous Cup?': Afternoon Tea in Australian Society, 1870–1914" (BA honors thesis, Department of Philosophical and Historical Inquiry, University of Sydney, October 2011). This is a remarkable thesis on a very understudied subject.

26. Mark Staniforth, *Material Culture and Consumer Society: Dependent Colonies in Colonial Australia* (New York: Kluwer Academic, 2003), 69–70, 92–93.
27. Griggs, "Black Poison," 25–26.
28. Ibid., 35.
29. Ibid., 28–30.
30. *Sydney Gazette*, 25 November 1826, as cited in Griggs, "Black Poison," 32.
31. Andrew Wells, *Constructing Capitalism: An Economic History of Eastern Australia, 1788–1901* (Sydney: Allen and Unwin, 1989); Philip McMichael, *Settlers and the Agrarian Question: Foundations of Capitalism in Colonial Australia* (Cambridge: Cambridge University Press, 1984).
32. Angela Woollacott, *Settler Society in the Australian Colonies: Self-Government and Imperial Culture* (Oxford: Oxford University Press, 2015), especially chap. 1.
33. This did not just apply to white settler colonies. See, for example, Richard Wilk's analysis in *Home Cooking in the Global Village: Caribbean Food from Buccaneers to Ecotourists* (Oxford: Berg, 2006).
34. Staniforth, *Material Culture*, 7–8.
35. Khamis, "Class in a Tea Cup," 13–26.
36. Martha Rutledge, "Inglis, James (1845–1908)," *Australian Dictionary of Biography*, National Centre of Biography, Australian National University, http://adb.anu.edu.au/biography/inglis-james-3834/text6087.
37. *First Annual Indian Tea Districts Association Annual Report* (February 1881), ITA Mss Eur F174/1. For a thorough analysis, see Peter H. Hoffenberg, *An Empire on Display: English, Indian, and Australian Exhibitions from the Crystal Palace to the Great War* (Berkeley: University of California Press, 2001), 118–20. Also see "British Grown Teas," *HCM*, 18 June 1886, iii.
38. *Indian Tea Districts Association Third Annual Report* (February 1883), 2, ITA Mss Eur F174/1.
39. *The Australian Grocer and Storekeeper and Oil Trade Review*, 27 October 1887, 82.
40. "The Battle of the Teas!" 73.
41. *Official Handbook and Catalogue of the Ceylon Court at the World's Columbia Exhibition* (Colombo: H. S. Cottle, 1893), 41.
42. Khamis, "Class in a Tea Cup," 22. Also see *The Tea Industry* (Melbourne: Economics Department, Australia and New Zealand Bank, 1970).
43. "The Tea Market in Australia," *The Tea Cyclopedia* (Calcutta: Indian Tea Gazette, 1881), 276.
44. "China vs. India in Australia," in *The Tea Cyclopedia*, 282.
45. Knight, "'A Poisonous Cup?,'" 16.
46. David Walker, *Anxious Nation: Australia and the Rise of Asia, 1850–1939* (Brisbane: University of Queensland Press, 1999).
47. "The Tea Market in Australia," *The Tea Cyclopedia*, 276–85.
48. Hoffenberg, *An Empire on Display*, 117.
49. Rutledge, "Inglis."

50. Michael Symons, *One Continuous Picnic: A Gastronomic History of Australia*, 2nd ed. (Melbourne: Melbourne University Press, 2007), 30–31.

51. Laksiri Jayasuriya, David Walker, and Jan Gothard, eds., *Legacies of White Australia: Race, Culture and Nation* (Crawley: University of Western Australia, 2003); Richard White, *Inventing Australia: Images and Identity, 1688–1980* (Sydney: Allen and Unwin, 1981), 157. Keith Windschuttle, *The White Australia Policy* (Sydney: Macleay Press, 2004) challenges the role of racism in the construction of Australian nationalism.

52. Symons, *One Continuous Picnic*, 93–94.

53. "The Combination against Indian Tea in Australia," *HCM*, 16 December 1881, iii. For a later assessment of the Tea Syndicate's successes in Australia in the 1880s, see Sir Edward Buck's remarks made at a meeting of Calcutta Tea Agency Houses held on 30 January 1903, ITA Mss Eur F174/922.

54. Griggs, "Black Poison," 29.

55. *Report of the Joint Committee of the Honorable Legislative Council and House of Assembly Upper Canada on the Importation of Tea into this Province* (York: John Carey, 1824), 2.

56. Leslie Holmes, "Westward the Course of Empire Takes Its Way through Tea," *Past Imperfect* 16 (2010): 66–88, 69–70.

57. Ibid., 73–74.

58. "Report on the Canadian Market—A New Market for Indian Tea," in *The Tea Cyclopedia*, 289. C. F. Amery divorced Leo's mother and reportedly took up farming in Canada. Deborah Lavin, "Amery, Leopold Charles Maurice Stennett (1873–1955)," in *Oxford Dictionary of National Biography*, ed. H. C. G. Matthew and Brian Harrison (Oxford: Oxford University Press, 2004), http://www.oxforddnb.com/view/article/30401.

59. Holmes, "Westward," 84–87.

60. William E. Van Vugt, ed., *British Immigration to the United States, 1776–1914*, vol. 4, *Civil War and Industry: 1860–1914* (London: Pickering and Chatto, 2009), xii.

61. Magee and Thompson, *Empire and Globalisation*, 68–69; Belich, *Replenishing the Earth*, 459.

62. Van Vugt, *British Immigration*, 4:xvi. Also see his *Britain to America: Mid-Nineteenth Century Immigrants to the United States* (Urbana: University of Illinois Press, 1999); C. Erickson, *Leaving England: Essays on British Emigration in the Nineteenth Century* (Ithaca: Cornell University Press, 1993); and Belich, *Replenishing the Earth*, chap. 9.

63. See Magee and Thompson, *Empire and Globalisation*, as well as Belich, *Replenishing the Earth*, for the most powerful arguments.

64. Van Vugt, *British Immigration*, 4:xiii.

65. *HCM*, 15 January 1897, v.

66. *HCM*, 26 November 1880, 3; "The American Market," in *The Tea Cyclopedia*, 286.

67. *HCM*, 14 January 1881, iii.

68. *Report of the Directors and Auditors made to the Shareholders at a General Meeting*, 19 June 1882, Ms. CLC/B/123/27,052/4, Assam Company Archives, London Metropolitan Archives.

69. *HCM*, 26 October 1888, iii.

70. "The Battle of the Teas!" 74.

71. *HCM*, 28 September 1888, iii.

72. "Pushing Ceylon in America," *HCM*, 28 September 1888, iii.
73. A. M. Ferguson, the editor of the *Ceylon Observer*, was Ceylon's tea commissioner at the Melbourne Exhibition. *Proceedings of the Planters' Association of Ceylon* (1883): 117.
74. H. R. Stimson, *Minutes of the Proceedings of a General Meeting of the Planters' Association in Ceylon* (21 September 1883) in *Proceedings of the Planters' Association of Ceylon* (1884), 66–67.
75. *Ceylon Observer*, 25 May 1886, 484.
76. Ibid., 17 May 1886, 454.
77. Ibid., 25 May 1886, 485.
78. Ibid., 2 November 1886, 483–84.
79. Ibid., 25 May 1886, 483.
80. Ibid., 17 May 1886, 454.
81. Ibid., 25 May 1886, 483.
82. "Ceylon Tea," *Ceylon Observer*, 4 September 1886, 820. At this time, Japan was becoming a key exporter of green teas so the anti-Chinese argument did not necessarily benefit British black teas. Indeed, Japanese advertising also stimulated the notion that Chinese teas were dirty and adulterated.
83. Tea Syndicate Circular published in *Ceylon Observer*, 20 August 1886, 769. *Planters' Association of Ceylon*; Denys Mostyn Forrest, *A Hundred Years of Ceylon Tea, 1867–1967* (London: Chatto and Windus, 1967), 193–212. In the early 1890s, publicity also began in Tasmania, Sweden, Germany, and Ceylon. *Planters' Association of Ceylon*, 118; "Ceylon's Tea Advertising," *TCTJ* (December 1925): 922.
84. *The Vocalist* (NY) 12, no. 4 (April 1896): 192.
85. *The Planting Directory for India and Ceylon* (Colombo: A. M. and J. Ferguson, 1878), 92, 294.
86. "Ceylon Tea in America," *Ceylon Observer*, 17 June 1887, 555; Ukers, *All about Tea*, 2:281; Forrest, *Hundred Years of Ceylon Tea*, 198.
87. "Ceylon Tea in America," *Ceylon Observer*, 17 June 1887, 555.
88. R. E. Pineo, *Ceylon Observer*, 23 April 1888, 382.
89. *Ceylon Observer*, 20 July 1888, 687.
90. Ibid., 25 April 1888, 392. May eventually patented several brands with Indian-inspired names such as Bungaloe and Tiffen. *Official Gazette of the United States Patent Office* 155 (June 1910): 478.
91. *Ceylon Observer*, 5 May 1888, 433.
92. See R. E. Pineo's discussion of growers' reactions in *Ceylon Observer*, 13 August 1888, 749.
93. *Report of the General Meeting of the Planters' Association of Ceylon*, held at Nuwara Eliya, published in the *Ceylon Observer*, 11 December 1888, 1187.
94. *Ceylon Observer*, 6 July 1889, 694 and 8 July 1889, 695.
95. "Ceylon Planters' Tea Company of New York," *Proceedings of the Planters Association of Ceylon*, 1893, ccxxxviii–ccxlv.
96. Ukers, *All about Tea*, 2:281. I would like to thank W. Bruce Reid, Charles Ker Reid's great-grandson, for providing me with information about his family and sending me two fascinating letters Reid wrote shortly after he had emigrated.
97. C. K. Reid to the editor, *Ceylon Observer*, 20 July 1888, 688.
98. See his letter quoted by Murray in *Ceylon Observer*, 20 July, 1888, 687 and his own letter published on 20 July 1888, 688.

99. *Ceylon Observer*, 4 April 1889, 333 and 6 April 1889, 340.

100. In-house history, dated 5 September 1983, Bin A2, Ty-Phoo Tea Archive, Moreton, UK.

101. David Wainwright, *Brooke Bond: A Hundred Years* (London: Brooke Bond, 1969), 14, 18.

102. *Ceylon Observer*, 7 June 1890; "Lipton versus the World—The Greatest Advertising Tea Grocer in the World," *Times of Ceylon*, 20 May 1890; Ceylon and Indian press notices from 20 May 1890 to 19 December 1894, Sir Thomas Lipton Collection, Mitchell Library, Glasgow.

103. *Ceylon Independent*, 9 June 1890.

104. "Lipton Agrees to 'Boom' Ceylon Tea in America," *Times of Ceylon*, 11 June 1890; "Mr. Lipton and the Tea Fund," *Overland Ceylon Observer*, 16 August 1890.

105. Letter to the editor, *Times of Ceylon*, 11 June 1890.

106. "The Romance of Tea Selling," *Ceylon Observer*, 12 June 1890.

107. J. J. Grinlinton, "Report on Ceylon Tea in America," *Proceedings of the Ceylon Planters Association* (1894), 28–29.

108. Thomas J. Lipton, *Lipton's Autobiography* (New York: Duffield and Green, 1932), 189–91.

109. Two distinct companies, T. J. Lipton Inc. (USA) and T. J. Lipton Ltd (Canada), demarcated the boundaries between these two "American" markets. Lipton, *Autobiography*, 192; Peter Mathias, *Retailing Revolution: A History of Multiple Retailing in the Food Trades based upon the Allied Suppliers Group of Companies* (London: Longmans, 1967), 342–46.

110. Lipton, *Autobiography*, 192.

111. His advertising budget had grown to approximately £40,000 annually, an enormous sum that foreshadowed things to come. Mathias, *Retailing Revolution*, 342–46.

112. J. L. Shand to H. K. Rutherford, *Ceylon Observer*, 11 June 1888, 545.

113. A. G. Stanton, *A Report on British-Grown Tea* (London: William Clowes, 1887), 6–7.

114. Forrest, *Hundred Years of Ceylon Tea*, 199.

115. "Ceylon Tea in San Francisco," *Proceedings of the Ceylon Planters Association* (1893): ccxlv–ccxlviii.

116. All told there were some 27,529,400 admissions. Robert W. Rydell, *All the World's a Fair: Visions of Empire at American International Expositions, 1876–1916* (Chicago: University of Chicago Press, 1984), 39–40.

117. William Cronon, *Nature's Metropolis: Chicago and the Great West* (New York: W. W. Norton, 1991).

118. Erika Diane Rappaport, *Shopping for Pleasure: Women in the Making of London's West End* (Princeton: Princeton University Press, 2000), 142–77.

119. Thorstein Veblen, *The Theory of the Leisure Class* (1899; New York: Penguin, 1994).

120. Upton Sinclair, *The Jungle* (1906; New York: Modern Library, 2002). Chicago was also important to the development of the American labor movement. Lizabeth Cohen, *Making a New Deal: Industrial Workers in Chicago, 1919–1939* (Cambridge: Cambridge University Press, 1990).

121. There is a huge literature on American consumer society in this era. Some key works include T. J. Jackson Lears, *No Place of Grace: Antimodernism and the Transformation of American Culture, 1880-1920* (Chicago: University of Chicago Press, 1983) and *Fables*

of Abundance: A Cultural History of Advertising in America (New York: Basic Books, 1994); William Leach, *Land of Desire: Merchants, Power, and the Rise of a New American Culture* (New York: Pantheon, 1993); Susan Porter Benson, *Counter Cultures: Saleswomen, Managers, and Customers in American Department Stores, 1890–1940* (Urbana: University of Illinois Press, 1988); Kathy L. Peiss, *Cheap Amusements: Working Women and Leisure in Turn-of-the-Century New York* (Philadelphia: Temple University Press, 1986) and *Hope in a Jar: The Making of America's Beauty Culture* (New York: Owl Books, 1998).

122. *Planters' Gazette,* 1 May 1893, 192.
123. Susan Strasser, *Satisfaction Guaranteed: The Making of the American Mass Market* (Washington: Smithsonian Institution Press, 1989), 181. For the importance of the 1893 Columbian Exposition to American business, see Nancy F. Koehn, *Brand New: How Entrepreneurs Earned Consumers' Trust from Wedgwood to Dell* (Boston: Harvard Business School Press, 2001), 45–47.
124. M. M. Manring, *Slave in a Box: The Strange Career of Aunt Jemima* (Charlottesville: University Press of Virginia, 1998), 75–78.
125. Rydell, *All the World's a Fair,* 49–51.
126. *HCM,* 1 January 1897, iii and 15 January 1897, iii. The fairs were especially important sites for the formation of American ideas of Japanese culture. On this point, see Neil Harris, "All the World a Melting Pot? Japan at American Fairs, 1876–1904," in *Mutual Images: Essays in American-Japanese Relations,* ed. Priscilla Clapp and Akira Iriye (Cambridge, MA: Harvard University Press, 1975), 24–54.
127. Ukers, *All about Tea,* 2:299–303.
128. Timothy Mitchell, *Colonising Egypt* (Berkeley: University of California Press, 1991), 33.
129. W. Brown, letter to the Indian Tea Cess Committee, 22 September 1906, ITA Mss Eur F174/926.
130. "The Ceylon Tea Fund," *Ceylon Observer,* 22 February 1888, 182. For a criticism of the government's lack of support, see David Reid's letter in the *Ceylon Observer,* 11 June 1888, 545.
131. Forrest, *Hundred Years of Ceylon Tea,* 198.
132. See the editorial in *Ceylon Observer,* 2 August 1892, 818.
133. "Ancient Ceylon Art and Modern Ceylon Tea," *Ceylon Observer,* 18 November 1892, 242.
134. *World's Columbian Exposition Hand Book and Catalogue: Ceylon Courts* (London: Cassell Brothers, 1893), 2.
135. Ibid., 2–6.
136. Ibid., viii.
137. "Indian Tea at Chicago," *HCM,* 7 April 1893, iii.
138. "The Battle of the Teas!" 74. A special committee from the Calcutta ITA "dispatched" this staff of Indian servants.
139. "Indian Teas at the World's Fair," *HCM,* 11 August 1893, iii.
140. "Indian Tea at Chicago," *HCM,* 14 April 1893, iii.
141. "The Battle of the Teas!" 74; "Indian Tea in America," *HCM,* 19 April 1895, iii.
142. "What the Americans Drink," *HCM,* 8 January 1897, iii.
143. J. J. Grinlinton, "Ceylon Tea in America," *Proceedings of the Planters Association* (1894), 26.
144. "Ceylon's Tea Advertising," *TCTJ* (December 1925): 925.

145. *1st Annual Report of the Indian Tea Cess Committee* (31 March 1904), 3, ITA Mss Eur F174/922.

146. This Act was seen as an "interesting experiment." See the short notice on its passage in the *Journal of Comparative Legislation and International Law* 6, pt. 2 (London: John Murray, 1905). In 1953, after Independence, a new Tea Act established that all teas, not just those geared toward export, would be subject to the cess. M. Halayya, *An Economic Analysis of the Indian Tea Industry and Public Policy* (Dharwar: Karnatak University, 1972), 9.

147. *2nd Annual Report of the ITCC* (31 March 1905), ITA Mss Eur F174/922.

148. ITCC to Sir Edward Buck, K.C.S.I., 8 July 1903, *Preliminary Report of the ITCC Executive Committee* (1 June to 31 December 1903), 32, ITA Mss Eur F174/922.

149. "Ceylon (and Japan) at St. Louis," *HCM*, 14 July 1904, 9.

150. "Indian Tea at St Louis," *HCM*, 1 July 1904, 9.

151. "Gotham Turns to Iced Tea," *Washington Post*, 19 August 1894, 10.

152. Marion Harland, *Breakfast, Luncheon and Tea* (New York: Scribner, 1875), 361.

153. *Preliminary Report of the ITCC Executive Committee* (1 June to 31 December 1903), 8, ITA Mss Eur F174/922.

154. W. Parsons, Secretary to the India and Ceylon American Advertising Fund, to the ITCC, 22 September 1906, ITA Mss Eur F174/926.

155. R. Blechynden to ITCC, 24 November 1903, 12, *Preliminary Report of the ITCC Executive Committee* (1 June to 31 December 1903), 10–11, ITA Mss Eur F174/922.

156. Ibid., 10.

157. R. Blechynden, "Memorandum Regarding Future Work in America for the Tea Cess Committee," in *Preliminary Report of the ITCC Executive Committee* (1 June to 31 December 1903), 12, ITA Mss Eur F174/922.

158. *2nd Annual Report of the ITCC*, 5–7.

159. Blechynden to ITCC, 27 September 1905, ITA Mss Eur F174/926.

160. Circular from R. Blechynden to Chicago Tea Houses, 14 August 1905, ITA Mss Eur F174/926.

161. "Indian and Ceylon Tea in the United States," *HCM*, 5 February 1897, iii.

162. "Taste for Tea in America," *HCM*, 20 April 1906, 9.

163. In 1912 the group changed its name to the Tea Association of the United States of America. *TCTJ* (September 1926): 321–22.

164. The journal is now published in digital form as well. See http://www.teaandcoffee.net/.

165. James P. Quinn, "The History of Mr. Ukers," *TCTJ* 170, no. 3 (1997): 94–102; Linda Rice Lorenzetti, "*Tea and Coffee Trade Journal*'s Rich History," *TCTJ* 17, no. 8 (August 2001): 16–25.

166. "Ceylon's Tea Advertising," *TCTJ* (December 1925): 926.

167. "Mr. Ukers in London," *TCTJ* (August 1928): 170–71; "Tea Book Researching," *TCTJ* (September 1928): 307.

168. Prohibition and the automobile aided the growth of this form of catering as well. Jan Whitaker, *Tea at the Blue Lantern Inn: A Social History of the Tea Room Craze in America* (New York: St. Martin's Press, 2002); Harvey A. Levenstein, *Revolution at the Table: The Transformation of the American Diet* (New York: Oxford University Press, 1988), 17, 62, 187; Wendy A. Woloson, *Refined Tastes: Sugar, Confectionery, and Consumers in Nineteenth Century America* (Baltimore: Johns Hopkins University Press, 2002), 88–102. For a general study of American drinking habits, see Andrew Barr, *Drink: A Social History of America* (New York: Carroll and Graf, 1999).

169. John T. Edge, ed., *The New Encyclopedia of Southern Culture,* vol. 7, *Foodways* (Chapel Hill: University of North Carolina, Press, 2007), 273.

170. "Tea Room Managers Wanted," *Good Housekeeping* (July 1928): 200.

171. Laura B. Starr, "Tea Drinking in Japan and China," *The Chautauqaun* 29, no. 5 (August 1899): 466–68 and her very similar "Tea-Drinking in Many Lands," *The Cosmopolitan* 27 (1899): 289–96.

172. Mari Yoshihara, *Embracing the East: White Women and American Orientalism* (Oxford: Oxford University Press, 2003); Kristin L. Hoganson, *Consumers' Imperium: The Global Production of American Domesticity, 1865–1920* (Chapel Hill: University of North Carolina Press, 2007); Elise Grilli, foreword to Okakura Kakuzo, *The Book of Tea* (1906; Boston, Charles E. Tuttle, 1956), xiv; Brian T. Allen and Holly Edwards, *Noble Dreams and Wicked Pleasures: Orientalism in America, 1870–1930* (Princeton: Princeton University Press with the Sterling and Francine Clark Art Institute, 2000).

173. *Ladies' Home Journal* 6, no. 8 (July 1889): 21.

174. *Ladies' Home Journal* 8, no. 2 (January 1891): 27.

175. Mrs. R. C. Haviland, "What to Do on Washington's Birthday: A Patriotic Tea Table," *Ladies' Home Journal* 22, no. 3 (February 1905): 28.

176. Lenore Richards and Nola Treat, *Tea Room Recipes* (Boston: Little, Brown, 1925); Alice Bradley, *Cooking for Fun and Profit: Catering and Food Service Management* (Chicago: American School of Home Economics, 1933).

177. Mrs. S. T. Rorer, "Foods That Are Enemies, and Why," *Ladies' Home Journal* 22, no. 3 (February 1905): 38; "What Should I Eat If I Had Headaches," *Ladies' Home Journal* 22, no. 9 (August 1905): 27.

178. Jennifer Scanlon, *Inarticulate Longings: The "Ladies' Home Journal," Gender and the Promises of American Consumer Culture* (New York: Routledge, 1995); Ellen Gruber Garvey, *The Adman in the Parlor: Magazines and the Gendering of Consumer Culture, 1880s to 1910s* (New York: Oxford University Press, 1996).

179. Agnes Repellier, *To Think of Tea!* (Boston: Houghton Mifflin, 1932), 194–95.

180. "British Tea in the States," *Tea* 1, no. 7 (October 1901): 193.

181. "Indian Markets for Indian Tea: How to Reach the Native Consumer," *Tea* 1, no. 4 (July 1901): 98.

182. Quoted in *Tea* 1, no. 1 (April 1901): 46.

183. Manu Goswami, *Producing India: From Colonial Economy to National Space* (Chicago: University of Chicago Press, 2004), 5.

184. On Indian consumption, see Gautam Bhadra, *From an Imperial Product to a National Drink: The Culture of Tea Consumption in Modern India* (Calcutta: Centre for Studies in Social Sciences, Calcutta and the Tea Board of India, 2005); Chatterjee, *A Time for Tea;* Philip Lutgendorf, "Making Tea in India: Chai, Capitalism, Culture," *Thesis Eleven* 113, no. 1 (December 2013): 11–31; Lizzie Collingham, *Curry: A Tale of Cooks and Conquerors* (Oxford: Oxford University Press, 2006), 187–214; A. R. Venkatachalapathy, "'In those days there was no coffee': Coffee-drinking and Middle-Class Culture in Colonial Tamilnadu," *Indian Economic and Social History Review* 39 (2002): 301–16.

185. Republished in *Tea* 1, no. 7 (October 1901): 200.

186. Kevin Grant, *A Civilized Savagery: Britain and the New Slaveries in Africa, 1884–1926* (New york: Routledge, 2005); Lowell J. Satre, *Chocolate on Trial: Slavery, Politics and the Ethics of Business* (Athens: Ohio University Press, 2005); Adam Hochschild, *King Leopold's Ghost: A Story of Greed, Terror, and Heroism in Colonial Africa* (New York: Mariner Books, 1999).

187. Judicial and Public Papers, 1903, Parliamentary Notice—File 603, IOR/L/PJ/6/630 and a letter from Lord George Francis Hamilton, Secretary of State for India, to Arthur Bain, 30 March 1903, Frances Hamilton's papers, Mss Eur F123/68.

188. *HCM*, 4 October 1901, iii.

189. *Tea* 1, no. 8 (November 1901): 324.

190. J. D. Rees, *Tea and Taxation*, reprinted from the *Imperial and Asiatic Quarterly* (Woking: Oriental Institute, 1904), 5.

191. On food in Indian culture, see K. T. Achaya, *Indian Food: A Historical Companion* (Delhi: Oxford University Press, 1994); Arjun Appadurai, "How to Make a National Cuisine: Cookbooks in Contemporary India," *Comparative Studies in Society and History* 30, no. 1 (January 1988): 3–24 and "Gastro-Politics in Hindu South Asia," *American Ethnologist* 8, no. 3 (August 1981): 494–511; Anita Mannur, *Culinary Fictions: Food in South Asian Diasporic Culture* (Philadelphia: Temple University Press, 2009); Krishnendu Ray and Tulasi Srinivas, *Curried Cultures: Globalization, Food, and South Asia* (Berkeley: University of California Press, 2012); and David Burton, *The Raj at the Table* (New Delhi: Rupa, 1995). Also see special issues on food in *South Asia Research* 24, no. 1 (May 2004) and *South Asia: Journal of South Asian Studies* 31, no. 1 (April 2008).

192. David Burton, *Raj at the Table: A Culinary History of the British in India* (New York: Faber and Faber, 1994), 192–93.

193. Petition from the Tea Planters of the Kangra Valley to the Hon. E. Cable, President of the Indian Tea Cess Committee, 1903, ITA Mss Eur F174/922.

194. *The Grocer*, 24 April 1880, 488.

195. Arun Chaudhuri, *Indian Advertising, 1780–1950, A.D.* (New Delhi: Tata McGraw-Hill, 2007), 144–46, 161. Also see Mishra Dasarathi, *Advertising in Indian Newspapers, 1780–1947* (Bhana Vhihar: Dasarathi Mishra, 1987), 61.

196. Ranabir Ray Choudhury, *Early Calcutta Advertisements, 1875–1925* (Bombay: Nachiketa Publications, 1992), 23.

197. Chaudhuri, *Indian Advertising*, 161.

198. Choudhury, *Early Calcutta Advertisements*, 23.

199. *HCM*, 6 May 1887, vii.

200. *The Grocer*, 11 June 1887, 1089.

201. *Colonial Empire and Star of India*, 16 December 1887, iii.

202. Choudhury, *Early Calcutta Advertisements*, 20–22, 26, 28, 34.

203. *Tea*, 1, no. 2 (May 1901): 34.

204. "Creating a Demand," *Tea* 1, no. 4 (July 1901): 98.

205. *Tea* 1, no. 8 (November 1901): 324.

206. *HCM*, 4 October 1901, iii and 20 July 1906, 9.

207. *Tea* 1, no. 5 (August 1901): 131.

208. *HCM*, 4 October 1901, iii.

209. *Tea* 1, no. 3 (June 1901): 74 and no. 4 (July 1901): 98.

210. "Produce, Planting, and Commercial Notes," *HCM*, 26 July 1901, iii.

211. Letter from Brooke Bond, and Co. to ITCC, 6 November 1903, ITA Mss Eur F174/922.

212. *8th Annual Report, ITCC*, 1911, 6, ITA Mss Eur F174/922.

213. Frank F. Conlon, "Dining Out in Bombay," in *Consuming Modernity: Public Culture in a South Asian World*, Carol A. Breckenridge, ed. (Minneapolis: University of Minnesota Press, 1995), 92.

214. *Tea* 1, no. 5 (August 1901): 131.

215. Conlon, "Dining Out in Bombay," 100–101, 106.

216. *Tea* 1, no. 6 (September 1901): 163.

217. *Tea* 1, no. 7 (October 1901): 202.

218. *Tea*, 1, no. 10 (December 1901): 360.

219. *Tea*, 1, no. 7 (October 1901): 201.

220. Ibid.

221. Packets were printed both in Hindi and Urdu and contained "circulars extolling the merits of Indian tea as a beverage." *Tea* 1, no. 6 (September 1901): 163.

222. *11th Annual Report, ITCC*, 1914, 7–9, ITA Mss Eur F174/923.

223. Frank Trentmann, *Free Trade Nation: Commerce, Consumption, and Civil Society in Modern Britain* (Oxford: Oxford University Press, 2008).

224. Martin Daunton, *Trusting Leviathan: The Politics of Taxation in Britain, 1799–1914* (Cambridge: Cambridge University Press, 2001), 332.

225. Circular to Sir Michael Hicks Beach, M.P., 10 December 1900, Peek Brothers and Winch, Ltd. Archives, Ms. CLC/B/177/31632, Newspaper Cuttings Book, 1896–1918. This collection moved from the Guildhall, London to the London Metropolitan Archives.

226. *Tea: The Injustice of the High Duty* (London: George Edward Wright, 1906).

227. Andrew S. Thompson, *Imperial Britain: The Empire in British Politics, c. 1880–1932* (Harrow: Longman, 2000), 2–3.

228. Here I am building especially on Trentmann's analysis in *Free Trade Nation*.

229. Andrew S. Thompson, "Tariff Reform: An Imperial Strategy, 1903–1913," *Historical Journal* 40, no. 4 (1997): 1045. There is a vast literature on this movement; see, for example, P. J. Cain and A. G. Hopkins, *British Imperialism: Innovation and Expansion, 1688–1914*, 2nd ed. (Harlow, England: Longman, 2002), 184–202 and Peter Cain, "Political Economy in Edwardian England: The Tariff-Reform Controversy," in *The Edwardian Age: Conflict and Stability, 1900–1914*, ed. Alan O'Day (Hamden, CT: Archon Books, 1979), 34–59.

230. *The Monthly Message of the Anti-Tea-Duty League*, 31 March 1905, 6–8.

231. Sir Roper Lethbridge, "The Tea Duties," reprinted from the *Asiatic Quarterly Review* (Woking: Oriental Institute, 1911), 3. On Lethbridge's tariff reform years, see Thompson, *Imperial Britain*, 100–101.

232. "Tea Must Be Free," *The Intermittent Message of the Free Tea League*, 24 March 1906, 2–3. On the ATDL's origins, see *Come to Tea with Us* (London: Anti-Tea-Duty League with Simpkin, Marshall, Hamilton, and Kent, 1906), chap. 9.

233. Trentmann, *Free Trade Nation*, 39; James Vernon, *Hunger: A Modern History* (Cambridge, MA: Belknap Press of Harvard University Press, 2007), 257.

234. "Tea Must Be Free," *The Intermittent Message of the Free Tea League*, 24 March 1906, 2–3.

235. The league also republished earlier essays such as J. D. Rees, "Tea and Taxation," which was originally from the *Imperial and Asiatic Quarterly* and then the Oriental Institute in 1904.

236. *Monthly Message*, 31 July 1905, 84. The league also reported to the ITCC in Calcutta and the Planters' Association of Ceylon. Compton to the ITCC, 16 August 1905, *ITCC Annual Report*, 1906, Mss Eur F174/926; *Minutes of Proceedings of a Meeting of the Committee of the Planters' Association of Ceylon* (9 March 1906), 3.

237. "Our Plan of Campaign," *Monthly Message*, 31 December 1905, 140; Compton, *Come to Tea with Us*, 18.

238. Compton, *Come to Tea with Us*, 111.

239. Trentmann, *Free Trade Nation*, 51.

240. These letters from December 1904 were reprinted in *What Started the League?* (London: Anti-Tea-Duty League, 1905), 11–14.

241. *Monthly Message*, 31 December 1905, 150.

242. *Monthly Message*, 30 September 1905, 107.

243. *Tea: The Injustice of the High Duty*, 6.

244. Compton, *Come to Tea with Us*, 14. See a similar reference in *Tea: The Injustice of the High Duty*, 13.

245. *Leeds Mercury*, 10 December 1904, printed in *What Started the League*, 9–10.

246. *Daily Mail*, 9 December 1904, printed in *What Started the League*, 10.

247. *Dundee Advertiser*, 25 January 1905, printed in *What Started the League*, 30.

248. Herbert Compton, "Tea Planters and Their Troubles," *Pall Mall Gazette*, 10 January 1905, printed in *What Started the League*, 45–47.

249. Arthur Bryans, *Bristol Times*, 19 December 1904, printed in *What Started the League*, 26.

250. *Tea: The Injustice of the High Duty*, 13.

251. Ibid., 7.

252. Ibid., 5.

253. *Monthly Message*, 31 August 1905, 97.

254. Ibid., 31 July 1905, 85.

255. Ibid., 122.

256. *Intermittent Message of the Free-Tea League*, 24 March 1906, 26.

257. Ibid., 5.

258. *Intermittent Message of the Free-Tea League*, 1 May 1906, 42. The Tea Buyers' Association formed in 1899. London Chamber of Commerce, Tea Buyers' Association Minute Books, Guildhall Manuscripts, 16,755 Guildhall, London.

259. Ukers, *All about Tea*, 2:127.

260. The ITCC reported that U.S. imports of Indian tea had increased by 97 percent in 1907. *7th Annual Report of ITCC* (31 March 1910), 5, ITA Mss Eur F174/922.

CHAPTER 7. "EVERY KITCHEN AN EMPIRE KITCHEN"

1. "The Assam Dinner," *HCM*, 15 June 1923, 201.

2. Mackay was an early investor and agent for tea estates all over Assam. Stephanie Jones, *Two Centuries of Overseas Trading: The Origins and Growth of the Inchcape Group* (Houndmills, Basingstoke: Macmillan, 1986), 48, 52; Geoffrey Jones, *Merchants to Multinationals: British Trading Companies in the Nineteenth and Twentieth Century* (Oxford: Oxford University Press, 2000), 55–56; Stephanie Jones, *Trade and Shipping: Lord Inchcape, 1852–1932* (Manchester: Manchester University Press, 1989); P. J. Griffiths, *A History of the Inchcape Group* (London: Inchcape and Co., 1977).

3. "The Assam Dinner," 201.

4. *Imperial Economic Committee Report on Tea* (1 June 1931), 1, NA C0 323/1142/18. The published version is *Empire Grown Tea: Report of the Imperial Economic Committee*

(London: Empire Tea Growers, 1932). For discussions, see *Indian Tea Cess Committee Report* (January 1932), appendix 2, 21, ITA Mss Eur F74/928.

5. *Minutes of the General Committee of the Planters' Association of Ceylon*, 13 May 1931, 5–6.

6. Virtually every political movement of the era sought to enlist the power of the consumer; see Erika Rappaport, "Consumption," in *The Ashgate Research Companion to Modern Imperial Histories*, ed. Philippa Levine and John Marriott (Farnham, Surrey: Ashgate, 2012). Also see Peter Gurney, *Co-Operative Culture and the Politics of Consumption in England, 1870–1930* (Manchester: Manchester University Press, 1996); James Vernon, *Hunger: A Modern History* (Cambridge, MA: Belknap Press of Harvard University Press, 2007); Frank Trentmann, *Free Trade Nation: Commerce, Consumption, and Civil Society in Modern Britain* (Oxford: Oxford University Press, 2008); Matthew Hilton, *Consumerism in Twentieth Century Britain: The Search for a Historical Movement* (Cambridge: Cambridge University Press, 2003); Kate Soper and Frank Trentmann, eds., *Citizenship and Consumption* (Houndmills, Basingstoke: Palgrave Macmillan, 2008); and Martin Daunton and Matthew Hilton, eds., *The Politics of Consumption: Material Culture and Citizenship in Europe and America* (Oxford: Oxford University Press, 2001).

7. The first of these questions is the central issue in Trentmann's *Free Trade Nation* and is explored in many of his publications, including "The Modern Genealogy of the Consumer: Meanings, Identities, and Political Synapses," in *Consuming Cultures, Global Perspectives: Historical Trajectories, Transnational Exchanges*, ed. John Brewer and Frank Trentmann (Oxford: Berg, 2006), 19–70.

8. David Thackeray, *Conservatism for the Democratic Age: Conservative Cultures and the Challenge of Mass Politics in Early Twentieth Century England* (Manchester: Manchester University Press, 2013) and his "Home and Politics: Women and Conservative Activism in Early Twentieth-Century Britain," *Journal of British Studies* 49, no. 4 (2010): 826–84, and "From Prudent Housewife to Empire Shopper: Party Appeals to the Female Voter, 1918–1928," in *The Aftermath of Suffrage: Women, Gender, and Politics in Britain, 1918–1945*, ed. Julie Gottlieb and Richard Toye (Houndmills, Basingstoke: Palgrave Macmillan, 2013), 37–53.

9. Charles F. McGovern, *Sold American: Consumption and Citizenship, 1890–1945* (Chapel Hill: University of North Carolina Press, 2006), 17. Also see Lizabeth Cohen, *A Consumers' Republic: The Politics of Mass Consumption in Postwar America* (New York: Knopf, 2003) and Meg Jacobs, *Pocketbook Politics: Economic Citizenship in Twentieth-Century America* (Princeton: Princeton University Press, 2005).

10. John Maitland to H. O. Wooten, 25 July 1917, Bin A6, Typhoo Archive, Moreton.

11. A. G. Kenwood and A. L. Lougheed, *The Growth of the International Economy, 1820–1990* (London: Routledge, 1992); Jones, *Merchants to Multinationals*, 84–115.

12. Ina Zweiniger-Bargielowska, Rachel Duffett, and Alain Drouard, eds., *Food and War in Twentieth Century Europe* (Farnham: Ashgate, 2011); Belinda J. Davis, *Home Fires Burning: Food, Politics, and Everyday Life in World War I Berlin* (Chapel Hill: University of North Carolina Press, 2000); Avner Offer, *The First World War: An Agrarian Interpretation* (Oxford: Clarendon, 1989); Carol Helstosky, *Garlic and Oil: Food and Politics in Italy* (Oxford: Berg, 2004), 39–51.

13. L. Margaret Barnett, *British Food Policy during the First World War* (London: George Allen and Unwin, 1985).

14. J. M. Winter, *The Great War and the British People* (Hampshire: Macmillan, 1985), 213–45.
15. Hilton, *Consumerism*, 53–78. For comparison, see Amy Bentley, *Eating for Victory: Food Rationing and the Politics of Domesticity* (Urbana: University of Illinois Press, 1998).
16. M. Todd, *Snakes and Ladders: An Autobiography*, quoted in Hilton, *Consumerism*, 58.
17. *Report of the General Committee of the ITA* (1916), 13–16, ITA Mss Eur F174/2A.
18. H. A. Antrobus, *The History of the Assam Company, 1839–1953* (Edinburgh: T. A. Constable, 1957), 188.
19. V. D. Wickizer, *Tea under International Regulation* (Palo Alto: Food Research Institute, Stanford University, 1921), 58.
20. Ibid., 59; Denys Forrest, *Tea for the British: The Social and Economic History of a Famous Trade* (London: Chatto and Windus, 1973), 201–3; John Burnett, *Liquid Pleasures: A Social History of Drinks in Modern Britain* (London: Routledge, 1999), 64.
21. *The Times*, 9 July 1918, 13; Barnett, *British Food Policy*, 140–42.
22. Barnett, *British Food Policy*, 142.
23. Alex J. Philip, *Rations, Rationing and Food Control* (London: Book World, 1918), 154.
24. Vernon, *Hunger*, 91–96; Mikuláš Teich, "Science and Food during the Great War: Britain and Germany," in *The Science and Culture of Nutrition, 1840–1940*, ed. Harmke Kamminga and Andrew Cunningham (Amsterdam: Rodopi, 1995), 213–34; Sally M. Horrocks, "The Business of Vitamins: Nutrition Science and the Food Industry in Inter-War Britain," in *Science and Culture of Nutrition*, 235–58. Also see Horrocks, "Nutrition Science and the Food Industry in Britain, 1920–1990," in *Food Technology*, ed. den Hartog, 7–18.
25. T. B. Wood, *The National Food Supply in Peace and War* (Cambridge: Cambridge University Press, 1917).
26. H. C., "Afternoon Tea in Hotels," *The Times*, 17 April 1917, 9.
27. Burton Chadwick, letter to the editor, *The Times*, 21 November 1916, 11 and "War Cakes: Afternoon Tea as a Needless Luxury," *The Times*, 31 March 1917, 3.
28. "Afternoon Tea: A Restaurant Manager's Defense," *The Times*, 23 November 1916, 11.
29. Ibid.
30. Ibid.
31. "Wheat and Sugar Saving: Afternoon Tea Order," *The Times*, 19 April 1917, 6; Georgiana H. Pollock, "Afternoon Tea in the Shops," *The Times*, 17 December 1917, 3.
32. William Ukers, *All about Tea* (New York: Tea and Coffee Trade Journal, 1935), 2:160.
33. "The Assam Dinner," 201.
34. "Brooke Bond Review of the Tea Trade, 1917," *Simmons Spice Mill* (January 1919): 47.
35. *Report of the General Committee of the ITA* (1919), 9–10, ITA MSS Eur F174/2A.
36. *14th Annual Report, ITCC* (1917), 6, ITA Mss Eur F174/923.
37. *15th Annual Report, ITCC* (1918), 5, ITA Mss Eur F174/923.
38. Meeting of the Executive Committee of the ITCC, Royal Exchange, Calcutta, 11 February 1921, 3, ITA Mss Eur F174/927.

39. *Subcommittee's Report on the Position in India, English and Scottish Co-Operative Wholesale Societies* (Manchester: CWS Printing Works, 1921), 25, CWS 1/35/32/23, CWS Archives, Mitchell Library, Glasgow.

40. D. L. LeMahieu, *A Culture for Democracy: Mass Communication and the Cultivated Mind in Britain between the Wars* (Oxford: Oxford University Press, 1988), 161–62.

41. Tea Association of the United States to the ITA (London), 21 April 1921, reprinted at the Executive Committee Meeting of the ITCC, 31 May 1921, ITA Mss Eur F174/927.

42. "Japan-Formosa Tea Outlook: How to Increase the Consumption of Tea," *TCTJ* (June 1925): 813–16. J. Walter Thompson conducted a five-year, $900,000 per year campaign. "A Tea and Coffee Chronology," *TCTJ* (September 1926): 304–13; William R. Rankin, "Can Tea Be Successfully Advertised in the United States?" *Twentieth Century Advertising* (January 1924): 74. In 1925 U.S. tea imports were as follows: Ceylon 27½ percent; Japan 21 percent; India 16½ percent; Formosa 11¼ percent; China 10¾ percent; Java 10 percent; Sumatra 2¼ percent; and blended Ceylon and India ¾ percent. India, Ceylon, and Java teas had increased at the expense of those from Japan, Formosa, and China. *TCTJ* (August 1925): 273. Growers were also motivated by a general desire to sell more British manufactured goods in the United States to offset Britain's war debt. See, for example, Charles Higham, "British Open Big Drive in World Markets," *Waukesha Daily Freeman* (Wisconsin), (19 January 1924): 4.

43. The Tea Cess Fund had nearly doubled since 1922. "Seeking New Tea Markets: Propaganda in the U.S. and Germany," *HCM*, 26 July 1928, 20.

44. "An Advertising King," *Planters' Chronicle*, 28 November 1925, 872. Over half of the teas drunk in the United States were now black Indian and Ceylon teas. "Tea Tastes," *Planters' Chronicle*, 29 August 1925, 652. On the *Financial Times*' criticisms and the planters' reactions, see "American Propaganda," *Planters' Chronicle*, 26 September 1925, 713.

45. In August 1925 Higham married the daughter of the famous baseball player John Charles Rowe, and the couple settled in Buckinghamshire. "Speaking of Sir Charles," *TCTJ* (September 1925): 453–54.

46. "Sir Charles Higham Visits 'Ad' Men Here," *New York Times*, 1 June 1922.

47. Ibid.

48. "Changing the Customs of a Continent," *Advertising World* (February 1925): 388–94.

49. Higham explained how he got the ITA's account after he had placed an advertisement in London newspapers describing his belief in "collective" advertising. William Ukers was also honored at this lunch. "Tea Men Give a Luncheon," *TCTJ* (April 1925): 469.

50. Roland Marchand, *Advertising the American Dream: Making Way for Modernity, 1920–1940* (Berkeley: University of California Press, 1986), 5.

51. T. R. Nevett, *Advertising in Britain: A History* (London: Heinemann, 1982), 155.

52. Sir Charles Higham, *Advertising, Its Use and Abuse* (London: William & Norgate, Ltd., 1924), 147.

53. "Changing the Customs of a Continent."

54. Radio broadcast, "India Tea and How to Make It," *Appleton Post-Crescent* (Wisconsin), 22 January 1924, 11.

55. *Charleston Gazette* (West Virginia), January 21, 1924, 1; *Star and Sentinel* (Gettysburg, PA), 26 January 1924, 1.
56. "Sir Charles on the U.S.A.," *TCTJ* (July 1926): 55.
57. "Goodbye to Sir Charles," *TCTJ* (April 1926): 461.
58. For the U.S. context, see Pamela Walker Laird, *American Business and the Rise of Consumer Marketing* (Baltimore: Johns Hopkins University Press, 1998).
59. "The US Campaign for India Tea," *Twentieth Century Advertising* (March 1924): 24.
60. "New Tea Advertising," *TCTJ* (October 1925): 582 and (November 1925): 806.
61. "The Years Between: A Chronological Record of the Activities of this Paper," *TCTJ* (September 1926): 383bb.
62. "Changing the Customs of a Continent," 390.
63. Ibid.
64. "Tea in the U.S.A.," *HCM*, 29 September 1927, 1.
65. Walter Chester, "How to Increase Tea Consumption," *TCTJ* (April 1925): 493–94.
66. Antonio Wakefield, "How to Increase Tea Consumption," *TCTJ* (May 1925): 649.
67. G. M. Gates, "Coffee Growing: Tea Losing. How to Increase the Consumption of Tea," *TCTJ* (August 1925): 267–68. For a similar point of view, see A. Raymond Hopper, "How Not to Advertise Tea," *TCTJ* (March 1927): 265–68.
68. Felix Koch, "Studying Local Tea Tastes: How to Increase Tea Consumption," *TCTJ* (July 1925): 85–86; also see "Tastes in Tea," *TCTJ* (June 1925): 820.
69. "India and Ceylon Teas Gain," *TCTJ* (September 1926): 337.
70. "Hard to Change Our Habits," *TCTJ* (October 1927): 1198; *HCM*, 28 April 1927, 4 and 19 May 1927, 20.
71. "New India Tea Commissioner," *TCTJ* (December 1927): 123–24; "Indian Tea Propaganda," *HCM*, 19 February 1928, 123–24; "India Tea Bureau," *HCM*, 8 March 1928, 1.
72. *Report of the American and Foreign Market Subcommittee to the ITA General Committee* (1928–1929), 11, ITA Mss Eur F174/3.
73. "Emblem for India Tea," *TCTJ* (March 1928): 382.
74. "India Tea Cess Renewed," *TCTJ* (April 1928): 507.
75. "American Women Shown How to Choose a Good Tea," *Sioux City Sunday Journal*, 3 June 1928, 31.
76. "India Tea Cess Renewed," *TCTJ* (April 1928): 507.
77. *Plan for Teaching a Million High School Students about India Tea*, 1929, memo from the India Tea Bureau (NY) to ITA, ITA Mss Eur F174/915.
78. *Report of the American and Foreign Market Subcommittee to the ITA General Committee* (1928–29), 11, 13.
79. *Report of the American and Foreign Market Subcommittee to the ITA General Committee* (1930–31), 11, ITA Mss Eur F174/3. By 1932, 178 brands used the emblem and 69 percent were pure India tea. *Report of the American and Foreign Market Subcommittee to the ITA General Committee* (1932–33), 15.
80. *Report by a Commission to the United States to the International Tea Committee (UK)*, 1934, ITA Mss Eur F174/949. I believe this survey was done by Elmo Roper; on his career and relationship to the tea industry, see chapter 8.
81. *Imperial Economic Committee Report on Tea*, 1931, 41, NA: C0323/1142/18.
82. Trentmann, *Free Trade Nation*, 229.

83. Philip Williamson, *National Crisis and National Government: British Politics, the Economy and Empire, 1926–1932* (Cambridge: Cambridge University Press, 1992); Basudev Chatterji, *Trade, Tariffs, and Empire: Lancashire and British Policy in India, 1919–1939* (Delhi: Oxford University Press, 1992); T. Rooth, *British Protectionism and the International Economy: Overseas Commercial Policy in the 1930s* (Cambridge: Cambridge University Press, 1994); Andrew S. Thompson, *Imperial Britain: The Empire in British Politics, c. 1880–1932* (Harrow: Longman, 2000); Forrest Capie, *Depression and Protectionism: Britain between the Wars* (London: George Allen and Unwin, 1983); Michael Kitson and Solomos Solomou, *Protectionism and Economic Revival: The British Inter-War Economy* (Cambridge: Cambridge University Press, 1990); Andrew Marrison, *British Business and Protection, 1903–1932* (Oxford: Clarendon, 1996).

84. Thackeray, *Conservatism for the Democratic Age*; Martin Pugh, *The Tories and the People, 1880–1935* (New York: Basil Blackwell, 1985); David Jarvis, "The Conservative Party and the Politics of Gender, 1900–1939," in *The Conservatives and British Society, 1880–1990*, ed. Martin Francis and Ina Zweiniger-Bargielowska (Cardiff: University of Wales Press, 1996); Stuart Ball, *Portrait of a Party: The Conservative Party in Britain, 1918–1945* (Oxford: Oxford University Press, 2013).

85. Michael Havinden and David Meredith, *Colonialism and Development: Britain and Its Tropical Colonies, 1850–1960* (London: Routledge, 1993), 144–45, 150; Stephen Constantine, "'Bringing the Empire Alive': The Empire Marketing Board and Imperial Propaganda, 1926–1933," in *Imperialism and Popular Culture*, ed. John M. MacKenzie (Manchester: Manchester University Press, 1986), 192–231; *Buy and Build: The Advertising Posters of the Empire Marketing Board* (London: HMSO, 1986); David Meredith, "Imperial Images: The Empire Marketing Board, 1926–32," *History Today* 37, no. 1 (January 1987): 30–36; Mike Cronin, "Selling Irish Bacon: The Empire Marketing Board and Artists of the Free State," *Eire-Ireland* 39, no. 3/4 (2004): 132–43; James Murton, "John Bull and Sons: The Empire Marketing Board and the Creation of a British Imperial Food System," in *Edible Histories, Cultural Politics: Towards a Canadian Food History*, ed. Franca Iacovetta, Valerie J. Korinek, and Marlene Epp (Toronto: University of Toronto Press, 2012), 225–48.

86. *H.M. Treasury Committee of Civil Research: Report of the Research Co-ordination Sub-Committee* (London: HMSO, 1928), 61–63, ITA Mss Eur F174/1089; Jacquie L'Etang, *Public Relations in Britain: A History of Professional Practice in the Twentieth Century* (Mahwah, NJ: Lawrence Erlbaum, 2004), 32–39; Scott Anthony, *Public Relations and the Making of Modern Britain: Stephen Tallents and the Birth of a Progressive Media Profession* (Manchester: Manchester University Press, 2013).

87. Gervas Huxley, *Both Hands: An Autobiography* (London: Chatto and Windus, 1970), 125–29.

88. *Report of the Research Co-ordination Sub-Committee* (London: HMSO, 1928), 61–63, ITA MSS Eur F174/1089, 61–63.

89. Anne Chisholm and Michael Davie, *Lord Beaverbrook: A Life* (New York: Knopf, 1993).

90. Lord Beaverbrook, *The Resources of the Empire* (London: Lane Publications, 1934), 11.

91. Chisholm and Davie, *Beaverbrook*, 275–82.

92. Stephen Constantine, "The Buy British Campaign of 1931," *European Journal of Marketing* 21, no. 4 (1987): 44–59.

93. Ibid., 54; Thackeray, *Conservatism for the Democratic Age*, 142–48.

94. Lord Beaverbrook, *My Case for Empire Free Trade* (London: The Empire Crusade, 1930), 15.

95. "Empire Meals on Empire Day," *Empire Production and Export* 187 (March–April 1932): 57–58.

96. Beatrix Campbell, *The Iron Ladies: Why Do Women Vote Tory?* (London: Virago, 1987), 60–61. For other national examples, see the special issue of *International Labor and Working-Class History* 77, no. 1 (2010); Victoria de Grazia, *How Fascism Ruled Women: Italy, 1922–1945* (Berkeley: University of California Press, 1992); and Nancy Ruth Reagin, *Sweeping the German Nation: Domesticity and National Identity in Germany, 1870–1945* (Cambridge: Cambridge University Press, 2007).

97. "Women's Buy British Campaign: Intelligent Demand," *Empire Production and Export* 186 (February 1932): 46–47.

98. "Every Kitchen an Empire Kitchen," manifesto of the League of Empire Housewives, 1927, ITA Mss Eur F174/1094.

99. "Labour and Empire Trade," *British Empire Annual* (May 1927), 4, ITA Mss Eur F174/1094; Mrs. Walrond Sweet, "How to Help the Empire in Your Shopping," *British Empire Annual* (May 1927), 3, ITA Mss Eur F174/109.

100. On the Tory view of the working-class consumer, see David Jarvis, "British Conservatism and Class Politics in the 1920s," *English Historical Review* 111, no. 440 (February 1996): 72–73.

101. Sir Percival Griffiths, *The History of the Indian Tea Industry* (London: Weidenfeld and Nicolson, 1967), 178.

102. *IEC Report on Tea*, 3–10.

103. *International Tea Committee: Fiftieth Anniversary, 1983* (London: Tea Broker's Publications, 1983), 2.

104. *IEC Report on Tea*, 11.

105. Ibid., 22.

106. B. R. Mitchell, *British Historical Statistics* (Cambridge: Cambridge University Press, 1988), 709–11.

107. For the working-class domestic economy, see Ross McKibbin, *Parties and People: England, 1914–1951* (Oxford: Oxford University Press, 2010), 41–42, and *Classes and Cultures: England, 1918–1951* (Oxford: Oxford University Press, 1998), 106–27.

108. "Buys a Tenth of the World's Tea," *TCTJ* (July 1927): 764; "Ready for a British Food War," *TCTJ* (February 1928): 288.

109. D. J. Richardson, "J. Lyons and Co., Ltd.: Caterers and Food Manufacturers," in *The Making of the Modern British Diet*, ed. Derek J. Oddy and Derek S. Miller (London: Croom Helm, 1976), 161–72.

110. "Tea Packeting in England," *TCTJ* (February 1927): 145. Lyons had recently purchased 8,000 acres in Nyasaland. *TCTJ* (April 1927): 454.

111. Various factors have shaped how power is exerted within food and other commodity chains. For two volumes that make such comparisons explicit, see Jennifer Bair, ed., *Frontiers of Commodity Chain Research* (Stanford: Stanford University Press, 2009) and Warren Belasco and Roger Horowitz, eds., *Food Chains: From Farmyard to Shopping Cart* (Philadelphia: University of Pennsylvania Press, 2009).

112. Finance Act, 1919, 9–10 Geo. V, chap. 32, quoted in Ian M. Drummond, *British Economic Policy and Empire, 1919–1939* (New York: Allen and Unwin, 1972), 52. Also see Ralph A. Young, "British Imperial Preference and the American Tariff," *Annals of the American Academy of Political and Social Science* 141 (1929): 204–11.

113. *Ceylon Planters' Association Yearbook* (Colombo: Planters' Association of Ceylon, 1932), 190.

114. Drummond, *British Economic Policy*, 17–25.

115. For a full discussion of the political economy of this idea, see Magee and Thompson, *Empire and Globalisation*, chap. 4.

116. *Board of Trade, Merchandise Marks Act, 1926. Report of the Standing Committee on Tea* (London: HMSO, 1929), Cmd. 3288, ITA Mss Eur F174/1094. Also see "The 'Marking' of Tea," *HCM*, 13 December 1928, 17–18, 20 December 1928, 5–6; 17 January 1929, 5; "Marking Tea in England," *TCTJ* (December 1928): 798; and "The Proposed Marking of Tea in England," *TJCJ* (January 1929): 135, 164–66.

117. Case for the Applicants in the matter of the Merchandise Marks Act 1926, ITA Mss Eur F174/1094.

118. Mr. Willink, *Minutes of the Proceedings before the Standing Committee on the Merchandise Marks Act, 1926,* (hereafter *BOT MMA Standing Committee*), 10 December 1928, ITA Mss Eur F174/1092.

119. Indian Tea Association, South India Association, and Ceylon Association to the Rt. Hon. Sir Philip Cunliffe-Lister, September 1928, ITA Mss Eur F174/1094.

120. "Statement of Opposition of the Tea Buyers' Association to the Application for the Marking of Tea under the Merchandise Marks Act, 1926," *BOT MMA Standing Committee*, ITA Mss Eur F174/1094.

121. Ibid.

122. "Précis of Evidence to be submitted to the Standing Committee under the Merchandise Marks Act against the proposal for the Marking of imported tea," *BOT MMA Standing Committee*, ITA Mss Eur F174/1094.

123. Evidence given by Henry Charles Johnston Barton, *BOT MMA Standing Committee*, 11 December 1928, ITA Mss Eur F174/1092.

124. Evidence given by Mr. John Douglas Garrett, *BOT MMA Standing Committee*, 11 December 1928, ITA Mss Eur F174/1092.

125. C. L. T. Beeching, *Salesmanship for the Grocer and Provision Dealer* (London: Institute of Certificated Grocers, 1924), 73–75; F. W. F. Staveacre, *Tea and Tea Dealing* (London: Sir Isaac Pitman, 1929), 104.

126. Many companies used the same label for years. Ridgways Wholesale Price List, 16 June 1924, Bin A2, Typhoo Archive, Company Headquarters, Moreton, UK; Guard Book of Labels, Banks and Co., BKS 11/11/3 (1932–34), BKS 11/11/4 (1933–35), BKS 11/11/5 (1934–39), Banks and Company Archive, University of Glasgow Archives.

127. William Saunders evidence, *BOT MMA Standing Committee*, 11 December 1928, ITA Mss Eur F 74/1092.

128. "Tea Interests Combine," *TCTJ* (January 1926): 97.

129. "Statement on Behalf of the British Tea Industry in Java and Sumatra, Merchandise Marks Act, 1926," *BOT MMA Standing Committee*, ITA Mss Eur F174/1094.

130. Ukers, *All about Tea*, 2:16–17.
131. Allister MacMillan, *Seaports of the Far East: Historical and Descriptive, Commercial and Industrial Facts, Figures, and Resources*, 2nd ed. (London: W. H. & L. Collingridge, 1925), 319.
132. Evidence of Major L. H. Cripps, *BOT MMA Standing Committee*, 11 December 1928, ITA Mss Eur F174/1092.
133. Evidence of Eric Madfadyen, *BOT MMA Standing Committee*, 11 December 1928, ITA Mss Eur F174/1092.
134. Evidence of Gordon Thomas H. Stampter, *BOT MMA Standing Committee*, 11 December 1928, ITA Mss Eur F174/1092.
135. Press ads and notices, 1919–1930, SA/MAR/ADV/1/3/3/1/2/9, #5636/2, ADV, Sainsbury Archive, Museum of the Docklands, London.
136. Mr. John Douglas Garrett, *BOT MMA Standing Committee*, ITA Mss Eur F174/1092.
137. H. M. Haywood, Secretary of ITA, Calcutta, to W. H. Pease, ITA London, 28 April 1921, Correspondence with Indian Tea Association, Calcutta, January–June 1921, Mss Eur F174/57.
138. D. K. Cunnison, Asst. Secretary to the Surma Valley Branch of ITA, to ITA, Calcutta, 23 April 1921, ITA Mss Eur F174/57.
139. Letter to the editor of *The Statesman*, 28 May 1921, ITA Mss Eur F174/57.
140. Rana Pratap Behal, "Forms of Labour Protest in Assam Valley Tea Plantations, 1900–1930," *Economic and Political Weekly* 20, no. 4 (January 1985): 19–26. Brooke Bond was also worried that the nationalist sentiment "awakening" in Ceylon was leading to land shortages. *TCTJ* (January 1927): 32–33.
141. *BOT Report of the Standing Committee on Tea* (London: HMSO, 1929).
142. Robert Boyce, *The Great Interwar Crisis and the Collapse of Globalization* (Hampshire: Palgrave Macmillan, 2009). For an excellent overview of how international business rode out this period of crisis, see Jones, *Merchants to Multinationals*, chap. 4.
143. "Rubber and Tea," *The Statesman* (20 March 1930), cutting in IOR: L/E/9/1294, file 1.
144. "Tea Consumption," *HCM*, 18 June 1931, 1.
145. Tea averaged just over 1s. 3d. per pound in early 1931. "Tea Prices: Report by the Food Council to the President of the Board of Trade," 30 July 1931, NA MAF 69/100. The value of Ceylon's exported tea fell by a third between 1929 and 1931. *Yearbook of the Ceylon Planters' Association*, 1932, 48.
146. Telegram from Indian Planters' Association to the Secretary of State for India, 4 September 1931, IOR: L/E/9/1294, file 1, Indian and African Collections, British Library.
147. "The Removal of the English Tea Duty," *HCM*, May 1929, 721–22.
148. "Minute Paper on Tea," IOR: L/E/9/1294, file 1; "Empire Tea: Inauguration of Notable Campaign," *HCM*, 9 September 1931, 1; *Report of the Empire Tea Sub-Committee to the Marketing Committee*, EMB, 13 July 1931, NA CO 758/88/4; S. S. Murray, "Advertising of Empire Tea in the United Kingdom," Bulletin No. 1, Department of Agriculture, Nyasaland Protectorate (Zomba: Government Printer, February 1932), 12. The EMB was reluctant to promote tea, but once they found that leading distributors were on board they agreed to engage in joint publicity. *Report of the Empire Tea Sub-Committee*.
149. "Empire Tea: Inauguration of Notable Campaign," *HCM*, 9 September 1931, 1.

150. Large tea estate proprietors who lived in London now joined those who lived in Ceylon to push the colonial government to revive the cess in 1932. *Minutes of the General Committee of the Planters' Association of Ceylon*, 13 May 1931, 81.

151. *Yearbook of the Planters' Association in Ceylon* (1932), 115.

152. Gervas Huxley, "Suggested Empire Tea Campaign," *Minutes of the Empire Tea Sub-Committee to the Marketing Committee*, EMB, 6 June 1931, NA CO 758/88/4.

153. Gervas Huxley's brother-in-law, Edward Harding, was the permanent head of the Dominions Office. On Elspeth's imperialism, see Phyllis Lassner, *Colonial Strangers: Women Writing the End of the British Empire* (New Brunswick, NJ: Rutgers University Press, 2004), 118–59. For the history of the WI, see Inez F. Jenkins, *The History of the Women's Institute Movement of England and Wales* (Oxford: Oxford University Press, 1953) and Maggie Andrews, *The Acceptable Face of Feminism: The Women's Institute as a Social Movement* (London: Lawrence and Wishart, 1997).

154. Huxley, *Both Hands*, 87–94; Scott M. Cutlip, *The Unseen Power: Public Relations, A History* (New York: Routledge, 1994), 662–759.

155. *ITCC Minutes*, 11 March 1932, 6 and 8 July 1932.

156. "EMPIRE GROWN TEA," 1931, ITA Mss Eur F174/854. This was reprinted in *The Grocer*, 16 May 1931, 1 and J. R. H. Pickney, "Empire Tea," letter to the editor of *HCM*, 26 February 1931, 13. Pickney was the director of nine tea-producing companies. On shareholder responses, see "Labelling Teas," *HCM*, 16 July 1931, 1.

157. Sir Charles C. McLeod, "A Plea for Empire Tea," speech first given at the Royal Empire Society, 17 November 1931, ITA Mss Eur F174/854. It was also published and/or discussed in trade papers, many dailies, and local newspapers. *ITCC Minutes*, January 1932, 6–7.

158. *The Grocers' Gazette*, 19 September 1931, collected in "Empire Marketing Board papers related to the advertising of Indian Tea," NA CO 758/88/4.

159. *ITCC Minutes*, 13 May 1932, 3, ITA Mss Eur F174/928.

160. *ITCC Minutes*, 10 June 1932, 2, ITA Mss Eur F174/928.

161. *ITCC Minutes*, 8 January 1932, 8, ITA Mss Eur F174/928.

162. Banks and Company Printing Guard Book of Labels (1932–34), BKS 11/11/3. Banks and Company Archive, University of Glasgow Archives.

163. Ridgways Circular, Bin A2, Typhoo Archive, Company Headquarters, Moreton, UK.

164. For a brief look at Romanne-James's career, see Maggie Andrews and Sallie McNamara, eds., *Women and the Media: Feminism and Femininity in Britain, 1900 to the Present* (New York: Routledge, 2014), 35.

165. *ITCC Minutes*, 9 December 1932, 2–3, ITA Mss Eur F174/928.

166. *ITCC Minutes*, 8 July 1932, 5, ITA Mss Eur F174/928.

167. Ibid.

168. Lidderdale report for September 1932, *ITCC Minutes*, 11 November 1932, 2–3, ITA Mss Eur F174/928.

169. Lidderdale to Harpur, August 1932, *ITCC Minutes*, 21 October 1932, 2, ITA Mss Eur F174/928.

170. *ITCC Minutes*, 9 September 1932, 14–15, ITA Mss Eur F174/928.

171. *ITCC Minutes*, 11 November 1932, 2–3, ITA Mss Eur F174/928.

172. *ITCC Minutes*, 12 February 1932, 6–8, ITA Mss Eur F174/928.

173. *ITCC Minutes*, 10 June 1932, 3, ITA Mss Eur F174/928.

174. Mahatma Gandhi, "Untruthful Advertisements," *Harijan* (24 August 1935), republished in M. K. Gandhi, *Drinks, Drugs and Gambling*, ed. Bharatan Kumarappa (Ahmedabad: Navajivan, 1952), 140–41. Also see Amitava Sanyal, "Mahatma Gandhi and His Anti-Tea Campaign," *BBC News Magazine*, 7 May 2012, http://www.bbc.com/news/magazine-17905975.

175. Gandhi, "Untruthful Advertisements," 141.

176. Douglas E. Haynes, "Creating the Consumer? Advertising, Capitalism and the Middle Class in Urban Western India, 1914–40," in *Towards a History of Consumption in South Asia*, ed. Douglas E. Haynes, Abigail McGowan, Tirthankar Roy, and Haruka Yanagisawa (New Delhi: Oxford, 2010), 185–223; Abigail McGowan, "Consuming Families: Negotiating Women's Shopping in Early Twentieth Century Western India, in *Towards a History of Consumption in South Asia*, ed. Haynes et al., 155–84; Harminder Kaur, "Of Soaps and Scents: Corporeal Cleanliness in Urban Colonial India," in *Towards a History of Consumption in South Asia*, ed. Haynes et al., 246–67.

177. Walter Benjamin, "The Work of Art in the Age of Mechanical Reproduction" was first published in 1936.

178. On Gandhi's theory of reading, self-rule, and sovereignty, see Isabel Hofmeyr, *Gandhi's Printing Press: Experiments in Slow Reading* (Cambridge, MA: Harvard University Press, 2013). On Gandhi's attitude toward food, see Parama Roy, "Meat-Eating, Masculinity and Renunciation in India: A Gandhian Grammar of Diet," *Gender and History* 14, no. 1 (2002): 62–91 and Tim Pratt and James Vernon, "'Appeal from This Fiery Bed . . .': The Colonial Politics of Gandhi's Fasts and Their Metropolitan Reception in Britain," *Journal of British Studies* 44, no. 1 (2005): 92–114.

179. Lisa N. Trivedi, *Clothing Gandhi's Nation: Homespun and Modern India* (Bloomington: Indiana University Press, 2007). Other important works include C. A. Bayly, "The Origins of Swadeshi (Home Industry): Cloth and Indian Society, 1700–1930," in *The Social Life of Things: Commodities in Cultural Perspective*, ed. Arjun Appadurai (Cambridge: Cambridge University Press, 1986); Bernard S. Cohen, "Cloth, Clothes and Colonialism: India in the Nineteenth Century," in *Cloth and the Human Experience*, ed. A. B. Weiner and J. Schneider (Washington, DC: Smithsonian Institution, 1989), 303–53; Susan Bean, "Gandhi and Khadi: The Fabric of Independence," in *Cloth and the Human Experience*, ed. Weiner and Schneider; Emma Tarlo, *Clothing Matters: Dress and Identity in India* (Chicago: University of Chicago Press, 1996), 23–128; Richard Fox, *Gandhian Utopia: Experiments with Indian Culture* (New York: Beacon, 1989); Sumit Sarkar, *The Swadeshi Movement in Bengal, 1903–1908* (New Delhi: Peoples' Publishers, 1973); and Parama Roy, *Indian Traffic: Identities in Question in Colonial and Postcolonial India* (Berkeley: University of California Press, 1998).

180. Trivedi, *Clothing Gandhi's Nation*, chap. 2; Manu Goswami, *Producing India: From Colonial Economy to National Space* (Chicago: University of Chicago Press, 2004), chap. 8.

181. Gautam Bhadra, *From an Imperial Product to a National Drink: The Culture of Tea Consumption in Modern India* (Calcutta: Centre for Studies in Social Sciences, Calcutta and the Tea Board of India, 2005); Lizzie Collingham, *Curry: A Tale of Cooks and Conquerors* (Oxford: Oxford University Press, 2006), 187–214; A. R. Venkatachalapathy, "'In those days there was no coffee': Coffee-drinking and Middle-Class Culture in Colonial Tamilnadu," *Indian Economic and Social History Review* 39 (2002): 301–16.

182. Mahatma Gandhi, *Third Class in Indian Railways* (Bhadarkali-Lahore: Gandhi Publications League, 1917), 4.
183. Extract included in a letter from John Harpur, *Meeting of the Executive Committee of the ITCC*, 31 May 1921, 4, ITA Mss Eur F174/927.
184. "Opium in Tea Stalls," *TCTJ* (October 1927): 1198.
185. Nabin Chandra Bordoloi, "The Non-Cooperation Movement," appendix 2, in C. F. Andrews, *Assam Opium Enquiry Report* (September 1925), 54–57.
186. *Young India*, 29 December 1921, 439.
187. Indian canvasser letter to John Harpur, *Meeting of the Executive Committee of the ITCC*, 12 August 1921, 3, ITA Mss Eur F174/927.
188. Report to Newby from the Punjab Superintendent and Re. Raichur from Southern India, *Meeting of the Executive Committee of the ITCC*, 8 April 1921, 4, ITA Mss Eur F174/927.
189. Reed Committee Report, April 1922, as cited in M.V. Kamath and Vishwas B. Kher, *The Story of Militant But Non-Violent Trade Unionism: A Biographical and Historical Study* (Ahmedabad: Navajivan, 1993). Many thanks to Abigail McGowan for alerting me to this source.
190. *ITCC Proceedings*, 8 January 1932, 11, ITA Mss Eur F174/928.
191. K. Venkatachary, Report on the Calicut Swadeshi Exhibition held 1–9 November 1932, *ITCC Proceedings*, 12 February 1932, 17, ITA Mss Eur F174/928.
192. *ITCC Proceedings*, 15 August 1932, 6, ITA Mss Eur F174/928.
193. Goswami, *Producing India*, 248–49.
194. Sri Prakasa, Legislative Assembly Debates, vol. 4, no. 8, New Delhi, 6 April 1935, 5, IOR/L/E/9/180, Collection related to the Tea Cess Acts, 1935–47, Indian and African Collections, British Library (hereafter Indian Tea Cess Debate).
195. James H. Mills, *Cannabis Britannica: Empire, Trade, and Prohibition, 1800–1928* (Oxford: Oxford University Press, 2003), 153.
196. Partha Chatterjee, *The Nation and Its Fragments: Colonial and Postcolonial Histories* (Princeton: Princeton University Press, 1993).
197. Mr. Ghanshiam Singh Gupta, Legislative Assembly Debates, vol. 4, no. 8, New Delhi, 6 April 1935, 9, Indian Tea Cess Debate.
198. On Chaliha's career, see Anuradha Dutta, *Assam in the Freedom Movement* (New Delhi: Darbari Prokasham, 1991), 56 and Anil Kumar Sharma, *Quit India Movement in Assam* (New Delhi: Mittal Publications, 2007), 22–24.
199. Harihar Mishra, *Pandit Nilakantha Das* (Delhi: Kanishka Publishers, 1994).
200. Pandit Nilakantha Das, Legislative Assembly Debate, vol. 4, no. 8, New Delhi, 6 April 1935, Indian Tea Cess Debate.
201. Pandit Nilakantha Das, Legislative Assembly Debates, vol. 9, no. 2, Simla, 10 October 1936, 14, Indian Tea Cess Debate.
202. Mohan Lal Saksensa, Legislative Assembly Debates, vol. 9, no. 2, Simla, 10 October 1936, 23, Indian Tea Cess Debate.
203. Ghanshiam Singh Gupta (Central Provinces, Hindi Division, vol. 4, no. 8, New Delhi, 6 April 1935, 9, Indian Tea Cess Debate.
204. Kuladhar Chaliha (Assam Valley, Non-Muhammadan), Legislative Assembly Debates, vol. 9, no. 2, Simla, 10 October 1936, 2, Indian Tea Cess Debate.
205. Abdul Matin Chaudhury (Assam, Mohammadan), Legislative Assembly Debates, vol. 9, no. 2, Simla, 10 October 1936, 7, Indian Tea Cess Debate. For Chaudhury's

career, see Artful Hye Shibley, *Abdul Matin Chaudhury (1895–1948): Trusted Lieutenant of Mohammed Ali Jinnah* (Dhaka: Juned A. Choudhury, 2011).

206. For Khan's vision of India's future, see Sir Muhammed Zafrullah Khan, "India's Place in the Commonwealth," in *Responsibilities of Empire* (London: George Allen and Unwin, 1937), 37–45.

207. Honorable Sir Muhammed Zafrullah Khan, Legislative Assembly Debates, vol. 9, no. 2, Simla, 10 October 1936, 13, Indian Tea Cess Debate.

208. Hon. Khan Bahadur (Bombay, nominated non-official), Extract from the Council of State Debates, vol. 1, no. 19, Council House New Delhi, 10 April 1935, 1, Indian Tea Cess Debate.

209. Amarendra Nath Chattopadhyaya (Burdwan Division, Non-Muhammadan), Legislative Assembly Debates, vol. 9, no. 2, Simla, 10 October 1936, 16–18, Indian Tea Cess Debate.

210. Griffiths, *History of the Indian Tea Industry*, 533.

211. Ram Narayan Singh (Chota Nagpur Division, Non-Muhammadan), Legislative Assembly Debates, vol. 9, no. 2, Simla, 10 October 1936, 21. Brohendra Narayan Chaudhury (Surma Valley, Non-Muhammadan) saw all these bodies as the political arm of European growers. Legislative Assembly Debates, vol. 6, no. 8, Simla, 20 September 1938, 2, Indian Tea Cess Debate.

212. Kuladhar Chaliha (Assam, Non-Muhammadan), Legislative Assembly Debates, vol. 6, no. 8, Simla, 20 September 1938, 3, Indian Tea Cess Debate.

213. Dr. Ziauddin Ahmed (United Provinces, Southern District, Muhammadan Rural), Legislative Assembly Debates, vol. 2, no. 10, New Delhi, 24 March 1942, 2–3, Indian Tea Cess Debate.

214. *Annual Report of the Indian Tea Market Expansion Board*, 1937, 55, ITA Mss Eur F174/924. For examples of some of this material, see Bhadra, *Imperial Product*, 10. Also see examples of two ads from *Muhammadi (Id)* Special Issue (1938), AM 22, 25–26, Colour Transparencies of Prints and Labels for Advertisement from the Collection of Indian Photo Engraving Company, Beniatola Lane, Kolkata, Courtesy Mr. Shymal Bhattacharya, Riddhi, Sanyal Memorial Collection, Centre for Studies in Social Sciences, Kolkata.

215. *Annual Report of the Indian Tea Market Expansion Board*, 1937, 54, ITA Eur Mss F174/924.

216. Bhadra, *Imperial Product*, 29.

217. Ibid., 31.

218. *Annual Report of the Indian Tea Market Expansion Board*, 1938, 12, ITA Mss Eur F174/924.

219. The problem of women's hesitancy to drink tea was a common refrain among tea promoters. See *Proceedings of the Indian Tea Cess Committee* (8 January 1932): 10, ITA Mss Eur F174/928.

220. *Annual Report of the Indian Tea Market Expansion Board*, 1937, 45, ITA Mss Eur F174/924.

221. Srishchandra Goswami, "Bangali Chhatroder swasthya gelo je," *Grishasthamangal*, no. 1 (4th Year, April/May 1930 [Baisakh 1337BS]): 1–5, as cited in Utsa Ray, *Culinary Culture in Colonial India: A Cosmopolitan Platter and the Middle Class* (Cambridge: Cambridge University Press, 2015), 88.

222. Hemantabala Debi cited in Ray, *Culinary Culture*, 90.

223. Venkatachalapathy, "'In those days there was no coffee,'" 301–16.

CHAPTER 8. "TEA REVIVES THE WORLD"

1. Cain and Hopkins argue that the new protectionist policies were not as much a departure as many have proposed. P. J. Cain and A. G. Hopkins, *British Imperialism, 1688–2000*, 2nd ed. (London: Longman, 2002), chap. 20.

2. Imperial rhetoric and imagery shifted in the interwar years. See Wendy Webster, *Englishness and Empire, 1939–1965* (Oxford: Oxford University Press, 2005); Stuart Ward, ed., *British Culture and the End of Empire* (Manchester: Manchester University Press, 2001); John M. MacKenzie, ed., *Imperialism and Popular Culture* (Manchester: Manchester University Press, 1986); and his *Propaganda and Empire: The Manipulation of British Public Opinion, 1880–1960* (Manchester: Manchester University Press, 1984).

3. John Stevenson and Chris Cook, *The Slump: Britain in the Great Depression*, 3rd ed. (London: Longman, 2010), 92–105. See, for example, the sociological study by H. L. Beales and R. S. Lambert, *Memoirs of the Unemployed* (1934; Yorkshire: E. P. Publishing, 1973).

4. Roland Marchand, *Advertising the American Dream: Making Way for Modernity, 1920–1940* (Berkeley: University of California Press, 1986), 336. Also see T. J. Jackson Lears, *Fables of Abundance: A Cultural History of Advertising in America* (New York: Basic Books, 1994), especially chap. 8 and William R. Leach, *Land of Desire: Merchants, Power, and the Rise of a New American Culture* (New York: Pantheon, 1993), 319–22, 352–58. Lizabeth Cohen also emphasizes the new arrangements between government and organized bodies of consumers, but she does not focus on how this shifted advertising per se in *A Consumers' Republic: The Politics of Mass Consumption in Postwar America* (New York: Alfred A. Knopf, 2003).

5. See, for example, Karl Gerth, *China Made: Consumer Culture and the Creation of the Nation* (Cambridge, MA: Harvard University Press, 2003); Irene Guenther, *Nazi Chic? Fashioning Women in the Third Reich* (Oxford: Oxford University Press, 2004); S. Jonathan Wiesen, *Creating the Nazi Marketplace: Commerce and Consumption in the Third Reich* (Cambridge: Cambridge University Press, 2011); Pamela Swett, *Selling under the Swastika: Advertising and Commercial Culture in Nazi Germany* (Stanford: Stanford University Press, 2014); and Karen Pinkus, *Bodily Regimes: Italian Advertising under Fascism* (Minneapolis: University of Minnesota Press, 1995).

6. John and Jean Comaroff, *Of Revelation and Revolution: The Dialectics of Modernity on a South African Frontier*, vol. 2 (Chicago: University of Chicago Press, 1993); Timothy Burke, *Lifebuoy Men, Lux Women: Commodification, Consumption, and Cleanliness in Modern Zimbabwe* (Durham: Duke University Press, 1996).

7. Jeffry A. Frieden, *Global Capitalism: Its Fall and Rise in the Twentieth Century* (New York: W. W. Norton, 2006), 188.

8. Ibid., 190–91.

9. *Annual Report Tea Growers' Association for the Netherlands East Indies* (1932), 22, ITA Mss Eur F174/2292.

10. V. D. Wickizer, *Tea under International Regulation* (Stanford: Food Research Institute, 1944); Bishnupriya Gupta, "Collusion in the Indian Tea Industry in the Great Depression: An Analysis of Panel Data," *Explorations in Economic History* 34 (1997): 155–73; and Bishnupriya Gupta, "The International Tea Cartel during the Great Depression, 1929–1933," *Journal of Economic History* 61, no. 1 (March 2001): 144–59.

Notes to Pages 267–270

11. Wickizer, *Tea under International Regulation*, 73.
12. "Tea Growing in East Africa," *HCM*, 24 November 1933, 4.
13. Wickizer, *Tea under International Regulation*, 72–96.
14. Maria Misra, *Business, Race and Politics in British India, 1850–1960* (Oxford: Clarendon, 1999), especially chap. 5.
15. For an excellent study on this issue, see Sarah E. Stockwell, *The Business of Decolonization: British Business Strategies in the Gold Coast* (Oxford: Clarendon, 2000).
16. Raj Chatterjee, oral interview, 17 March 1974, 2/9, Mss Eur T.15, African and Indian Collections, British Library.
17. Silences are significant in the colonical archive; see Ann Laura Stoler, *Along the Archival Grain: Epistemic Anxieties and Colonial Common Sense* (Princeton: Princeton University Press, 2009).
18. Sir Percival Griffiths, *The History of the Indian Tea Industry* (London: Weidenfield, 1967), 2:614–29. Griffiths became vice chairman of the board in 1937.
19. Canada and British Honduras were in the dollar bloc. Cain and Hopkins, *British Imperialism*, 466–67.
20. Sir Robert Graham, opening remarks at the first meeting of what was then called the International Tea Propaganda Board, 15 July 1935, held at 59 Mark Lane, London, ITA Mss Eur F174/958.
21. Précis of the Explanatory Note by the International Tea Market Expansion Board to be sent to editors of national and provincial newspapers, 26 November 1935, ITA Mss Eur F174/959.
22. Gervas Huxley, speech at the 43rd Annual General Meeting of the Ceylon Association in London, 25 April 1932, *Planters' Association of Ceylon Year Book* (1932), 125–28.
23. Report of the Ceylon Association in London, 1933, *Planters' Association of Ceylon Year Book* (1933), 80–81; "Tea in the U.S.A.," *HCM*, 6 April 1934, 5.
24. The Indian Tea Cess Act was passed by the Indian legislature and given assent by the governor-general in council in October 1936. The cess now also covered tea exported via sea or land. *Annual Report of the Indian Tea Market Expansion Board* (1937), 1, ITA Mss Eur F174/924.
25. Gervas Huxley, *Both Hands: An Autobiography* (London: Chatto and Windus, 1970), 158.
26. *Annual Report Tea Growers' Association for the Netherlands East Indies* (1933), 29 and (1936), 66–67, ITA Mss Eur F174/2292.
27. *Report of the General Committee of the ITA* (1936–37), ITA Mss Eur F174/4. The members of the first Executive Committee were J. S. Graham as chairman, P. J. Griffiths as vice chairman, N. W. Chisholm, N. C. Datta, D. C. Ghose, J. Jones, C. K. Nicholl, I. B. Sen, and J. C. Surrey. *ITMEB Annual Report*, 1937, 5, ITA Eur Mss F174/924.
28. Huxley, *Both Hands,* 162.
29. *HCM*, 3 June 1932, 14; Ukers, *All about Tea*, 1:170.
30. Sir Alfred D. Pickford, "India's Interests and the Empire," speech given at the Canada Club of Toronto, 25 April 1938, http://www.canadianclub.org/Events/EventDetails.aspx?id=1053.
31. *Annual Report of the General Committee of the ITA* (1935–36), 19, ITA Mss Eur F174/4.
32. Allister MacMillan, *Seaports of the Far East: Historical and Descriptive, Commercial and Industrial, Facts, Figures and Resources* (London: W. H. Collingridge, 1925), 306.

33. Arjun Appadurai, *Modernity at Large: Cultural Dimensions of Globalization* (Minneapolis: University of Minnesota Press, 1996), 42.
34. Searle Austin, "Twelve-Year-Olds Design for Lyons," *Advertising Display*, 1935, Acc. #3527/414, J. Lyons and Company Papers, London Metropolitan Archives (LMA).
35. Peter Bird, *The First Food Empire: A History of J. Lyons and Co.* (West Sussex: Phillimore, 2000). Also see Erika D. Rappaport, *Shopping for Pleasure: Women in the Making of London's West End* (Princeton: Princeton University Press, 2000), 103–5; Judith R. Walkowitz, *Nights Out: Life in Cosmopolitan London* (New Haven: Yale University Press, 2012) chap. 6. On Lyons's defense of its "British" identity, see Stephanie Seketa, "Spectacle Men and Tea Agents in London: The Conflict between International Networks and Rising Nationalism at the Turn of the Twentieth Century" (unpublished research paper, University of California, Santa Barbara, 2015).
36. See, for example, Lisa Jacobson, *Raising Consumers: Children and the American Mass Market in the Early Twentieth Century* (New York: Columbia University Press, 2004).
37. Bernard Porter made this argument in *The Absent-Minded Imperialists: Empire, Society and Culture in Britain* (Oxford: Oxford University Press, 2004), 34–35.
38. For the sheer volume of national symbols in British advertising, see Robert Opie, *Rule Britannia: Trading on the British Image* (Harmondsworth: Viking, 1985).
39. Much of this debate has focused on corporate size and management structures. See Alfred D. Chandler, *Scale and Scope: The Dynamics of Industrial Capitalism* (Cambridge: Cambridge University Press, 1990). For a different take, see Leslie Hannah, *The Rise of the Corporate Economy* (Baltimore: Johns Hopkins University Press, 1976). Also see Sue Bowden and Paul Turner, "The Demand for Consumer Durables in the United Kingdom during the Interwar Period," *Journal of Economic History* 53, no. 2 (1993): 244–58 and Peter Scott, "Marketing Mass Home Ownership and the Creation of the Modern Working-Class Consumer in Inter-War Britain," *Business History* 50, no. 1 (January 2008): 4–25.
40. For the postwar years, see Sean Nixon, *Hard Sell: Advertising, Affluence and Transatlantic Relations, c. 1951–69* (Manchester: Manchester University Press, 2013).
41. For the debate on mass culture as unifying or creating notions of difference in interwar Britain, see D. L. Le Mahieu, *A Culture for Democracy: Mass Communication and the Cultivated Mind in Britain between the Wars* (Oxford: Oxford University Press, 1988); Ross McKibbin, *Classes and Cultures: England 1918–1951* (Oxford: Oxford University Press, 1998); Robert James, *Popular Culture and Working-Class Taste in Britain: A Round of Cheap Diversions, 1930–39?* (Manchester: Manchester University Press, 2010); and Joanna Bourke, *Working-Class Cultures in Britain, 1890–1960: Gender, Class and Ethnicity* (London: Routledge, 1984).
42. Charles S. Gulas and Marc G. Weinberger, *Humor in Advertising: A Comprehensive Analysis* (London: M. E. Sharpe, 2006). On film, see Morris Dickstein, *Dancing in the Dark: A Cultural History of the Great Depression* (New York: W. W. Norton, 2009), 394 and Joanna E. Rapf, "What Do They Know in Pittsburgh?: American Comic Film in the Great Depression," *Studies in American Humor*, nos. 2/3 (1984): 187–200.
43. Steven Watts, "Walt Disney: Art and Politics in the American Century," *Journal of American History* 82, no. 1 (1995): 84–110.
44. Thomas Richards, *The Commodity Culture of Victorian England: Advertising and Spectacle, 1851-1914* (Stanford: Stanford University Press 1990), especially chap. 4.
45. Ian Gordon, *Comic Strips and Consumer Culture, 1890–1945* (Washington, DC: Smithsonian, 1998), 89–90.

46. Ibid., 94–105.
47. Le Mahieu, *A Culture of Democracy*, 161. On humor and Victorian and Edwardian mass culture, see Peter Bailey, *Music Hall: The Business of Pleasure* (Milton Keynes: Open University Press, 1986) and his *Popular Culture and Performance in the Victorian City* (Cambridge: Cambridge University Press, 1998).
48. Karl Marx, *Capital: A Critique of Political Economy*, ed. Frederick Engels (1867; New York: Random House, 1906), 81.
49. Ibid.
50. Victoria de Grazia distinguished between New World advertising, which emphasized the "product's personality, highlighting outward charms that compensated the viewer for not knowing its place of origin or intrinsic values," and Old World merchandising that stressed the product's character or intrinsic qualities. Victoria de Grazia, *Irresistible Empire: America's Advance through Twentieth-Century Europe* (Cambridge, MA: Belknap Press of Harvard University Press, 2005), 198. This builds on Warren Susman's classic formulation about character versus personality in his 1977 essay "Personality and the Making of Twentieth Century Culture," republished in *Culture as History: The Transformation of American Society in the Twentieth Century* (Washington, DC: Smithsonian, 2003). Both modes of advertising were regarded as modern in their day, and both were popular in the New World and the Old.
51. Winston Fletcher, *Powers of Persuasion: The Inside Story of British Advertising* (Oxford: Oxford University Press, 2008), 42.
52. Stanley Pigott, *OBM: A Celebration: One Hundred and Twenty Five Years in Advertising* (London: Ogilvy and Benson, 1975), 21–22.
53. As cited in ibid., 33.
54. David Hughes, *Gilroy Was Good for Guinness* (London: Liberties Press, 2014).
55. Frederick Clairmonte and John Cavanagh, *Merchants of Drink: Transnational Control of World Beverages* (Malaysia: Third World Network, 1988).
56. Tania M. Buckrell, *Tea and Taste: The Visual Language of Tea* (Atglen, PA: Shiffler Publishing, 2004), 47–58; Huge Pearman, "Living: Design Classics, Brown Betty Tea Pot," *The Times*, 29 September 2002, http://www.thetimes.co.uk.
57. Jed Esty, *A Shrinking Island: Modernism and National Culture in England* (Princeton: Princeton University Press, 2004).
58. Peter Mandler, *The English National Character: The History of an Idea from Edmund Burke to Tony Blair* (New Haven: Yale University Press, 2006).
59. As cited in ibid., 165.
60. Alison Light, *Forever England: Femininity, Literature and Conservatism between the Wars* (Oxford: Clarendon, 1988), 11.
61. Kenneth Lunn, "Reconsidering 'Britishness': The Construction and Significance of National Identity in Twentieth Century Britain," in *Nation and Identity in Contemporary Europe*, ed. Brian Jenkins and Spyros A. Sofos (London: Routledge, 1996), 87; Simon Featherstone, *Englishness: Twentieth Century Popular Culture and the Forming of English Identity* (Edinburgh: University of Edinburgh Press, 2009).
62. *HCM*, 28 September 1934, 4.
63. *ITMEB Annual Report* (1936), 9, ITA Mss Eur F174/961. For tea at the holiday camp, see "The Camper's Cup of Tea" (London: Empire Tea Bureau, 1947), ITA Mss Eur F174/963. The camps were a very important part of working-class leisure.

Sandra T. Dawson, *Holiday Camps in Twentieth Century Britain: Packaging Pleasure* (Manchester: Manchester University Press, 2011).

64. *HCM,* 27 September 1935, 5.

65. Marcia Landy, "The Extraordinary Ordinariness of Grace Fields: The Anatomy of a British Film Star," in Bruce Babington, *British Stars and Stardom: From Alma Taylor to Sean Connery* (Manchester: Manchester University Press, 2001), 56–67.

66. Quoted in Jeffrey Richards, *The Age of the Dream Palace: Cinema and Society in Britain, 1930–1939* (London: Routledge and Kegan Paul, 1984), 171.

67. From "Lancashire Blues" (1930), quoted in Featherstone, *Englishness*, 94.

68. McKibbin, *Classes and Cultures*, 154.

69. Dawson, *Holiday Camps*, 101.

70. Peter Lowe, *English Journeys: National and Cultural Identity in 1930s and 1940s England* (Amherst, NY: Cambria Press, 2012).

71. ITMEB display material, c. 1935. I would like to thank Gavin Brain, who generously gave me this rare foldout that his father, Mike Brain, acquired while working at Waddingtons, a printing and packaging firm in Leeds. Luckily Mike and his friends understood its value and kept it and other material in his basement.

72. *Gilroy Is Good for You: A Celebration of the Life and Work, of the Artist John Gilroy* (Norwich: History of Advertising Trust, 1998).

73. Gillian Dyer, *Advertising as Communication* (London: Routledge, 1996), 46.

74. Paul R. Deslandes, "Selling, Consuming and Becoming the Beautiful Man in Britain: The 1930s and 1940s," in *Consuming Behaviours: Identity, Politics and Pleasure in Twentieth Century Britain*, ed. Erika Rappaport, Sandra Trudgen Dawson, and Mark J. Crowley (London: Bloomsbury, 2015), 53–70; Matthew Thomson, *Psychological Subjects: Identity, Culture, and Health in Twentieth Century Britain* (Oxford: Oxford University Press, 2006).

75. Ana Carden-Coyne, *Reconstructing the Body: Classicism, Modernism, and the First World War* (Oxford: Oxford University Press, 2009); Ina Zweiniger-Bargielowska, *Managing the Body: Beauty, Health and Fitness in Britain, 1880s–1939* (Oxford: Oxford University Press, 2010); Charlotte Macdonald, *Strong, Beautiful, and Modern: National Fitness in Britain, New Zealand, Australia and Canada, 1935–1960* (Vancouver: University of British Columbia Press, 2011); Joanna Bourke, *Dismembering the Male: Men's Bodies, Britain and the Great War* (Chicago: University of Chicago Press, 1996); Michael Hau, *The Cult of Health and Beauty in Germany: A Social History, 1890–1930* (Chicago: University of Chicago Press, 2003).

76. Lee Grieveson, "The Cinema and the (Common) wealth of Nations," in *Empire and Film*, ed. Lee Grieveson and Colin MacCabe (London: Palgrave Macmillan, 2011), 73–113.

77. *Life in India and Ceylon: Programme of Sound and Talking Films*, correspondence related to films belonging to the Empire Tea Market Expansion Board, 1935–38, NA, INF 17/44/99648.

78. There has been a great deal of scholarship on *The Song of Ceylon*, which was paid for by the Ceylon Tea Propaganda Board. For the broader context and legacy of the EMB, see Scott Anthony, "Imperialism and Internationalism: The British Documentary Movement and the Legacy of the Empire Marketing Board," in *Empire and Film*, 135–48. Also see J. Hoare, "'Go the Way the Material Calls You': Basil Wright and *The Song of Ceylon*," in *The Projection of Britain: A Complete History of the GPO Film*

Unit, ed. Scott Anthony and James Mansell (London: BFI, 2011) and William Guynn, "The Art of National Projection: Basil Wright's *Song of Ceylon*," in *Documenting the Documentary: Close Readings of Documentary Film and Video*, ed. Barry Keith Grant and Jeannette Sloniowski (Detroit: Wayne State University Press, 2014), 64–80.

79. New trade papers, such as the *Luncheon and Tea Room Journal*, explained the merits of modern ovens, electric grills, self-generating pudding, and vegetable steamers. Yet feature articles on furniture, menus, and decor insisted that modern tea shops should have an "old world" feel or, as an article on "the tea shops of Rye" put it, a "modern outlook in an Old World setting." Beryl Heitland, "The Tea Shops of Rye: Modern Outlook in an Old World Setting," *Luncheon and Tea Room Journal* (July 1936): 221; "The Oak Café and the Oak Lounge," *Luncheon and Tea Room Journal* (March 1937): 83; "Lavender Cottage," *Luncheon and Tea Room Journal* (September 1938): 275.

80. There is a vast literature on this topic. Especially helpful are Raphael Samuel, *Theatres of Memory: Past and Present in Contemporary Culture* (London: Verso, 1994); Patrick Wright, *On Living in an Old Country: The National Past in Contemporary Britain* (London: Verso, 1985); George K. Behlmer and Fred M. Leventhal, *Singular Continuities: Tradition, Nostalgia and Identity in Modern British Culture* (Stanford: Stanford University Press, 2000).

81. Pierre Dubois, *How to Run a Small Hotel or Guest House, with a Chapter on Running a Tea Room* (London: Vawser and Wiles, 1946), 72. For a similar vision, see *A New Essay upon Tea: Addressed to the Medical Profession* (London: Empire Tea Market Expansion Board, 1936); "Russell E. Smith," "Tea in English Literature," *TCTJ* (March 1920): 316–18; and William Lyon Phelps, *Essays on Things* (New York: Macmillan, 1930), 80–84.

82. "Scottish Catering: Give Your Room a National Atmosphere," *Luncheon and Tea Room Journal* (January 1936): 29.

83. Arjun Appadurai, "How to Make a National Cuisine: Cookbooks in Contemporary India," *Comparative Studies in Society and History* 30, no. 1 (January 1988): 3–24; Warren James Belasco and Philip Scranton, eds., *Food Nations: Selling Taste in Consumer Societies* (New York: Routledge, 2002); Jeffrey M. Pilcher, *Que Vivan Los Tamales!: Food and the Making of Mexican Identity* (Albuquerque: University of New Mexico Press, 1998); Carol Helstosky, *Garlic and Oil: Politics and Food in Italy* (Oxford: Berg, 2006); Donna R. Gabaccia, *We Are What We Eat: Ethnic Food and the Making of Americans* (Cambridge, MA: Harvard University Press, 1998); Krishnendu Ray and Tulasi Srinivas, eds., *Curried Cultures: Globalization, Food, and South Asia* (Berkeley: University of California Press, 2012). For the international context of the British diet and cuisine, see Sidney W. Mintz in *Sweetness and Power: The Place of Sugar in Modern History* (New York: Penguin, 1985); Elizabeth Buettner, "'Going for an Indian'": South Asian Restaurants and the Limits of Multiculturalism in Britain," *Journal of Modern History* 80, no. 4 (December 2008): 865–901 and Panikos Panayi, *Spicing up Britain: The Multicultural History of British Food* (London: Reaktion, 2008).

84. B. W. E. Alford, "New Industries for Old? British Industry between the Wars," in *The Economic History of Britain since 1700*, vol. 2, *1860s–1970s*, ed. Roderick Floud and Donald McCloskey (Cambridge: Cambridge University Press, 1981), 318. Some important works include Thomas A. B. Corley, "Consumer Marketing in Britain,

1914–1960," *Business History* 29, no. 4 (1987): 65–83; Hartmut Berghoff, Philip Scranton, and Uwe Spiekerman, eds., *The Rise of Modern Market Research* (New York: Palgrave Macmillan, 2012); Richard S. Tedlow, *New and Improved: The Story of Mass Marketing in America* (Cambridge, MA: Harvard Business School Press, 1996); Richard S. Tedlow and Geoffrey G. Jones, eds., *The Rise and Fall of Mass Marketing* (London: Routledge, 1993); Geoffrey G. Jones and Nicholas J. Morgan, eds., *Adding Value: Brands and Marketing in Food and Drink* (London: Routledge, 1994); August W. Giebelhaus, "The Pause That Refreshed the World: The Evolution of Coca-Cola's Global Marketing Strategy," in *Adding Value*, ed. Jones and Morgan, 191–214; Roy Church and Andrew Godley, eds., *The Emergence of Modern Marketing* (London: Routledge, 2003); Kerstin Brückweh, ed., *The Voice of the Citizen Consumer: A History of Market Research, Consumer Movements, and the Political Public Sphere* (Oxford: Oxford University Press, 2011); Stephen L. Harp, *Marketing Michelin: Advertising and Cultural Identity in Twentieth-Century France* (Baltimore: Johns Hopkins University Press, 2001); Uwe Spiekermann, "Understanding Markets: Information, Institutions, and History," *Bulletin of the German Historical Institute* 47 (Fall 2010): 93–101; and Yavuz Köse, "Nestlè: A Brief History of the Marketing Strategies of the First Multinational Company in the Ottoman Empire," *Journal of Macromarketing* 27, no. 1 (2007): 74–85.

85. Stefan Schwarzkopf, "Discovering the Consumer: Market Research, Product Innovation, and the Creation of Brand Loyalty in Britain and the United States in the Interwar Years," *Journal of Macromarketing* 29, no. 1 (February 2009): 8–20.

86. D. Lageman, "Norway Report," (August 1935), 4, ITA Mss Eur F174/958 (June 1935).

87. D. Lageman, "Belgium Report," (June 1935), ITA Mss Eur F174/958.

88. Alfred N. Pickford, *Tea Tells the World* (London: ITMEB, 1937), 4, ITA Mss Eur F174/925. A second copy is in the special collections, Shields Library, UC-Davis.

89. Joyce Appleby, *The Relentless Revolution: A History of Capitalism* (New York: W. W. Norton, 2010).

90. Pickford, *Tea Tells the World*, 2.

91. Huxley, *Both Hands*, 176.

92. Ibid., 179.

93. "Reid, Helen Miles Rogers (1882–1970), Newspaper Publisher," in *Encyclopedia of American Women, Colonial Times to the Present*, vol. 2, *M–Z*, ed. Carol H. Krismann (Westport, CT: Greenwood, 2005), 457–59.

94. Huxley, *Both Hands*, 180–81.

95. Ibid., 187–94; Scott M. Cutlip, *The Unseen Power: Public Relations, A History* (New York: Routledge, 1994), 662–759.

96. Sarah E. Igo, *The Averaged American: Surveys, Citizens and the Making of a Mass Public* (Cambridge, MA: Harvard University Press, 2007), 115.

97. Ibid.

98. Ibid., 104.

99. This was by no means only an "American" project. Sherene Seikaly has written that such methods "conjured markets as the definition of the social" and made consumption "the obligatory act of the normative social subject." Sherene Seikaly, *Men of Capital: Scarcity and Economy in Mandate Palestine* (Stanford: Stanford University Press, 2015), 39.

100. Benjamin Wood, a former executive with Scripps-Howard newspapers and the *Saturday Evening Post*, was New York's managing director. Memorandum from Newsom to K. P. Chen, "The Tea Bureau and Its Operation," 4 April 1946, 1, Newsom Papers, Box 48/20, Wisconsin Historical Society, Madison.

101. *Report by a Commission to the United States to the International Tea Committee* (1934), ITA Mss Eur F174/949.

102. Earl Newsom to Gervas Huxley, 11 January 1937, Box 47, File 46, Newsom Papers.

103. Ibid.

104. Quoted in Gervas Huxley to Earl Newsom, 13 January 1937, Box 47, File 46, Newsom Papers.

105. *ITMEB Annual Report* (1936), 4, ITA Mss Eur F174/961.

106. Tom Pendergrast, *Creating the Modern Man: American Magazines and Consumer Culture, 1900–1950* (Columbia: University of Missouri Press, 2000), 134.

107. The classic account of this version of American history is Alan Trachtenberg, *The Incorporation of America: Culture and Society in the Gilded Age* (New York: Hill and Wang, 1982).

108. Earl Newsom to Gervas Huxley, 7 July 1936, Box 47, File 46, Newsom Papers.

109. See, for example, Earl Newsom to Gervas Huxley, 12 June 1936, Box 47, File 46, Newsom Papers.

110. Susanne Freidberg, *Fresh: A Perishable History* (Cambridge, MA: Belknap Press of Harvard University Press, 2009), 23; Jonathan Rees, *Refrigeration Nation: A History of Ice, Appliances and Enterprise in America* (Baltimore: Johns Hopkins University Press, 2013).

111. As cited in Freidberg, *Fresh*, 23.

112. Ibid., 39.

113. Douglas Cazaux Sackman, *Orange Empire: California and the Fruits of Eden* (Berkeley: University of California Press, 2005), 7.

114. Alice Bradley, *Sunkist Recipes: Oranges-Lemons* (Los Angeles: California Fruit Growers' Exchange, 1916), 57, https://archive.org/details/sunkistrecipesor00bradiala.

115. Ibid., 84–116. Sackman concentrates on oranges (pun intended), but Sunkist's lemon campaign was equally significant. See Toby Sonneman, *Lemon: A Global History* (London: Reaktion Books, 2012), 85–94.

116. As cited in Deborah Jean Warner, *Sweet Stuff: An American History of Sweeteners from Sugar to Sucralose* (Washington, DC: Rowman and Littlefield, 2011), 25. For an excellent new history of sugar, see April Merleaux, *Sugar and Civilization: American Empire and the Cultural Politics of Sweetness* (Chapel Hill: University of North Carolina Press, 2015).

117. *ITMEB Annual Report* (1936), 4, ITA Mss Eur F174/961.

118. "Tea Peps You Up," billboard, Atlantic City, July 1939, R. C. Maxwell Digital Collection, #4686, Duke University Special Collections.

119. Russell Z. Eller, "Sunkist—Tea's Working Partner," *Coffee and Tea Industries and the Flavor Field* (formerly *Spice Mill*) 79, no. 5 (May 1956): 69–73. For an example of this advertising in the 1950s, see ibid., 56–57.

120. Joe Gray Taylor, *Eating, Drinking, and Visiting in the South: An Informal History* (Baton Rouge: Louisiana State University Press, 1982).

121. "Tea Revives You," *Winnipeg Free Press, Magazine Section* (11 February 1939), 16.

122. Franca Iacovetta, Valerie J. Korinek, and Marlene Epp, eds., *Edible Histories, Cultural Politics: Towards a Canadian Food History* (Toronto: University of Toronto Press, 2012).

123. *Tea Tells the World*, 30.

124. Ibid.

125. Lageman, "Belgium Report" (June 1935), ITA Mss Eur F174/958.

126. "Tea Propaganda on the Continent of Europe," *ITMEB Quarterly Report*, January–March 1936, appendix 3, published in *Indian Tea Cess Committee Report* (22 June 1936), ITA Mss Eur F174/958.

127. *ITMEB Annual Report*, 1936, 6–7, ITA Mss Eur F174/961.

128. Ibid.

129. *Report of the Tea Propaganda Committee, 1936*, 83, ITA Mss Eur F174/2292.

130. Ibid., 70–73.

131. D. K. Fieldhouse, *Unilever Overseas: The Anatomy of a Multinational, 1895–1965* (London: Croom Helm, 1978), 96–122 and his *Merchant Capital and Economic Decolonization: The United Africa Company, 1929–1987* (Oxford: Oxford University Press, 1994); Burke, *Lifebuoy Men, Lux Women*; Brian Lewis, *"So Clean": Lord Leverhulme, Soap and Civilization* (Manchester: Manchester University Press, 2008), 154–98; and Bianca Murillo, *Market Encounters: Consumer Cultures in Twentieth Century Ghana* (Athens: Ohio University Press, 2017).

132. Jeremy Prestholdt, *Domesticating the World: African Consumerism and the Genealogies of Globalization* (Berkeley: University of California Press, 2008); Stanley B. Alpern, "What Africans Got for Their Slaves: A Master List of European Trade Goods," *History in Africa* 22 (1995): 5–43; George E. Brooks, *Yankee Traders, Old Coasters and African Middlemen: A History of American Legitimate Trade with West Africa in the Nineteenth Century* (Boston: Boston University Press, 1970).

133. For an analysis of this debate, see Mehita Iquani, *Consumption, Media and the Global South: Aspiration Contested* (New York: Palgrave Macmillan, 2016), and for an earlier treatment, see Jerry K. Domatob, "Sub-Saharan Africa's Media and Neocolonialism," *Africa Media Review* 3, no. 1 (1988): 149–74. Some studies have built on work on African American consumerism, such as Davarian L. Baldwin, *Chicago's New Negroes: Modernity, the Great Migration, and Black Urban Life* (Chapel Hill: University of North Carolina Press, 2007).

134. Lynn M. Thomas, "The Modern Girl and Racial Respectability in 1930s South Africa," *Journal of African History* 47, no. 3 (November 2006): 472.

135. Jean M. Allman, ed., *Fashioning Africa: Power and the Politics of Dress* (Bloomington: Indian University Press, 2004); Hildi Hendrickson, *Clothing and Difference: Embodied Identities in Colonial and Post-Colonial Africa* (Durham: Duke University Press, 1996).

136. James McDonald Burns, *Flickering Shadows: Cinema and Identity in Colonial Zimbabwe* (Athens: Ohio University Press, 2002), 25–26, 53; Lee Grieveson and Colin MacCabe, eds., *Film and the End of Empire* (Houndmills: Palgrave Macmillan, 2011); Peter J. Bloom, *French Colonial Documentary: Mythologies of Humanitarianism* (Minneapolis: University of Minnesota Press, 2008); Rosaleen Smyth, "Film as an Instrument of Modernization and Social Change in Africa: The Long View," in *Modernization as Spectacle in Africa*, ed. Peter J. Bloom, Stephan Miescher, and Takyiwaa Manuh (Bloomington: Indiana University Press, 2014).

137. Huxley, *Both Hands*, 166.

138. Roger B. Beck, *The History of South Africa* (London: Greenwood, 2000), 37.

139. Alan Lester, *Imperial Networks: Creating Identities in Nineteenth Century South Africa and Britain* (London: Routledge, 2001), 74–75. Also see Robert Ross, *Status and*

Respectability in the Cape Colony, 1750–1870: A Tragedy of Manners (Cambridge: Cambridge University Press, 1999).

140. P. J. van der Merwe, *The Migrant Farmer in the History of the Cape Colony, 1657–1842*, trans. Roger B. Beck (Athens: Ohio University Press, 1995), 182.

141. Comaroff and Comaroff, *Of Revelation and Revolution*, vol. 1. There is a great deal of work on this topic; see, for example, Elizabeth Elbourne, *Blood Ground: Colonialism, Missions, and the Contest for Christianity in the Cape Colony, 1799–1853* (Montreal: McGill-Queen's University Press, 2002) and Richard Elphick and Rodney Davenport, eds., *Christianity in South Africa: A Political, Social, and Cultural History* (Berkeley: University of California Press, 1997).

142. Comaroff and Comaroff, *Of Revelation and Revolution*, 2:187.

143. As cited in Nancy Rose Hunt, "Colonial Fairy Tales and the Knife and Fork Doctrine in the Heart of Africa," in *African Encounters with Domesticity*, ed. Karen Tranberg Hansen (New Brunswick, NJ: Rutgers University Press, 1992), 144.

144. Richard Parry, "Culture, Organisation and Class: The African Experience in Salisbury, 1892–1935," in *Sites of Struggle: Essays in Zimbabwe's Urban History*, ed. Brian Raftopoulos and Tsuneo Yoshikuni (Harare: Weaver Press, 1999), 58; Mhoze Chikowero, *African Music, Power, and Being in Colonial Zimbabwe* (Bloomington: Indiana University Press, 2015), 93–97. For a general analysis, see Michael O. West, *The Rise of an African Middle Class: Colonial Zimbabwe, 1898–1965* (Bloomington: Indiana University Press, 2002).

145. Tera W. Hunter, *To 'Joy My Freedom: Southern Black Women's Lives and Labors after the Civil War* (Cambridge, MA: Harvard University Press, 1997), 162–67; Evelyn Brooks Higginbotham, *Righteous Discontent: The Women's Movement in the Black Baptist Church, 1880–1920* (Cambridge, MA: Harvard University Press, 1993), especially chap. 7; Laura Moore, "'Don't tell me there is nothing in appearance: Thee's everything in it': African American Women and the Politics of Consumption, 1862–1920" (PhD diss., University of California, Santa Barbara, forthcoming).

146. Quoted in Comaroff and Comaroff, *Of Revelation and Revolution*, 2:236.

147. William Beinart, *Twentieth-Century South Africa* (Oxford: Oxford University Press, 2001), 119.

148. "Tea in South Africa's History," *Die Burger*, 3 February 1937, 5. Dr. Jean Smith translated all the Afrikaans-language advertisements.

149. "Tea Had Restored His Energy," *Die Burger*, 17 March 1937, 17.

150. "Can You Make Delicious Tea?" *Die Burger*, 21 January 1937, 4.

151. "Mr. T. Pott—Always a Welcome Visitor," *Die Burger*, 26 May 1937, 9.

152. "Tea Is Good for Children," *Die Burger*, 2 June 1937, 4.

153. "Tea—The World's Most Popular Drink," *Die Burger*, 6 January 1937, 12.

154. Les Switzer and Donna Switzer, *The Black Press in South Africa and Lesotho: A Descriptive Bibliographic Guide to African, Coloured and Indian Newspapers, Newsletters and Magazines, 1836–1976* (Boston: G. K. Hall, 1979), 7. For a detailed analysis of the advertising and editorial policies of the paper, see Les Switzer, "*Bantu World* and the Origins of a Captive African Commercial Press in South Africa," *Journal of Southern African Studies* 14, no. 3 (April 1988): 351–70. Also see Thomas, "The Modern Girl and Racial Respectability in 1930s South Africa," 461–90 and Nhlanhla Maake, "Archetyping Race, Gender and Class: Advertising in *The Bantu World* and

The World from the 1930s to the 1990s," *Journal for Transdisciplinary Research in Southern Africa* 2, no. 1 (July 2006): 1–22.

155. Switzer, "*Bantu World* and the Origins," 352.

156. Ibid., 353–54.

157. Switzer and Switzer, *The Black Press*, 8.

158. Switzer, "*Bantu World* and the Origins," 351.

159. For this point about gender struggles, see Thomas, "The Modern Girl and Racial Respectability," 461–62. Two key studies include Stephan Miescher, *Making Men in Ghana* (Bloomington: Indiana University Press, 2005) and Lisa Lindsay and Stephan Miescher, eds., *Men and Masculinities in Modern Africa* (Portsmouth: Heinemann, 2003). For an overview of the South African industrial economy in this period, see Charles H. Feinstein, *An Economic History of South Africa: Conquest, Discrimination and Development* (Cambridge: Cambridge University Press, 2005), 121–27.

160. Switzer, "*Bantu World* and the Origins," 357.

161. Switzer and Switzer, *The Black Press*, 8. Switzer also cites the fact that the Tea Board began a children's supplement in 1936, which appeared in the weekly newspapers of the Bantu Press, *Umteteli wa Bantu*, and at least two other religious newspapers (20-21). Also see A. J. Friedgut, "The Non-European Press," in *Handbook on Race Relations in South Africa*, ed. E. Hellman (Cape Town: Oxford University Press, 1949).

162. Switzer, "*Bantu World* and the Origins," 366–68.

163. *ITMEB Annual Report* (1936), 14, ITA Mss Eur F174/961.

164. *Bantu World* (hereafter *BW*), 30 November 1937, 13, for example.

165. Ibid.

166. *BW*, 1 January 1938, 3.

167. Ibid., 7.

168. On the global history of the modern girl, see Weinbaum et al., ed., *The Modern Girl around the World: Consumption, Modernity, and Globalization* (Durham: Duke University Press, 2008). On the consumer housewife, see Abigail McGowan, "Consuming Families: Negotiating Women's Shopping in Early Twentieth Century Western India," in *Towards a History of Consumption in South Asia*, ed. Douglas E. Haynes, Abigail McGowan, Tirthankar Roy, and Haruka Yanagisawa (New Delhi: Oxford University Press, 2010), 155–84 and Seikaly, *Men of Capital*, 53–76.

169. For an example of the column, see *BW*, 28 November 1936, 9, 5 December 1936, 9, and 19 December 1936, 9.

170. Paul La Hausse, "The Message of the Warriors: The ICU, the Labouring Poor and the Making of a Popular Political Culture in Durban, 1925–1939," in *Holding Their Ground: Class, Locality and Culture in 19th and 20th Century South Africa*, ed. Philip Bonner, Isabel Hofmeyr, Deborah James, and Tom Lodge (Johannesburg: Witwatersrand University Press, 1989), 20–21.

171. Anne Kelk Mager, *Beer, Sociability, and Masculinity in South Africa* (Bloomington: Indiana University Press, 2010), 4.

172. Ibid., 13.

173. Chikowero, *African Music*, 175, and especially chap. 7. Also see La Hausse, "The Message of the Warriors," 23 and Mager, *Beer, Sociability*.

174. La Hausse, "The Message of the Warriors," 36.

175. Chikowero, *African Music*, 187.
176. Ibid., 188.
177. *Tea Tells the World*, 32.
178. *Tea Times of Africa* (September 1948): 1, 4–5, 7.
179. *Report of the ITMEB Board* (1946), 9, ITA Mss Eur F174/961.
180. This is a point nearly every author makes in Grieveson and MacCabe, *Film and the End of Empire*.
181. "Tea Ventures . . . Up Country," *Tea Times of Africa Quarterly* (Summer 1953): 2–5.
182. "Tea Films for Africans," *Tea Times of Africa* (January 1949): 7.
183. "Three New Tea Films," *Tea Times of Africa Quarterly* (Summer 1952): 22; "Films for Africans," *Tea Times of Africa Quarterly* (May 1955): 17.
184. "South Africa Bureau Makes Good Progress in Service Drive," *Tea Times of Africa* (September 1948): 5.
185. *Tea Times of Africa* (September 1948): 1–2.
186. *Tea: The Worker's Drink* (Johannesburg: The Tea Bureau, 1950), 1.
187. Ibid.
188. "Distributing Tea and Food to African Estate Workers," *Tea Times of Africa* (September 1948): 2.
189. "Tea Pluckers' Tea," *Tea Times of Africa* (December 1948): 4.
190. "Free Tea for Workers Who Arrive on Time," *Tea Times of Africa* (September 1948): 4.
191. Burke, *Lifebuoy Men, Lux Women*, 127.
192. "Too Much Water with It . . . ?: Findings of Recent Research on Beverage Trends in South Africa," *Tea Times of Africa Quarterly* (Summer 1953): 13–16.
193. "Per Capita Tea Consumption of Union's Total Population, 1911–1954," *Tea Times of Africa Quarterly* (December 1955): 9.
194. A study the following year added "Asiatics" to the three previous categories. "Tea Consumption by Racial Group," *Tea Times of Africa Quarterly* (August 1954): 26.
195. For a discussion of this map and Gill's work, see "MacDonald 'Max' Gill: A Digital Resource 2011," http://arts.brighton.ac.uk/projects/macdonald-gill/max-gill. Reproductions are available, however, from www.oldhousebooks.co.uk.
196. "Tea Ventures . . . Up Country," *Tea Times of Africa* (Summer 1953): 3–4.
197. I witnessed the poster hanging in the gift shop when I visited the estate in February 2015. For information about Happy Valley, see http://www.darjeelingteaboutique.com/happy-valley-tea-estate/.

CHAPTER 9. "HOT DRINKS MEAN MUCH IN THE JUNGLE"

1. Magnus Pyke, *Food and Society* (London: John Murray, 1968), 48; Derek Cooper, *The Beverage Report* (London: Routledge and Kegan Paul, 1970), 24–25. Pyke had been a member of the Scientific Advisers Department in the Ministry of Food during the war. For an example of this sort of propaganda, see *Tea on Service* (London: The Tea Centre, 1947).
2. Joanna Mack and Steve Humphries, *The Making of Modern London, 1939–45: London at War* (London: Sidgwick and Jackson, 1985), 58, 61; Peter Stansky, *The First Day of the Blitz: September 7, 1940* (New Haven: Yale University Press, 2007), 44–45, 137–38, 161. For an excellent analysis of the role of tea in wartime cinema,

see Richard Farmer, *The Food Companions: Cinema and Consumption in Wartime Britain, 1939–45* (Manchester: Manchester University Press, 2011), 185–216.

3. For an overview of the People's War debate, see Mark Connelly, *We Can Take It! Britain and the Memory of the Second World* War (Harlow: Longman, 2004). Key studies include Angus Calder, *The People's War: Britain, 1939–45* (New York: Pantheon, 1969); Angus Calder, *The Myth of the Blitz* (London: Jonathan Cape, 1991); Sonya O. Rose, *Which People's War: National Identity and Citizenship in Wartime Britain, 1939–1945* (Oxford: Oxford University Press, 2003); and Malcolm Smith, *Britain and 1940: History, Myth and Popular Memory* (London: Routledge, 2000). For the importance of air raids in creating this view of the war, see Susan R. Grayzel, *At Home and under Fire: Air Raids and Culture in Britain from the Great War to the Blitz* (Cambridge: Cambridge University Press, 2012)

4. George Orwell, *The Lion and the Unicorn: Socialism and the English Genius* (London: Secker and Warburg, 1941), 15.

5. Lizzie Collingham, *The Taste of War: World War II and the Battle for Food* (New York: Penguin, 2012), chap. 5.

6. Peter Lewis, *A People's War* (London: Thomas Methuen, 1986), 157.

7. On the Bengal Famine, see Madhusree Mukerjee, *Churchill's Secret War: The British Empire and the Ravaging of India during World War II* (New York: Basic Books, 2010) and sources in notes 106 and 107, below. For nutritional improvements in the UK, see Sir John Boyd Orr, *The Nation's Food* (London: Labour Party Pamphlets, 1943); John Burnett, *Plenty and Want: A Social History of Food in England from 1815 to the Present Day*, rev. ed. (1966; London: Scolar Press, 1979), 322–32; Christopher Driver, *The British at Table, 1940–1980* (London: Hogarth Press, 1983), 18. More recent work has complicated this picture; see Ina Zweiniger-Bargielowska, *Austerity in Britain: Rationing, Controls and Consumption, 1939–1955* (Oxford: Oxford University Press, 2000), 36–45, and for responses to global scarcity, see Frank Trentmann, "Coping with Shortage: The Problem of Food Security and Global Visions of Coordination, c. 1890s–1950," in *Food and Conflict in Europe in the Age of the Two World Wars*, ed. Frank Trentmann and Flemming Just (London: Palgrave Macmillan, 2006), 13–48. Peter J. Atkins, "Communal Feeding in Wartime: British Restaurants, 1940–1947," in *Food and War in Twentieth Century Europe*, ed. Zweiniger-Bargielowska, Duffett, and Drouard, 139–53. England's situation is in sharp contrast with that of the Soviet Union, Greece, the Netherlands, and other occupied countries.

8. Farmer, *The Food Companions*, 3. For the U.S. case, see Amy Bentley, *Eating for Victory: Food Rationing and the Politics of Domesticity* (Urbana: University of Illinois Press, 1998).

9. Zweiniger-Bargielowska, *Austerity in Britain*, 6. The most detailed account of the rationing system is Richard J. Hammond's three-volume study on food and the war. It is generally titled *Food* (London: HMSO and Longman and Green, 1951–62). Each volume has a unique subtitle, see below.

10. Zweiniger-Bargielowska, *Austerity in Britain*; James Vernon, *Hunger: A Modern History* (Cambridge, MA: Belknap Press of Harvard University Press, 2007), 223–35.

11. "Inequality of Sacrifice," Home Intelligence Report, 25 March 1942, NA INF 1/292, quoted in Harold L. Smith, ed., *Britain in the Second World War: A Social History* (Manchester: Manchester University Press, 1996), 48.

12. Paul Brassley and Angela Potter, "A View from the Top: Social Elites and Food Consumption in Britain, 1930s–1940s," in *Food and Conflict in Europe in the Age of the Two World Wars*, ed. Trentmann and Just, 223–42. Also see Mark Roodhouse, "Popular Morality and the Black Market in Britain, 1939–55," in *Food and Conflict in Europe in the Age of the Two World Wars*, ed. Trentmann and Just, 243–65; and his *Blackmarket Britain 1939–1955* (Oxford: Oxford University Press, 2013).

13. Zweiniger-Bargielowska, *Austerity in Britain*, especially. chap. 5.

14. "Ministry of Food: Food Defence Plans Department of the Board of Trade: Feeding of Greater London in an Emergency. Bulk Supplies of Bread, Flour, Yeast, Milk, Tea, Sugar, etc. . . ." (1938), NA MAF 72/9.

15. Wickizer, *Tea under International Regulation* (Stanford: Food Research Institute, 1944), 97.

16. Denys M. Forrest, *Tea for the British: The Social and Economic History of a Famous Trade* (London: Chatto and Windus, 1973), 224–26.

17. R. D. M. Morrison, *Tea: Memorandum Relating to the Tea Industry and Tea Trade of the World* (London: International Tea Committee, 1943), 57. Morrison was one of the directors of the Ceylon Tea Propaganda Board during the war. For a discussion of tea controls in the United States, see Wickizer, *Tea under International Regulation*, 103–5.

18. Morrison, *Tea*, 57, 218.

19. V. D. Wickizer, *Coffee, Tea and Cocoa: An Economic and Political Analysis* (Stanford: Stanford University Press, 1951), 217.

20. Home Publicity Division minutes, 1 September 1939, NA INF 1/316, cited in Ian McLaine, *Ministry of Morale: Home Front Morale and the Ministry of Information in World War II* (London: George Allen and Unwin, 1979), 27.

21. Huxley, *Both Hands*, 187, 194–95.

22. Ibid., 202–10.

23. Hammond, *Food: The Growth of Policy* (London: HMSO, 1951), 1:125.

24. Charles Smith, *Food in Wartime* (London: Fabian Society, 1940), 5.

25. Quoted in Hammond, *Food: Studies in Administration and Control* (London: HMSO, 1956), 2:740.

26. *Tea on Service*, 75.

27. One expert proposed that the "separate identities of soft drink manufacturers were almost completely obliterated." *Food*, vol. 1, *The Growth of Policy*, 339.

28. Ibid., 2:699–749.

29. Morrison, *Tea*, 43. The Indian Tea Association publicized this episode with the publication of Geoffrey Tyson, *The Forgotten Frontier* (Calcutta: W. H. Targett and Co., 1945).

30. Yet, most work on consumption and wartime has remained incidental and anecdotal. Zweiniger-Bargielowska, *Austerity in Britain*, 61.

31. McLaine, *Ministry of Morale*. On methods developed in the 1920s and 1930s, see Stefan Schwarzkopf, "Discovering the Consumer: Market Research, Product Innovation, and the Creation of Brand Loyalty in Britain and the United States in the Interwar Years," *Journal of Macromarketing* 29, no. 1 (2009): 8–20. Also see Stefan Schwarzkopf, "A Radical Past?: The Politics of Market Research in Britain, 1900–1950," in *The Voice of the Citizen Consumer: A History of Market Research,*

Consumer Movements, and the Political Public Sphere, ed. Kerstin Brückweh (Oxford: Oxford University Press, 2011), 29–50.

32. Scholars are increasingly interrogating how M-O provided a new context in which individuals narrated the self and the social. James Hinton, *Nine Wartime Lives: Mass Observation and the Making of the Modern Self* (Oxford: Oxford University Press, 2010); Tony Kushner, *We Europeans? Mass-Observation, "Race" and British Identity in the Twentieth Century* (Aldershot: Ashgate, 2004); Nick Hubble, *Mass-Observation and Everyday Life: Culture, History, Theory* (Basingstoke: Palgrave Macmillan, 2006). For a full history of the organization, see James Hinton, *The Mass Observers: A History, 1937–1949* (Oxford: Oxford University Press, 2013).

33. Interview #9, 45-year-old man, M-O Typed Directives on Tea Rationing carried out in Stepney on 13 July 1940, Topic Collection—Food 67/2/E, Mass Observation Archive, University of Sussex, Special Collections.

34. Interview #14, 35-year-old woman, M-O Typed Directives on Tea Rationing carried out in Stepney on 13 July 1940, Topic Collection—Food 67/2/E, Mass Observation Archive, University of Sussex, Special Collections.

35. 60-year-old man, M-O Typed and Hand Written Directives on Tea Rationing carried out in Bourne End, 11–13 July 1940, Topic Collection—Food 67/2/E, Mass Observation Archive, University of Sussex, Special Collections.

36. Interview #6, 70-year-old man, M-O Typed and Hand Written Directives on Tea Rationing carried out in Bourne End, 11–13 July 1940, Topic Collection—Food 67/2/E, Mass Observation Archive, University of Sussex, Special Collections.

37. Interview #7, 20-year-old woman, M-O Typed and Hand Written Directives on Tea Rationing carried out in Bourne End, 11–13 July 1940, Topic Collection—Food 67/2/E, Mass Observation Archive, University of Sussex, Special Collections.

38. Food Facts No. 15, Week of 4 November 1940, quoted in Farmer, *The Food Companions*, 189.

39. Quoted in Lewis, *A People's War*, 160.

40. Interview #15, 50-year-old woman, M-O Topic Collection—Food 67/2/E.

41. Interview #16, 45-year-old woman, M-O Topic Collection—Food 67/2/E.

42. Interviews #6 and 7, 70-year-old man and 20-year-old woman. So, for example, in 1936–37, 43.4 percent of those with an income over £1,000 per year drank coffee at breakfast while only 8.1 percent with an income over £250 did so; of those with an income under £125, a mere 1.2 percent drank tea with their morning meal. Sir W. Crawford and H. Broadley, *The People's Food* (1938), quoted in John Burnett, *Liquid Pleasures: A Social History of Drinks in Modern Britain* (London: Routledge, 2001), 88.

43. Wickizer, *Coffee, Tea and Cocoa*, 104.

44. Burnett, *Liquid Pleasures*, 89.

45. Cocoa consumption increased by 30 percent during the war. Gervas Huxley, "The Consumption of Tea," a lecture given to the City of London College, 2 December 1948 (London: International Tea Market Expansion Board, 1948), 12.

46. *Report on the Work of the Ceylon Tea Propaganda Board* (1940), 24, ITA Mss Eur F174/793.

47. John Burnett, *England Eats Out: A Social History of Eating Out in England from 1830 to the Present* (Harlow, England: Pearson/Longman, 2004); Rachel Rich, *Bourgeois Consumption: Food, Space and Identity in London and Paris, 1850–1914* (Manchester:

Manchester University Press, 2011); Brenda Assael, "Gastro-Cosmopolitanism and the Restaurant in Late Victorian and Edwardian London," *Historical Journal* 56, no. 3 (September 2013): 681–706; Judith R. Walkowitz, *Nights Out: Life in Cosmopolitan London* (New Haven: Yale University Press, 2012), especially chap. 4. Working-class consumers also had their public eating culture; see, for example, John K. Walton, *Fish and Chips and the British Working Class, 1870–1940* (Leicester: Leicester University Press, 2000). For an excellent study of the French origins of the modern restaurant, see Rebecca L. Spang, *The Invention of the Restaurant: Paris and Modern Gastronomic Culture* (Cambridge, MA: Harvard University Press, 2000). Exhibitions were also critical; see Nelleke Teughels and Peter Scholliers, eds., *A Taste of Progress: Food at International and World Exhibitions in the Nineteenth and Twentieth Centuries* (London: Routledge, 2015).

48. Derek J. Oddy, *From Plain Fare to Fusion Food: British Diet from the 1890s to the 1990s* (Suffolk: Boydell, 2003), 158–59. Also see Nadja Durbach, "Communal Feeding Centre to British Restaurant: Food and the State during World War II" (unpublished paper presented at the NACBS, Little Rock, Arkansas, November 2014).

49. Robert MacKay, *Half the Battle: Civilian Morale in Britain during the Second World War* (Manchester: Manchester University Press, 2002); Daniel Ussishkin, "Morale and the Postwar Politics of Consensus," *Journal of British Studies* 52, no. 3 (July 2013): 722–43. On school lunches, see Vernon, *Hunger,* 161–66 and Susan Levine, *School Lunch Politics: The Surprising History of America's Favorite Welfare Program* (Princeton: Princeton University Press, 2010).

50. Quoted in Hammond, *Food,* 2:383; Atkins, "Communal Feeding in Wartime."

51. Hammond, *Food,* 2:393.

52. Ibid., 411.

53. Vere Hodgson, *Few Eggs and No Oranges: A Diary Showing How Unimportant People in London and Birmingham Lived through the War Years, 1940–45* (London: Dennis Dobson, 1976), 176.

54. Quoted in Jane Pettigrew, *A Social History of Tea* (London: The National Trust, 2001), 161.

55. Quoted in Perilla Kinchin, *Tea and Taste: The Glasgow Tea Rooms, 1875–1975* (Oxford: White Cockade, 1991), 159.

56. During the war, Kardomah controlled 2.12 percent of all British coffee sales. "Brief Survey of the Café Trade," included in the Report of the Directors for the year ending 25 September 1943, Kardomah Ltd., Minute Book, no. 4, 1940–44, Typhoo Archive, Moreton.

57. Ibid.

58. Managing director's report to the Board of Directors, October and November 1940, Kardomah Ltd., Minute Book, no. 4, 1940–44, Typhoo Archive, Moreton.

59. The chairman's speech, annual meeting, 30 December 1940, 2, Kardomah Ltd., Minute Book, no. 4, 1940–44, Typhoo Archive, Moreton.

60. Managing director's review of the year ending 27 September 1941, 2, Kardomah Ltd., Minute Book, no. 4, 1940–44, Typhoo Archive, Moreton.

61. "All Lyons Teashops Converted to Cafeteria Service," *Caterer and Hotel Keeper* (28 August 1942): 7; report of the Board of Directors for the year ending 26 September 1942, 2, Kardomah Ltd., Minute Book, no. 4, 1940–44, Typhoo Archive, Moreton.

62. Huxley, "The Consumption of Tea," 11.
63. Hammond, *Food*, 2:714.
64. Griffiths, *History of Indian Tea*, 367.
65. Drummond, *Food*, 2:714.
66. Huxley, "Consumption of Tea," 11.
67. "Movements of Members of the Technical Department," *Report of the ITMEB* (December 1940), 3, ITA Mss Eur F74/961.
68. T. R. Nevett, *Advertising in Britain: A History* (London: Heinemann, 1982), 169–70.
69. Siân Nicholas, *The Echo of War: Home Front Propaganda and the Wartime BBC, 1939–1945* (Manchester: Manchester University Press, 1996), 2–3.
70. Ibid.
71. Huxley, *Both Hands*, 187.
72. Ibid., 188–89.
73. Charles F. McGovern, *Sold American: Consumption and Citizenship, 1890–1945* (Chapel Hill: University of North Carolina Press, 2006), 260, 265. Also Roland Marchand, "Customer Research as Public Relations: General Motors in the 1930s," in *Getting and Spending: European and American Consumer Societies in the Twentieth Century*, ed. Susan Strasser, Charles McGovern, and Matthias Judt (Cambridge: Cambridge University Press, 1998), 85–109.
74. Stefan Schwarzkopf, "Who Said 'Americanization'? The Case of Twentieth-Century Advertising and Mass Marketing from a British Perspective," in *Decentering America*, Jessica C. E. Gienow-Hecht (New York: Berghahn Books, 2007), 23–72. For Britain, see Scott Anthony, *Public Relations and the Making of Modern Britain: Stephen Tallents and the Birth of a Progressive Media Profession* (Manchester: Manchester University Press, 2012); Jacquie L'Etang, *Public Relations in Britain: A History of Professional Practice in the 20th Century* (London: Lawrence Erlbaum, 2004); John Ramsden, *The Making of the Conservative Party Policy: The Conservative Research Department since 1929* (London: Longman, 1980); and Philip M. Taylor, *The Projection of Britain: British Overseas Publicity and Propaganda, 1919–1939* (Cambridge: Cambridge University Press, 1981).
75. Schwarzkopf, "A Radical Past?" 44.
76. The Labour Party promoted a similar vision. See Laura Beers, *Your Britain: Media and the Making of the Labour Party* (Cambridge, MA: Harvard University Press, 2010), especially 139–85.
77. This quote was cited in a letter Ernest Gourlay sent to Earl Newsom, 19 March 1941, Tea Bureau Correspondence, Newsom Papers, Box M96–2, Gourlay File, Wisconsin Historical Society. Madison.
78. Ibid.
79. Ibid.
80. *Report of the ITMEB*, 1940, 12.
81. ITMEB advertisement, *The West Australian* (Perth), 10 June 1941, 9.
82. Postcard, 1942, Australian Military, Acc. No. H97, 248/367—pc001196, State Library of Victoria.
83. Natal's production accounted for only about 5 percent of domestic needs. Average imports for 1935–39 were 7,580 tons and in 1943 they reached 9,700 tons, but in 1944–45 they dropped to 6,200 tons. J. M. Tinley, *South African Food and Agriculture in World War II* (Stanford: Stanford University Press for the Stanford Food Research Institute, 1954), 66.

84. *BW*, 2 May 1942.

85. Industries sold their products in different ways, however, even though they all used national appeals. See Lisa Jacobson, "Beer Goes to War: The Politics of Beer Promotion and Production in the Second World War," *Food, Culture and Society* 12, no. 3 (2009): 275–312.

86. Johnston Birchall, *Co-op: The People's Business* (Manchester: Manchester University Press, 1994), 136.

87. Ibid.

88. Ibid.

89. A truck driver, for example, enjoyed his tea in a garage canteen in "This Is a Good Cup of Tea!" 8 August, no year but likely 1941. CWS 1/14/4, CWS Archive, Mitchell Library, Glasgow.

90. Advertisement, 1 August, CWS 1/14/4, CWS Archive, Mitchell Library, Glasgow.

91. Advertisement, 15 August, CWS 1/14/4, CWS Archive, Mitchell Library, Glasgow.

92. Advertisement, 25 July, CWS 1/14/4, CWS Archive, Mitchell Library, Glasgow.

93. "Tea Sense," 11 April, CWS 1/14/4, CWS Archive, Mitchell Library, Glasgow.

94. *Report of the ITMEB* (1941), 10–11. Also see the 1942 *Report*, 4–5, ITA Mss Eur F174/961.

95. *Report of the ITMEB* (1943), 4, ITA Mss Eur F174/961.

96. *Report of the ITMEB* (1944), 4, ITA Mss Eur F174/961.

97. *Tea Centre Publications*, ITA Mss Eur F174/802. See, for example, James Laver's, *Eating Out*; *The Camper's Cup of Tea*; *Tea for the Services*; *A Portfolio of Canteen Kitchen Services*; *The English Tea Pot*; *Serving Tea in Industry*; *Tea and Tea Cakes*; a children's coloring book titled *Boodoo and Sookoo*, which depicted life on an Indian tea garden; Osbert Lancaster, *The Story of Tea* and his *Tea on Service*; and several other publications of this kind.

98. C. G. Gardiner, *Canteens at Work* (Oxford: Oxford University Press, 1941), ix–x.

99. Indeed, I suspect this wartime and postwar tea campaign influenced Sidney Mintz's interpretation of the brew in *Sweetness and Power*. Mintz was from New Jersey, but his mother was a labor organizer who may have encountered such rhetoric about tea during and after the war.

100. *Feeding the Young Worker* (London: Empire Tea Bureau, 1944), Bin A4, Typhoo Archive, Moreton. *Feeding the Young Worker*, which was funded by the National Catering Service, the Factory Department of the Ministry of Labour and National Service, the Air Ministry, Ministry of Food and Board of Education, the Industrial Health Research Board, National Whitley Council, and the Scottish Special Housing Association, never explicitly mentions tea but emphasizes health and efficiency and the value of collective feeding in factories and other industrial settings.

101. Empire Tea Bureau advertisement, "Tea for the Workers: How It Helps Keep up Production Level," 1946/47, Ogilvy and Mather Misc. Client's Guard Book, 1931–57, HAT/OM (L) 32, History of Advertising Trust, Norwich.

102. *Report of the ITMEB* (1940), 48, ITA Mss Eur F174/924.

103. Ibid. 48–50.

104. "Appendix II: Annual Report on Propaganda Operations in India during the period April 1, 1942 to March 31, 1943," *Report of the ITMEB* (1943), 28–30, ITA Mss Eur F174/924.

105. Amritananda Das, Peter Philip, and S. Subramanian, *The Marketing of Tea: Report on a Study Undertaken by a Team of Experts Sponsored by the Tea Industry* (Calcutta: Consultative Committee of Plantation Associations, 1975), 58; Rowland Owen, *India: Economic and Commercial Conditions in India: Overseas Economic Surveys* (London: HMSO, September 1952), 176.

106. Amartya Sen, *Poverty and Famines: An Essay on Entitlement and Deprivation* (Oxford: Clarendon, 1981), 52–85; Debarshi Das, "A Relook at the Bengal Famine," *Economic and Political Weekly* 43, no. 31 (2–8 August 2008): 59–64; Paul R. Greenough, *Prosperity and Misery in Modern Bengal: The Famine of 1943–1944* (New York: Oxford University Press, 1982).

107. Sugata Bose, "Starvation Amidst Plenty: The Making of Famine in Bengal, Honan, and Tonkin, 1942–45," *Modern Asian Studies* 24, no. 4 (1990): 709–11.

108. *CTPB Report*, 1941, 33, ITA Mss Eur F174/793.

109. Ibid., 28–32.

110. *Report of the ITMEB* (1939), 11, ITA Mss Eur F174/924.

111. "Appendix II: Report by the Commissioner on Propaganda Operations in India during the year April 1, 1938," in ibid., 48.

112. Ibid., 50.

113. Ibid., 53.

114. Ibid., 55.

115. Jan Breman, *The Making and Unmaking of an Industrial Working Class: Sliding Down the Labour Hierarchy in Ahmedabad, India* (New Delhi: Oxford University Press, 2004), 74.

116. "Appendix III, Report on Propaganda Operations in India during the Period April 1, 1939 to March 31, 1940," *Report of the ITMEB* (1940), 59–65, ITA Mss Eur F174/924.

117. "Appendix II, Report on Propaganda Operations in India during the Period April 1, 1940 to March 31, 1941," *Report of the ITMEB* (1941), 62, ITA Mss Eur F174/924.

118. *Report of the ITMEB* (1944), 33, ITA Mss Eur F174/924.

119. *Tea at Work* (London: Gas Council and the Tea Bureau, c. 1950s); *Tea for the Workers* (London: Tea Centre, c. 1950s), Bin A7 Typhoo Archive, Moreton.

120. Huxley, *Both Hands*, 196.

121. Morrison, *Tea*, 55.

122. Huxley, *Both Hands*, 197.

123. Ibid., 198.

124. *CTPB Report*, 1940, 22, ITA Mss Eur F174/793.

125. I suspect in reality there were many tensions around this service, as there were in these voluntary agencies in general. Nella Last, the famous wartime housewife who kept a diary of Mass Observation, described how her mobile canteen turned away soldiers and only served civilians. See her discussion in Patricia Malcolmson and Robert Malcolmson, *Women at the Ready: The Remarkable Story of the Women's Voluntary Services on the Home Front* (London: Little, Brown, 2013), 90. For these tensions, see James Hinton, *Women, Social Leadership, and the Second World War: Continuities of Class* (Oxford: Oxford University Press, 2002).

126. Forrest, *Tea for the British*, 232.

127. R. L. Barnes, *Tea Times* (December 1951), quoted in Forrest, *Tea for the British*, 232.

128. *CTPB Report*, 1940, 24, ITA Mss Eur F174/793.

129. "Third List of Gifts and Promises: National Y.M.C.A. War Service Fund," *The Times*, 13 February 1940, 5.
130. "Y.M.C.A Tea Cars en Route Overseas," *Montreal Gazette*, 11 July 1941, 13.
131. Ibid.
132. J. Mallet, East African Committee, YMCA, South African War Work Council to the National Secretary, SAWAS, Pretoria, 2 April 1941, W Box 12, DR 12/58, SAWAS, Canteens, Mobile and Otherwise, South African Women's Auxiliary Archive, South African National Defence Force Archive, Pretoria, South Africa.
133. *CTPB Report*, 1941, 11, ITA Mss Eur F174/793.
134. Ibid., 23.
135. "A Day in the Life: Girls of the Blitz Canteen," *Picture Post*, 1941.
136. *Report of the ITMEB* (1940), 12, ITA Mss Eur F174/924.
137. Children's supplement, *BW*, 9 May 1942.
138. "Hot Drinks Mean Much in the Jungle," *Cairns Post* (Queensland), 27 April 1944, 3.
139. Griffiths, *History of the Indian Tea Industry*, 369.
140. Farmer, *Food Companions*, 185–216.
141. For the cars' visit to Buckingham Palace, see www.britishpathe.com, ID #588.13. Huxley was present at this event and describes it in *Both Hands*, 198.
142. "Tea for Tommy Atkins," (1939), www.britishpathe.com, ID #1029.06.
143. Newsreel of Gracie Fields serving tea in France (1940), www.britishpathe.com, ID #1655.17.
144. *CTPB Report*, 1941, 22, ITA Mss Eur F174/793.
145. *CTPB Report*, 1941, 17, ITA Mss Eur F174/793.
146. *Report of the ITMEB* (1943), 4, ITA Mss Eur F174/924.
147. *Report of the ITMEB* (1944), 32, ITA Mss Eur F174/924.
148. For a broader discussion of such images, see Rose, *Which People's War* and Wendy Webster, *Englishness and Empire, 1939–1965* (Oxford: Oxford University Press, 2005), chap. 2. Several essays in Stuart Ward, ed., *British Culture and the End of Empire* (Manchester: Manchester University Press, 2001) are also helpful.
149. See, for example, the photograph of British officers sitting in the shade of a garden, likely in Tunisia, Catalogue #TR 44, Ministry of Information, Second World War Colour Transparency Collection, Imperial War Museum, London.
150. See, for example, Mary Louise Roberts, *What Soldiers Do: Sex and the American G.I. in World War II France* (Chicago: University of Chicago Press, 2013). For two other important new books, see Yasmin Khan, *India at War: The Subcontinent and the Second World War* (Oxford: Oxford University Press, 2015) and Judith Byfield and Carolyn Brown, eds., *Africa and World War II* (Cambridge: Cambridge University Press, 2015).
151. On how such images are created and circulated in British consumer culture, see Frank Mort, *Cultures of Consumption: Masculinities and Social Space in Late Twentieth-Century Britain* (London: Routledge, 1996).
152. Orwell made a similar point in "A Nice Cup of Tea," *Evening Standard*, 12 January 1946, reprinted in George Orwell, *Essays*, ed. John Carey (New York: Knopf, 1946), 991.
153. *Report of the ITMEB* (1940), 1, ITA Mss Eur F174/924.

CHAPTER 10. LEFTOVERS

1. Broadcast script of talk given on the Home Service, 7 April 1954, by Philip Witham, Tetley Group Archive (TGA), London Metropolitan Archive (LMA), 4364/01/006. In 1954 foreign (primarily British) companies controlled 86 percent of the 776,898 acres planted with tea in India. Sunat Kumar Bose, *Capital and Labour in the Indian Tea Industry* (Bombay: All-India Trade Union Congress, 1954), 46. For an overview of the industry in 1954, see Anthony Hyde, *New Global Strategy for Trade and Tea: The Dynamics of an Expanding Market* (New York: Tea Association of the United States, 1954).

2. In fact, many white and Eurasian planters and their wives continued to enjoy this colonial lifestyle. See, for example, Iris Macfarlane, "Memoirs of a Memsahib," in Alan Macfarlane and Iris Macfarlane, *Green Gold: The Empire of Tea* (London: Ebury Press, 2003), 1–27; Edward Bramah, *Tea and Coffee: A Modern View of Three Hundred Years of Tradition* (London: Hutchinson and Co., 1972), 8–10, 53–66; Beryl T. Mitchell, *Tea, Tytlers and Tribes: An Australian Woman's Memories of Tea Planting in Ceylon* (Adelaide, Australia: Seaview Press, 1996); "Kelavan" (Charles T. Brooke-Smith), *Two Leaves and a Bud: Tales of a Ceylon Tea Planter* (Colchester: Bloozoo Publishing, 2000); Navarathnam Uthayakumaran, *Life on Spring Valley: A Magnificent Tea Estate in Uva, Sri Lanka* (Castle Hill, Australia: Navarathnam Uthayakumaran, 2011); and Tony Peries, *George Steuart & Co. Ltd., 1952–1973: A Personal Odyssey* (Kohuwala, Nugegoda, Sri Lanka: Wasala Publications, 1973).

3. V. D. Wickizer, *Coffee, Tea, and Cocoa: An Economic and Political Analysis* (Stanford: Stanford University Press, 1951), 169.

4. Witham, BBC broadcast.

5. Bill Schwarz, *Memories of Empire*, vol. 1, *The White Man's World* (Oxford: Oxford University Press, 2011).

6. For an excellent summary, see the introduction to Christopher J. Lee, ed., *Making a World after Empire: The Bandung Moment and Its Political Afterlives* (Athens: Ohio University Press, 2010).

7. D. K. Fieldhouse, *Black Africa: Decolonization and Arrested Development* (London: Allen and Unwin, 1986); Josephine F. Milburn, *British Business and Ghanaian Independence* (Hanover, NH: University Press of New England, 1977); B. R. Tomlinson, *The Political Economy of the Raj, 1914–1947* (London: Macmillan, 1979); S. E. Stockwell, *The Business of Decolonization: British Business Strategies in the Gold Coast* (Oxford: Clarendon Press, 2000); and Maria Misra, *Business, Race, and Politics in British India, c. 1850-1960* (Oxford: Clarendon Press, 1999); Frank Heinlein, *British Government Policy and Decolonisation, 1945–1963: Scrutinising the Official Mind* (London: Frank Cass, 2002).

8. P. J. Cain and A. G. Hopkins, *British Imperialism, 1688–2000*, 2nd ed. (New York: Longman, 2002). Also see Raymond E. Dummett, ed., *Gentlemanly Capitalism and British Imperialism: The New Debate on Empire* (London: Longman, 1999) and Shigeru Akita, ed., *Gentlemanly Capitalism, Imperialism and Global History* (Houndmills, Hampshire: Palgrave Macmillan, 2002). On the multinational, see, for example, D. K. Fieldhouse, *Unilever Overseas: The Anatomy of a Multinational* (London: Croom Helm, 1978) and his *Merchant Capital and Economic Decolonization: The United African*

Company, 1929–1987 (Oxford: Clarendon, 1994) and Robert Tignor, *Capitalism and Nationalism at the End of Empire: State and Business in Decolonizing Egypt, Nigeria, and Kenya, 1945–1963* (Princeton: Princeton University Press, 1998), 16. For an introduction to this literature, see Alfred D. Chandler Jr. and Bruce Mazlish, eds., *Leviathans: Multinational Corporations and the New Global History* (Cambridge: Cambridge University Press, 2005); Geoffrey Jones, *The Multinational and Global Capitalism from the Nineteenth to the Twenty-First Century* (Oxford: Oxford University Press, 2005); Geoffrey Jones, *British Multinationals: Origins, Management and Performance* (Aldershot: Gower, 1986); Mira Wilkins, *The Emergence of Multinational Enterprise* (Cambridge, MA: Harvard University Press, 1970) and *The Maturing of the Multinational Enterprise* (Cambridge, MA: Harvard University Press, 1974).

9. Anne Orde, *The Eclipse of Great Britain: The United States and British Imperial Decline, 1895–1956* (New York: St. Martin's Press, 1996). On continuities, see Joseph Morgan Hodge, *Triumph of the Expert: Agrarian Doctrines of Development and the Legacies of British Colonialism* (Athens: Ohio University Press, 2007), 207–76.

10. Goutam K. Sarkar, *The World Tea Economy* (Delhi: Oxford University Press, 1972); *Tea: UN FAO Commodity Report*, August 1953 (Rome: UN FAO, 1953); Dieter Elz, *Report on the World Tea Economy* (Washington, DC: World Bank, 1971).

11. Nicholas J. White, "Decolonisation in the 1950s: The Version According to British Business," in *The British Empire in the 1950s: Retreat or Revival?* ed. Martin Lynn (Houndmills, Basingstoke: Palgrave Macmillan, 2006).

12. Jayeeta Sharma, *Empire's Garden: Assam and the Making of India* (Durham: Duke University Press, 2011), 238–41.

13. Yasmin Khan, *The Great Partition: The Making of India and Pakistan* (New Haven: Yale University Press, 2007). Also see Urvashi Butalia, *The Other Side of Silence: Voices from the Partition of India* (Durham: Duke University Press, 2000) and Gyanendra Pandey, *Remembering Partition: Violence, Nationalism and History in India* (Cambridge: Cambridge University Press, 2001); for an excellent recent collection, see Amritjit Singh, Nalini Iyer, and Rahul K. Gairola, eds., *India's Partition: New Essays on Memory, Culture, and Politics* (Lanham, MD: Lexington Books, 2016).

14. J. L. Llewellyn to Sir Percival Griffiths, "Notes on the Political Situation in India and Pakistan and Its Implications for the Tea Industry," 28 June 1948, 5–6, ITA Mss Eur F174/1124.

15. Ibid., 13.

16. Ibid., 16.

17. Llewellyn, "Indian Tea Association Adviser's Note," no. 3, 4 March 1948, 1, ITA Mss Eur F174/1124.

18. For some of the impact of this, see H. A. Antrobus, *A History of the Assam Company, 1839–1953* (Edinburgh: T. and A. Constable, 1957), 236–37.

19. *Tea Marketing Systems in Bangladesh, China, India, Indonesia and Sri Lanka* (New York: United Nations, 1996), 14; Willem van Schendel, *The Bengal Borderland: Beyond State and Nation in South Asia* (London: Anthem, 2005), 148.

20. Anthony G. Tasker, "The Problem of U.S. Tea Promotion," *The Spice Mill* (June 1948): 41.

21. Sir Percival Griffiths, *The History of the Indian Tea Industry* (London: Weidenfeld and Nicolson), 218–19. Pakistan banned the transport of goods through its

territory, cutting off Assam from Calcutta in early 1950. *Tea Times of Africa* (January 1950): 1.

22. K. L. Khaitan, Chairman's Address, annual meeting of the Cachar Branch of the Tea Association of India, *The Tea* (January 1965): 9.

23. Van Schendel, *Bengal Borderland*, 148.

24. K. M. deSilva, "Sri Lanka in 1948," *Ceylon Journal of Historical and Social Studies* 4, n.s. (1974): 107. Also see W. David McIntyre, *British Decolonization, 1946–1997* (New York: St. Martin's Press, 1998), 28–29.

25. Kumari Jayawardena, *Nobodies to Somebodies: The Rise of the Colonial Bourgeoisie in Sri Lanka* (London: Zed Books, 2002), 192–93.

26. Patrick Peebles, *The Plantation Tamils of Ceylon* (London: Leicester University Press, 2001), 225–26.

27. P. Kanapathypillai, *The Epic of Tea: Politics in the Plantations of Sri Lanka* (Colombo: Social Scientists' Association, 2011); Nira Wickramasinghe, *Ethnic Politics in Colonial Sri Lanka, 1927–1947* (New Delhi: Vikas, 1995).

28. Minutes of a Meeting of the Board of Directors, 17 July 1947, Kardomah Ltd. Minute Book, no. 5, Bin A15, Typhoo Archives, Moreton.

29. Bramah, *Tea and Coffee*, 99.

30. Assorted press cuttings on price campaigns, including tea (1955), Tweedy Papers, Accession 98/17/14, National Archives, Dublin, Ireland.

31. *Financial Times*, 28 July 1955; *Sunday Express*, 31 July 1955; Peter David Shore Papers, file titled "Labour Party and Consumer Policy, 1952–53," SHORE/3/57, London School of Economics.

32. Managing Director Report, Kardomah and Company, *Minutes of a Meeting of the Board of Directors*, 14 September 1955, Bin A15, Typhoo Archives, Moreton.

33. Bramah, *Tea and Coffee*, 151.

34. "Brief on Nationalisation of Tea and Rubber Plantations in Ceylon for Meeting with S. de Zoysa, Ceylon Minister of Finance," NA: DO 35/8580.

35. Mr. L. J. D. Mackie's speech before the 70th Annual General Meeting of the Ceylon Association reported in *The Times*, 5 January 1959, NA: DO 35/8580. Also see "Brief for Mr. Alport's meeting with representatives of the Ceylon Association," 22 October 1958, NA: DO 35/8580.

36. Louis Stephens, *Tea Share Manual, 1952* (London: Jones and Cornelius, 1953).

37. Stockwell, *Business of Decolonization*, 124. Also see Jacquie L'Etang, *Public Relations in Britain: A History of Professional Practice in the Twentieth Century* (London: Lawrence Erlbaum, 2004), 153.

38. E. D. Obrien, "Report on Ceylon," directed to the Special Committee of the Ceylon Association, London, Ceylon Association Minutes (1954–59), 6 May 1959, 2, NA: DO 35/8580.

39. Ibid., 5.

40. Ibid., 7.

41. Ibid., 8.

42. E. D. O'Brien, "Annex 'A': Publicity in Ceylon: Benefits of Company Ownership," NA: DO 35/8580.

43. N. Ramachanadran, *Foreign Plantation Investment in Ceylon, 1889–1958* (Colombo: Central Bank of Ceylon Research Series, 1963); Kidron, *Foreign Investments*;

M. Habibullah, *Tea Industry of Pakistan* (Dacca: Bureau of Economic Research, University of Dacca, 1964); Sarkar, *World Tea Economy*.

44. George Schwarz, "A Nice Cup of Tea," *Sunday Times*, 7 May 1950, cuttings on tea and coffee issues, 1950–52, LMA 4364/02/023, TGA, LMA.

45. S. A. Dange, introduction to Bose, *Capital and Labour*.

46. McFarlane, *Green Gold*, 228–32, 236–41.

47. Priyadarsshini Sharma, "Patriotism Is Needed Today," *The Hindu*, 8 August 2006, online edition. Fearing nationalization, British companies were selling off estates, spending very little on maintenance, and sending profits back to Britain. Roy Moxham, *Tea: Addiction, Exploitation, and Empire* (New York: Carroll and Graf, 2003), 207.

48. Piya Chatterjee, *A Time for Tea: Women, Labor and Post/Colonial Politics on an Indian Plantation* (Durham: Duke University Press, 2001); K. Ravi Ramen, *Global Capital and Peripheral Labour: The History and Political Economy of Plantation Workers in India* (London: Routledge, 2010). For Ceylon, see, for example, Ronald Rote, *A Taste of Bitterness: The Political Economy of Tea Plantations in Sri Lanka* (Amsterdam: Free University Press, 1986); Kanapathypillai, *Epic of Tea*; Ridwan Ali, Yusuf A. Choudhry, and Douglas W. Lister, *Sri Lanka's Tea Industry: Succeeding in the Global Market* (Washington, DC: World Bank Discussion Paper, 1997); and Youngil Lim, "Impact of the Tea Industry on the Growth of the Ceylonese Economy," *Social and Economic Studies* 17, no. 4 (1 December 1968): 453–67.

49. Sidney Pollard, *The Development of the British Economy, 1914–1950* (London: Edward Arnold, 1962), 356–410; David Kynaston, *Austerity Britain, 1945–51* (London: Bloomsbury, 2007); Arthur Marwick, *British Society Since 1945*, 4th ed. (London: Penguin, 2003), especially 3–73. For other interpretations of this period, see Peter Hennessy, *Having It So Good: Britain in the Fifties* (London: Penguin, 2007) and Avner Offer, *The Challenge of Affluence: Self-Control and Well-Being in the United States and Britain since 1950* (Oxford: Oxford University Press, 2006).

50. Heinlein, *British Government Policy*, 27; Allistair Hinds, *Britain's Sterling Colonial Policy and Decolonization, 1939–1958* (London: Greenwood, 2001); Gerold Krozewski, *Money and the End of Empire: British International Economic Policy and the Colonies, 1947–58* (Basingstoke: Palgrave, 2001); Toyin Falola, *Development Planning and Decolonization in Nigeria* (Gainesville: University Press of Florida, 1996); Michael Havinden and David Meredith, *Colonialism and Development: Britain and Its Tropical Colonies, 1850–1960* (New York: Routledge, 1993).

51. Philip Murphy, *Party Politics and Decolonisation: The Conservative Party and British Colonial Policy in Tropical Africa, 1951–1964* (Oxford: Oxford University Press, 1995).

52. Heinlein, *British Government Policy*, 56–58.

53. Caroline Elkins, *Imperial Reckoning: The Untold Story of Britain's Gulag in Kenya* (New York: Henry Holt, 2005); David Anderson, *Histories of the Hanged: Testimonies from the Mau Mau Rebellion in Kenya* (London: Phoenix, 2006).

54. Michael Lipton and John Firn, *The Erosion of a Relationship: India and Britain since 1960* (London: Oxford University Press, 1975), 19–28.

55. For the compromises India made between the 1950s and 1970s, see B. R. Tomlinson, *Economy of Modern India, 1860–1970* (Cambridge: Cambridge University Press, 1993). Hiranyappa Venkatasubbiah, *Indian Economy since Independence* (New York: Asia, 1961); Dwijendra Tripathi, *The Oxford History of Indian Business* (New Delhi: Oxford University Press, 2004), 282–325. For a brief but globally-oriented

overview of this period, see Jeffry A. Frieden, *Global Capitalism: Its Fall and Rise in the Twentieth Century* (New York: W. W. Norton, 2006), chap. 13.

56. Dennis. J. Encarnation, *Dislodging Multinationals: India's Strategy in Comparative Perspective* (Ithaca: Cornell University Press, 1989); V. N. Balasubramanyam and V. Mahambare, "FDI in India," *Transnational Corporations* 12, no. 2 (2003): 45–72.

57. J. S. Graham, Chairman of the ITMEB, *Report*, 1949, 5, ITA Mss Eur F174/961; *Report of the Plantation Inquiry Commission, 1956: Part I: Tea* (Delhi: Government of India Press, 1956), 1–12; G. D. Banerjee and Srijeet Banerji, *Global Tea Trade: Dimensions and Dynamics* (Delhi: Abhijeet Publications, 2008) and their study *Export Potential of Indian Tea* (Delhi: Abhijeet Publications, 2008).

58. United Nations Conference on Trade and Development, *Studies in the Processing, Marketing and Distribution of Commodities* (New York: United Nations, 1984), 3; Maxwell Fernando, *The Geography of Tea* (Colombo: Standard Trading Co., 2001).

59. Banerjee and Banerji, *Global Tea Trade*, 303; "The South American Way," *The Tea Flyer: "Two Leaves and a Bud": The Newspaper of the Brooke Bond Group* 11, no. 6 (May 1958): 1. Stalin encouraged production for domestic consumption in the USSR; the state did as well in Turkey and Argentina. Elz, *Report on the World Tea Economy*, 35–36.

60. *The Tea Industry* (Melbourne: Economics Department, Australia and New Zealand Bank, 1970), 24–25.

61. Fernando, *Geography of Tea*, 88–119.

62. A. W. Lovatt, "Tea in Malawi," *Marga* 3, no. 4 (1976): 123; John McCracken, *A History of Malawi, 1859–1966* (Surrey: James Currey, 2012), 167.

63. McCracken, *Malawi*, 167, 194–97; Robin Palmer, "The Nyasaland Tea Industry in the Era of International Restrictions, 1933–1950," *Journal of African History* 26, no. 2 (1985): 215–39, 220; Robin Palmer, "White Farmers in Malawi: Before and after the Depression," *African Affairs* 84, no. 334 (1985): 211–45.

64. Peter Bird, *The First Food Empire: A History of J. Lyons Co.* (London: Butler and Tanner, 2000), 160.

65. *Tea from British Africa* (London: Tea Bureau, 1950).

66. David Wainwright, *Brooke Bond: A Hundred Years* (Brooke Bond Liebig, Ltd.), 30–31.

67. *James Finlay & Company Ltd.: Manufacturers and East India Merchants, 1750–1950* (Glasgow: Jackson and Son, 1951), 108.

68. D. M. Etherington, "An Econometric Analysis of Smallholder Tea Growing in Kenya" (PhD diss., Stanford University, 1970), 8–9. For a comparison with coffee, see W. G. Clarence-Smith and Steven Topik, eds., *The Global Coffee Economy in Africa, Asia, and Latin America, 1500–1989* (Cambridge: Cambridge University Press, 2003), 11.

69. Charles Hornsby, *Kenya: A History since Independence*, reprint ed. (New York: I. B. Tauris, 2012), 49.

70. Etherington, *Smallholder Tea Growing in Kenya*, 5–6.

71. Hornsby, *Kenya*, 134–35, 302.

72. *Kenya's Tea Estates: The Story of the Kenya Growers' Association* (1986), Bin A7, Typhoo Company Archive, Moreton.

73. *The Tea* 15, no. 3 (February 1965): 76; Denys Mostyn Forrest, *A Hundred Years of Ceylon Tea, 1867–1967* (London: Chatto and Windus, 1967), 248.

74. Ali, Choudhry, and Lister, *Sri Lanka's Tea Industry*, 50. In 2003 smallholders produced 46 percent of Sri Lanka's tea. Deepananda Herath and Alfons Weersink, "Peasants and Plantations in the Sri Lankan Tea Sector: Causes of the Change in Their Relative Viability," *Australian Journal of Agricultural and Resource Economics* 51, no. 1 (1 March 2007): 77. Sri Lanka's tea industry was restructured again in 1977. Sunil Bastian, *The Tea Industry since Nationalisation* (Colombo: Centre for Society and Religion, 1981).

75. Bastian, *Tea since Nationalisation*, 53. Pakistan absorbed 16.2 percent of Ceylon's tea.

76. Ibid., 19.

77. Ali, Choudhry, and Lister, *Sri Lanka's Tea Industry*, 45–46. Much higher taxes, including the cess, transport, and other costs, made Sri Lanka's tea more expensive to produce than that of India or Kenya, Bastian, *Tea since Nationalisation*, 70, 91–92.

78. Hans-Joachim Fuchs, "'Ceylon Tea': Development and Changes," in *Sri Lanka Past and Present: Archaeology, Geography, Economics*, ed. Manfred Domrös and Helmet Roth (Weikersheim: Margraf Verlag, 1998), 152–67. In 1996, 1.2 million workers labored in the industry; 40 percent of the tea is plantation grown and the rest is cultivated by smallholders (156).

79. In 1947 India produced 592.5 million pounds, while Ceylon produced 298.5 million pounds. Rowland Owen, *India: Economic and Commercial Conditions in India: Overseas Economic Surveys* (London: HMSO, March 1949), 84. Griffiths, *History of the Indian Tea Industry*, especially chaps. 17–19. These statistics don't include tea traded directly for wheat with the Soviet Union. Also, India was the first country to protest South Africa's racial politics by severing trade relations on 12 March 1946. T. G. Ramamurthi, *Fight against Apartheid: India's Pioneering Role in the World Campaign against Racial Discrimination in South Africa* (New Delhi: ABC Publishing House, 1984), 57.

80. Amritananda Das, Peter Philip, and S. Subramanian, *Marketing of Tea: Report on a Study Undertaken by a Team of Experts Sponsored by the Tea Industry* (Calcutta: Consultative Committee of Plantation Associations, 1975), 58.

81. P. N. Agarwala, *The History of Indian Business: A Complete Account of Trade Exchanges from 3000 B.C. to the Present Day* (New Delhi: Vikas, 1985), 347.

82. Das, Philip, and Subramanian, *Marketing of Tea*, 58.

83. Ibid., 61.

84. Dan M. Etherington, "The Indonesian Tea Industry," *Bulletin of Indonesian Economic Studies* 10, no. 2 (1974): 87–89.

85. Ibid., 89.

86. Ibid., 94.

87. Dan M. Etherington and Keith Forster, *Green Gold: The Political Economy of China's Post-1949 Tea Industry* (New York: Oxford University Press, 1993).

88. Ibid., 85–86.

89. Ibid., 203–5.

90. Henry Benjamin Wheatley, *London Past and Present: Its History, Associations and Traditions* (1891; Cambridge: Cambridge University Press, 2011), 2:546.

91. "Moreton—Production Center for Cadbury Biscuits and Typhoo Tea, prepared in February 1983," Bin #A9, Typhoo Company Archives, Moreton.

92. *Report of the Executive Committee of the Tea Buyers' Association*, 1955.

93. Denys Mostyn Forrest, *Tea for the British: The Social and Economic History of a Famous Trade* (London: Chatto and Windus, 1973), 256–57.

94. *Marketing and Distribution of Commodities*, 3–7.

95. *Marketing and Processing of Tea*, 7. The use of container ships also altered the geography of tea distribution. See *Retail Business, Special Issue on Tea*, no. 320 (October 1984): 28.

96. Papers related to the Chettur Ad Hoc Committee, 1949–50, 6 September 1949, ITA Mss Eur F174/829; *Report of the Committee of the Bengal Chamber of Commerce, 1950*, 26, ITA Mss Eur F174/2203.

97. *Tea Marketing Systems*, 24; Llewellyn, "Indian Tea Association Adviser's Note, no. 3," 3, ITA Mss Eur F174/1124.

98. "Tea Notes, produced by Thomson, Smithett and Ewart, Ltd., c. 1963," ITA Mss Eur F174/2296.

99. *Tea Digest* (Calcutta: Calcutta Tea Traders Association, 1975), 13.

100. Lipton's opened a new packing facility in West Punjab. *Proceedings of the Tea Conference held at Sylhet, 26 and 27 January 1949* (Karachi: Governor General's Press, 1949), 4. 54 (PAK) 4, London School of Economics-Government Publications. Lyons opened a new packing factory at Pinetown near Durban, which it named Cadby Hall. *Tea Times of Africa* (September 1948): 5. Also see "Prosperity for Kenya: This Is What the Tea Industry Means," *The Tea Flyer* 6, no. 1 (January 1962): 3.

101. *The Times*, 30 January 1937, 9.

102. Harry Kissin, "Commodity Traders' Role in Exports," *The Times*, 13 April 1970, 9; John Dunning and Victor E. Morgan, eds., *An Economic Study of the History of London* (London: George Allen and Unwin, 1971), 340–41, 351.

103. Forrest, *Tea for the British*, 262.

104. John Sutherland Hamilton, *Tea: The Colonial Legacy* (Cambridge: Cambridge World Development Action Group, 1975), 1.

105. Ibid., 5.

106. Quote from 1953 F.A.O. Report cited in Hamilton, *Tea*, 5.

107. Hamilton, *Tea*, 7.

108. In 1977, prices were half of what they had been in 1962. *Report on the Fourth Intergovernmental Group on Tea to the Committee on the Commodity Problems* (London: UN FAO Report, 1977), 1. On tea and development politics, see Banerjee and Banerji, *Global Tea Trade* and their *Export Potential of Indian Tea*.

109. Minutes of the 74th Annual Meeting of the ITMEB, London, 25 September 1947, ITA Mss Eur F174/961.

110. F. E. B. Gourlay, "Developments of the Board's Work in Africa: Confidential, for the use of the Directors and Representatives Only (5 June 1947)," in ibid.

111. Ibid., 3. Gourlay didn't mention or was unaware that due to economic sanctions Indian tea could no longer be sold in South Africa after 1946.

112. Ibid., 5.

113. Ibid.

114. Ibid.

115. Verbal report by C. J. Harpur at the 74th ITMEB Annual Meeting, 8 October 1947, 6.

116. Ibid., 9.
117. Mark Pendergrast, *For God, Country and Coca-Cola*, rev. ed. (New York: Basic Books, 2000), 233. Coke established beachheads in South Africa, Australia, and Trinidad in the late 1930s. Giebelhaus, "The Pause That Refreshed the World: The Evolution of Coca-Cola's Global Marketing Strategy," in *Adding Value: Brands and Marketing in Food and Drink*, ed. Geoffrey Jones and Nicholas Morgan (London: Routledge, 1994), 199–200. Consumers changed the meanings and nature of the drink; see Daniel Miller, "Coca-Cola: A Black Sweet Drink from Trinidad," in *Material Cultures: Why Some Things Matter*, ed. Daniel Miller (Chicago: University of Chicago Press, 1998).
118. H. W. Brands, "Coca-Cola Goes to War," *American History* 34, no. 3 (August 1999): 30–36; Robert J. Foster, *Coca-Globalization: Following Soft Drinks from New York to New Guinea* (New York: Palgrave Macmillan, 2008), 37–38.
119. Pendergrast, *For God, Country and Coca-Cola*, 201.
120. John Burnett, *Liquid Pleasures: A Social History of Drinks in Modern Britain* (London: Routledge, 1999), 104; Derek Cooper, *The Beverage Report* (London: Routledge and Kegan Paul, 1970), 49.
121. Cooper, *Beverage Report*, 50.
122. Burnett, *Liquid Pleasures*, 107.
123. "Tea and Soft Drinks," *Tea Times of Africa* (October 1948): 6.
124. Richard Kuisel, *Seducing the French: The Dilemma of Americanization* (Berkeley: University of California Press, 1993), 52–69.
125. Victoria De Grazia, *Irresistible Empire: America's Advance through Twentieth-Century Europe* (Cambridge, MA: Belknap Press of Harvard University Press, 2005).
126. Gervas Huxley, "International Newsletter, #4—Functions and Organization of a Bureau," *The International Tea Market Expansion Board Proceedings*, 1947, 1, ITA Mss Eur F174/961.
127. *Report of the ITMEB*, no. 14 (1949), 2, ITA Mss Eur F174/961.
128. *Report of the Tea Buyers' Association, 1952–53*, 14.
129. Memorandum from Newsom to K. P. Chen, "The Tea Bureau and Its Operation," 4 April 1946, 1, Newsom Papers, Box 48/20, Wisconsin Historical Society, Madison.
130. Jones, *Merchants to Multinationals*, 270.
131. "The International Tea Market Expansion Board," *Tea Trade and Industry* (April 1952): 195–97.
132. Habibullah, *Tea Industry of Pakistan*, 31.
133. Pakistan's Tea Board helped develop the domestic market, but in 1955 it intensified work in foreign markets with the hope of increasing foreign exchange earnings. *Proceedings of the Tea Conference Held at Sylhet, 26 and 27 January 1949* (Karachi: Governor General's Press, 1949); 54 (PAK) 41, London School of Economics-Government Publications; Habibullah, *Tea Industry of Pakistan*, 126, 264, 267.
134. "Comments by the Tea Brokers' Association of London, on the Questionnaire issued by the Government of India's Ministry of Commerce and the Ad Hoc Committee on Tea," papers related to the Chettur Ad Hoc Committee, 1949–50, 6 September 1949, ITA Mss Eur F174/829. On the purpose and function of the committee, see *Central Tea Board, First Annual Report* (Calcutta, 1951), 22–24.

135. Tea and Coffee Association of Canada, Responses, 6 June 1949, and the Tea Association of the United States Responses, 28 July 1949, papers related to the Chettur Ad Hoc Committee, 1949–50, ITA Mss Eur F174/829.
136. ITMEB replies to questionnaire, 30 May 1949, papers related to the Chettur Ad Hoc Committee, 1949–50, ITA Mss Eur F174/829.
137. "The International Tea Market Expansion Board," *Tea Trade and Industry* (April 1952): 197.
138. *Report of the Work of the CTPB* (1949), 19, ITA Mss Eur F174/793.
139. *Central Tea Board, First Annual Report* (1951), 3–4, 7–15.
140. Owen, *India*, 177.
141. "New Campaigns," *Tea Promotion* 2 (January 1950): 4, 10; "Tea Promotion in West Africa," *Tea Promotion* 3 (May, 1950): 2–5; *Tea Times of Africa, 1948–1951* (September 1948): 1.
142. These numbers are based on the estimates of expenditures given in *ITMEB Report*, no. 16 (1951): 6.
143. *Tea Trade and Industry* (January 1952): 15.
144. Huxley, *Both Hands*, 211.
145. *ITMEB Report* (1946), 7, ITA Eur F174/961.
146. On Regent Street's commercial culture in particular, see Erika Rappaport, "Art, Commerce, or Empire? The Rebuilding of Regent Street, 1880–1927," *History Workshop Journal* 53 (Spring 2002): 73–94.
147. Judith R. Walkowitz, *Nights Out: Life in Cosmopolitan London* (New Haven: Yale University Press, 2012); Frank Mort, *Cultures of Consumption: Masculinities in Late Twentieth-Century Britain* (London: Routledge, 1996) and his recent *Capital Affairs: London and the Making of the Permissive Society* (New Haven: Yale University Press, 2010); Justin Bengry, "Peacock Revolution: Mainstreaming Queer Styles in Post-War Britain, 1945–1967," *Socialist History* 36 (2010): 55–68.
148. Hugh Casson, as cited in Becky E. Conekin, *"The Autobiography of a Nation": The 1951 Festival of Britain* (Manchester: Manchester University Press, 2003), 35.
149. L'Etang, *Public Relations in Britain*, 81.
150. Conekin, *Autobiography of a Nation*, 35.
151. Huxley, *Both Hands*, 211.
152. *Tea Times* (November 1948): 2; "Verbal Report by the Commissioner, The Tea Bureau, U.K.," *ITMEB Minutes*, meeting 11 December 1947, ITA Mss Eur F174/963; "Planning—Tea Services," *Tea Promotion*, no. 3 (May 1950): 5–8; "Equipment for Tea," *Tea Promotion* (January 1950): 5–9.
153. I remember my family enjoyed a cup of tea at the Regent Street Tea Centre on a trip to London in 1973.
154. *Library Catalogue of the Tea Bureau* (London: Tea Centre Publication, 1951).
155. *A Good Cup of Tea* (London: The Tea Centre, 1946), 1; "Tea-Making for Caterers," *Tea Times* (December 1949); "Tea Making Courses for Industry," *Tea Times* (August 1949): 11; "The Bureau at Glasgow and Liverpool," *Tea Times* (November 1949): 6; "Tea in Hospitals," *Tea Times* (November 1948): 10.
156. "'Projects' on Tea," *Tea Times* (November 1948): 12.
157. The first two exhibitions, "The English Tea-Table" and "Tea Round the World—With B.O.A.C.," emphasized tea's Englishness and its cosmopolitan modernity. *ITMEB Report*, 1946, 7, ITA Mss Eur F174/961.

158. *Tea: A Progressive Industry* (London: The Tea Centre, 1950), 24.

159. *Tea Promotion* (November 1951): 2–5.

160. Oliver Warner, *Tea in Festival* (London: The Tea Centre, 1951), 12. For examples of this material, see Inner London Educational Authority, Schools Department, Catering Branch, ILEA/S/CS/10/031, LMA.

161. *Tea Times* (October 1949): 2.

162. *Tea Leaf: Display Ideas about Tea and the Things That Go with It*, August/September 1959, July 1961, and June 1960.

163. Exhibition pamphlet, "The Romance of Tea," 13 January to 8 February 1949, ITA Mss Eur F174/963.

164. See, for example, Huxley, *Talking of Tea*.

165. *ITMEB Report* (1949), 25, ITA Mss Eur F174/961.

166. "Tea as a Beverage for West Africans," *Crown Colonist* (August 1950): 479. I'd like to thank Bianca Murillo for bringing this article to my attention.

167. Ibid.

168. "The International Tea Market Expansion Board," *Tea Trade and Industry* (April 1952): 195–97.

169. Huxley, *Both Hands*, 214.

170. "Propaganda for Tea," *Tea Trade and Industry* (July 1953): 329.

171. *Times of Ceylon,* 10 January 1952, TGA, LMA/4364 02/024.

172. Huxley, *Both Hands*, 214.

173. *Tea Leaf*, October 1957.

174. *Tea Leaf*, April 1960.

175. *Glasgow Herald*, 4 August 1961, 5.

176. *Tea Leaf*, April 1963; *Birmingham Post*, 27 May 1963,

177. *Tea Leaf*, January 1964.

178. *Tea Leaf*, November 1965.

179. *Tea Leaf*, June 1961.

180. *Tea Leaf*, December 1958, 2.

181. *Tea Leaf*, May 1956 and July 1956; Ceylon Tea Centre ads, *Punch*, 1 December 1965; *Daily Mail*, 6 December 1965; *Grocery Marketing*, January 1966; *Grocers' Gazette*, 29 January 1966.

182. *Tea Leaf*, December 1958.

183. *Tea Leaf*, June 1961.

184. *Tea Leaf*, June 1960.

185. "How (and Why) Ceylon Teas Will Make Selling Profitable Again," *The Grocer*, 30 July 1966.

186. Ogilvy and Mather, *Survey of High Quality Tea: A Report Prepared for the Tea Council*, 21 September 1966, ITA Mss Eur F174/802.

187. "Notes on the Scheme for the Development of Tea Propaganda in India," 29, Central Tea Board of India, January 1955, 9–10, ITA Mss Eur F174/928.

188. *Central Tea Board Third Administrative Report* (1956–57), 47, ITA Mss Eur F174/2114.

189. Gautam Bhadra, *From an Imperial Product to a National Drink: The Culture of Tea Consumption in Modern India* (Kolkata: Centre for Studies in Social Sciences in association with Tea Board India, 2005).

190. Chatterjee, *A Time for Tea*, 108–14.

191. "Tea Propaganda in India," ITA Mss Eur F174/928.

192. Ibid., 34.

193. Ibid., 31.

194. *Central Tea Board Second Administrative Report*, 49.

195. *Indian Tea* (Calcutta: Tea Board of India, 196?), n.p.

196. Tea was not in fact a national drink but it was ubiquitous in Bengal. Studying a Gujarat village, sociologist A. R. Desai commented that while "formerly hardly a family was tea prepared daily. Now tea is drunk in almost all families, and some have it twice every day." A. R. Desai, *Rural Sociology in India*, 4th ed. (Bombay: Popular Prakashan, 1969), 366.

197. *Report on the Work of the CTPB* (1962), 5, ITA Eur MSS F174/793; "Notes on India," *The Tea* 14, no. 3 (March 1964): 87.

198. Michael Butterwick, *Prospects for Indian Tea Exports* (Oxford: Oxford University Press, 1965), 206–9.

199. Private companies sustained advertising and propaganda within India to expand their market share but also because advertising budgets offset taxable profits. A. S. Bam, "Indian Tea Industry and the Tea Board," *The Tea: A Monthly Journal on World Tea Plantation and Trade* 14, no. 6 (June 1964): 212–17.

200. Merchandising and Marketing Ltd., "Review of Advertising and Sales Promotion 1964/5," 3, presented to the Tea Board of India, ITA Mss Eur F174/2052.

201. "Financial Assistance for Export Houses," *The Tea* 14, no. 2 (February 1964): 52–53.

202. *Tea Board Fourth Administrative Report* (1959), 47–48, ITA Mss Eur F174/2114.

203. *Sri Lanka Tea Board Report for the Year 2002*, 48–49.

204. B. K. Goswami, "Indian Tea: A Bright Prospect in the Offing," *Capital* [Supplement] (12 April 1979): 98.

205. In 1965 the national average was still two-thirds of a pound per person. Butterwick, *Prospects*, 215.

206. Afshan Yasmeen, "Chai, Everyone's Cup of Joy," *The Hindu* (1 March 2002), http://www.thehindu.com/thehindu/lf/2002/03/01/stories/2002030100010200.htm.

207. "Tea Promotion in the USA," *Tea Trade and Industry* (November 1952): 569; Sir Percival Griffiths, *Report of the Indian Tea Delegation to the USA and Canada* (September/October 1954): 3, ITA Mss Eur F174/1275.

208. "Centre of Ceylon's Tea Propaganda Passes from London to United States," *Tea Trade and Industry* (April 1953): 202.

209. Huxley, *Both Hands*, 213.

210. "Tea Today in the USA," memo from U.S. Tea Bureau, 1951, Accession 2407, Subject Files, Box 6/ file 102e, Dichter Papers, Hagley Museum and Archives; "Tea Council of the USA," *Tea Trade and Industry* (July 1953): 357.

211. "Anthony Hyde," biography, http://prabook.com/web/person-view.html?profileId=365868.

212. "Tea Council of the USA," *Tea Trade and Industry* (July 1953): 357.

213. S. C. Datta, "A Visit to the United States," *Tea Trade and Industry* (August 1953): 420. Fred Rosen was the founder of Fred Rosen Associates, which in the 1950s worked for India and Italy, among other places. In 2000 his clients included American Express, Goldman Sachs, and the *New York Times*. See "Fred Rosen, 84, Dies," *New York Times*, 21 June 2000, http://www.nytimes.com/2000/06/21/nyregion/fred-rosen-84-dies-led-a-publicity-firm.html.

214. Datta, "A Visit to the United States," 425.

215. Anthony Hyde, "The Dynamics of an Expanding Market," in *New Global Strategy for Trade and Tea*, 1.

216. There were considerable tensions between the British and Americans who forged these agreements; John Maynard Keynes complained that Americans wanted to "pick out the eyes of the British Empire." Quoted in Frieden, *Global Capitalism*, 259.

217. Philip Mason, "Obituary: Sir Percival Griffiths," *The Independent*, 20 July 1992. Sir Percival's son, John Griffiths, was once president of the Liberal Party and is also a prolific writer who published *Tea: The Drink That Changed the World* (London: Andre Deutsch, 2007).

218. Griffiths argued for the renewal of the tea cess in the debate discussed on pages 256–59 above.

219. *Report of the ITMEB*, 1948, 1, ITA Mss Eur F174/961.

220. Sir Percival Griffiths, *Report of the Indian Tea Delegation to the USA and Canada* (September/October 1954). Annexure "A" listed formal functions and meetings but did not include private events or affairs. ITA Mss Eur F174/1275.

221. Ibid.

222. Ibid.

223. Griffiths, *Indian Tea Delegation to the USA and Canada*, 1954.

224. Ibid.

225. This was even true in the 1920s. See Katherine J. Parkin, *Food Is Love: Advertising and Gender Roles in Modern America* (Philadelphia: University of Pennsylvania Press, 2006), 2.

226. Tracey Deutsch, *Building a Housewife's Paradise: Gender, Politics and American Grocery Stores in the Twentieth Century* (Chapel Hill: University of North Carolina Press, 2010).

227. D. H. Kay, "Zeisel, Hans (1905–1992)," in *Encyclopedia of Law and Society: American and Global Perspectives*, ed. D. Clark (New York: Sage, 2007), 3:1599–1600.

228. Griffiths, *Report of the Indian Tea Delegation to the United States and Canada*, 1954, 6.

229. Daniel Horowitz, *The Anxieties of Affluence: Critiques of American Consumer Culture, 1939–1979* (Amherst: University of Massachusetts Press, 2004), 52.

230. Ibid.

231. Ibid., 54.

232. Quoted in Stefan Schwarzkopf and Rainer Gries, "Ernest Dichter, Motivation Research and the 'Century of the Consumer,'" in *Ernest Dichter and Motivation Research: New Perspectives on the Making of Post-War Consumer Culture*, ed. Stefan Schwarzkopf and Rainer Gries (Houndmills, Hampshire: Palgrave Macmillan, 2010), 9.

233. Letter summarizing a phone conversation between Dichter and Henry Starr, Research Director, Leo Burnett, Accession 2407, Box 6/file 102A, Dichter Papers, Hagley Museum and Archive, Delaware.

234. Ernest Dichter, "Can We Build a New 'Tea Culture' in the United States?" summary of speech to Annual Convention of the Tea Association of the USA, White Sulphur Springs, Virginia, 20 September 1955, Subject Files, Box 176, Dichter Papers, Hagley Museum and Archive, Delaware.

235. Ernest Dichter, "How to Make People Drink Tea: A Psychological Research Study," April 1951, Subject Files, Box 6, Dichter Papers, Hagley Museum and Archive.

236. Ibid., 15.

237. Ibid., 36.

238. Ibid., 44.

239. Ibid., 49.

240. Ibid., 32.
241. Ibid., 55.
242. Ibid., 14.
243. Dichter, "Can We Build a New 'Tea Culture,'" 3.
244. "Tea Goes to Town," *Tea Promotion* (March 1952): 3.
245. *Report on the Work of the CTPB* (1954), 23, ITA Mss Eur F174/793.
246. *Report on the Work of the CTPB* (1960), 26, ITA Mss Eur F174/793.
247. *Report on the Work of the CTPB* (1957), 26, ITA Mss Eur F174/793.
248. Ernest Dichter, "A Proposal for a Motivational Research Study on Lyons Tea," submitted to J. Lyons and Co., by the Motivational and Social Research Centre, Ltd., London office, April 1958, 2, 7, Dichter Papers, Hagley Museum and Archives, Delaware.
249. Ibid., 2.
250. Griffiths, *Indian Tea Delegation to the USA and Canada*, 1962, 8, ITA Mss Eur F174/1276.
251. Quoted in "Tea in the U.S.A.," *The Tea* 14, no. 2 (February 1964): 52.
252. Griffiths, *Indian Tea Delegation to the USA and Canada*, 1962, 3–4, ITA Mss Eur F174/1276.
253. Between 1946 and 1950 India had 38.4 million pounds, while Ceylon had 35.6. Between 1956 and 1960 India was down to 28.9 million and Ceylon had risen to 45.3 million (ibid.).

CHAPTER 11. "JOIN THE TEA SET"

1. The source of the chapter epigraph is: "Advice to the Tea Trade," *The Grocer*, 3 March 1962, Scrapbook J. Lyons Company Archive, Acc. 3527, London Metropolitan Archives (LMA) (hereafter Lyons Archive). Peter Mathias, *Retailing Revolution: A History of Multiple Retailing in the Food Trades Based upon the Allied Suppliers Group of Companies* (London: Longmans, 1967), chap. 18.
2. William Hardcastle, "The Cup of Tea, Another Valued Tradition Seems to Be Dying," BBC *Today Programme*, 20 May 1965, Telex Report, Telex Monitors Ltd., ITA Mss Eur F174/800.
3. Ibid.
4. *Financial Times*, 13 January 1958, LMA/4364/03/004, Tetley Group Archive (TGA), LMA. Also see "Suez! Brooke Bond in Egypt," *Tea Flyer: Two Leaves and a Bud* 1 (January 1957): 4 and "Brooke Bond in Egypt" (January 1957): 2; Minutes of a Meeting of the Board of Directors, 16 March 1956 and "Managing Directors' Report on Trading," 27 October 1956, Kardomah Ltd., Minute Book no. 8, Bin A15, 1955–58, Typhoo Archives, Moreton, UK. Another major issue was the political changes going on in Indonesia in this period.
5. John Burnett, *Liquid Pleasures: A Social History of Drinks in Modern Britain* (London: Routledge, 1999), 67.
6. Ibid., 90.
7. Roberto A. Ferdman, "Where the World's Biggest Tea Drinkers Are," *Quartz* (20 January 2014), http://qz.com/168690/where-the-worlds-biggest-tea-drinkers-are/; Lauren Davidson, "Is Britain Falling out of Love with Tea?" *The Telegraph* (5 August 2015), http://www.telegraph.co.uk/finance/newsbysector/retailandconsumer/11782555/Is-Britain-falling-out-of-love-with-tea.html.

8. Kaison Chang, *World Tea Production and Trade: Current and Future Development* (Rome: FAO, 2015).

9. Ridwan Ali, Yusuf Choudhry, Douglas W. Lister, *Sri Lanka's Tea Industry: Succeeding in the Global Market* (Washington, DC: World Bank Discussion Paper, 1997), 8–11.

10. There is a growing body of work on the cultural and social histories of decolonization. See, for example, Elizabeth Buettner, *Europe after Empire: Decolonization, Society, and Culture* (Cambridge: Cambridge University Press, 2016); Ruth Craggs and Claire Wintle, eds., *Cultures of Decolonisation: Transnational Production and Practices, 1945–70* (Manchester: Manchester University Press, 2016); Stuart Ward, ed., *British Culture and the End of Empire* (Manchester: Manchester University Press, 2001); Jordanna Bailkin, *The Afterlife of Empire* (Berkeley: Global, Area and International Archive and University of California Press, 2012).

11. *Evening Standard*, 11 April 1951, LMA/4364/01/005, TGA, LMA.

12. See headlines from the *Financial Times, Daily Telegraph, Daily Mirror*, and others in Cuttings Book II on General Tea and Coffee Issues, 1952–54, LMA/4364/02/024, TGA, LMA. For the history of rationing and its impact on 1950s politics, see Ina Zweiniger-Bargielowska, *Austerity in Britain: Rationing, Controls, and Consumption, 1939-1955* (Oxford: Oxford University Press, 2000). Other countries lifted controls much earlier. Holland, for example, ended tea rationing on 1 January 1949. *Tea Times* (February 1949): 9.

13. Tea Bureau ad, *Daily Telegraph*, 8 September 1952, LMA/4364/02/023, TGA, LMA.

14. *Newark Sunday News* (Newark, NJ), 12 October 1952, LMA/4364/02/023, TGA, LMA.

15. Brooke Bond ad, LMA/4364/02/024, TGA, LMA.

16. Central Tea Board of India ad, *The Times*, 12 October 1953, LMA/4364/02/023, TGA, LMA.

17. Becky Conekin, Frank Mort, and Chris Waters, eds., *Moments of Modernity: Reconstructing Britain, 1945–1964* (London: Rivers Oram Press, 1999), 1. Also see Becky Conekin, *The Autobiography of a Nation: The 1951 Festival of Britain* (Manchester: Manchester University Press, 2003) and Peter H. Hansen, "Coronation Everest: The Empire and Commonwealth in the 'Second Elizabethan Age,'" in *British Culture and the End of Empire*, ed. Stuart Ward (Manchester: Manchester University Press, 2001), 57–72.

18. Eric Wainwright, "Mash Me a Hot Sweet Brew," *Daily Mirror*, October 1952, LMA/4364/02/024, TGA, LMA.

19. Dudley Barker," *Daily Herald*, August 1952, LMA/4364/02/024, TGA, LMA.

20. *Daily Mirror*, 1 November 1952, LMA/4364/02/024, TGA, LMA.

21. *Tea Bureau: Third Consumer Survey among Housewives* (London: Tea Bureau, 1953), 3–4. The survey was conducted in April 1953, six months after derationing.

22. Petula Clark with Tony Osborne, "Anytime Is Tea Time Now," Polygon records, 1952, *The Caterer and Hotel Keeper*, 1 November 1952.

23. Black and Green advertisement, 1967, Press Cuttings and Advertisements, 1950–1969, LMA/4364/02/025, TGA, LMA.

24. Elizabeth Ho, *Neo-Victorianism and the Memory of Empire* (London: Continuum International Publishing, 2012); Antoinette Burton, "India, Inc.? Nostalgia, Memory and the Empire of Things," in *British Culture at the End of Empire*, ed. Ward, 217–32.

25. Co-op tea ad, *Daily Herald*, 2 February 1954, 5, LMA/4364/02/024, TGA, LMA.

26. Ridgways advertisement, *Evening Standard*, 7 July 1953, LMA/4364/02/024, TGA, LMA.
27. Horniman's advertisement, *Middlesex Hospital Concert*, 1953, LMA/4364/01/006, TGA, LMA.
28. Horniman's advertisement, *Sunderland Echo*, November 1952. For similar examples, see *Sunday Times*, 3 July 1966 and *Woman's Realm*, 12 November 1966. Even in the late 1960s Horniman ads joked about keeping tea in a 140-year-old tea caddy. See *South Wales Argus*, *South Wales Echo*, *Merthyr Express*, *Ponty Pridd Observer*, and others. Cuttings file for Horniman's Dividend Tea, 1961–67, LMA/4364/01/008, TGA, LMA.
29. Twinings ad, *The Caterer and Hotel Keeper*, 1 April 1961, 16.
30. *Leicester Evening Mail*, 22 September 1958, Tea Press Cuttings, 1958, LMA/4364/02/026, TGA, LMA.
31. "Saving the Cutty Sark," *Evening Standard*, 15 December 1952, 4. J. Lyons, the Tea Centre, Tea Trade Committee, and the advertising firm S. H. Benson contributed, for example. *Cutty Sark: A Brief Description of the Ship, Her Voyages and How She Came to Greenwich* (London: Cutty Sark Society, 1957).
32. *Tea Digest* (Calcutta: Calcutta Tea Traders Association, 1975), 29.
33. See, for example, *Norwood News*, 9 February 1954, and similar ads in the *Streatham News* and *Balham and Tooting News*. Tetley cuttings book regarding teabags, LMA/4364/03/004, TGA, LMA.
34. *Muswell Hill Record*, 1 April 1955, LMA/4364/03/004, TGA, LMA.
35. Tetley ad, 1954, no specific date given, LMA/4364/03/004, TGA, LMA.
36. Tetley ad, spring 1954, LMA/4364/03/004, TGA, LMA.
37. Lyons Quick Brew ad, *Woman's Realm*, 2 December 1963, Quick Brew Press Cuttings, LMA/4364/02/030, TGA, LMA.
38. *The Tea* 15, no. 4 (April 1965): 102.
39. Winston Fletcher, *Powers of Persuasion: The Inside Story of British Advertising, 1951–2000* (Oxford: Oxford University Press, 2008), 23–61.
40. Ibid., 27.
41. Ibid., 29–30.
42. "Chimpanzees Drinking Tea," *Tea Times of Africa* (March 1951): 1.
43. "The Chimps Have Been Invited to Butlin's," *The Tea Flyer* (May 1958): 1 and (August 1958): 5.
44. Tetley Tea Folk Facebook Page, 1 May 2015, https://www.facebook.com /TheTetleyTeaFolk?fref=ts.
45. A. Vinter, Ltd., "Tea Board of India: Summary of Sales Promotion Policy for the UK," 1967, 1, ITA Mss Eur F174/806.
46. "Tea in an Instant," *Retail Business* 23 (January 1960): 497.
47. A. Vinter, Ltd., "Tea Board of India: Summary of Sales Promotion Policy for the UK" (1966), marked confidential, ITA Mss Eur F174/806.
48. Vinter, "Summary of Sales Promotion Policy for the UK" (1967).
49. "Tea and Coffee in Canada," *Tea Times* (November 1948): 6.
50. Tea Association of Canada response to Chettur Ad Hoc Committee Questionnaire, 6 June 1949, ITA Mss Eur F174/829.
51. Sir Percival Griffiths, *Report of the Indian Tea Delegation to the U.S.A. and Canada, 1954*, pt. 2, 23, ITA Mss Eur F174/1275.
52. *The Tea Industry* (Melbourne: Economics Department, Australia and New Zealand Bank, 1970), 55–60.

53. Ibid., 56, 59. Also see *The Coffee Industry in Papua-New Guinea: An Economic Survey* (Canberra: Bureau of Agricultural Economics, 1951).

54. *The Tea Industry*, 55.

55. Ibid., 60.

56. "Market Appreciation and Brief for the Period October 1966 to September 1967, prepared for the Tea Council by Ogilvy and Mather Ltd., 1967," ITA Mss Eur F174/803.

57. "The Young Idea," *Tea Flyer* 9, no. 7 (July 1965): 1.

58. On the postwar consumer housewife, see Bianca Murillo, "Ideal Homes and the Gender Politics of Consumerism in Postcolonial Ghana, 1960–1970," *Gender and History* 21, no. 3 (November 2009): 560–75. Also see her *Market Encounters: Consumer Cultures in Twentieth Century Ghana* (Athens: University of Ohio Press, 2017); Judy Giles, *The Parlour and the Suburb: Domestic Identities, Class, Femininity and Modernity* (Oxford: Berg, 2004), chap. 3; Erica Carter, *How German Is She? Postwar West German Reconstruction and the Consuming Woman* (Ann Arbor: University of Michigan Press, 1997); Victoria de Grazia, *Irresistible Empire: America's Advance through Twentieth-Century Europe* (Cambridge, MA: Belknap Press of Harvard University Press, 2005), chap. 9 and Lizabeth Cohen, *A Consumers' Republic: The Politics of Mass Consumption in Postwar America* (New York: Knopf, 2003).

59. Following Dick Hebdige's interpretation, I see "youth culture as a politics of metaphor: it deals with the currency of signs and is, thus always ambiguous." "Hiding in the Light: Youth Surveillance and Display," in *Hiding in the Light* (London: Routledge, 1988), 35. For historical studies of this phenomenon, see Penny Tinkler, *Constructing Girlhood: Popular Magazines for Girls Growing Up in England, 1920–1950* (London: Taylor and Francis, 1995); David Fowler, *The First Teenagers: The Lifestyle of Young Wage-earners in Interwar Britain* (London: Woburn Press, 1995); David Fowler, *Youth Culture in Modern Britain, c. 1920–1970: From Ivory Tower to Global Movement— A New History* (London: Palgrave Macmillan, 2008); Jon Savage, *Teenage: The Creation of Youth Culture, 1875–1945* (New York: Viking, 2007); and Melanie Tebbutt, *Being Boys: Youth, Leisure and Identity in the Inter-War Years* (Manchester: Manchester University Press, 2012).

60. Harry Hopkins, *The New Look: A Social History of the Forties and Fifties in Britain* (Boston: Houghton Mifflin, 1964), 423.

61. Ibid., 424.

62. Ibid., 425–26.

63. Adrian Horn, *Juke Box Britain: Americanisation and Youth Culture, 1945–60* (Manchester: Manchester University Press, 2009), 171–78; Markman Ellis, *The Coffee House: A Cultural History* (London: Weidenfeld and Nicolson, 2004), 225–45; Joe Moran, "Milk Bars, Starbucks and the *Uses of Literacy*," *Cultural Studies* 20, no. 6 (2006): 552–73.

64. Christina Hardyment, *Slice of Life: The British Way of Eating since 1945* (London: BBC Books, 1995), 80.

65. Ian Samwell, "The History of the 2 i's Coffee Bar," Musicstorytellers Blog, http://musicstorytellers.wordpress.com. Also Anthony Clayton, "2i's," http://www.sohomemories.org.uk/index.aspx.

66. David Wainwright, *Brooke Bond: A Hundred Years* (London: Brooke Bond, 1969), 30–31.

67. For a film clip of Sutch performing "Jack the Ripper" in London in 1964, see https://www.youtube.com/watch?v=c2ZsWENob1s. For the place of Jack the Ripper in Victorian culture, see Judith R. Walkowitz, *City of Dreadful Delight: Narratives of Sexual Danger in Late-Victorian London* (Chicago: University of Chicago Press, 1992).

68. Key works include Stuart Hall and Tony Jefferson, eds., *Resistance through Rituals: Youth Subcultures in Post-war Britain* (London: Hutchinson, 1976); Dick Hebdige, *Subculture: The Meaning of Style* (London: Methuen, 1979); and Angela McRobbie, *In the Culture Society: Art, Fashion and Popular Music* (London: Routledge, 1999).

69. For the politics of the journal and its early history, see "A Brief History of *New Left Review*, 1960–2010," https://newleftreview.org/history.

70. Richard Hoggart, *The Uses of Literacy: Aspects of Working-Class Life with Special Reference to Publications and Entertainments* (London: Penguin, 1957), 246.

71. Ray Gosling, *Personal Copy: A Memoir of the Sixties* (London: Faber and Faber, 1980), 22.

72. Fowler, *Youth Culture*, 117, 122–44.

73. Gosling, *Personal Copy*, 24–25.

74. Ray Gosling, quoted in Hardyment, *Slice of Life*, 73.

75. Ray Gosling, *Sum Total* (London: Faber and Faber, 1962), 62.

76. Kate Bradley, "Rational Recreation in the Age of Affluence: The Café and Working-Class Youth in London, c. 1939–65," in *Consuming Behaviours: Identity, Politics and Pleasure in Twentieth-Century Britain*, ed. Erika Rappaport, Sandra Trudgen Dawson, and Mark J. Crowley (London: Bloomsbury, 2015), 71–86.

77. Gosling, *Personal Copy*, 65.

78. Peter Bird, *The First Food Empire: A History of J. Lyons & Co.* (London: Phillimore, 2000), 192–96.

79. "An Abstract of Non-Confidential Research Findings from Motivational Investigations Concerning Consumer Attitudes towards Tea and Coffee," submitted to J. Lyons and Co., London (London: Ernest Dichter Association, 1962), Accession 2407 (Box 49), 64, Dichter Papers, Hagley Museum and Archive.

80. Ibid., 56.

81. Ibid.

82. Ibid., 64.

83. Ibid.

84. "An Advertising and Public Relations Campaign for the Maintenance and Expansion of Tea Consumption in the U.K." (1964), 7, report produced by Mather and Crowther, Ltd., to the Tea Trade Committee, ITA Mss Eur F174/800. Also see "Market Appreciation and Brief for the Period, October 1966–September 1967 prepared for the Tea Council by Ogilvy and Mather Ltd., 1967," ITA Mss Eur F174/803.

85. Mather and Crowther, "Advertising and Public Relations Campaign," (1964), 15.

86. "Special Report on Coffee, Market and Prospects," *Retail Business* 21 (November 1959): 385.

87. *The Grocer*, 22 May 1965, 40.

88. *Sun*, 20 May 1965.

89. *The Times*, 21 May 1965. For a discussion of some of these changes, see E.J.T. Collins, "The 'Consumer Revolution' and the Growth of Factory Foods: Changing Patterns of Bread and Cereal Eating in Britain in the Twentieth Century," in *The Making of*

the Modern British Diet, ed. Derek J. Oddy and Derek S. Miller (London: Croom Helm, 1976), 26–43.

90. During 1965–66 these included the National Drinks Survey, a Tea Attitude Survey, the Attwood Catering Survey, and a Survey of High Quality Tea. See "Summary of Market Research Programme, 1965/66," prepared for the Tea Council by Ogilvy and Mather's Research Department, 3 March 1966, ITA Mss Eur F174/802.

91. *Report on the First Tea Attitude Survey, 1965*, prepared for the Tea Council by Ogilvy and Mather, 1965, ITA Mss Eur F174/802.

92. Various housewives' responses quoted in *Survey of High Quality Tea: A Report on the First Stage*, prepared for the Tea Council by Ogilvy and Mather, September 1966, ITA Mss Eur F174/802.

93. Ibid.

94. Ibid.

95. Ibid.

96. Ibid.

97. Ibid.

98. Mather and Crowther, "An Advertising and Public Relations Campaign, 1964."

99. Ibid.

100. See, for example, "Tea and Coffee in Canada," *Tea Times* (November 1948): 6; "Tea News from Africa," *Tea Times* (February 1949): 6–9; "Australia—A Great Tea Market," *Tea Times* (April 1949): 10–12; "Africa as a Potential Market," *Tea Times* (July 1949): 5–6.

101. "Join the Tea Set," *The Tea Flyer* 9, no. 9 (September 1965): 2.

102. "Propaganda for Tea in the United Kingdom," *Report of the General Committee of the Indian Tea Association* (1962–63), 2. For brief discussions of this body and the Join the Tea Set Campaign, see Denys Mostyn Forrest, *Tea for the British: The Social and Economic History of a Famous Trade* (London: Chatto and Windus, 1973), 279; Edward Bramah, *Tea and Coffee: A Modern View of Three Hundred Years of Tradition* (London: Hutchinson & Co. Ltd., 1972), 140; and Burnett, *Liquid Pleasures*, 68.

103. B. C. Ghose, presidential address, 49th Annual General Meeting of the Indian Tea Planters' Association, 16 May 1964; *The Tea: Monthly Journal on World Tea Plantation and Trade* 14, no. 5 (May 1964): 141.

104. "Britain in 1964—Expansion without Inflation," *The Tea* 14, no. 1 (January 1964): 29–31.

105. Vinter, "Summary of Sales Promotion Policy for the U.K. (1967)," 3.

106. Gervas Huxley, *Both Hands: An Autobiography* (London: Chatto and Windus, 1970), 215.

107. Fletcher, *Powers of Persuasion*, 42, 44; Stanley Pigott, *OBM: A Celebration: One Hundred and Twenty-five Years in Advertising* (London: Ogilvy Benson and Mather, 1975), 58. Ogilvy and Mather report, "Presentation to the U.K. Tea Trade," held at the Baltic Exchange, 20 September 1967, 114–15, ITA Mss Eur F174/805. On the milk campaign, see Deborah M. Valenze, *Milk: A Local and Global History* (New Haven: Yale University Press, 2011), 263. Also see Derek J. Oddy, *From Plain Fare to Fusion Food: British Diet from the 1890s to the 1990s* (Woodbridge: Boydell Press, 2003), 107–9.

108. Fletcher, *Powers of Persuasion*, 45.

109. Pigott, *OBM*, 61. The two firms kept their distinct names for a year.

110. *Tea Campaign News* 2 (January 1966): 11, ITA Mss Eur F174/2053. D. M. Forrest, who had been head of Ceylon's U.K. Tea Centres, retired in July 1965. *The Tea Flyer* 9, no. 7 (July 1965): 5.

111. Ray Culverhouse, biographical insert, *Tea: The Journal of the UK Tea Council* 1 (Autumn 1967): 1.

112. The Tea Trade Committee Drink More Tea Campaign memo, 10 August 1965, Tea Trade Committee Minutes, 1964–65, ITA Mss Eur F174/1299.

113. Minutes of an Emergency Meeting of the Tea Trade Committee held in London, 4 August 1965, Tea Trade Committee Minutes, 1964–65, ITA Mss Eur F174/1299.

114. Tea Campaign Bulletin #1, September 1965, Tea Trade Committee Minutes, 1964–65, ITA Mss Eur F174/1299.

115. Press and TV advertising expenditures in 1966, for example, stood at: beer £3,999,000, wines £3,156,000, health beverages and foods £2,525,000, tea (including Tea Council) £2,511,000, soft drinks £2,329,000, milk £1,824,000, and coffee and coffee extracts £1,650,000. See U.K. Advertising Expenditures, *Ogilvy and Mather Report Presented to the U.K. Tea Trade* (20 September 1967), 8, ITA Mss Eur F174/805. For percentage of overall sales, see page 7.

116. A. E. Pitcher, "Room in the Tea Set—An Advertising Appraisal," *Tea* 1 (Autumn 1967): 12; *Report of the Management Committee of the Tea Council Ltd* (November 1967), 7, ITA Mss Eur F174/1274.

117. "Notes on India," *The Tea* 14, no. 5 (May 1964): 153; ITA Report, *International Tea Promotion* (March 1971), 5–7, ITA Mss Eur F174/2213.

118. S. Guha, Editorial, *The Tea* 14, no. 2 (February 1964): 37.

119. "£2 Million over Three Years to Encourage Tea Drinking," *World Press News and Advertisers' Review*, 24 September 1965, 50.

120. Quoted in the article "Encourage the Younger Generation to Drink Tea," *The Tea* 14, no. 5 (May 1964): 157.

121. J. R. Hugh Sumner, *Ty-Phoo Tea (Holdings) Ltd. Report and Accounts, 1964*, 2 March 1965, Bin A9, Ty-Phoo Archives, Moreton.

122. "Whether You're 16 or 60 Join the Tea Set," *The Tea Flyer* 9, no. 8 (August 1965): 4.

123. Julian Palacios, *Syd Barrett & Pink Floyd: Dark Globe* (London: Plexus, 2010), 66.

124. I suspect that this band was created by the Dutch tea interests but haven't found evidence that supports my hunch.

125. *Tea Campaign News* 2 (January 1966): 2, ITA Mss Eur F174/2053.

126. "List of Singles Chart Number Ones of the 1960s," http://en.wikipedia.org/wiki /List_of_UK_Singles_Chart_number_ones_of_the_1960s.

127. "The Ivy League Official Website," http://www.theivyleague.co.uk.

128. *Tea Campaign News* 2 (January 1966): 3.

129. "A Time for Tea," report prepared by Ogilvy and Mather presented to the U.K. Tea Trade at the Baltic Exchange on 20 September 1967, ITA Mss Eur F174/805.

130. *New Musical Express* (7 February 1967), HAT OM (L) 02, Ogilvy and Mather Archive, History of Advertising Trust, Norwich.

131. "Meet the Tea Set Group," *The Tea Flyer* 10, no. 7 (July 1966): 6, ITA Mss Eur F174/2053.

132. *Tea Campaign News* 1 (November 1965): 1, ITA Mss Eur F174/2053.

133. "For a Teenage Party," *The Tea Flyer* 9, no. 9 (September 1965): 4; "Brooke Bond Has an Eye on the Younger Generation," *The Tea Flyer* 9, no. 9 (September 1965): 1.

134. "Top of the Pops," *The Tea Flyer* 9, no. 1 (January 1965): 1; *The Tea Flyer* 9, no. 5 (May 1965): 5.

135. *Tea Campaign News 2* (January 1966): 4, ITA Mss Eur F174/2053.

136. "A Time for Tea," ITA Mss Eur F174/805.

137. *The United Kingdom Tea Council Limited Annual Report* (1973/74), 5–10, ITA Mss Eur F174/804.

138. "Get to Know the Tea Set Tea Bar—It's a Swinging Place," *Slough Observer*, 22 November 1966.

139. *UK Tea Council Report*, 1973/74, 5–10, ITA Mss Eur F174/804.

140. Ibid., 10.

141. David Gray and Peter Watt, *Giving Victims a Voice: A Joint MPS and NSPCC Report into Sexual Allegations Made against Jimmy Savile* (January 2013), https://www.nspcc .org.uk/globalassets/documents/research-reports/yewtree-report-giving-victims -voice-jimmy-savile.pdf.

142. Eight of the original ads can be viewed on YouTube: https://www.youtube.com /watch?v=PMZ4Ztpybcw. Also see *Tea Council Annual Report*, 1969, 7, ITA Mss Eur F174/804.

143. *Tea Campaign News* 1 (November 1965): 1, Mss Eur F174/2053.

144. Tea Campaign Bulletin #1, September 1965, Tea Trade Committee Minutes, 1964–65, ITA Mss Eur F174/1299.

145. *Tea Campaign News* 1 (November 1965): 10, ITA Mss Eur F174/2053.

146. *Caterer and Hotel Keeper*, final proof of ad, 27 September 1968, HAT/OM (L) 30, Tea Council Ads, Ogilvy and Mather Archive, History of Advertising Trust, Norwich.

147. S. S. Jayawickrama, "The System of Marketing Tea—Improvements or Alternatives," *Marga* 3, no. 4 (1976): 72.

148. *Tea Buyers Association: Report of the Committee* (1969), 11, ITA Mss Eur F174/1263.

149. Michael Lipton and John Firn, *The Erosion of a Relationship: India and Britain since 1960* (London: Oxford University Press, 1975), 50.

150. "Tea Promotion: A New Approach," memo submitted to the Government of India by the Indian Tea Association and the United Planters of Southern India, 1972, 2, ITA Mss Eur F174/805.

151. Ibid., 7.

152. Paul Gilroy, *After Empire: Melancholia or Convivial Culture?* (London: Routledge, 2004), especially chap. 3.

153. Sidney W. Mintz, *Sweetness and Power: The Place of Sugar in Modern History* (New York: Penguin, 1985).

154. "Old and New Ethnicities," in *Culture, Globalization and the World System: Contemporary Conditions for the Representation of Identity*, ed. Anthony D. King (Minneapolis: University of Minnesota Press, 1997), 48–49.

155. Bailkin, *Afterlife of Empire*.

156. Joint CTC/ESCAP Unit on Transnational Corporations, *Transnational Corporations and the Tea Export Industry of Sri Lanka* (Bangkok: UN Economic and Social Commission for Asia and the Pacific, 1982), 12.

157. Ali, Choudhry, and Lister, *Sri Lanka's Tea Industry*, 17.

158. Dwijendra Tripathi and M. Mehta, *Business Houses in Western India: A Study in Entrepreneurial Response, 1850–1956* (New Delhi: Manohar, 1999); http://www.tataglobalbeverages.com.
159. On tea tourism, see Lee Joliffe, *Tea and Tourism: Tourists, Tradition and Transformations* (Buffalo: Channel View Publications, 2007); Indrani Dutta, "Harvesting Tourist Dollars in Tea Gardens," *The Hindu*, 26 October 2005; "Recrowning the Queen of Hills," *Hindu Sunday Magazine*, 27 April 2003; and R. Ramabhadran Pillai, "A Museum for Tea," *The Hindu*, 20 March 2004. For key industry websites, see UK Tea and Infusions Association, http://www.tea.co.uk; Tea Association of the USA, http://www.teausa.com/index.cfm; Sri Lanka Tea Board, http://www.pureceylontea.com; Indian Tea Association, http://www.indiatea.org; and Tea Association of Canada, http://www.tea.ca. The listing of current associations involved in tea promotion can be found on the website of the International Tea Committee, http://www.inttea.com/member_details.asp. Former tea factories have also been turned into museums and tourist sites. See, for example, the Dodabetta Tea Factory Museum in Nilgiris, Tamil Nadu, http://www.teamuseum-india.com/index.html. Tata Tea recently opened a tea museum on an estate in Munnar, Kerala; see http://www.keralatourism.org/destination/destination.php?id=191979895. Kerala's industry was particularly hard hit by another crisis in 2003. "A Bitter Brew in the High Ranges," *The Hindu*, 28 September 2003. See also the Ceylon Tea Museum in Kandy, http://www.ceylonteamuseum.com/about.html. In London this imperial history used to be chronicled at the Brahma Tea and Coffee Museum, but the museum closed in 2008. Twinings' shop in the Strand is still open to purchasers and tourists and exhibits the early modern and domestic history of tea in Britain; see http://twinings.co.uk/our-stores/twinings,-216,-strand,-london.
160. "India Tea Strikes Gold at London Olympics Village," *Hindustani Times*, 11 August 2012, http://www.hindustantimes.com/StoryPage/Print/912131.aspx#. See also "Indian Tea to Be Promoted during the London Olympics," *The Hindu*, 6 July 2012, http://www.thehindubusinessline.com/industry-and-economy/agri-biz/indian-tea-to-be-promoted-during-london-olympics/article3610253.ece.

ILLUSTRATIONS

MAPS

TABLES

INDEX

2i's coffee bar, 384–85, 388

abolitionism, 51, 65–66, 69, 80–81, 87, 120
Abrams, Mark, 315
Accum, Friedrich, 122–23
Adams, Abigail, 54
Adams, John, 54–55
Adams, John Quincy, 81
addiction, 112, 132, 253, 256
adulteration: in Australia, 189; as a
    consequence of free trade, 121–29, 337;
    and the creation of a negative image of
    Chinese tea, 51, 120–21, 129–43, 391;
    in India, 258, 261; and the promotion of
    Indian tea, 164–65,; in U.S., 204; and the
    Victorian food system, 121–25
advertising, 9, 14–15; and adulteration,
    120–21, 133–40; agencies, 184, 229–33,
    235, 273, 365, 282–83, 377, 389–94,
    477n42; American approach to, 228–29,
    365–73, in Australia, 188–90, 268, 281,
    289, 314, 316, 327, 357; brand-name,
    15, 178–81, 189, 210, 308, 379–80; in
    Canada, 190–91, 289, 315–16; Ceylon's
    approach to, 171–72, 185–86, 192–95;
    and decline of Chinese market, 133–40,
    147–82; generic (collective), 15, 268–82,
    292, 393, 410; global campaigns in, 183,
    268–71, 314, 280–304, 313–30, 349–61,
    in Great Britain, 39, 133–40, 147–48,
    151–52, 158, 163–82, 241–52, 264–65,
    271–80, 377–81, 389–403; and history,
    use of by, 11, 161, 173–75, 358, 363,
    367, 408, 414–15n33; and humor, 272,
    278–79, 400–401; impact of, 390–92,
    402; in India, 207–13, 252–62, 321–22,
    361–64, 517n19; as industry, 272, 310,
    365–73, 393, 468n111, 525n115; in
    South Africa, 290–304, 316–17, 349–52;
    as stimulating imperialism; 133–35, 158,
    159, 163–82, 235–37, 241–52, 313–31;
    and "Tea Revives You" campaign,
    264–304, 316, 327; in U.S., 15, 192–207,
    228–34, 284–88, 365–67; in wartime,
    314–34; to youth market, 389–404. *See
    also* branding; film; posters; television;
    and specific brands and marketing
    boards
Afghanistan, 211
Africa: consumer culture in, 290–304,
    316–17, 349–52, 359, 362; middle classes
    in, 294–304; tea markets in, 347; tea
    production in, 2, 14, 111, 114, 240, 243,
    335, 345, 348. *See also* specific cities and
    countries
African American consumer culture, 291
Afrikaner consumer culture, 293–94, 301
afternoon tea: decline of, 386–68; in India,
    256; invention of, 83–84; and neo-
    Victorianism, 409; as social ritual in
    Victorian England, 153–56; and the
    tea shop business, 168–69; in the U.S.
    205–6, 231; during World War I, 224–27
agency houses, 9, 87, 162, 211, 215, 222,
    340
Ahmed, Ziauddin, 259
All about Tea, 204, 414n33
Allied Suppliers, 308, 375
American Chain Stores Organization, 230
American business: and advertising
    industry, 272–73, 282–88, 365–73; as
    part of the British World, 191–207,
    228–34; selling British imperialism,
    316; and the tea trade, 114–16. *See also*
    United States Tea Association; United
    States Tea Council; and under specific
    companies
American tea culture. *See under* United
    States
American market empire, 184, 204, 366–68,
    372–73. *See also* Americanization
American Revolution, 40, 53–55, 190, 218,
    370, 407
American Temperance Society, 69
Americanization, 12, 184, 231, 314–15
    349–52, 365–72, 375, 382, 386–88,
    404–5. *See also* American market empire
Amery, Charles Frederick, 190, 466n58

Smith, Miss Lucinda, 114–15
Smith, Mrs. Nancy, 132
Smith, Sydney, 67
smuggling, 29, 40, 44–46, 48,
    50–51, 54, 64
Society of Public Analysts, 448n28
soda consumption, in UK, 351. *See also*
    Coca-Cola
soft power, 358
Soho, 384
soldiers, as market, 1–3, 212, 225–29,
    238, 305–6, 312–13, 316–18, 323–31,
    402, 406
Song of Ceylon, 247, 279, 491n78
South Africa, 79, 265, 290–301, 316–17,
    349–52
South African Tea Board, 324
South African War (Anglo-Boer War),
    134, 213
South African Women's Auxiliary Service,
    324–25
South Indian Association, 240, 266
South Sea Islands, 79–80
South-South trade relations, 364
Southern Rhodesia, 267, 291, 299, 313,
    344–45, 353
Soviet Union, 340, 345–46, 364.
    See also Russia
spice trade, 26–27
Sri Lanka. *See* Ceylon
Sri Lankan Freedom Party, 340
St. Katharine's Dock, 149–50
Stamford (Connecticut), 372–74
Stamp Act (1765), 53
Stanton, A. G., 215
Starbucks, 408
Starr, Henry, 370
Stimson, H. R., 192
Stringfellow, H. K., 367
Suez Canal, 115, 128, 150, 376, 379
sugar: and adulteration, 124–25, 254; and
    afternoon tea, 83, 154, 206; boycotts of,
    40, 51; in the global economy, 11–12,
    17, 24, 406; as mass commodity, 48–50,
    56; rates of increase in consumption
    of, 239; rationing of, 309–10, 351; sale
    of, 47; in South Africa, 292, 298–300;
    taxation of, 66 , 214, 240; in tea, 32, 38,
    284–88, 328, 332, 372; and temperance

movement 68, 74–75; threatening
    nationalization of, 341; trade in, 37,
    41, and working-class diet, 56–63, 176;
    during World War I, 227
Sumatra, 33, 88, 237, 241–42, 332,
    477n42
Sumner, J. R., 396
Sunkist, 286–88
supermarket, 369, 383
Surat, 32–33, 209
surpluses, 15, 183–85, 191, 244
Susman, Warren, 490n50
swadeshi, 253–56, 261
Sweden, 268, 281, 289–90
Sylhet, 97–98, 111, 166, 338–39, 353

Tagore, Dwarkanath, 103
Taiping Rebellion, 128
Taiwan. *See* Formosa (Taiwan)
Tallents, Stephen, 235
Tamilnadu, 261
Tamils, 172, 269, 339, 341, 359
Tanzania, 14, 345, 388, 394
Tariff Reform League, 214–15, 234, 240
tariff reform, 214–16, 234–37, 240,
    244–51. *See also* imperial preference;
    protectionism
taste: and advertising, 15, 18, 23; of
    Ceylon tea, 188; for Coca-Cola, 351,
    and colonial encounter, 79; as cultural
    practice, 33, 36, 154; decline of for tea,
    375–78, 381–84, 388; and food scares,
    121; global production of, 25; and green
    tea, 140–41, 190; imperialism and the
    shaping of, 56, 147, 176, 181, 185, 19;
    of Indian tea, 156–60, 164, 166, 168–69,
    173, 183, 189, 210–12; and market
    research, 232; as social construction,
    23, 418n56; of tea, 33–34, 39, 193–94,
    207, 284, 372–73, 391; and tea business,
    150, 167; and temperance, 77; and the
    workplace, 228, during World War II,
    332, 407
Tata Global Beverages, 408
taxation, 41, 53–54, 59, 66, 126–27, 137,
    213–20, 226, 240, 245, 251, 256–62, 268,
    313–314, 337, 340–348, 395, 430n51. *See
    also* cess; tea duties
Taylor, Vince, 384–385